UNDERSTANDING COLLEGE AND UNIVERSITY ORGANIZATION

Volume II—Dynamics of the System

UNDERSTANDING

COLLEGE AND

UNIVERSITY

ORGANIZATION

Theories for Effective Policy and Practice

James L. Bess and Jay R. Dee

Foreword by D. Bruce Johnstone

Volume II—Dynamics of the System

STERLING, VIRGINIA

COPYRIGHT © 2008, 2012 BY
STYLUS PUBLISHING, LLC.

Published by Stylus Publishing, LLC
22883 Quicksilver Drive
Sterling, Virginia 20166-2102

A hardcover edition of this book was published in 2008 by
Stylus Publishing, LLC.

**The Library of Congress has cataloged the hardcover
edition as follows:**
Bess, James L.
   Understanding college and university organization :
theories for effective policy and practice / James L. Bess and
Jay R. Dee ; foreword by D. Bruce Johnstone.
      p.   cm.
   Includes bibliographical references and index.
   ISBN 1-57922-131-9 (v. 1 : alk. paper)
   ISBN 1-57922-132-7 (v. 2 : alk. paper)
   1. Universities and colleges—Administration.
2. Organizational sociology.   I. Dee, Jay R.   II. Title.
LB2341.B4769   2007
378.1′01—dc22   2006033065

Volume I
ISBN: 978-1-57922-131-7 (cloth)
ISBN: 978-1-57922-768-5 (paper)
ISBN: 978-1-57922-771-5 (library networkable e-edition)
ISBN: 978-1-57922-773-9 (consumer e-edition)

Volume II
ISBN: 978-1-57922-132-4 (cloth)
ISBN: 978-1-57922-769-2 (paper)
ISBN: 978-1-57922-772-2 (library networkable e-edition)
ISBN: 978-1-57922-774-6 (consumer e-edition)

Two-Volume Sets
ISBN: 978-1-57922-197-3 (cloth)
ISBN: 978-1-57922-770-8 (paper)

Printed in the United States of America

All first editions printed on acid-free paper
that meets the American National Standards Institute
Z39-48 Standard.

Bulk Purchases

Quantity discounts are available for use in workshops
and for staff development.
Call 1-800-232-0223

First Paperback Edition, 2012

CONTENTS

VOLUME II: DYNAMICS OF THE SYSTEM

PROBLEM-TO-THEORY APPLICATION TABLE   *xiii*

FOREWORD   *xxiii*
D. Bruce Johnstone

ABOUT THE AUTHORS   *xxvii*

ACKNOWLEDGMENTS   *xxix*

PREFACE   *xxxi*

1   OVERVIEW   *463*
Overview of Volume I, 464
Organizational Theory, 466
Organizational Paradigms, 467
Overview of Systems Theory, 471
Key Concepts in Systems Theory, 472
Contents of Volume II, 474
Summary, 482
References, 484

2   CONFLICT IN ORGANIZATIONS   *487*
Open and Closed Systems, 493
History of the Development of Conflict Theory, 498
Conflict as Structure, 501
Conflict as Process, 503
Social Constructionist Perspectives on Conflict, 522
Postmodern Perspectives on Conflict, 524
Gender Issues in Conflict Management, 526
Summary, 527
Review Questions, 527
Case Discussion Questions, 529
References, 530

3 POWER AND POLITICS IN HIGHER EDUCATION
   ORGANIZATIONS   535
   Some Definitions: Power, Authority, and Politics, 541
   Power and Rationality, 546
   Organizational Versus Personal Determinants of Power, 548
   Organizational Determinants of Power, 549
   Horizontal Power: Strategic Contingencies Theory, 551
   Vertical Power: Partisans and Authorities, 554
   Personal Power, 561
   Social Constructionist Perspectives on Power, 568
   Empowerment, 571
   Marxist and Postmodern Alternatives, 572
   Power, Politics, and Unions, 574
   Summary, 575
   Review Questions, 576
   Case Discussion Questions, 578
   References, 578

4 ORGANIZATIONAL DECISION MAKING   583
   Decision Making as a Process, 594
   Decision Making as Structure, 597
   Participation Theories, 605
   Risky Shift, Polarization, and Social Loafing in Group Decision Making, 615
   Social Constructionist Perspectives on Group Decision Making, 617
   Summary, 620
   Review Questions, 620
   Case Discussion Questions, 622
   References, 622

5 INDIVIDUAL DECISION MAKING   628
   Garbage Can Model, 634
   Decisions as Role Playing, 637
   Decisions as Personality Manifestations, 639
   Decisions and Information Utilization, 643
   Risk and Uncertainty: The Gambling Metaphor, 646
   Decision Trees, 649
   Non-Decision Making, 650
   Postmodern Perspectives on Individual Decision Making, 653
   Summary, 655
   Review Questions, 655
   Case Discussion Questions, 657
   References, 657

6 ORGANIZATIONAL LEARNING   *660*
   Conceptualizations of Organizational Learning, 665
   Processes and Stages of Organizational Learning, 670
   Linking Individual and Organizational Learning, 678
   Cultural Conceptualizations of Organizational Learning, 686
   Dialectical Perspectives on Cultural Learning, 689
   Postmodern Interpretations of Organizational Learning, 693
   Contingencies Governing the Use of Alternative Learning Models, 694
   The Learning Organization, 696
   Summary, 698
   Review Questions, 699
   Case Discussion Questions, 700
   References, 701

7 ORGANIZATIONAL STRATEGY   *706*
   Strategy and the External Environment, 714
   The Linear Model of Strategy, 723
   The Adaptive Model of Strategy, 726
   The Emergent Model of Strategy, 730
   The Symbolic Model of Strategy, 732
   Postmodern Models of Strategy, 734
   Curriculum as Strategy: Application of the Five Models, 736
   Heuristics for Choosing a Model of Strategy, 738
   Summary, 741
   Review Questions, 742
   Case Discussion Questions, 744
   References, 745

8 ORGANIZATIONAL GOALS, EFFECTIVENESS, AND
   EFFICIENCY   *750*
   Conceptualizations of Effectiveness and Efficency, 755
   Model 1: The Goal Model, 758
   Model 2: The System Resource Model, 764
   Model 3: The Internal Process Model, 765
   Model 4: Strategic Constituencies Model, 766
   Model 5: Phase Models, 767
   Model 6: Fit Models, 767
   Model 7: Competing Values Model, 770
   Model 8: Quality Model, 772
   Model 9: Other Models of Effectiveness, 772
   The Social Construction Model of Organizational Effectiveness, 774
   Postmodern Perspectives on Effectiveness, 777
   Organizational Efficiency, 779

Summary, 781
Review Questions, 781
Case Discussion Questions, 783
References, 784

9　ORGANIZATIONAL CHANGE IN HIGHER
　　EDUCATION　　　　　　　　　　　　　　　　　　　　　790
　　Defining Change, 796
　　Planned Change Models, 798
　　Emergent Change Framework, 808
　　Synthesis of the Change Models, 810
　　Contingency Framework for Change, 813
　　Postmodern and Critical Perspectives on Change, 816
　　Summary, 819
　　Review Questions, 820
　　Case Discussion Questions, 821
　　References, 822

10　LEADERSHIP　　　　　　　　　　　　　　　　　　　　826
　　Defining Leadership, 830
　　A History of the Study of Leadership, 835
　　Idiographic Leadership Theories, 838
　　Nomothetic Approaches to Understanding Leadership, 843
　　Behaviorist Theories of Leadership, 847
　　Interactive Theories of Leadership, 852
　　Matching Traits, Contingencies, and Behaviors for Effective Leadership, 854
　　Other Approaches to Leadership, 864
　　Social Construction and Leadership, 866
　　Summary, 875
　　Review Questions, 875
　　Case Discussion Questions, 876
　　References, 877

11　THE END AND THE BEGINNING: FRESH
　　THOUGHTS ABOUT ORGANIZATIONAL THEORY
　　AND HIGHER EDUCATION　　　　　　　　　　　　　886
　　Purposes of the Book—A Reprise, 887
　　The Complexity of Higher Education, 888
　　Perspectives of and Challenges to the Postmodern Paradigm, 889
　　The Contributions of Social Constructionist Theory, 890
　　Emerging Organizational Challenges in Higher Education, 890
　　Conclusions, 891
　　References, 892

SUBJECT INDEX   *895*

AUTHOR INDEX   *919*

VOLUME I: THE STATE OF THE SYSTEM

PROBLEM-TO-THEORY APPLICATION TABLE   *xiii*

FOREWORD   *xxiii*
D. Bruce Johnstone

ABOUT THE AUTHORS   *xxvii*

ACKNOWLEDGMENTS   *xxix*

PREFACE   *xxxi*

INTRODUCTION   *xxxv*

1   THE APPLICATION OF ORGANIZATIONAL THEORY
    TO COLLEGES AND UNIVERSITIES   *1*
    Colleges and Universities as Complex Organizations, 2
    Objectives of the Book, 5
    Theory, 7
    Organizational Theory, 10
    Three Perspectives on Organizational Theory, 12
    Summary, 16
    References, 17

2   COLLEGES AND UNIVERSITIES AS COMPLEX
    ORGANIZATIONS   *18*
    Roles and Functions of Colleges and Universities, 20
    College and University National Organization, 21
    Internal Organization of Colleges and Universities, 21
    Budget Making in Academic Institutions, 28
    Personnel Decisions, 29
    Tenure and Academic Freedom, 34
    Student Participation in Decision Making, 35
    Summary, 36
    References, 36

3   APPROACHES TO ORGANIZATIONAL ANALYSIS:
    THREE PARADIGMS   *38*
    Paradigms Defined, 42

Approaches to Paradigmatic Use, 43
Three Paradigms: An Overview, 46
Positivist Paradigm, 50
The Social Construction Paradigm, 54
Postmodern Perspectives on Organizations, 65
Applying the Three Paradigms, 77
Summary, 78
Review Questions, 80
Case Discussion Questions, 81
References, 82

4 GENERAL AND SOCIAL SYSTEMS THEORY   87
History of Systems Theory, 91
General Systems Theory, 93
Social Systems Theory, 109
The Social Systems Model, 111
Expanded Social Systems Model, 113
Proportionate Contribution of Idiographic versus Nomothetic, 114
The "Fit" Between and Among System Components, 116
Extensions of Systems Theory: Alternative Paradigms, 118
Summary, 120
Review Questions, 120
Case Discussion Questions, 121
References, 122

5 ORGANIZATIONAL ENVIRONMENTS   126
Systems Theory and Organizational Environments, 130
Positivist Theories of Organization-Environment Relations, 134
Social Construction Perspectives on Environment, 152
Postmodern Perspectives on Environment, 158
Summary, 161
Review Questions, 163
Case Discussion Questions, 165
References, 166

6 CONCEPTUAL MODELS OF ORGANIZATIONAL
   DESIGN   170
A Brief Definition of Organizational Design, 174
Description and Overview of This Chapter, 175
A Brief Review of a Typical College or University Design, 175
Differentiation and Integration: Basic Issues in Organizational Design, 176

Alternative Modes of Designing an Organization: Mechanistic and
    Organic, 178
Determinants of Organizational Design, 181
Summary, 194
Review Questions, 195
Case Discussion Questions, 196
References, 197

7 BUREAUCRATIC FORMS AND THEIR LIMITATIONS   *200*
Bureaucratic Structure, 203
Centralization, Decentralization, and Participation, 212
Common Bureaucratic Forms, 214
Social Construction of Organizational Structure, 222
Postmodern Views on Organizational Design, 228
Summary, 231
Review Questions, 232
Case Discussion Questions, 234
References, 235

8 ORGANIZATIONAL ROLES   *239*
Organizational Benefits and Detriments of Precise Role Definition, 245
Role Theory in Organizations, 246
Roles as Functional Positions in Bureaucracies, 247
Role as Expected Behavior, 249
Social Construction Conceptualizations of Roles, 258
Postmodern and Feminist Perspectives on Roles, 260
Role Conflict, 262
Role Ambiguity, 265
Supplementary Role Concepts, 267
Summary, 270
Review Questions, 270
Case Discussion Questions, 272
References, 272

9 MOTIVATION IN THE HIGHER EDUCATION
WORKPLACE   *278*
Need Theories, 284
Process Theories, 294
Social Construction and Motivation Theory, 306
Feminist Theory and Motivation, 307
Management and Motivation, 309
Summary, 309

Review Questions, 310
Case Discussion Questions, 312
References, 313

10 GROUPS, TEAMS, AND HUMAN RELATIONS　317
A Brief History of Human Relations Theory, 321
The Study of Groups, 325
Informal Organization, 329
Group Norms, 338
Teams as Groups, 345
Social Construction, Groups, and Teams, 346
Postmodern Perspectives on Groups and Teams, 349
Summary, 350
Review Questions, 351
Case Discussion Questions, 352
References, 353

11 ORGANIZATIONAL CULTURE　358
Conceptualizations of Culture, 362
Schein's Framework, 364
Organizational Culture and Organizational Functions, 372
Positivist Research on Organizational Culture, 375
Cultural Typologies in Higher Education, 376
Social Constructionist Perspectives on Organizational Culture, 381
Organizational Subcultures, 382
Critical and Postmodern Perspectives on Organizational Culture, 385
Culture and Difference, 388
Using Positivist, Social Constructionist, and Postmodern Approaches, 389
Organizational Climate, 390
Summary, 393
Review Questions, 394
Case Discussion Questions, 395
References, 396

12 CONCLUSIONS: UNDERSTANDING THE SHAPE OF
HIGHER EDUCATION　400

APPENDIX: APPLYING ORGANIZATIONAL THEORY　407

SUBJECT INDEX　425

AUTHOR INDEX　449

PROBLEM-TO-THEORY APPLICATION TABLE

The following are organizational problems college and university administrators typically encounter in their work. For each problem listed, reference is given to directly relevant theory and to conceptual frameworks that have been found to be effective by researchers and administrators.

We have presented these problems as illustrations of the utility of organizational theories. We do not, however, claim that the list of problems is comprehensive. Readers who seek theoretical solutions to problems not listed below should consult the index, whose entries provide access to the wide range of administrative issues and theoretical approaches covered by this book.

Organizational Problem	Related Theory or Conceptual Framework	Vol/Chap/Page
1. Competition and External Relations		
Need to conduct a comprehensive environmental scan.	General and Proximate Environments	V1, C5 (pp. 131–134)
	SWOT Analysis	V2, C7 (pp. 728–729)
Competition with other colleges and universities is intensifying.	Population Ecology Theory	V1, C5 (pp. 138–141)
	Adaptive Model of Strategy (including determining the organization's core competencies)	V2, C7 (pp. 726–729)
Pressures from external agencies (e.g., state government) demand a response.	Institutional Theory	V1, C5 (pp. 141–144)
	Planned Change Models	V2, C9 (pp. 798–808)
Organization is not well known or understood by external groups.	Organizational Image and Identity	V1, C5 (pp. 155–158)
	Symbolic Model of Strategy	V2, C7 (pp. 732–734)
Accreditation issues, standards from the professional associations (e.g., law, nursing, education, social work)	Institutional Theory	V1, C5 (pp. 141–144)

(continued)

Organizational Problem	Related Theory or Conceptual Framework	Vol/Chap/Page
Need to improve external relations	Identifying Stakeholders	V2, C7 (pp. 715–716)
	Boundary Spanning Personnel	V2, C7 (pp. 721–722)
Organization needs to demonstrate accountability to external agencies.	Goal Model of Effectiveness	V2, C8 (pp. 758–763)
2. Planning and Budgeting		
Resources are scarce (e.g., declining state revenue for public university and college budgets).	Resource Dependence Theory	V1, C5 (pp. 148–152)
	System Resource Model of Effectiveness	V2, C8 (pp. 764–765)
Plans and forecasts have failed to serve as an accurate guide for institutional decision making.	Chaos Theory	V1, C5 (pp. 158–161)
	Postmodern and Critical Perspectives on Change	V2, C9 (pp. 816–819)
Declining enrollment	Resource Dependence Theory	V1, C5 (pp. 148–152)
	Population Ecology Theory	V1, C5 (pp. 138–141)
The organization needs to make decisions regarding program expansion and/or contraction.	Decision Trees	V2, C5 (pp. 649–650)
Budget uncertainties	Strategic Contingencies Theory	V2, C3 (pp. 551–554)
Decisions are made too quickly without sufficient analysis of the problem.	Decision Making as a Process	V2, C4 (pp. 594–597)
	Group versus Individual Decision Making	V2, C4 (pp. 606–608)
	Shared Decision Making	V2, C4 (pp. 608–614)
Decisions are made too slowly; not all decisions require extensive discussion and analysis.	Modes of Decision Making in Organizations	V2, C4 (pp. 602–605)
	Group versus Individual Decision Making	V2, C4 (pp. 606–608)
	Shared Decision Making	V2, C4 (pp. 608–614)

Organizational Problem	*Related Theory or Conceptual Framework*	*Vol/Chap/Page*
The use of formal decision-making procedures does not improve the quality of decisions made within the organization.	Garbage Can Model of Decision Making	V2, C5 (pp. 634–637)
	Nondecision Making	V2, C5 (pp. 650–653)
	Postmodern Perspectives on Individual Decision Making	V2, C5 (pp. 653–655)
The organization struggles to find the "right" people to make different kinds of decisions under different types of circumstances; decision makers' skills are not a good match for the types of decisions that typically come to them.	Information Accessing Preferences and Information Processing Preferences	V2, C5 (pp. 639–643)
	Decisions and Information Use	V2, C5 (pp. 643–646)
Top-level leaders are too controlling of the planning process.	Dialectical Perspectives on Cultural Learning	V2, C6 (pp. 689–693)
	Postmodern Interpretations of Organizational Learning	V2, C6 (pp. 693–694)
	Postmodern Perspectives on Strategy	V2, C7 (pp. 734–736)
	Emergent Change Framework	V2, C9 (pp. 808–810)
Organization has difficulty using data to demonstrate its effectiveness; data are misunderstood or distorted, or too few data are used.	Social Construction Model of Organizational Effectiveness	V2, C8 (pp. 774–777)
3. Organizational Structure and Core Processes		
Organization is slow to respond to changes in the external environment.	Contingency Theory	V1, C5 (pp. 145–148)
	Adaptive Model of Strategy	V2, C7 (pp. 726–729)
Rules and procedures are interfering with the organization's ability to respond to changes in the external environment.	Matching Organizational Design and External Environment	V1, C6 (pp. 183–184)
Core organizational processes are not yielding effective outcomes.	Matching Organizational Design and Technology	V1, C6 (pp. 184–189)

(continued)

Organizational Problem	Related Theory or Conceptual Framework	Vol/Chap/Page
Student services (e.g., financial aid, advising) are too scattered across campus; the services are not convenient or well coordinated.	Functional Forms of Organization	V1, C7 (pp. 215–217)
Leaders of specialized units complain that centralized administrative functions (e.g., budget, fund raising) are not addressing their needs.	Product Forms of Organization	V1, C7 (pp. 217–219)
Interdisciplinary initiatives are difficult to implement.	Matrix Forms of Organization	V1, C7 (pp. 220–222)
	Loose Coupling Theory	V1, C7 (pp. 223–226)
Collaboration between student affairs and academic affairs divisions is rare.	Matrix Forms of Organization	V1, C7 (pp. 220–222)
	Loose Coupling Theory	V1, C7 (pp. 223–226)
	Collaborative Leadership	V2, C10 (pp. 869–871)
Restructuring initiatives have failed to improve organizational performance.	Structuration Theory	V1, C7 (pp. 226–228)
	Postmodern Views on Organizational Design	V1, C7 (pp. 228–231)
Formal procedures for resolving conflict do not improve unit or organizational performance.	Social Constructionist Perspectives on Conflict	V2, C2 (pp. 522–524)
	Postmodern Perspectives on Conflict	V2, C2 (pp. 524–526)
Organization fails to detect service problems until they reach near-crisis proportions.	Single- and Double-Loop Learning	V2, C6 (pp. 674–678)
Effective practices are concentrated in only a few units within the organization; good ideas to improve performance do not spread across the organization.	Shared Mental Models: The Nexus between Individual and Organizational Learning	V2, C6 (pp. 680–686)
	Adoption of Innovations	V2, C9 (pp. 800–801)
4. Managing Departments and Institutional Units		
Departments do not coordinate their work with other units, leading to unnecessary duplication.	Differentiation and Integration	V1, C6 (pp. 176–178)
	Pooled, Sequential, and Reciprocal Interdependence	V1, C6 (pp. 191–194)

Organizational Problem	*Related Theory or Conceptual Framework*	*Vol/Chap/Page*
Information is not being exchanged among units that need to coordinate their efforts.	Division of Labor	V1, C7 (pp. 205–206)
Lack of clear rules and procedures has led to inconsistent performance within and across units.	Procedural Specification	V1, C7 (pp. 206–208)
Too many people report to one supervisor.	Hierarchy–Span of Control	V1, C7 (pp. 210–212)
Organizational members report they receive mixed messages or conflicting instructions from their supervisors about how to do their jobs.	Role Conflict	V1, C8 (pp. 262–265)
Organizational members report they do not receive clear instructions from their supervisors.	Role Ambiguity	V1, C8 (pp. 265–266)
Lack of focus on task accomplishment; too much socializing among organizational members interferes with performance.	ERG Theory–Frustration-Regression Hypothesis	V1, C9 (pp. 292–294)
	Optimum Levels of Conflict	V2, C2 (pp. 498–500)
Competition among departments for resources	Organizational Sources of Conflict	V2, C2 (pp. 496–497)
	Structural Approaches to Conflict Management	V2, C2 (pp. 517–518)
	Process Approaches to Conflict Management	V2, C2 (pp. 518–521)
Conflict between individuals	Conflict of Interest, Conflict of Understanding, Conflict of Ideology	V2, C2 (p. 497)
	Structural Approaches to Conflict Management	V2, C2 (pp. 517–518)
	Process Approaches to Conflict Management	V2, C2 (pp. 518–521)

(continued)

Organizational Problem	*Related Theory or Conceptual Framework*	*Vol/Chap/Page*
Organizational units continue to make the same errors repeatedly; they fail to improve over time.	How Organizational Learning May Be in Error	V2, C6 (pp. 667–668)
	Single- and Double-Loop Learning	V2, C6 (pp. 674–678)
Leaders do not do a good job of delegating responsibilities; too much micromanagement.	Situational Leadership	V2, C10 (pp. 852–853)
	Collaborative Leadership	V2, C10 (pp. 869–871)
Leaders tend to give projects to people who are not prepared to handle them; lack of mentoring.	Situational Leadership	V2, C10 (pp. 852–853)
5. Managing Groups and Teams		
Team members disagree about who should be in charge.	Authority of the Situation	V1, C10 (pp. 322–323)
Group/team/committee meetings tend to accomplish little.	Personal Roles in Groups	V1, C10 (pp. 333–334)
	Stages of Group Function and Development	V1, C10 (pp. 336–338)
	Social Construction, Groups, and Teams	V1, C10 (pp. 346–349)
Team members are not contributing equally toward group performance; a few members are doing most of the work.	Free Riding and Social Loafing	V1, C10 (pp. 342–343)
Groups and teams tend to shoot down new ideas.	Groupthink	V1, C10 (pp. 344–345)
Groups and teams tend to avoid tough decisions.	Groupthink	V1, C10 (pp. 344–345)
Groups and teams have difficulty making decisions.	Decision Making as a Process	V2, C4 (pp. 594–597)
	Symbolic Convergence Theory	V2, C4 (pp. 617–620)

Organizational Problem	Related Theory or Conceptual Framework	Vol/Chap/Page
6. Change Management and Organizational Growth		
Need to plan for organizational growth and expansion	Matching Organizational Design and Size	V1, C6 (p. 191)
Current values and assumptions impede organizational growth and development.	Cultural Typologies in Higher Education	V1, C11 (pp. 376–380)
Faculty and staff members often resist decisions by organizational leaders.	Downward Influence: How Authorities Attempt to Influence Partisans	V2, C3 (pp. 559–561)
	Zone of Acceptance	V2, C4 (pp. 614–615)
Organization is not innovative.	Dialectical Perspectives on Cultural Learning	V2, C6 (pp. 689–693)
	Implementing a Learning Organization	V2, C6 (pp. 696–698)
	Emergent Model of Strategy	V2, C7 (pp. 730–732)
	Adoption of Innovations	V2, C9 (pp. 800–801)
	Sociotechnical Theories of Change	V2, C9 (pp. 801–805)
	Emergent Change Framework	V2, C9 (pp. 808–810)
Change initiatives get stalled, lose momentum, and fail to accomplish their intended goals.	Central Problems in the Management of Change	V2, C9 (pp. 796–797)
	Planned Change Models	V2, C9 (pp. 798–808)
Organization needs to implement new technology more extensively in distance education; need to encourage more faculty members to use the technology.	Planned Change Models	V2, C9 (pp. 798–808)
	Adoption of Innovations	V2, C9 (pp. 800–801)
Faculty and staff are resistant to changing their behaviors.	Force Field Analysis of Change	V2, C9 (pp. 805–807)

(continued)

Organizational Problem	Related Theory or Conceptual Framework	Vol/Chap/Page
7. Personnel Management		
Orientation programs do not prepare new employees effectively to be successful in their jobs.	Role Socialization	V1, C8 (pp. 258–260)
The organization needs to improve faculty development and evaluation systems.	Job Characteristics Theory	V1, C9 (pp. 302–306)
Salary ratcheting issues: Senior faculty and staff complain that incoming junior-level faculty and staff are earning nearly as much as (or more than) they do.	Equity Theory	V1, C9 (pp. 299–302)
Demands for higher salaries	Upward Influence: How Partisans Attempt to Influence Authorities (Influencing, Shaping, and Determining Others' Objectives)	V2, C3 (pp. 557–559)
Unions and collective bargaining difficulties	Upward Influence: How Partisans Attempt to Influence Authorities	V2, C3 (pp. 557–559)
	Downward Influence: How Authorities Attempt to Influence Partisans	V2, C3 (pp. 559–561)
8. Mission, Vision, and Goals for the Organization		
Need to develop new goals for department, unit, or whole organization	Matching Organizational Design and Goals	V1, C6 (pp. 189–190)
	Goal Model of Effectiveness	V2, C8 (pp. 758–763)
New leaders (e.g., a newly hired president) need to learn as much as possible about the organization.	Schein's Organizational Culture Framework	V1, C11 (pp. 364–372)
	Using Positivist, Social Constructionist, and Postmodern Approaches for Analyzing Organizational Culture	V1, C11 (pp. 389–390)

Organizational Problem	Related Theory or Conceptual Framework	Vol/Chap/Page
Inefficiency: Organizational efforts are not clearly linked to the institution's mission; too many disconnected initiatives	Linear Model of Strategy	V2, C7 (pp. 723–726)
Organizational drift: The institution's key values and purposes are not known or not clearly articulated.	Symbolic Model of Strategy	V2, C7 (pp. 732–734)
9. Diversity and Quality of Work Life		
Women and racial/ethnic minorities report that their contributions are not valued as highly.	Postmodern and Feminist Perspectives on Roles Sex and Gender Issues in Leadership	V1, C8 (pp. 260–262) V2, C10 (pp. 871–874)
Organizational morale is low; job dissatisfaction is high.	Two-Factor Theory	V1, C9 (pp. 289–291)
Organizational members lack motivation; they experience high levels of burnout and frustration.	Expectancy Theory Goal Theory Job Characteristics Theory Path-Goal Theory	V1, C9 (pp. 294–296) V1, C9 (pp. 296–299) V1, C9 (pp. 302–306) V2, C10 (pp. 854–859)
Organizational members complain they are treated unfairly and other people in the organization receive more rewards for the same or less effort.	Equity Theory	V1, C9 (pp. 299–302)
Organization is not as welcoming as it should be for students, faculty, and staff from traditionally underrepresented groups.	Critical Theory and Organizational Culture Postmodern Perspectives on Organizational Culture Culture and Difference	V1, C11 (pp. 385–386) V1, C11 (pp. 386–388) V1, C11 (pp. 388–389)
Lack of trust between administration and faculty, or between administration and staff	Continuum of Trust	V2, C3 (pp. 556–557)

I n this monumental two-volume study, *Understanding College and University Organization*, Jim Bess and Jay Dee have produced a reference (really, a text) that is highly theoretical, eminently practical, and like no other work to date on the complex topic of how and why colleges and universities behave as they do and how to lead (and follow) for a more humane, appropriately responsive, and cost-effective institution. The sweep of their coverage draws on decades of theoretical and empirical work, not just on colleges and universities, but on organizations of all forms and from the disciplinary vantages of sociology, psychology, management, and organizational behavior as well as the extensive and growing body of literature on higher education itself, to which both authors have made major contributions.

If there can be an overriding theme to a work of this scope, it is found in their subtitle: *Theories for Effective Policy and Practice*. Theory, however abstract and increasingly contested (that is, between positivist, social-constructionist, and post-modern paradigms), is essential not only for understanding these complex organizations, but also for their more effective design and leadership. Although the paradigmatic tilt is definitely positivist, the authors provide sympathetic, learned, and nuanced explanations of the more recent social constructionist and postmodern approaches and illustrate the fundamental complementarities of these ontologically and epistemologically different strands of scholarship.

Whether a graduate student given these two volumes as a text in a doctoral level course on higher education organization and governance or a scholar aspiring to an administrative career will become a *better* college dean or university president is beside the point. Anyone caring to become immersed in the nature of organizational theory, liberally illustrated by realistic cases, will better understand from these volumes what has happened—not only to a particular college or university at a point in time, but to the public's and politician's important and not always favorable perceptions of, and behaviors toward, the more than four thousand U.S. colleges and universities.

As a former college and university administrator (vice president for administration at the University of Pennsylvania, president of Buffalo State College, and chancellor of the State University of New York system, and for the most recent thirteen years as University Professor of higher and comparative education, I have attempted to fathom answers to questions such as:

- Why is it that many or most presidents (and virtually all members of college and university boards) lament what they perceive to be the excessive power of the faculty, especially to thwart the president's efforts to change the institution in directions that are more fiscally prudent and responsive to the changing needs of the students and the society that is to be served, while most faculty lament the fact that they have little or no *real* authority and that sooner or later the president (or the dean or the board) will have their way?

- And why is it that politicians and the press are convinced that colleges and universities "almost never change," which they invariably perceive as a kind of organizational pathology, while by most measures, the institutions that truly need to change do so quite profoundly (e.g., from a Roman Catholic liberal arts college for women to a co-educational college serving largely part-time and nontraditional students in preparation for careers in business and the health professions) and those institutions that are most resistant to change (e.g., a well-endowed, selective liberal arts college or university with a deep applicant pool and considerable socioeconomic and ethnic diversity in the entering classes) probably do not and almost certainly should not?

- Why do large lectures and smaller "discussion" classes continue to meet for two or three sessions a week for two annual semesters of thirteen weeks (mainly from mid-morning to mid-afternoon Monday through Thursday) in spite of advances in instructional technology that could provide synchronous and asynchronous learning opportunities for students to move at their own paces at home or elsewhere?

- Why do politicians and the press (and more than a few students and parents) see nothing but waste and incompetence in average yearly tuition increases that exceed the prevailing rates of inflation when a rate of inflation is nothing but an average of many price increases, roughly one-half of which perforce will be above the average, and when whether a price increase is in the "above" or the "below" half is a function mainly of the degree to which capital can replace labor—which is rarely the case in traditional higher education?

I read many books in my administrative career and gave more than a few lectures and wrote many chapters and articles for the edification of other higher education leaders, all in an attempt not so much to figure out what to do, but to better understand what happened when I did what I did and why other people seem to so misunderstand us. Later in my career as a professor of higher and comparative education, specializing in higher education finance, governance, and policy in both domestic and international comparative perspectives, I searched for works that would help my students better understand the wonderful complexities of these organizations we term "colleges and universities." Alas, I was never quite satisfied. I wish Professors Bess and Dee had completed this work, say, thirty years earlier. But then, it would have missed the last three decades' worth of theoretical and empirical work that the authors so adroitly draw on. So I will never know, and perhaps it is just as well, what I might have done differently had I had the advantage of Jim Bess's and Jay Dee's learning earlier in one of my careers in higher education. But I predict that many years will pass before these two volumes are surpassed.

D. Bruce Johnstone
Buffalo, New York

ABOUT THE AUTHORS

James L. Bess is professor emeritus at New York University and a consultant to colleges and universities throughout the world. He conducts research on organizational and faculty issues and is completing several books and papers on matters of higher education policy.

Dr. Bess's education includes degrees from Cornell, Harvard, New York University, and the University of California at Berkeley. He has written or edited eight books, including *Collegiality and Bureaucracy in the Modern University* and, most recently, *Teaching Alone/Teaching Together: Transforming the Structure of Teams for Teaching*. He has published more than 60 articles and book chapters, many on the organization of colleges and universities, faculty motivation, and issues of tenure.

Dr. Bess has received grants from the U.S. Department of Education, Exxon Education Foundation, TIAA-CREF, and a number of organizations in Japan, where he and his family spent two sabbatical years and subsequent shorter periods with the support of a Fulbright research grant.

Jay R. Dee is associate professor at the University of Massachusetts, Boston, where he also directs the doctoral program in higher education administration. He earned a Ph.D. from the University of Iowa, and his research interests include organizational change, faculty development, and governance. He has published more than twenty studies of college and university organization and leadership with particular attention to how institutional cultures and external accountability pressures shape organizational behavior.

In 2004, Dr. Dee received a grant from the Ford Foundation to work with colleges and universities in New England to improve faculty development programs. Under the auspices of this grant, he worked with faculty at eight institutions to create the New England Center for Inclusive Teaching, a faculty development network that promotes pedagogical and curricular change to serve diverse student populations.

Dr. Dee also teaches in the Leadership in Urban Schools Doctoral Program at the University of Massachusetts, Boston, and he has written extensively on teams and teamwork in school organizations.

ACKNOWLEDGMENTS

Writing books is no picnic except when the readers find the intellectual "food" tasty and nutritional and the "conversation" with the author stimulating. We hope that our readers will find sustenance and enjoyment from reading this book. But preparing for a picnic is also no picnic, and in this case, we owe to many our deep thanks for making important, substantive contributions of different kinds.

Both authors are grateful for the generosity of the reviewers whose names appear at the beginning of each chapter. We also owe a special debt of gratitude to Sharon McDade at George Washington University, who provided a thorough and thoughtful critique of the cases presented in each chapter. In addition, we are especially appreciative of our conversations with Adrianna Kezar at the University of Southern California and Joseph Berger at the University of Massachusetts, Amherst. Both of these colleagues shared with us insights and observations on organizational theory—and on the teaching of organizational theory—that enriched our perspectives for the book.

We also thank the doctoral students and graduates from the University of Massachusetts, Boston who provided equally insightful reviews of many of the chapters in this book: Mirtha Crisostomo (Emmanuel College), Cheryl Daly (University of New Hampshire), Paul DiFrancesco (Massachusetts College of Pharmacy and Health Sciences), Roxanne Gonzales (Colorado State University), Ralph Kidder (Newbury College), and Helen Page (Harvard University).

We are especially grateful to Bruce Johnstone for a generous and informative foreword. We owe debts as well to the many unnamed colleagues, mentors, students, and contributors to the body of literature from which we liberally borrowed ideas, old and new. Finally, together, we thank our publisher, John von Knorring, whose demeanor and tact matched his command of our field and led us to avoid many false steps that he anticipated with great insight.

Individually, James L. Bess would like to acknowledge the 35-year "gift" of his spouse, Nancy Moore Bess, who permitted him to be himself, despite his frequent idiosyncratic, irascible departures from reason and obligations to family life. How she managed her own professional life (she's a textile craftsperson) while tending to me is a wonderful mystery. She had help from our two sons, Isaac and Ivan, whose own professional and personal lives distracted me felicitously from my cocoon and enlivened my days. To them and other family and friends, I give my grateful thanks.

Jay Dee extends sincere thanks and gratitude to family, friends, and colleagues who have been patient and supportive during the writing process, including but not limited to Steve Backhaus, Alan Henkin, and Tim and Cinda Dee.

Authors' Disclaimer: We have conscientiously endeavored to cite and give credit to the many sources of ideas and theories used in the book. If there are instances where an author may not have been appropriately credited with authorship for either a published work or a phrase in the text, the error was completely unintentional and accidental. We do not believe that such is the case, but we sincerely apologize for any possible omission.

This book was written with two audiences in mind. The first audience comprises graduate students studying to become upper-level administrators, leaders, and policy makers in higher education. The second includes those persons currently employed in institutions of higher learning as administrative and faculty leaders.

The reason we felt such a book was necessary was not that there are insufficient resources in the literature that are relevant to contemporary practice. Rather, we believe that the literature is fragmented and not well organized. Readers of this book, probably as a regular practice, read the *Chronicle of Higher Education* and perhaps some other highly regarded periodicals, such as *Academe, Change, About Campus,* and other high-quality newsletters and periodicals of a more specialized nature. Relatively little of this literature, however, is grounded in **organizational theory**—the knowledge base that informs the practice of leadership and management.

Theory, as social psychologist Kurt Lewin said, is the best practice. Without theory, organizational leaders are forced to treat each problem that they encounter as unique—as if it were encountered for the first time. While leaders may have some experience with a particular problem, their solutions are usually not informed by the accumulated wisdom of others who have already encountered and solved similar problems, perhaps with much greater efficiency and effectiveness. Building theory in higher education results in a heuristic approach to problem solving that uses validated, proven theoretical relationships among independent and dependent variables (which are often causes and effects of phenomena). Having theory in mind, organizational leaders can determine whether the extant theory works for them. We hope with this book to provide a large number of systematically organized theories that can be applied in many typical situations. Ours is a pragmatic approach. Here are some possible answers to organizational problems that are suggested by theory. Try them out.

On the other hand, we hasten to add that the book is not a "how to" guidebook for managers. Many such management texts offer the latest techniques in organizational efficiency. Instead, we offer deeper, more sophisticated theories that will allow readers to develop their *own* management techniques and to evaluate intelligently contemporaneous approaches that are put forth regularly in magazines and management workshops.

In an effort to provide initial linkages between established theories and pressing problems being experienced by readers, we offer a **Problem-to-Theory Application Table** (see pages xiii–xxi). The table offers a range of typical problems (by no means an exhaustive list) with references to chapters and pages in the book where applicable theories can be found.

We have attempted as far as possible to speak plainly, avoiding jargon wherever possible. This is difficult when dealing with theory, since its linguistic mode tends to be abstract. Nevertheless, we hope that the reader will be able to follow our reasoning about the theories. In virtually all cases, we support our own explanations with references to literature that either amplifies what we have written or offers alternative perspectives. For pedagogical purposes, we also provide case material to which the theories can be applied and discussions of the application modes conducted. Working with theory requires practice, and skill development is cumulative. It is difficult at the start, but it becomes somewhat easier as one learns how to make the theory relevant to problems at hand.

The reader will discover quickly that we have approached the theory of the organization and administration of colleges and universities from three quite different perspectives, each relying on different assumptions about how human beings apprehend reality—or believe they do. Readers should be able to learn about their organizations from all three perspectives. On occasion, the approaches may appear to yield contradictory directives about which actions to take. We believe that this conclusion is largely a result of the fundamental philosophic assumptions about the most important characteristics of human life that underlie all behavior and projections of behavior in organizations, including colleges and universities. Each perspective—we call them paradigms rather than perspectives—has its own validity, but each does not automatically lead to immediately practical solutions to problems. They do, however, highlight phenomena that require attention if the institution is ultimately to be considered successful. We also argue that success needs to be measured in many ways, including not only the traditional criteria of student, faculty, and administrative achievement, but also the social and ethical goals of the larger society.

Indeed, we wish finally to underline our commitment to these goals. Individual human behavior in all domains—for example, home, market, school, work—is driven at least partially by each individual's underlying and often unexamined, deeply held beliefs about human nature, about the morality of interpersonal interactions in general, and about the meaning and purposes of human life. While we cannot examine all of the assumptions and presumptions that lie behind each of the theories we present in this book about the application of organizational theory in colleges and universities, we do wish to make explicit our view about the ethical posture to which all organizations, including those in our field—perhaps especially those—should adhere.

We take as an essential good the integrity and worth of each human being—each organizational member—regardless of position or authority in the organizational structure. Such a perspective requires the organization to deal with each individual with dignity and respect. It recognizes the need for each person to be enabled to continue to develop and grow in different ways—intellectual, practical, and psychological. The organization thus represents an environment for learning and personal growth. It means, in addition, that organizations do not have a reason for being in and of themselves in which they intentionally or unintentionally use employees as mechanical tools to further either alleged organizational goals or the goals of the organizations' more powerful executives.

We are not, however, so naïve as to ignore the practical necessity for organizations to be "in the real world." Every organization must be able to survive, especially to compete successfully. To do so, it must be perceived by clients as making meaningful contributions to them, individually and collectively. This sustained pressure on organizations from the external, competitive environment places great burdens on leaders who must transform that force, often transmitted downward in the organization, into the need to be efficient and effective—requirements for sustained successful competition.

Our aim in this book is to elucidate how administration can be made more efficient and effective through rational decision making, but not at the risk of sacrificing humanistic values. There may be occasions when demands for efficiency or effectiveness of organizational outcomes appear to give priority to dehumanization of workers. Our own ethical standards suggest, however, that morally conscious and conscientious administrators must be persistently and diligently sensitive to such proclivities and must exercise their power and influence to create a strong cultural norm with action consequences that uphold the integrity and dignity of every human being. Our presentation of multiple alternative paradigms should give conceptual support and moral grounding for these orientations and actions.

What the reader will find, therefore, in each of the chapters in this book are theories drawn from the literature that address the human condition in organizational life. It will invariably be the case that the theories will be cast at least as having the potential for providing organizational members with opportunities for becoming more active, energetic, enthusiastic, and satisfied with their organizational lives. We believe that such an objective can readily be accomplished within the parameters of achieving with sustained high quality the important goals of colleges and universities.

I

OVERVIEW

CONTENTS

Overview of Volume I   464
Organizational Theory   466
Organizational Paradigms   467
Overview of Systems Theory   471
Key Concepts in Systems Theory   472
Contents of Volume II   474
Summary   482
References   484

Overview of Volume I

This book is the second of a two-volume set dealing with the organization and administration of colleges and universities. Volume I addressed the important, continuing issues facing leaders of all organizations. On a rather predictable basis, organizational leaders will encounter challenges associated with external environments, internal organizational design, bureaucratic procedures, work roles, worker motivation, groups and teams, and organizational culture. In Volume II, we turn to somewhat more dynamic conditions of organizations—conditions that arise less predictably and that often challenge the status quo. Here, we examine conflict, power, decision making, organizational learning, strategy, assessments of effectiveness, change, and leadership.

Though much of the material in Volume II refers to and utilizes concepts and theories introduced in the first volume, it is possible to read and understand Volume II without having absorbed all of the ideas in Volume I. In this introduction, we outline the basic content of Volume II. First, however, for readers who may not have read the first volume, we present an abbreviated recapitulation of some of the basic assumptions and paradigms that we employed there and that will undergird the discussions of the topics in Volume II. As we noted in Volume I, in an effort to provide initial linkages between established theories and pressing problems being experienced by readers, we offer a Problem-to-Theory Application Table (see pages xiii–xxi). This table offers a range of typical problems (by no means an exhaustive list) with references to chapters and pages in the book where applicable theories can be found.

In Volume I, we considered in some depth the variety of **organizational environments** faced by colleges and universities, followed by a discussion of many different ways of understanding how institutions address those environments. Some environments, for example, are predictable and stable; others are more chaotic. Institutions must deal with each using different design and intervention strategies in order to be effective.

Also discussed in Volume I is the subject of **organizational design.** The ways in which organizations choose to create units with different functions and then relate those units to one another are dependent on a number of conditions—for example, the external environment, technology of research and teaching, goals of the organization, the organization's size, and organizational culture. Each of these elements must be taken into account in the design of the organization if the institution is to be effective and efficient.

The organizational designs of colleges and universities are at least in part bureaucratic. They are so because, under certain conditions, bureaucracies tend to be the most efficient organizational design. Many people complain about bureaucratic red tape—a seemingly endless stream of forms and procedures that must be followed in all circumstances. What causes the red tape, however, is not the **bureaucracy** per se, but its misuse. In Volume I, we considered alternative forms of bureaucratic structures and their advantages and disadvantages.

Organizations comprise roles and role players. A separate chapter in Volume I considered **organizational roles** and the ways that they are created and played out. We also discussed role conflict and role ambiguity, which are the sources of many problems in institutions of higher education.

In addition, the subject of how organizational members can become more productive and satisfied is covered in our chapter on **motivation.** There we discussed a variety of theories that should help leaders understand the sources of low and high motivation and associated levels of productivity. For example, we discussed job characteristics theory (Hackman & Oldham, 1980), which considers several psychological states that organizational members experience. This theory points to working conditions that are related to the psychological states so that the latter can be positively related to high motivation, productivity, and satisfaction.

As in most organizations, organizational members in colleges and universities work frequently in **groups.** In Volume I we examined the nature of groups—how they are formed, how they function, the impact of group dynamics on individual members, and the dangers of overly homogeneous thinking by members (groupthink).

A final substantive chapter in Volume I examined **organizational culture**—the unseen but experienced and felt ambience of an organization that includes a large variety of norms about work and other behavior of organizational members. The chapter explored the different types of norms found in organizations and the ways that people find out about them. Organizational members must conform to normative expectations of colleagues and leaders or find themselves ostracized, if not sabotaged, in their work. Different organizations have varying degrees of tightness or looseness of norms. The chapter describes the impact of these conditions on the options that workers have to either conform to or deviate from organizational norms.

Before outlining the contents of the chapters in Volume II, we describe some basic underlying notions about organizations that are critical to understanding the chapters in both volumes. First, since this is a book about organizational theory, we will explain briefly what we mean by this concept. We then examine three prominent paradigms used in contemporary organizational theory—positivist, social constructionist, and postmodernist—that reflect different sets of assumptions about theory and organizational life. We follow that discussion with an examination of systems theory, which is a wide-ranging "grand" theory that undergirds many of the positivist organizational theories described in this book.

Organizational Theory

Most people, for practical reasons, make hypothetical cause-effect predictions about their past behavior or proposed actions. That is, most people have at least tentative ideas that one action or event is likely to lead to another or that among different possible actions, one is more likely to have the desired effect. While it is tempting to call such individual conjectures "theory," they are not. **Theory** has a more precise meaning in the natural and social sciences. It refers to a relationship between two or more **concepts**—abstract ideas that, in turn, have referents in the real world. Importantly, to be called a theory, the relationship between or among the concepts must be confirmed as valid by virtue of many empirical measurements carried out with appropriate scientific methods (Kaplan, 1964). Kerlinger (1979), for example, defined theory as "a set of interrelated constructs (variables), definitions, and propositions that presents a systematic view of phenomena by specifying relations among variables, with the purpose of explaining natural phenomena" (p. 64).

To be called a theory, related constructs must be empirically verified and supported by evidence gathered over time by different researchers. The theory must also be parsimonious; that is, it must explain phenomena of interest with the fewest possible concepts or variables. There should be no extraneous explanations. In addition, theories vary in the breadth of phenomena to which they refer. As Creswell (1994) notes, "grand theories attempt to explain large categories of phenomena and are most common in the natural sciences (e.g., Darwin's theory of evolution). Middle-range theories fall between minor working hypotheses of everyday life and the all-inclusive grand theories (e.g., life span development theories). Substantive theories are restricted to a particular setting, group, time, population, or problem (e.g., math anxiety)" (p. 83). In this book, we deal with a wide range of theories (grand, middle range, and substantive), but all are associated with college and university organization and administration.

Theories are highly valuable tools for organizational leaders. Using theory takes advantage of the long periods of scientific study of others and thus provides more informed and usually more accurate guides to policy and practice than relying on guesswork, intuition, or seat-of-the-pants judgments. A common error of organizational leaders is to consider local and immediate problems as unique to themselves and/or to specific campuses.

Almost invariably, however, there are comparable situations elsewhere and precedents that have been examined scientifically and used to develop practical theories. Paradoxically, theories are practical because they are abstract; that is, they are not specific to a particular organization. This quality makes them applicable to a wide variety of situations (Reynolds, 1971).

Organizational theory comprises a body of knowledge about how and why organizations function. Obviously, not all organizations are alike—for example, differences exist among religious, business, scientific, athletic, and educational organizations. And within the educational sector, there are significant differences between elementary and secondary school organizations and colleges and universities. And with still more specification, there are important differences between different kinds of colleges and universities, depending on such factors as size, age, control (public, private, or for-profit), and mission. Despite these differences, however, there are many commonalities. All organizations have goals with members who serve those goals to one degree or another. They usually have a division of labor, often a hierarchy of authority, and modes of conflict resolution, among other structural features. In this book, we have gathered the wisdom of many scholars who present theories about these phenomena that in general can be applied to virtually any organization and hence can be used to understand, predict, and intervene to improve organizational performance. We have attempted to show in particular how the theories have been or can be applied to colleges and universities.

Organizational Paradigms

All organizational theories make assumptions about organizations and the people in them. These assumptions can be grouped into different perspectives about the nature of reality (ontological assumptions) and the nature of knowledge (epistemological assumptions). These different perspectives are called **paradigms**. A paradigm is a set of assumptions that guides a research community or a community of practice such as college administrators (Lewis & Grimes, 1999). Paradigms suggest which problems are important to solve, which methods are appropriate for research, and which conclusions are legitimate and valid (Creswell, 1994). In this section, we briefly describe three paradigms that are prominent in organizational research: positivist, social constructionist, and postmodernist.

Some theories assume that organizational phenomena such as structure and culture are objective entities that can be observed and measured consistently through well-specified research procedures. Through objective research, the "true" characteristics of an organization can be discovered. People may differ in their views of what organizational reality is, but they can resolve their disagreements through scientific methods of reason, logic, and empirical inquiry.

In this perspective, the individual is assumed to be separate from the reality he or she is attempting to discover or understand. If reality is separate from the person attempting to study it, then researchers can obtain objective, positive knowledge (rather than subjective views and opinions). This view of the way we come to know our world is called the **positivist** paradigm and has been the dominant philosophy of inquiry and practice virtually since the period of the Enlightenment in the 18th century. The impact of such thinking on modern organizations stems from the correlated belief in the possibility of linking the present with the future and in the belief that by constructing and using theory, organizational leaders can make accurate predictions about how their behavior will affect the organization's future. To give a practical example, an admissions director can make predictions about the likelihood of the persistence of the class admitted in a particular year if he or she knows certain of their characteristics that have been shown in the past to be predictive of college student success.

The purpose of positivist research is threefold:

1. To explain scientifically the phenomenon of interest—for example, individual or group behavior, beliefs, or attitudes. Such explanations permit reasoned and valid conclusions as to the probable causes of organizational problems.
2. To predict what is likely to follow from observations. For example, positivist theories can help leaders anticipate future conditions of the organization. Positivist theories give organizational leaders a good chance of making accurate predictions, since the theories are based on extensive research.
3. To control or intervene. Positivist theories give organizational participants confidence that they can judiciously and efficiently control relevant organizational variables and make changes that will benefit the organization.

Positivist theory argues for careful scientific study of the various contingencies that enter into good decision making. If we can accurately explain the various dimensions of an organizational problem, then we are more likely to identify the factors that contributed to the problem. With this knowledge, we can predict that if we alter those factors, then the problem may be alleviated. Thus, we can intervene in ways that are likely to improve organizational performance.

Positivist research holds significant advantages for informing organizational leadership and decision making, but its limitations are also becoming more evident. Cracks in what appeared to be a knowable environment with stable relationships have made positivist prediction and control somewhat problematic. Organizations and their environments have become increasingly complex, unpredictable, and even chaotic. Seemingly solid and reliable connections between and among phenomena have become suspect.

In recent years, alternative paradigms have emerged, partly in recognition of the increasing complexity and diversity of organizations and the environments in which they operate. One of the prominent alternatives to the positivist paradigm is **social constructionism.** This paradigm suggests that the organizational world is not an independent reality separate from the observer. Rather, human beings construct reality individually and through interactions with one another (Berger & Luckmann, 1967; Neumann, 1995). Theory, in this view, does not reflect the consensus of scientific observations about what is "true" in the "real" world. Instead, it represents a cognitive and affective reality derived from the minds of organizational members. Social constructionism, therefore, makes no claim to absolute truth. Instead, these theorists examine the multiple meanings that organizational members construct about their work and their interactions together.

From a social constructionist perspective, organizational life tends to be more ambiguous, with information seen as less reliable and having multiple interpretations (Weick, 2001). This is especially true for institutions of higher education. Social constructionism as a paradigm for thinking about organizations explores the ways that members of those organizations together create a vision of a viable view of reality that can be useful in their work. It conceives of the search for reality as an ongoing, dynamic process of continuous interaction and reshaping of meaning. This reshaping is not so much an attempt to get at some universal truth, but to arrive at a position in which people can agree sufficiently to be able to carry out their roles. The alternative assumptions of social constructionism argue for the need to foster more trust and communication among colleagues, as well as more sharing of leadership roles (Kezar, Carducci, & Contreras-McGavin, 2006).

A third paradigm that has achieved some considerable prominence in organizational thinking is called **postmodernism.** Like social constructionists, postmodernists do not adhere to an epistemological determinism that requires a search for the one true reality. In contrast to social constructionists, however, postmodernists claim that contemporary human experience is so disjointed and disconnected that knowledge about it cannot be logically connected with any degree of certainty. This condition has been brought on by the proliferation of information technology, trends toward globalization, and the rise of a consumer-driven economy, which collectively have "undermined traditional conceptions of knowledge and legitimacy" (Dickens & Fontana, 1994, p. 5).

Postmodernists pay close attention to semiotics—that is, the signs and symbols in the use of language. Attention to language and meaning in understanding how organizations operate has raised critical questions about the dangers of intentional or unintentional distortion and manipulation of words to empower certain groups (e.g., top management) and to disadvantage other less powerful groups and persons. Ambiguity of language may lead to conditions where organizations exploit less powerful members, but most postmodernists also valorize ambiguity and fragmentation as potentially liberating. They reject totalizing claims and generalizations that seek to establish a formalized knowledge base. Instead, postmodernists emphasize difference, plurality, and instability over uniformity, universality, and stability (Dickens & Fontana, 1994). Organizations that embrace diverse perspectives, encourage dissent, and empower people at-all levels can achieve a high degree of creativity, innovation, and personal fulfillment for their members (Hirschhorn, 1997). Clearly, the postmodern position creates unique and different kinds of challenges for the organization and administration of colleges and universities.

Our aim in this book is not to compare the three paradigms and attempt to determine which is a more valid or accurate way to analyze an organization. Instead, we seek to promote a pluralism of perspectives that emanates from multiple paradigms. Rather than stick with one dominant paradigm, we encourage readers to employ several paradigmatic lenses in their analyses of organizational problems. We argue, therefore, that a balance among the different paradigms (rather than a selection of the "best" paradigm) will generate more sophisticated understandings of college and university organization. In this volume, then, the reader will find numerous theories and frameworks that enable the organization to develop a balance between rationality and intuition, power and trust, and precision and ambiguity. While this volume demonstrates the utility of positivist theory, it also shows that in loosely coupled and postmodern organizations, broader, more amorphous goals and higher priorities for encouraging cooperation and trust can be introduced and employed effectively. An increasing number of scholars and practitioners argue for these organizational characteristics (Bensimon, 2004; Bergquist, 1993; Cutright, 2001; Del Favero, 2003; Kezar, 2000). Research reveals, however, that higher education leaders are increasingly being frustrated by externally generated demands for greater accountability and efficiency. These are orchestrated through a managerialist mentality (Bess,

2006) that pushes for centralization, oversight, and standardization of outputs—often at the expense of shared decision making, autonomy, and creativity. Robust responses are needed to address, correct, and sometimes counteract the weight of external pressures toward heavy-handed management. We argue that the use of theories from multiple paradigms offers leaders a wider assortment of options and alternative futures that they can enact both to remain accountable to external constituencies and to facilitate the achievement of the goals and aspirations of organizational members.

Overview of Systems Theory

Among the three paradigms described above, the positivist position is most commonly followed in college and university administration. It lends itself most easily to rapid decision making and action, even if flawed. The danger is that organizational leaders may accept positivist theories without question, partly because they want to avoid the delay and administrative conflict that may threaten efficiency. The alternative paradigms, social constructionism and postmodernism, offer checks and balances against the perpetuation of the status quo and against the abuse of power by those who would use the status quo to advance their personal agendas.

Those caveats having been stated, however, it is important to understand the scope and dimensions of the central tenets of the positivist position, which has guided the vast majority of research on organizations, including colleges and universities. The basic principles of positivist theories derive primarily from systems theory, an integrated set of propositions about the ways that participants in social systems are inextricably linked with one another. Many positivist organizational theories were developed in the 1960s by researchers who found consistent connections between configurations of organizational structure and the external environment (Burns & Stalker, 1961; Lawrence & Lorsch, 1967; Thompson, 1967). These theories were based, in large part, on principles from systems theory.

The central theme of systems theory is the notion that a change in any part of a system has implications for all other parts of the system. For example, the introduction of a new curriculum in a university's college of liberal arts, while seemingly bounded within that college, will have an impact on other parts of the institution such as admissions, registrar, physical plant, and advising. The changes will also be observed by those outside the institution—such as employers and graduate schools who need to be clear on the nature and qualifications of the graduates.

Systems theory is a "grand" theory that explains a wide variety of biological, sociological, and psychological phenomena. Given this broad scope, systems theory cannot be used to make predictions about organizational behavior. Other, more specific theories are needed to make such predictions (e.g., theories of work motivation or theories of organizational culture). The concepts in systems theory, therefore, are primarily "markers" that allow observers to utilize a common vocabulary in discussing organizational phenomena. Below are some of the concepts and brief definitions. For the most part, the definitions are drawn from Berrien (1968). We also reproduce from Volume I a figure that displays the relationships among several variables in systems theory (Figure 1.1).

Key Concepts in Systems Theory

1. **System**—"a set of components interacting with each other and a boundary which possess the property of filtering both the kind and rate of flow of inputs and outputs to and from the system" (pp. 14–15).
   a. Open systems—systems "which accept and respond to inputs (stimuli, energy, information, and so on)" (p. 15).
   b. Closed systems—"are assumed to function 'within themselves'" (p. 15). That is, they maintain vitality via their own energy, resources, and dynamic interactions.
2. **Boundary**—"that region separating one system from another; it can be

FIGURE 1.1
Elements in a Systems Framework

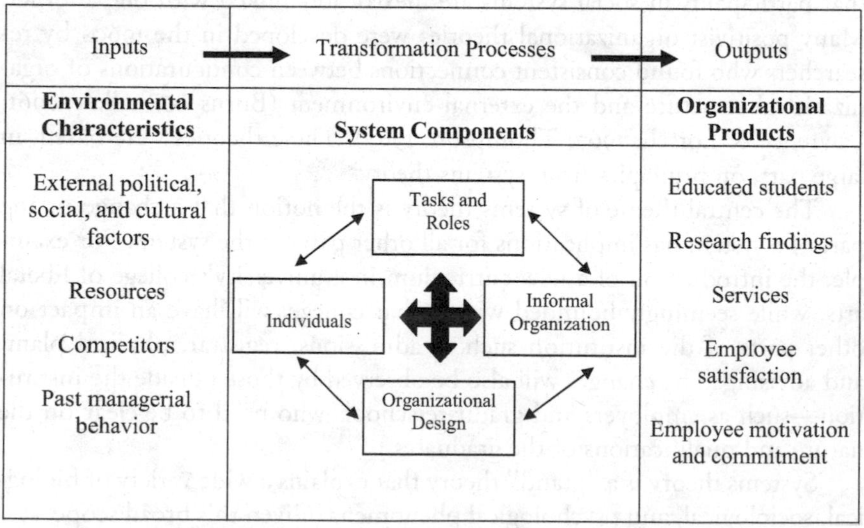

Inputs	Transformation Processes	Outputs
Environmental Characteristics	**System Components**	**Organizational Products**
External political, social, and cultural factors	Tasks and Roles · Individuals · Informal Organization · Organizational Design	Educated students Research findings
Resources		Services
Competitors		Employee satisfaction
Past managerial behavior		Employee motivation and commitment

Based on Hills (1968) and Nadler and Tushman (1977).

identified by some differentiation in the relationships existing between the components inside the boundary and those relationships which transcend the boundary" (p. 21).

3. **Interface**—"the region between the boundaries of two systems" (p. 24); the size and quality of the space (physical or psychological) through which exchanges between systems must pass.

4. **Environment** (suprasystem)—everything that is outside of the boundary of the system.

5. **Inputs**—"the energies absorbed by the system or the information introduced into it" (p. 24).

   a. Maintenance inputs—inputs "which energize the system and make it ready to function" (p. 25).

   b. Signal inputs—inputs "which provide the system with information to be processed" (p. 25).

6. **Memory**—"any relatively permanent record of inputs to a system that subsequently affects the processing of other inputs" (p. 40).

7. **Components or subsystems**—"a unit that in combination with other system units (subsystems) functions to combine, separate, or compare the inputs to produce the outputs" (p. 17).

8. **Structure**—the set of "components that . . . function with each other to combine, separate, or compare inputs to produce outputs" (pp. 54–55).

9. **Differentiation**—the tendency of growing systems to develop more specialized units to perform different required system functions.

10. **Transformations**—the technological and human processes that change inputs into finished outputs ready to be sent to the environment.

11. **Black box**—the condition "when faced with any system which we cannot describe, either because it is inconvenient and tedious or because the internal structure of a system is unknown" (p. 17).

12. **State of the system**—the "components of a system being arranged in a given pattern at one moment of time and in another way at another moment" (p. 24).

13. **Homeostasis**—"a condition brought about by feedback" that tends to restore the system to its original state (p. 37).

14. **Equifinality**—the principle that there is no one way to organize that is necessarily the most efficient and effective mode.

15. **Outputs**—"those energies, information, or products that the components discharge from the system into the suprasystem" (p. 27).

16. **Feedback**—information returned to the system about its impact on the external environment.

17. **Entropy**—the tendency for closed systems to lose energy and to dissolve

into less differentiated internal structures with less predictable functions.

A theory closely related to systems theory that we also use in the following chapters is **social systems theory**. Its basic premise is that all human behavior is a function of the interaction of a person with his or her environment, or $B = f(P,E)$ (Lewin, 1938). This seemingly simple notion is often overlooked by administrators who try to explain organizational phenomena solely in terms of the individual or the environment. For example, if faculty members in a university receive few national research fellowships in a particular year, some academic administrators may question whether faculty worked hard enough to secure such grants; others may suggest that research funding has dried up and that there is not much that can be done to improve the situation. Instead, it is necessary to take into account both individual *and* environmental conditions together. The former in social systems theory is called the **idiographic** dimension, while the latter is labeled the **nomothetic**. Social systems as a whole vary in their emphasis on one dimension versus the other. In some systems, the pressure on the nomothetic side overrides the idiographic. In military units, for example, individual personality will not usually be a strong determinant of behavior. In research groups, on the other hand, the idiographic explanation of behavior will predominate.

Systems theory serves as the basis for many of the positivist theories that we consider in the chapters that follow. Below we provide an overview of each of these chapters.

Contents of Volume II

The next chapter in this volume, chapter 2, covers the subject of **conflict** in organizations. We begin by explaining how conflict can have either positive or negative connotations and consequences. The proper management of conflict (rather than its elimination) can have salubrious effects on organizational outcomes. Conflict can be explained as a process and as a structure. That is, conflict can be seen as an unfolding dynamic process with recognizable stages or episodes that permit intervention at appropriate times and in appropriate ways, and conflict can typically be traced to a breakdown in the decision-making structure of an organization. Often both structural and process-oriented approaches are involved in the resolution of conflict.

Conflict exists at many levels in college and university organizations—intrapersonally, interpersonally, within a group, between groups or units, and between the institution and outside agencies. Typical modes of addressing conflict include competition, avoidance, compromise, collaboration, and accommodation. The most debilitating kind of conflict occurs when it remains latent—lying beneath the surface of daily organizational life and causing distrust and a lack of cooperation among organizational members.

In chapter 3, we consider **power** and **politics** in higher education organizations. Power tends to be viewed as illegitimate authority, because it can connote an attempt by an individual or group to gain an advantage that is not sanctioned by the authority of the organization. The exercise of power is usually inversely related to the amount of trust that exists in the organization. In the absence of trust, malevolent conflict tends to increase and organizational effectiveness and personal satisfaction suffer. Power is often seen as a tendency of the organization to depart from rationality, again with deleterious consequences for organizational productivity. A college or university with blatant evidence of the exercise of power will likely be immersed in internecine battles over turf, authority, and funding, with a strong undercurrent of distrust and disharmony among the workers.

In the chapter, however, we clarify how power can also be legitimate. Organizations like colleges and universities can be conceived not only as bureaucratic organizations, but at least in part as polities (i.e., as democratically governed communities). Hence, the ways that decisions are made are frequently subject to political as well as bureaucratic influences. Indeed, the status of colleges and universities as partial polities results in their having more diffuse and competing sources of power. It is useful to consider how members of colleges and universities respond to these influences. In chapter 3, we use the theories of William Gamson to explicate the sources of power of what he calls *potential partisans* and the targets of those partisans— those who have the authority to make decisions. In the chapter, we outline Gamson's conceptualization of the tools that potential partisans use to influence authorities. He labels them as constraints, inducements, and persuasion. The authorities, on the other hand, depending on the situation, use other tactics, such as persuasion, sanctions, and insulation. They also engage in strategies of co-optation and participation, which are intended to involve potential partisans in the decision-making process. On occasion, this is a devious device used to suppress dissent; at other times, it is a powerful tool for garnering the ideas and cooperation of potential partisans.

Chapter 4 in this volume addresses issues of **organizational decision making**—a subject of constant concern and consternation by organizational members in colleges and universities. We start the chapter with a simple but useful definition of decision making. It is the process commonly portrayed as occurring early in a problem-solving process—the sensing, exploration, and definition of problems and opportunities—as well as the generation, evaluation, and selection of solutions (Huber, 1986). An important distinction is made in the chapter between routine and nonroutine decision making, with a danger associated with selecting the inappropriate mode—for example, assuming that a problem is unique when it is not, or assuming that a problem is routine when it is novel. For reasons of presumed efficiency, organizations try to treat most problems as routine. Such tendencies, however, may be ineffective if the problem is not well understood or if the problem affects different areas of responsibility within the organization (e.g., academic affairs and the budget office). In these instances, decisions may be avoided out of fear that conflict will arise around different definitions of the problem or due to jurisdictional battles regarding who has the authority to make the decision.

Most complex decisions in organizations take place in group settings because individuals have bounded rationality, that is, they simply cannot gather all of the information needed to make an intelligent decision in the time available. A typical sequence in the process of decision making involves decision recognition, diagnosis, development of solutions, selection, screening, evaluation and choice, and authorization. We also consider a typology of decisions that is a function of the degree of agreement on goals and the means to achieve those goals. Hence, as Thompson and Tuden (1959) point out, there are four different modes of decision making in organizations: by computation, compromise, consensus, and inspiration. It is useful to understand the conditions that determine when each of these is likely to occur.

A major portion of the chapter is devoted to detailing the contingencies that managers should consider before deciding under what conditions decision-making authority should be shared with subordinates. Four possibilities are: (1) not at all (i.e., autocratically), (2) with full consultation, (3) with consultation, but with final decision by the chief executive, or (4) by complete delegation of authority to the group. The chapter concludes with a discussion of risk taking by decision-making groups and with the phenomenon of polarization, which pits group members against one another for avoidable reasons that are explained in the chapter.

In chapter 5, we turn from decision making at the organizational level to the subject of how and why individuals make different kinds of decisions in organizations. The focus is on what individuals bring to decision-making activities—that is, their predispositions, preferences, and styles. We are also concerned in this chapter with how people make decisions, in particular with the cognitive processes they go through in the course of deciding among alternative choices and the impact of emotion or affect on their thinking. In this chapter, we consider five prominent approaches in the research literature addressed to these issues: the garbage can process (Cohen, March, & Olsen, 1972), decisions as role playing (Mintzberg, Raisinghari, & Theoret, 1976), decisions as personality manifestations (Mitroff & Kilmann, 1976), decisions and information utilization (Driver, 2003), and decisions as a gamble (various authors).

According to Cohen et al. (1972), there are four independent streams that enter into decision making. These include the nature of the problem, possible solutions, participants who enter and leave the process, and choice opportunities. Cohen et al. describe how these four ingredients interact over time as problems and decision opportunities become separated from one another until conditions change (e.g., the problem goes away or a new leader arrives).

Three groups of managerial roles comprise the conceptual framework for Mintzberg's (1973) outline of decision making: interpersonal roles, informational roles, and decisional roles. Within these three groupings are 10 different roles (e.g., figurehead, leader, liaison, monitor), each of which is called for under different circumstances, which Mintzberg (and we) describe.

Information and its use is a fundamental ingredient of all organizational functioning and, quite obviously, enters critically into the decision-making process. Too much or too little information or the wrong kind of information can result in poor decision making and inefficiency in operations. Different organizational members have different needs for information and have limitations on the ways that they can use it, even if it is available. Driver (2003) suggests that there are four basic types of decision makers who operate more effectively in different types of information-rich or information-poor environments. These four decision-making types are created by juxtaposing two dimensions of information processing: (1) the amount of information used and (2) the number of solutions generated. They are labeled as the following: decisives, hierarchics, flexibles, and integrators, each of which is described in the text.

For Mitroff and Kilmann, decision making is a function of the personality dispositions of decision makers. Using Jung's theory of archetypes, Mitroff and Kilmann suggest that there are four different kinds of problem-solving styles. The styles are determined by two personality characteristics that every individual possesses in different strengths: (1) information accessing preferences and (2) information processing preferences. The combination of these two personality dimensions results in four distinctive styles of decision-making preferences that are described at length in the chapter.

Decisions are often made under varying degrees of uncertainty. The gambling metaphor (Goldstein & Weber, 1995) explores these conditions. There are three main categories of decision making with varying levels of risk associated with them: certainty, risk, and uncertainty. We consider in this chapter the factors that decision makers must take into account under these conditions.

In the next chapter, we shift from the individual to the organization and its relationship to the environment surrounding it. **Organizational learning** has attained critical importance for gaining a competitive advantage in the higher education marketplace. Learning organizations display high levels of both cultural and structural adaptation and can quickly accommodate new ways of thinking and organizing. Chapter 6 discusses cognitive conceptualizations of organizational learning, which rely on rational assessments of intentional experiments and trial-and-error occurrences. Huber (1996), for example, identifies five cognitive processes through which organizations learn: congenital learning, experiential learning, vicarious learning, grafting, and searching and scanning. Many of these approaches focus on learning from other organizations within a focal organization's sector. Colleges and universities, for example, may benchmark their practices in comparison to a set of peer institutions and, in turn, seek to adopt new ideas that have been successful elsewhere. Similarly, they may learn from failures of practice in comparable institutions or, indeed, from organizations out of their own field.

In contrast, cultural conceptualizations of organizational learning—based in the social constructionist paradigm—rely on developing a deeper understanding of core values and shared commitments among organizational members. Social constructionists suggest that organizational culture is the means through which organizations learn. Organizational learning in this framework entails the development and maintenance of language, artifacts, and routines that give meaning to work. This type of learning occurs through socialization processes that make organizational members more aware of the culture in which they work. In the higher education context, each campus is characterized by a collectively shaped *web of meaning,* which reflects the shared history of the college. As webs of meaning are further elaborated, new meanings are incorporated into the collective practices of the college. In this way, organizational cultures change and evolve over time. Organizational cultures, therefore, reflect prior learning and produce opportunities for new learning.

This chapter also examines postmodern perspectives on organizational learning, which draw attention toward the underlying chaos and disorganization that must be apprehended and accepted before learning can occur. Postmodernists claim that organizational life is too fragmented for any generalized insights to be derived as guidance for future action (Bloland, 1995). Hence, postmodernists claim that the organization as a whole cannot learn. Those in positions of power, however, may make claims about what they view to be the important lessons that all members of the organization must learn and incorporate into their practice (Foucault, 1976/1986). Organizational leaders may learn how to leverage the organizational system so that it maintains their status and power, and groups and individuals may learn how to gain a larger share of organizational resources through more skillful political maneuvering. But at the organizational level, there is no learning, only political games and efforts to resist or enforce compliance with organizational directives and policies. This view of learning, however, need not be nihilistic. Even if organizations cannot learn, postmodernists argue that individual organizational members can learn how to take more critical stances toward organizational practices and beliefs. These learning processes can engender an ongoing critique of the organization and destabilize any effort by an individual or group to institutionalize a particular insight as the correct or only way that the organization should think and act.

In chapter 7, the focus is on **organizational strategy**, a subject of considerable interest in the organizational theory literature as well as in higher education. Strategy is largely concerned with the alignment of the internal resources and goals of organizations so that they are congruent with the nature of the environment in which the organization is immersed. Strategy requires continuous scanning and assessment of the external environment and the subsequent use of this information to adapt internal processes accordingly. Organizations that are better able to adapt to their environments are said to have a competitive advantage over other organizations in the same field or industry (Day & Schoemaker, 2005; Porter, 1985). Strategic planning can involve the entire organization in aggressive learning so that it can change its posture and adapt its structures quickly and appropriately (Chaffee, 1985; Hatch, 1997).

While most practitioners and organizational theorists conceive of strategy as proactive and forward thinking, others conceive of it as a retrospective appraisal of an organization's actions. That is, since so many variables are involved in planning and implementing strategies, an organization's net or actual strategy can be known only after the fact—that is, after some time has passed and the organization's total stance can be appraised. In this chapter, we discuss this "emergent model," proposed by Mintzberg and Waters (1985).

In their strategic activities, organizations rely heavily on boundary spanners—personnel who link the organization to the external environment and provide critical information for planning purposes. Clearly, each boundary spanner makes an interpretation of the conditions identified as external to the organization and will attempt to make sense of that confusing and complex external world. Given the information resources to which they have access, boundary spanners can shape how other organizational members view the external environment, which in turn may yield organizational strategies that reflect a particular interpretation of that environment. Boundary spanners from subunits with more internal power can disproportionately influence how organizational decision makers view the environment. As noted earlier, there is some danger in this outcome (Bloland, 2005; Gordon & Grant, 2005; Grandy & Mills, 2004) because of the potential bias of those boundary spanners who actively or unintentionally distort both the organization and the environment.

Chapter 8 focuses on assessing the **effectiveness** of colleges and universities. This process is central to demonstrating institutional accountability, but the complexities of conceptualization and measurement make effectiveness a controversial topic in higher education circles. We delineate a large number of effectiveness models that emphasize concepts such as goals, benchmarking, internal processes, and congruence. The competing values model is one of the most comprehensive (Quinn & Rohrbaugh, 1983). This model takes into account the need to balance internal and external demands, and consider needs for flexibility as well as control.

Assessments of effectiveness can also be viewed as a social construction, which reflects the values and beliefs of those conducting the assessment. The social construction paradigm emphasizes the importance of perceptual measures rather than written records for demonstrating effectiveness. This is not to suggest that data are unimportant in the social constructionist interpretation of effectiveness. Instead, the social construction of data—that is, what the data mean to different people—affects how the organization creates its own interpretation of effectiveness. Postmodernists, however, raise concerns that dominant coalitions—either within the organization or imposed from the outside—control the criteria used to interpret data in assessments of organizational effectiveness. These criteria may marginalize the interests of less powerful groups or less prestigious institutions.

Processes associated with organizational learning, strategy formation, and the assessment of effectiveness may stimulate a desire for **change.** Emerging insights, new strategies, and discrepancies between desired and observed outcomes may motivate change agents within the organization to modify structures, policies, and practices, or even attempt to overhaul the core competencies and values of the organization. Chapter 9 examines the complexities and challenges associated with organization-wide change. We explore a planned change framework, which is guided by positivist assumptions regarding change as an intentional act that is driven by specific goals and plans.

Research on planned change examines the effects of different organizational designs and decision-making structures on desired organizational outcomes. Flexible, loosely coupled organizational designs, for example, stimulate individual and subunit innovation, but may make organization-wide changes more difficult to implement. In contrast, when structures are centralized, large-scale changes can be implemented from the top down, but the motivation and capacity for individual and department-level change becomes constrained.

In this chapter, we also discuss an emergent change framework, which is based on social constructionist assumptions that emphasize nonlinear and nonhierarchical forms of change. Social constructionists note that changes are occurring on an ongoing basis at every level of the organization. Changes emerge when organizational members respond to the day-to-day practical challenges of their work. These local adaptations do not deliberately seek to change the entire organization. Nevertheless, over time, their cumulative effects can reveal a fundamental shift in the direction of the organization.

Finally, chapter 10 examines a range of theories that suggest that different kinds of **leadership** are required for different organizational circumstances. We discuss two major approaches to understanding leadership: transactional and transformational. Transactional leaders identify what organizational members desire from their work environments and then attempt to provide those features, if performance warrants it. Their focus is on developing a reward system that motivates high-level performance. Transformational leaders, in contrast, encourage organizational members to transcend self-interest and focus on higher order collective goals. This form of leadership may transform followers into leaders and leaders into change agents.

Several leadership theories examine the characteristics of and relationships between leaders and followers. Contingency theories suggest that the characteristics of followers—such as their maturity and skill levels—must be taken into account in leader behavior. Similarly, path-goal theory argues that effective leaders are those who can assist workers in understanding how the achievement of organizational objectives can provide them with desirable rewards and satisfactions. In leader-member exchange theory, leaders and followers evolve through a series of interactions that results, if effective, in networks of collaboration between leaders and followers and among followers.

In addition to positivist theories that emphasize leader and follower characteristics and organizational contingencies, the chapter offers a social constructionist alternative that highlights the importance of organizational culture, images, and symbols. Within this conceptualization, leadership depends on the processes of sensemaking and reframing. Issues of leadership and power are also considered in this chapter from the vantage point of feminist theory, which notes that leadership constitutes a gendered relationship that may be characterized by the corrosive effects of patriarchy.

Our goal in this volume is to provide readers with a wide range of theories and concepts that they can apply in their own colleges and universities in order to understand and navigate dynamic systems. These theories can serve as lenses to the organizational world and promote new ways of seeing and new modes of relating. Application of organizational theories can strengthen the capacity of colleges and universities to navigate turbulent external conditions, as well as empower all organizational members to contribute to the academic, social, economic, moral, and civic aims of higher education. Our basic argument, reinforced in the following chapters, is that there is increasing research evidence that higher education organizations fulfill their aims more effectively when leaders reject excessive managerialism and no longer resign themselves to the notion that their fates are externally controlled. We offer a theory-based approach to leadership, which not only relies on extensive research but also taps into the capacities of each individual for growth, development, and insight; capacities that will be necessary in the future for higher education leaders to guide some of the most complex and consequential organizations in human history.

Summary

This introductory chapter to Volume II provided a brief recapitulation of the contents of Volume I and an overview of the central social science tenets that undergird the specific organizational theories used in the book to explain various phenomena in colleges and universities. The topics that were treated here included the meaning and uses of organizational theory in general. We also introduced the idea of paradigms and described the three that are used in this book: positivist, social constructionist, and postmodernist. Each makes important and different assumptions about the nature of reality in organizations, and each is used differently in different organizations. We pointed out that positivism is the most common paradigm used in higher education, but we attempted to show how its biases can be at least partially offset by the conjoint use of the other two paradigms. Social constructionism and postmodernism tend to be more attentive to the changing state of society, especially its disconnectedness in both human and economic spheres. With its epistemological underpinning, social constructionism argues for the need of more consensual decision making about what is real and important to higher education, while postmodernism cautions against the seduction of believing that there is more connection than truly exists.

FIGURE 1.2*
Organization of the Book by Chapters

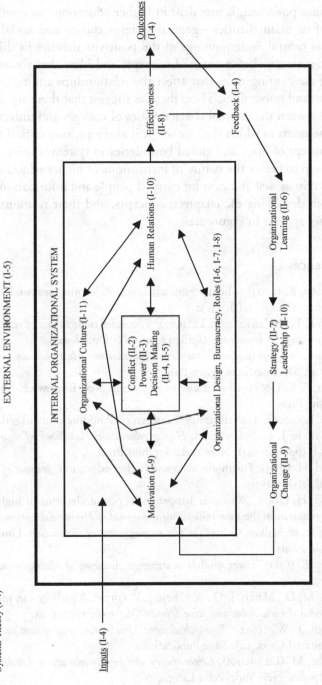

EXTERNAL ENVIRONMENT (I-5)

INTERNAL ORGANIZATIONAL SYSTEM

Systems Theory (I-4)

Inputs (I-4)

Outcomes (I-4)

Effectiveness (II-8)

Feedback (I-4)

Human Relations (I-10)

Organizational Culture (I-11)

Organizational Design, Bureaucracy, Roles (I-6, I-7, I-8)

Conflict (II-2)
Power (II-3)
Decision Making (II-4, II-5)

Motivation (I-9)

Organizational Change (II-9)

Organizational Learning (II-6)

Strategy (II-7)
Leadership (II-10)

*Volume and chapter numbers appear in parentheses. Arrows refer to interactions among components.

Since positivism is prevalent in higher education, we continually utilize two of its main theories—general systems theory and social systems theory—as central underpinnings of the positivist theories in this book. Both offer decision makers a range of concepts and ideas that are useful in recognizing the contingencies that affect the relationships among components of colleges and universities. These theories suggest that there are strong connections between the internal characteristics of colleges and universities and the environments in which they are set. It is also especially critical to understand the concept of open and closed boundaries in systems theory, since boundaries help to define the nature of institutions of higher education by providing screens as well as means for entry of people and information. A schematic diagram describing the chapters, concepts, and their relationships for both volumes appears in Figure 1.2.

References

Bensimon, E. (2004). The diversity scorecard: A learning approach to institutional change. *Change, 36*(1), 45–52.

Berger, P. L., & Luckmann, T. (1967). *The social construction of reality: A treatise in the sociology of knowledge.* Garden City, NY: Doubleday.

Bergquist, W. (1993). *The postmodern organization: Mastering the art of irreversible change.* San Francisco: Jossey-Bass.

Berrien, F. K. (1968). *General and social systems.* New Brunswick, NJ: Rutgers University Press.

Bess, J. L. (2006). Toward strategic ambiguity: Antidote to managerialism in governance. In J. C. Smart (Ed.), *Higher education: Handbook of theory and research* (XXI) (pp. 491–543). New York: Agathon Press.

Bloland, H. (1995). Postmodernism and higher education. *Journal of Higher Education, 66*(5), 521–559.

Bloland, H. (2005). Whatever happened to postmodernism in higher education?: No requiem in the new millennium. *Journal of Higher Education, 76*(2), 121–150.

Burns, T., & Stalker, G. (1961). *The management of innovation.* London: Tavistock Publications.

Chaffee, E. (1985). Three models of strategy. *Academy of Management Review, 10*(1), 89–98.

Cohen, M. D., March, J. G., & Olsen, J. P. (1972). A garbage can model of organizational choice. *Administrative Science Quarterly, 17*(1), 1–25.

Creswell, J. W. (1994). *Research design: Qualitative and quantitative approaches.* Thousand Oaks, CA: Sage Publications.

Cutright, M. (Ed.) (2001). *Chaos theory and higher education: Leadership, planning, and policy.* New York: Peter Lang.

Day, G., & Schoemaker, P. (2005). Scanning the periphery. *Harvard Business Review, 83*(11), 135–148.

Del Favero, M. (2003). Faculty-administrator relationships as integral to high-performing governance systems: New frameworks for study. *American Behavioral Scientist, 46*(7), 902–922.

Dickens, D. R., & Fontana, A. (1994). Postmodernism in the social sciences. In D. R. Dickens & A. Fontana (Eds.), *Postmodernism and social inquiry* (pp. 1–22). New York: Guilford Press.

Driver, M. (2003). Decision style and organizational behavior: Implications for academia. In J. L. Bess (Ed.), *College and university organization: Insights from the behavioral sciences* (pp. 149–168). Amherst, MA: I & I Occasional Press.

Foucault, M. (1986). Disciplinary power and subjection. In S. Lukes (Ed.), *Power* (pp. 229–242). New York: New York University Press. (Reprinted from M. Foucault, *Power/knowledge: Selected interviews and other writings, 1972–1977*, C. Gordon, Ed., 1976, New York: Random House)

Goldstein, W. M., & Weber, E. U. (1995). Content and discontent: Indications and implications of domain specificity in preferential decision making. *The Psychology of Learning and Motivation, 32*, 83–136.

Gordon, R., & Grant, D. (2005). Knowledge management or management of knowledge? Why people interested in knowledge management need to consider Foucault and the construct of power. *TAMARA: Journal of Critical Postmodern Organization Science, 3*(2), 27–38.

Grandy, G., & Mills, A. (2004). Strategy as simulacra? A radical reflexive look at the discipline and practice of strategy. *Journal of Management Studies, 41*(7), 1153–1170.

Hackman, J. R., & Oldham, G. R. (1980). *Work redesign.* Reading, MA: Addison-Wesley.

Hatch, M. (1997). *Organization theory: Modern, symbolic, and postmodern perspectives.* New York: Oxford University Press.

Hills, R. J. (1968). *Toward a science of organization.* Eugene, OR: Center for the Advanced Study of Educational Administration, University of Oregon.

Hirschhorn, L. (1997). *Reworking authority: Leading and following in a postmodern organization.* Cambridge, MA: MIT Press.

Huber, G. (1996). Organizational learning: The contributing processes and the literatures. In M. Cohen & L. Sproull (Eds.), *Organizational learning* (pp. 124–143). Thousand Oaks, CA: Sage.

Huber, O. (1986). Decision making as a problem solving process. In B. Brehmer, H. Jungermann, P. Louvens, & G. Sevon (Eds.), *New directions in research on decision making* (pp. 108–138). New York: Elsevier.

Kaplan, A. (1964). *The conduct of inquiry: Methodology for behavioral science.* San Francisco: Chandler Publishing.

Kerlinger, F. N. (1979). *Behavioral research: A conceptual approach.* New York: Holt, Rinehart & Winston.

Kezar, A. (2000). Pluralistic leadership: Incorporating diverse voices. *Journal of Higher Education 71*(6), 722–743.

Kezar, A., Carducci, R., & Contreras-McGavin, M. (2006). *Rethinking the "L" word in higher education: The revolution of research on leadership*. San Francisco: Jossey-Bass.

Lawrence, P., & Lorsch, J. (1967). *Organization and environment: Managing differentiation and integration*. Boston: Harvard Business School Press.

Lewin, K. (1938). *The conceptual representation and measurement of psychological forces*. Durham, NC: Duke University Press.

Lewis, M., & Grimes, A. (1999). Metatriangulation: Building theory from multiple paradigms. *Academy of Management Review, 24*(4), 672–690.

Mintzberg, H. (1973). *The nature of managerial work*. New York: Harper & Row.

Mintzberg, H., Raisinghari, D., & Theoret, A. (1976). The structure of "unstructured" decision processes. *Administrative Science Quarterly, 21*(2), 246–275.

Mintzberg, H., & Waters, J. A. (1985). Of strategies, deliberate and emergent. *Strategic Management Journal, 6*(3), 257–272.

Mitroff, I., & Kilmann, R. (1976). On organizational stories: An approach to the design and analysis of organizations through myths and stories. In R. H. Kilmann, L. R. Pondy, & D. P. Slevin (Eds.), *The management of organization design*. Dordrecht, Holland: North Holland.

Nadler, D. A., & Tushman, M. L. (1977). A diagnostic model for organizational behavior. In J. R. Hackman, E. E. Lawler III, & L. W. Porter (Eds.), *Perspectives on behavior in organizations* (pp. 85–98). New York: McGraw-Hill.

Neumann, A. (1995). On the making of hard times and good times: The social construction of resource stress. *Journal of Higher Education, 66*(1), 3–31.

Porter, M. E. (1985). *Competitive advantage: Creating and sustaining superior performance*. New York: Free Press.

Quinn, R. E., & Rohrbaugh, J. (1983). A spatial model of effectiveness criteria: Toward a competing values approach to organizational analysis. *Management Science, 29*, 363–367.

Reynolds, P. D. (1971). *A primer in theory construction*. Indianapolis, IN: Bobbs-Merrill Company.

Thompson, J. D. (1967). *Organizations in action*. New York: McGraw-Hill.

Thompson, J. D., & Tuden, A. (1959). *Comparative studies in administration*. Pittsburgh, PA: University of Pittsburgh Press.

Weick, K. E. (2001). *Making sense of the organization*. Malden, MA: Blackwell Publishers.

2

CONFLICT IN ORGANIZATIONS

CONTENTS

Preview	488
Case Context	489
Introduction	491
Open and Closed Systems	493
History of the Development of Conflict Theory	498
Conflict as Structure	501
Conflict as Process	503
Social Constructionist Perspectives on Conflict	522
Postmodern Perspectives on Conflict	524
Gender Issues in Conflict Management	526
Summary	527
Review Questions	527
Case Discussion Questions	529
References	530

The authors are most grateful for the critical comments on an early draft of this chapter by Christopher Morphew, University of Georgia. The final version, of course, is our own and may or may not reflect the perspective of the reviewer.

Preview

- Conflict can have both positive and negative connotations and consequences.
- How conflict is managed is crucial to the effectiveness and efficiency of the organization.
- There are numerous kinds of conflict within and across larger organizational and subunit borders.
- Typically, conflict is the result of a breakdown in the standard mechanisms of decision making.
- When organizations are seen as open systems, there needs to be a match or fit of the internal conditions to those outside. Lack of fit generates conflict.
- The most prominent causes of conflict are: a lag in perception of needs for change, lack of internal fit and/or lack of internal-external fit, disagreements about the ways that perceived differences should be resolved, and persistent efforts to suboptimize goals.
- For purposes of analysis and leadership intervention, it is useful to divide conflict into two domains: conflict as a process, and conflict as a structure.
- Understanding conflict as an unfolding, dynamic process with recognizable stages permits propitious and effective intervention. The stages include frustration, conceptualization, intervention, behavior and analysis of reactions, and outcomes.
- Considering conflict as a structure permits the identification of organizational design features that interfere with timely and effective decision making.
- Many conflict outcomes depend on the orientations of the parties toward conflict resolution, particularly the strength of their desires to satisfy their own versus their opponent's needs, as well as their stake in the outcome. A range of these orientations includes: competition, accommodation, compromise, collaboration, and avoidance.
- Conflict that is most harmful to organizations is latent—conflict that simmers below the surface of daily organizational behavior, yet interferes significantly with organizational performance.
- Social constructionists locate the source of conflict in multiple constructions of reality within the organization.
- Postmodernists note that rational arguments used to justify certain resolutions of conflict may be biased in favor of those who seek to preserve the status quo. This perspective highlights the need to disrupt conflict management practices that reinforce power and status differences.

———————————— **CASE CONTEXT** ————————————

Conflict Over Articulation Agreements at Pacific Shores Community College

Pacific Shores Community College (PSCC) had an active Transfer Advising Office, which worked with faculty and admissions staff at 4-year institutions to develop articulation agreements for nearly every major. The maintenance of dozens of agreements with both public and private institutions, however, was too much for the small transfer office to address. Articulation agreements needed to be updated continually, but staff time in the office needed to be devoted primarily to providing transfer counseling services to students. Over time, administrators at PSCC received complaints from students who transferred and found that not all of their credits were accepted by the receiving institution. These students discovered that they had transferred to another institution where the articulation agreement was no longer current in their major.

In response to this problem, PSCC hired a new dean for curriculum, Lois Van Cleve, who would have as part of her responsibilities oversight for articulation agreements. However, staff in the transfer office, including Transfer Director Don McCay, continued to view articulation agreements as their prerogative. They argued that they had the most direct contact with the 4-year sector, and they persisted in negotiating agreements without including the new dean in the process. The tension between the dean and the transfer office erupted into open conflict when Transfer Director McCay negotiated a controversial articulation agreement with a nearby private university.

"I will not sign that agreement," declared Dean Van Cleve after reviewing a proposed criminal justice articulation agreement with Royalston University. "You had no right to negotiate this agreement with Royalston, and I don't want you speaking with them on behalf of the college."

"Quite frankly, I am shocked by your reaction," replied Transfer Director McCay. "My office has been developing articulation agreements for decades, long before you were hired. My transfer counselors are in regular communication with admissions officers at Royalston, so we have a real strong sense of what they want on the 4-year side of things. And our sociology faculty have been working with my office and with Royalston faculty to put all of this together."

"Well, the chair of sociology has been in touch with me," Dean Van Cleve responded. "And he is not in favor of this. It would require a complete overhaul of the curriculum to get it aligned with Royalston's program, and there is no way that I am going to let this go through. Besides, we have a perfectly good articulation agreement with State University, so there is no need to work with Royalston."

"The curricular adjustments would be minor," Transfer Director McCay replied. "And Royalston would give our students opportunities that State University simply cannot provide. Our faculty have great relationships with the faculty at Royalston. This could be a win-win for both institutions."

"Well, the department chair wants nothing to do with this, and neither do I," indicated the dean.

"Yeah, that makes perfect sense, since you appointed that chair. It is no wonder that you two think alike," the transfer director curtly replied.

"OK, this conversation is over," noted the dean, who left the conference room and immediately went to see the vice president for academic affairs. The transfer director returned to his office and immediately composed an e-mail to the vice president, blasting the dean for her behavior.

"I can't deal with that hothead," Dean Van Cleve noted, referring to the transfer director. "He had no right to go over my head with this. He is impossible to deal with, and you have got to do something about him."

"Let's sort this out," the vice president replied. "From what I can gather, this seems to be more than a personality clash. I need some time to gather some information about this. Let's meet again later this week, along with folks from the transfer office."

"I refuse to meet with him or his staff," Dean Van Cleve replied.

"Well, that's how we're going to handle it," the vice president explained. "I am not dealing with this behind people's backs. That's how this whole thing got started in the first place."

After Dean Van Cleve left the office, the vice president called Transfer Director McCay. "I read your e-mail. This agreement with Royalston sounds like a good idea. Our criminal justice enrollments would certainly support this, and the connection to Royalston would probably attract even more students to the program. But Dean Van Cleve has a point. You completely cut her out of the loop on this."

"You know that we have been doing things this way for years," Transfer Director McCay replied. "Then you hired her [the dean] last year, and she puts up every road block she can. And then she appoints department chairs who see it her way. She just wants to order people around, and that's not right."

"Hold on, Don, hold on," the vice president replied. "You're making some pretty strong allegations, here, and it's not going to do anyone any good just to blame one person for this problem. Let me get on the phone with the department chair in sociology and get his take on things."

"He's an idiot," Transfer Director McCay replied. "I have been working with the faculty over there who really do the work, the faculty who are really entrepreneurial and student focused, the faculty who want to try new things for their program."

"I promise that I will talk with them, too," the vice president explained. "But the department chair is not an idiot. Remember it is the dean *and* the vice president who appoint chairs. Don, you have to respect the people I appoint to these positions."

After talking with the department chair and faculty in sociology, the vice president met with the dean and the transfer director. "I talked with the sociology chair, and he was not aware of the details of what you were working on with Royalston. As it turns out, the curricular changes would be less than he assumed, and he was not aware that Royalston was willing to do a joint marketing campaign with us to promote the program. But he is still worried that one of the course changes would interfere with the articulation agreement that we already have with State University."

"Well, I will have one of my staff go back to Royalston, and see if they can compromise on that one course," Transfer Director McCay replied.

"No," the vice president continued. "From now on, all of these decisions will be made by a new transfer and articulation team that will be chaired by Dean Van Cleve and composed of staff from the transfer office and a group of department chairs. This will give us a clear communication path between the people who work with the 4-year colleges and the people with responsibility for developing the curriculum."

"And Don, I want to apologize for my initial reaction to the agreement," explained Dean Van Cleve. "I should have sought out more information before jumping to conclusions. This really looks like a good thing for our students. And I promise to respect the work of your staff."

Transfer Director McCay replied, "And I understand why you and the department chairs need to be informed about what's going on out there. If we're not all on the same page, we could end up making a whole bunch of articulation agreements that we can't sustain, and that wouldn't be good for the students either."

"Well, let's schedule the first meeting for the team," Dean Van Cleve replied. "What else do you have for the agenda?"

Introduction

Conflict is one of the most dynamic subjects in organizational theory. Disagreements and disputes between individuals, groups, and organizations have long intrigued observers of the human condition.

Conflict calls up images of heroism, underdogs, underhandedness, victory, and defeat. It is important that we understand this topic in the higher education setting, because there are some sources of conflict in college and university organizations that can and should be generated because they are functional, while other kinds need to be avoided. Some kinds of manifested conflict are good, some bad, some moments of intervention are propitious, some awkward, and some end products of conflict should be recognized and others ignored.

Conflict evokes positive or negative connotations and results in different consequences based partly on whether institutions are manifested as bureaucratic organizations or political entities. If colleges and universities are conceived primarily as political entities, then we should not be surprised to find conflict among the constituents on a campus, since by definition, politics involves entities with competing interests. Such conflict can thus be viewed as expected—a typical occurrence in the everyday life of the organization. If, on the other hand, colleges and universities are addressed primarily as bureaucratic organizations, then conflict would seem to reflect a failure on the part of the leadership to unify the members under a consensus-based, rational set of prerequisites—for example, agreement on educational goals and the means to achieve them. What we find typically in higher education, however, is an ambiguous combination of political and bureaucratic organization (Barsky, 2002). Hence, conflict is viewed by some constituents as a reflection of failed leadership and by others as a normal concomitant of decision making.

Conflict can be defined as a condition that is perceived to need remediation in order to correct one or more misfits in the system (Losey, 1994). Internally, this might be an individual-task misfit or a task-structure misfit (Brown, 1979). As one example, the departmental structure of most colleges and universities may not fit the tasks associated with interdisciplinary research and hence serve as a source of conflict between department chairs and directors of interdisciplinary research centers regarding the allocation of financial and staff resources. In addition to internal misfit, conflict may arise due to incongruence between the internal components of an organization and external elements. Outmoded processes for assessing student learning outcomes, for example, may generate a misfit between the internal structure of a public college and external expectations communicated by a state board of higher education.

Misfits between and among components of organizations and misfits across organizational boundaries usually result in a person or group perceiving a situation that prevents an unequivocal decision from being made within the time frame required. Organizational members cognitively apprehend and comprehend that there is a problem, the solution for which is not readily apparent from existing bureaucratic or other known organizational problem solving processes (de Dreu & Van de Vliert, 1997; March & Simon, 1958).

Conflict itself often consumes time and energy and may be costly. Patient and appropriate effort at conflict management, however, often has long-term payoffs (Wall & Callister, 1995). In contrast, arbitrary decisions that resolve short-term conflicts may be deleterious to the culture, climate, and motivational states of organizational members.

We begin this chapter with a systems perspective, taking first the organization as the system and looking at its internal conflicts, then, considering the individual as a system, determining his or her conflicts. At both the organizational and individual levels, we consider conflict in terms of structure and process, and conceptualize conflict as both a cognitive and affective (emotional) phenomenon.

Open and Closed Systems

Two contrasting views of conflict reflect some underlying assumptions about whether organizations are open or closed systems.

1. *The closed system metaphor.* In a closed system, internal organizational coordination and efficiency are impaired by conflict. Different subunits of the organization can be compared to different parts of a machine. To work properly, the parts must be coordinated so that they mesh efficiently. Even if each of the individual parts (each subsystem) is working properly, when the parts are not well connected with each other the machine as a whole will not operate efficiently. Using this metaphor, conflict is defined as a misfit where the interdependence among elements in the system is malfunctioning. When conflict occurs, then, it is symptomatic of the failure of some parts of the system to be synchronous with the others. Conflict under this model is usually characterized as dysfunctional and to be avoided, if possible (Amason, 1996).

2. *The open system metaphor.* This approach assumes some permeability in the boundaries of an organization and suggests that conditions in the external environment affect the types of conflict that emerge within organizations. Under conditions of external stability—for example, steady annual budgets—most internal conflicts are power based, as different constituents strive to improve their positions

within a framework of a fixed amount of inputs from the environment. A dean or director with a no-increase budget for the succeeding year must adjudicate among competing needs and demands for limited funds. Thus, when the environment is simple and stable, a struggle for internal power takes precedence. In such a case, conflict can be considered as arising over issues of control of key resources available inside the organization (Hickson, Hinings, Lee, Schneck, & Pennings, 1971; Hinings, Hickson, Pennings, & Schneck, 1974).

Under conditions of a dynamic external environment, on the other hand, the system must respond to changing outside stimuli, and there is a need to match or fit the internal parts to new external circumstances. When the external environment changes or when leaders project a need to change the organization-environment relationship (e.g., finding a new market niche or expanding services to a new geographical area), the organization/environment match will be temporarily out of alignment. To restore fit with the environment, different components of the organization will change their relationships to external conditions as well as to each other. The result, however, will be some degree of internal tension—some conflict—about how to proceed. For example, if a new university is created across the river from an old one, the latter may have to abandon some practices and policies that were efficient when the university did not have such competition. Decisions about which practices and policies to abandon are likely to generate conflict, especially as those with vested interests in the status quo seek to maintain their programs. Under these conditions, leaders are in a position to reverse the naturally occurring entropic forces that may have led to organizational decline and allocate new funds to departments whose promise toward achieving the organization's goals is highest.

In the open system metaphor, conflict is not, by definition, bad; it is expected, even inevitable. It can even be healthy if adaptations can be made expeditiously. The open systems argument, then, is that such temporary imbalances are necessary for the organization to continue to develop.

Unit of Analysis

It is important to note that regardless of the unit in which conflict takes place, the conceptual nature of the conflict—either its structure or its process—is the same (Hermann, 2004; Sandole, 1987, 1993). Systems theory applies equally both to the system as a whole and to all the components of a larger system. We can, therefore, look at conflict in all levels of these systems in two ways: (1) in terms of the structural characteristics that influence it and result from it and (2) as a sequence of events that unfolds in reasonably predictable stages (Allison, 1971; Janis, 1989). The process of managing conflict, however, is likely to differ in each case depending on the setting in which the conflict originates (Costantino & Merchant, 1996). As Table 2.1 reveals, there are five settings for conflict in any organizational system (Hellriegel, Slocum & Woodman, 1995).

When the individual is the unit of analysis, conflict will be either intrapersonal or interpersonal. **Intrapersonal conflict** occurs *within* an individual and is characterized by cognitive and/or affective dimensions. A decision about whether to report a colleague's inappropriate financial practices, for example, may generate an intrapersonal conflict between a value for justice and accountability and a value for loyalty and friendship toward the colleague. **Interpersonal conflict**, in contrast, takes place in a social context *between* individuals—for example, conflicts with others in the individual's workplace.

When the organization is the unit of analysis, conflict can be categorized as intragroup, intraorganizational, or interorganizational. Rahim (2001) notes that **intragroup conflict** "refers to the incompatibility, incongruence, or disagreement among the members of a group or its subgroups regarding goals, functions, or activities of the group" (p. 143). Some examples include conflict among coaches in an athletics department, conflict among cardiology faculty in a university hospital, and conflict among students who are members of an undergraduate student senate. The conflict is centered within the group and may have few consequences for those who are not members of that group, although such conflicts could have a detrimental impact on

TABLE 2.1
Conflict Settings in Organizations

Focal System	Kind of Conflict	Description
Person	Intrapersonal	Values issues, cognitive dissonance, psychic disorders
People in a Department	Interpersonal	Between individuals in a dyadic relationship
Group	Intragroup	Within a group
Organization	Intraorganizational	Between groups; between individuals in different groups
Multiple Organizations	Interorganizational	Between different organizations

overall organizational effectiveness if they are not managed well. **Intraorganizational conflict,** in contrast, involves disagreements between (rather than within) organizational subsystems. Cardiology faculty may disagree with pediatrics faculty regarding priorities for ordering new medical equipment. In this case, the conflict involves multiple departments or units of the organization. Colleges and universities often have formal venues for addressing intraorganizational conflict. Budget committees, for example, can adjudicate conflicting claims for resources. In other instances, however, intraorganizational conflict remains unregulated—sometimes with damaging consequences. Finally, **interorganizational conflict** is manifest in relationships between organizations. A group of colleges may be in competition for the same types of resources—students, research grants, prestige—and interactions between those colleges could erupt into open conflict. In the public higher education sector, state coordinating boards were created, in large part, to minimize conflict between institutions. Coordinating boards seek to ensure that public colleges and universities are not competing with each other for limited resources. Interorganizational conflict may also occur between higher education institutions and other types of organizations. A university may encounter conflict with neighborhood associations and community organizations over the location of a new residence hall or research facility.

Sources of Conflict

Within open systems, there are four primary organizational sources of conflict (Pneuman & Bruehl, 1982):

1. The lag in the organization as a whole in perceiving needed changes in the direction of the organization. Here, the feedback loop in the system is remiss.
2. Lack of internal fit among the components of the organization and/ or lack of internal-external balance (Darkenwald, 1971). External conditions do not uniformly affect internal units, especially when the organization is highly differentiated and decentralized. Therefore, some units may perceive a need for organizational change, while others see no reason to deviate from the current strategy.
3. Disagreements about the ways that differences should be resolved. Even after a need for change has been identified, organizational members may dispute how the change should be implemented.
4. Suboptimization. Residual or persistent power struggles within the organization focus on maximizing current subunit goals at the expense of overall organizational objectives.

We can understand conflict in colleges and universities as a result of inattention to, misperception of, or disagreements about organizational fit with the external environment and/or internal organizational unit interactions. These result in a perception of inadequacy of the standard decision-making apparatus to allow action alternatives to be chosen propitiously.

Sources of organizational conflict can also be traced to the individuals within the organization. Druckman (1993) suggests that there are three main sources of conflict that are manifested by individuals in organizations: (1) **conflict of interest**—a discrepancy between individuals regarding preferred outcomes, (2) **conflict of understanding**—interpersonal disagreements about the best way to accomplish a shared goal, and (3) **conflict in ideology**—differences in the values held by the disputants.

Is Conflict Inevitable?

Goals and objectives of higher education are often assumed to be held in common by all members of the college or university. Of course, they are not, and conflicts thought to be based on divergence of interests (e.g., should sociology or psychology get a new faculty position) or different understandings may, in fact, reflect conflicts over basic values. Given the frequency of conflicts of interest, understanding, and ideology, it is appropriate to ask whether conflict is inevitable in higher education organizations. Conflict is inevitable if we assume the inevitability of variety in organizational members' backgrounds and values and differences of opinion about goals and means to accomplish them. Conflict can be useful when individuals with diverse perspectives are engaged creatively in decision-making processes. In contrast, homogenization of individuals at the departmental level may result in less intradepartmental conflict, but perhaps more interdepartmental conflict if the set of departments is heterogeneous. If the whole organization is homogeneous, there may be less interdepartmental conflict, but there may also be less vitality and less innovation. Recruitment of new organizational members too often addresses the need for departmental comity, without recognizing the equally important need for variety of opinion and perspective.

Latent Versus Manifest Conflict

Many conflicts in higher education are latent. They remain dormant, hidden from view. Members of higher education organizations like to believe that they are above conflict and politics, and that they are governed by **rationality**—that is, the belief that good-willed people can reason together and find commonly accepted solutions. This is one explanation why manifested, open conflict may feel so uncomfortable and why it is often avoided in colleges and universities.

Latent conflict is sometimes called the "defective pressure cooker" syndrome. If conflict is left unresolved and allowed to percolate, largely unrecognized, pressures build up that get in the way of functional activity. Such was the practice in higher education throughout much of the 19th and early 20th centuries. As Graff (1998) notes, paraphrasing Rudolph (1977), "the modern bureaucratic university typically dealt with conflicts 'by walking away' from the choices over which college authorities had agonized throughout the century" (p. 16). Structural differentiation into relatively autonomous academic departments had the effect of creating separate domains of influence that pre-empted many disputes from arising. These structural barriers, however, are now being regularly breeched as research (and to some extent, teaching) has demanded more integration of formerly separated domains. In addition, resource constraints and pressures for accountability may preclude departments from going their own way and instead subject their decisions to institution-wide scrutiny through budget hearings and academic program evaluations. Under these circumstances, walking away from conflict may no longer be a viable option.

Conflict avoidance, in fact, may damage the overall effectiveness of colleges and universities. Indeed, Simmel (1955) points out that conflict "may exert a quieting influence, produce a feeling of virtual power, and thus save relationships whose continuation often puzzles the observers. In such cases, opposition is an element in the relation itself; it is intrinsically interwoven with the other reasons for the relation's existence" (p. 19). Thus, conceivably, the occasionally adversarial relationship between faculty and administrators could provide a stabilizing social function by making their interactions more predictable. When disagreements emerge, faculty and administrators use well-known scripts and tactics for airing their disputes (e.g., faculty referring to academic freedom or administrators arguing for more accountability); each side can predict fairly accurately how the other will respond, thus stabilizing the relationship between them.

Research indicates that a moderate level of conflict results in more positive organizational outcomes (Brown, 1986). Less favorable outcomes are associated with both lower and higher conflict intensities (see Figure 2.1). The major organizational challenge is how to structure interunit and interpersonal exchanges that allow conflict to be expressed in sufficient strength, but permit it to be translated into more dispassionate discussions of the causes of the conflict. This type of conflict management, however, requires time and patience.

History of the Development of Conflict Theory

Historically, three main conceptualizations have guided studies of organizational conflict and its management: traditional, behavioral, and interactionist

FIGURE 2.1
Optimum Levels of Conflict

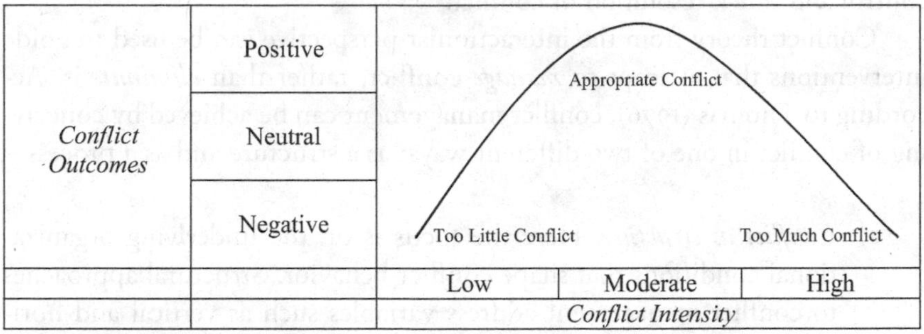

Conflict Outcomes	Positive	Appropriate Conflict
	Neutral	
	Negative	Too Little Conflict Too Much Conflict
		Low	Moderate	High
		Conflict Intensity		

Adapted from Brown (1986).

(Robbins, 1974). In the first era, roughly from the late 19th century through the middle 1940s (though some such thinking persists today), the belief was that all conflict is destructive and hence must be eliminated from all organizations. The second philosophy, behavioral, which was prevalent from the mid-1940s to the present time, holds that conflict must be accepted as inevitable, but it is not necessarily bad. It may, in fact, facilitate the achievement of some important organizational goals (Bennis, Benne, & Chin, 1969).

Robbins (1974) notes, however, that organizational leaders who have applied this second philosophy have directed their efforts toward *resolving* organizational conflicts. The philosophy thus has the flavor of rationalizing the positive value of conflict in organizations while continuing to seek its elimination. That is, the underlying assumption is that conflict is dysfunctional.

The third philosophy, the interactionist, has achieved prominence in more recent years. Its underlying assumption is that conflict is inevitable and potentially useful, and it takes the logical next step of recommending the *stimulation* of appropriate conflicts while seeking to prevent or manage others (Amason & Schweiger, 1994; Jehn, 1994; Jehn, Northcraft, & Neal, 1999; Tjosvold, 1991). The interactionist approach suggests that some conflicts are beneficial and hence can be creatively encouraged, while other, less functional conflicts can be handled through prevention, resolution, and suppression.

The newer, interactionist ways of thinking actually reflect much older ideas about conflict, which were first advanced by Mary Parker Follett (1924). She argued that conflict could facilitate socially valuable expressions of difference, which she viewed as essential to a healthy democracy. Follett also applied this principle to conflict in organizations, and her views became influential among business leaders in the United States and Great Britain.

Following her death in 1933, however, Follett's ideas about organizational management were overshadowed by approaches that emphasized the tight control and quick resolution of conflict.

Conflict theory from the interactionist perspective can be used to guide interventions that attempt to *manage* conflict, rather than *eliminate* it. According to Thomas (1976), conflict management can be achieved by conceiving of conflict in one of two different ways: as a structure and as a process.

1. *Conflict as structure.* Here the focus is on the underlying organizational conditions that shape conflict behavior. Structural approaches to conflict management address variables such as vertical and horizontal coordination, power, authority, and organizational climate—as well as the characteristics of the parties in conflict. Organizational analysts examine the structures that give rise to conflict, as well as the structures through which conflict is adjudicated. One example of structural conflict is the tension over policy and authority among administration, faculty, and trustees (Birnbaum, 1988; Del Favero, 2003; McGee, 1971). Shared governance entails decision-making participation among these three groups, but the degree of authority for each group is often unclear and may be in dispute. Thus, the structure of shared governance generates some degree of conflict.

2. *Conflict as a process.* Here, analysts seek to address problems in decision making through an observation of the sequence of events that unfold in a conflict. In general, conflict can be analyzed as a dynamic process that comprises different phases or stages of development. This approach is useful for understanding *when* and *how* to intervene in a conflict episode. (For a detailed description of conflict as a process in a higher education setting, see Bartos & Wehr, 2002; Coffman, 2005; and Sturnick, 1998.)

    Structure and process are not completely separate and distinct modes for understanding conflict. They are related in important ways. For example, as the conflict process unfolds, structural conflict varies. Further, both of these approaches to conflict analysis—as a process and as a structure—must be understood from two perspectives representing the major modes by which individuals experience organizational stimuli: *cognitively* (i.e., through the play of ideas) and *affectively* (i.e., through feelings; see Guetzkow & Gyr, 1954). More specifically, each of these modes is defined as follows:

    a. *Cognitive conflict*—in which ideas or thoughts within or between individuals are thought to be incompatible (Hellriegel et al.,

1995). For example, one person believes the other is simply wrong in holding that a particular option is a reasonable goal for the organization.

b. *Affective conflict*—when feelings or emotions within or between individuals are unable to coexist (Hellriegel et al., 1995). When people dislike each other and have difficulty working together, affective conflict is likely to occur.

Conflict as Structure

By considering conflict as structure, we point to organizational design features that give rise to difficulties experienced by organizational members to make decisions effectively (Collins, 1975). A number of structural conditions can cause decision-making mechanisms to break down. These types of conflict can occur, cognitively or affectively, at multiple system levels. We examine three kinds of structural conflict in greater detail: goal conflicts, means conflicts, and procedural conflicts.

1. *Goal conflicts* occur when the preferred objectives of organizational members are different and appear to be incompatible or irreconcilable. These kinds of conflicts can occur among individuals or subunits in the organization. To illustrate goal conflict at different system levels, here are two examples (Steers, 1991).

    a. *Intrapersonal goal conflict*—this conflict occurs when it appears to an individual that it is impossible to achieve two (or more) goals because they seem to be incompatible. Moreover, his or her mechanism for reconciling the conflict is apparently inadequate. The psychic dilemma takes the following three forms:

        i. **Approach-approach conflict**—where the individual feels a necessity to choose among two or more alternatives, both of which have positive valences.

        ii. **Approach-avoidance conflict**—where the individual is required to decide among alternatives that can have both positive and negative valence.

        iii. **Avoidance-avoidance conflict**—the perception by the individual that he/she must choose among two or more alternatives with negative valence.

    b. *Interpersonal/intergroup conflict*—this conflict emerges from the incompatibility of goals between or among two or more people. For example, two individuals may have mutually exclusive goals.

Or two departments may have apparently incompatible educational objectives—for example, faculty who argue that the curriculum should emphasize the development of skilled technicians versus another group of faculty who focus on producing morally educated persons.

It should be noted that what appears to be mutually exclusive incompatibility may not actually be so. A college, for example, could educate skilled technicians who are morally and ethically grounded. Incompatibility of goals, therefore, may be a social construction among individuals, rather than an objective state of affairs. In this instance, more objective data and information are unlikely to address the conflict (Van Slyke, 1999). Instead, the conflicting parties would need time to communicate, develop trust, and identify shared commitments that could lead to the identification of compatible goals. Faculty who once viewed technical education and moral development as competing curricular goals could reconstruct their conceptualizations and identify modes for promoting both objectives; for example, a community-based, service-learning course that enhances both technical skills and moral reasoning.

2. *Means conflicts* are differences with respect to the methods for achieving goals. These differences could revolve, for example, around questions of which recruitment methods should be used to attract more students, how to set up a curriculum, what pedagogy to use, or what kinds of organizational designs are best.

3. *Procedural conflicts* emerge when the resolution procedures preferred by the interacting parties differ from one another. For example, two faculty members may recognize that they differ both about the goals of an academic program and about the means for achieving goals. In addition, they do not agree on a procedure for resolving their differences—for example, appealing to the department chair, putting the issue to a vote of the faculty, or trying to find a compromise position.

This framework constitutes a useful diagnostic to analyze conflict situations because the three types of conflict can take place in various settings and at various points in the conflict cycle. The three types of conflict can also vary in their levels of intensity, pervasiveness, and duration (Mintzberg, 1983). This variability of conflict can be characterized in terms of:

- *Intensity*: intense to moderate
- *Pervasiveness*: pervasive to confined
- *Duration*: brief (transient) to enduring (stable)

A union protest, for example, may be intense, pervasive, and brief, if it brings the parties back to the bargaining table. An ongoing contract negotiation, however, may be characterized by conflict that is moderate (lengthy discussion precludes the maintenance of high intensity conflict), confined (limited to those responsible for negotiating the contract), and enduring (if the parties engage in tactics to delay the process).

Conflicts related to goals, means, and procedures can arise due to various structural design characteristics. A few of the structural sources of conflict that might be found in institutions of higher education include the following:

1. Differentiation—the division of labor and suboptimization
2. Interdependence—reliance on other units
3. Lack of common performance standards
4. Scarce resources—competition for limited resources
5. Uncertainty—technological ambiguity
6. Jurisdictional ambiguities and overlaps
7. Power distribution—improper use of authority
8. Communication problems
9. Unequal rewards for achievements and status

Division of labor and interdependence are purely structural sources of conflict, but they also significantly shape the stages of the conflict process. Structural differentiation, for example, may generate competition among units for scarce resources. In this case, structural conflict provides an opportunity for conflicting units to exercise power and attempt to influence the course and outcomes of conflict. Some units within the organization possess more power than others, but the amount of power is often ambiguous. Therefore, units test their relative power positions as the conflict process unfolds. In this way, the structure of the organization shapes conflict as a process.

Conflict as Process

By understanding the unfolding of conflict as a *process* we can see how and why the decision-making apparatus of an organization breaks down and what kinds of conflict can occur as a result. Equally important, we can make decisions about what junctures (times and situations) are best suited for mediation and conflict management.

Conflict in organizations occurs episodically. That is, it takes place over time with distinctive phases or stages. Typically (though not inevitably), each stage leads to an escalation to the next, more serious stage. Further, different kinds of conflict assume more or less salience as the organization as a whole moves through different phases of development. A university may experience *goal conflict* during a period of expansion (e.g., conflicting priorities for using new resources), but *means conflict* during a recessionary stage (e.g., disagreements about how to pursue the same goals with fewer resources).

To manage conflict effectively, it is important for organizational members to understand the stages in a conflict episode and the reasons for escalation from one stage to another. The following discussion of conflict process stages is a modification of the work of Kenneth Thomas (1976). (See also McCaffery, 2004. Earlier theorists are Pondy, 1967; Walton & Dutton 1969; and Deutsch, 1973. The stages are also related to conceptualizations of problem solving by Dewey, 1910.) The five stages in Thomas's model include the following:

- **Frustration** with organizational and/or interpersonal conditions
- **Conceptualization** of the problem
- **Behavioral intentions or plans**
- **Interactions**
- **Outcomes**

In the following sections, we describe each of these stages in detail. Remember that conflict can take place at any system level (e.g., organization, subunit, or individual). However, in this discussion of the conflict sequence, we examine the process as it develops at the individual level.

Phase One: Frustration

The perception that another party is responsible for the lack of achievement of one's own needs, desires, formal objectives, and standards of behavior is one type of frustration. This phase of conflict is largely affective, rather than cognitive, and entails a number of possible proximate causes, such as denial of a request, violation of an agreement, insults, active interference with performance, vying for scarce resources, breaking a norm, diminishing a person's status, and ignoring a person's feelings (Bartos & Wehr, 2002). Frustration derives from a perceived inadequacy of the system (or parts of it) to provide either the satisfactions or the rewards of achievement of desired goals. It also stems from the failure of the system to provide the means for achieving those goals.

According to Thomas (1976), three kinds of frustration lead to conflict.

1. *Goals-oriented frustration*—when extrinsic or intrinsic rewards that can be derived from goal achievement are perceived to be withheld by other parties. The other party referred to in the definition can withhold extrinsic rewards such as pay or promotions, or the work itself may not provide the intrinsic satisfactions that it might (e.g., the work is not challenging enough or does not provide sufficient autonomy). In this case, frustration arises because the system is not focused on the goals that the focal person desires.

2. *Means-oriented frustration*—when the system prevents the accomplishment of goals. Organizational leaders, for example, may deny adequate funding and/or personnel to certain departments. Hypothetically, the greater the shortage of funds, the greater the frustration; the greater the frustration, the greater the conflict.

3. *Ambiguity-oriented frustration*—when there is lack of clarity about how to resolve a problem. A common dilemma in many organizations, particularly colleges and universities, is who handles the issue or problem. The complex decision-making structure of many higher education institutions, which includes both faculty and administrative governance bodies, generates jurisdictional ambiguity regarding where to route various disputes and disagreements. Unionization adds another level of complexity. Should a party in a conflict file a grievance and seek the intervention of union representatives, or should they attempt to resolve the issue through administrative channels—for example, by appealing to a higher level supervisor? The answer, in many instances, is not clear and, hence, a source of frustration.

Phase Two: Conceptualization

Conceptualization is the second phase in the sequence of the conflict episode. After a perceived frustration, a person seeks to define the conflict in terms of possible action alternatives and their likely outcomes. This phase is more cognitive than affective and has two parts:

1. *Defining the issue:* A person cognitively assesses the primary concerns of the parties in the dispute. An assistant professor, for example, may want a raise, but her chair wants to reduce departmental expenditures. The assistant professor may define the issue in terms of pay equity. The department chair, on the other hand, could view the issue as a conflict over fixed resources. Faculty salaries can be raised only at the expense of other important priorities. Class sizes may need to be increased or student advising services may need to be reduced

in order to reallocate funds for faculty raises. From the chair's perspective, the conflict is defined in terms of competing priorities.
2. *Calculation of salient alternatives*: In this part of the conceptualization phase, the organizational member conceives of how the "pie" can be split, imagining the options of the rewards being solely his or hers, divided in some way, or allocated to another person.

Knowing how a person conceives of the possible conflict outcomes can help determine appropriate forms of intervention. The intervention will be different depending on whether the person sees the possibility for mutual satisfaction or views the conflict as one where only one party can obtain their desired outcome. In other words, the very definition of the conflict issue and the understanding of the *possibilities* of resolution critically affect the nature of the conflict management that can be attempted.

It is possible to be somewhat more diagnostic about issue definition and calculation of alternatives. Four scenarios describe the processes by which people perceive conflict outcomes or determine tentatively where the alternatives lie: (1) **either/or**, (2) **zero-sum**, (3) **indeterminate**, and (4) **unresolvable**. These are presented in figures 2.2–2.5 in joint outcomes space, where alternatives are juxtaposed in terms of the satisfactions of the parties in the conflict.

The either/or scenario is captured by two dimensions depicting the strength of the satisfaction of two parties in competition for good or services (Figure 2.2). Note that there are only two possible outcomes presented in this scenario—either win or lose. Whoever wins, takes all. There is no division of the benefits. Consider, for example, two faculty members competing for one travel grant. One faculty member will win the grant, and the other will not. In figure 2.2, X represents an outcome where faculty member A receives the grant and is highly satisfied, but faculty member B does not win the grant and has a low level of satisfaction. In contrast, Y represents the outcome where faculty member B wins the grant and is satisfied, and where faculty member A loses the competition and is dissatisfied.

The second scenario, zero-sum, constitutes a conceptualization of the outcomes as having the possibility of being shared. The diagonal line in Figure 2.3 represents a continuum of satisfaction, which varies from zero to all. Participants, in other words, see the possibility of sharing the spoils. For example, the travel grant could be split between the two competing faculty—either evenly (a 50–50 split) or proportionally based on some criterion (e.g., a larger award for the faculty member attending the more expensive conference). Cooperative negotiation—communication of the dimensions of the

FIGURE 2.2
Either/or Joint Outcome Space

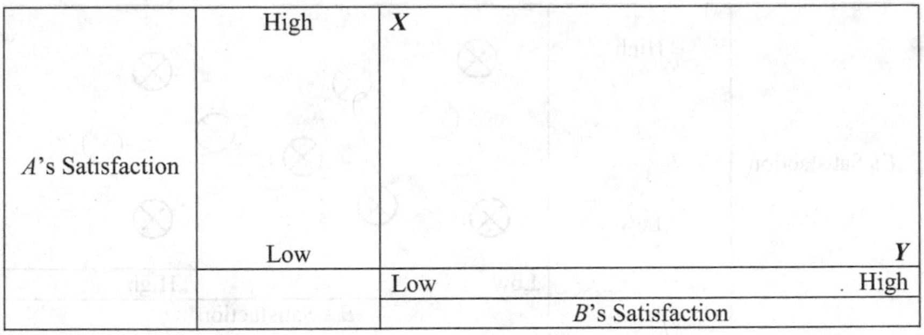

	High	X	
A's Satisfaction			
	Low		Y
		Low	High
		B's Satisfaction	

Based on Thomas (1976).

FIGURE 2.3
Zero-Sum

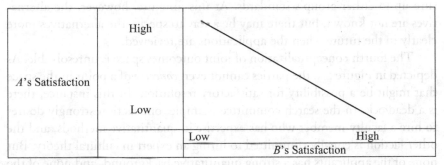

	High		
A's Satisfaction			
	Low		
		Low	High
		B's Satisfaction	

Based on Thomas (1976).

give and take among various options—is often used in such situations (Lulofs & Cahn, 2000).

The third conceptualization of joint outcomes space is indeterminate. In this scenario, the alternatives are unknown (randomly distributed in Figure 2.4). At the time of conflict conceptualization, the possible outcomes are not known. Importantly, however, there is an assumption that at a point in the future, some resolution will be discovered. Imagine, for example, two factions of a newly formed faculty search committee. One faction is concerned most with the research skills of the person to be hired (e.g., qualitative, quantitative, or mixed methods), while the other faction is focused primarily on the candidates' knowledge of different theories. The possible solution to this

FIGURE 2.4
Indeterminate Joint Outcome Space

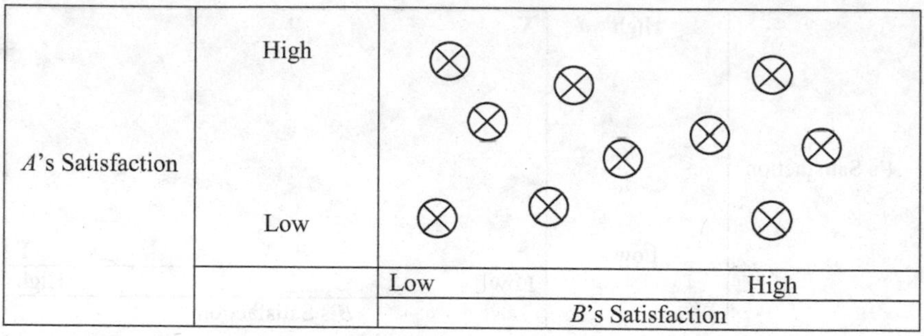

Based on Thomas (1976).

conflict is not immediately apparent. Perhaps an applicant will emerge who addresses both groups' expectations; perhaps none of the applicants will measure up to either group's standards. At this juncture, however, the alternatives are not known, but there may be a way to specify the alternatives more clearly in the future when the applications are reviewed.

The fourth conceptualization of joint outcomes space is unresolvable. As depicted in Figure 2.5, the parties cannot even *conceive* of a point in the space that might be a possibility for satisfactory resolution. In this instance, there is a deadlock. In the search committee example, one faction strongly desires to hire a faculty member who has expertise in quantitative methods, and the other faction is equally committed to hiring an expert in cultural theory. But none of the applicants has a strong quantitative background, and none of the

FIGURE 2.5
Unresolvable Joint Outcome Space

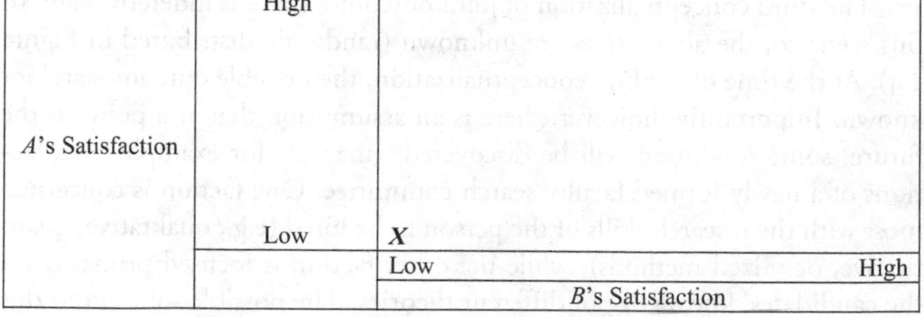

Based on Thomas (1976).

applicants is sufficiently knowledgeable about cultural theory. At this point, neither party can conceive of an alternative that would be satisfactory. The problem may be seen as not having a solution, even in the long run.

This set of four conceivable joint outcome spaces (either/or, zero-sum, indeterminate, and unresolvable) is useful for categorizing the perspectives of conflicting parties; however, this set is not an exhaustive array of all possible conflict outcomes. The assumption of these four models is that the size of the payoffs (i.e., the "pie") is fixed. We could, however, conceive of *changing the size of the pie* such that satisfactions for each party would increase. Expanding the size of potential payoffs could allow both parties to achieve their goals. Take, for example, the physics and psychology departments in a university. Each wants the statistics department to gear its courses toward their students. The conflict could be conceptualized as either/or: Either the statistics courses are geared toward the physics students or toward the psychology students. Alternatively, the conflict could be viewed as zero-sum: The statistics courses incorporate some of what the physics faculty want and some of what the psychology faculty desire. But neither department is completely satisfied with that outcome. Instead, expanding the size of the pie could allow both departments to hire their own methodologists who would teach statistics in ways deemed appropriate within each discipline. Or, absent new resources, the departments could work together to develop a new statistics curriculum that would accommodate the needs of both departments. New resources or creative thinking could expand the size of the pie for both parties and allow them both to achieve desired outcomes.

In sum, conceptualization is the phase in the conflict episode when the parties to a dispute imagine what the outcomes might be. Effective conflict management may depend on how organizational leaders imagine the parties conceiving of the situation. Leaders may (1) clarify an indeterminate situation, (2) mediate in a way that turns an either/or into a zero-sum situation, or (3) reconceive the situation so that the potential payoffs are increased for both parties.

Phase Three: Behavior

We turn now to behavior, the third phase in the conflict episode. (Thomas might more properly have labeled it "planning" or "projection of behavior options," because some conflicts are not manifested in overt behaviors.) This phase refers to how a party in a conflict *plans* his or her objectives in dealing with the other party. After frustration and conceptualization, planning of action is usually taken. In what follows, we first consider the planning of behavior on an individual level and then examine the organizational level.

Individual planning consists of three components: (a) orientation, (b) strategic outcomes assessment, and (c) tactics development. Each affects the range of conflict management behaviors to be utilized.

Orientation Toward Conflict

After feeling frustrated and then ascertaining what the problem is, an individual tries to solve the problem. This process usually begins when people are able to recognize their affective condition—that is, by considering their feelings about the other person and their own desire for satisfaction in this instance. Five distinct orientations (Table 2.2), depend on the degree to which organizational members differ on two variables: (1) the party's desire to satisfy his or her own concerns and (2) the party's desire to satisfy the other's concerns. Given the value of these two variables, the behavior of each person in a conflict situation can be categorized as either **competitive, avoidant, compromising, collaborative,** or **accommodative.** Thomas (1976) suggests that these orientations represent temporary attitudes determined by contextual factors. Conflict orientation is not a personality disposition.

TABLE 2.2
Orientation Toward Conflict Resolution

Party's Desire to Satisfy Party's Own Concern	**Highly Assertive**	Competitive (dominating or forcing)		Collaborative (integration)
			Compromising (sharing)	
	Highly Unassertive	Avoidant (neglect)		Accommodative (appeasement)
		Very Uncooperative		**Very Cooperative**
		Party's Desire to Satisfy Other's Concern		

Based on Thomas (1976).

Key:
- **Competitive:** desire to win one's own concerns at the other's expense; to dominate in win-lose power struggles.
- **Accommodative:** desire to satisfy the other's concerns, attending less to one's own concerns.
- **Compromising:** preference for moderate but incomplete satisfaction for both parties; split the difference.
- **Collaborative:** desire to satisfy the concerns of both parties as much as possible; to integrate their concerns; a problem-solving orientation.
- **Avoidant:** indifference to concerns of self and other party; withdrawal, isolation, or reliance on fate; evasion, flight, or apathy.

Nevertheless, here, we will adopt the position that both circumstances and personality affect one's orientation toward self and others.

The question relevant to effective conflict management is: What influences the preferred modes of conflict behavior among organizational members? The answer may lie in the confluence of organizational conditions and individual personality. In other words, behavior may be a function of personal and environmental variables, represented in the social systems formula: $B = f(P,E)$ (Lewin, 1938). If leaders can operationally define P (personality) and E (environment) for individual workers, then they may be able to predict and explain (at least to a limited extent) the behavior of the conflicting parties. Further, to the extent that E—the work environment—is a variable subject to change, the behavior of conflicting parties can be influenced.

Considering the work environment, if organizational norms emphasize politics, then competitive behavior is likely to dominate the conflict episode. If, on the other hand, the culture reflects concern for human growth and development, then compromise and collaboration are more likely to prevail.

In fact, a number of newer approaches to conflict management behavior have emerged in recent years. One is called **alternative dispute resolution** (ADR) (Lipsky, Seeber, & Fincher, 2003; Phillips, 2000). Alternative dispute resolution programs emerged in response to the dissatisfactions of management, outside consultants, and the participants themselves with traditional conflict management methods. According to Costantino and Merchant (1996), "ADR is any method of dispute resolution other than formal adjudication such as court litigation or administrative proceedings" (p. 33). The purpose of ADR is to head off the kinds of conflict that can lead to expensive litigation in federal and state courts. From an individual's perspective, ADR allows the conflict participants to shape the conflict management process. The disputants choose which ADR method is most likely to meet their goals.

Typically, ADR takes place through three increasingly formal methods. The first is **negotiation** in which the parties attempt a resolution interpersonally. The second is **mediation,** which involves an outside person who acts as a facilitator (without power to impose a solution). The most formal form of ADR is **arbitration** in which the mediator by agreement of the disputants is given the power to impose resolution of the disagreement (Lulofs & Cahn, 2000).

A continuum describes the evolution of ADR techniques (Figure 2.6) in terms of three kinds of methods (power-based, rights-based, and interest-based) and three kinds of conflict management designs (similarly, power-based, rights-based, and interest-based). The arrows in the diagram represent the typical evolutionary sequence. In each of the quadrants, different participants are involved, with different methods and foci. For example, in

FIGURE 2.6
Conflict Resolution Continuum

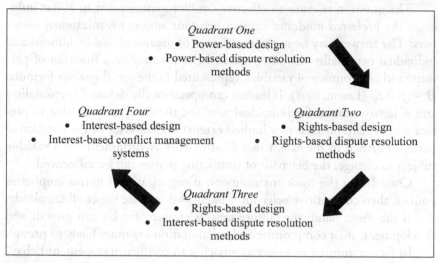

Adapted from Costantino and Merchant (1996).

Quadrants Two and Three, the focus is on individual cases of conflict, rather than on the institution as a whole. But as the organization evolves toward Quadrant Four, ADR methods become institutionalized across the entire organization. Rather than deal with conflict on a case-by-case basis, the organization maintains an ongoing network to deal with conflicts as they emerge and to assess the reasons why conflicts develop in the first place. For example, a college may hire an ombudsperson whose role is to use ADR methods to address common academic disputes and grievances (Hebein, 1999). Costantino (1996) notes that interest-based conflict management (Quadrant Four) has the strongest potential to produce practical, long-term solutions to organizational conflict.

Strategic Outcomes Assessment

This is the second part of the behavior phase of the conflict episode. Whereas conflict orientation represents an affective condition, this second part—strategic outcomes assessment—is more cognitive. It consists of an examination of the possibilities for conflict resolution, given one's conceptualization of the conflict and the affective preferences noted above. That is, once he or she conceives of the situation (in joint outcomes space) and determines what the preferences for conflict resolution are (conflict orientation), a strategy for action must be planned. In other words, given the situation, what are the realistic options?

To give an example, a middle manager in a registrar's office may view a problem as an either/or conflict and be oriented toward competition. However, there may be a powerful same-rank peer involved in the conflict. Thus, the middle manager's strategy must take into account not only the situation and his or her own preferences, but the real interpersonal issues that are likely to emerge.

One activity in strategic outcomes assessment is determining the size of the pie (the desired outcome) and the slice that exists or might exist for the focal person or group (Harinck, de Dreu, & Van Vianen, 2000; Pinkley, Griffith, & Northcraft, 1995). This determination depends in part on an assessment of the other's power, degree of commitment, and stake in the outcome. Walton and McKersie (1991) have suggested that this assessment often takes place in the context of labor-management relations and collective bargaining in one of two ways (Figure 2.7). If disputants believe that the size of the pie is fixed, then the size of the slice is calculated along a **distributive dimension** (a zero-sum orientation). In this case, the conflict behaviors run from competing to compromising, to accommodating. If the amount of power, degree of commitment, and stake in the outcome are roughly equal among the disputing parties, then competition is likely to be the most probable strategy. A party with less power, lower commitment, and/or a limited stake in the outcome, however, may simply accommodate and give in to the wishes of the other party.

On the other hand, if the disputants conceive of the size of the pie as changeable, they will calculate the size of their slice along an **integrative dimension** (running from avoidance, to compromising, to collaborating).

FIGURE 2.7
Integrative and Distributive Dimensions of Conflict Management

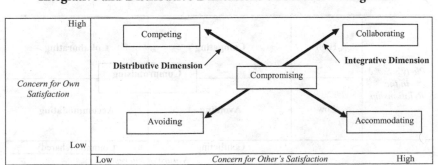

Again, if power, commitment, and stake in the outcome are nearly equal among the disputing parties, then there is a strong incentive for the disputants to pursue a collaborative strategy where an increase in the size of the pie can result in the satisfaction of *both* parties. A party with little power, commitment, or interest in the outcome, however, may not wish to invest the significant amount of time needed to forge a collaborative solution and instead may simply avoid dealing with the issue.

Tactical Plan

In this third part of the behavior phase, the question is how the actor plans to behave. Now that the individual knows what his or her strategy will be (integrative or distributive), how will he or she act to accomplish it? In our discussion above, we noted that amount of power, degree of commitment, and stake in the outcome affected individuals' positions on the integrative and distributive dimensions. In addition, Thomas (1976) noted that there are two critical variables that also determine choices regarding tactical plans: the actor's **stake in the relationship** with the other party in the conflict; and the degree of **congruence of interests** between the parties (Figure 2.8).

If an individual has common interests with another person, but a *low* stake in the relationship with that person, then he or she will tend to accommodate. When both parties share interests, whatever happens is likely to be in the interest of both; therefore, accommodating the other party is likely to satisfy the focal person's interests, too. Consider two academic department chairs who seldom interact and are unlikely to work together in the future. Neither party has a high stake in the relationship. One chair disagrees with a new college-wide admissions policy proposed by the second chair. Both

FIGURE 2.8
Conflict Behavior Reflecting Stake in Outcomes and Congruence of Interests

Party's Stake in the Relationship		Competing	Collaborating
	High		Compromising
	Low	Avoiding	Accommodating
		Conflicting	Common (shared)
		Nature of Interests	

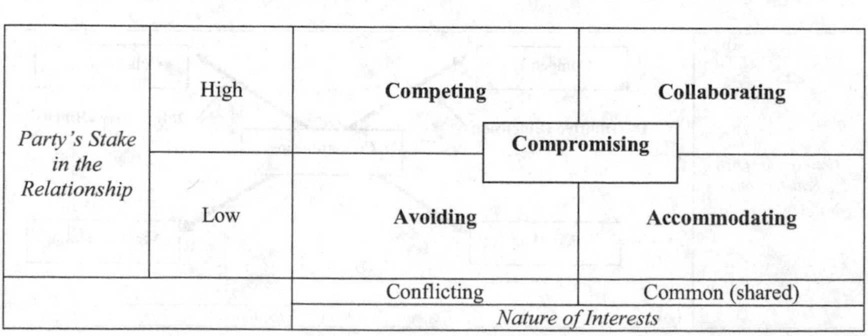

Adapted from Thomas (1977).

chairs, however, share a common interest in maintaining access for low-income students. It is likely that the first chair will accommodate the second chair's position, knowing that ultimately the second chair will continue to work toward their shared goal—access for low-income students.

In the case of common interests and a *high* stake in the relationship, the parties are more likely to collaborate. When people have a high stake in maintaining good working relationships, they are more likely to invest time in collaborative conflict management approaches. A dean of students and a residential housing director have many common interests and must work together frequently in planning and implementing programs for students. Given their common interests and important relationship, they are likely to collaborate to find solutions to their disagreements.

On the other hand, if the parties have *high* stakes but conflicting interests, they tend to partake in competitive behavior. If the dean of students and the housing director have radically different philosophies about college student development, they would likely compete with one another. The consequences of an opposing view carrying the day are simply too high to allow someone with conflicting interests to determine the outcome.

Under conditions of conflicting interests and *low* stakes, however, avoidance is the more likely tactic. People are unlikely to devote energy to fierce competition if they perceive the stakes to be low (e.g., unlikely to work with that person again in the future).

Thomas (1976) does not completely lay out the entire theory, so some interpolations and extrapolations must be offered. In reality, high stakes must be combined with an assertive personality to result in competitive behavior. Although a person may have a high stake and see conflicting interests, it may still be that he does not compete. His personality may simply be non-assertive. Another important consideration is that individuals are attracted to and tend to remain employed at institutions where their personalities can be accommodated. Further, organizations recruit and hire people who fit the culture. A competitive organization will likely hire competitive people, and these people are more likely to feel comfortable in that setting.

Phase Four: Interaction

So far, we have discussed the first three phases in the conflict cycle: frustration, conceptualization, and behavior (orientation, strategy, and tactics). We turn next to the fourth phase.

In this phase, the domain under scrutiny is expanded. Whereas previously, it was the perspective of the individual before us, we now consider organizations as the unit of analysis. Assuming that there has been frustration, conceptualization, and behavior, some action is next in order, and insofar as the individual is a member of an organization, it is likely that his or her action will be felt in some other part of the organization. Thus interaction, Thomas's fourth stage, includes organizational responses to conflict.

First, we examine how conflict is most frequently dealt with in organizations. A common mode is to ignore it or to address it in secret (Kolb & Bartunek, 1992; March & Simon, 1958). Conflict is unpleasant for individuals and is perceived to be dysfunctional for organizations. Indeed, it is alleged that

> A high proportion of people who get to the top are conflict avoiders. They don't like hearing negatives, they don't like saying or thinking negative things. They frequently make it up the ladder in part because they don't irritate people on the way up. (cited in Robbins, 1998, p. 447)

As a result of the propensity for conflict avoidance, organizations develop formal mechanisms to defuse conflict and the allegedly damaging interpersonal emotional exchanges that accompany it.

A second common response to conflict is to postpone its resolution in the hope that it will simply disappear. Indeed, the length of time taken in addressing critical problems (known as **problem latency**) is sometimes used as an index of organizational health (Cyert & March, 1963). The longer it takes the organization to address the conflict, the less healthy the organization is.

A third mode is for leaders to suppress conflict; that is, to prevent it from arising in the first place. And a fourth is to try to make the system work in spite of the conflict, however inefficient the system may be. Instead of attempting to uncover the sources of the conflict, this approach takes the form of developing more organizational structures to deal with it—such as grievance committees and formal adjudication procedures. It is possible, however, that if the deeper issues causing conflicts can be addressed, not only will new structures become unnecessary, but the problems themselves will likely be reduced in their severity.

Yet a fifth possible response to conflict is to engage in secret (i.e., not through official offices), informal arrangements among powerful alliances that the public is not permitted to see. Bartunek, Kolb, and Lewicki (1992) in their description of a search for a new chancellor at the University of Illinois at Chicago note the nonrational, emotional, and often acrimonious conditions that are typical in a high-stakes search, but also identify the latent benefits of behind-the-scenes conflict management; for example, the ventilation of feelings that would be politically and socially unpalatable if made public.

Almost invariably, conflict generates politics, and politics result in the use of power games that create winners and losers. A more constructive mode is to develop a comprehensive, organization-wide approach to conflict management. Such approaches, however, require long-term investments of energy and commitment, which people may be unwilling to devote (or lack the skills to carry out). Instead, the orientation toward short-term outcomes tends to displace both movements toward organizational health and the functional use of conflict.

In contrast to short-term fixes, organizational leaders can use a range of conflict management strategies, which we classify in three ways: (1) structural, (2) processual, and (3) mixed. This framework for understanding conflict management is consistent with our conceptualization of conflict as structure and as a process.

Structural Approaches to Conflict Management

As noted earlier, conflict arises from perceptions that are created, in part, by the structural conditions of the organization, including differentiation, scarce resources, interdependence, uncertainty, and perceived inequity in power distribution (Aldrich, 1979). If these elements can be changed, the resulting conflict and perceptions of it can be moderated.

Lawrence and Lorsch (1967) argued that differentiation and integration, the opposing centrifugal and centripetal forces of organization, must go hand in hand in order for conflict to be managed effectively. That is, when organizational members are divided into specializations (such as academic departments and student affairs divisions), there must be ways to connect and integrate their work, or conflict (and inefficiency) will result. The creative management of the tension between differentiation and integration often distinguishes successful from unsuccessful organizations.

Organizations change their structures in many ways to manage this conflict. One is by physically separating the disputing parties (Daft & Steers, 1986; Neilson, 1972). For example, physically relocating one academic department known to be frequently feuding with another may reduce the intensity of the conflict, but it may not address the underlying causes that impede effective integration of these departments. An opposite approach is to create one department from two, thus, encompassing the conflicting groups in a larger unit. This strategy reduces differentiation and thus minimizes the problems associated with integrating organizational units. The merger of two units may engender new goals, new loyalties, and new orientations toward the larger department. Further, propinquity (closeness of work stations) would likely strengthen emotional bonds among members.

Another mode of conflict management is through role separation. The formal designation of clearly distinct roles removes the ambiguity that is often a source of conflict. Job rotation, still another strategy, can promote understanding and comity by establishing friendships (or at least acquaintances) across departmental boundaries. Rotating staff among admissions and student services offices, for example, can strengthen the collaborative relationships between these units.

When units are mildly differentiated in process or function, a shared supervisor or director can resolve conflicts. An academic dean, for example, can adjudicate disputes among departments. On the other hand, when units are widely separated in function, it is wiser to use a new unit to provide the mediating services (Sheppard, 1984). For example, a conflict between the registrar and an academic dean can best be managed through a third party to whom neither reports. In some organizations, this ADR mediating role has become a new formal role in the organizational chart.

Since perceived inequity in resource allocation is a significant cause of conflict, the use of clearly articulated budget criteria and reward systems provides a formal organizational rationale for the differential distribution of scarce resources. Still another strategy for conflict management is to change the decision-making procedure and/or structure. For example, student protests may cause institutions temporarily to move to a more democratic decision-making process, which may ameliorate some of the student perceptions of disenfranchisement.

Process Approaches to Conflict Management

In addition to structural approaches to conflict management, there are a variety of processes that are used in organizational and interpersonal conflict management. March and Simon (1958), for example, identify two alternative processual approaches to conflict management—analytical and bargaining modes, which result in integrative or distributive (zero-sum) solutions, respectively (Lewicki & Litterer, 1985). They say that when conflict is interpersonal more analytical modes are used, but when conflict is group based bargaining modes tend to predominate (see Table 2.3). That is, when individuals are engaged in conflict, they tend to use analytical modes. The reason is first that conflict is usually unpleasant, and second that organizations typically wish for a commonality of goals, often in the hope that organizational members will rally around a common mission and share a loyalty base. Rather than disrupt this image, organizational leaders may assume (and adopt a posture) that all conflict is interpersonal and that it can be resolved analytically. They are then able to say that the conflict is not organizational but only a dispute between individuals, probably with some personality clash. Further, conceiving of conflict as organizationally based would require

TABLE 2.3
Organizational Conflict Management

Analytical Modes of Conflict Management		
Perceived Outcome Space Regarding Goals	*Conceptualization and Behavior*	*Behaviors and Tactics*
Goals are shared (assumes shared objectives are possible)	Integrative Solution	Problem solving. Identify a solution that will meet a shared goal. Rationality is the means.
Goals may be different	Integrative Solution	Test goals for consistency. Appeal to superordinate goals. Use flexible persuasion. Some emotional appeals involved.

Bargaining Modes of Conflict Management		
Perceived Outcome Space Regarding Goals	*Conceptualization and Behavior*	*Behaviors and Tactics*
Goals are assumed to be different	Distributive Solution (e.g., bargaining)	Disagreement conceived to be inevitable. Appeals are made to fairness. Bargaining mode can be identified by threats, falsification of positions.
Goals are assumed to be different	Distributive Solution (e.g., politics)	Use outside arena. Find allies.

Adapted from March and Simon (1958).

admitting the existence of a heterogeneity of goals. Goal conflict reduces the possibility of united, focused effort and leads to the replacement of some bureaucratic authority with political power—a shift that may upset the status quo.

Of course, interpersonal conflict and organizational conflict are not unrelated. Indeed, interpersonal conflict often has a negative influence on the ability of individuals and groups to achieve organizational goals. Organizational members are forced to devote significant amounts of time to responding to threats, maintaining and expanding power bases, and building cohesive coalitions, rather than working on tasks and achieving performance goals (Jehn, 1997).

To reiterate, when the conflict is interpersonal, the mode of conflict management tends to be analytical, which relies upon integrative solutions. In contrast, when conflict is conceptualized as group-based or organizationally based, the mode of conflict management tends to be bargaining and the solutions arrived at through distributive processes.

The following are some tactics that Thomas (1976) notes are distributive rather than integrative:

- re-evaluation—changing the definition of the situation and the preferred alternatives ("I thought it was *his* job, not mine.")
- self-fulfilling prophecies—reinforcing one's own perception ("My work is exceptional, especially under the circumstances in which I am forced to work.")
- underestimating commonalities
- oversimplification and other communication distortions
- communication breakdowns that increase hostility and distrust
- elevating the importance of winning, not even just to achieve a goal, but simply for the sake of winning itself
- spreading conflict to other issues
- communicating the perception of incompatibility ("We simply cannot work together.")

Integrative conflict management processes, in contrast, have been shown to be effective when certain organizational conditions are present (Fisher & Ury, 1981; Robbins, 1974). If the conflict can be made visible, for example, it may be possible for participants to vent feelings in the open, thereby identifying foci for potential solutions. In order to make conflict visible, organizations can provide safe spaces for people to examine disagreements without fear of repercussion or reprisal. Safe spaces require extensive trust among organizational members and a normative context where diversity of opinion and perspective is valued.

It may also be important to try to establish common goals and to institutionalize shared commitments. Recall the physics and psychology departments that engaged in an either/or conflict regarding the pedagogical focus of statistics courses. Assume for the moment that faculty in both departments convened a committee to identify common goals for quantitative instruction. This process could lead to the identification of new teaching techniques that neither department had considered previously, but which ultimately may contribute to higher student performance in both departments. The process of identifying common goals could reveal new directions and insights that neither conflicting party would have identified independently; an outcome frequently referred to as synergy.

Similarly, the identification of shared commitments can also result in integrative solutions to conflict, and, in fact, serve as the basis for future collective action among previously conflicting parties. Shared commitments can be defined as intentional public statements that reveal mutually agreed upon motivations and justifications for action (Staw, 1980). Shared commitments are action oriented, but do not require a common set of values; therefore, even conflicting parties with widely different value systems may be able to identify shared commitments (Spender & Grinyer, 1995). For example, one group of faculty and staff may be committed to civically engaged learning due to a commitment to social justice, while another group may be committed to the same pedagogy but for financial reasons (e.g., stronger retention of students and more applications from prospective students who want that type of learning experience).

Open, but civil, expression of conflict, formation of common goals, and identification of shared commitments can each contribute to integrative conflict management processes, which are more likely to result in solutions that benefit all parties. These integrative processes suggest several implications for organizational leadership. Leaders can mediate divisive forces by sharing information, facilitating communication, encouraging collaboration, and building trust and confidence among organizational members (Henkin, Cistone, & Dee, 2000).

Mixed Approaches (Structural and Processual) to Conflict Management
Some approaches to conflict management evoke ideas from both structural and processual traditions. Organizational leaders, for example, can engage in a sequential strategy in which they first clarify the structural parameters for conflict management and then address the substance of the conflict through various processes. Depending on the type of organization, it is often useful to address procedural conflict first. Establishing rules for working out conflicts and specifying procedures and boundaries for action serves as an initial regulator of conflict. Without this step, inappropriate actions are likely to exacerbate the conflict situation. Further, the formalization of conflict management procedures renders conflict less personal. As noted earlier, treatment of conflict as merely a personal squabble tends to avoid the underlying issues of conflict.

Another mixed approach is to make third party conciliators available at all times to manage conflicts. **Ombudspersons** can be constituted to be

readily available to deal with grievances of individuals across the entire organization. Interdepartmental teams, task forces, and formal integrators can
also be useful mechanisms for adjudicating disputes.

Phase Five: Outcomes

The final phase in Thomas's conflict cycle—outcomes—is the immediate
aftermath of the conflict (e.g., satisfaction or more frustration). The long-
term effects can be a perpetuation or even escalation of the conflict, the institutionalization or changing of existing conflict management modes, and/or
a redefinition of the conflict and the modes for its management.

Creative conflict management will often result in the reduction of interpersonal tensions that draw attention and energy away from tasks and valued
activities (Jehn, 1997). The diffusing of emotional, interpersonal conflict can
result in the stimulation of new and better ideas, increased curiosity and innovative behavior, openness to solving organizational problems, and greater
organizational and group cohesiveness (Coser, 1956).

Social Constructionist Perspectives on Conflict

In several ways, the social constructionist paradigm reinforces the interactionist perspective on conflict within positivism, which suggests that conflict
can be beneficial to the organization. To reiterate, the interactionist perspective proposes that conflict can stimulate change, innovation, and the emergence of new leadership that challenges a stagnant status quo (Pondy, 1967;
Robbins, 1974). Social constructionists also view conflict as a driving force
for organizational change, but their conceptual focus differs from positivism
in some important ways.

First, social constructionists locate the source of conflict in multiple constructions of reality (Baxter & Montgomery, 1996; Benson, 1977). They
argue that reality is enacted through ongoing social processes that produce
and reproduce the context in which people work. Organizational reality is a
manifestation of the perceptions, mental models, dispositions, and values of
organizational members—all of which are shared to greater or lesser degrees.
Through patterned behaviors and adherence to organizational norms, reality
gets constructed in similar ways, day after day. Conflict emerges, however,
when different units of the organization begin to construct reality in different ways. Given high levels of differentiation in most complex organizations,
different departments and units begin to construct reality in ways that differ
from other departments and units. As an example, because of structural differentiation into separate units, people working in student affairs divisions

may construct organizational reality differently than people working in academic affairs divisions.

Multiple constructions of reality, according to social constructionists, are the source of most conflicts in organizations. These forms of conflict reveal previously hidden **contradictions** in how the organization operates. A contradiction is an opposition within a social system that does not present a ready-made solution. A college may want to restrict intolerant speech, yet maintain academic freedom. A university may espouse a commitment to teaching, yet emphasize research in its evaluation of faculty. As Tierney (1992) notes, colleges and universities are filled with such contradictions. Again, the source of these conflicts and contradictions is multiple constructions of reality, engendered in part through structural differentiation but also through a pluralism of ideas and a diversity of backgrounds that characterize organizational membership in higher education.

Another important difference between the positivist and social constructionist perspectives involves approaches to managing conflict. Positivist views on conflict management suggest that organizational leaders can identify the sources of conflict, assess the condition of the organization (e.g., the degree of consensus on organizational goals and the means to achieve them), and then select a conflict management approach (e.g., collaboration or compromise) that is the best fit for the contingencies of the situation. In contrast, social constructionists claim that conflict may not be amenable to such rational assessments. First, the positivist view assumes that the conflict is overt; that is, behaviors can be identified as conflict or as potentially conflicting. However, as political scientist Stephen Lukes (1974) notes, many important conflicts remain latent. Contradictions may not be explored, because their discussion could be too painful for organizational members. Consider, for example, the emotions triggered by discussions of affirmative action and the allegedly competing values of access and merit. Alternatively, conflicts may be suppressed by overt force or more subtle norms that favor the status quo. Conflicts may never be expressed because organizational members fear to bring up issues that may result in retaliation, or organizational members may be so homogeneous in their backgrounds and philosophies that challenging the status quo simply does not occur to them (Bachrach & Baratz, 1962; Kolb & Putnam, 1992; Lukes, 1974).

Second, even when conflict is overt, attempts to manage conflict may be based on some faulty assumptions. Organizational leaders who intervene in a conflict may think that they have assisted the disputants in arriving at an appropriate resolution, such as a compromise or an agreement to collaborate. But as organizational members return to their day-to-day activities, it may become apparent that the disputants did not embrace the organizational leader's interpretation of the situation, and they do not intend to adhere to the resolution that was developed during the leader's intervention. In the absence of constant direct oversight, disputants could simply return to their previously conflicting behaviors, and organizational leaders may remain unaware that the conflict was not actually resolved until ineffective performance was eventually noticed again by those in charge.

The social constructionist perspective does not offer a clear alternative for leaders to address organizational conflict. One implication from social constructionist research, however, is that in order to deal with conflict, disputing parties will need to begin to construct reality in ways that are more similar than different. Different communication venues may be necessary to promote this type of social construction. Opportunities for open communication and informal interaction, for example, can enable organizational members to construct common frames of reference for interpreting their problems and for enacting solutions to them (Bormann, 1996). Van Maanen (1992), in a study of police departments, noted how conflicts were often addressed informally over drinks at a local bar. The conflict was physically removed from the workplace, which led to a de-escalation of emotion and a focus on common interests. These less structured means of communication may be more effective than formal, organizationally based approaches to conflict management that emphasize intervention and rational problem solving.

Postmodern Perspectives on Conflict

Conflict and contradiction are also central elements in the postmodern conceptualization of organizations. The postmodern perspective notes that organizational life is fragmented, shared meanings are elusive, and a clear sense of purpose may be missing for many organizational members. Under these conditions, conflict is inevitable. Rational approaches to conflict management, however, may be unsustainable as language and word meanings are constantly shifting. The very meanings of compromise, collaboration, and competition, for example, are in flux.

The French literary critic Jacques Derrida (1976) claimed that people deal with contradictions by erecting binary oppositions that exclude alternative ways of thinking. In colleges and universities, these binary distinctions may include:

- research that is scientific versus nonscientific
- an academically qualified student versus one who is not

- a legitimate academic credential versus one that is not
- a text that is part of the literary canon versus one that is not

These binary distinctions resolve conflicts that emerge in higher education organizations. A conflict over the future direction of an academic field of study, for example, is resolved through a peer review process that determines which ideas are scientifically valid and suitable for publication in prominent journals and which ideas are not suitable. Conflicts over who should be admitted to institutions of higher education are often resolved on the basis of allegedly objective criteria such as standardized test scores. Derrida noted that these binary distinctions, as a means for dealing with conflict, relegate some people, issues, and ideas to the margins of organizations (and by extension, to the margins of society).

In addition, some postmodernists claim that rational arguments used to justify certain resolutions of conflict are biased in favor of those who benefit from existing status hierarchies. Rational arguments are based on criteria that guide the judgments of those who adjudicate conflict. These criteria must be created by someone, and postmodernists argue that any set of criteria will serve the interests of one group or coalition better than others. Inevitably, those who determine the criteria for resolving conflict are also those who hold the highest status positions in the organization. Bloland (1995, 2005), for example, questioned why certain administrators and professors, rather than others, are able to benefit from existing academic hierarchies. An example can illustrate Bloland's point. Academic programs in the hard sciences often receive more funding than humanities disciplines. Allegedly rational criteria can be used to justify resolving resource conflicts in favor of the hard sciences; for example, research in the hard sciences can lead to more socially useful discoveries. But alternative criteria that emphasize aesthetic and cultural impact could be used to justify giving more funds to faculty in the arts. Again, postmodernists argue that allegedly rational criteria for adjudicating conflicts are constructions of high-status groups in organizations, and members of those groups work to maintain those criteria in order to retain their high status.

Again, like the social constructionists, postmodernists do not offer concrete practices as alternatives to the positivist paradigm. Replacing one set of conflict-resolving criteria with another would simply create new status hierarchies to govern future conflicts. The "in" and "out" groups would change, but the underlying force of exclusion would remain. Bloland (1995) instead calls for the "harsh questioning" of hierarchy in higher education organizations and the ongoing scrutiny of who benefits from and who is disadvantaged by existing policies and practices.

Postmodernists argue that exclusionary hierarchies can be identified and dismantled. They offer alternatives to hierarchy, which can minimize the status differences that cause many conflicts to arise in the first place. Decentralized authority, personalized relationships, and a culture of trust and openness can facilitate more authentic communication in the organization and disrupt tendencies to resolve conflict based on power and status differences. As Hirschhorn (1997) notes, this type of organizational arrangement requires a significant investment of psychological energy. People must learn the viewpoints of others, take more risks in their thinking and actions, and commit themselves to ongoing self-reflection and critique. Moreover, each conflict episode would need to be treated as unique; again, the application of uniform criteria for resolving conflict would merely replicate the status hierarchy currently operating in the organization. Given these types of investments of time and energy, however, organizational members can deal with conflict openly and not rely on status and power differences as means to resolve conflict.

Gender Issues in Conflict Management

Accumulating evidence suggests that problems in organizations tend to be "drawn from the experience of men, especially those who are white and of the middle class and, in the case of organization theory, those who manage corporations" (Kolb, 1992, p. 67). As Lulofs and Cahn (2000) note:

> Clearly, what men and women deem as competent communication behavior differs, and this will have important consequences for conflict behavior. Whereas a woman will expect competence in the form of attentiveness and other "personal" behaviors, a man might expect attention to the issues of conflict. Both are likely to be disappointed in opposite-sex conflicts. (p. 51)

Communication difficulties, therefore, are likely to shape the course and outcomes of gender-based conflict.

Feminist theorists share the postmodernist concern with hierarchy and power as it relates to conflict. Rosabeth Moss Kanter (1977), for example, was among the first to note that women often lack power in organizations because they are underrepresented in formal leadership positions. College presidents, as one example, remain an overwhelmingly (79%) male group (Chronicle of Higher Education, 2005, p. 25). In organizations that lack gender diversity in upper-level leadership, women occupy subordinate positions in the organizational hierarchy (Martin, 1990). By virtue of their subordinate position, women are less able to voice disagreements and shape the conflict management process. As a result, gender conflict may remain suppressed (unvoiced), and male-oriented conflict management behaviors such as competition may predominate. Gender differences in the perception of and management of conflict complicate organizational solutions, but the exploration of the gendered sources of conflict can illuminate issues that may have been hidden by dominant male biases. As Martin (1990) notes, "If feminist perspectives were fully incorporated, the usual emphases on rationality, hierarchy, competition, efficiency, and productivity would be exposed as only a very small piece of the organizational puzzle" (p. 357).

Summary

In this chapter, we examined the different kinds of conflict, conflict's course, and the behaviors associated with each phase in the conflict episode. At the start of the chapter, two approaches to understanding conflict were suggested—conflict as structure and conflict as process. We then examined a range of organizational approaches to conflict management, which leaders can use to harness the productive functions of conflict. As Rahim (1992) notes,

> Organizational conflict now is considered as legitimate, inevitable, and even a positive indicator of effective organizational management. It is now recognized that conflict within certain limits is essential to productivity. (p. 10)

Finally, we explored social constructionist, postmodernist, and feminist perspectives on conflict, which raise important considerations regarding multiple constructions of reality, hierarchy, and power.

Review Questions

1. A member of a board of trustees strongly believes that a prayer should precede all basketball games at the university. The college president thinks otherwise. If the issue comes to a head, what kind of conflict is likely to result?
    a. Cognitive goal conflict
    b. Cognitive means conflict
    c. Affective goal conflict
    d. Procedural conflict
    e. Two of the above

2. An annual award to the best teacher of the year by a college carries a value of $500. Each of the two finalists conceives of the situation in which of the following terms:
   a. Either/or
   b. Zero-sum
   c. Indeterminate
   d. Unresolvable

3. A dean threatens to assign a faculty member Friday and Saturday classes, despite the faculty member's objections. Which of the following is the likely effect on the faculty member?
   a. Cognitive dissonance
   b. Approach-approach conflict
   c. Approach-avoidance conflict
   d. Avoidance-avoidance conflict
   e. Cognitive conflict

4. The perception by an individual of the desirability of collaboration is, in part, a function of:
   a. The degree of overlapping interests with the other person in the conflict
   b. The potential costs or benefits to the individual
   c. Both a and b
   d. Neither a nor b

5. Faculty members in the departments of psychology, economics, and education were in conflict over what should be taught in the basic statistics courses in the university. The vice president for academic affairs, in consultation with the faculty, created a new university-wide statistics department staffed by members of each of the three departments where statistics was taught. This approach to conflict management is called:
   a. Structural
   b. Processual
   c. Mixed (both structural and processual)
   d. Interventionist

6. In a college with declining resources, the opportunities for horizontal conflict among academic departments increase when:
   a. There are fewer buffers between departments
   b. There is less functional interdependence between departments

c. There is lower dependence on common resources between departments
d. None of the above

7. The social constructionist perspective on conflict differs from positivist conceptualizations in which of the following ways?
    a. Viewing multiple constructions of reality (rather than misfits between system components) as the source of conflict
    b. Emphasizing integrative rather than distributive forms of conflict management
    c. Noting that ADR methods merely replicate the status hierarchies that currently exist in the organization
    d. All of the above

8. Postmodernists suggest that organizational members often deal with contradictory conditions in the workplace in which of the following ways?
    a. By surfacing latent conflicts through ADR methods
    b. By questioning harshly the hierarchy of the organization
    c. By erecting binary (either/or) oppositions that resolve the contradiction
    d. By forcing the conflicting parties into mediation

Case Discussion Questions

Consider again the Pacific Shores Community College case presented at the beginning of this chapter.

1. What steps did the vice president take for depersonalizing the conflict?
2. Analyze this conflict episode in terms of the five stages of conflict development: frustration, conceptualization, behavior, interaction, and outcomes.
    • What was the source of **frustration** (goal oriented, means oriented, ambiguity oriented)?
    • Plot in joint outcome space the dean's and the director's initial **conceptualizations** of the conflict.
    • Categorize the dean's and the director's **behaviors**—assertive or unassertive, cooperative or uncooperative (see Table 2.2).
    • How did the vice president facilitate **interactions** that led to an integrative, rather than a distributive approach to conflict management?

- What are the likely long-term **outcomes** of this conflict? Did the vice president's conflict management approach enhance the likelihood for functional responses to future conflict, or did his approach increase the chances for more dysfunctional conflicts in the future?

References

Aldrich, H. E. (1979). *Organizations and environments*. Englewood Cliffs, NJ: Prentice-Hall.

Allison, G. (1971). *Essence of decision: Explaining the Cuban missile crisis*. Boston: Little, Brown.

Amason, A. C. (1996). Distinguishing the effects of functional and dysfunctional conflict on strategic decision making: Resolving a paradox for top management teams. *Academy of Management Journal, 39*, 123–148.

Amason, A. C., & Schweiger, D. M. (1994). Resolving the paradox of conflict, strategic decision making, and organizational performance. *International Journal of Conflict Management, 5*, 239–253.

Bachrach, P., & Baratz, M. (1962). The two faces of power. *American Political Science Review, 56*, 947–952.

Barsky, A. E. (2002). Structural sources of conflict in a university context. *Conflict Resolution Quarterly, 20*(2), 161–176.

Bartos, O. J., & Wehr, P. (2002). *Using conflict theory*. Cambridge, England: Cambridge University Press.

Bartunek, J. M., Kolb, D. M., & Lewicki, R. J. (1992). Bringing conflict out from behind the scenes: Private, informal, and nonrational dimensions of conflict in organizations. In D. M. Kolb & J. M. Bartunek (Eds.), *Hidden conflict in organizations* (pp. 209–228). Newbury Park, CA: Sage Publications.

Baxter, L., & Montgomery, B. (1996). *Relating: Dialogues and dialectics*. New York: Guilford Press.

Bennis, W., Benne, K., & Chin, R. (1969). *The planning of change: Readings in the applied behavioral sciences* (2nd ed.). New York: Holt, Rinehart, & Winston.

Benson, J. K. (1977). Organizations: A dialectical view. *Administrative Science Quarterly, 22*(1), 1–20.

Birnbaum, R. (1988). *How colleges work: The cybernetics of academic organization and leadership*. San Francisco: Jossey-Bass.

Bloland, H. (1995). Postmodernism and higher education. *Journal of Higher Education, 66*(5), 521–559.

Bloland, H. (2005). Whatever happened to postmodernism in higher education?: No requiem in the new millennium. *Journal of Higher Education, 76*(2), 121–150.

Bormann, E. (1996). Symbolic convergence theory and communication in group decision making. In R. Hirokawa & M. Poole (Eds.), *Communication and group decision making* (2nd ed., pp. 81–113). Thousand Oaks, CA: Sage.

Brown, L. D. (1979). Managing conflict among groups. In D. A. Kolb, I. M. Rubin, & J. M. McIntyre (Eds.), *Organizational psychology: A book of readings* (pp. 377–389). Englewood Cliffs, NJ: Prentice-Hall.

Brown, L. D. (1986). *Managing conflict at organizational interfaces*. Reading, MA: Addison-Wesley Publishing.

Chronicle of Higher Education. (2005, August 26). Characteristics of college presidents, 2001. *The Chronicle of Higher Education, 52*(1), 25.

Coffman, J. R. (2005). *Work and peace in academe: Leveraging time, money, and intellectual energy through managing conflict.* Bolton, MA: Anker Publishing.

Collins, R. (1975). *Conflict sociology.* New York: Academic Press.

Coser, L. (1956). *The functions of social conflict.* New York: The Free Press.

Costantino, C. A. (1996). Using interest-based techniques to design conflict management systems. *Negotiation Journal, 12*(3), 207–215.

Costantino, C. A., & Merchant, C. S. (1996). *Designing conflict management systems: A guide to creating productive and healthy organizations.* San Francisco: Jossey-Bass.

Cyert, R. M., & March, J. G. (1963). *A behavioral theory of the firm.* Englewood Cliffs, NJ: Prentice-Hall.

Daft, R., & Steers, R. (1986). *Organizations: A micro/macro approach.* Glenview, IL: Scott, Foresman and Company.

Darkenwald, G. (1971). Organizational conflict in colleges and universities. *Administrative Science Quarterly, 16*(4), 407–412.

de Dreu, C., & Van de Vliert, E. (Eds.). (1997). *Using conflict in organizations.* Thousand Oaks, CA: Sage.

Del Favero, M. (2003). Faculty-administrator relationships as integral to high-performing governance systems: New frameworks for study. *American Behavioral Scientist, 46*(7), 902–922.

Derrida, J. (1976). *Of grammatology.* Baltimore: Johns Hopkins University Press.

Deutsch, M. (1973). *The resolution of conflict: Constructive and destructive processes.* New Haven, CT: Yale University Press.

Dewey, J. (1910). *How we think.* Boston: D.C. Heath.

Druckman, D. (1993). An analytical research agenda for conflict and conflict resolution. In D. Sandole & H. Van Der Merwe (Eds.), *Conflict resolution theory and practice: Integration and application.* New York: Manchester University Press.

Fisher, R., & Ury, W. (1981). *Getting to yes: Negotiating agreement without giving in.* New York: Penguin Books.

Follett, M. P. (1924). *Creative experience.* London: Longman and Green.

Graff, G. (1998). Administration in an age of conflict. In S. A. Holton (Ed.), *Mending the cracks in the ivory tower: Strategies for conflict management in higher education.* Bolton, MA: Anker Publishing.

Guetzkow, H., & Gyr, J. R. (1954). An analysis of conflict in decision making groups. *Human Relations, 7,* 367–382.

Harinck, F., de Dreu, C., & Van Vianen, A. (2000). The impact of conflict issues on fixed-pie perceptions, problem solving, and integrative outcomes in negotiation. *Organizational Behavior and Human Decision Processes, 81*(2), 329–358.

Hebein, R. (1999). The prevention and cure of campus disputes. *New Directions for Teaching and Learning, Vol. 77* (pp. 87–95). San Francisco: Jossey-Bass.

Hellriegel, D., Slocum, J. W., Jr., & Woodman, R. W. (1995). *Organizational behavior* (7th ed.). Minneapolis, MN: West Publishing Company.

Henkin, A., Cistone, P., & Dee, J. (2000). Conflict management strategies of principals in site-based managed schools. *Journal of Educational Administration, 38*(2), 142–158.

Hermann, T. (2004). Reconciliation: Reflections on the theoretical and practical utility of the term. In Y. Baar-Siman-Tove (Ed.), *From conflict resolution to reconciliation* (pp. 39–60). New York: Oxford University Press.

Hickson, D. J., Hinings, C. R., Lee, C. A., Schneck, R. E., & Pennings, J. M. (1971). A strategic contingencies theory of interorganizational power. *Administrative Science Quarterly, 16*(2), 216–229.

Hinings, C. R., Hickson, D. J., Pennings, J. M., & Schneck, R. E. (1974). Structural conditions of intraorganizational power. *Administrative Science Quarterly, 19*(1), 22–44.

Hirschhorn, L. (1997). *Reworking authority: Leading and following in a postmodern organization.* Cambridge, MA: MIT Press.

Janis, I. (1989). *Crucial decisions.* New York: Free Press.

Jehn, K. A. (1994). Enhancing effectiveness: An investigation of advantages and disadvantages of value-based intragroup conflict. *International Journal of Conflict Management, 4*, 223–238.

Jehn, K. A. (1997). A qualitative analysis of conflict types and dimensions in organizational groups. *Administrative Science Quarterly, 42*(3), 530–557.

Jehn, K. A., Northcraft, G. B., & Neal, M. A. (1999). Why differences make a difference: A field study of diversity, conflict, and performance in workgroups. *Administrative Science Quarterly, 44*(4), 741–763.

Kanter, R. M. (1977). *Men and women of the corporation.* New York: Basic Books.

Kolb, D. M. (1992). Women's work: Peacemaking in organizations. In D. M. Kolb & J. M. Bartunek (Eds.), *Hidden conflict in organizations* (pp. 63–91). Newbury Park, CA: Sage Publications.

Kolb, D. M., & Bartunek, J. M. (Eds.). (1992). *Hidden conflict in organizations.* Newbury Park, CA: Sage Publications.

Kolb, D. M., & Putnam, L. (1992). The dialectics of disputing. In D. M. Kolb & J. M. Bartunek (Eds.), *Hidden conflict in organizations* (pp. 1–31). Newbury Park, CA: Sage.

Lawrence, P., & Lorsch, J. (1967). *Organization and environment.* Cambridge, MA: Harvard University Press.

Lewicki, R. J., & Litterer, J. A. (1985). *Negotiation.* Homewood, IL: Irwin.

Lewin, K. (1938). *The conceptual representation and measurement of psychological forces.* Durham, NC: Duke University Press.

Lipsky, D. B., Seeber, R. L., & Fincher, R. D. (2003). *Emerging systems for managing workplace conflict: Lessons from American corporations for managers and dispute resolution professionals.* San Francisco: Jossey-Bass.

Losey, M. R. (1994). Managing in an era of workplace violence. *Managing Office Technology, 39,* 27–28.

Lukes, S. (1974). *Power: A radical view.* London: Macmillan.

Lulofs, R. S. & Cahn, D. D. (2000). *Conflict: From theory to action* (2nd ed.). Boston: Allyn and Bacon.

March, J. G., & Simon, H. A. (1958). *Organizations.* New York: Wiley.

Martin, J. (1990). Deconstructing organizational taboos: The suppression of gender conflict in organizations. *Organization Science, 1*(4), 339–359.

McCaffery, P. (2004). *The higher education manager's handbook: Effective leadership and management in universities and colleges.* New York: Routledge Falmer.

McGee, R. J. (1971). *Academic Janus.* San Francisco: Jossey-Bass.

Mintzberg, H. (1983). *Power in and around organizations.* Englewood Cliffs, NJ: Prentice-Hall.

Neilson, E. H. (1972). Understanding and managing conflict. In J. Lorsch & P. Lawrence (Eds.), *Managing group and intergroup relations.* Homewood, IL: Irwin.

Phillips, F. P. (2000). *Employment dispute resolution systems: An empirical survey and tentative conclusions.* New York: CPR Institute for Conflict Resolution.

Pinkley, R. L., Griffith, T. L., & Northcraft, G. B. (1995). Fixed pie a la mode: Information-availability, information-processing, and the negotiation of suboptimal agreements. *Organizational Behavior and Human Decision Processes, 62*(1), 101–112.

Pneuman, R. W., & Bruehl, M. E. (1982). *Managing conflict: A complete process-centered handbook.* Englewood Cliffs, NJ: Prentice-Hall.

Pondy, L. R. (1967). Organizational conflict: Concepts and models. *Administrative Science Quarterly, 12,* 296–320.

Rahim, M. A. (1992). *Managing conflict in organizations* (2nd ed.). Westport, CT: Praeger.

Rahim, M. A. (2001). *Managing conflict in organizations* (3rd ed.). Westport, CT: Quorum Books.

Robbins, S. P. (1974). *Managing organizational conflict: A nontraditional approach.* Upper Saddle River, NJ: Prentice Hall.

Robbins, S. P. (1998). *Organizational behavior: Concepts, controversies, applications* (8th ed.). Upper Saddle River, NJ: Prentice Hall.

Rudolph, F. (1977). *Curriculum: A history of the American undergraduate course of study since 1636.* San Francisco: Jossey-Bass.

Sandole, D. (1987). Conflict management: Elements of generic theory and practice. In D. Sandole & I. Sandole-Staroste (Eds.), *Conflict management and problem solving: Interpersonal to international applications.* New York: New York University Press.

Sandole, D. (1993). Paradigms, theories, and metaphors in conflict and conflict resolution: Coherence or confusion? In D. Sandole & H. Van Der Merwe (Eds.), *Conflict resolution theory and practice: Integration and application* (pp. 3–24). New York: Manchester University Press.

Sheppard, B. H. (1984). Third party conflict intervention: A procedural framework. In L. L. Cummings & B. M. Staw (Eds.), *Research in Organizational Behavior, Vol. 6* (pp. 41–90). Greenwich, CT: JAI Press.

Simmel, G. (1955). *Conflict and the web of group affiliations.* Glencoe, IL: The Free Press.

Spender, J.-C., & Grinyer, P. (1995). Organizational renewal: Top management's role in a loosely coupled system. *Human Relations, 48*(8), 909–926.

Staw, B. (1980). Rationality and justification in organizational life. In L. Cummings & B. Staw (Eds.), *Research in organizational behavior, Vol. 2* (pp. 45–80). Greenwich, CT: JAI Press.

Steers, R. M. (1991). *Introduction to organizational behavior* (4th ed.). New York: Harper Collins Publishers.

Sturnick, J. A. (1998). And never the twain shall meet: Administrator-faculty conflict. In S. Holton (Ed.), *Mending the cracks in the ivory tower: Strategies for conflict management in higher education* (pp. 97–112). Bolton, MA: Anker Publishing.

Thomas, K. W. (1976). Conflict and conflict management. In M. D. Dunnette (Ed.), *Handbook of industrial and organizational psychology* (pp. 889–935). Chicago: Rand McNally.

Thomas, K. W. (1977). Toward multidimensional values in teaching: The example of conflict behaviors. *Academy of Management Review, 2*(3), 484–490.

Tierney, W. (1992). Cultural leadership and the search for community. *Liberal Education, 78*(5), 16–21.

Tjosvold, D. (1991). Rights and responsibilities of dissent: Cooperative conflict. *Employee Responsibilities and Rights Journal, 4,* 13–23.

Van Maanen, J. (1992). Drinking our troubles away: Managing conflict in a British police agency. In D. M. Kolb & J. M. Bartunek (Eds.), *Hidden conflict in organizations* (pp. 32–62). Newbury Park, CA: Sage.

Van Slyke, E. J. (1999). *Listening to conflict: Finding constructive solutions to workplace disputes.* New York: AMACOM.

Wall, J. & Callister, R. R. (1995). Conflict and its management. *Journal of Management, 21,* 515–558.

Walton, R. E., & Dutton, J. M. (1969). The management of interdepartmental conflict: A model and review. *Administrative Science Quarterly, 14*(1), 73–84.

Walton, R. E., & McKersie, R. B. (1991). *A behavioral theory of labor negotiations: An analysis of a social interaction system.* Ithaca, NY: Industrial and Labor Relations Press, Cornell University.

3

POWER AND POLITICS IN HIGHER EDUCATION ORGANIZATIONS

CONTENTS

Preview   536
Case Context   537
Introduction   540
Some Definitions: Power, Authority, and Politics   541
Power and Rationality   546
Organizational Versus Personal Determinants of Power   548
Organizational Determinants of Power   549
Horizontal Power: Strategic Contingencies Theory   551
Vertical Power: Partisans and Authorities   554
Personal Power   561
Social Constructionist Perspectives on Power   568
Empowerment   571
Marxist and Postmodern Alternatives   572
Power, Politics, and Unions   574
Summary   575
Review Questions   576
Case Discussion Questions   578
References   578

The authors are most grateful for the critical comments on an early draft of this chapter by Benjamin Baez, Florida International University. The final version, of course, is our own and may or may not reflect the perspective of the reviewer.

Preview

- Power is a potential or kinetic force that enables one organizational unit (e.g., department, individual) to influence others in ways that benefit the power holder(s).
- Politics arises when there is uncertainty or disagreement about important choices.
- To make policy decisions, colleges and universities combine the structures of rational bureaucracy and democratic polity.
- Authority is legitimated power. The design of an organization serves to constrain power through the use of authority.
- A heterogeneity of organizational norms and values is likely to evoke political activity unless there is a strong set of counternorms toward common goals and unity.
- According to strategic contingencies theory, subunit power is derived from a unit's ability to provide critical resources to other units when there is scarcity, uncertainty, workflow centrality, and nonsubstitutability.
- According to William Gamson, organizations can contain multiple subgroups with varying degrees of visibility and interest in pressing self-serving agendas.
- The exercise of power is inversely related to the presence of trust among organizational participants.
- Authorities and workers (potential partisans) engage in a variety of efforts to influence each other with the choice of tactic being partly a function of the degree of trust among participants.
- Potential partisans use constraints, inducements, and persuasion, while authorities use insulation, sanctions, and persuasion to influence each other.
- French and Raven proposed five different modes by which individuals exercise power: reward power, coercive power, legitimate power, referent power, and expert power.
- Organizations with different emphases on centralization and individualism/collectivism use different strategies for employing power.
- The social construction paradigm notes that organizational symbols convey and maintain power.
- Empowerment is based on the idea that each person has an internal drive for autonomy and meaningful work. Organizational members are empowered when power and authority are decentralized and workers believe that they have control over meaningful work.

--------------------- CASE CONTEXT ---------------------

Organizational Politics at Bryson College

Bryson College, a private institution in the Midwest, had a long-standing reputation as a highly political work environment. Factions within the college would squabble over resources. Disgruntled parties would routinely take their grievances to the media. The board of trustees became so dissatisfied with faculty behavior that they voted to eliminate tenure, only to restore it 1 year later after large numbers of faculty threatened to leave.

This unwieldy campus was held together by the dominant personality of its previous president. He had been a faculty member at Bryson prior to becoming its president. His smooth-talking charm and tact were always able to bring the factions (faculty, trustees, students) back from the brink of outright warfare. "And he knew where all the bodies were buried," joked a senior faculty member. "He had been at Bryson forever, and if you crossed him, he knew how to take you down."

Recently, however, the trustees had appointed a new president, Janice Briggs, who was entering her first presidency. President Briggs was ambitious and wanted to bring national attention to Bryson College. The trustees were wary of her ideological beliefs (she had a reputation as a liberal activist), but they were impressed with her vision for national prominence.

The faculty were initially receptive to President Briggs. Women faculty, in particular, were hopeful that she would brush away the good old boys' network that tended to prevail during her predecessor's tenure. Briggs, however, met extensively with the former president and decided to adopt many of his practices, including limiting faculty access to her office and relying on only a few trusted advisors when making decisions. "Keep it close to the vest," the former president advised. "Otherwise, they will eat you alive. I still have the teeth marks to prove it!"

It was not long before President Briggs encountered her first major crisis. It occurred at the beginning of her first full year in office, and it was displayed across the front page of the local newspaper: "Bryson College President Blasts U.S. Counter-Terrorism Effort."

"Everything about this article is a distortion," complained President Briggs to her chief of staff. In her opening day convocation speech, Briggs had focused her remarks on civil liberties and national security. She had asked students to consider how much control over their personal lives they were willing to sacrifice in order to give the federal government more authority to monitor and regulate personal behavior. Then, she referred to pending federal legislation to give the FBI and CIA more authority to intercept telephone conversations without prior approval by a judge. President

Briggs's next remark earned her the front page headline: "Those in Congress who vote without reservation to restrict civil liberties in the name of counter-terrorism may do more damage to the Constitution than the terrorists themselves."

This statement prompted a swift response from the chair of the college's board of trustees, who happens to be a major financial contributor to the political party currently in power. "In no way does the board support President Briggs's remarks. Her comments were irresponsible and disrespectful to anyone who has worn the military uniform of this country." Another member of the board expressed similar outrage: "We pay her to have an academic policy, not a foreign policy. That was not the thing to say when we are in the middle of a capital campaign. It's going to hurt fund raising."

For her part, President Briggs was bewildered. "When did college presidents stop being public intellectuals, and morph into professional fund raisers?" she asked her academic vice president, a long-time friend and colleague. "Our students ought to have the courage to stand for an unpopular position, and if I don't set that example, who will?"

"Certainly not the trustees," answered the vice president. "Well, on the bright side, this will probably make the *Chronicle*," he noted, referring to the *Chronicle of Higher Education*'s weekly coverage of higher education news.

"This isn't the way I wanted to make the *Chronicle*," the president replied.

Meanwhile, across campus, several members of the faculty senate convened an informal gathering to discuss President Briggs's situation. Last spring, senate members expressed displeasure with several of Briggs's actions. For example, faculty members were not included in her recent decision to make admissions standards more selective and "rebrand" the institution as an elite educational experience. There had been some talk that the senate would take a vote of no confidence in the president in September.

"I agree with everything that she said, but what was she thinking? We all know the politics of the board. Is she trying to get fired?" asked the chair of the English department.

"Well, this whole thing could be a blessing or a curse," noted the chair of the faculty senate. "It seems like bad timing to vote against her when she said some things that most of the faculty would agree with," continued the senate chair. "But at the same time, this controversy weakens her standing with the board, and our vote of 'no confidence' could be enough to push her aside."

"But our goal is not necessarily to push her aside," replied the English department chair. "Who knows who the board would hire to replace her—probably someone even worse. Let's wait on this no confidence vote. What we want instead is to overturn this crazy selective admissions policy and get more faculty influence back in decision making. She is relying on outside consultants and completely disregarding us."

The senate members agreed that they would draft a memo to both President Briggs and the chair of the trustees. The memo would attempt to persuade them that the new admissions standards were inconsistent with the mission of college and that the college should appoint a new faculty committee to address any future major policy changes.

Before the senate members even began to draft the memo, however, President Briggs had already assembled another coalition of faculty who rallied to her defense. This coalition included faculty who supported the higher admissions standards, as well as faculty for whom civil liberties was the driving force in how they viewed the entire issue. "I am willing to put aside my current feelings about the admissions policy," noted a professor of religious studies, "because I have such strong feelings about what I see as the erosion of liberty and democracy in this country. I am with Briggs on this one."

President Briggs also rallied to her side academics, celebrities, and political figures who supported her position and who lobbied board members to tone down their criticism. Before the senate's memo reached the chair of the board of trustees, he had already been lobbied by two college presidents and had received a telephone call from a Hollywood celebrity whose movies he enjoyed a great deal. Following that conversation, the board chair did not even read the faculty senate's memo. "Those crazy faculty can't influence me," the chair proudly proclaimed to a fellow board member. "Those faculty are the reason why I wanted to get rid of tenure in the first place."

Two weeks later, the senate took a vote of no confidence, but by that time, the board had relented and the controversy had subsided. A narrow majority of the senate voted 'no confidence' in the president, but the trustees reaffirmed their support for Briggs in their next meeting. President Briggs then sought to remove several members of the senate whom she claimed had not been duly elected by their respective departments. New senate elections were scheduled. During the election period, President Briggs announced that a new faculty travel fund would be established,

which would provide extra money for departments deemed particularly innovative. Briggs announced that she would name those departments following
the election. Perhaps it was not a coincidence, then, that many of the new
members elected to the senate were those same faculty members who
backed the president during the crisis. Following the election, departments
that elected supporters of Briggs were awarded the additional travel funds.

Introduction

F aculty argue with deans, deans with vice presidents, the president's
staff with the president, the president with the trustees, and, within
these groups, members and clusters of members with each other.
Who wins these battles is often (though not always) a reflection of who has
the most power. Wishes for power, the exercise of power, and the results
of using power pervade higher education, as they do in virtually all
organizations.

Power as an important force in higher education tends to be denigrated
by organizational members, since institutions of higher education wish to be
perceived as citadels of rationality, hence, presumably, more bound by logic,
truth, and manifested humanistic values than by the excessive self-interest
alleged to be commonly found in the profit-making sector (Brown, 1982;
Wolff, 1969). Uses of certain kinds of power by persons or groups in colleges
and universities are, however, an inevitable result of a democratic, participative ethos in higher education and must be understood and managed
carefully. Excessive uses of power, on the other hand, sometimes arise ille-
gitimately—that is, without community acceptance—and are deleterious to
the accomplishment of the missions of institutions. Distinguishing between
legitimate and illegitimate uses of power requires careful analysis if appropriate policies and actions are to be taken.

Recall that in the previous chapter, we examined some of the sources of
conflict in colleges and universities. We noted that in systems terms, when
there is a mismatch or misfit of organizational components, self-preservation
or suboptimization at the unit level takes place. That is, groups and individuals seek to maximize their local advantage, even at the expense of others
within the system. In this chapter, we explore somewhat further this distributive dimension of conflict in organizations where goals are diverse, resources
are fixed or declining, and comity and trust are low. We move into a somewhat shady domain of organizational activity—the infighting, backbiting,
and nonrational means of influence that are employed behind the scenes to
a greater or lesser degree in most organizations. In this chapter, we examine

how power is a form of control and how the extent and manner of its exercise are affected by the structures and culture of the organization (Tushman, 1977). The chapter considers power from both organizational and personal perspectives. In other words, we look at the manifestations of power as the resultant of organizational conditions as well as the product of individual choice (i.e., through autonomous action).

Some Definitions: Power, Authority, and Politics

Though power has long been the subject of thought and research, there is notable disagreement both about its specific definition and the related concepts used to study this phenomenon in organizations. We start, therefore, with some basic definitions. As a first step toward a definition, we can distinguish the meaning of power from that of influence and authority. Specifically, authority is one type of power, and power is one form of influence.

The political scientist Robert Dahl (1961) defined power as the ability to get others to do something that they would not otherwise do. In this definition, a dean has power if she is able to get faculty to change their teaching practices if the faculty had no desire to do so themselves. Power reflects not only the ability to provoke changes in others, but also the *potential* ability to do so. Thus, if the faculty believe that the dean has the capacity to make them change their teaching practices in spite of their desire not to, then the dean can be said to possess power. In this case, power reflects an influence relationship—that is, the potential or actual ability to change others.

Power, however, is only one form of influence. Other types of influence can occur without the exercise of power. Recommendations, advice, and rational arguments, for example, can convince people to change their views and actions. The argument may be powerful, but the individual making the argument cannot be said to have exercised power, since the others willingly accepted the argument.

Thus, power connotes the ability to get people to do something against their will or against their interests. Power is an exercise of control that diminishes the autonomy of the other party. Max Weber (1924/1947), in fact, defined power in terms of the probability that one actor can influence another to do his/her will despite the other's resistance. One problem with this definition, however, is that it suggests that resistance must be manifest in order to know when power has been exercised. Yet power can be used to suppress or pre-empt resistance. Moreover, power can be used to shape the outlooks of others so that they do not resist. Some people exercise power over others by fostering alienation and a feeling of helplessness; resistance, from this vantage point, is futile. This is a form of power. The tyrannical leader who creates a work environment where resistance seems pointless has induced people to do something (i.e., refrain from resisting) that they otherwise would not have done. Under other circumstances, they *would* have resisted.

Steven Lukes (1974, 2005) provides a useful categorization of the different definitions of power. The first camp, which he calls the **one-dimensional view of power,** adopts Dahl's basic definition—getting people do to something that they otherwise would not. More specifically, this definition assumes that people act in accordance with their own interests. A person's interests can be equated with those features of the environment that advance his or her well-being. Labor unions emerged, for example, to advance individuals' interests in wages and working conditions. Power is revealed through conflicts of interest; for example, a conflict between management's desire to keep costs low and employees' interest in obtaining better wages. "To exercise power is to prevail over the contrary preference of others, with respect to key issues" (Lukes, 1986, p. 9). Power is thus equated with those who are able to force others to accept an outcome that is not in their interest. A union has power, for example, if it is able to get management to provide raises that it otherwise would not have given.

The **two-dimensional view of power** extends this analysis and suggests that power is exercised not only through direct conflicts of interest, but also through the ability to control agendas, to decide which issues come up for discussion, and to exclude ideas that might be dangerous to the interests of the powerful. Under this conceptualization, overt conflicts of interest (e.g., labor-management disputes) are not necessary concomitants of power. Power is also exercised through the ability to exclude certain issues from decision-making forums. Bachrach and Baratz (1962) referred to this phenomenon as the "two faces" of power. The first face is the ability to make direct and visible change. The second face refers to the capacity to erect or maintain barriers to the decision-making process itself. A college president facing a potentially controversial issue, for example, may route the decision to a committee known to be supportive of his or her views. Other committees where alternative views and interests might be expressed are shut out of the process.

Finally, Lukes offers a **three-dimensional view of power** that builds on the previous two. In addition to overt control (the one-dimensional view) and more subtle exclusion (the two-dimensional view), power is also manifest when it shapes and modifies the desires and beliefs of others in ways that are contrary to their interests. "To put the matter sharply, A may exercise power over B by getting him to do what he does not want to do, but he also exercises power over him by influencing, shaping and determining his very wants" (Lukes, 1974, p. 23). This conceptualization of power is slightly different from the example of a tyrannical leader who forces an organization into submission, where resistance is viewed as futile. Instead, the level of control is more insidious; the members of the organization do not think to resist because they do not perceive any conflict of interest.

Consider, for example, a college where the dean has traditionally mandated a certain type of curriculum for the faculty—the books to use, the lessons to teach. On most campuses, such an effort would evoke resistance and retaliation by faculty who expect to make their own curricular decisions. Here we would have a genuine conflict of interest: the dean's interest in control and the faculty's interest in academic freedom. But on the campus that we are considering, the faculty do not even think to question the dean's decision. Through processes of selection and socialization, the interests of the faculty have been shaped and determined by the administrators of the college. These faculty do not want what faculty elsewhere typically want. No grievances are raised; no pockets of potential opposition can be detected. The administration has exercised the power to control what the faculty want.

Of course, this definition assumes that we can determine the "real" interests of a particular group and ascertain when those real interests have been supplanted by contrary interests. In the example above, we assume that faculty have an interest in academic freedom, and when they act and think in ways that are contrary to those interests we assume that power has been exercised over them. Lukes (1974) acknowledges that these assumptions may be difficult to operationalize; that is, how can we determine a group's real interests if the group itself is unaware of them? If we substitute our own views for those of the group, then we are making a normative decision about what a group's interests *ought* to be, rather than what they actually are.

Lukes does, however, point to some examples such as air quality that are incontrovertible public goods. Lukes refers to a study by political scientist Matthew Crenson (1971), which examined how different cities in the United States responded to poor air quality during the 1950s and 1960s. Some cities witnessed active regulatory movements. In other cities, specifically those that were "one-company" towns with a single political party in charge, very little activity occurred. When one company dominated the economic base of a city, its power reputation thwarted attempts to raise the air quality issue. Citizens did not engage in activities that could damage the viability of the company that provided for the livelihood of so many. In contrast, in cities where the economic base was more diversified, attacks on a particular polluting factory were not viewed as jeopardizing the entire community. The political composition of city government also played a role in determining the scope of regulatory activity. With a dominant political party in the city, policy makers perceived no need to identify issues for reform. Instead, political actors sought stability and attempted to curry favor with the dominant company in town. In some cities, it was several decades before the clear air issue even surfaced in the regulatory actions of municipal government. This example demonstrates "how political systems prevent demands from becoming political issues or even from being made" (Lukes, 1974, p. 38).

Two additional points can be made regarding definitions of power. First, the exercise of power is not necessarily good or evil. Power can effect positive change as well as oppress and alienate. Even Lukes's three-dimensional view of power can be seen to have potentially positive implications. In fact, transformative leadership is often defined in terms of the ability of a leader to get people to move beyond their interests and adopt a different set of wants (Burns, 1978). (The problem, of course, is that the leader gets to determine what those wants should be. Thus, the more likely scenario of the three-dimensional view of power is exploitation, or at the very least paternalism.)

Second, power is not restricted to top-down, superior-subordinate relationships. All organizational members have power (or potential power). As Foucault (1976/1986) noted:

> Power must be analyzed as something which circulates, or rather as something which only functions in the form of a chain. It is never localized here or there, never in anybody's hands, never appropriated as a commodity or piece of wealth. Power is employed and exercised through a net-like organization. And not only do individuals circulate between its threads; they are always in the position of simultaneously undergoing and exercising this power. (p. 234)

Thus, lower level organizational members can exercise power over colleagues and even over their supervisors. Several authors, in fact, argue that most influence attempts in organizations move upward; that is, lower level employees attempt to change the actions and beliefs of upper level managers (Porter, Angle, & Allen, 2003). This is not to suggest that all organizational members have equal power. As Foucault also noted, power is not "the best distributed thing in the world" (p. 234). There are vast disparities in power in organizations and in society at large. But people are not powerless. Small acts of resistance, for example, can trigger a tipping point that reshapes the balance of power.

A specific type of power, however, is exercised in a formal hierarchical relationship. **Authority** is conceived as legitimated power. That is, when the exercise of power is accepted by organizational members as reasonable and proper, it is labeled "authority." Lower level members accept the authority of higher level members to determine what constitutes appropriate action. Deans of academic colleges typically accept the authority of the chief academic officer to determine various policies. Similarly, a dean of residence life may accept the authority of the vice president for student affairs to request data on the quality of services provided by his or her unit. When authority is exercised, the communication that an organizational member receives is viewed as appropriately governing the action that he or she has been asked to take (Barnard, 1938). The communication stems from a source in the organization conceived by the recipient to be valid.

Thus authority is one type of power—one that is organizationally endorsed. In contrast, **politics** can be defined as the use of influence in ways *not* officially sanctioned by the organization. Pfeffer (1981) reports that within most organizational settings, politics refers to "those activities taken to acquire, develop, and use power and other resources to obtain one's preferred outcomes in a situation in which there is uncertainty or dissensus about choices" (p. 7). The key words here are "uncertainty" and "dissensus," since it is under these conditions that politics is more likely to arise.

Sometimes politics involves an abuse of authority; for example, a twisting of official rights by a department chair to make a politically desirable decision; other times, it involves the formation of power coalitions, which serve as a stimulus for positive change. Secretaries in an admissions office, for example, may band together to protest a newly imposed mandatory after-hours assignment for which they are not compensated (White, 1989). At still other times, politics involves the use of underhanded, if not illegal methods. The dominant coalition in the organization (i.e., the one that possesses the most aggregated power) controls the structures and processes through which most organizational decisions are made; therefore, members of that coalition are in positions to make decisions that preserve their power base and maintain their dominant status. The self-serving behaviors of dominant coalitions are the focus of much research from critical and postmodern perspectives (Deetz, 1992).

Politics in a **polity** (i.e., a democratically organized governance system), on the other hand, is not necessarily viewed as devious manipulation, but as part of the processes of democratic conflict resolution in a community that involves persons and units with different goals and interests—for example, governance in an institution of higher education (Cohen & March, 1974; Easton, 1965). Gareth Morgan (1998) suggests that all organizations can and should be viewed through the lens of politics. He notes:

> Organizational politics arise when people think differently and want to act differently. This diversity creates a tension that must be resolved through political means . . . there are many ways in which this can be done: autocratically ("We'll do it this way"); bureaucratically ("We're supposed to do it this way"); technocratically ("It's best to do it this way") or democratically ("How shall we do it?"). In each case the choice between alternative

paths of action usually hinges on the power relations between the actors involved. (p. 152)

Power and Rationality

Colleges and universities are combinations of rational organization and polity. As rational organization, higher education institutions rely primarily on hierarchical authority relations to accomplish collective goals. As polity, colleges and universities are characterized by political behaviors such as bargaining and negotiation, which seek to advance individual or subunit goals. Daft (2001) has identified the differences between the rational and political models of organization (Table 3.1).

Depending in part on such factors as mission, goals, size, and institutional history, one or the other form tends to predominate. Further, the proportional influence of rational organization versus polity varies substantially across organizations. Sometimes the entire organization constitutes a mixture; other times, different sectors of the organization manifest more rational hierarchy or more polity characteristics. Different constituencies across the organization, moreover, will view the use of power differently. Some will see power as a legitimate tool that can be used to advance organizational goals, but others will see power as a perversion of the noble aims of higher education. Finally, even the same individual in an organization will likely gravitate between using the tools of hierarchy and polity. A college president may criticize a group of faculty who protest a recent cut in their department's budget. He may claim that rational criteria such as enrollment data were used in the budget process. But that same president may use political pressure tactics when a state legislature or a governing board fails to act on one of his funding priorities. In order to understand more fully the relative balance between hierarchy and polity, we explore the relationship between rationality and power.

Rational organizational behavior can be defined as behavior aimed at the effectiveness of the organization as a whole, even at the possible cost of some diminution of individual or group benefit. When high value is attached to an institution's goal achievement by organizational members, they are more willing to sacrifice personal goals to the common good. In a perfectly rational bureaucracy, it is assumed that members will work toward organizational aims under two conditions: when there is a high degree of homogeneity in personal backgrounds and attitudes and when there is a strong organizational culture. More homogeneous organizations tend to experience less conflict among workers, thus reducing the need for power or authority to adjudicate among competing claims. When organizations recruit and select employees,

TABLE 3.1
Comparison of Rational and Political Models of Organizational Behavior

Organizational Characteristics	Rational/Bureaucratic	Political
Goals and preferences	Consistent across participants	Inconsistent, pluralistic
Role orientation	Maximize organizational goal achievement, which is assumed to be homogeneous across participants	Suboptimization; realize individual goals and desires, often at the expense of the collective good
Power and control	Centralized, bureaucratic	Decentralized, shifting coalitions and interest groups
Rules and norms	Little deviance from organizational mandates	Deviance is subject to constraints of manifested power
View of discontent and dissatisfaction	A problem that must be addressed to increase motivation among organizational members	Basis for self-serving behavior designed to increase power and influence
Information	Extensive, systematic	Ambiguous; information used and withheld strategically
Beliefs about cause-effect relationships	Believed to be known, at least to a probability estimate	Disagreements about causes and effects
Decisions	Based on rational optimization of total organizational goals	Outcome of bargaining, interplay among interests
Ideology	Efficiency and effectiveness of organization	Struggle, conflict, winners and losers among factions
Focus of theory and research	Regulation of conflict; how organizations can keep workers "in line" with expectations	Who succeeds and why; under what conditions do certain individuals and groups get their own way (e.g., unions, academic departments)

Adapted from Daft (2001, p. 446).

they tend to look for people who share backgrounds and perspectives with others already employed by the organization. This recruitment strategy will bring in workers who are predisposed to link their own personal and professional objectives with extant organizational goals.

Similarly, when the culture of an organization is quite strong, people are attracted and recruited on the basis of the organization's known values, objectives, and style of activity. Under these conditions, there is usually less use of politics and power. The downside risk of excessive homogeneity and strong cultures, however, is "groupthink"—a condition in groups when continuing agreement and civility among members are viewed as more important than arriving at a high-quality decision. Under these conditions, organizational members may attain a quick consensus and thereafter fail to question the correctness of their position. This rigidity in thinking can lead to less innovation within the organization and to the development of poorly informed decisions (Hirokawa, Gouran, & Martz, 1988; Janis, 1982). A continuing problem for leaders, therefore, is the extent to which they can and will as a matter of policy accept some degree of conflict and power use in order for organizational members not to fall into too uniform a pattern of thinking and problem solving.

Note that we are considering rationality from the perspective of an outside observer of organizational efficiency. From the point of view of an individual, maximization of personal goals is also "rational," even if it violates organizational rationality. However, this perspective may not be functional for the organization in the long run, since, as Harden (1968) observes, the system suffers a "tragedy of the commons." That is, the exploitation of common organizational resources by each person seeking to maximize his or her benefits will result, ultimately, in a scarcity of resources for everyone.

When assumptions of rationality break down, self-interests or group interests take over—either in self-defense or in an effort to advance a particular agenda. Departures from organizational rationality, therefore, can be defined as political or power-based behavior. Extensive division of labor and scarce resources are likely to diminish organizational members' focus on organization-wide goals and thus contribute to the breakdown of rational behavior. As a result, political behavior can be expected. Indeed, as Pettigrew (1973) notes, "as long as organizations continue as resource sharing systems where there is an inevitable scarcity of those resources, political behavior will occur" (p. 20).

Organizational Versus Personal Determinants of Power

A significant debate in the literature is concerned with the extent to which power in organizations is derived primarily from *structural* characteristics of the organization or largely from *individual* strengths and distinctiveness (Pfeffer, 1992; Welsh & Slusher, 1986). In the case of organizational determinants, power gravitates to certain units in the organization based on their position in the organizational design—horizontally, vertically, and across the organizational boundary (Brass & Burkhardt, 1993). In the case of individual determinants, power accrues to individuals on the basis of their personal characteristics. We will examine theories in both of these camps.

First, we employ strategic contingencies theory to explain the distribution of horizontal power in the organizational structure. Second, we explore William Gamson's (1968) theory of partisans and authorities to describe the tactics associated with exercising vertical power. We then consider individual determinants of power from the perspectives of French and Raven's (1960) sources of power framework and Mintzberg's (1983) analysis of political games in organizations.

Organizational Determinants of Power

Potential power is generated structurally because of the division of labor both horizontally and vertically and the consequent need to coordinate the differentiated parts. In colleges and universities, units are separated into schools, departments, and programs. Who ultimately comes to have the capacity to coordinate these divisions is at least partly a power question.

Decision-making systems are another structural source of potential power. Higher education institutions have both bureaucratic and consensual/collegial systems of decision making (Birnbaum, 1988). The administration and the faculty structure are separate but linked. Both have hierarchical characteristics (vertical relationships among operating units) that require approval of decision makers in successively higher offices. But lower entities that operate in a political democracy are generally resistant to disenfranchisement and reluctant to yield final authority upward. Consider, for example, a college curriculum committee that has representatives from all academic departments. The committee may decide to recommend a particular software package for online courses but resist when higher level administrative authorities—for example, the college's chief information officer—attempt to negotiate a site license with a different software firm. This tension in the exercise of vertical authority is adjudicated partly through bureaucratic authority and partly through the use of political power.

From a practical standpoint, it is necessary to look, therefore, at the ways that subunits acquire and use power both rationally and politically and at the structural explanations for that phenomenon. For any set of organizational units in a relationship, we can then conceive of the structural conditions of power in terms of their strength and distribution in three dimensions:

(1) horizontal power *within* the organization, (2) vertical power *within* the organization, and (3) power *across* the organization's boundaries.

Horizontal power is concerned with lateral relationships across units at the same or near the same level in the organizational hierarchy. In a college or university, such relationships might include school-to-school or department-to-department connections. The law school in a university, for example, may compete with the school of education for additional library resources. Both units would likely employ horizontal power to advance their interests. Within an organizational subunit itself, the horizontal power relationships might be among individual faculty members and/or staff of a department.

Vertical power is expressed in organizations through relationships between workers at different levels of responsibility. In these relationships, power is exercised both up and down the hierarchy. An academic dean may pressure faculty members to utilize a specific math skills assessment instrument to guide placement decisions for incoming students. In this example, vertical power is exerted downward—from a high ranking dean to a relatively lower ranking faculty unit. In contrast, vertical power may also be exerted upward. Entry-level staff in an admissions office, for example, may lobby their supervisor for more flexible work hours.

Vertical power reflects the legitimate power of authority that is expressed through the bureaucratic hierarchy and the deviations from authority that are the result of political behavior in an organization. It may refer also to underhanded and unethical political behavior that would not be deemed legitimate in any organization.

Cross-boundary power relationships also determine who has power in an organization. Power is likely to accrue to the units or people who can best deal with the environmental pressures that happen to be most crucial at the moment. Consider, for example, a vice president for administration and finance at a public university who is in frequent contact with the governor's office regarding budget projections for next year. She would have considerable power in the university, given her knowledge of and ability to deal with external financial pressures.

In the following sections, we examine two structural theories of power in organizations. The first—**strategic contingencies theory**—explains the horizontal distribution of power among subunits in an organization. The theory also incorporates cross-boundary relationships in its predictions of who will likely hold power in an organization. Second, we consider William Gamson's theory of the ways that organizational members exercise and mutually adjust to vertical (upward and downward) influence processes.

Horizontal Power: Strategic Contingencies Theory

Strategic contingencies theory is one of the most widely referenced structural theories of power in organizations (Goltz & Hietapelto, 2002; Hickson, Hinings, Lee, Schneck, & Pennings, 1971; Hinings, Hickson, Pennings, & Schneck, 1974; Salancik & Pfeffer, 1977). Hickson et al. suggest that subunits gain power when other organizational components (e.g., a department or an individual person) depend on that subunit for critical information, services, or resources. Dependencies arise when one unit is in a position to provide needed inputs to another and the second unit is not able to reciprocate (Pettigrew, 1973). As Hardy and Clegg (1996) note:

> Strategically contingent sub-units are the most powerful because they are the least dependent on other sub-units and can cope with the greatest systemic uncertainty, given that the sub-unit is central to the organization system and not easily substitutable. (p. 626)

For example, if the athletics department of a university produces resources in excess of its needs, and the institution comes to rely on that income, then the athletics department will become powerful. In another situation, if an organizationally desirable condition lies in the control of a particular subunit, other subunits will become dependent on that subunit, giving it power. Hickson et al. list four key contingencies that predict which organizational subunits will be most powerful: **scarcity, uncertainty, workflow centrality,** and **nonsubstitutability.**

1. **Scarcity.** Any subunit that is in a position to obtain resources that are especially critical to the effective functioning of the larger organization is likely to acquire and maintain power (Pfeffer & Salancik, 1974; Salancik & Pfeffer, 1974; Schick, Birch, & Tripp, 1986). Certain departments in colleges, for example, will be seen to be more powerful than others if they can procure more of the following: students (who provide tuition), parental and alumni approval, grants, and prestigious recognition such as top rankings in *U.S. News and World Report*. A subunit becomes powerful due to its ability to attract these resources, and, because of its power, the subunit can command other desired benefits. If an academic department acquires a major grant, for example, the college may reward this outcome with additional investments in that unit (e.g., a larger budget for the following academic year). The downside, however, may be a "rich get richer" phenomenon where subunits that are in control of scarce resources, in turn, command a disproportionately large share of an institution's

budget. As a result, the other, relatively poor units find themselves not only without power, but with reduced capacity to compete for resources in the future, thus leading to an ongoing cycle of disproportionate resource allocation.

2. **Uncertainty.** A critical source of power is the ability of any subunit to help other subunits deal with their uncertainties (Miles, 1980). If a subunit can provide needed information or resources to another subunit that allows better prediction of future events, then the other subunit will be dependent on the original unit. Hence, the original subunit will have power over the second unit.

Another form of uncertainty reduction can take place when one unit absorbs the pressures of another; for example, by taking on some of its roles or anticipating its needs. If an institutional research office, as one instance, is able to predict with reasonable accuracy how many students a department is likely to have registered in the forthcoming semester, it can reduce the uncertainty of that department, allowing it to plan better, hire the appropriate number of instructors and teaching assistants, and allocate the right number of classrooms.

As another example, if the institutional research office can predict for the college as a whole how many students will transfer from local community colleges and how many current students will drop out, the research office can reduce the uncertainty of the environment for the entire college, rendering the research office more powerful. The greater the uncertainty, the more powerful the unit can become (Pfeffer & Moore, 1980).

Power can also be predicted on the basis of whether a person's role spans across the boundary of the organization or is focused internally. Whether "boundary spanners" or "internals" are more powerful depends on external and internal conditions. Boundary spanners (e.g., enrollment specialists, marketing directors, directors of government relations) will be more powerful when the environment is turbulent, uncertain, complex, and competitive, since their role in reducing the organization's uncertainty is crucial. When external environments are simple and stable, on the other hand, internals (e.g., computer technicians, classroom schedulers) will be more powerful because they possess needed skills that are critical to effective organizational performance. In sum, when environments are unstable, boundary spanners can reduce uncertainty about inputs. When environments are stable, internal personnel can reduce uncertainty about processes and outputs.

3. **Workflow centrality.** A third contingency in determining power

holders is centrality to the workflow of the organization as a whole. There are two parts to this concept. Workflow **pervasiveness** refers to the degree to which the work of a subunit is connected to other units, particularly those that are critical to the key outputs of the organization. For example, if units are connected sequentially, then the "feeder" unit will have power over the receiving unit, since the latter is dependent on the quality, quantity, and timely delivery from the former. Further, if the receiving unit is central to the main mission of the organization, then the sending feeder unit will gain additional power. The information technology (IT) office in a university is powerful, because it pervades the organization and is critical to its success. Similarly, a large science department in a university contributes significantly to the university's success (reputation), thus giving it power over other units. However, if the science department is working on a project (e.g., superconductivity) that is likely to have a heavy impact on the institution's infrastructure, then other university subunits that have the capacity to control the success of the science department (e.g., the university's grants administration office) may gain additional power.

The second category of workflow centrality is **immediacy,** which refers to the capacity of a unit to provide rapid attention to organizational needs. If, for example, a unit is able to satisfy emergency service requirements, it will have more power than another unit that takes more time to do so. Thus, if there is a disturbance at an invited lecture on campus, security personnel who can respond quickly will be seen to have more power than others who must go through bureaucratic channels or who are physically more distant from the altercation.

4. **Nonsubstitutability.** The last category in strategic contingencies theory refers to the capacity of units to find substitute resources either inside or outside of the organization. If a subunit (either its personnel or its function) cannot be replaced, then it will acquire more power. As another example, if there is no substitute for the outputs that a department provides to other subunits (e.g., an information technology office that is the only supplier of technical support for the university's computers), then the original subunit will gain power.

Power, therefore, accrues to units or individuals who can deal with scarcity and uncertainty, who are central to the organization's key processes or outputs, and whose services cannot be substituted for.

Scarcity, uncertainty, workflow centrality, and nonsubstitutability constitute the major organizational factors that explain horizontal power—that is, the relative power of organizational subunits. We turn next to vertical power—specifically, influence tactics up and down the organizational hierarchy.

Vertical Power: Partisans and Authorities

To explore vertical power in colleges and universities, we turn to the work of William Gamson (1968). As a political and social scientist, Gamson was primarily concerned with sorting out the play of power among different constituencies and with understanding how to improve management effectiveness in a context of competing, and often self-serving, subunits. Gamson's theories can be used to reveal a number of vertical power relationships; for example, how faculty and administrators work out their power conflicts or how faculty and student power relationships can change depending on circumstances.

Gamson's theory seeks to understand how the actors in an organizational system react to the availability of power, how they seek to acquire power, and how the conflict over power is adjudicated. In Gamson's theory, there is no optimum functional form or design toward which the organization tends to strive—no overriding goal or structure to which the organization aspires. Instead, temporary coalitions arise to forward their own more limited and temporal aims (Alt & Alesina, 1996). This temporary, in-flux notion of power is consistent with several postmodern conceptualizations that emphasize the chaotic, disjointed, and fragmentary characteristics of power use (Martin, 1992).

Organizational "discontent" (part of the title of Gamson's book) is viewed, therefore, as an opportunity or as a threat for a particular subgroup, rather than simply as a problem of social control for organizational leaders. For example, when considering the effects of a decision by the state to hold public university salaries at current levels without granting raises, Gamson would have us consider the issues likely to arise not only as a problem for the administration, but also as an occasion for increased participation among the affected subgroups and the anticipation of action on their part.

Note that the assumptions of this model are quite different from those of a hierarchical, bureaucratic perspective. First, it assumes that there is no single, unifying organizational goal. Indeed, different subgroups in the organization have their own goals and tend to suboptimize. Second, it assumes that individuals are interested in being active and taking control; they are not passive, lazy, and unmotivated. If we begin with these different perspectives, the use of influence or control takes on a different tone. The major source of energy lies not in formal hierarchical authority, but instead in groups of organizational members (coalitions) who desire to exert some influence over their lives.

Organizational members in Gamson's theory are called **potential partisans**—actors who are affected by the decisions and actions of authorities. Set against these partisans are **organizational authorities** who are the targets that the partisans hope to influence. Authorities are those agents of the system who have the authority—legitimate power—to make binding decisions for others. Authorities in colleges and universities are organized into offices, boards, committees, administrations, councils, and senates, among other forms.

Potential partisans in a political system are more than simply aggregates of organized individuals (Etzioni, 1961). They are defined as "that set of actors who, for a given decision, are affected by the outcome in some significant way" (Gamson, 1968, p. 32). Gamson conceptualizes three kinds of potential partisans. The first is called a **solidary group**—a loose collection of workers who are attracted to each other initially for social reasons, but who have the potential to become involved in issues and to exercise influence. In a solidary group, members are aware of the views of others and identify with their concerns. There is a strong sense of collective belonging among members of a solidary group. Some examples of solidary groups include affiliations based on occupational specialties, a shared ethnic or linguistic heritage, or a shared status within the organization. In a college or university, for example, adjunct faculty members can be considered a solidary group (unless they are formally organized—see below).

By definition, solidary groups are not formally or legally constituted. If they are, then they comprise Gamson's second category of potential partisans: **interest groups.** An interest group has a clearly stated mission or purpose, as well as formalized procedures to delineate its membership. Unions, student organizations, and faculty committees can function as interest groups that seek to influence higher level authorities such as college presidents and trustees.

A third category of potential partisans is labeled by Gamson as a **quasi group.** Such a group is not necessarily oriented toward a common goal within the organization, nor do its members necessarily interact. Members of a quasi group are linked by common social characteristics. Female employees at an institution might be considered members of a quasi group. They constitute a latent arena for recruiting members for formal interest groups. For example, if a group of organizational members wished to create a committee to press for equal pay for women faculty and staff, then female employees as a quasi group could serve as the initial recruitment base for members for this new interest group.

Trust and Power

Relationships between authorities and partisan groups vary widely depending on the amount of **trust** that the partisans have in the authorities and in the organization in general. Trust can be viewed as faith or confidence that others will act in ways that are beneficial or at least not detrimental to the focal person (Mayer, Davis, & Schoorman, 1995). People also exhibit varying degrees of trust toward organizations and social institutions such as schools, churches, and government agencies. The subject of trust is of profound significance in all organizations, especially educational institutions (see for example, Fukuyama, 1995; Kramer & Tyler, 1995; Tierney, 2006; Tschannen-Moran & Hoy, 2000; Yamagishi & Yamagishi, 1994).

As Gamson explains, potential partisans' attitudes toward authorities range along a **continuum of trust**. Potential partisans' attitudes can range from high trust (**confidence**) to moderate trust (**neutrality**) to low trust (**alienation**). To the extent that potential partisans have trust in institutional authorities, according to Gamson's theory, they are less likely to engage in individual or collective partisan activities intended to influence those authorities on their behalf. To the extent that organizational members trust their authorities, they will find less need to try to influence them. In the organizational members' minds, the authorities are *already* acting in their behalf.

The theory, however, gives trust a neutral value. For example, when trust is high, authorities could make new commitments and take actions that are actually deleterious to organizational members' interests. Thus, there may be perils associated with high trust. Indeed, complacent acceptance of authorities' actions may impede innovation and hinder organizational growth and development (Minor & Tierney, 2005). Further, when trust is low or declining, authorities may find it difficult to meet existing commitments and to govern effectively. Thus neither high trust nor low trust are likely to contribute to long-term organizational effectiveness. Rather, neutrality toward others in the system or moderate confidence in the system as a whole (not only the authorities but in the whole system of decision making) will contribute to more effective organizational performance.

Gamson's theory assumes that a single, unitary organizational goal is unrealistic and/or mythical. Organizations and their members have many subgoals, often in competition with one another. If colleges and universities are viewed as democratically governed polities, Gamson's theory suggests that there must inevitably be some level of discontent among the constituencies—some frustration in losing out in the competition for satisfaction of competing goals. Given finite resources, at least *some* of the constituents' goals must be in conflict. Thus, if all subunits are supremely confident in the authorities, then some must surely be deceiving themselves (or are being deceived). Organizational effectiveness as a whole will *not* be maximized under conditions of universal maximum trust, according to Gamson, because the latent conflicts across constituencies are being masked.

In a typical decentralized academic system, different groups vary widely on the continuum of trust—some confident in the administration, some neutral, some alienated. For example, faculty may feel that the administrators are unfairly distributing pay raises and will try to influence them. If faculty members are successful in getting the administration to change the distribution of pay raises, then there may be fewer funds available for compensating other personnel (e.g., mid-level administrators such as department chairs) who, in turn, may lose confidence in the leadership of the organization. Institutional leaders, therefore, will have difficulty managing the discontent that inevitably arises in some groups.

On the other hand, if there is a common trust orientation among the members of the organization (even if it is not at the highest level), the sense of *equity* for the organization as a whole is not violated and interest groups may remain active or inactive at different times and under different circumstances. They will perceive that over time, on average, all parties will receive their just desserts.

In sum, neither complete confidence by all parties nor unequal confidence among parties will be effective. A narrow range of moderate confidence in the authorities is best, and authorities need to understand that some degree of distrust is perhaps essential in a healthy organization. Moreover, attempts to correct perceived inequities by deception will not be effective in the long run.

Upward Influence: How Partisans Attempt to Influence Authorities

We turn next to Gamson's analysis of the objects of influence—the authorities—and the modes by which partisans attempt to influence them. According to Gamson, there is no unified "them"—the "bad" authorities. Potential partisans often develop different attitudes toward many types of authorities: incumbent officials, institutional entities (e.g., a human resources office), institutional philosophies (e.g., the mission of the institution), and governance and decision-making procedures. For example, groups could be alienated with respect to a particular authority (an overbearing dean), but feel quite positively toward the institution's decision-making structure per se.

The politics of "upward influence" in organizations has received increasing attention in the literature. Some authors (Porter et al., 2003), in fact, suggest that the vast majority of political influence tactics in organizations is directed up the hierarchy. Workers learn how to work the system by absorbing and abiding by the norms of political behavior within each organization—a difficult task, since these informal guides to behavior are subtle and rarely articulated openly.

Gamson notes that there are three modes by which upward influence is exercised in organizations: constraints, inducements, and persuasion. Which are used most often and which are effective under different circumstances are key questions to understanding power in organizations.

1. **Constraints** are the addition of (or the threat of adding) new disadvantages to the authorities' behavior. Any resource can be used as a constraint. Partisans, for example, may simply imply that a new weapon will be used against authorities, and under certain circumstances that threat alone will be effective. For example, students may threaten to boycott, or union members may threaten to strike.
2. **Inducements** are the addition of new advantages that will accrue to the authorities or the promise to add them. A specific good or service, for example, can be transferred from partisans to authorities in exchange for some other good or service. This quid pro quo can be explicit or implicit. For example, workers may take a cut in salary in exchange for more job security.
3. **Persuasion** entails changing the minds of authorities without adding anything new to their situation; that is, convincing them to prefer some outcomes that are actually in the interests of the potential partisans. University faculty, for example, may persuade an academic vice president that research and teaching performance are highly correlated and that additional investments in research infrastructure will not be detrimental to the teaching mission of the institution. In this case, the faculty may change the mind of a vice president who was initially predisposed toward addressing concerns about the quality of teaching in undergraduate courses.

Usually groups will employ multiple types of influence. Oftentimes, a combination is used and no single approach will predominate. In fact, Gamson proposes a *matching* of influence strategies with particular situations depending on where the group lies on the continuum of trust noted earlier. In other words, according to Gamson's schema, different upward influence tactics are used when levels of trust vary. As noted in Table 3.2, when the trust level is high (confident), persuasion is most effective; when trust is neutral, inducements are used; and when partisans are alienated, constraints are likely to be employed.

Downward Influence: How Authorities Attempt to Influence Partisans

We shift now from the upward influence modes of the partisans to the downward tactics of the authorities. Authorities make **binding decisions** for the organization. A decision is binding if (1) it is accepted for whatever reason, (2) legitimate force can be used to implement it, and (3) it is not subject to review by others. Effective authority, then, is compliance in the absence of the necessity for control. That is, potential partisans do what leaders want without the leaders needing to exercise continual monitoring and control (Barnard, 1938).

Authorities exercise their influence through three basic methods. First, they can attempt to persuade potential partisans that decisions are actually in their long-term collective interest (e.g., no pay raise now to avoid layoffs later). Second, authorities can offer rewards for compliance and penalties for noncompliance (e.g., not granting the vacation request of a troublesome employee). Third, authorities can insulate themselves from potential partisans by limiting access to the decision-making system of the organization. All three approaches serve to emphasize stability and allow authorities to govern. Table 3.3 reveals Gamson's analysis of the relative effectiveness of different influence tactics by authorities depending on circumstances.

Two other somewhat overlapping control activities fall under more than one of these categories of downward influence. Co-optation and participation are mixed modes of social control by authorities intended to establish trust by involving potential partisans in decision making. **Co-optation** is the process of absorbing partisan elements into the leadership or policy-determining structure of the organization. An example is appointing a faculty member known to have views *opposing* the authorities to an administrative committee. Once a discontented person or group is co-opted, there is a greater likelihood of control by authorities, as the co-opted person is influenced by the increased contact with authorities and is likely to carry the authorities' message more positively and convincingly to fellow potential partisans.

Participation is the process of allowing potential partisans access to the formal decision-making apparatus itself. From the social control perspective,

TABLE 3.2
Effective Influence Tactics Under Varying Degrees of Trust

When trust level is:	Influence type used is:	Rationale
Confident	**Persuasion**	Used by a confident partisan group. Reason: These persons already believe that authorities are committed to goals that they can support. Persuasion tactics: Communications, media, reputation of the authority figure for wisdom and skills; personal charisma of the authority figure. Problems with other tactics: If threat is used, it might have an adverse effect on the authority-partisan relationship. Retaliation may result. For example, if a confident group (e.g., a campus security union) threatens a strike, authorities are likely to react negatively.
Neutral	**Inducements**	Used by a neutral partisan group. Reason: Persons in this group are not fully convinced of the authorities' benevolence, but they do not believe that authorities will take advantage of them. Inducement tactics: Offer something to authorities in exchange for which authorities will give something back; a quid pro quo. Problems with other tactics: Other means of influence might backfire. For example, persuasion is not perceived to be effective, because authorities are viewed as having different goals. And constraints might create hostility between the partisans and the authorities.
Alienated	**Constraints**	Used by an alienated partisan group. Reason: The group does not worry about resentment from authorities in the form of unfavorable outcomes, because outcomes were anticipated to be unfavorable prior to the use of influence. Constraint tactics: Work restriction, circumvention of authority, threats.

When trust level is:	Influence type used is:	Rationale
		Problems with other tactics: Alienated partisans who engage in persuasion will not be believable by untrusting authorities, and the partisans usually have nothing to offer as inducements—or are unwilling to offer them because of their distrust of authorities.

Adapted from Thomas (1976).

it is reasoned that a feeling of legitimate participation will increase commitment to the organization and acceptance of decisions even if outcomes are not always particularly satisfying.

It is important to recognize that Gamson's political approach is different from a social control perspective. In the latter, advocates tend to take the side of management and try to determine how to sustain commitment to work and compliance to management-determined work rules. The agents of social control are authorities in organizations acting in their capacity as agents of the system. The targets of control are the workers who can disrupt the orderly functioning of the system. Gamson's political perspective, on the other hand, is an influence perspective, rather than a control perspective (though the difference is subtle). Gamson's focus is on subordinates and their legitimate or illegitimate claims of influence. The targets of influence in this case are the very authorities in control; that is, those actors who are in a position to make binding decisions governing the workers. Gamson views organizations as comprising actors with individual goals and/or group goals, and he is interested in seeing how upward and downward influence tactics result in one or another party gaining or losing power.

Personal Power

Thus far, we have considered organizational subunits and nonformalized groups and their power orientations and behaviors, both horizontal and vertical. Next we turn to individuals as units of analysis to see how they exercise power—or attempt to. Here, we can examine organizations as congeries of different kinds of people and groups, each seeking to maximize their own self-interest within the constraints of the system (Pfeffer, 1981).

A number of theorists have expanded our understanding of personal power. Perhaps the most well known is the approach of French and Raven

TABLE 3.3
Downward Influence Tactics by Authorities

When trust level is:	Influence type used is:	Rationale
Confident	**Persuasion**	Serves to control the desire and influence of partisans or persuade them that the decisions are in their interest or that decisions serve the larger interest. Tactics: Education, socialization, indoctrination, manipulation, propaganda. For example, convince faculty and staff that the good of the college is at stake.
Neutral	**Sanctions**	Rewards and punishments. Tactics: Reward the responsible; punish the irresponsible. Establish penalties. Bestow or withdraw authority.
Alienated	**Insulation**	Controlling potential partisans by limiting access to authorities. Allow potential partisans differential access to authorities and to positions that involve control of resources that can be brought to bear on authorities. There are four types: 1. Selective entry. Keep those who might cause problems out of the decision-making network. For example, a dean may decide not to see certain student leaders who are disruptive on campus. 2. Self-selection. Build an image of organizational exclusivity. For example, Ivy League universities have a reputation for high-level intellectual skills that reduces the range of student applicants. 3. Recruit people with consistent educational perspectives. That is, seek and find faculty, staff, and students with philosophies similar to those on campus. 4. Selective exit. Fire persons whose attitudes and behavior are inconsistent with those of the authorities.

Adapted from Thomas (1976).

(1960) who identified five major ways that individual power is exercised in organizations. **Reward power** induces compliance for obvious reasons; there is a positive benefit for addressing the expectations of authorities. **Coercive power,** the opposite, encourages compliance on the basis of threat and fear. **Legitimate power** calls for obedience because its holder has formal authority in the hierarchy of an organization. The fourth kind of power is **referent power** (sometimes called charismatic power), which induces followers who wish to model their actions on the power holder and behave in ways that are consistent with the power holder's desires. Finally, **expert power** invokes action out of recognition of the power holder's special skills and competencies, which may be useful at some time in the future. Each of these sources of power can be exercised maliciously or benevolently.

Yukl (2002) examined the outcomes that each form of power is likely to elicit from organizational members (Table 3.4). The use of reward power, for example, is likely to generate compliance. Workers engage in the desired behavior simply to obtain the reward and may have little commitment to the goals and purposes related to that behavior. If compliance is all that is desired, then reward power will probably lead to task completion with little resistance from organizational members. An academic dean, for example, may want faculty and staff to comply with the expectations of an accreditation review such as assessing student learning outcomes. The dean may use rewards to get faculty and staff involved in assessment activities, but if reward power is the sole motivation for behavior, then organizational members will be unlikely to develop a strong commitment to the accreditation process. Simple monetary rewards may result in satisfactory compliance with organizational needs, but not necessarily optimum performance.

TABLE 3.4
Likely Responses to Different Sources of Power

	Most Likely Outcome	*Less Likely Outcome*	*Least Likely Outcome*
Reward	Compliance	Commitment	Resistance
Coercive	Resistance	Compliance	Commitment
Legitimate	Compliance	Commitment	Resistance
Referent	Commitment	Compliance	Resistance
Expert	Commitment	Compliance	Resistance

Based on Yukl (2002).

The use of coercive power is likely to result in high levels of resistance (especially in colleges and universities), and, if used frequently, it may corrode workplace relationships and erode the effectiveness of other forms of power. Most effective leaders avoid the use of coercive power, but its exercise may be necessary at times; for example, in response to continual violation of rules, stealing, sabotage, or behaviors that could pose physical harm to others.

Legitimate power involves the use of positional authority and may be expressed in directives, instructions, and policies. The likely outcome is compliance. Organizational members acknowledge the authority of the office holder to exercise power within a *zone of acceptance* (Simon, 1947). This zone includes actions that organizational members view as legitimate obligations to the organization. For example, faculty members are likely to comply with administrative requests for the timely submission of grades. Submitting grades is viewed as a legitimate faculty obligation. Ordering a faculty member to change a student's grade, however, is likely to fall outside the faculty member's zone of acceptance and will not be deemed legitimate (Hoy & Miskel, 2005).

In contrast to legitimate power, the use of referent and expert power is likely to engender commitment to the leader and his or her goals for the organization. When referent power is prevalent, leader-follower relationships are characterized by mutual respect, trust, and affection. Under these circumstances, organizational members are likely to identify with and display personal loyalty to leaders; however, if referent power is the predominant form of power in an organization, then the basis for power may collapse if there is substantial turnover in leadership positions. Goodwill and positive regard may dissipate quickly if leaders do not remain in office for very long.

Expert power generates commitment when organizational members value the knowledge offered by a particular leader. The leader's expertise must be relevant to the work of organizational members, and leaders must display their expertise in ways that demonstrate its utility. Leaders may have broad and relevant experience, but if they never interact with subordinates, then their knowledge is seldom on display for workers to assess.

French and Raven's (1960) sources-of-power framework has served as the basis for additional theory building. A useful refinement of French and Raven's work, provided by Bacharach and Lawler (1980), distinguishes among sources, types, and bases of power (Table 3.5). **Sources** are the circumstances that give rise to power. The four alternative sources of power are structure (e.g., an office held), personality (e.g., charisma, verbal skills), expertise (e.g., specialized information), and opportunity (e.g., being in the

TABLE 3.5
Relationships of Sources, Types, and Bases of Power

Source	Type	Base
Structure	Authority	Coercion Remunerative Normative Knowledge
Personality	Influence	Normative Knowledge
Expertise	Influence	Normative Knowledge
Opportunity	Influence	Coercion Knowledge

Based on Bacharach and Lawler (1980), p. 36.

right place at the right time). Any organizational member may possess one or more of these sources of power.

In an organizational context, the sources can be exercised through two **types** or modes. One of the two types of power is *authority,* defined as formally mandated organizational rights. According to Bacharach and Lawler, possessing authority is essentially a dichotomous condition; a person either does or does not have authority to act. Note, however, that in ambiguous settings like colleges and universities, even formal authority is often unclear. The other type of power is *influence.* Parties can have mutual influence, using various techniques to cause decisions to be made more in their favor than others.

There are also four **bases** of power—that is, the means through which power is exercised. **Coercion** is the control of punishment (e.g., dismissal). **Remuneration** is directed at control over rewards (e.g., pay). **Normative** power offers control through symbols (e.g., awards, recognition), and **knowledge** as a power base is exercised through the control of information (i.e., giving or withholding it).

As indicated in Table 3.5, authority has only one source—**formal organizational structure**—while influence has three sources—**personality, expertise,** and **opportunity.** Further, the bases for exercising power differ depending on the combinations of sources and types. Thus, for example, the type of influence whose source is expertise can only be exercised normatively or through a knowledge base. In different colleges and universities, all of these combinations may be found.

Bacharach and Lawler (1980) also suggest that there is an optimum match among source, type, and base that yields effective power use. To illustrate, suppose a student affairs vice president attempted but failed to change the goals of her division. How can we understand her inability to accomplish this task? If she tried to *influence* her staff by demonstrating her *expertise* (a source), but also threatened penalties (a *coercive* base) when they did not respond, we can see that the match of source, type, and base of power was inappropriate and likely to be ineffective. Using *expertise* to influence workers only works with a *normative* or *knowledge* base. If she wanted to use her *expertise* as *influence,* the most effective action she could take would be to share her *knowledge.*

It is possible to relate this schema to Gamson's theory and by so doing make a prediction of which of the bases of power are likely to be used under different political conditions. For example, when partisans are predominantly confident on the continuum of trust, influence is more likely to be exercised and interactions among organizational members are based on norms and knowledge. In a condition of neutrality, on the other hand, remunerative bases of influence will tend to be more salient; while a campus that is alienated will find coercion the major power base being used.

Personal Power Tactics in Organizations

Personal power in organizations is exercised in a wide variety of ways. The approaches have been characterized by Mintzberg (1983) as *games.* According to Mintzberg, members of an organizational coalition engage in a set of power games that are intended to advance their interests. These are noted in Table 3.6. The names of the games are fairly self-explanatory.

Different games are played by coalitions and individuals for different purposes, primarily: (1) to resist orders and defend positions from intrusions from above, (2) to counter resistance from lower levels in the organizational hierarchy, (3) to build additional power from all sources, (4) to defeat competitors at the same horizontal level who are seeking power in a zero-sum relationship, and (5) to change the organization to favor the coalition. Mintzberg points out that the games can coexist and even reinforce the formal organizational authority system, but they can also undermine the system or be used as substitutes for an inadequate or poorly performing system.

It is useful to be able to recognize the conditions under which one or another of the games might be employed. Based on Gamson's theory, one can speculate that when the potential partisans reflect a position of confidence (i.e., a high level of trust in authorities), few if any of these games would be seen as necessary. When partisans fall predominantly in the area of neutrality or alienation on the continuum of trust, however, it is likely that

TABLE 3.6
Games Played by Organizational Coalition Participants

Purpose	*Games*
1. To resist orders from authorities	The **insurgency game** (IG). Played by lower level partisans and coalitions of them.
2. To counter resistance to authority	The **counterinsurgency game** (CI). Played by those in authority fighting back.
3. To build power bases	The **sponsorship game** (with superiors) (SP). Played by subordinates who seek mentors. The **alliance-building game** (with peers) (AB). Played by equal status workers to build mutually supportive coalitions. The **empire-building game** (EB). Played by individuals seeking to boost their power and influence. The **budgeting game** (with resources) (BG). Played largely by managers attempting to expand their resources (e.g., personnel), often by distorting real needs for those resources. The **expertise game** (with knowledge and skills) (EX). Played often by professionals who flaunt their skills or by nonprofessionals who feign them. The **lording game** (with authority) (LG). Played by authorities who use their power in illegitimate ways or by lower level participants by wielding bureaucratic rules for their own ends.
4. To defeat a rival	The **line versus staff game** (LS). A zero-sum game played by both line and staff persons to defeat rivals, often in a clash of formal and informal power. The **rival camps game** (RC). Played by established power centers to gain superiority.
5. To effect organizational change	The **strategic candidates game** (SC). Played by decision makers pushing pet projects who identify with powerful players. The **whistle blowing game** (WB). Played by insiders who publicize others' violations of formal or informal rules. The **young Turks game** (YT). Usually played by persons relatively high in the hierarchy who seek to make significant changes in the direction of the organization.

Based on Mintzberg (1983), pp. 187–212.

organizational members will engage simultaneously in multiple games in their efforts to influence authorities.

Power Use in Different Kinds of Organizations

Since not all organizations have the same organizational designs or cultures, it is important to be able to predict when and in what form power will appear in organizations with different structures and cultures. By integrating Mintzberg's power games with an organizational typology developed by Jeffrey Pfeffer (1981), we can predict the probable sources, types, and bases of power and the kinds of games likely to be used in different types of organizations (Table 3.7). Pfeffer's typology is based on two variables: degree of centralization in the organization (i.e., the extent to which power is concentrated in only a few hands) and degree of consensus among organizational members regarding goals and the means to achieve them.

From Table 3.7, it is possible to predict either the games played or the type of organization. More concretely, in an organization characterized as a professional model (low centralization, high degree of consensus on goals and means to achieve them), it is likely that expertise will be the primary source of power, used to influence organizational members through normative and knowledge means. Similarly, in the same kind of professional organization, the most likely political games will be alliance building, expertise, and young Turks. Since colleges and universities vary in characteristics across these models, readers might benefit from predicting the games being played in their organizations based on this model.

Identifying Power Holders

It is sometimes quite clear who holds power in colleges and universities, but oftentimes appearances are inaccurate as apparent power holders may be merely figureheads and those with no formal authority may actually exercise significant influence. It is important, therefore, to be able to identify accurately the true power holders. Bacharach and Lawler (1980) have suggested a number of methods that facilitate this process. These are noted in Table 3.8.

It is likely, of course, that no one person or coalition is identified through all of these modes. In many cases, depending on the issue, power may be either widely dispersed or, in the instance of particularly controversial issues, even fragmented.

Social Constructionist Perspectives on Power

Foucault's (1976/1986) notion of power as something that "circulates" through a "net-like organization" (p. 234) is an appropriate metaphor for

TABLE 3.7
Organizational Types, Power, and Power Games

Organizational Type	Most Prevalent Sources of Power	Most Prevalent Types of Power	Most Prevalent Bases of Power	Most Prevalent Power Games
Bureaucratic organization High degree of centralization, high degree of means/ends consensus	Structure	Authority	Remunerative Normative	Insurgency Counterinsurgency Budgeting Line versus staff
Professional organization Low degree of centralization, high degree of means/ends consensus	Expertise	Influence	Normative Knowledge	Alliance building Expertise Young Turks
Centralized organization High degree of centralization, low degree of means/ends consensus	Structure Opportunity	Authority	Coercion	Sponsorship Budgeting Lording Line versus staff
Political organization Low degree of centralization, low degree of means/ends consensus	Personality Opportunity	Influence	Coercion	Alliance building Rival camps Strategic candidates Whistle blowing Young Turks Empire building

Based on Bacharach & Lawler (1980), Mintzberg (1983), and Pfeffer (1981).

understanding the social constructionist perspective on power. In contrast to some positivist conceptualizations that suggest power is something that individuals possess (e.g., French and Raven's sources of power framework), the social construction perspective emphasizes the relational aspects of power. Social constructionists assert that power cannot exist outside of the context of a relationship—either between two coworkers, two departments, or two organizations. Relationships are the means through which power is

TABLE 3.8
Modes of Identifying Power Holders

Direct Observation Measures	Indirect Observation Measures
1. Observe the users of sources of power. 2. Identify the beneficiaries of contested decisions. For example, how are budgets and positions allocated? 3. Study cultural symbols. For example, who is accorded informal accoutrements of high status such as reserved parking spaces, larger offices?	1. Use reputation indicators. When asked, what do workers in the organization say about power, power use, and power holders? 2. Use representational indicators. Who holds memberships on influential boards and committees, and who holds key administrative posts?

Based on Bacharach and Lawler (1980).

exercised. As Foucault (1976/1986) put it, "individuals are the vehicles of power, not its points of application" (p. 234).

Some positivist perspectives also employ this relational aspect of power. Again, Gamson's theory of partisans and authorities suggests that power is an influence relationship that permeates the organizational hierarchy and moves in both upward and downward directions. Given this type of multidirectional circulation, power becomes increasingly difficult to control or redistribute. Specifically, if the circulation of power does not necessarily follow formal organizational lines of authority, then organizational restructuring efforts may not actually affect how power is exercised within the organization (Pondy, 1977). For example, attempts to flatten the organizational structure and distribute decision-making power more evenly among organizational members may fail if the circulation of power does not change course. Conversely, efforts to centralize power in the hands of a few organizational leaders may also fail if interpersonal interactions in the organization are still characterized by both the upward *and* downward influence attempts that Gamson claims are characteristic of most organizations.

One important contribution that social constructionists add to views on power is the suggestion that symbols convey and maintain power. Reserved parking spaces for upper level administrators, luxurious offices for certain faculty members, and expectations that people address supervisors by their formal titles (e.g., professor, director, president) reinforce hierarchical flows of power. Strong values, beliefs, and expectations can maintain flows of power that are difficult (though not impossible) to change (Pondy, 1977).

From this vantage point, changing the distribution of power in an organization becomes associated with cultural change (Martin, 1992). Symbols, rituals, and norms sustain the current circulation of power. When those cultural artifacts are altered, power may begin to flow in different directions. Consider, for example, a new college president who abolishes reserved parking spaces and insists that people address each other by first name, rather than title. Through these actions, the president has changed the *symbols* that reinforced hierarchical power distinctions. Over time, power may become more evenly distributed among organizational members.

Empowerment

Other strategies for changing the flow and distribution of power involve efforts to empower people at all levels of the organization. Empowerment is based on the notion that each person has "an internal drive for self-determination and a need to cope with environmental demands" (Conger & Kanungo, 1988, p. 474). Empowerment has long been a buzzword in the field of management, but it is important to distinguish between two quite different conceptualizations of this term: (1) a structural/managerial perspective and (2) a psychological/cognitive frame (Dee, Henkin, & Duemer, 2003). Structural empowerment is viewed as a process by which a leader shares power with his or her subordinates. The outcome is a transfer of power from higher to lower organizational echelons (Conger & Kanungo, 1988; Hollander & Offerman, 1990). The implication is that empowerment is something that management does to employees (i.e., "management has empowered you to address this problem"). This perspective reflects the positivist view that power can be redistributed through structural change.

Structural transitions to more empowering work environments often necessitate the introduction of new, flexible organizational designs that reduce pressures for conformity (Belasco & Strayer, 1994). But these new organizational designs may not fundamentally alter the culture of the institution; thus, the organization's dominant values and assumptions may remain intact (Deetz, 1992). Therefore, although the structure of the organization may be designed for empowerment, the workers themselves may not experience the organization as empowering. Traditionally marginalized and underrepresented groups, in particular, may experience a disconnection between an allegedly empowering organizational design and work conditions that continue to silence alternative voices and perspectives.

The psychological frame, in contrast, is conceptualized as a mind-set that organizational members have about the organization. Within this framework, empowerment is defined as "a subjective state of mind where an employee perceives that he or she is exercising efficacious control over meaningful work" (Potterfield, 1999, p. 51). Thus, psychological empowerment may engender a sense of connectedness to the organization and may affect an employee's decision to stay or depart the organization (Ko, 1996).

Psychological empowerment necessitates a shift in the culture of the organization. Openness, trust, and diversity become central to the organization's overall value system (Nyhan, 2000). Psychological empowerment suggests that organizations need to change not only their structures but also their underlying ideologies and belief systems in order to facilitate empowerment (Ko, 1996).

Marxist and Postmodern Alternatives

Marxism and postmodernism offer additional alternatives to the positivist view of power, yet they represent very different conceptualizations. Marxists view power in terms of class struggle. Postmodernists such as Foucault focus on localized power relations, rather than power at the level of nation states or social classes.

Marxists define power as the ability of a social class to achieve its interests (Braverman, 1974; Poulantzas, 1973). They argue that the interests of social classes are incompatible and that history reflects a series of class struggles that reveal tensions between oppressors and the oppressed. For example, Marx (1818–1883) identified the tension between labor and management as the defining element of capitalism. Those who own the means of production are able to dominate those who provide the labor. This tension merely replicates previous class struggles in social history such as feudalism (lord, serf) and slavery (master, slave).

From the Marxist perspective, social class is the locus of power. Individuals do not exercise power. Instead, they are the bearers of class power; individual actions are the means through which class interests are promulgated. For example, a factory owner busting a union is not an act of individual power; instead, it is a manifestation of class power. Poulantzas (1973), in fact, argues that "the concept of power cannot be applied to inter-individual relations" (p. 105). Power is exercised across social classes, rather than among individuals.

The Marxist perspective assumes homogeneity of interests within social classes and may underestimate the effects of localized action as a result of its focus on macrolevel class struggle. In contrast, postmodernists see power as "being diffused more broadly in the environment and among individual organizational members" (Martin, 1992, p. 159). Postmodernists are more likely to locate power in the routine social relations of everyday life.

Foucault was concerned with micropolitics—the politics of everyday life, which occur in social institutions, organizations, professions, and academic disciplines. One of the foundational elements of Foucault's perspective is that power and knowledge are inextricably linked. Those who are in positions of power control the means through which knowledge is created—for example, journal editors who decide what is published and what is not, grant and foundation officers who decide what research is funded and what is not, and faculty members who decide which books are assigned to students and which are not. Moreover, power is exercised through the production of knowledge (i.e., the process by which people generate claims about what is "true"). Specifically, Foucault (1976/1986) argued that "we are subjected to the production of truth through power and we cannot exercise power except through the production of truth" (pp. 229–230).

Scientific knowledge in the positivist tradition is equated with attempts to identify a true or accurate understanding of a particular phenomenon (i.e., a *truth claim*). Knowledge becomes equated with a truth claim, as research attempts to get progressively closer to an objective assessment of a phenomenon. Foucault, however, argues that truth claims are produced through the exercise of power, rather than through objective claims of accuracy and verifiability. Each scientific discipline, Foucault argues, establishes its own criteria for assessing the accuracy and verifiability of knowledge. These criteria are established through consensus among the researchers in that field. Therefore, accuracy (truth) is a product of social consensus, rather than a reflection of some incontrovertible standard of evidence. The processes associated with achieving consensus are inherently political (Kuhn, 1970). Thus the production of knowledge is a function of power, and power is used to uphold certain truth claims and to discount others.

Equating knowledge and power may be a troubling or controversial idea for those who believe that research entails the objective pursuit of truth. Similarly, the idea that power is used to discount alternative truth claims may be disheartening for those who aspire to change the dominant way of thinking within a particular profession or field of study. On the other hand, if we view truth and knowledge as the products of consensus, rather than the outcomes of objective indisputable procedures, then fields of study become open to significant change. Kuhn (1970) explained how fields of study periodically undergo paradigm shifts that alter the fundamental processes through which knowledge is created.

Power, Politics, and Unions

How do these various theories help us unravel the mysteries of power use in colleges and universities? We can illustrate by examining the power that is played out on campuses where collective bargaining is a significant force in decision making. Unions have long been powerful forces in public colleges and universities and to a lesser extent in private institutions. Approximately 25% of full-time faculty members are unionized (Clery & Lee, 2002). The percentage is highest in community colleges (51.6%) and lowest in private universities (3.1%). In Gamson's terms, unions are interest groups that are visible manifestations of a kind of power that is both outside and inside the formal organizational authority structure. That is, unions do not report to any administrative office; yet, through negotiation of union contracts, their decision-making power is legitimated (Chaison & Bigelow, 2002).

Many would assert that unions served valuable functions in the late 19th and early 20th centuries by creating a legal power base for disenfranchised, unorganized, lower level employees. This new power to some extent has been able to offset the arbitrary and capricious power concentrated in the formal authorities. Today, however, the existence of unions has come to institutionalize what appear to be contrasting values of two or more powers (e.g., faculty and administrators), even if those values may not be directly antithetical to each other. The preservation of power and its prerogatives by each side (labor and management) frequently interferes with rational problem solving or even agreement to submit to mediation or arbitration of the issues.

In sum, whether unions have positive or negative benefits is still being debated (Blum, 1990; Wasley, 2006). Some argue that unionization often stultifies relationships among different constituencies, reduces communication possibilities, and creates a climate of distrust. Unions, it is alleged, also threaten the professionalism of faculty. As Mintzberg (1983) notes:

> Unionization, by paving over professional and departmental differences and, more importantly, challenging individual control of the work, seriously damages professional autonomy and individual responsibility. And collective responsibility can never replace individual responsibility in these kinds of organizations. Unionization also damages a second characteristic key to the effective functioning of these organizations—collegiality, which means in part professional control of administrative decision making, either directly by the operating professionals or through their representatives in the administrative positions. Collegiality assumes that operating professionals and administrators work together, in common interest. Unionization, in contrast, assumes a conflict of interest between the two. (p. 414)

On the other hand, other contemporary observers of governance are more positive about the effects of unionization. Unions, they say, protect the freedom and autonomy of the faculty from insidious intrusions by the administration. Unions can and do negotiate contracts that protect faculty members' due process rights in grievance procedures and that protect their rights to discuss and write about unpopular ideas, thus enhancing academic freedom and autonomy, particularly at institutions with the support of the American Association of University Professors and where these freedoms are under attack (DeCew, 2003). Whether the protections for less powerful groups offered by unions are needed depends in large part on the skills of leaders in creating climates of trust.

Summary

We have seen in this chapter that power and influence are omnipresent in nearly all organizations. Moreover, their exercise, even in moderation, is often perceived as a malfunction of the organization—that is, a deviation from the more rational behavior that would ordinarily lead to efficiency and effectiveness for the entire organization. Whether power and influence are viewed negatively can be explained in part by the nature of the organization itself—for example, the degree to which its decision-making structure is purely bureaucratic, purely political, or some combination of the two. Bureaucracies are ideally driven by pure rationality; hence, political influences that interfere with rational decision making will make the organization less efficient. On the other hand, in democratically governed polities, politics and the play of power are both natural and inevitable. Whether power in polities severely interferes with efficiency depends on the modes by which it is exercised. Some would argue that while bureaucracies can be efficient, in external environments that are turbulent, bureaucracies close off unstructured interaction and the creativity necessary to adapt to external contingencies. Polities, similarly, have their advantages and disadvantages. They can encourage useful exchanges of ideas that stimulate the entire organization. On the other hand, they can deteriorate into power-dominated oligarchies whose beneficiaries are largely those with self-serving political skills.

From a positivist perspective, research has made clear that at least some of the power-driven behavior can be explained by organizational conditions and some by individual agency or personality. In this chapter, we demonstrated how certain strategic contingencies result in the accretion of power by certain groups. We also showed how power is exercised up and down the hierarchy in different ways using different instruments of power. Indeed, a classification of the political games that organizational members play can reveal much about the ways that organizational subunits and individual actors gain power.

The modes by which power is manifested vary depending on the issue and on the trust that organizational members have in the organization's beneficence and in its leadership. As we demonstrated through the explication of Gamson's theory, neither complete trust nor complete alienation constitute the optimum condition for leadership in a polity. In colleges and universities, there is a perpetual conflict between the forces of bureaucratic authority, with its legitimated power lodged at the top, and the dispersed power of the lower level participants who use power tactics to influence authorities. To some extent, the strength and acerbity of the conflict depends on the success of the institution in assembling personnel in both bureaucracy and polity who share values and are willing to sacrifice for the good of the institution. It depends also on the wisdom of leaders in promulgating and maintaining those values.

Review Questions

1. A newly hired expert demonstrates her ability to predict with some considerable reliability the university students' daily demand on the computer registration system. Using strategic contingencies theory, which of the following explains the new power she finds herself in possession of?
   a. Scarcity
   b. Uncertainty
   c. Workflow centrality
   d. Nonsubstitutability

2. At a prestigious university whose reputation is based on its prowess in the sciences, the budget of the Department of Mathematics invariably exceeds that of the Department of English. Using strategic contingencies theory, which of the following variables explains this phenomenon?
   a. Scarcity
   b. Uncertainty
   c. Workflow centrality
   d. Nonsubstitutability

3. Workers in a university bookstore promise to work longer hours if their salaries are increased. According to Gamson's theory, which of the following modes of influence is being used?
   a. Constraints

    b. Inducements

    c. Persuasion

4. A confident partisan group will be unlikely to use constraints as an influence tactic because:

    a. The authorities have more power

    b. The authorities might respond in kind

    c. Constraints are generally less effective

    d. Partisan groups frequently do not have constraints available as an influence tactic

5. A dean reveals completely the nature of his budget to faculty who are demanding a larger raise. This convinces the faculty of the futility of pressing their case. The dean has used which of the following methods of social control?

    a. Insulation

    b. Sanctions

    c. Persuasion

6. In a newly formed private university with faculty and administrators carefully recruited for their uniformity of beliefs and capacity for making independent professional decisions, the dean of the school of arts and sciences was happy to receive news of a small budget surplus at his disposal. Which of the following games are more likely to be played in the decision to allocate the funds?

    a. Alliance building, expertise, young Turks

    b. Insurgency, counterinsurgency, budgeting, line versus staff

    c. Alliance building, rival camps, strategic candidates, whistle blowing, young Turks

    d. Sponsorship, budgeting, lording, line versus staff

7. The ability of a college leader to modify the desires and beliefs of faculty and staff in ways that are contrary to their interests (but are in service to the leader's interests) is an example of:

    a. The one-dimensional view of power

    b. The two-dimensional view of power

    c. The three-dimensional view of power

8. The social constructionist perspective notes that:

    a. Power is enacted through relationships among individuals

    b. Organizational restructuring may not necessarily change the distribution and flow of power in an organization

   c. Changing the distribution and flow of power in an organization occurs through changes in the organizational culture

   d. All of the above

Case Discussion Questions

Consider the Bryson College case presented at the beginning of this chapter.

1. Based on her conversations with the former president, President Briggs selected downward influence tactics such as limiting access (Table 3.3), which assumed that faculty were an alienated group and that the trust level between administration and faculty was low. Which strategies could Briggs have adopted to increase trust levels? If these trust-building efforts were successful, which influence tactics could Briggs have employed with faculty members?

2. Which upward influence tactics (Table 3.2) did President Briggs use in her efforts to regain the support of the trustees? Which upward influence tactics did the faculty senate use in their communications with the trustees? Why were President Briggs's tactics more effective than the faculty senate's tactics?

3. On which sources of power (Table 3.4) does President Briggs rely? What are the likely outcomes of her continued use of these power sources? Consider her relationships with faculty and trustees.

4. Bryson College is a highly politicized organization (Table 3.7). What changes in the organization of the college would be necessary for Bryson to become a professionalized organization? A bureaucratized organization? A centralized organization? How would each of those changes affect the sources, types, and bases of power available to President Briggs?

References

Alt, J. E., & Alesina, A. (1996). Political economy: An overview. In R. E. Goodin & H-D. Klingemann (Eds.), *A new handbook of political science* (pp. 645–674). New York: Oxford University Press.

Bacharach, S., & Lawler, E. J. (1980). *Power and politics in organizations*. San Francisco: Jossey-Bass.

Bachrach, P., & Baratz, M. (1962). The two faces of power. *American Political Science Review, 56*, 947–952.

Barnard, C. (1938). *The functions of the executive*. Cambridge, MA: Harvard University Press.

Belasco, J., & Strayer, R. (1994). Why empowerment doesn't empower: The bankruptcy of current paradigms. *Business Horizons, 37*(2), 29–42.

Birnbaum, R. (1988). *How colleges work: The cybernetics of academic organization and leadership.* San Francisco: Jossey-Bass.

Blum, D. E. (1990, January 31). Merits of academic unionism still hotly debated 10 years after high court limited faculty bargaining. *The Chronicle of Higher Education, 36,* A15–A16.

Brass, D. J., & Burkhardt, M. E. (1993). Potential power and power use: An investigation of structure and behavior. *Academy of Management Journal, 36*(3), 441–470.

Braverman, H. (1974). *Labor and monopoly capital: The degradation of work in the twentieth century.* New York: Monthly Review Press.

Brown, W. R. (1982). *Academic politics.* Tuscaloosa: University of Alabama Press.

Burns, J. M. (1978). *Leadership.* New York: Harper & Row.

Chaison, G., & Bigelow, B. (2002). *Unions and legitimacy.* Ithaca, NY: Cornell University Press.

Clery, S., & Lee, J. (2002). Faculty salaries: Recent trends. In C. Lehane (Ed.), *The NEA 2002 Almanac of Higher Education* (pp. 11–20). Washington, DC: National Education Association.

Cohen, M. D., & March, J. G. (1974). *Leadership and ambiguity: The American college president.* New York: McGraw Hill.

Conger, J., & Kanungo, R. (1988). The empowerment process: Integrating theory and practice. *Academy of Management Review, 13*(1), 371–482.

Crenson, M. A. (1971). *The un-politics of air pollution: A study of non-decision-making in the cities.* Baltimore: Johns Hopkins University Press.

Daft, R. L. (2001). *Organization theory and design* (7th ed.). Cincinnati, OH: South-Western College Publishing.

Dahl, R. A. (1961). *Who governs? Democracy and power in an American city.* New Haven, CT: Yale University Press.

DeCew, J. W. (2003). *Unionization in the academy: Visions and realities.* Lanham, MD: Rowman & Littlefield Publishers.

Dee, J., Henkin, A., & Duemer, L. (2003). Structural antecedents and psychological correlates of teacher empowerment. *Journal of Educational Administration, 41*(3), 257–277.

Deetz, S. (1992). *Democracy in an age of corporate colonization: Developments in communication and the politics of everyday life.* Albany: State University of New York Press.

Easton, D. (1965). *A framework for political analysis.* Englewood Cliffs, NJ: Prentice-Hall.

Etzioni, A. (1961). *A comparative analysis of complex organizations: On power, involvement, and their correlates.* New York: The Free Press.

Foucault, M. (1986). Disciplinary power and subjection. In S. Lukes (Ed.), *Power* (pp. 229–242). New York: New York University Press. (Reprinted from M. Foucault, *Power/knowledge: Selected interviews and other writings, 1972–1977,* C. Gordon, Ed., 1976, New York: Random House).

French, J., & Raven, B. (1960). The bases of social power. In D. Cartwright & A. F. Zander (Eds.), *Group dynamics* (pp. 607–623). Evanston, IL: Row, Peterson.

Fukuyama, F. (1995). *Trust: The social virtues and the creation of prosperity.* New York: The Free Press.

Gamson, W. A. (1968). *Power and discontent.* Homewood, IL: Dorsey Press.

Goltz, S., & Hietapelto, A. (2002). Using the operant and strategic contingencies models of power to understand resistance to change. *Journal of Organizational Behavior Management, 22*(3), 3–22.

Harden, G. (1968). The tragedy of the commons, *Science, 162,* 1243–1248.

Hardy, C., & Clegg, S. R. (1996). Some dare call it power. In S. R. Clegg, C. Hardy, & W. R. Nord (Eds.), *Organizational studies* (pp. 622–641). Thousand Oaks, CA: Sage Publications.

Hickson, D. J., Hinings, C. R., Lee, C. A., Schneck, R. E., & Pennings, J. M. (1971). A strategic contingencies theory of interorganizational power. *Administrative Science Quarterly, 16*(2), 216–229.

Hinings, C. R., Hickson, D. J., Pennings, J. M., & Schneck, R. E. (1974). Structural conditions of intraorganizational power. *Administrative Science Quarterly, 19*(1), 22–44.

Hirokawa, R. Y., Gouran, D. S., & Martz, A. E. (1988). Understanding the sources of faulty group decision making: A lesson from the Challenger disaster. *Small Group Behavior, 19,* 411–433.

Hollander, E., & Offerman, L. (1990). Power and leadership in organizations. *American Psychologist, 45*(2), 179–189.

Hoy, W., & Miskel, C. (2005). *Educational administration: Theory, research, and practice* (7th ed.). New York: McGraw-Hill.

Janis, I. L. (1982). *Groupthink* (2nd ed.). Boston: Houghton Mifflin.

Ko, J. (1996). *Assessments of Meyer and Allen's three component model of organizational commitment in South Korea.* Unpublished doctoral dissertation, University of Iowa, Iowa City.

Kramer, R. M., & Tyler, T. R. (Eds.). (1995). *Trust in organizations: Frontiers in theory and research.* Thousand Oaks, CA: Sage.

Kuhn, T. S. (1970). *The structure of scientific revolutions* (2nd ed.). Chicago: University of Chicago Press.

Lukes, S. (1974). *Power: A radical view.* London: Macmillan.

Lukes, S. (1986). Introduction. In S. Lukes (Ed.), *Power* (pp. 1–9). New York: New York University Press.

Lukes, S. (2005). *Power: A radical view* (2nd ed.). New York: Palgrave Macmillan.

Martin, J. (1992). *Cultures in organizations: Three perspectives.* New York: Oxford University Press.

Mayer, R. C., Davis, J. H., & Schoorman, F. (1995). An integrative model of organizational trust. *Academy of Management Review, 20*(3), 709–734.

Miles, R. (1980). *Macro organizational behavior.* Glenview, IL: Scott, Foresman.

Minor, J., & Tierney, W. (2005). The danger of deference: A case of polite governance. *Teachers College Record, 107*(1), 137–156.

Mintzberg, H. (1983). *Power in and around the organization.* Englewood Cliffs, NJ: Prentice-Hall.

Morgan, G. (1998). *Images of organization: The executive edition.* Thousand Oaks, CA: Sage Publications.

Nyhan, R. (2000). Changing the paradigm: Trust and its role in public sector organizations. *The American Review of Public Administration, 30*(1), 87–109.

Pettigrew, A. M. (1973). *The politics of organizational decision-making.* London: Tavistock.

Pfeffer, J. (1981). *Power in organizations.* Marshfield, MA: Pitman.

Pfeffer, J. (1992). *Managing with power: Politics and influence in organizations.* Boston: Harvard Business School Press.

Pfeffer, J., & Moore, W. L. (1980). Power in university budgeting: A replication and extension. *Administrative Science Quarterly, 25*(4), 637–653.

Pfeffer, J., & Salancik, G. (1974). Organizational decision-making as a political process: The case of a university budget. *Administrative Science Quarterly, 19,* 135–151.

Pondy, L. (1977). The other hand clapping: An information processing approach to organizational power. In T. H. Hammer & S. B. Bacharach (Eds.), *Reward systems and power distribution* (pp. 56–91). Ithaca, NY: School of Industrial and Labor Relations, Cornell University.

Porter, L. W., Angle, H. L., & Allen, R. W. (Eds.). (2003). *Organizational influence processes* (2nd ed.). Armonk, NY: M.E. Sharpe.

Potterfield, T. (1999). *The business of employee empowerment.* London: Quorum Books.

Poulantzas, N. (1973). *Political power and social classes.* London: New Left Books, Sheed and Ward.

Salancik, G. R., & Pfeffer, J. (1974). The bases and use of power in organizational decision making: The case of a university. *Administrative Science Quarterly, 19,* 453–473.

Salancik, G. R., & Pfeffer, J. (1977). Who gets power—and how they hold on to it: A strategic contingency model of power. *Organizational Dynamics, 5*(3), 3–21.

Schick, A. G., Birch, J. B., & Tripp, R. E. (1986). Authority and power in university decision making: The case of a university personnel budget. *Canadian Journal of Administrative Sciences, 3,* 41–64.

Simon, H. (1947). *Administrative behavior.* New York: Macmillan.

Thomas, K. W. (1976). Conflict and conflict management. In M. D. Dunnette (Ed.), Handbook of industrial and organizational psychology (pp. 889–935). Chicago: Rand McNally.

Tierney, W. (2006). *Trust and the public good: Examining the cultural conditions of academic work.* New York: Peter Lang Publishing.

Tschannen-Moran, M., & Hoy, W. K. (2000). A multidisciplinary analysis of the nature, meaning, and measurement of trust. *Review of Educational Research, 70*(4), 547–593.

Tushman, M. L. (1977). A political approach to organization: A review and rationale. *Academy of Management Review, 2,* 206–216.

Wasley, P. (2006). Lawmakers intervene in labor dispute. *Chronicle of Higher Education, 52*(26), A24.

Weber, M. (1947). *The theory of social and economic organizations* (A. M. Henderson & T. Parsons, Trans.). New York: Free Press. (Original work published 1924.)

Welsh, M. A., & Slusher, E. A. (1986). Organizational design as a context for political activity. *Administrative Science Quarterly, 31*(3), 389–402.

White, G. (1989, July 17). Secretaries are in the driver's seat. *Los Angeles Times,* pp. 4–5.

Wolff, R. P. (1969). *The ideal of the university.* Boston: Beacon Press.

Yamagishi, T., & Yamagishi, M. (1994). Trust and commitment in the United States and Japan. Trust and Distrust: Psychological Dimensions [Special issue]. *Motivation and Emotion, 18*(2), 129–166.

Yukl, G. A. (2002). *Leadership in organizations* (5th ed.). Upper Saddle River, NJ: Prentice Hall.

4

ORGANIZATIONAL DECISION MAKING

CONTENTS

Preview   584
Case Context   584
Introduction   588
Decision Making as a Process   594
Decision Making as Structure   597
Participation Theories   605
Risky Shift, Polarization, and Social Loafing in Group Decision
   Making   615
Social Constructionist Perspectives on Group Decision Making   617
Summary   620
Review Questions   620
Case Discussion Questions   622
References   622

The authors are most grateful for the critical comments on an early draft of this chapter by Jason Lane, University of North Dakota. The final version, of course, is our own and may or may not reflect the perspective of the reviewer.

Preview

- Decisions in organizations are typically either routine or require individual or group judgments about novel circumstances.
- All decisions have implicit value assumptions.
- Decisions are the result of the application of rationality, but they are modulated by considerations of risk and individual personality.
- Organizations tend to program as many decisions as possible, since such procedures are efficient in the short run.
- Because it is impossible for workers to know all of the relevant information needed for a decision, they tend to *satisfice.*
- A typical sequence of steps in the decision process includes decision recognition, diagnosis, development of solutions, selection, screening, evaluation and choice, and authorization.
- Organizational decisions can be classified as strategic, tactical, or operational. They vary on a variety of dimensions.
- All organizations must make decisions that address four functional prerequisites: adaptation, goal attainment, integration, and latency.
- Decisions in organizations vary according to a number of contingencies, including the degree of consensus on both goals and the means to achieve them.
- When decisions should be made by individuals versus groups is a function of the complexity of the problem and the distribution of the talent available in the group.
- Willingness of workers to take risks in group decision making depends in part on their risk-taking propensities.
- Decisions in groups are often a result of polarization of positions within the group.
- Symbolic convergence theory explains how decisions are socially constructed through dramatizing themes and other creative communication processes.

—————————— CASE CONTEXT ——————————

Financial Concerns at Eastern State University

The fiscal realities at Eastern State University were bleak. Reductions in funding by the state led to higher tuition levels and a subsequent drop in enrollment. Meanwhile, basic operating costs continued to escalate, and faculty and staff salaries were scheduled for substantial increases due to a union contract that was negotiated under more favorable economic conditions.

One year ago, the university implemented a hiring freeze and laid off a large number of nonunionized staff who worked in academic advising, residence life, facilities, and maintenance. As the new state budget was released, however, university leaders realized that more drastic measures were necessary.

"We are at a point now where we either raise tuition to stratospheric levels, or we cut programs," announced the president to her senior administrative team. "As you know, the trustees were extremely reluctant to approve our last tuition increase, and I simply cannot go back to them again in less than a year, and ask for another increase."

"I think the faculty are starting to see the handwriting on the wall," noted the provost. "I have had a lot of calls in the past couple weeks from people wanting to know what's going on with this budget cycle. Faculty are worried, and the rumors are flying."

"To this point, the academic programs have largely been spared," explained the chief financial officer. "We really gutted a lot of student services last year, and if we cut any more, we would basically have to eliminate all of those services and close down the residence halls. I don't know if we are willing to do that. We already took a great deal of heat from students and in the media for what happened last year." The room fell silent for a moment, as the administrators remembered the student protests from last spring and the very vocal resignation of the vice president for student affairs, whose position remained unfilled.

"Well, how do we proceed with this?" asked the provost. "Should we bring together the leadership from the faculty senate and get a task force going?"

"I am not sure if the routine decision-making bodies are up for this," the president responded. "The faculty senate does not have the best reputation; too much squabbling and too much petty political infighting. If we went through the senate, I don't think people would take this seriously."

"So we will work this through the academic deans?" asked the chief financial officer.

"No, not exactly," answered the president. "You know, we have the data that we need to make these decisions ourselves. You know, we have the enrollment data. We have all of the program evaluation reports that we require everybody to do every 5 years. So we have some sense of quality, some sense of what the market supports, some sense of where we have real strengths, and some understanding of the weaknesses. But if we don't proceed carefully, we risk tearing apart the whole university. People are really on edge. Morale is down, and we have already lost a few really good faculty members who have gone to other institutions. We cannot afford to have this process become divisive and bring everybody down with it."

Two weeks later the president appointed the Committee on Restructuring for Excellence (CORE). She selected faculty members from each college in the university. These faculty were not necessarily involved in the traditional governance committees, but they were viewed by many as trusted, reasonable colleagues who did not have an overt political agenda. The president also appointed two undergraduate students, two graduate students, and three professional staff members to CORE, which was co-chaired by the provost and the chief financial officer.

As an initial step, CORE cosponsored an open meeting with the faculty senate. The meeting was dominated by interest group politicking. Faculty and students from programs that perceived themselves to be vulnerable engaged in strong lobbying to prevent their programs from being closed. In one case, faculty members brought in a local state legislator who was a graduate of their program; the legislator spoke of the benefits of the program to the state and hinted that his colleagues in the legislature would not take kindly to its closure.

The CORE committee and the faculty senate convened three more of these meetings over the course of an entire semester. "These meetings showed that we were correct in not delegating program closure directly to the senate," the president explained to the provost. "It would have been total chaos, and no decisions would have been made. But these meetings have been important in terms of identifying where we might find the most political opposition."

At the end of the semester, CORE developed a set of criteria to be used in program closure decisions. The document, *Guidelines for Reorganization,* was disseminated via e-mail to the entire campus community. The document identified five principles to be considered in program closure decisions: (1) mission centrality, (2) program quality, (3) student demand, (4) service to the state, and (5) cost. The committee refrained from assigning numeric weights to the five criteria, nor did they create a formula for making such decisions. "We wanted to provide some flexibility, some amount of discretion for the next level of review," noted one of the faculty members on the committee. "These are relatively subjective criteria. We wanted to allow for some degree of choice."

As a next step, the president requested that all academic deans submit a reduction plan for their college. "I asked the deans to describe what their college would look like if we had to cut their budgets by 15%," explained the president. "Ultimately, I don't think that we will be looking at 15% cuts, but I wanted to get a sense of their real priorities."

Finally, the president and her senior staff decided that it would be the CORE committee that would make recommendations to the president and trustees regarding which programs to cut. "The real decision was about where the decisions will be made," noted the provost. "We decided to keep the CORE committee around beyond its initial charge, and ask them to make some tough decisions. We gave them all of the data that we had—enrollments, accreditation reports, program evaluations. We gave them the deans' reduction plans. And we, the president's cabinet, I mean, we just sat back and hoped for the best. We could have micromanaged the process, but I guess we trusted them to make decisions."

"Ultimately, I would say that there was about an 80% match in terms of what CORE recommended to close and what I had on my initial list before the process began," noted the president. "They didn't go quite as far as I would have, but they recommended the closure or merger of many of the same programs that my cabinet had discussed."

"CORE stuck by their criteria pretty well," noted the chief financial officer. "But they were also really sensitive to political pressures both inside the university and outside. More so than I thought they would be. We did not get a single complaint from a legislator. And I am convinced that CORE is the reason why we did not get a bunch of faculty protests either. Since the committee was mostly faculty members, they kind of accepted those decisions more than if they would have come from the cabinet. You know, we could have gone to them with the same decisions, and the faculty would have raked us over the coals. But they were a little more accepting when it came from their own colleagues."

Before sharing CORE's recommendations with the trustees, the president convened a meeting with the academic deans. In two cases, deans were able to convince the president to merge rather than close a particular program. But in no instance was a dean able to convince the president or the other deans to reinstate a program that had been slated for closure. "At that point, the perspective of most deans was that we all have to take our poison," noted one dean. "In other words, we all realized that each of us had to make some sacrifices. And once that became clear to the group, it became almost impossible for any of the deans to reinstate anything."

The trustees ultimately approved all but one of CORE's recommendations. A program that had been slated for closure was saved through alumni pressure and the receipt of a state grant for student scholarships in this field——the direct result of powerful alumni lobbying the legislature. Otherwise, the program closures were implemented without much fanfare. Some faculty in the merged or closed programs departed for other institutions. Adjunct faculty in the closed programs were not rehired, and some tenure track faculty in those programs were not renewed through the tenure decision year.

"Was it a completely rational process?" the president asked rhetorically. "No, some programs that probably deserved to be cut were spared due to political pressure. But was it a good process? And by that, I mean, did we make wise decisions that will eventually strengthen our areas of excellence? Well, only time will tell, but we avoided the chaos and infighting that we've seen at some of our peer institutions in other states. And we kind of stopped the bleeding regarding the departure of some of our best faculty. Undoubtedly, some people were unhappy with the outcomes. That's understandable. But I think everyone had confidence in the process."

Introduction

D ecisions are made individually, in groups, and in formal offices at all levels of institutions of higher education. The decisions almost invariably have ramifications beyond the decision maker him- or herself. As McLaughlin (1995) notes, decisions are the "core transactions" of an organization. But the decisions may not completely solve the issues that they were intended to address. Indeed, most decisions are partial solutions at best. As might be expected, decisions are often flawed in some way. Paul Nutt (1999), in fact, reports that half of all organizational decisions fail.

Decisions also vary in their complexity. Some decisions are routine—for example, when the need for a decision is recognized as familiar, when there is a known and rehearsed procedure for choosing among alternative responses, and when responsibility for the choice is clear. We can partially judge the effectiveness of routine decision making simply in terms of the time it takes for the decision maker to identify correctly the nature of the decision and to take action. This phenomenon is often referred to as **decision latency.** Many routine decisions are made quickly and efficiently—for example, by faculty advisors who approve courses for registering students on the basis of the faculty member's knowledge of prerequisite courses and expected distribution requirements. Decision latency is low in this instance.

On the other hand, many decisions in higher education do not lend themselves to routinization, either because they require individual and/or group judgments about novel circumstances or there are uncertainties about inputs, transformation processes, and outcomes. The effectiveness of a decision to begin a new degree program, as one example, must be judged not only on the speed with which the decision can be made, but also on the degree to which available knowledge was secured from and utilized by the right persons in the time available (Lopes, 1996). Valid evaluations of non-routine decision-making effectiveness, in fact, require sufficient time for the full impact of the decision to become known.

Oftentimes in higher education, there is ambiguity not so much about the decision at hand but about who is responsible for making the decision—in essence, decisions about decision-making authority itself. These kinds of decisions involve long-term considerations of the decision-making system in the organization and about the motivation and commitment consequences of including or excluding different constituencies in the process. Whether students should have a formal position on boards of trustees, for example, is a question that requires judicious judgments about complex questions of organizational culture as well as organizational design.

Finally, it is important to note that all decisions are value laden (Jacob, Flink, & Schuchman, 1962; Posner & Schmidt, 1993). Implicit in all decisions are assumptions about human values and about the goals and objectives of human systems. As critical theorists have noted, issues of equality, power, and dignity are often hidden in seemingly simple decisions (Deetz, 1992). In higher education organizations, values frequently come to the fore. Decisions about access to higher education, for example, involve questions not only about efficiency and effectiveness but about whether traditional definitions and criteria need to be reframed in order to satisfy moral imperatives (Bensimon, 2004).

Recall that in discussing systems theory (see chapter 1), we noted that the same framework and concepts may be applied to systems at any domain or level—from physical to biological to human to organizational to collections of organizations. So, when considering decision making, we must examine how it takes place from the perspective of the individual, as well as the organization, and how the individual and organizational systems interact.

Decision Making Defined

We begin this chapter with two definitions of decision making:

> the process commonly portrayed as occurring early in "problem-solving processes"—the sensing, exploration, and definition of problems and opportunities—as well as the generation, evaluation, and selection of solutions. (Huber, 1986)

and,

> the process of developing a commitment to a course of action. (Mintzberg, 1979, p. 58)

Note that these definitions presume that high-quality decisions are the result of maximum rationality—that is, applying intelligence to an assessment of alternatives and leaving emotion aside. The origins of decision making theory are alleged to lie in the quantitative, statistical treatment of utility theory, particularly the work of von Neumann and Morgenstern (1944) and Luce and Raiffa (1957). They are normative in character, meaning that the valued, correct decision can be discerned through reason (Allison, 1971). Recently, however, increasing attention has been devoted to the role of emotion and bias in explaining how decisions are made (Keren, 1996; Medin & Bazerman, 1999; Zey, 1992). Other theorists approach organizational decision making as largely a matter of the allocation and use of power (Kakabadse, 1987; Pettigrew, 1973). Still others include philosophical, psychological, sociological, political, and legal factors in their definitions (Harrison, 1999). In fact, while decision making appears to be a fairly simple phenomenon, the process is quite complex and there are many approaches and theories surrounding it. In this chapter and the next we will examine some of the most important of them.

Decision Making Contrasted with Problem Solving

Many decisions are made in answer to perceived problems. Indeed, the processes of decision making are often tied together with problem solving (Gray, 2001; Huber, 1986). However, many decisions are not answers to problems so much as responses to routine stimuli requiring a rather structured, programmed response (Simon, 1960). They are rule-based, rather than choice-based, decisions (March, 1994; Mintzberg, Raisinghani, & Theoret, 1976).

When organizations respond to situations, they employ a variety of simplifying measures. Some of these are structural; some procedural. The first of these measures is **routinization.** In general, members of human systems, especially organizations, feel uncomfortable dealing with problems that are not of their own intentional making—for example, situations that have no precedent in known decision-making repertoires. These kinds of decisions take time, are subject to human error, and may be anxiety producing. Hence, organizations attempt as much as possible to "program" decisions—that is, to circumscribe the problem so that it can be recognized (or labeled) as routine and therefore subject to routine decision-making protocols (Bachrach & Baratz, 1962). Thus, problems that are identified as programmable can be assigned to specialists whose knowledge and skills are appropriate to their solution and who can prepare standardized procedures and practices for managing recognizable and more repetitive issues. Institutional review boards on university campuses are one example of an organizational structure designed to routinize decisions—in this case, decisions regarding research ethics and protections for human subjects.

This is not to say that all decisions *should* be programmed, but that there is a tendency in all organizations toward trying to isolate the parts of decisions that can be programmed, leaving only the really uncertain parts to be addressed through the more time-consuming processes of problem solving. Most organizational designs are created primarily to facilitate the process of making organizational decisions more routine (Huber & McDaniel, 1986). The result, however, of overutilizing routine decision-making processes can be self-deception and complacency (Sutcliffe & McNamara, 2001). When organizational members view all decision opportunities as routine, they miss the novel and nuanced dimensions of their changing external environments. The *over-efficient* organization that attempts to program all of its decisions may not be responsive to external circumstances. Excessive focus on decision-making efficiency may be especially harmful for colleges and universities with a high degree of unpredictability in their external environments (Duncan, 1972). The most effective and efficient organizations have not, needless to say, programmed all of their decisions.

Routinization of decision making also accounts for some of the allegations of red tape that are expressed in many organizations. Red tape derives from excessive routinization that cannot truly handle the real complexity and diversity of decisions that the organization faces (Gouldner, 1952). Further, organizations may elect to engage in risk-taking enterprises of varying strength (Bazerman, 1990; Shapira, 1995). The greater the risk, the less valid programmed decisions will be. Indeed, it could be argued that given an organization's appraisal of its desired market and the concomitant levels of resource dependence, there is an optimum amount of risk to be taken and a concomitant uncertainty about the decisions to be made (Baird & Thomas, 1990; McNamara & Bromiley, 1999). Routinization under these circumstances may produce ineffective decisions that are not responsive to changing external conditions.

A second process to simplify organizational decision making is the use of **technology.** Organizational members often make assumptions about the inputs entering the organization and the technology required to transform them. Colleges typically use the past to make simplifying assumptions about the qualifications, character, and needs of entering students. For example, academic policies may follow from the assumption that "since all freshmen are reasonably homogeneous in learning styles and readiness for complex material, they will be assigned to large lecture classes." Such assumptions obviate the need for continual reevaluation and give the impression of addressing organizational needs for efficiency. While these approaches do render decisions more efficient, some question whether the educational processes and outcomes that result from these assumptions are appropriate. Recent vociferous complaints of parents and students about the quality of undergraduate education give evidence of the danger of making erroneous assumptions.

A third simplifying measure has been called **satisficing**—in other words, choosing the first available satisfactory solution to a problem, even if it may not be the optimum solution (Simon, 1955). Because of the constraints of time and of human capability, most individuals and most organizations find that they cannot afford to pursue the perfect or optimum answer to problems encountered. Most decision makers seek solutions to problems by examining alternatives one at a time, sequentially. They often make do with the first reasonable solution to a problem without seeking an optimum one. Usually the solution is similar to those adopted in the past.

Herbert Simon (1955, 1957; cf. Radner, 1997) noted that there is a limit to rationality; it is bounded. That is, for the most part, at any particular decision-making time, no one person has all the information necessary to make nonroutine decisions, nor can the necessary information usually be secured in the time available (Ackoff, 1981). Further, while on some occasions, the information may actually be obtainable or even on hand in the organization, it is so formidable in scope and complexity as to be incomprehensible in the time frame required. What organizations try to do, therefore, is to obtain just the right amount of information at the right time for only those individuals who need it so that they can rationally deal with it within the limits of their existing or accessible knowledge in the time frame allowed.

Yet a fourth simplifying measure used in organizations is **decision avoidance**. In most organizations, a class of problems never reaches the decision stage (Bachrach & Baratz, 1962). The issues surrounding these problems are so conflict ridden that they remain submerged in the unseen "iceberg" of neglected organizational problems. In many ways, however, these submerged problems drive the more visible decisions that can be observed. A college that is unwilling or unable to come to grips openly with issues of race, for example, may make decisions that satisfy certain constituencies (e.g., hiring more faculty of color) but are inadequate to resolve the underlying educational and moral problems that require more substantive resolution (e.g., the persistent use of curricula that are not inclusive of diverse perspectives).

Key Questions in Decision Making

Two major approaches have been used to understand key questions in organizational decision making—process and structure. The process approach addresses questions such as, What is the sequence of stages in decision making? and Is it necessary to modify the sequence to yield higher quality decisions in a shorter time? Structure questions, on the other hand, are associated with a range of variables that researchers use to explain decision-making effectiveness. They include such queries as, Which organizational and individual characteristics affect decision making? Some of these structural questions and variables are summarized in Table 4.1 and are discussed later in the chapter.

Not all decision-making theories incorporate both process and structural approaches. However, both must be taken into account for the decision to be effective. As March (1997) notes,

> Students of organizational decisions [try] to understand conflict and consciousness as embedded in social relations, rules, norms, and constraints . . . They focus on decision-making processes, trying simultaneously to identify the ways in which decisions unfold within them and to understand the processes as forms of social drama and locales for creating stories. (pp. 9–10)

First, we take up decision making as a social process. Later in the chapter, we focus on structural issues.

TABLE 4.1
Structural Questions and Associated Decision-Making Variables

Structure Questions	Selected Variables Involved
Unit of analysis	Individual, group, organization, polity
Nature of problem	Simple/complex, availability of information
Qualities of the decision maker	Expertise, personality
Qualities of followers	Expertise, stake in decision
Organizational conditions	Environmental complexity/stability, time and money constraints, significance of the decision
Nature of the decision	Information availability, certainty or ambiguity of the information, risk to organization or individual, irreversibility, accountability

Decision Making as a Process

Much organizational decision making is conducted over time through "seat-of-the pants" methods. Charles Lindblom (1959) has labeled this phenomenon *disjointed incrementalism* in his imaginatively titled article, "The Science of 'Muddling Through.'" Others have given different names to this phenomenon. Quinn (1980) calls it *logical incrementalism.* Behn's (1988) label is *management by groping along,* as is Straussman's (1993). Lindblom notes that significant or revolutionary changes in organizational routines are rarely formally conceptualized as important problems to be solved. The usual approach instead is to adapt existing structures and processes to accommodate new needs without examining fundamental questions of organization. As one example from higher education, in the late 19th century, some American colleges began to conduct research, partly in response to the needs of the industrial revolution and partly as a result of the arrival of American scholars who were educated in European universities where scientific research was being carried out. Rather than create a European model of separate research institutes, however, the research role was gradually included as an additional legitimate function of existing faculty in traditional academic teaching departments in many American colleges. Thus, research was incrementally added to teaching as part of the formal role for faculty (Parsons & Platt, 1973). While often this successive additive approach works quite well, it may on occasion result in putting multifunctional structures in place that become entrenched by tradition and are difficult to change even when it becomes evident that they are inefficient (Bess, 1982).

Although incremental approaches to decision making appear rather unplanned, unsystematic, and even chaotic, social scientists continue to seek new ways to explain them. Therefore, many models have been developed for understanding the evolving phases in the processes of decision making (Bass, 1983; Hellriegel, Slocum, & Woodman, 2004; McCall & Kaplan, 1990). An adapted version of the Mintzberg et al. (1976) model is produced in Figure 4.1.

Commonly included in models of decision-making phases are the following: (1) intelligence gathering activities that recognize and clarify the problem or issue—this activity usually involves making distinctions among problems, opportunities, and crisis decisions; (2) interpretation or analysis—a diagnosis routine that sorts through the ambiguous and/or conflicting relevant stimuli and searches for and identifies alternative solutions; (3) establishing criteria for an effective solution; (4) designing and developing alternative plans; (5) evaluating the pros and cons, especially the risks, of alternatives; (6) selecting a plan; and (7) initiating action. Each of these

FIGURE 4.1
Model of the Decision-Making Process

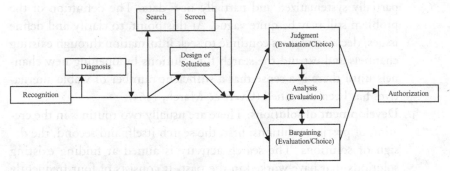

Adapted from Mintzberg et al. (1976).

stages is described below. Though each is discussed in sequence, some re-searchers have suggested that the process is often not quite so linear but can be sporadic, fluid, and constricted (Cray, Mallory, Butler, Hickson, & Wilson, 1988; Hickson, Butler, Cray, Mallory, & Wilson, 1986; Hogarth, 1980; Huber & McDaniel, 1986).

1. **Decision recognition.** Problems, opportunities, and immediate critical decisions are identified in the recognition phase. Since organizational behavior, in part, consists of routines, it is important for organizational leaders to recognize problems both in the routines themselves and in those situations that are unique. Leaders may recognize a need for changing routine decision-making procedures if they perceive a breakdown in effectiveness or efficiency. If routine decisions to approve research studies do not result in the protection of human subjects, for example, then leaders may call for changes in the decision-making procedures utilized by the university's institutional review board. Alternatively, novel situations may evoke recognition of the need for a decision that takes new external circumstances into account. External changes often take place over time and with some subtlety. For some colleges and universities, the changing expectations of their student bodies may call for shifts in the curriculum, but the need for such shifts may be ignored by status quo minded faculty unless the failure to address students' expectations is recognized as a problem—hopefully before the situation reaches crisis proportions.

2. **Diagnosis routine.** Once the need for a decision has been recognized,

a decision-making sequence is begun and resources are gathered to address the problem. The decision maker is then faced with a set of partially systematized and partially new data. The definition of the problem still may be quite vague. At this point, to clarify and define issues, decision makers continue to seek information through existing channels and expand the search for solutions by opening new channels until there is a sense that a sufficient number of viable alternatives has been identified (Cyert & March, 1963).

3. **Development of solutions.** There are usually two routines in the creation of possible solutions: first, the search itself; and second, the design of solutions. The search activity is aimed at finding existing solutions that have worked in the past. It consists of four frequently overlapping approaches: (1) **memory search**—scanning the organization's memory (including institutional memories personified in long-term employees); (2) **passive search**—waiting for alternatives to appear; (3) **trap search**—making potential problem solvers outside of the organization aware of the issue and inviting solutions; and (4) **active search**—direct seeking of alternatives through intraorganizational initiatives. A university, for example, may appoint a task force to search actively for solutions to its problems with undergraduate student retention.

   The subsequent development of solutions varies according to technology. For example, when the problem requires only minor adjustments in product or process, a search is generated to narrow down already available solutions. In manufacturing industries, relatively minor design problems lend themselves to rapid solutions. On the other hand, when the system requires custom-made solutions, the search process typically is iterative. That is, the solution is not in focus and both the search and the solution proceed together, working from vague to concrete, without really knowing what the solution looks like until the search is completed. Colloquially, we will know the solution when we see it.

4. **Selection/analysis.** This next phase usually comprises many steps in an interactive process that goes deeper into the examination of alternatives. Committees in higher education institutions, especially ad hoc committees, constitute one type of mechanism for carrying out the selection/analysis process. Committees tend to bring together persons from organizational units whose members usually do not interact frequently, thus helping to provide some unifying orientation toward wider institutional goals.

5. **Screening.** This stage is evoked when the search is expected to generate more alternatives than can be intensively evaluated in a reasonable period of time. Screening requires a rank ordering of alternatives, followed by the elimination of what is not feasible and then by a determination of what is most desirable.

6. **Evaluation and choice.** Depending on the unit charged with making the decision, the choice routine takes place in different ways. When individuals must make choices, the decision can be made (according to this model) either by judgment or intuition—that is, cognitively or on the basis of feeling. At the group or larger organizational level, decisions are often made through bargaining, since group goals often differ. Alternatively, in a bureaucracy, the decision is taken first through factual evaluation, followed by managerial choice or judgment.

7. **Authorization.** After the choice has been determined, it must be authorized for action.

In Mintzberg et al.'s (1976) conception of the decision-making process, the quality of performance in each stage can reduce or enhance the effectiveness of the organization. Performance at each stage constitutes an independent variable that has the potential to affect outcomes (quality and/or quantity of decisions): the dependent variable.

Decision Making as Structure

While the stages in the decision-making process are more or less similar regardless of the organizational unit where the decision takes place, there are important differences in the mechanics of the process. We turn now to the structural conditions that influence the organizational mechanics of decision making. These structural conditions are shaped, in large part, by decision type and organizational function served.

Classification of Decisions at the Organizational Level

At the organizational level, it is useful to distinguish among three types of typical decisions—**strategic, tactical,** and **operational** (Parsons, 1951). They differ from one another in terms of time frame, organizational locus, information, risk, number of people involved, idea versus thing orientation, nature of constraints, and repertories employed. Strategic decisions are concerned with the long-term orientation and design of the organization vis-à-vis its environment. Tactical decisions refer to choices about the transformation of products and services to make them ready for export across system boundaries, while operational decisions have to do with concrete questions of timing, efficiency of linkages among units, personnel selection, technology, and equipment.

Since all three types of decisions are common at the organizational level, it is useful to understand the dimensions of and constraints on each. As Table 4.2 shows, the structural conditions are different for each of the three types of decisions. When organizational members understand the structural conditions that are likely to accompany different types of decisions, they will be better able to anticipate the course and outcomes of decision making. If we are considering a strategic decision of a board of trustees—for example, dealing with a college's history of budget deficits over the previous 10 years—we can identify the character of the decision that will be made in terms of the eight structural dimensions and can anticipate the behaviors of the decision makers with some predictive validity.

Classification of Decisions by Organizational Function Served

All three kinds of decisions can be made at different organizational levels when any of the structural components of the system is itself considered as a system. Thus, an office of student affairs can and does engage in strategic, tactical, and operational decisions. But there is one further helpful descriptive characteristic of decisions, no matter what level, that needs to be

TABLE 4.2
Organizational Decisions

Variables	Strategic Decisions	Tactical Decisions	Operational Decisions
Time	Long-term	Short-term	Daily
Organizational locus	Upper levels	Middle management	Line personnel; task specific
Information	Varying	More reliable	Technological
Risk	Varying	More predictable	Most predictable
Number of people/units affected	Large numbers	Fewer numbers	Fewest numbers
Ideas/things	Ideational	Conceptual and practical	Things
Constraints	Future uncertainty	Time and resources	Tradition
Repertoires	Forecasting, brainstorming	Well-known repertories	Routine

Adapted from the work of Parsons (1951).

added—namely, the organizational function of the decision. Knowing the organizational functions served by a decision permits a prediction of the effects of the decision on different constituencies and of the orientations of the actors making the decision.

One omnibus theory that efficiently classifies the organizational functions that decisions serve is the AGIL approach of Talcott Parsons (1951), who suggests that all systems must make decisions that address four basic functional prerequisites (**adaptation, goal attainment, integration,** and **latency**) for the system to survive and be effective. Two dimensions define the two-by-two Parsonian framework. One dimension consists of instrumental (focused on means/processes) versus consummatory (focused on end results) functions; the other, internal versus external functions. The prerequisites are defined in Table 4.3, and their relationships are displayed in Table 4.4.

To summarize, strategic, tactical, and operational decisions are constantly being made at *all* levels of the organization for different purposes—that is, to perform the four different functions listed in Parsons's framework.

The Utility of Identifying Levels and Functions

Understanding how to classify decisions properly helps to reduce conflict, since the latter, at least in part, results from different members of the organization seeing the same phenomena differently, especially at the early stages or phases in the decision-making process described earlier. A dean, for example, may see salary policy as a strategic decision serving an adaptation function, while the faculty may see it as a tactical, latency-directed decision. That

TABLE 4.3
Definitions of Parsons's Functional Prerequisites

Adaptation	Acquiring resources from the environment; also, distributing resources among organizational units (e.g., budget decisions)
Goal Attainment	Achievement of the objectives of the organization as a whole; decisions involve establishment of organizational identity, strategies of competition, delivery of goods
Integration	Coordinating/linking units and people. Requires interpersonal skills that motivate people to collaborate
Latency	Pattern maintenance and tension reduction—setting up symbols and mechanisms to establish stability, assure continuity

Adapted from Parsons (1951).

TABLE 4.4
Parsons's Framework of Organizational Decisions

	Instrumental (means)	*Consummatory* (ends)
External	Adaptation	Goal attainment
Internal	Latency (pattern maintenance and tension reduction)	Integration

Adapted from Parsons (1951).

is, the dean may see the problem as a long-term question of how to attract employees efficiently and to compensate them equitably. But the faculty may debate among themselves about salary policy in terms of bargaining positions to maximize the funds available for faculty compensation.

Importance of Solving the "Right" Problem

Not only may there be conflict among levels or units in the organization but also potential misinterpretations of problems. A dean, for example, may attach the wrong meaning to the problems to be solved—strategic, tactical, or operational and AGIL. If a dean determines that the problem is that faculty need more chalk in their classrooms to be able to write on the chalkboards, but the real problem is that chalkboards are not the proper teaching technology to be used, then the immediate problem may be solved but not the more important one (Nutt, 1989).

Another oft-cited example is a person whose car has a flat tire but no jack to raise the car. The definition of the problem here is critical. Some would say that the problem is to locate a substitute jack to change the tire, another to find some substitute way to raise the car (or lower the ground) in order to change the tire, while still another to find an alternative means of transportation (or even to avoid the need for transportation). So also in higher education, defining the problem and establishing consensus on its definition are critical to achieving efficient and effective solutions.

A brief summary of the chapter to this point is in order. Here is what we have considered about decision structures to this point:

1. All organizations have four prerequisites that describe important decisions to be made.
2. Three different kinds of decisions—strategic, tactical, and operational—are associated with each of the prerequisites at all levels of the organization.

3. Decision making in the twelve possible cells (four prerequisites by three kinds of decisions) is seldom optimal, and, because of bounded rationality, individuals usually must satisfice.

The discussion thus far has been largely descriptive and classificatory. We are working our way into the question of *how* decisions are made in organizations. We continue with several additional contingencies that must be taken into account.

Organizational Decision-Making Procedural Models

Understanding decision making is complicated by the fact that different kinds of organizations address problems quite differently and thus make strategic, tactical, and operational decisions in different ways. Hence, the very same problem in one organization may be examined and addressed quite differently in another. Different organizational designs—organic compared to mechanistic, for example—may lead to different decision-making patterns. Organizations with organic designs make decisions through informal information exchange, collaboration, and democratic decision making. Decision making in a mechanistic organization occurs through more hierarchical and bureaucratic means.

This simple dichotomy, however, does not adequately describe the varieties of organizations in which decisions take place. For a more comprehensive typology, we turn to the theories of James Thompson (Thompson, 1967; Thompson & Tuden, 1959). Thompson and Tuden describe four different types of organizations. Successful organizations tend to drift toward one of these four prototypes because a particular model is found to be more effective, given the contingencies of their external environments and internal work conditions. The four prototypical organizations are created by juxtaposing two dimensions describing their cultures and belief systems:

1. *Consensus on means*—the degree of agreement or disagreement among system/unit participants about appropriate technology and processes to be used—that is, the relationship of means to desired effects. How much agreement is there in the organization about whether the methods selected to accomplish goals will indeed lead to their achievement? In the case of higher education institutions, organizational members may or may not agree about the effects of certain types of teaching—for example, distance education courses. Some say it is an effective approach to the attainment of institutional goals; others may disagree.

2. *Consensus on goals*—the degree of agreement or disagreement about preferred possible outcomes. That is, to what extent do members of the organization (or group) agree about the goals of the system? Again, considering higher education institutions, how much agreement is there about what the aims of the institution should be? The multifaceted missions of many colleges and universities may generate some degree of disagreement regarding appropriate priorities for the institution. Community college faculty, for example, may disagree regarding the relative emphasis on transfer programs versus career-oriented programs.

Thompson suggests that when these two dimensions—means consensus and goals consensus—are juxtaposed, the result is a classification of decision-making procedures into four distinct modes of organizational decision making. These are displayed in Table 4.5. Thompson notes that each of these four decision-making modes is usually associated with one of the four types of organizations, because the specific decision-making mode helps that particular type of organization survive in the environment in which it is nested. Next, we discuss the ways that decisions are made in these four kinds of institutions.

Modes of Decision Making in Organizations

1. **Decision by computation** is typically found in a bureaucratic structure. In the ideal bureaucratic form, organizational participants are presumed to be in agreement about both means and goal preferences.

TABLE 4.5
Four Modes of Decision Making in Organizations

		Preferences About Goals	
		Agreement	Disagreement
Preferences About Means	Agreement	*Computational*	*Compromise*
	Disagreement	*Consensus*	*Inspiration*

Adapted from Thompson (1967).

The organizational hierarchy is understood and the sources of knowledge needed for decision making are known. Knowledge and skill specialists are clustered in identifiable units, and decisions by superiors are accepted as legitimate. Decision making, then, is a technical or mechanical matter.

We can consider an example from a college administrative function that is bureaucratized: when most faculty and administrators agree that end-of-semester grades must be made available to students on time and there is adequate knowledge about how the registrar's computer system should be programmed to distribute them. Here the decisions involve making sure that the data are accurate, that the software programs are in place, and that full and accurate communication occurs.

2. **Decision by consensus**—usually is found in a collegial organization. In this case, although preferences about goals are clearly known and shared, the appropriate technology is uncertain or disputed, requiring an adjudication of differences about how to proceed (Loke, 1995). In this kind of organization, the resolution of differences is not accomplished hierarchically, but through direct input and negotiation. Thus, parties participate equally until consensus is reached. For instance, when faculty are not sure whether a certain teaching technology (e.g., a team taught, interdisciplinary approach) will lead to a mutually agreed-upon educational outcome, then the *collective* wisdom and judgment of the decision makers must be utilized.

3. **Decision by compromise**—this mode predominates in political organizations. Organizational members agree on the effects that certain actions will have, but they lack consensus over goals. Different factions try to reach agreement so that resources can be properly allocated to the producing units. Bargaining is a common conflict resolution mechanism. Formal decisions are made through a representative body, such as a faculty senate, with much informal jockeying for influence and power.

Since colleges and universities are partially political organizations, this mode of decision making can very often be found, especially in larger institutions. Imagine, for example, an institution where there may be substantial agreement about appropriate means of teaching students, but faculty and administrators do not agree on whether cognitive or psychosocial development needs of students should predominate. That is, there is no disagreement on how to address either cognitive or psychosocial needs, but consensus is lacking on which should have higher priority. Competing factions on campus will dispute the issue, with resolution probably based on some compromise in the goal priorities (though the dominant coalition will usually hold sway). A debate such as this, over the goals of education, is usually never completely resolved, but decisions nevertheless must be made. For example, decisions about the allocation of resources often have deadlines.

4. **Decision by inspiration** is the mode of decision making in an anarchic organization. In this case, there is disagreement on both means and goal preferences. The result is usually a decision (or an indecision) not to face the issue. Individuals tend to be independent actors, and incentives and means for regularized sharing of needed information are not in place. When an inspiration for solving a problem strikes any particular organizational member, action is usually taken on that basis alone. Intermittent brainstorming and outsider insight (e.g., from consultants) is also used to produce inspiring ideas that may work.

When faculty and administration cannot agree on whether to adopt a goal of inculcating multicultural competence in students, and when they also cannot agree on how the college might seek to carry out its educational practices, usually no decision can be taken. Each faculty member decides independently whether to include that goal in his or her courses, and, if so, determines independently how to teach it. Or, if an organizational decision results, it evolves from an inspiration by one individual, not by rational discussion. Here Mintzberg and Waters (1982) suggest that the idea of a decision is no longer coherent enough to permit its use as a valid explanation of organizational phenomena.

To summarize, Thompson and Tuden identify four different types of organizations that evolve in response to degrees of consensus about goals and means. Each of these organizations has a different decision-making style as noted in Table 4.6.

These four types of decision-making modes have a history of success in different organizational contexts. Hence, two directional hypotheses can be generated from the variables. First, if an organization is observed to have a decision-making style that is computational (in contrast to the other three), then its organizational design should be bureaucratic if it is to succeed. Conversely, if the organization is bureaucratic, then its decision-making style should be computational. If organizational leaders discover a mismatch in

TABLE 4.6
Organizational Type and Decision-Making Style

Type of Organization	Effective Decision-Making Style
Bureaucracy	Computation/calculation
Collegium	Consensus through interpersonal means
Polity	Compromise with majority ruling
Anarchy	Inspiration produced by individual hunches

Adapted from Thompson & Tuden (1959).

their own organizations—for example, many decisions being made by compromise in a bureaucratic organization—they can develop change strategies that will move their systems into better matched positions, which will lead to success. Note, however, that such hypotheses deal exclusively with internal organizational design and ignore both the external environment and culture of the organization. Thus, for example, if a university is seen to be making computational decisions, the hypothesis that follows would argue that bureaucratic organizational design would be most efficient. Such a conclusion, however, ignores the professional credentials of the faculty and the culture necessary to support it.

A Brief Recapitulation

Thus far, in this chapter, we have discussed the following:

1. Kinds of decisions—strategic, tactical, and operational
2. Organizational functions served by decisions—AGIL
3. Modes of decision making—computational, compromise, consensus, and inspiration—and associated organizational designs that are more effective

Now that we have mapped out the decision-making modes that might be followed depending on beliefs in the organization about goals and the means to achieve them, we turn to consider who participates in different types of organizational decisions.

Participation Theories

Within all organizations, the structure permits some decisions to be made by individuals alone without utilizing the decision-making apparatus that brings in other persons. That is, individuals often make at least some, and frequently many, kinds of decisions by themselves in bureaucracies, collegiums, and political units—and certainly in anarchies. When is it appropriate, however, for a decision to be made unilaterally versus through a group structure? Many theories examine the ways that decision making is and should be shared (Heller, Pusic, Strauss, & Wilpert, 1998; Leana, Locke, & Schweiger, 1990; Olsen, 1976). We next take up three theories that address this issue. (For early literature on this subject, see Marrow, Bowers, & Seashore, 1967; Mulder, 1971; and Patchen, 1970. A review of more current research on decision making in groups appears in Kerr & Tindale, 2004.)

Group Versus Individual Decision Making

Understanding the nature of decision making in groups is increasingly important as the use of teams in organizations increases (Ilgen, Major, Hollenbeck, & Sego, 1995). Thibaut and Kelley (1986), early researchers on this subject, consider the question of when group versus individual decision making is more effective. In particular, they wished to determine under what conditions individual versus group decision making is more accurate and rapid. They proposed two criteria for selection of the most appropriate mode:

1. *The nature of the problem to be solved*—is it simple or complicated? Simple problems require only a few steps to reach a solution. A complicated problem, on the other hand, necessitates proceeding sequentially or in parallel through many steps.

2. *The distribution of talent in the group*—do most members possess more or less the same skills and abilities? That is, is the group relatively homogeneous, with virtually all members equally capable of performing all of the tasks? Or are the many required talents dispersed uniquely among different group members? In a heterogeneous group, no one person has a monopoly on skills, and the skills that different people have complement each other.

Putting these two dimensions together results in prescriptions for group versus individual decision making. These are illustrated in Table 4.7. The general hypothesis is that the simpler the task (versus complex) and the more that talent is homogeneously (versus heterogeneously) distributed, the more effective individual (versus group) decision making will be. In cell 1, when the problem is very simple and the solution is highly verifiable by all persons in possession of the original facts, individual decision making is called for. Here, groups will perform only at the level of the most proficient single member, no higher. There is no benefit in bringing people together for joint

TABLE 4.7
Conditions Predicting the Efficiency of Group
Versus Individual Decision Making

		Problem Type	
		Simple	Complex
Distribution of Talent	Homogeneous	Individual (1)	Individual (2)
	Heterogeneous	Individual (3)	Group (4)

Adapted from Thibaut and Kelley (1986).

decision making, since each person is equally skilled and knowledgeable about the decision domain at hand. Hence, it is more efficient (i.e., less costly) to let any one individual make the decision alone. The decision outcome would likely be the same, regardless of which member was selected to make it. The decision about how many parking lots to open for guests to a university's graduation ceremony, for example, can be determined readily by one person who obtains the number of guests and the number of parking spaces available in each of the university's lots.

Cell 2 describes a task that requires many different steps, but again no one person is better than any other at each step. Here once more, it is more efficient to allow one person to make the decision alone. If more than one person is involved in the decision, the memory of each participant's activity must be passed along to the next decision maker. The problem of accurate communication, especially of heavily nuanced matters, suggests that sequential decision making will result in lost or distorted information. On the other hand, if one person handles all steps of the decision alone, he or she can keep in mind all the prior steps in the sequence. The decision to close a university due to weather conditions may require reviewing forecasts, contacting state highway and transportation officials, and speaking with campus police and maintenance staff (e.g., snow removal). This multistage decision is likely to be handled more effectively by a single person. If a committee were assigned to make this decision, information from various sources may not be integrated effectively and a poor decision would be made.

In other words, where the solution requires thinking through a series of interrelated steps or stages, applying a number of rules at each point, and always keeping in mind the conclusions reached at earlier points, groups will do less well because the thinking processes and the logic are not well articulated between individuals. A similar situation occurs in cell 3. Even though there is much talent distributed throughout the organization, since the task is simple, once again group participation is not needed.

The conditions in cell 4, however, are quite different. Since the task is complex, different talents are needed to complete it, and that talent resides among different members of the group—not just one person. Hence, group decision making maximizes the use of the available expertise. Search committees are often appointed to select new faculty members, because the decision is complex and the perspectives of multiple members are necessary to assess accurately the qualifications of applicants. When complex problems must be solved, whoever in the group has the relevant expertise is called upon. This principle was first identified by Mary Parker Follett (1924) in her conceptualization of the **authority of the situation,** which suggests that organizations will be more effective when decisions are made by those who have the most expertise required by the demands of the current situation. Expertise relative to the situation, rather than formal title or position in the organization, should determine who makes decisions.

In short, individuals perform better than groups on tasks that are structured, sequential, connected tightly to other tasks, and do not require creativity. Groups are better than individuals when pooling of diverse talents is needed to manage complex tasks.

Shared Decision Making (Vroom and Yetton)

For Thibaut and Kelley, the independent variables that answered the question of group versus individual decision making were the *complexity of the problem* and the *distribution of talent.* But there are other variables or contingencies that may need to be taken into account. The next two theories suggest several. The theories translate the question of decision sharing into issues of who has final authority for the decision.

To some extent, the mode of authority is determined by the contingencies discussed by Thompson and Tuden—that is, agreement about goals and about the means to achieve them (i.e., technology). The source of formal decision-making authority differs in bureaucracies, polities, and collegiums. Bureaucratic authority is vested in the position. Political authority is generated by election or negotiation, and collegial authority finds its backing in professional norms of consensus. In each of these, however, delegation rights exist. Authorities can distribute rights to make decisions under certain circumstances.

Indeed, researchers Vroom and Yetton (1973) and later Vroom and Jago (1988) say that even in hierarchical systems like bureaucracies, the question of participation is central to understanding effective decision making. In colleges and universities, participation in decision making is an especially critical issue, since the organizational structure is overlaid with a democratic ethos, thus placing normative pressures on the system and seemingly making widespread participation almost an ethical obligation of the institution.

According to Vroom and Yetton (1973) and Vroom and Jago (1988), there are seven kinds of decision making with varying degrees of participation. They are arrayed on a continuum from complete leader **autonomy**, to **sharing** with subordinates or colleagues, to complete **delegation** to subordinates or colleagues. They include:

Autocratic Mode

AI—The leader makes the decision alone with currently available information.

AII—Necessary information is obtained from subordinates, but the leader still decides alone. The role of subordinates is to provide data only; they have nothing to do with generating or evaluating alternatives.

Consultative Mode

CI—The leader discusses problems with relevant subordinates *individually.* Then, without bringing them together, the leader makes a decision that may or may not reflect their input.

CII—The leader shares the problem with subordinates in a *group* setting. The leader alone then makes the decision that may or may not take the input from the group meeting into account.

Group Mode

GI—The leader shares the problem with one subordinate and together they analyze the problem. The two arrive at a mutually satisfactory solution in an atmosphere of free and open exchange of information and ideas. Both contribute to the resolution of the problem with the relative contribution of each being dependent on knowledge rather than on formal authority.

GII—The leader shares the problem with a group of subordinates. The leader functions in a participatory mode. His/her role is to provide information and facilitate the group's determination of its own solution, rather than his or her own.

Delegative Mode

DI—The leader delegates the problem to one of the subordinates, providing the person with any relevant information, but giving the subordinate full responsibility for solving the problem alone. Any solution that the person reaches will receive the leader's support.

Vroom and Jago (1988) suggest that eight contingencies need to be taken into account in determining which of the above seven decision-making modes is likely to be most effective. The contingencies—the independent variables—to be considered are:

1. Quality Requirement: importance of the technical quality of the decision
2. Commitment Requirement: importance of subordinate commitment to the decision
3. Leader Information: whether the leader has sufficient information to make the decision
4. Structure of the Problem: degree to which the problem has known alternative solutions and clear criteria for evaluating those alternatives
5. Commitment Probability: likelihood that subordinates will accept the leader's unilateral decision
6. Goal Congruence: whether subordinates support the organizational goals to be achieved through solving the problem
7. Conflict Among Subordinates: likelihood of conflict among subordinates over preferred solutions
8. Subordinate Information: whether subordinates have sufficient information to decide

We can now explore the contingencies in greater detail.

1. **Quality Requirement**: If technical quality does not matter, then any acceptable alternative will be satisfactory to solve the problem.
2. **Commitment Requirement**: This variable represents the extent to which acceptance or commitment on the part of subordinates is critical to the effective implementation of the decision. Acceptance becomes more critical and necessary under two conditions:
   a. If the effective execution of the decision requires initiative, judgment, or creativity on the part of subordinates.
   b. When conditions for obtaining compliance break down (e.g., the leader cannot communicate with subordinates—as when there is no time for a meeting but the subordinates are needed to carry out a directive).
3. **Leader Information**: Two types of information are needed:
   a. Information about preferences of subordinates. Does the leader know the preferences of subordinates for various types of solutions to the problem?
   b. Information about the grounds for judging the quality of alternatives. Does the leader have enough information and expertise to be able to assess alternative solutions?

4. **Structure of the Problem**: Structured problems are those for which known alternative solutions and criteria for evaluating those alternatives are available. The organization may have specific procedures for handling these types of problems.

5. **Commitment Probability**: Will the leader's unilateral decision be accepted by subordinates? Here, the question of legitimacy is raised. In some organizations, subordinates may accept the leader's decision because they believe that it is his or her legitimate right to make that decision by virtue of the position he or she occupies, or because he or she is the acknowledged expert and the only one capable of taking all the necessary factors into account.

6. **Goal Congruence**: This variable refers to the extent to which subordinates are motivated to attain the organization's goals. Do subordinates have the same goals as management? Further, do informal goals coincide with formal goals? If not, energies will likely be misdirected and organizational goals may be sacrificed if not sabotaged.

7. **Conflict Among Subordinates**: To what extent are subordinates likely to be in disagreement over preferred solutions? Subordinates may agree on a common goal but disagree on how to achieve it. Subordinates may disagree among themselves because of different gains or losses from an alternative or because of differences in values or other critical factors.

8. **Subordinate Information**: This variable represents the extent to which subordinates, taken collectively, have the necessary information to generate a high-quality decision. (Note that this is related to Thompson and Tuden's variable, distribution of talent.) In some situations, subordinates may lack the technical knowledge needed. On the other hand, it could be that in complex decisions, input from subordinates is critical.

How to Use the Shared Decision Making Model

Figure 4.2 provides a decision tree for determining when to use different decision-making strategies. To apply the decision tree to a particular problem, the user starts at the left-hand side and works to the right by answering the question in each box that is encountered. Following a line all the way to the right reveals the particular kind of decision-making process that is called for.

We illustrate the utility of this framework with an example from higher education. The director of a teacher education program is attempting to determine whether to offer an online degree program. You can trace the program director's answer to each question through the decision tree in Figure 4.2.

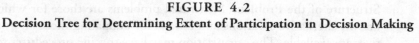

FIGURE 4.2
Decision Tree for Determining Extent of Participation in Decision Making

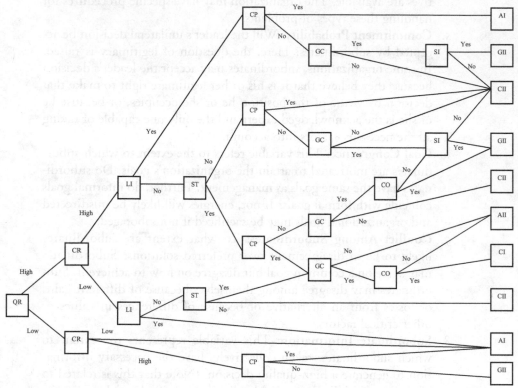

Adapted from Vroom and Jago (1988).

Key to Questions: QR—Quality Requirement; **CR**—Commitment Requirement; **LI**—Leader Information; **ST**—Structure of the Problem; **CP**—Commitment Probability; **GC**—Goal Congruence; **CO**—Conflict Among Subordinates; **SI**—Subordinate Information

Key to Decision-Making Modes: AI—Leader makes decision alone; **AII**—Leader obtains information from subordinates and decides alone; **CI**—Leader discusses problem with subordinates individually and makes a decision that may or may not reflect their input; **CII**—Leader discusses problem with subordinates as a group and makes a decision that may or may not reflect their input; **GI**—Leader shares problem with one subordinate and together they develop the solution; **GII**—Leader shares problem with subordinates as a group and the group determines the solution; **DI**—Leader delegates the problem to subordinates.

1. Quality Requirement (QR): Yes, the quality of the decision is critical, given the need to invest new resources in equipment and personnel to implement an online program, as well as the tuition revenue implications of such a decision.

2. Commitment Requirement (CR): Yes, it is important that faculty members in the program are committed to the decision, since they will likely be the ones teaching in the program.

3. Leader Information (LI): No, in this case, the program director does not have sufficient information about the market for such a program, nor expertise in developing online courses.

4. Structure of the Problem (ST): Yes, the alternatives are known and the criteria for assessing alternatives (pedagogical soundness, student demand for online programs) are clear.

5. Commitment Probability (CP): No, it is unlikely that the faculty would accept the program director's unilateral decision. They expect to be involved in program development decisions.

6. Goal Congruence (GC): Yes, the faculty share the institution's goal of providing access through a wide variety of formats and delivery modes.

7. Conflict Among Subordinates (CO): No, the faculty have not expressed strong preferences regarding online courses or program expansion, and there is no reason to believe that positions in favor or against the idea have been solidified.

8. Subordinate Information (SI): Yes, the faculty have extensive information about pedagogy, technology, and the market for teacher education programs.

In this case, the decision tree leads the program director to GII—share the problem with the faculty as a group and allow the program faculty as a whole to make the decision.

Often it is not necessary to consider all eight contingencies in order to arrive at an appropriate decision-making mode. Consider, for example, a parking manager who needs to decide how many parking lots to open for guests to the university's graduation ceremony. The quality requirement (QR) for this decision is low; the decision does not require technical expertise. The decision tree in Figure 4.2 takes the manager next to commitment requirement (CR), which in this case is low. The parking attendants will monitor whichever lots are opened; their commitment to the decision about how many lots to open is not necessary. Based on the answers to these two questions, the parking manager moves directly to the appropriate decision-making mode—in this case, AI, make the decision alone with the currently available information.

Note that Figure 4.2 represents a general decision tree that can be used to obtain the appropriate decision-making mode for any decision—not just the answers to the examples that we provided in the text. For an additional example, you can trace through the figure a recent decision that you made in the workplace. You can determine if you used an appropriate mode for decision making.

The Zone of Acceptance (Hoy and Miskel)

Another contingency-based approach that also accounts for the timing and extent of participation in decision making is offered by Hoy and Miskel (1996), who borrow heavily from the early and important work of Chester Barnard (1938) in his groundbreaking book, *The Functions of the Executive.* Hoy and Miskel suggest that organizational members encounter decisions that they either accept routinely as legitimately belonging to their supervisor *or* they do not accept them and want some rights of participation. Whether and how they should get those rights is a critical managerial decision in its own right.

Hoy and Miskel, building on previous theories and research (especially Edward Bridges, 1967), suggest that there are two tests that can be employed to see if organizational members should be involved in a particular decision: the **test of relevance** and the **test of expertise**. The first asks whether subordinates have a high personal stake in the decision. If yes, they will want to participate. The second question asks whether the expertise of the subordinates is needed to make a better decision. Whether they *want* to participate and whether they *should* participate are two different, though related, questions. They deal respectively with motivation and effectiveness. Here are the procedures suggested by Hoy and Miskel:

1. Determine whether the decision falls *inside* the subordinates' **zone of acceptance.** If the leader's unilateral decision is likely to be accepted as legitimate by subordinates, then participation will not be necessary and, in fact, will be less efficient because it will consume extensive amounts of time.
2. Determine if the subordinates have a personal stake in the outcome (the test of relevance).
3. Determine if the subordinates have expertise related to the decision (the test of expertise).

With the answers to these three questions, the manner of involvement of subordinates can be determined so that the decision will be made effectively. The decision rules about participation are as follows:

1. For decisions *outside* the zone of acceptance, where both stake and expertise are high, subordinates should be involved very early in the decision-making process.
2. For decisions *outside* the zone, where there is a high personal stake but no expertise, occasionally involve subordinates, but make sure they know that management will make the final decision. The main purpose is to communicate the rationale for the decision and to lower resistance to management's decision.
3. For decisions *outside* the zone, where there is a low personal stake and high expertise, again occasionally involve subordinates. In this case, the expertise is needed.
4. For decisions clearly *inside* the zone, do not involve the subordinates. There is no need.

A brief example can illustrate the use of the Hoy and Miskel heuristic. Suppose a decision is needed regarding how faculty should accommodate the test-taking needs of dyslexic students. In this case, a unilateral decision by a dean would fall outside the faculty's zone of acceptance; the faculty would not view the dean as the legitimate decision maker regarding testing procedures for their courses. It is clear that the faculty have a personal stake in the decision, but it is probably not the case that they have sufficient expertise in learning disabilities to understand what the requirements of the accommodation should be. In sum, this seems to require faculty involvement in the decision but with a clear understanding that administrators will set the policy.

Note that the timing of involvement is also important. When to bring subordinates into the process depends on what the purpose is.

1. If it is important to improve the quality of decision, then early involvement of subordinates in problem solving is important.
2. If it is important to improve morale and/or lower resistance, then leaders should involve subordinates later in the decision sequence and concentrate on the rationale for the decision, not on the processes for making the decision.

Risky Shift, Polarization, and Social Loafing in Group Decision Making

Another major question in decision making theory has to do with the degree to which people in groups are willing to take risks and whether individuals or groups are more willing to take risks in their decision making (van Knippenberg, van Knippenberg, & van Dijk, 2000). When problems are posed in ways that reveal positive gains, both individuals and groups tend to shy *away* from taking risks—preferring options that are more likely to assure their obtaining the gains. In contrast, when losses rather than gains are stressed, individuals and groups tend to take *more* risks in order to avoid the losses (Kahneman & Tversky, 1984).

Do groups usually make more risky decisions than their individual members because each member can hide from individual responsibility via "free riding" (Albanese & Van Fleet, 1985; Ostrom, 1998)? Or does the necessity for groups to develop a commonly accepted agreement make it more likely that they will rule out decisions that appear risky to some members?

The research on this subject is interesting and relevant. Groups tend to shift to more risky decisions in the course of discussion and decision making (Kogan & Wallach, 1967; Stoner, 1961, 1968). Further, a group as a whole is more likely to come to a more risky decision than any one member (Kogan & Wallach, 1964). However, later studies found also that some groups experience a *conservative* shift toward *less* risky options.

What determines the direction? It appears to be the initial positions of the members before they begin discussion of the problem. The group will move in the direction of the initial predominant values of the group, risky or conservative. Group discussion opens up new ideas that are perceived according to initial predispositions.

Other trends in group decision making suggest that groups over time tend to **polarize**—that is, to solidify positions in opposition to other groups (Doise, 1969; Moscovici & Zavalloni, 1969). Further, a dominant member emerges in the group if consensus does not form after some period. Often this member is more conservative than the group and through that orientation instills a norm of cohesiveness that bends the group toward compromise.

In groups, some members may be less motivated to work hard than others, since it is possible to hide from individual responsibility when individual work output is submerged in the group's productivity (George, 1992; Hart, Karau, Stasson, & Kerr, 2004; Latane, Williams, & Harkins, 1978). Such **social loafing** represents a serious problem for organizations concerned with maximizing individual motivation and commitment to the institution (Comer, 1995).

To summarize, when considering the assignment of tasks with somewhat ambiguous goals to individuals or groups, it is important to consider the risk propensities and motivation levels of the individual members and the history and character of the group. Since so much decision making in academia takes place in ad hoc committees, administrators must use sophisticated judgments in assigning responsibility.

Social Constructionist Perspectives on Group Decision Making

Social constructionist theories offer additional frameworks for understanding how groups, teams, and committees make decisions. These theories focus on the development of a group consciousness or a collective mind that shapes decision-making processes and outcomes (Bormann, Cragan, & Shields, 2001; Cragan & Shields, 1998; Weick & Roberts, 1993).

Ernest Bormann's (1996) **symbolic convergence theory** suggests that recurring forms of communication (e.g., group members seeking task-related information or committee members sharing office gossip) demonstrate the presence of a shared group consciousness. Group members form a shared consciousness when their separate cognitive worlds begin to resemble each other more closely. As a result, the group members begin to socially construct reality in ways that are more similar than different.

Bormann noted that certain types of communication are likely to trigger the formation of a shared group consciousness. Dramatizing messages, for example, can energize a group and pull members together around common communicative themes. When a group member tells a captivating story or when a committee member offers a particularly harsh critique of a policy, the other group members may be stimulated by the ideas and emotions conveyed by the speaker and, in turn, add their own contributions that extend and modify the theme of the original communication. Bormann (1996) conceptualizes this process as a chain reaction.

> The flow of communication in consciousness-creating segments of meetings is not from the speaker to the listeners. Instead, a chain is triggered by the first dramatizing message and is then picked up and elaborated by other members. Soon a number of people are deeply involved in the discussion, excitedly adding their emotional support, and often modifying the ongoing script. (p. 104)

Bormann refers to this type of chain reaction as a **fantasy theme**. Here, Bormann is not using the term "fantasy" in the way that it is commonly used; that is, as something that is imaginary and not grounded in reality. In Bormann's (1996) theory, fantasy refers to "the creative and imaginative shared interpretation of events that fulfills a group psychological or rhetorical need" (p. 88). Fantasy themes are often based in the real life events of the group members or are grounded in their interpretations of events occurring elsewhere in the organization. In addition, themes may emerge around anticipated future events. An information technology team, for example, may have constructed an apocalyptic theme around Y2K computer problems (i.e., all computers will crash at the beginning of the year 2000), only later to dis-cover that the group's fears were largely unfounded.

Not all dramatizing messages will produce a fantasy theme. A joke, story, or anecdote may be met with apathy or criticism rather than enthusiasm. In such cases, the communication episode reveals dimensions of consciousness *not* shared by the group members. This information is important for group decision makers, as it reveals the extent of subcultures or cliques within the group and can uncover differences in values and perspectives that may need to be addressed in the course of decision making and problem solving.

Groups and teams adopt different types of fantasy themes, depending on the initial predispositions of the members, the members' prior interaction history, and the organizational circumstances with which they are con-fronted. Some groups are characterized by **mastery themes,** which pertain to the goals of gaining and using power. Consider, for example, a diversity task force that is continually underfunded by the college administration. Its members may form a fantasy theme related to being an "underdog" in the struggle for resources. Others in the organization may expect the task force to lose to more powerful interests in the competition for resources, but when task force members are able to secure additional funding for their programs, they view themselves as achieving against the odds. They have triumphed over adversity.

In contrast, other groups are defined by **affiliation themes,** where the desire for social interaction and fun predominates. Members of an enroll-ment management team, for example, may enjoy each other's company and share stories about their family members, hobbies, and vacations. The themes that emerge from these conversations fulfill important psychological needs for attachment and belonging. A third type of fantasy is found in groups that cohere around **achievement themes.** These themes direct atten-tion to tasks and problem solving. A story about how the group addressed a particularly challenging problem in the past, for example, would likely rein-force the group's motivation to address similarly complex issues in the future.

Fantasy themes can have a significant impact on group decision making, because they frame group members' perspectives about what constitutes a good decision. In a team characterized by mastery fantasies, for example, de-cisions may be made on the basis of how the likely outcome will affect the relative power of the group. Will the decision enhance the power of the group vis-à-vis other groups and units within the organization? Mastery fan-tasies, in some instances, may generate an "us versus them" mentality that can rally strong internal group support for a decision; however, it can also reinforce tendencies to suboptimize—that is, to make decisions that advance the group's goals rather than those of the larger organization.

Groups that share affiliation fantasies, in contrast, may be afraid to make controversial decisions that could generate strong emotional responses. Members of this type of group value harmony and good interpersonal relationships, which they do not wish to jeopardize. As a result, these groups may seek to avoid some decisions or seek quick solutions that avert the possibility of open conflict. Finally, achievement fantasies can focus the decision-making process on improving quality and productivity. Group members, in this instance, are likely to emphasize rational, data-based procedures for decision making. These emphases, however, are not a guarantee of success, especially when external conditions are unpredictable. Research on the Johnson administration's decision to escalate the war in Vietnam in the 1960s, for example, revealed shared themes of rationality, fact finding, and computerized decision making. Yet conditions on the ground in the war zone did not follow the assumptions made in the administration's decision-making models (Ball, 1992).

Symbolic convergence theory does not attempt to match fantasy themes with different types of organizational decisions; it does not offer hypotheses regarding which type of theme would be most likely to generate effective decisions. Bormann (1996) explains that symbolic convergence theory is not positivist in its assumptions: "The theory does not provide prediction and control of group decision making, but it does allow for understanding after the event and for anticipating possible developments" (p. 112). Therefore, Bormann recommends that organizational members use symbolic convergence theory to enhance group members' awareness of the symbolic convergence process and its effects on decision making.

First, groups can assess whether or not their shared group consciousness facilitates coping fantasies or disabling fantasies. Bormann (1996) notes that shared fantasies can help group members adapt to a changing external environment, as well as deal with internal conflicts. Other fantasies, however, "may be so dysfunctional that they can be compared to psychologically disturbed thinking in individuals" (p. 108). Groups may share utopian, apocalyptic, or paranoid fantasies that damage group productivity and social development. Consider, for example, a group of graduate students who have been assigned a team research project. This group has constructed a fantasy theme that suggests that the instructor is "out to get them." They believe that regardless of their efforts, the instructor will give them a poor grade. Hence, the team members do not devote much time to the project, do not challenge each other with new ideas, and do not accept responsibility for the outcome.

If an assessment of the current prevailing themes reveals a need for change, then group members can generate new fantasy themes through creative, open-ended communication processes. Bormann (1996) suggests that groups can take a "fantasy vacation and think and talk about something completely removed from the problem" on which they are working (p. 111). This activity frees the group from the cognitive and emotional constraints under which it had been operating. Brainstorming and other forms of free association can stimulate new fantasy themes, reignite energy for task accomplishment, and stimulate imaginative solutions to problems.

Summary

Many theories deal with decision making. They include process theories, theories about types of decisions, about participation, and about individual predispositions. Understanding the decision-making process allows propitious intervention by organizational leaders. Understanding the decision-making structure permits judicious allocation of different types of decisions to decision makers (groups or individuals) who are best able to make the decision effectively and efficiently.

Given the prevalence of groups and teams in organizations, collaborative approaches to decision making have become increasingly important to overall organizational effectiveness. If organizations delegate decision-making authority to groups and teams, then members need well-developed communication skills and an awareness of the existing and emergent themes that characterize the group's communication patterns. Symbolic convergence theory and other social constructionist perspectives on decision making suggest that careful attention must be paid to the group dynamics that shape decision-making processes and outcomes.

Review Questions

1. Which of the following reflects the need in every college and university to make decisions to secure adequate resources and assure their efficient distribution (e.g., via budgeting) across various organizational units?
   a. Adaptation
   b. Goal attainment
   c. Integration
   d. Pattern maintenance and tension reduction (latency)

2. A large community college has recruited faculty carefully to assure their agreement with the goals of the college. Many rules and regulations have

been developed to direct faculty in the conduct of their classes. In Thompson's framework, most decisions are likely to be made by:

a. Consensus
b. Coalition
c. Judgment
d. Computation

3. In some colleges or universities, there may be much disagreement about the institution's objectives (e.g., transmit knowledge to students versus change their values) and about how to achieve them (e.g., through lectures, discussion, or electronic media). According to Thompson, how are most decisions usually made in such organizations?

a. By compromise
b. Through power
c. By hierarchical referral
d. By inspiration

4. According to Vroom and Yetton, to determine how much and what kind of involvement of subordinates is appropriate to a particular decision, a manager should consider which of the following?

a. Whether the organization is structured by function or product
b. Leadership style
c. Amount of information possessed by subordinates
d. Whether the organization is unionized

5. A vice president for information technology is told by members of her department that the brand of computers the college has been buying are more expensive but do not differ in quality from a less expensive brand. Before deciding to switch to the cheaper brand, she is thinking about consulting the faculty who use the computers. According to Vroom and Yetton, should she ask for input from the faculty?

a. Yes
b. No

6. An eight-member curriculum committee comprising faculty members from various liberal arts departments is faced with the problem of deciding whether to include two years of a foreign language in the required curriculum. According to Thibaut and Kelley, which of the following decision-making modes should be used?

a. Discussion and decision by the committee
b. A decision by one faculty member

   c. A decision by a knowledgeable outside consultant
   d. A decision by the chair of the committee without having to consult
       with the committee

7. A decision-making group is fixated on advancing its power position
    within the organization. According to symbolic convergence theory,
    which types of themes are likely to characterize communication in this
    group?
    a. Mastery themes
    b. Affiliation themes
    c. Achievement themes

Case Discussion Questions

Consider again the Eastern State University case presented at the beginning
of this chapter.

   1. The provost noted that one of the most important decisions involved
       the locus of decision making; that is, who should make decisions re-
       garding program closure. Ultimately, the president decided that the
       routine decision-making channels would not be utilized. What were
       the reasons for this decision?
   2. In what ways did the program closure process follow a linear model
       (i.e., decision recognition, diagnosis, development of solutions, se-
       lection/analysis, screening, evaluation and choice, authorization), and
       in what ways did the process deviate from these rational, linear
       procedures?
   3. College leaders ultimately chose group decision making rather than
       individual decision making. How might this decision be explained
       using Thibaut and Kelley's theory of participation? How might this
       decision also relate to the zone of acceptance?
   4. Consider the open meetings convened by CORE and the faculty sen-
       ate. Did these meetings address any of Parsons's functional prerequi-
       sites? If so, explain how.
   5. The CORE committee decided against using a computational for-
       mula for making program closure decisions. How might this decision
       be explained using Thompson's four modes of decision making?

References

Ackoff, R. L. (1981). The art and science of mess management. *Interfaces, 11*(1),
    20–26.

Albanese, R., & Van Fleet, D. D. (1985). Rational behavior in groups: The free-riding tendency. *Academy of Management Review, 10*(2), 244–255.

Allison, G. T. (1971). *Essence of decision: Explaining the Cuban Missile Crisis.* Boston: Little, Brown.

Bachrach, P., & Baratz, M. S. (1962). The two faces of power. *American Political Science Review, 56,* 947–952.

Baird, I., & Thomas, H. (1990). What is risk anyway? Using and measuring risk in strategic management. In R. Bettis & H. Thomas (Eds.), *Risk, strategy, and management.* Greenwich, CT: JAI Press.

Ball, M. A. (1992). *Vietnam on the Potomac.* New York: Praeger.

Barnard, C. I. (1938). *The functions of the executive.* Cambridge, MA: Harvard University Press.

Bass, B. M. (1983). *Organizational decision making.* Homewood, IL: Richard D. Irwin.

Bazerman, M. (1990). *Judgment in managerial decision making* (2nd ed.). New York: Wiley.

Behn, R. D. (1988). Management by groping along. *Journal of Policy Analysis and Management, 7,* 643–663.

Bensimon, E. (2004). The diversity scorecard: A learning approach to institutional change. *Change, 36*(1), 45–52.

Bess, J. L. (1982). *University organization.* New York: Human Sciences Press.

Bormann, E. (1996). Symbolic convergence theory and communication in group decision making. In R. Hirokawa & M. Poole (Eds.), *Communication and group decision making* (2nd ed., pp. 81–113). Thousand Oaks, CA: Sage.

Bormann, E., Cragan, J., & Shields, D. (2001). Three decades of developing, grounding, and using symbolic convergence theory. In W. B. Gudykunst (Ed.), *Communication yearbook, volume 25* (pp. 271–313). Mahwah, NJ: Lawrence Erlbaum.

Bridges, E. M. (1967). A model for shared decision making in the school principalship. *Educational Administration Quarterly, 3,* 49–61.

Comer, D. R. (1995). A model of social loafing in real work groups. *Human Relations, 48*(6), 647–667.

Cragan, J. F., & Shields, D. C. (1998). *Understanding communication theory: The forces for human action.* Boston: Allyn and Bacon.

Cray, D., Mallory, G. R., Butler, R. J., Hickson, D. J., & Wilson, D. C. (1988). Sporadic, fluid and constricted processes: Three types of strategic decision-making in organizations. *Journal of Management Studies, 25*(1), 13–39.

Cyert, R. M., & March, J. G. (1963). *A behavioral theory of the firm.* Englewood Cliffs, NJ: Prentice-Hall.

Deetz, S. (1992). *Democracy in an age of corporate colonization: Developments in communication and the politics of everyday life.* Albany: State University of New York Press.

Doise, W. (1969). Intergroup relations and polarization in individual and collective judgments. *Journal of Personality and Social Psychology, 12,* 136–143.

Duncan, R. B. (1972). Characteristics of perceived environments and perceived environmental uncertainty. *Administrative Science Quarterly, 17,* 313–327.

Follett, M. P. (1924). *Creative experience.* London: Longman and Green.

George, J. M. (1992). Extrinsic and intrinsic origins of perceived social loafing in organizations. *Academy of Management Journal, 35*(1), 191–202.

Gouldner, A. (1952). Red tape as a social problem. In R. K. Merton, A. P. Gray, B. Hockey, & H. C. Selvin (Eds.), *Reader in bureaucracy* (pp. 410–418). Glencoe, IL: Free Press.

Gray, P. H. (2001). A problem-solving perspective on knowledge management practices. *Decision Support Systems, 31*(1), 87–102.

Harrison, E. F. (1999). *The managerial decision-making process* (5th ed.). Boston: Houghton Mifflin.

Hart, J. W., Karau, S. J., Stasson, M. F., & Kerr, N. A. (2004). Achievement motivation, expected coworker performance, and collective task motivation: Working hard or hardly working? *Journal of Applied Social Psychology, 34*(5), 984–1000.

Heller, F., Pusic, E., Strauss, G., & Wilpert, B. (1998). *Organizational participation: Myth and reality.* Oxford, England: Oxford University Press.

Hellriegel, D., Slocum, J. W., Jr., & Woodman, R. W. (2004). *Organizational behavior* (10th ed.). Cincinnati, OH: South-Western College Publishing.

Hickson, D. J., Butler, R. J., Cray, D., Mallory, G. R., & Wilson, D. C. (1986). *Top decisions: Strategic decision-making in organizations.* San Francisco: Jossey-Bass.

Hogarth, R. M. (1980). *Judgment and choice.* New York: Wiley.

Hoy, W., & Miskel, C. (1996). *Educational administration: Theory, research, and practice* (5th ed.). New York: McGraw-Hill.

Huber, G. P., & McDaniel, R. R. (1986). The decision-making paradigm of organizational design. *Management Science, 32*(5), 572–589.

Huber, O. (1986). Decision making as a problem solving process. In B. Brehmer (Ed.), *New directions in research on decision making* (pp. 108–138). New York: North Holland.

Ilgen, D. R., Major, D., Hollenbeck, J. R., & Sego, D. J. (1995). Raising an individual decision-making model to the team level: A new research model and paradigm. In R. A. Guzzo, E. Salas, & Associates (Eds.), *Team effectiveness and decision making in organizations* (pp. 113–148). San Francisco: Jossey-Bass.

Jacob, P. E., Flink, J. J., & Schuchman, H. L. (1962). Values and their function in decision making. *Supplement to the American Behavioral Scientist, 5,* 5–38.

Kahneman, D., & Tversky, A. (1984). Choices, values, and frames. *American Psychologist, 39,* 341–350.

Kakabadse, A. (1987). Organizational politics. *Management Decisions, 25,* 33–37.

Keren, G. (1996). Perspectives of behavioral decision making: Some critical notes. *Organizational Behavior and Human Decision Processes, 65*(3), 169–178.

Kerr, N. L., & Tindale, R. S. (2004). Group performance and decision making. *Annual Review of Psychology, 55,* 623–655.

Kogan, N., & Wallach, M. A. (1964). *Risk taking: A study in cognition and personality.* New York: Holt, Rinehart and Winston.

Kogan, N., & Wallach, M. A. (1967). Group risk taking as a function of members' anxiety and defensiveness levels. *Journal of Personality, 35*(1), 50–64.

Latane, B., Williams, K., & Harkins, S. (1978). Many hands make light the work: The causes and consequences of social loafing. *Journal of Personality and Social Psychology, 37,* 822–832.

Leana, C. R., Locke, E. A., & Schweiger, D. M. (1990). Fact and fiction in analyzing research on participative decision making: A critique of Cotton, Vollrath, Froggart, Lengnick-Hall, and Jennings. *Academy of Management Review, 15,* 137–146.

Lindblom, C. E. (1959). The science of "muddling through." *Public Administration Review, 19*(2), 79–88.

Loke, W. H. (Ed.). (1995). *Perspectives on judgment and decision making.* Lanham, MD: Scarecrow Press.

Lopes, L. L. (1996). When time is of the essence: Averaging, aspiration, and the short run. *Organizational Behavior and Human Decision Processes, 65*(3), 179–189.

Luce, R. D., & Raiffa, H. (1957). *Games and decisions: Introduction and critical survey.* New York: John Wiley & Sons.

March, J. G. (1994). *A primer on decision-making: How decisions happen.* New York: Free Press.

March, J. G. (1997). Understanding how decisions happen in organizations. In Z. Shapira (Ed.), *Organizational decision making* (pp. 9–32). New York: Cambridge University Press.

Marrow, A. J., Bowers, D. G., & Seashore, S. E. (1967). *Management by participation.* New York: Harper & Row.

McCall, M. W., & Kaplan, R. E. (1990). *Whatever it takes: The realities of managerial decision making* (2nd ed.). Englewood Cliffs, NJ: Prentice-Hall.

McLaughlin, D. J. (1995). Strengthening executive decision making. *Human Resource Management, 34*(3) 443–461.

McNamara, G., & Bromiley, P. (1999). Risk and return in organizational decision making. *Academy of Management Journal, 42*(3), 330–339.

Medin, D. L., & Bazerman, M. H. (1999). Broadening behavioral decision research: Multiple levels of cognitive processing. *Psychonomic Bulletin and Review, 6*(4), 533–546.

Mintzberg, H. (1979). *The structuring of organizations.* Englewood Cliffs, NJ: Prentice-Hall.

Mintzberg, H., Raisinghani, D., & Theoret, A. (1976). The structure of "unstructured" decision processes. *Administrative Science Quarterly, 21*(2), 246–275.

Mintzberg, H., & Waters, J. A. (1982). Tracking strategy in an entrepreneurial firm. *Academy of Management Journal, 25*(3), 465–499.

Moscovici, S., & Zavalloni, M. (1969). The group as a polarism of attitudes. *Journal of Personality and Social Psychology, 12,* 125–135.

Mulder, M. (1971). Power equalization through participation? *Administrative Science Quarterly, 16*(1), 31–38.

Nutt, P. C. (1989). Errors in sizing up the situation. In P. C. Nutt (Ed.), *Making tough decisions: Tactics for improving managerial decision making* (pp. 51–69). San Francisco: Jossey-Bass.

Nutt, P. C. (1999). Surprising but true: Half the decisions in organizations fail. *Academy of Management Executive, 13*(4), 75–90.

Olsen, J. P. (1976). University governance: Non-participation as exclusion or choice. In J. G. March & J. P. Olsen (Eds.), *Ambiguity and choice in organizations* (pp. 277–313). Bergen, Norway: Universitetsforlaget.

Ostrom, E. (1998). A behavioral approach to the rational choice theory of collective action. *American Political Science Review, 92*(1), 1–22.

Parsons, T. (1951). *The social system.* Glencoe, IL: The Free Press.

Parsons, T., & Platt, G. (1973). *The American university.* Cambridge, MA: Harvard University Press.

Patchen, M. (1970). *Participation, achievement, and involvement on the job.* Englewood Cliffs, NJ: Prentice-Hall.

Pettigrew, A. (1973). *The politics of organizational decision-making.* London: Tavistock.

Posner, B. Z., & Schmidt, W. H. (1993). Value congruence and differences between the interplay of personal and organizational value systems. *Journal of Business Ethics, 12,* 341–347.

Quinn, J. B. (1980). *Strategies for change: Logical incrementalism.* Homewood, IL: Irwin.

Radner, R. (1997). Bounded rationality, indeterminacy, and the managerial theory of the firm. In Z. Shapira (Ed.), *Organizational decision making* (pp. 324–352). New York: Cambridge University Press.

Shapira, Z. (1995). *Risk taking: A managerial perspective.* New York: Russell Sage.

Simon, H. A. (1955). A behavioral model of rational choice. *Quarterly Journal of Economics, 69,* 99–118.

Simon, H. A. (1957). *Administrative behavior.* New York: The Free Press.

Simon, H. A. (1960). *The new science of management decision.* New York: Harper & Row.

Stoner, J. A. F. (1961). *A comparison of individual and group decisions involving risk.* Unpublished master's thesis, Massachusetts Institute of Technology, School of Industrial Management, Boston.

Stoner, J. A. F. (1968). Risky and cautious shifts in group decisions: The influence of widely held values. *Journal of Experimental Social Psychology, 4,* 442–459.

Straussman, J. D. (1993). Management by groping along: The limits of a metaphor. *Governance: An International Journal of Policy and Administration, 6*(2), 154–171.

Sutcliffe, K. M., & McNamara, G. (2001). Controlling decision-making practice in organizations. *Organizational Science, 12*(4), 484–501.

Thibaut, J. W., & Kelley, H. H. (1986). *The social psychology of groups.* New Brunswick, NJ: Transaction Books.

Thompson, J. D. (1967). *Organizations in action: The social science bases of administration.* New York: McGraw-Hill.

Thompson, J. D., & Tuden, A. (1959). *Comparative studies in administration.* Pittsburgh, PA: University of Pittsburgh Press.

van Knippenberg, D., van Knippenberg, B., & van Dijk, E. (2000). Who takes the lead in risky decision making? Effects of group members' risk preferences and prototypicality. *Organizational Behavior and Human Decision Processes, 83,* 213–234.

von Neumann, J., & Morgenstern, O. (1944). *Theory of games and economic behavior.* Princeton, NJ: Princeton University Press.

Vroom, V. H., & Jago, A. G. (1988). *The new leadership.* Englewood Cliffs, NJ: Prentice-Hall.

Vroom, V. H., & Yetton, P. W. (1973). *Leadership and decision-making.* Pittsburgh, PA: University of Pittsburgh Press.

Weick, K., & Roberts, K. (1993). Collective mind in organizations: Heedful interrelating on flight decks. *Administrative Science Quarterly, 38*(3), 357–381.

Zey, M. (1992). *Decision making: Alternatives to rational choice.* London: Sage.

5

INDIVIDUAL
DECISION MAKING

CONTENTS

Preview   629
Case Context   629
Introduction   633
The Garbage Can Model   634
Decisions as Role Playing   637
Decisions as Personality Manifestations   639
Decisions and Information Utilization   643
Risk and Uncertainty: The Gambling Metaphor   646
Decision Trees   649
Non–Decision Making   650
Postmodern Perspectives on Individual Decision Making   653
Summary   655
Review Questions   655
Case Discussion Questions   657
References   657

The authors are most grateful for the critical comments on an early draft of this chapter by Marietta Del Favero, University of New Orleans. The final version, of course, is our own and may or may not reflect the perspective of the reviewer.

Preview

- Decision making is a "choice opportunity" that takes place in ambiguous situations.
- At least four "streams" of ingredients usually enter into decision making: problems, solutions, participants, and choice opportunities.
- Managerial decision making comprises three types of roles: interpersonal, informational, and decisional.
- Individuals exhibit styles of decision making depending in part on the balance in their personalities between thinking versus feeling and sensing versus intuition.
- Decisions are made by different individuals as a result of their preferences for using some or all of the information available and their needs to reach solutions in a given time frame.
- There is an optimum information "load" for efficient decision making.
- Some decisions can be subjected to mathematical calculations of risk probability and likely rewards.
- Individual decision makers are often engaged in a "gamble" in which they estimate expected rewards and calculate the probabilities of achieving them.
- Critical theory focuses attention on "nondecisions" that suppress or thwart latent and manifest desires to challenge the status quo.
- Postmodern conceptualizations of organizational fragmentation suggest that it may not be possible to assume the existence of stable sets of problems, known alternatives, and consistent levels of participation and interest in decision making.

---------------------------- CASE CONTEXT ----------------------------

Academic Planning at Adams County Community College

The academic planning group at Adams County Community College meets twice each month to discuss curriculum and program development. The group consists of five division deans (to whom the department chairs report), the dean of curriculum and instruction (who is responsible for faculty professional development and instructional technology), and the vice president for academic affairs (who chairs the meetings). The group is primarily advisory to the vice president, though occasionally the vice president will use the group as a sounding board for his own ideas before making a decision.

Traditionally, each meeting begins with round-robin sharing by the deans regarding major initiatives and accomplishments within their units.

Typically, each dean takes about 5 minutes to highlight a few issues in his or her division. But at the first meeting of the academic year, the dean of the division of social sciences, Elizabeth Kimball, violated that norm and launched into a 20-minute presentation on the merits of interdisciplinary learning communities. Dean Kimball was one of only two female deans at Adams County Community College, and she was often frustrated by the slow pace of change at the college.

Dean Kimball had just returned from a national conference on learning communities, and she wanted her college to commit to adopting this pedagogical and curricular innovation. As she spoke, she distributed to the academic planning group a wide assortment of handouts, copies of PowerPoint slides, research studies, and brochures of learning community programs at other colleges. Her colleagues, however, scarcely looked up from their agendas as she spoke, and few even bothered to glance at the materials she was distributing.

Finally, the academic vice president interrupted. "Well, I can see that this is something that has really kindled an interest for you," he told Dean Kimball. "But we need to move along to our other agenda items. Maybe we can discuss this more extensively when I meet with you and your department chairs next month."

"Well, no, actually, we would need to move on this right away," Dean Kimball replied, "if we want to do this on an experimental basis in the spring semester."

"I am in no position to make a decision on this today," the vice president responded. "Something like this would require significant resources for faculty training and curriculum development, not to mention big changes in the spring course schedule, which is already well on its way to being finalized."

"Well, this is not the first time that I have brought this idea to the group," Dean Kimball noted. Slowly the other deans remembered that in fact at the last meeting of the previous academic year, Dean Kimball had indicated that she planned to attend the national learning communities conference and would report back to them in the fall.

"You've given us a lot to think about today," the vice president replied.

"Yeah, maybe too much," joked one of the other deans.

"We would need a specific proposal," the vice president explained. "And even then, I am not sure if the timing is right."

"That's right," the dean of curriculum and instruction added. "We have a major technology initiative planned for this year, and a lot of your social sciences faculty are already signed up for the workshop series. We have a lot of our resources tied up in the teaching-with-technology initiative."

"But I feel that our students really need these types of learning communities," Dean Kimball continued. "We could really improve our developmental courses if we grouped, say, a writing course with one of our introductory literature courses, or a developmental math course with one of our introductory biology courses. And we could do some of the same things with our honors courses. A whole cohort of students could take honors classes together for an entire semester. These studies," she pointed to the materials that she distributed, "show that it improves student success and retention."

"Okay, I think we understand the importance of it," the vice president noted. "As I said, maybe this is something that you want to talk over with your chairs and get back to me with a proposal."

Four months later, Dean Kimball had not responded with a proposal. Instead, she moved forward with a small pilot project that paired two developmental writing courses with literature courses and linked together the honors courses for students majoring in criminal justice. She did not check with the academic vice president before making these changes, because these courses required few additional resources, and the four participating faculty members had volunteered their time to develop the new courses. Instead of returning to the academic planning group with a larger proposal, Dean Kimball was focused on other pressing issues, including the renewal of two articulation agreements with nearby universities. The other deans were similarly occupied by other matters, and the academic planning group focused largely on routine issues, as well as the teaching-with-technology initiative.

At the beginning of the spring semester, however, the academic vice president received some disappointing, though not unexpected, news. Enrollment figures were down for the fourth consecutive semester, student departure rates were approaching an all-time high, and failure rates in developmental courses were climbing at an alarming pace.

"The trustees and the state Board of Higher Education are going to be all over us," the president confided to the vice president. "They are tired of the bad press we have been getting. I don't think they realize that we are getting squeezed at both ends. Our strong students are leaving us earlier to transfer to four-year colleges, and our academically weaker students are arriving from high school with even poorer skills. So the universities are cherry-picking our best students, and the high schools are giving us students who need so much remedial work that they may never be college ready."

"We've got to do something about this, and fast," the president continued. "I've already had run-ins with two of the trustees that the new governor appointed. I can't afford another showdown with the board. So I will need something big from you." He looked directly at the vice president. "Give me something by next Monday. I don't care what it is. I just need something so that I can tell the trustees that we are doing something about this."

While the president spent the rest of the day at a charity golf event, the vice president went back to his office to search through institutional data reports on student performance. As he was moving a stack of papers on his desk to make room for more reports, he noticed a pile of materials on learning communities that Dean Kimball had provided months ago. By chance, the study on top of that pile was titled "Learning Communities Improve Retention and Strengthen Remedial Outcomes." The vice president put the data reports aside and spent the next several hours reading research studies on the outcomes of learning communities and then pondering the implications for Adams County Community College. Then, he called Dean Kimball to invite her to dinner, over which they discussed what it would take for Adams County Community College to implement learning communities for its developmental courses and its honors program.

Two weeks later, the academic vice president and Dean Kimball presented their learning communities plan to the board of trustees. They explained how enhancing the honors program through learning communities could keep the transfer-oriented students at Davis for a full two years and how learning communities would improve instruction in the developmental courses. And they described the pilot project that was already in progress in the social sciences division. After the meeting, the president called both of them into his office.

"The trustees just loved your presentation," the president gushed. "That this stuff is backed up with real research. That other community colleges are doing this stuff. They just ate it up. And to think that you already had a pilot project going to address these problems."

Actually, they hadn't. The pilot project started without the vice president's approval and was not initiated in response to the diminished enrollment numbers or the declining student performance in developmental courses. In fact, the social sciences dean was unaware of these data until the vice president met with her over dinner. But at this point, that fact did not seem to matter.

"I am going to go along with your decision and redirect a lot of resources to this learning communities thing," the president continued. "I will just slow down implementation on the technology initiative. You guys can wait a couple more years for new laptops, right?" the president laughed. "Just let the chief financial officer know that I approved your resource request, and you are all set to go. Next week, I'm going to be in Santa Barbara for a conference of community college presidents, but call me on my cell, if the financial officer gives you a hard time. And again, great stuff in there with the trustees. It was an excellent presentation."

Introduction

In chapter 4, we considered the topic of decision making from a collective perspective. Our concern there was with the way decision making takes place in organizational contexts involving more than one person, especially those in which organizational members at different levels and positions share responsibility for decisions. In this chapter, we turn to theories of decision making that explain what individuals bring to those collective decision-making activities—that is, their predispositions, preferences, and styles (Nord & Fox, 1996). This chapter is concerned, in other words, with the psychology of decision making and argues that human beings in managing their lives are driven to achieve and maintain control over themselves in their environments. More specifically, they have needs to exercise **agency** (i.e., a state of action that utilizes one's autonomy).

We are also concerned in this chapter with *how* people make decisions. The mode by which decisions are made often affects the outcome of those decisions (Weber, Ames, & Blais, 2005). Decision modes can be separated into three categories. The first, **calculation-based decision making,** involves a determination of the value of alternative choices and the selection of the one that maximizes benefits and minimizes costs. In the second, **recognition-based decision making,** the decision maker approaches problems in one of three modes: a *rule-based mode* in which he or she refers to procedural manuals; a *case-based mode,* which depends on recalling similar conditions from the past; or a *role-based mode,* which invokes an awareness by the decision maker of extant rules of conduct (without calculating explicitly the likely benefits or detriments). The third category, **affect-based decision making,** recognizes that many people base their decisions on immediate, emotional responses to alternative decision choices. A faculty recruitment and selection committee, for example, may narrow its choices down to the three top candidates and then make decisions simply on whether they like a candidate and see that person as a compatible colleague. Which of these categories and sub-categories would be employed in any decision is a function of the particular situation. For example, instrumental decisions would probably involve more use of the calculation-based mode, while relationship-related decisions would be made primarily by a role-based or affect-based mode (Weber et al., 2005).

Brehmer (1999) suggests that "despite nearly 50 years of decision research, we do not know very much about what people actually do when making decisions" (p. 10). In this chapter, we consider five different approaches that have been suggested to rectify this gap:

1. The garbage can process (Cohen, March, and Olsen)
2. Decisions as role playing (Mintzberg)
3. Decisions as personality manifestations (Mitroff and Kilmann)
4. Decisions and information utilization (Driver)
5. Decisions as a gamble (Goldstein and Weber)

In accordance with the central principle of the book, in our discussion of these approaches, we view decision-making behavior as a function of the interaction of individual and environment. Thus, ultimately all five approaches aim at understanding how the individual must fit into the needs of the organization for the system to be efficient and effective and how the organization must make adaptations to the needs of the individual.

The Garbage Can Model

Cohen, March, and Olsen (1972) suggest that colleges and universities may be described as **organized anarchies** where there is little agreement about goals and the means to achieve them and where key individuals are only sporadically involved in decision-making processes. In organized anarchies, problems and potential solutions are ambiguous and not well understood and decision makers are continually bombarded with new demands that prohibit them from devoting prolonged attention to a particular issue. Under these conditions, rational models of decision making may not be appropriate. Thus, rather than assume that decisions will unfold in a rational, linear process, higher education leaders can anticipate that decisions will emerge in a more random, haphazard fashion. Cohen, March, and Olsen describe this phenomenon as the "garbage can" model of decision making. They note that:

> Although it may be convenient to imagine that choice opportunities lead
> first to the generation of decision alternatives, then to an examination of

their consequences, then to an evaluation of those consequences in terms of objectives, and finally to a decision, this type of model is often a poor description of what actually happens. In the garbage can model, on the other hand, a decision is an outcome or interpretation of several relatively independent streams within an organization. (pp. 2–3)

Imagine that all of the ingredients surrounding a decision have been dumped into a metaphorical garbage can. These ingredients include four central, independent streams. The first is the set of **problems** that occupy the attention of organizational members. These problems may be related to internal working conditions, personal concerns, or changes in the external environment. The second is the set of possible **solutions** that have priority for different workers or groups of workers. In this model, it is important to think of solutions *not* as ideas that people generate in order to solve a particular problem. Instead, solutions flow continuously throughout the organization, and those who promulgate certain types of solutions are constantly looking for problems to which they can attach their favorite solutions. As Cohen et al. (1972) note, a solution "is an answer actively looking for a question" (p. 3). The third stream is **participants,** whose time, interest, and commitment change depending on what is salient in the short and long run. They move in and out of the process as circumstances change and make their involvement less or more important. The last stream is **choice opportunities.** These are occasions when the organization is expected (by its own leaders or by external stakeholders) to produce a decision that will result in a change in behavior or outcomes.

The intersection of these streams produces a decision, but how the streams become intertwined is often random and unpredictable. Again, the garbage can model is not linear. Organizational problems do not clearly present themselves. Solutions are not offered in response to specific circumstances. Choice opportunities such as budget meetings and hiring decisions do not always coincide with the times when problems need to be solved. As Hatch (1997) notes, "Choices may be made without solving a problem, some problems are never solved, and solutions may be proposed where no problem exists" (p. 278). Consider, for example, a committee where a computer specialist continually offers new technology as the solution to all of the organization's problems, where a faculty member raises new problems at each meeting but never follows through with proposing specific changes, and where choices are made that have little to do with the problems at hand.

Nevertheless, some decisions get made and some problems are solved, even if only by chance. In a particular meeting, the faculty member in the example above may complain about the amount of time he needs to devote to advising students about which courses to take. The computer specialist may interject to describe a new software package that permits much advising to be done online. The solution does not actually pertain to the faculty member's problem, since online advising takes nearly as much time as in-person advising, but the chair of the committee notes that the college will make budget decisions in three weeks and suggests that the committee put in a proposal to purchase the online advising software package. In this case, a problem (student advising) became linked to a solution (online advising) in the context of a choice opportunity (budget decisions). Again, the solution was not offered as a direct response to the faculty member's problem; it was not an exact match for a problematic situation. Other solutions, such as streamlining the course schedule or convening group advising sessions, may have solved the problem more efficiently. But in this instance, those solutions were not available in the "stream" of that particular meeting, and if they would be brought up at next month's meeting, the choice opportunity (the budget decision) will have passed.

The outcomes of the garbage can process are affected by "the mix of choices available at any one time, the mix of problems that have access to the organization, the mix of solutions looking for problems, and the outside demands on the decision makers" (Cohen et al., 1972, p. 16). In addition, the timing of the arrival of problems, choices, solutions, and decision makers affects how the streams intersect. For example, if a problem is introduced after a choice opportunity has passed, it will likely go unsolved. Finally, the energy levels of the decision makers in the participants stream will be critical, especially if the situation is new, unique, and complex. How and when organizational members become involved in decisions is a function of their personal needs, goals, values, and the opportunities for participation available to them. If organizational members' energy is scattered among too many decision domains, then focused attention cannot be brought to bear on any of the problems plaguing the organization. In times of especially heavy decision activity, problems tend to be ignored (intentionally or inadvertently). Similarly, if organizational members are disinterested in particular types of problems and solutions, then related decisions are likely to be avoided or postponed.

Perhaps the key feature of the garbage can framework for understanding decision making is the decoupling of problems and choices. Leaders in colleges and universities work on salient problems that appear to have alternative solutions, but the choice of the most appropriate solution will not become truly viable until there is a shift in the combination of problems, solutions, and decision makers. For example, a dean who plans to retire may not be in a position to make a decision that his or her successor will find less difficult, especially if circumstances—budget, personnel, and other priorities—have shifted.

In sum, the garbage can theory provides a useful diagnostic tool for identifying the central features of decision making and for understanding how they interact. This context for decision making also reveals some of the dilemmas faced by individuals as they struggle to understand the complexities of the shifting environment in which they are asked to make decisions.

Decisions as Role Playing

In Henry Mintzberg's pioneering work (1976), he recognized that most managers are likely to gather information and make decisions quickly on the basis of limited data and that this condition limits the range and possibilities of their actions. Managers rarely have a great deal of time for thinking or planning. Often they are as likely to use intuition as systematic data analysis (Agor, 1989). Indeed, individuals almost invariably employ **heuristics,** or rules of thumb that they have found to have been reasonably successful in dealing with similar situations in the past.

Mintzberg was concerned with understanding how these heuristics are employed in the three central managerial roles where important decisions are made: **interpersonal roles, informational roles,** and **decisional roles** (Mintzberg, 1973). Within these three groupings are ten different roles, each of which calls for different kinds of decisions. Problems of decision making can often be traced to the failure of an organization to recognize the need for each role to be played and/or the need for selecting a person with the talent to perform it.

There are three interpersonal managerial roles. The first is **figurehead,** which pertains to the ceremonial and symbolic roles that managers must fulfill on a regular basis. "Because of his formal authority, the manager is a symbol, obliged to perform a number of duties. Some of these are trite, others are of an inspirational nature" (Mintzberg, 1973, p. 59). Signing official documents and presiding over ceremonial events are two examples of figurehead duties. Managers must perform these duties, which convey to organizational members and external constituents the legal and organizational authority of the head of the organization.

The second interpersonal role is **leader.**

> In analyzing the activities that make up the *leader* role, we must note first that leadership permeates all activities; its importance would be underestimated if it were judged in terms of the proportion of a manager's activities that are strictly related to leadership. (p. 61)

A third interpersonal role in Mintzberg's typology is the **liaison** role, which refers to the significant set of relationships that managers develop with individuals and groups *outside* the organization. College presidents, for example, tend to be engaged, both formally and informally, with fairly large collegial networks of similarly ranked individuals in other organizations. Their decisions in the liaison role function to establish and maintain stable organization-environment relationships.

Informational roles comprise the second category of decision-making roles in Mintzberg's theory. These relate to the flow of information in and out of the organization. There are three such roles. The first is the manager as **monitor.** The manager makes decisions that result in the generation of new information and in the identification of new problems and opportunities. The availability of these new data lead to the exercising of a second informational role—**disseminator.** Decisions made to satisfy this role relate to the manager's efforts to ensure that critical information reaches subordinates and others in a timely and accurate way. Yet another informational role in Mintzberg's schema is that of **spokesperson.** Making decisions in this role entails transmitting information to stakeholders in the organization's environment (e.g., a department chair deciding how to present the strengths of academic programs to prospective students).

The third category of decision-making roles is called "decisional" by Mintzberg. They "involve the making of significant decisions—handling requests for authorization, scheduling his own time, holding meetings to make strategies and handle problems, and negotiating with other organizations" (1973, p. 77). Essentially, these roles revolve around issues of organizational strategy. The first decisional role is **entrepreneur.** According to Mintzberg, managers can engage in entrepreneurial decision making, which begins with monitoring the internal organization and external environment and seeks to uncover and anticipate problems as well as opportunities.

> The chief executive questions subordinates at random, holds functional review sessions, takes the occasional unannounced tour, searches for possible problems in the mail and in the comments of deputies and others, all the time looking for areas of possible improvement. (p. 78)

The second decisional role is **disturbance handler.** The decisions taken in this capacity are reactive, rather than proactive as in the entrepreneurial role. Innumerable and varied disturbances occur daily in colleges and universities—protests, undelivered goods and services, unexpected demands from the outside, the resignation of a key staff member. These types of disturbances may require quick decisions to prevent the spread of problems.

The third decisional role is **resource allocator**—especially resources such as money, time, material, equipment, personnel, and reputation. In this capacity, managers are responsible for scheduling, programming work, and taking authorizing actions (e.g., signing off on budgets).

The last of the decisional roles is **negotiator,** which reflects the manager's role in representing his or her unit in working out conflicts among persons and subunits within the organization and engaging them in mutually beneficial resolutions of problems.

To recapitulate Mintzberg's ten key managerial decision-making roles, they include interpersonal actions (figurehead, leader, and liaison), informational actions (monitor, disseminator, and spokesperson), and decisional actions (entrepreneur, disturbance handler, resource allocator, and negotiator). As Mintzberg notes, these are key managerial roles; hence, it is incumbent on leaders to be sure that they are properly attended to. We turn next from the description of individual decision-making roles to the intrapersonal, psychological sources of those decisions.

Decisions as Personality Manifestations

As we will see in chapter 10 on the subject of organizational leadership, Fred Fiedler (1967) has developed a theory suggesting that a leader's personality is critical to effective decision making. Fiedler suggests that it is necessary to find a fit among leader personality, situational constraints, and decision-making opportunities. Fiedler's concept of personality is relatively simplistic, however. Individuals are, in his view, either people oriented or task oriented. Researchers have suggested that a more sophisticated conceptualization is necessary, especially one with better predictive validity (Barrick & Ryan, 2002). Given the variety of decision-making settings, it is important to be able to identify a range of people with more diverse personalities than a simple task versus person orientation.

Mitroff and Kilmann (1976) theorized that if it is possible to classify different kinds of people, the kinds of decisions that they would be most competent in making can be more easily and accurately determined. They incorporated the theories of an important person in the history of psychology—Carl Jung—and his theory of archetypes (Jung, 1935/1959). Borrowing from Jung, Mitroff and Kilmann suggested that there are four different kinds of problem solving styles. The styles are determined by two personality characteristics that every individual possesses in different strengths: information-accessing preferences and information-processing preferences.

Information-accessing preferences reflect how a person takes in information from the outside—that is, how he or she perceives the data. There are two basic ways:

1. *Sensation* (S)—a perceptual orientation that focuses on details and facts, particularly in a "now" orientation to the situation. Such people tend to absorb information in discrete bits and pieces.
2. *Intuition* (N)—a perceptual orientation that is holistic and global. People with this orientation tend to absorb information in large clumps—intuitively, as a gestalt, the whole at once. They make fewer contextual distinctions.

Information-processing preferences, the second dimension, reflects the predilections of people to deal with the data once it has been received. Different people react differently to available data. Some prefer a primarily cognitive approach that entails thinking about the data; others have a more affective response.

1. *Thinking* (T)—is a judgmental function concerned with formulating rules, procedures, and analytical approaches for decision making. People who think about data work through logic to make it organized and sensible to them.
2. *Feeling* (F)—is concerned with individual cases and with subjective value judgments associated with decision making (Kilmann & Herden, 1976).

The two personality dimensions of information processing and information accessing can be juxtaposed in a two-by-two table that explains to a significant degree the ways in which organizational decision makers are motivated. As noted in Table 5.1, four types of decision makers emerge: STs, SFs, NTs, and NFs. Jung has suggested that people have both primary and secondary orientations. A leader may, for example, have NT (intuition and thinking) as a primary orientation, but will draw from the other three dimensions on occasion as warranted by different situations. Within any organization, there are needs for all four of these different kinds of decision makers.

TABLE 5.1
Decision-Making Style and Dispositions

		Information Processing	
		Thinking (T)	Feeling (F)
Information Accessing	Sensation (S)	ST	SF
	Intuition (N)	NT	NF

Adapted from Kilmann & Herden (1976); Mitroff & Kilmann (1975).

Mitroff and Kilmann also attach descriptive labels to these four dimensions and identify the decision-making characteristics of the persons who possess them.

Systematics (STs) take in small bits of data (S) and then think about them (T). They like quantitative measures. An example of a systematic decision maker would be a director of institutional research who collects student outcomes data (many small bits of data) and then develops recommendations for improving the accuracy and quality of data within the college.

Judicials (SFs) also take in small bits of data (S) but then relate to them affectively (F). The information used by these decision makers comes from the immediate or current situation or circumstances. An example here might be a residence life counselor who deals on an individual level with students.

Speculatives (NTs) take in data in large clumps (N) and then think about them (T). Information about future options forms the basis of their decision making. A university vice president for planning might exemplify this orientation. He or she might look at a large number of factors in the ecology of the university's environment and then attempt to determine by careful thought the strategies that the university should follow in managing external relationships.

Heuristics (NFs) take in data in large clumps (N) and then relate to them affectively (F). Using contextualized hunches or cues about people, these decision makers then apply their own values as the basis for their action choices (Nutt, 1989). A college vice president for human resources might assess the ambience or climate of his or her campus and then propose general approaches to humanize it. Other examples are offered in Table 5.2.

Another way of understanding the utility of Mitroff and Kilmann's framework is to consider how different kinds of decision makers can best be utilized as organizations undergo different phases in their evolutionary or developmental life cycles. As Parsons, Bales, and Shils (1953) observe, organizational systems go through successive phases in which different goals, objectives, and performance criteria are more prominent than others. Colleges and universities, for example, may at different times be more focused on external fund raising than internal organizational efficiency (Cameron, Sutton, & Whetten, 1988; Cameron & Whetten, 2003). It is reasonable to assume, therefore, that in different phases of organizational development, workers are needed whose competencies in decision making meet the needs of that phase.

Different phases, for example, may generate needs for different types of information-accessing skills. During a period of strong regulatory pressure from state governments, colleges and universities need to be able to interpret

TABLE 5.2
Comparison of Decision-Maker Types in Profit-Making Versus College and University Organizations

	Profit-Making Organization	*College or University*
ST	Data processors	Budget makers Institutional researchers Applied academic research
SF	Personnel	Student personnel Teaching
NT	Advertising	Original research New program market research
NF	Long-term planning	Identification of community needs for educational services

large amounts of information about new policies and procedures. Under these conditions, the skills of speculatives (NT) and heuristics (NF)—those who prefer to work with large aggregates of data—become more important to effective organizational decision making. Other times, however, colleges and universities need to process many small bits of discrete information; for example, during an accreditation review when data from multiple programs and offices need to be synthesized. During this period of internal assessment, the abilities of systematics (ST) and judicials (SF) fit the needs of the organization.

Different organizational phases may also emphasize different types of information-processing skills. A major fund-raising campaign will need people who can convey decisions to key constituencies (such as alumni and corporate foundations) in terms of emotional and values-based appeals. In this phase of external resource acquisition, the skills of people who affectively relate to data—judicials (SF) and heuristics (NF)—will address important organizational needs. In contrast, during an expansionary phase, decisions about program growth will need to consider market surveys, demographic trends, and the behaviors of competitor institutions. Under these conditions, the skills of systematics (ST) and speculatives (NT), who cognitively process data, will become more critical. It is important to note, of course, that all kinds of decision makers are needed in each organizational phase. However, in a particular phase, organizational leaders must be sure to utilize sufficient numbers of decision makers whose personalities best match that phase.

Mitroff and Kilmann's theory provides a framework for understanding how different information-accessing and information-processing preferences are applied in organizational decision making. In the next section, we consider how information availability and its use affect the decision-making process.

Decisions and Information Utilization

Information is the lifeblood of colleges and universities. It is an essential element in teaching, learning, and research. It is also a critical part of decision making, since both long-term and short-term planning and the execution of actions to achieve institutional aims rely on information. It is important, therefore, to understand how information is utilized and can be more effectively employed in college and university organizational life. For this, we focus on the amount of information available for decision making.

We saw in chapter 4 how Vroom and Yetton and Hoy and Miskel deal with some parts of this issue when they indicate the importance of the question of *who* has the information necessary for the decision—the leader, subordinates, or both. With Driver, we deal with the question of information in general. Too much, too little, or the wrong kinds of information can lead to inefficient and ineffective decision making. A dean seeking to make a tenure decision, for example, needs relevant information in the right amount and format and at the right time.

For efficient decision making to take place, there is an optimum *amount* of information, and that quantity may differ depending on the nature of the decision maker. Too much information for one kind of decision maker can overload the person; too little can cause incorrect decisions to be made.

Driver (2003) suggests that there are four basic types of decision makers who operate more efficiently and effectively in different types of environments: **information rich** or **information poor**. Driver presents what is basically an information-processing model with two dimensions: the amount of information used and the number of solutions generated.

Information use refers to the amount and complexity of information that is actually used in decision making. Some organizational members use all of the information that is available to them. Others use just enough information to get one or two acceptable solutions. Most are somewhere in between. The first type is called a **maximizer;** the second, a **satisficer.**

Solutions generated is sometimes called "focus" by Driver. Some people look for one solution only; others keep their options open and are pluralistic. The **unifocus** person seeks the one right answer, while the **multifocus** person never closes off options. There are always several possible answers, and the expected returns on them are varied.

Table 5.3 presents four decision-making styles that are derived from Driver's two variables, information use and solutions generated. We describe these types a bit more fully.

> *Decisives* use a small amount of information to generate a "good enough" decision. They favor speed, efficiency, and achievement of results. They tend to dislike committees and personal interaction in decision making.
>
> *Flexibles* continually absorb new data and generate new solutions. They prefer adaptability, speed, and efficiency.
>
> *Hierarchics* practice the use of all available information to get the one best solution. They emphasize rigor, precision, and long-range planning.
>
> *Integratives* want much information and generate many solutions. Theirs is a creative synthesis, rather than purely logical activity. They are inventive and enjoy team building and participation.

When or under what conditions of information availability will each of these types thrive? The answer is that each type operates best under different conditions (Svenson & Maule, 1993). The flexible and decisive types never use all of the available information, especially if given too much. Moreover, the integrative and hierarchic types become much less efficient when too much information is available. Their circuits become overloaded. Therefore, it is important to match decision makers with appropriate decision-making

TABLE 5.3
Driver's Four Decision Styles

		Information Use	
		Moderately Low (satisficer)	High (maximizer)
Focus (number of alternatives generated)	Unifocus	**Decisive**	**Hierarchic**
	Multifocus	**Flexible**	**Integrative**

Adapted from Driver (2003).

opportunities. A classification is offered in Table 5.4, which suggests that hierarchics are well suited for strategic decision making, decisives excel in making operational decisions, and integratives are effective with tactical decisions. Flexibles are particularly adept at brainstorming and developing new solutions to novel problems.

Driver suggests that there are qualitative as well as quantitative dimensions of optimum information availability. He further diagnoses the information available to decision makers in terms of **environmental load**, which comprises four related environmental factors: information **complexity, noxicity, eucity,** and **uncertainty.** Information complexity refers to the amount of data in the situation. Noxicity is the amount of negative input (e.g., stress) present. Eucity, in contrast, measures the amount of positive input (e.g., praise) present, while uncertainty is concerned with the unpredictability of the situation. Some degree of uncertainty is inevitable in organizational decision making. Information can add or reduce uncertainty, depending on the decision maker's style (Kahneman, Slovic, & Tversky, 1980).

There is an *optimum* amount of environmental load that can be handled for efficient decision making. For most people, not unexpectedly, a moderate load results in the maximum use of information available, while at very high or very low loads, information use declines. This conclusion holds in general, but there are differences depending on individual focus (as defined above). Unifocus workers, for example, tend to dominate in underload or overload conditions.

Finally, Driver reminds us that most people have primary and secondary decision-making styles, with the secondary style taking over under certain extremes. Over the long run, there is a continuing shift in organizational circumstances and needs for different kinds of decision makers. Hence, the

TABLE 5.4
Effective Styles for Different Organizational Decisions

Style	Classification of Organizational Decisions
Hierarchic	Long-range, strategic planning; need much information but seek one ultimate solution
Decisives	Short-run scheduling; operational level decisions
Integratives	Continuous, tactical-level participatory planning; much information is used to create several solutions
Flexibles	Brainstorming; improvisation

Adapted from Driver (2003).

most effective choice of decision maker for the organization may be a combination of at least *two* leaders with different styles—one attending to the dominant issue of the moment and the other prepared to deal with the next phase. Self-aware college leaders can recognize their personal decision-making style and note the need to identify colleagues with complementary styles.

Risk and Uncertainty: The Gambling Metaphor

It is rare that decisions in organizations are made under conditions of complete certainty, since this would require that the decision maker be completely informed about the problem, sensitive to external conditions, and able to act completely rationally. As we have noted earlier, however, nearly all decisions involve some measure of perceived uncertainty or risk, partly because decision makers operate under bounded rationality—the virtual impossibility of having all of the necessary information to make an optimum decision.

A body of theory has arisen to help decision makers deal with conditions of uncertainty and risk. Sometimes called the *gambling metaphor* (Goldstein & Weber, 1995), this theoretical framework examines the costs and benefits associated with different decision alternatives, and it assesses the probability of the outcomes that may occur if certain alternatives are chosen. Below we have listed the different categories of decisions.

Certainty—when all of the alternatives for a decision are known and it is possible to choose any one of them without error. When there is certainty, the decision maker knows all the alternatives and has no doubt that the choice will lead to a specific outcome (Taylor, 1965). There is no element of chance. An athletics department, for example, may receive bids from three well-known vendors to provide concessions at sporting events on campus. The three alternatives are known, and the bids provided by the vendors indicate the cost of each option. Moreover, the services to be received by the university are specified in the concessions contract. All elements of the decision—the alternatives, costs, and benefits—are known, and the outcomes are specified in advance of the decision.

Risk—when available "alternatives are known and in which each alternative leads to one of a set of possible specific outcomes, each outcome occurring with a known probability" (Taylor, 1965, p. 50). Under conditions of risk, decision makers know the alternatives, but they are not certain what the outcomes will be for each option. Therefore, they need to assign probabilities of success for each alternative. The director of a continuing education division, for example, can assess the likelihood of enrollment growth if more courses were offered in the evenings. In this case, the alternatives are known (more, fewer, or the same number of evening courses), and the probability for enrollment growth under each scenario can be determined. The risk, of course, is in making a decision that ultimately does not pay off. Even if the director determines that there is a 90% chance that adding more courses will lead to enrollment growth, there is still a 10% chance that it will not. Therefore, the director is not certain that enrollment growth will occur, but the high probability for growth—perhaps based on market research and prior performance of similar programs—suggests that expansion is a risk worth taking.

Uncertainty—when the alternatives are ambiguous and the payoffs from any alternative are unknown and impossible to predict. Imagine a president of a public university faced with the prospect of dealing with the forthcoming visit of a speaker whose controversial opinions could result in some unknown degree and type of reaction (such as alumni withholding financial support, negative media attention, or even a large-scale protest on campus). In this case, the president's alternatives are ambiguous. Due to free speech concerns in public institutions, the president may be unsure if he has the legal authority to cancel the presentation or move the event to an off-campus location. Moving the event may not even be a viable alternative, if other venues of appropriate size are not available. Moreover, reactions to the presentation (or reactions to the cancellation of the presentation) cannot be predicted; students and alumni may do nothing, or they may engage in actions damaging to the institution. No probabilities can be assigned to these possible outcomes; they defy prediction given the limited information available. Thus, the president is not aware of all possible alternatives, nor is he aware of the likely results of his deciding on any one of them. Under conditions of uncertainty, decision makers frequently attempt to obtain more information so that the range of alternatives becomes clearer and the probabilities of various outcomes can be assessed more accurately. In other words, decision makers attempt to move from a position of uncertainty to a position where a calculated risk can be made.

Early theorists in the area of risk and uncertainty (e.g., von Neumann & Morgenstern, 1944) were working in a field that ultimately became known as "management science." Their work involves game theory, decision trees, probabilities, and expected utility. Goldstein and Weber (1995) note:

> In 1947, von Neumann and Morgenstern published the second edition of their book, *Theory of Games and Economic Behavior,* in which they listed conditions under which a person's choices among gambles could be used to infer a "utility function" for the outcomes of the gambles, which in turn could be used to describe the person's choices. That is, if the conditions

were satisfied, people's choices could be described as if they were choosing so as to maximize the expected utility of choice outcomes. (p. 84)

Expected utility is the likelihood that an individual will obtain personal benefits from a particular choice. More specifically, expected utility is "a weighted average of future pleasures and pains, where the weights are the probabilities of attaining these outcomes" (Einhorn & Hogarth, 1982, p. 34). The idea of a gamble can be used to describe the expected utility of decisions where the outcomes are not completely certain (Rettinger & Hastie, 2003). Organizational decisions under these conditions can be subjected to the same kind of reasoning that is involved in gambling with a monetary outcome. The theory suggests that decision makers enter into a mental, though not necessarily cognitive, calculation of the probabilities and values associated with various decision alternatives. Decision making involves the estimation of the likelihood of different outcomes, matching them up with the personal value of each outcome, and selecting the choice that maximizes the subjective expected value—that is, the product of the probability that the outcome (monetary or personal) will occur.

In the example in Table 5.5, a reasonable decision would be to choose alternative #1, since one can expect a higher reward. The subjective expected value, in other words, is higher. It is important to recognize, however, that the decision also depends on the risk-taking propensity of the decision maker. Risk-averse individuals, for example, tend to assign more importance to potentially negative outcomes and in this example, would be likely to express preferences for alternative #2.

Since groups also have risk-taking propensities, the question arises as to when to assign a decision to a single individual versus a group. (See our consideration of this in the discussion of Vroom and Yetton in chapter 4.) One answer to this question lies in whether individuals or groups are more willing to make risky decisions. Research has found, not unexpectedly, that it depends on the particular individual (Streuffer, 1986) and the dynamics of the group. A particularly charismatic, risk-taking faculty member in a small department may sway the department toward one decision option, while in a department with equally strong and dynamic members, the risk-taking

TABLE 5.5
Risk Taking and Rewards in Decision Making

	Reward	*Probability*	*Expected Utility of Receipt*
Alternative #1	$1,400	$p = .25$	$350
Alternative #2	$400	$p = .75$	$300

propensity of any one member will be mitigated by the collective propensities of the whole group.

Decision Trees

The apparent simplicity of the argument for assigning probabilities to actions and outcomes belies the reality of decision making in organizations, which is typically quite complex. As Goodwin and Wright (1991) note, "Any attempt at clear thinking can be frustrated by the large number of interrelated elements which are associated with the problem so that, at best, the unaided decision maker can have only a hazy perception of the issues involved" (p. 102). One answer to unraveling the complexity in decision making involves the construction of a decision tree. (We saw a limited example of such a tree in the Vroom and Yetton model in the previous chapter.) Such practical aids permit the splitting of problems into discrete parts so that each can be viewed separately and quantification of values and probabilities can be calculated.

Decision trees can be used to identify the most desirable policy for an administrator. In the case that follows, on page 650, a provost faces the problem of deciding whether to expand the biology or nursing programs. There are funds for only one. Figure 5.1 illustrates how the problem can be addressed using a decision tree.

FIGURE 5.1
Decision Tree

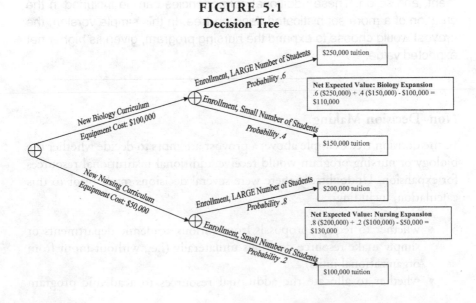

───────────── DECISION TREE ─────────────

Expansion for Biology or Nursing?

The provost at a private university must decide whether to expand the biology or nursing programs. The biology equipment would cost $100,000; the nursing equipment costs $50,000. She is uncertain about the tuition that would be generated from the two programs, so she makes estimates of the tuition under both favorable and unfavorable circumstances and places probability estimates for each. (The probability estimates—signified by the decimals in each branch on the decision tree—would be informed by market research.)

In this instance, market research showed higher probability for strong enrollment growth in nursing over biology (.8 probability for high enrollment in nursing compared to .6 probability in biology). However, in this institution, biology is a larger program than nursing, and strong enrollment growth in a large program would yield more additional tuition dollars ($250,000) than strong enrollment growth in a relatively smaller program such as nursing ($200,000).

The objective of decision tree analysis is to derive a "net expected value" for each programmatic alternative. The decision tree displays the data and the calculations for each alternative. Needless to say, there is information missing from this simplified diagram—for example, the length of time to build the equipment and recruit the students, more concrete data on the numbers of students, the faculty costs, the durability of the equipment, and so on. These additional contingencies can be included in the creation of a more sophisticated decision tree. In this simple version, the provost would choose to expand the nursing program, given its higher net expected value.

Non–Decision Making

In the decision tree example above, a provost attempts to decide whether the biology or nursing program would receive additional institutional resources for expansion. Undoubtedly there were several decisions made prior to this calculation, including:

- whether to request proposals from various academic departments or simply make resource decisions unilaterally (i.e., without input from organizational units)
- whether to allocate the additional resources to academic program

expansion or to some other institutional aim such as research or community service

- whether decisions about academic program expansion would be based on revenue projections or some other criterion such as social justice needs or external political pressures

These types of decisions may be made with little conscious consideration. Requesting resource proposals from academic departments, for example, may be so ingrained in the culture of a university that the decision to do so becomes automatic. Similarly, enrollment pressures may be so strong at an institution that nearly all decision alternatives are considered in terms of attracting and retaining students and, in turn, generating revenue. As a matter of course, organizational members in these types of institutions accept that enrollment and revenue generation will be the driving force behind most decisions.

We can refer to these implicit limits on decision making as the decision context. The decision context is shaped by the organization's external environment, history, and culture. This context, in turn, confines the scope of decisions that people can make within an organization (Giddens, 1984). In the example in Figure 5.1, if the provost wanted to allocate additional resources based on her own judgment rather than on the basis of proposals submitted by departments, it is likely that her attempts at unilateral decision making would be opposed and resisted by faculty members who would view such actions as inconsistent with the culture of the college. Similarly, faculty in low-enrollment programs such as theater arts and dance may decide not to submit a proposal, realizing that such efforts would be futile if the decisions were ultimately to be made on the basis of potential for revenue generation.

Thus, the decision context restricts the scope of decisions that individuals can make. The culture of the university, in effect, prevents the provost from making unilateral budget decisions. And the university's resource limitations prevent the theater arts and dance faculty from even entering the competition for funds.

In this example, the decision context appears to be shaped by cultural and economic forces that are beyond the ability of any single decision maker to change. Collegial cultures foster values and expectations for shared governance; unilateral decision making would be viewed as antithetical to such cultures. Economic constraints may suggest that even if decision makers wanted to use alternative criteria such as aesthetic impact for allocating resources, they could not.

Some critical theorists suggest, however, that theories of decision making

may overstate the extent to which the decision context is determined by impersonal forces beyond the control of decision makers (Deetz, 1992; Lukes,
2005). They suggest that powerful interest groups within the organization
(e.g., top-level managers) shape the decision context so that it leads to decisions that reinforce the status quo and suppress or thwart potential opponents. Feminist theorists, in addition, suggest that patriarchal organizations
are characterized by decision contexts that rely upon masculine-oriented criteria (Martin, 1990). Decision-making venues, for example, may be constructed in ways that emphasize competition among units, rather than
collaborative approaches to problem solving. In the biology/nursing example
in Figure 5.1, the decision context included competition among academic
departments as the means to determine how resources would be allocated.
The provost could have utilized a different method for making decisions, but
she chose not to.

Bachrach and Baratz (1970) refer to these events as **nondecisions**; that
is, "a decision that results in suppression or thwarting of a latent or manifest
challenge to the values or interests of the decision maker" (p. 44). The provost in this case may not have intentionally decided to exclude collaborative
approaches to decision making, but the effect of her action was to reinforce
competition as the means for deciding. Competition also reinforces the provost's position, because it retains her power for making a choice among competing proposals. She gets to determine the winners and losers; it reinforces
her power.

Critical theorists acknowledge the economic, structural, and cultural
constraints on decision making, but they also recognize how individual decision makers construct and reconstruct those constraints over time. Political
scientist Steven Lukes (2005), for example, notes that the lack of affordable
housing can be attributed to economic and structural problems that are:

> the uncoordinated and unintended outcome of the independent actions of
> large numbers of actors pursuing their varied respective interests—renters,
> home buyers, mortgage lenders, real-estate brokers, developers, land-use
> regulators, transport planners, and so on. But insofar as individuals or
> groups lack access because of the actions or inactions of other identifiable
> individuals or groups, who by acting otherwise could make a difference,
> then it makes sense to see the latter as powerful because [they are] responsi-
> ble. So, of course, at the individual level, discriminatory landlords and cor-
> rupt officials have power; but, at the city, corporate or national levels,
> politicians and others in "strategic positions," who individually or in alli-
> ance could make a difference, can be viewed as powerful to the extent that
> they fail to address remediable problems. (p. 67)

Thus, decision makers are powerful not only when they make a decision
(e.g., invest in biology or nursing), but also when they fail to make decisions

that would remedy problems encountered by the less powerful (e.g., failing to promote collaboration and instead encouraging competition among departments, which reinforces resource disparities among programs). The provost could have structured the decision context in a way that encouraged departments to develop collaborative resource proposals. In this case, even the faculty in theater arts and dance could become engaged in the process as collaborators with other units. As an example, nursing faculty and dance faculty could develop a proposal for a dance therapy program, which would tap into the talents of faculty and students in both departments. This example illustrates that colleges and universities still must recognize that the decision context is constrained by enrollment and associated financial pressures; these external pressures cannot be ignored. But it also suggests that the decision context is not completely determined by outside forces. Critical and feminist theorists emphasize the power that organizational leaders have to shape the decision context. Such power can be used to reinforce the status quo or employed to embrace alternative forms of decision making that widen the circle of participants as well as increase the range of alternative solutions considered.

Postmodern Perspectives on Individual Decision Making

Both the positivist and critical/feminist perspectives assign some degree of agency to individual decision makers who, it is asserted, can make decisions and shape the decision context for organizations. Postmodernists, however, offer an important caveat to these perspectives. They suggest that organizations and decision contexts are so fragmented and chaotic that individual efforts toward rational decision making (positivism) or attempts at more collaborative forms of decision making (an implication of feminist and critical perspectives) may be doomed to fail. Put simply, the ability to make changes through decision making is limited by an organizational context that is ambiguous and nearly impossible to control. As Martin (1992) notes, "Many connections among employees can only be explained by sheer contiguity or random effects" (p. 131).

The fragmented organization that Martin describes can be seen in colleges and universities that employ significant numbers of part-time and adjunct faculty and in institutions that outsource functions such as food service and building maintenance. Structural differentiation also plays a role in fostering fragmentation. In a community college, faculty who teach in transfer-oriented programs may seldom interact with colleagues who teach in vocational programs. Similarly, residential housing staff members in a large university may have only superficial connections with faculty members.

In a fragmented, postmodern organization, decision makers cannot assume the existence of stable sets of problems, known alternative solutions, and consistent levels of participation and interest. Rational decision making would be incredibly difficult (and perhaps incredibly ineffective) in such a context. Thus the random and unpredictable processes associated with the garbage can model of decision making (Cohen et al., 1972) may be aligned more closely with the conditions found in postmodern organizations. The unplanned confluence of streams of problems, solutions, participants, and choice opportunities is more likely to describe how decisions get made in the context of fragmented interests and fluctuating temporal and spatial boundaries.

Not only are organizations fragmented, but the identities of individual decision makers are in flux and cannot be categorized easily. Martin (1992) describes individual identity as "a fluctuating composite of partial allegiances" (p. 156). Individuals hold multiple, simultaneous identities that affect their decision-making roles (Putnam & Stohl, 1996). Gender, ethnic, and class identities intersect and shape professional and organizational identities that themselves are multifaceted and complex.

Occasionally, organizational leaders may attempt to shape the decision context based on assumptions of unitary rather than fragmented identities. For example, a dean may appoint an African American faculty member to a committee in order to bring racial diversity to the decision-making context. But this approach denies other components of individual identity that may be important to this faculty member. The result may be to pigeonhole this faculty member's contributions to decision making (i.e., influential only when decisions regarding a racial issue need to be made).

This is not to suggest that individual identity is irrelevant to decision making. As Putman and Stohl (1996) note, "asking a female faculty member to comment on how a particular concern affects retention of women professors calls for this member to wear a representative hat that may alter decision-making dynamics in subtle yet complex ways" (p. 151). Instead, what is needed is a more complex way of understanding individual identity as a multifaceted phenomenon that is constantly in flux. Rather than view individual identities as an input to the decision-making context (e.g., putting more ethnic minorities on committees), organizational leaders can view identity and decision making as constructs that evolve and shape each other. Individual identities are expressed and modified through decision-making processes, which themselves are shaped by the multiple identities of those engaged in decision making.

The involvement of White organizational members in decisions involving race, for example, can enhance participants' understandings of White racial identity and the privileges that often (though not always) are associated with it. Through the decision-making process, the decision makers become more aware of their own racial identities. Decisions resulting from such involvement, in turn, may reflect greater awareness of the racial dynamics in the organization (McDermott & Samson, 2005; Miller & Harris, 2005). In this way, greater awareness of racial identity shapes the decision outcome.

Summary

Colleges and universities represent communities of action comprising individuals who make myriad decisions both alone and in groups. In this chapter, we have discussed a variety of influences on individual decision making. These range from (1) an analysis of the complex factors that individuals must encounter as they consider alternative solutions, to (2) the constraints on their decisions by virtue of their organizational roles, to (3) the ways in which their personalities may affect their decisions, to (4) the form and amount of information that is available and then utilized in the decision, and to (5) the modes by which individuals deal with uncertainty. Organizational leaders act both rationally and intuitively in coming to decisions, depending usually on rules and precedents, time constraints, authority, and collegial norms. All decision makers encounter pressures to act quickly and efficiently, especially at lower levels in the hierarchy of authority. Largely because of hiring practices, most college and university workers are employed in positions that are well suited to their styles of dealing with information and with coworkers. As colleges and universities become more managerial (Bess, 2006), however, there is some cause for concern about their capacity to tolerate or, to put it more kindly, incorporate decision-making styles that are different, yet needed for institutional efficiency and effectiveness.

Review Questions

1. A college of engineering has been experiencing a decline in enrollments for the previous five years. What combination of Parsons and Kilmann and Mitroff characteristics should the dean look for in his search for a new enrollment management executive?
   a. Adaptation and ST
   b. Goal attainment and NF
   c. Latency and NT
   d. Integration and SF

2. The dean of a college has asked for a report in no more than six months from a new committee on general education requirements. He has appointed a chair for the committee, who is considering what kinds of faculty should be appointed as members. Using Driver's theory, faculty with which of the following decision styles should be chosen to serve on the committee:
   a. Decisives
   b. Hierarchics
   c. Flexibles
   d. Integratives
   e. Some combination of these four: which? _____

3. A student about to take a final exam does not know with any degree of reliability what will be on the test, nor does he know the professor's likely weighting of the answers given to the various questions. The student is suffering from the ambiguity of:
   a. Risk
   b. Uncertainty
   c. A combination of the two

4. In what way is the garbage can model of decision making consistent with the postmodern paradigm?
   a. Both acknowledge the fragmentation present in organizational life and the inability to assume that there are stable sets of problems, known alternative solutions, and consistent levels of participation
   b. Both acknowledge that decision making often reflects a random amalgamation of problems, solutions, participants, and choices that is neither rational nor linear
   c. Both A and B
   d. Neither A nor B

5. Which of the following statements is associated with the garbage can model of decision making?
   a. Decisions are *not* typically made through careful searches for problems, rational assessments of alternatives, and deliberate choice processes carried out by a stable set of decision makers
   b. Problems and choices are decoupled; organizational members may not be aware of a problem until they encounter new choices that can be made, and they may not be aware of potential choices until there is a shift in the type of problems considered
   c. The confluence of problems, solutions, participants, and choice opportunities is often unplanned; due to happenstance, luck, or accident
   d. All of the above

Case Discussion Questions

Consider again the Adams County Community College case presented at the beginning of this chapter.

1. Analyze the learning communities decision through the application of Cohen, March, and Olsen's garbage can theory. Describe the participants stream, the solution stream, the problem stream, and the choice opportunity.

2. The solution stream (i.e., adoption of a learning communities instructional model) was presented prior to the emergence of the problem stream (i.e., downturns in enrollment, retention, and student performance). Through what mechanisms and processes did these two streams come to be linked? To what extent did these processes reflect a rational analysis of problems and alternatives? To what extent did happenstance and individual agency play a role in the decision?

3. Use Mitroff and Kilmann's framework (Table 5.1) to characterize the information-accessing and information-processing preferences of Dean Kimball and the academic vice president. How might their different preferences explain why the academic vice president was not initially receptive to Dean Kimball's presentation to the academic planning group? Also, explain how their different preferences may have contributed to the favorable reception that they both received from the board of trustees.

4. Consider the cool reception that Dean Kimball received when she presented her ideas to the mostly male academic planning group. Consider the warmer reception that the same ideas received when the male academic vice president was presenting them with Dean Kimball at the board of trustees meeting. How might gender have affected the decision-making process in this case? Why may decision makers perceive ideas differently based on the gender of the person who presents the ideas?

5. Consider the role of Adams County Community College's president in this decision. Where would you locate him on Driver's four decision-making styles (see Table 5.3)? Is the president's decision-making style likely to be effective in similar circumstances (i.e., strategic responses to external pressures) in the future (see Table 5.4)?

References

Agor, W. H. (1989). *Intuition in organizations.* Newbury Park, CA: Sage.

Bachrach, P., & Baratz, M. S. (1970). *Power and poverty: Theory and practice.* New York: Oxford University Press.

Barrick, M. R., & Ryan, A. M. (Eds.). (2002). *Personality and work: Reconsidering the role of personality in organizations.* San Francisco: Jossey-Bass.

Bess, J. L. (2006). Toward strategic ambiguity: Antidote to managerialism in governance. In J. C. Smart (Ed.), *Higher education: Handbook of theory and research, Vol. XXI* (pp. 491–594). Dordrecht, the Netherlands: Springer.

Brehmer, B. (1999). Reasonable decision making in complex environments. In P. Juslin & H. Montgomery (Eds.), *Judgment and decision making: Neo-Brunswikian and process-tracing approaches* (pp. 9–21). Mahwah, NJ: Lawrence Erlbaum.

Cameron, K. S., Sutton, R. I., & Whetten, D. A. (1988). *Readings in organizational decline: Frameworks, research, and prescriptions.* Cambridge, MA: Ballinger Publishing.

Cameron, K. S., & Whetten, D. A. (2003). Models of the organizational life cycle: Applications to higher education. In J. L. Bess (Ed.), *College and university organization: Insights from the behavioral sciences* (pp. 31–61). Amherst, MA: I & I Occasional Press.

Cohen, M. D., March, J. G., & Olsen, J. P. (1972). A garbage can model of organizational choice. *Administrative Science Quarterly, 17*(1), 1–25.

Deetz, S. (1992). *Democracy in an age of corporate colonization: Developments in communication and the politics of everyday life.* Albany: State University of New York Press.

Driver, M. (2003). Decision style and organizational behavior: Implications for academia. In J. L. Bess (Ed.), *College and university organization: Insights from the behavioral sciences* (pp. 149–168). Amherst, MA: I & I Occasional Press.

Einhorn, H. J., & Hogarth, R. M. (1982). Behavioral decision theory: Processes of judgment and choice. In G. R. Ungson & D. N. Braunstein (eds.), *Decision making: An interdisciplinary inquiry* (pp. 15–47). Boston: Kent.

Fiedler, F. E. (1967). *A theory of leadership.* New York: McGraw Hill.

Giddens, A. (1984). *The constitution of society.* Berkeley: University of California Press.

Goldstein, W. M., & Weber, E. U. (1995). Content and discontent: Indications and implications of domain specificity in preferential decision making. *The Psychology of Learning and Motivation, 32,* 83–136.

Goodwin, P., & Wright, G. (1991). *Decision analysis for management judgment.* Chichester, England: John Wiley & Sons.

Hatch, M. (1997). *Organization theory: Modern, symbolic, and postmodern perspectives.* New York: Oxford University Press.

Jung, C. G. (1959). *The archetypes and the collective unconscious* (R. F. C. Hull, Trans.). New York: Pantheon Books. (Original work published 1935.)

Kahneman, D., Slovic, P., & Tversky, A. (Eds.). (1980). *Judgment under uncertainty: Heuristics and biases.* Cambridge, England: Cambridge University Press.

Kilmann, R. H., & Herden, R. P. (1976). Towards a systematic methodology for evaluating the impact of interventions on organizational effectiveness. *Academy of Management Review, 1*(3), 87–98.

Lukes, S. (2005). *Power: A radical view* (2nd ed.). New York: Palgrave Macmillan.

Martin, J. (1990). Deconstructing organizational taboos: The suppression of gender conflict in organizations. *Organization Science, 1*(4), 339–359.

Martin, J. (1992). *Cultures in organizations: Three perspectives.* New York: Oxford University Press.

McDermott, M., & Samson, F. L. (2005). White racial and ethnic identity in the United States. *Annual Review of Sociology, 31*(1), 245–261.

Miller, A. N., & Harris, T. M. (2005). Communicating to develop white racial identity in an inter-racial communication class. *Communication Education, 54*(3), 223–242.

Mintzberg, H. (1973). *The nature of managerial work.* New York: Harper & Row.

Mintzberg, H. (1976, July/August). Planning on the left side and managing on the right. *Harvard Business Review, 54,* 51–63.

Mitroff, L., & Kilmann, R. (1975). Stories managers tell: A new tool for organizational problem solving. *Management Review, 64*(7), 18–28.

Mitroff, I., & Kilmann, R. (1976). On organizational stories: An approach to the design and analysis of organizations through myths and stories. In R. H. Kilmann, L. R. Pondy, & D. P. Slevin (Eds.), *The management of organization design.* Dordrecht, Holland: North Holland.

Nord, W. R., & Fox, S. (1996). The individual in organizational studies: The great disappearing act. In S. R. Clegg, C. Hardy, & W. R. Nord (Eds.), *Handbook of organizational studies* (pp. 148–174). Thousand Oaks, CA: Sage Publications.

Nutt, P. C. (1989). Errors in sizing up the situation. In P. C. Nutt, *Making tough decisions: Tactics for improving managerial decision making* (pp. 51–69). San Francisco: Jossey-Bass.

Parsons, T., Bales, R. F., & Shils, E. A. (1953). Phase movement in relation to motivation, symbol formation, and role structure. In T. Parsons, R. F. Bales, and E. A. Shils (Eds.), *Working papers in the theory of action* (pp. 163–269). New York: The Free Press.

Putnam, L., & Stohl, C. (1996). Bona fide groups: An alternative perspective for communication and small group decision making. In R. Hirokawa & M. S. Poole (Eds.), *Communication and group decision making* (2nd ed., pp. 147–178). Thousand Oaks, CA: Sage Publications.

Rettinger, D. A., & Hastie, R. (2003). Comprehension and decision making. In S. L. Schneider & J. Shanteau (Eds.), *Emerging perspectives on judgment and decision research* (pp. 165–200). New York: Cambridge University Press.

Streuffer, S. (1986). Individual differences in risk taking. *Journal of Applied Social Psychology, 16,* 482–497.

Svenson, O., & Maule, A. J. (Eds.). (1993). *Time pressure and stress in human judgment and decision making.* New York: Plenum Press.

Taylor, D. W. (1965). Decision making and problem solving. In J. G. March (Ed.), *Handbook of organizations* (pp. 48–86). Chicago: Rand McNally.

von Neumann, J., & Morgenstern, O. (1944). *Theory of games and economic behavior.* Princeton, NJ: Princeton University Press.

Weber, E. U., Ames, D. R., & Blais, A-R. (2005). "How do I choose thee? Let me count the ways": A textual analysis of similarities and differences in modes of decision-making in China and the United States. *Management and Organization Review, 1*(1), 87–118.

6

ORGANIZATIONAL LEARNING

Contents

Preview   661
Case Context   661
Introduction   664
Conceptualizations of Organizational Learning   665
Processes and Stages of Organizational Learning   670
Linking Individual and Organizational Learning   678
Cultural Conceptualizations of Organizational Learning   686
Dialectical Perspectives on Cultural Learning   689
Postmodern Interpretations of Organizational Learning   693
Contingencies Governing the Use of Alternative Learning Models   694
The Learning Organization   696
Summary   698
Review Questions   699
Case Discussion Questions   700
References   701

The authors are most grateful for the critical comments on an early draft of this chapter by Lisa Petrides, Institute for the Study of Knowledge Management in Education. The final version, of course, is our own and may or may not reflect the perspective of the reviewer.

Preview

- Organizational learning can provide a competitive advantage to organizations.
- Learning takes place at different rates throughout the organization and depends in part on the magnitude of the difference between the new and old ideas.
- Four constructs are important to understanding the process of organizational learning: knowledge acquisition, information distribution, information interpretation, and organizational memory.
- The sum of individual learning in an organization is not the same as organizational learning if the learning has not been institutionalized.
- There are two main approaches to understanding organizational learning: cognitive/behavioral conceptualizations and cultural conceptualizations.
- Organizations learn from trial and error and by intentional, organized self-education efforts.
- Huber identifies five cognitive processes through which organizations learn: congenital learning, experiential learning, vicarious learning, grafting, and searching and scanning.
- Single-loop learning occurs when organizations recognize the need to make ongoing, often incremental, adaptations to processes that need adjustments; double-loop learning addresses larger issues and conditions of the organization that require fundamental reorganization and reorientation.
- The social constructionist perspective suggests that organizational learning involves the development and maintenance of shared meanings.
- Weick and Westley argue for a greater understanding of the conflict or dialectical tension between the order of the past (tradition) and the disorder that accompanies the change that follows learning.
- Postmodernists suggest that there is more underlying chaos and disorganization in organizations that must be both apprehended and accepted as inevitable before learning can take place.
- According to Senge, there are five disciplines that guide the learning organization: systems thinking, personal mastery, mental models/cognitive maps, shared vision, and team learning.

--- CASE CONTEXT ---

Student Recruitment at Outback Community College

Outback Community College, a rural institution in the West, was once a thriving campus, serving personnel at a local air force base and offering degrees in agriculture and natural resources for those working in farming, forestry, and mining. In the early 1990s, however, the air force base closed as part of a national realignment in defense spending. The local mines had already begun to close prior to the air force's departure, leaving the small communities in Outback Community College's service area with few large employers. Thus began a steady population decline, which significantly affected Outback's enrollment.

Outback Community College, in fact, experienced five consecutive years of enrollment decline. The decline was not due to lower retention rates. Outback had the highest retention and program completion rates within the state's community college system. Instead, the decline was associated with increasingly small entering classes. Each year that college leaders detected a decline in the size of the entering class, the college invested more money the following year in recruitment and marketing. But still no signs of improvement had been noted.

"We are doing what we are supposed to be doing," explained the director of admissions. "We have increased our high school visit programs. We are doing more marketing toward adult students. We even put some commercials on radio and TV. But nothing seems to work. Regardless of what we do, we seem to get a relatively fixed percentage of the population, and that population is declining."

"We need to rethink our whole approach," noted the president. "Our budget continues to be tight, and the state won't let us increase tuition. If we lay off any more staff, then I am afraid that the quality of education will suffer."

The president convened a two-day retreat for the senior administrators to rethink the college's approach to recruitment. From that meeting emerged the idea that the college could build residence halls to attract out-of-state students.

"Even though our admissions office was doing a hell of a good job, it became apparent that the same old way of doing business was inadequate," explained the president. "We needed a different vision for the future."

"We have one of the best forestry programs of any community college in the nation," noted the vice president for academic affairs. "We have great articulation agreements for students to go on for a four-year degree. There are many recreational opportunities in the region for students. We have skiing in the winter, hiking in the summer. We could definitely recruit nationally."

The board of trustees reacted favorably to the request and agreed to take up the issue of financing the construction of residence halls at their next meeting. Meanwhile, however, the faculty voiced serious opposition.

"What does this guy think he is doing?" a faculty member asked, referring to the president. "We are a community college, and our mission is to serve the local community. He thinks residence halls are going to bring in young, affluent students from out of state who want to get a cheap education so that they can spend all of their money on skiing all winter. Well, what about our adult students? What about our low-income students from our own communities? Are they suddenly less important?"

"I worry that this will take the 'community' out of the community college," added the president of the faculty union. "Our focus has always been on the two counties in our service area. In fact, they have voted for tax levies to support us time and time again. If we change that focus, who is to say how the voters will react in the future?"

The faculty union, along with several student organizations, staged a public protest against the plan. In light of these complaints, the board of trustees tabled discussion of the financing plan, and the president convened several open meetings to hear from faculty, staff, and students.

"I am still relatively new to this college," the president confided to the vice president for academic affairs. "But I am now strongly aware that this college believes in access for low-income students in our two-county region, and I can see now how people could think that our residence hall plan would have changed that. And it would have skewed the campus demographics younger, when we have a strong commitment to older students. I learned that those commitments need to be at the heart of whatever plan we come up with."

"But what the faculty learned through these meetings," added the vice president, "is that we have a dramatically different demographic and financial picture than a decade or two ago. We have to figure out how to maintain those strong commitments but do so in ways that recognize that we are not living in the 1980s anymore."

After the open meetings, the president appointed a task force of faculty and administrators to rethink the residence hall plan. He noted that the task force was given the freedom to abandon the plan, but if the members decided to do so, then they would be obligated to develop a viable alternative.

Following several meetings, the task force presented a proposal that would build several small residence halls for *both* in-state and out-of-state students. At least one of the units would be designated for single mothers with a need for child care. Finally, the task force endorsed the idea of recruiting out-of-state students but shifted the recruitment emphasis toward low-income students.

"If we are going to have our admissions staff go out-of-state, then we want them to go where the need for access is the greatest," explained a faculty member on the task force. "Instead of going off to affluent suburban high schools, we want the admissions staff recruiting low-income students who may never have thought about going to college."

"We had to change. The demographics dictated it," noted the faculty union president. "But we didn't have to change *who* we are. The new plan reflects who we are as a college. The whole process made us get really clear about what we value."

"I am delighted with this plan," noted the admissions director. "This is exciting. We get to go out there and be entrepreneurial. But we are doing it in a way that is consistent with who we are as a college. I am very proud of our college, and I can't wait to carry our message to new states."

Introduction

Colleges and universities would appear to be optimally positioned to be learning organizations, given a continual influx of new students, faculty, and knowledge to refresh the information base of the institution. In fact, the absorption and construction of new ideas constitutes the very substance of higher education. Students grow and develop cognitively and socially. Faculty members create new knowledge through the weaving and reweaving of old and new material. Student affairs professionals develop and learn new approaches for facilitating student success.

Note, however, that in these examples the use of new data, ideas, and information occurs at the individual level of analysis. That is, individual students learn as they respond to new modes of thinking and behavior. Faculty members learn as they remap their cognitive appreciations of their subject matter territory for the purposes of teaching and publication. Student affairs professionals learn when they encounter and apply new conceptualizations of student development.

In point of fact, however, these are not examples of learning at the organizational level. For organizational learning to occur in colleges and universities, the entire organization must be receptive toward and ready to utilize new knowledge to improve core processes (Dill, 1999; Starbuck, 1992). Learning organizations are able to shift both culturally and structurally to accommodate new ways of thinking and organizing.

Capacity for learning may enable a college or university to respond rapidly and effectively to changing circumstances (Slater & Narver, 1995), thus providing a competitive advantage in the recruitment of students and highly qualified faculty and in the acquisition of resources, prestige, and legitimacy. Moreover, colleges and universities—as learning organizations—are likely to have closer relationships with key external stakeholders due to the institution's commitment to continual environmental scanning activities and its values of open communication and information sharing (Kontoghiorghes, Awbrey, & Feurig, 2005; Roome & Wijen, 2006). As a result of organizational learning, colleges and universities can provide enriched learning environments for the people who work and study in these institutions (Bensimon, 2005; O'Banion, 1997). The decentralized structure of most colleges and universities, however, may reduce the likelihood of engaging in the open communication and information sharing necessary for the entire organization to be engaged in learning. Individual departments and units may learn, but the organization as a whole may not acquire new knowledge that can be used and shared.

Fortunately, a rapidly expanding body of research on organizational learning can be utilized in the study of colleges and universities (Bapuji & Crossan, 2004). In this chapter, we begin with a broad conceptualization of organizational learning and an explanation of its relationship to organizational behavior in general and to the administration of colleges and universities in particular. We describe the processes and stages through which organizations learn and examine the linkage between individual learning and organizational learning. Then we consider social constructionist and postmodern perspectives on learning and offer a diagnostic framework that organizational leaders can use to determine when to apply different models of organizational learning. In the final section, we discuss the characteristics of a learning organization and the actions that college and university leaders can take to initiate support for organizational learning on their campuses.

Conceptualizations of Organizational Learning

Learning by an organization as a whole should not be equated with the individual learning that occurs within an organization. Even though individuals may learn new ideas, and leaders may then make organization-wide changes, such activity is not (yet) *organizational* learning. That is, although organizations provide venues for individual members to learn, grow, and develop, the organization as a whole may not be learning. While it might be assumed that collectively, the sum of the individual learning is equivalent to organizational learning, it is not. As Balbastre and Moreno-Luzón (2003) note, "it would be a mistake to consider that organizational learning is only the accumulated result of individual learning" (p. 372). Organizational learning instead is an interactive process that creates and recreates a shared knowledge base, which guides behavior, shapes meaning and experience, and institutionalizes learning that occurs at the individual and group levels (Crossan, Lane, & White, 1999). Through organizational learning, the knowledge generated by individuals and groups becomes embedded within the structures, strategies, routines, and culture of the entire organization.

Many colleges and universities, for example, have centers for teaching and learning that promote individual faculty development and instructional improvement. These centers help faculty members learn new teaching practices and may assist entire departments in developing new measures for assessing student learning. If the effects of the center's activities remain at the individual or departmental level, it does not generate organizational learning. In contrast, if the center reframes how the entire college views teaching (e.g., facilitating a shift in assumptions about how students learn), then it has produced organizational learning (Lieberman, 2005). In this way, the center affects not only those faculty who participate in its programs, but all faculty who work in the college.

Many conceptualizations of organizational learning are based in cognitive perspectives. The underlying assumption is that the organization as a whole has cognitive capabilities as well as the capacity to store what it learns in order to inform future behaviors and practices. Gareth Morgan (1986), for example, offers the brain as one metaphor for understanding organizations, and Senge (1990) refers to the collective mind of the organization—both relying on an underlying cognitive perspective for understanding organizations. Shrivastava (1983), connecting knowledge and cognition, defined organizational learning as a process through which the organizational knowledge base is developed and refined.

From a systems theory perspective, organizational learning entails information acquisition, processing, and storage. Huber (1991), for example, suggests that there are four constructs related to organizational learning: **knowledge acquisition,** the process by which knowledge is obtained; **information distribution,** the process by which information is shared, leading to enhanced knowledge; **information interpretation,** when information is accorded some meaning; and **organizational memory,** the mechanisms by which information is retained in the organization for future use.

Most cognitive definitions of organizational learning have behavioral implications. According to this branch of cognitive theories, unless what is learned and processed leads to changes in the behavioral repertories of organizational members, it cannot be said to be organizational learning. As Fiol and Lyles (1985) note, organizational learning means "improving actions through better knowledge and understanding" (p. 803). Similarly, Huber (1991) states that an organization can be said to have learned when "the range of its potential behaviors is changed" (p. 89).

These definitions suggest that cognition guides behavior—our thoughts shape our actions. But as social constructionists note, behavior also shapes cognition (Seely-Brown & Duguid, 1991). Sometimes we act in order to understand what we think. Organizational members act individually and collectively and then attempt to make sense of the outcomes of their efforts (Weick, 1995). They assign meaning to their activities. Social constructionists argue that cognition alone may be insufficient to stimulate organizational learning; it may be necessary for organizational members to take actions and experiment with new ideas *first* in order to generate new meanings and interpretations of organizational life. Thus, organizational learning is not restricted merely to the acquisition, processing, and storage of information; it also involves the creation of meaning and knowledge by interpreting prior actions and putting them into an informative context.

How Organizational Learning May Be in Error

It is important to caution here that organizational learning is not always associated with improvement or effectiveness. Organizations "can incorrectly learn, and they can correctly learn that which is incorrect" (Huber, 1991, p. 89). Levitt and March (1988), for example, suggest that superstitious learning, the ambiguity of success, and competency traps can lead to negative learning outcomes.

Superstitious learning occurs when cause-effect relationships are attributed incorrectly. A college, for example, may incorrectly attribute an enrollment increase to a new strategic plan. The college may believe that it has learned that its strategic plan has been effective, but other causes (e.g., population growth in the region) may actually account for the enrollment increase. The college then may overestimate its ability to control the environment and as a result make poor decisions in the future.

The absence of obvious or salient success is a further inhibiter of organizational learning. The **ambiguity of success** and the difficulties associated with measuring success render accurate gauges of effectiveness problematic. Colleges and universities tend to have broad and general goals that are difficult to make operational. As a result, indicators of success are not universally agreed upon either within the institution or by stakeholders (Birnbaum, 1988). As Hatch (1997) noted, "when success is difficult to pinpoint, it is tough to learn on the basis of what has worked in the past" (p. 370). Especially in higher education, even when new methods have been successful elsewhere outside of the organization (or even inside, when institutions are large and decentralized), they may not be recognized as successful. As a result, the innovations may remain local, and the organization as a whole may not learn. As Hargadon (2002) notes, organizational learning entails disentangling the knowledge being used in one context and analyzing the possibilities for transfer of that knowledge to new situations. Organizational learning takes place when those possibilities are realized.

Competency traps occur when organizations invest in improving a "tried and true" process. Success with the current process may diminish motivation to experiment with new processes. Meanwhile, if competitors are developing new and potentially more effective techniques, then the organization may be caught in a trap created by its own past success. A community college that invests heavily in its successful on-campus continuing education programs, for example, may be caught flat-footed when its competitors expand into distance education.

In addition to the decline in search behavior owing to early innovation and success, competency traps may arise because learning does not necessarily take place at the same rates throughout the entire organization. When there are reasonably similar learning rates across an organization, different units can more readily accommodate changes in adjacent units. But when learning rates differ, inferior procedures and policies tend to persist and inhibit changes at other levels (Herriott, Levinthal, & March, 1985). In loosely coupled, decentralized organizations, learning usually proceeds at different rates in different units.

Additional learning traps include the **familiarity trap**, the **maturity trap**, and the **propinquity trap** (Ahuja & Lampert, 2001). These traps are summarized in Table 6.1.

The Trap of Success—Learning Through Failure

Despite the seductiveness of these learning traps, it is both possible and essential that organizational members individually and collectively learn to learn from their failures. Organizations must constantly be alert to the dangers of learning traps as well as the complacency brought on by success. Successful organizations are often the long-term victims of their success because they lose their learning edge. The rewards of success can inure an organization to the possibilities of even greater success and/or to the need for change to ensure continued success (Sitkin, 1996). The way to overcome this complacency is to develop criteria for "intelligent failure."

While all failures cannot—and should not—be predictable, organizations that wish to learn from them are better able to do so when they establish a feedback loop that provides information not only about the impact of

TABLE 6.1
Organizational Learning Traps

Learning Trap	Definition
Superstitious learning	Incorrect attribution of cause-and-effect
Ambiguity of success	Difficulty in pinpointing when success has occurred
Competency trap	Ongoing investments in effective procedures may reduce the motivation to innovate
Familiarity trap	Tendency to use solutions that are well known in a particular field or industry
Maturity trap	Tendency to rely on the solutions that have worked for the organization in the past
Propinquity trap	Tendency to use solutions that are similar to those employed in the past

Based on Levitt & March (1988) and Ahuja & Lampert (2001).

an organization's programs and services but also about the success or failure of organizational change (de Geus, 1996). Changes in organizations are frequently buried in a maze of background noise that makes their impact difficult to discern or gauge. Organizations that have intelligent failures are usually able to identify them quickly through carefully organized feedback systems and mechanisms that allow propitious remedial action.

Properly promulgated failure legitimizes the kinds of failures that the organization deems valuable and thus removes the stigma attached to individuals who might otherwise be embarrassed into not risking future failures. Indeed, the absence of visible failure can be taken as a signal of inertia, risk aversion, or an inability to adapt (Sitkin, 1996), in turn leading to a culture with norms that tolerate such behavior (Barrett, 1995).

Learning as an organization does not come easy (Chickering, 2003). Leaders and other organizational members must understand that learning may challenge cherished beliefs, relationships, and accustomed patterns of behavior. Hence, a learning organization must comprise both courageous individuals and trusting ones. The courage to learn carries with it the obligation to change. But courageous behavior in organizations demands a culture of trust and a toleration of failure by colleagues. Indeed, learning requires collegial support that creates positive norms within the organization and the strength to resist the imposition of undesirable demands from those who would stifle risk taking to preserve the status quo.

Challenges Associated With Organizational Learning

Organizational learning need not be left to happenstance. An architecture of organization-led learning can be created that sustains the "learning, training, development and education processes that an organization, either deliberately or unintentionally, puts in place to encourage and stimulate learning at work" (Heraty, 2004). Colleges and universities can develop a medium for learning that envelops and shapes all goals, persons, activities, interactions, and sentiments in the organization (Watkins, 2005).

The daily grind of getting work done, however, may conflict with the attention and energy required for learning and innovating. As Seely-Brown and Duguid (1991) note:

> working, learning, and innovating are closely related forms of human activity that are conventionally thought to conflict with each other. Work practice is generally viewed as conservative and resistant to change; learning is generally viewed as distinct from working and problematic in the face of change; and innovation is generally viewed as the disruptive but necessary imposition of change on the other two. (p. 40)

Organizations that neglect organizational learning as a necessary, if disruptive, counterpart of work and change often pay the price of stunted growth. In order to stimulate and support learning, organizational members can apply insights from several theories and frameworks. In the following sections, we examine the processes and stages of organizational learning and discuss the linkage between individual and organizational learning.

Processes and Stages of Organizational Learning

Organizations learn primarily from direct experience—by intentional experimentation or by accident from trial and error efforts—and secondarily from organized programs of self-education—for example, institutionalized programs for regular environmental scanning. More specifically, Huber (1991) delineated five processes through which organizations learn. By "process" we mean the mode by which information is acquired, interpreted, and placed in an implementation queue.

Organizational Learning Processes

Huber begins with the internal sources of extant organizational knowledge. Hence, the first process is labeled **congenital learning**, which refers to knowledge that is passed down by the organization's founders. A new branch campus of a community college, for example, is likely to inherit knowledge from the main campus, or at least to adopt its parent group's knowledge through conscious information sharing or exchange of personnel.

Second, organizations learn through experience. **Experiential learning** can occur through organizational experiments, such as pilot projects, or through reflection on routine organizational behaviors. As an organization gains more experience with a process, it typically becomes more efficient and effective at executing that process. This increase in efficiency is sometimes displayed graphically as a **learning curve.** A steep learning curve indicates that an organization would need long-term experience with a new process before achieving significant gains in efficiency or effectiveness (Arthur & Huntley, 2005; Reagans, Argote, & Brooks, 2005). In Figure 6.1, curve A indicates a lengthy period of time before the organization becomes effective in executing a particular process, whereas curve B notes a relatively brief period culminating in high-level effectiveness. The learning curve for implementing a new curriculum, for example, may be fairly steep, as there are many complex, interdependent components that need to be implemented. In contrast, the learning curve for a new admissions policy may be relatively brief, as faculty and admissions counselors adjust the criteria (e.g., required high school GPA and SAT scores) that they use to evaluate applications.

FIGURE 6.1
Learning Curves

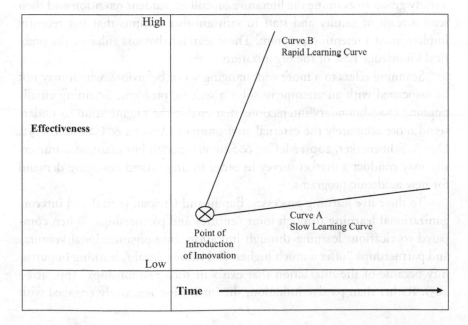

Third, Huber states that organizations can learn **vicariously** through the experience of other organizations. Colleges and universities often adopt the same practices as their peer institutions. They learn about the success of a program at another institution through literature or word of mouth and mimic that practice on their own campus. Many years ago, David Riesman (1958) referred to this mimetic proclivity in higher education as the "academic procession." Some researchers, however, caution that imitation as a form of learning may not be viable over the long term; vicarious learning promotes a passive, reactive stance toward the environment and does not encourage organizational members to be sufficiently reflective on their own experiences (Bourgeois & Eisenhardt, 1988).

Fourth, Huber suggests that organizations can learn through **grafting**. In this instance, the organization acquires new members or units that possess knowledge not previously contained in the organization. Consider, for example, a large university acquiring a previously stand-alone college of nursing. If the university did not previously have a nursing program, then it has acquired a new area of expertise.

Finally, organizations learn through **searching and scanning**. Search behaviors include active efforts to identify solutions to specific problems (Siggelkow & Levinthal, 2005; Siggelkow & Rivkin, 2005). If a community college has identified student retention as a problem, organizational members can search for practical solutions to this problem. The college may form a study group to examine the literature on college student retention and then send a team of faculty and staff to visit another campus that has recently implemented a retention program. These search behaviors enhance the practical knowledge base of the organization.

Scanning refers to a more wide-ranging set of behaviors, which may not be associated with an attempt to solve a specific problem. Scanning entails ongoing cross-boundary interactions that enable the organization to understand more accurately the external environment (Ancona & Caldwell, 1992; Day & Schoemaker, 2005; McGee & Sawyerr, 2003). For example, a university may conduct a market survey in order to understand emerging demand for new academic programs.

To these five learning processes, Bapuji and Crossan (2004) add **interorganizational learning** through joint ventures and partnerships. When compared to vicarious learning through imitation, interorganizational ventures and partnerships "offer a much higher, and more relevant, learning opportunity because of the interaction that exists in such relationships" (pp. 404–405). Rather than passive imitation, the institution is actively engaged with other organizations in its environment. Collaborative interaction creates knowledge that would not have been generated by any of the partnering organizations acting independently. Thus, external partnerships represent a significant opportunity for organizational learning. Multi-institutional consortia, collaboration with K–12 schools, and articulation agreements between two-year and four-year institutions are only a few examples of partnerships that can be oriented toward learning.

Stages of Organizational Learning

As organizations learn through different processes, they may also be progressing through various stages of organizational learning—some of which produce only superficial insights, while others surface deep-level assumptions and values for more critical examination. Carroll, Rudolph, and Hatakenaka (2002) offer a useful model for categorizing these developmental stages.

Typically (but not invariably), organizations go through four stages of learning, ranging from reactive operation on known memory and traditional inputs to proactive systems that move beyond the routine. These are indicated in Table 6.2.

Many organizations begin as small entrepreneurial enterprises where learning operates in the **local** stage. Knowledge is housed primarily in the minds of the original organizational members and is mostly tacit (unspoken) rather than explicit (Nonaka & Takeuchi, 1995). It tends to be organization-specific and task-specific knowledge that is often not codified or written; this knowledge tends to fit the local circumstances only.

In the **constrained learning** stage, learning takes place within a defined organizational structure—usually a bureaucracy—that is guided by accumulated assumptions, habits, and routines that have been codified. Most learning at this stage is directed at finding solutions to immediate problems by searching in procedural manuals that describe standard operating practices. There is little research or deep analysis and little challenge to extant systems.

TABLE 6.2
Four Stages of Organizational Learning

Local	*Constrained*	*Open*	*Deep Learning*
Deny problems	Comply with rules	Benchmark the best	Systems models
Bounded know-how	Fix symptoms	Communicate	Challenge assumptions

Adapted from Carroll et al. (2002).

Here, the old saying applies: "If it ain't broke, don't fix it." At the constrained stage, however, there is a danger of competency traps and other erroneous forms of learning.

In the **open learning** stage, organizations become less constrained by bureaucratic rules and regulations and the norms that accompany them. What was once tacit knowledge in the local stage becomes more explicit. Indeed, new norms of openness to diverse viewpoints will emerge. Human relationships that recognize the uniqueness of individuals and the emotional content of their personalities are taken into account in the institutionalization of new opportunities and even new structures for learning. The danger at this stage is that good social relationships displace the need for high productivity. Ongoing exploration of new ideas with like-minded colleagues may be stimulating, but if those activities do not result in concrete improvements in organizational practices, then overall effectiveness is likely to suffer.

In Carroll et al.'s model, organizational learning reaches a fourth stage, **deep learning**, when openness to learning becomes linked to professional practice. Authority shifts from structural bases to expert bases. The underlying linkages that connect units to one another become open for examination, instead of being accepted as pragmatic adaptations. Tolerance for failure is taken as a signal for improved learning rather than an occasion for punitive action. Organizational members learn not only the skills for collaboration but also the systemic rationale for engaging in collective action across the entire organization. Deeper understanding of the systemic basis for collective action allows recognition of new levels of collaboration and fosters the implementation of innovations that can be mutually beneficial.

Carroll et al.'s (2002) model suggests that organizations progress through developmental stages that lead from superficial learning to deep-level assessments of practices and their underlying assumptions. Argyris and Schön's (1978) theory of single- and double-loop learning also posits differing depths of organizational learning.

Single- and Double-Loop Learning

Argyris and Schön's (1978) theory of **single-loop learning** and **double-loop learning** is one of the most prominent cognitive theories of organizational learning. Single-loop learning is defined as the learning that occurs from feedback generated by monitoring the effects of ongoing organizational processes and behaviors. Feedback on past routines and present policies is used to correct errors in performance. Monthly budget reports, for example, may show that a department is expending its resources at an alarmingly fast rate. In future months, the department can take corrective action so that it does not deplete its budget prior to the end of the fiscal year. Budget reports provide feedback that the organization can use to correct its behavior. Similarly, enrollment data may show that a college has a declining retention rate and that a larger than average number of students does not plan to return to campus next semester; therefore, the college may choose to admit more transfer students if it wishes to keep its enrollments fairly constant.

Single-loop learning occurs through cybernetic feedback loops that allow an organization to make ongoing adjustments in its basic functions and processes. The organization establishes monitoring devices that provide constant feedback, which can be used to correct errors. Cybernetic feedback loops operate in ways similar to a thermostat. When the temperature falls below a certain level, the thermostat activates the furnace to produce more heat. Similarly, when an organization's performance slips below an acceptable range, feedback mechanisms trigger organizational activities that seek to return the college or university to the desired level.

Single-loop learning attempts to correct mistakes but does not explore why the mistakes occurred in the first place. Moreover, single-loop learning makes use of a relatively limited set of feedback mechanisms. Organizations cannot possibly develop feedback mechanisms for every possible behavior or process; efforts to collect and process the data would simply overwhelm the organization. As Birnbaum (1988) noted, "cybernetic systems can respond only to stimuli to which they are sensitive . . . other potentially important data, which have no focused feedback channels, are not observed at all" (p. 188).

In response to the limitations of single-loop learning, Argyris and Schön (1978) offered a double-loop model, which suggests that organizations not only monitor and correct behavior but also assess and, if necessary, change the policies, goals, and plans that support those behaviors (see Figure 6.2). In other words, rather than simply attempting to make the same techniques

FIGURE 6.2
Single- and Double-Loop Learning

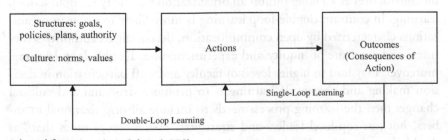

Adapted from Argyris & Schön (1978).

more efficient (single-loop), the organization reexamines the basic assumptions and principles of its operations (double-loop). As a result of questioning the organization's foundational beliefs and assumptions, organizational leaders may identify inadequacies in existing goals, policies, and behavioral routines. Leaders come to realize that organizational performance problems lie not in the performances per se, but in performing the wrong tasks or pursuing the wrong goals. In these cases, structural and cultural changes may be necessary in order to improve performance. Double-loop learning, therefore, "manifests itself as a transformation process, that is, changes in the organization's knowledge and competency base by collectively reframing problems and developing new policies, objectives and mental maps" (Romme & van Witteloostuijn, 1999, p. 440).

The assessment of student learning outcomes, for example, represents one opportunity for colleges and universities to learn from direct measures of teaching effectiveness (Alfred, 2000; Dill, 1999). Assessment results can generate single-loop learning that entails a change in the activity itself (e.g., a change in pedagogical practices based on assessment results). Double-loop learning may occur if the results cause the institution to reexamine and reform its learning goals for students.

Interorganizational collaboration may also serve as an impetus for single- and double-loop learning. In the case of articulation agreements, the two-year institution is able to learn the curricular expectations of the four-year setting and incorporate those insights into its own thinking about learning goals and outcomes (an example of double-loop learning). Meanwhile, the four-year institution can learn about the preparation and background of likely transfer students and adjust advising and tutoring services accordingly (an example of single-loop learning). As a result of its interactions with the two-year campus, the four-year institution may also reexamine its entire approach to recruiting transfer students (an example of double-loop learning).

Argyris's (1990, 1999) research showed that many organizations resist double-loop learning. Resistance to change, fear of failure, and an emphasis on control over risk taking inhibit an organization's capacity for double-loop learning. In contrast, double-loop learning is more likely to occur in organizations characterized by open communication, decentralized authority structures, and a culture of inquiry and experimentation. Double-loop learning, moreover, may lead to higher levels of faculty and staff participation in decision making and change. If learning is to promote structural and cultural change, then the learning process needs to include all organizational members, not just top-level leaders and strategists. Hatch (1997) notes that "as double-loop learning diffuses, organizational stability is replaced by chaos and new organizational orders emerge from the internal dynamics of the organization rather than at the behest of top management" (p. 372). In this way, double-loop learning is consistent with the postmodern desire to deconstruct hierarchy and empower people at all levels of the organization (Bokeno, 2003).

Some researchers, however, have noted that double-loop learning may lead to further organizational errors (Blackman, Connelly, & Henderson, 2004). If organizational members have limited skills and knowledge, then double-loop learning may be unreliable and, in fact, may blind the organization to new lines of thought. Goals, policies, and structures may be changed, but in ways that are ill informed or not well suited to emerging trends and issues in the field. Additionally, double-loop learning can contribute to tendencies toward overthinking. When an organization becomes too introspective, thinking displaces doing, and the organization generates a deficiency of practical experiences from which it can learn (Lewis & Moultrie, 2005).

In response, some researchers have proposed "triple-loop" learning as a mechanism for dealing with the cognitive limitations of organizations (Flood & Romm, 1996). The third loop in triple-loop learning refers to the development of an organizational infrastructure for managing the learning that occurs. The infrastructure links together all units of the organization and promotes a collective mindfulness toward how organizational members and their predecessors have facilitated or impeded learning (Romme & van Witteloostuijn, 1999). Thus, the third loop promotes metacognitive understandings about organizational learning; that is, learning about how the organization learns. This type of self-awareness can ensure that organizational members are capable of dealing with cognitive complexity, and that they are not spending too much time thinking at the expense of action.

Argyris and Schön's theory, as well as other cognitive approaches to organizational learning, has been criticized for not specifying the mechanisms through which individual learning is retained at the organizational level (Balbastre & Moreno-Luzón, 2003; Kim, 1993). Most theorists agree that organizational learning must start at the individual level. Organizations cannot see, sense, scan, and detect; they need people to interact with the environment. Moreover, as we noted, organizational learning is not simply the sum total of individual learning within the organization; additional processes are needed to convert individual learning into organizational learning. It is important, therefore, to understand the ways in which individual learning becomes organizational learning. In the next section, we examine the connection between individual learning and organizational learning. First, we explore David Kolb's theory of experiential learning to provide some background on how individuals learn. We then describe a conceptual model developed by Crossan, Lane, and White, which links learning at three levels: individual, group, and organization.

Linking Individual and Organizational Learning

A substantial body of literature addresses multilevel research on organizations (Klein, Dansereau, & Hall, 1994; Klein, Tosi, & Cannella, 1999; Rousseau, 1985; Yammarino, Dionne, Chun, & Dansereau, 2005). This literature is important in its focus on bridging the divide between micro-organizational and macro-organizational behavior; that is, exploring how what happens at the individual level affects the larger organization—and the converse.

Unfortunately, the research on organizational learning is lacking in sophistication about the mutual impacts of entities at different levels of the organization (Kim, 1993). Nevertheless, it seems clear that there is some intimate connection between how individuals learn and how they use what they learn and how that same information is acquired and used by the larger entities of which they are a part. We present below several conceptualizations of learning at both the individual and organizational level and make some speculative generalizations about how both are related to each other and to the development of a learning organization—that is, an organization in which knowledge and values are shared and utilized in the service of organizational effectiveness.

Kolb's Theory of Experiential Learning

We begin at the individual level. David Kolb's (1976, 1984) model, based in part on the learning theories of John Dewey, suggests that learners go through four modes of learning that are defined by the juxtaposition of two axes of thought and action (see Figure 6.3). Learners first undergo **concrete experiences** that they can draw on later. These concrete experiences entail a range of internal and external interactions such as a college president's communications with potential donors, a faculty member's interactions with students, and a technology director's conversations with vendors. Next, learners engage in **reflective observations** that give them insights into the complexities and nuances of those experiences and the results of their own involvements. A college president, for example, may observe that potential donors are particularly attracted to opportunities to endow scholarships for students. The third of Kolb's stages is called **abstract conceptualization.** Here learners extract from their observations generalizations or principles that can be used to generate new ideas that can be used in or by the organization. The college president in the example above may conclude that donors want to have direct impact on students' lives. Lastly, Kolb suggests that learners engage in

FIGURE 6.3
Kolb's Model of Experiential Learning

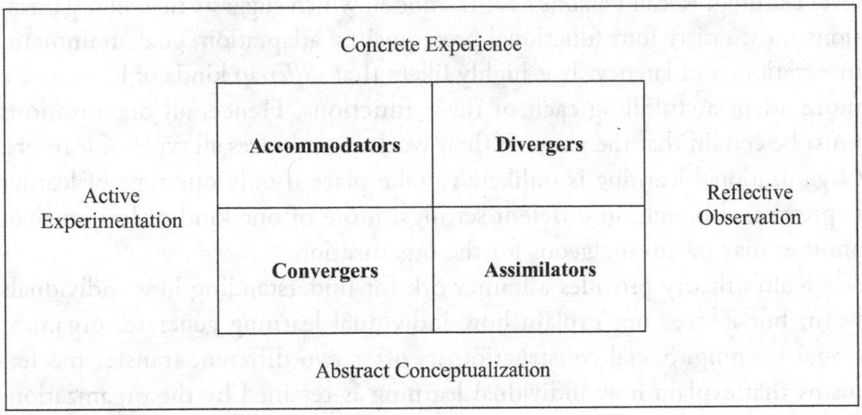

Adapted from Kolb (1984).

active experimentation, during which phase they introduce innovations that have been informed by the learning that preceded them in the three earlier phases. The president in our example may seek to experiment with the "direct impact" concept by inviting donors to campus to meet student recipients of previous scholarships awards.

Kolb's model dichotomizes the two dimensions created by concrete experience versus abstract conceptualization and active experimentation versus reflective observation, in turn resulting in four quadrants. Since learners have preferences for different styles of learning, four distinct approaches are created by the juxtaposition of the categories in the learning model (Figure 6.3).

Divergers gain experience directly and then transform it by reflecting on it. These learners are especially good at generating ideas and brainstorming (Claxton & Murrell, 1987). **Assimilators,** on the other hand, see life (organizational life) through abstract conceptualization and then rework their conclusions through reflective observation. These types of learners are skilled at putting information into concise, logical forms. The **convergers,** on the other hand, absorb information through abstract conceptualization and are inclined to transform their understandings by active involvement in their work—through experimentation. They excel at technical tasks and problem solving. Finally, **accommodaters** learn through concrete experience and apply it through experimentation. These are risk takers who adapt ideas to new circumstances. Each type of learner, according to Kolb, has a distinctive personality disposition and preferred style of learning.

The central point of this theory for understanding organizational learning is that all four types of learners may be needed to stimulate organization-level learning. Recall Parsons's AGIL model, which suggests that all organizations must satisfy four functional prerequisites: adaptation, goal attainment, integration, and latency. It is highly likely that *different* kinds of learners are more adept at fulfilling each of these functions. Hence, all organizations must be certain that the range of their workers embraces all types of learners. Organizational learning is unlikely to take place if only one type of learner is present, although, in different settings, more of one kind of learner than another may be advantageous for the organization.

Kolb's theory provides a framework for understanding how individuals learn, but it does not explain how individual learning generates organizational learning. Social constructionists offer two different transfer mechanisms that explain how individual learning is retained by the organization. One explanation is that individual learning becomes organizational learning through the construction of shared mental models (Kim, 1993; Senge, 1990). A second, related explanation is that organizational culture serves as the means through which individual and organizational learning shape each other (Cook & Yanow, 1996).

Shared Mental Models: The Nexus Between Individual and Organizational Learning

Mental models are thought constructs that shape how people see the world (Senge, 1990). These deeply held images (or cognitive maps) affect what people notice as well as what they fail to see. As Weick (1979) noted, people are more likely to see something when they believe it, rather than believe it when they see it. For example, a manager may not see conflict if he believes that he works in a harmonious organization. Another manager in that *same organization* may see conflict in every organizational action if she believes that the organization is basically driven by the political games of powerful coalitions. Mental models shape what people see and limit their range of sight.

As a result, "individuals will interpret the same stimulus differently, based on their established cognitive maps" (Crossan et al., 1999, p. 528). These different interpretations are not necessarily due to uncertainty about the information received. Even clear information may hold multiple, and sometimes conflicting, meanings. Thus, people may learn different things from the same set of data. In order to facilitate organization-level learning, therefore, the mental models of different individuals need to overlap—to some degree—in order to construct and share knowledge.

Crossan et al. (1999) offer a theory that explains the development of shared mental models as a means for producing organizational learning. This model is based on earlier work by March (1991) who noted that organizational learning entails a balance between exploration (the search for new ideas) and exploitation (the application of what has already been learned). According to March, exploration occurs through **feed-forward** processes that transmit information from individuals to groups and then to the organization as a whole. A new idea for improving student recruitment, for example, may be fed-forward by an admissions recruiter to an enrollment management team and then disseminated to all faculty and staff. Exploitation, in contrast, involves **feedback** mechanisms that return information to groups and individuals so that they can adjust their activities according to information about the outcomes of applied learning. If the new recruitment strategy generates more applicants but does not affect the yield rate (i.e., the number of admitted applicants who actually enroll), then individuals and groups may need to modify their actions (e.g., by making financial aid packages more attractive for admitted applicants). Information about the outcomes of the learned strategy shapes subsequent behaviors.

Crossan et al. (1999) suggest that feed-forward and feedback mechanisms are linked through four social and psychological processes: intuiting, interpreting, integrating, and institutionalizing. These processes explain how individual and group learning is fed-forward to the organization and how organizational learning is fed-back to shape individual and group behavior.

Intuition refers to the recognition of a pattern that yields insight on personal experience. One form of intuition is manifest in expertise. Olympic skiers, for example, may not have to think consciously about every action. They can respond intuitively to conditions on the slopes. "Having been in the same, or similar, situations and recognizing the pattern, the expert knows, almost spontaneously, what to do" (Crossan et al., 1999, p. 526). They act intuitively and improvise their behavior on the spot.

Another form of intuition entails the identification of a novel insight that holds the key to new possibilities. Entrepreneurs, for example, are able to make connections between ideas that previously had not been considered. In the early years of Apple Computer, Steve Jobs utilized an "appliance" metaphor for describing his vision for the personal computer. Like other household appliances, the Macintosh would be easy to use, affordable, and come in a variety of colors. This appliance metaphor continues to influence product development at Apple, including products such as the iPod and other computer-based forms of entertainment.

Intuition is a uniquely individual process. Crossan et al. (1999) argue that groups and organizations do not possess the capacity to intuit. More-over, intuition is incredibly difficult to share with others. Professional ath-letes may not be able to explain the actions that led to a spectacular performance. Experienced factory workers may not be able to articulate why they pulled a particular product off the assembly line, perhaps other than to say that it didn't "look right" or "feel right" (Cook & Yanow, 1996). An intuitive sense of quality cannot be communicated easily to others. Hence, there is a need for imagery and metaphor. The appliance metaphor, for ex-ample, helped others at Apple understand Steve Jobs's vision for the personal computer. Such metaphors need not be tremendously groundbreaking. Even a seemingly commonplace insight can cause others to see the organization in a different way.

Metaphors and images facilitate a second process in organizational learn-ing: **interpretation.** Interpretation is a collective activity that "creates and refines a common language, clarifies images, and creates shared meaning and understanding" (Crossan et al., 1999, p. 528). The result of this process is a shared mental model that can guide future collective action. Faculty in a teacher education department, for example, may develop a shared mental model regarding outreach and service to local school districts. The mental model would include a common language for describing the work (e.g., co-operating schools, lead principals, teacher teams, site-based management) as well as shared meanings and understandings regarding the significance of the work (e.g., promoting reform, improving inner-city schools).

Communication is a key component of interpretation, but Crossan et al. are not referring to the type of communication in which one person trans-mits an idea to others. Instead, communications that provoke organizational learning are complex, and ideas flow among multiple individuals. Someone may share an intuitive insight through metaphor or imagery, but others add to it, shape it, and modify it in an ongoing dialogue. Interpretation is diffi-cult work, because it challenges people to make their own mental models explicit while being open to alternative points of view and expressing a readi-ness to change one's own viewpoint (Kim, 1993).

Shared interpretations often lead to shared practices. Group members frequently desire to put their ideas into action. **Integrating**—the third proc-ess in Crossan et al.'s model—involves coordinated action by a work group. The members integrate new, shared mental models into their work together.

Seely-Brown and Duguid (1991) refer to this process as the development of a **community of practice** where knowledge is put back and tested in the contexts in which it has meaning. Rather than viewing organizational learn-ing as merely transmitting knowledge up and down the organization, the idea of a community of practice suggests that learning is enacted in a particular context.

> Learners do not receive or even construct abstract, objective, individual knowledge; rather, they learn to function in a community—be it a community of nuclear physicists, cabinet makers, high school classmates . . . They acquire that particular community's subjective viewpoint and learn to speak its language. (Seely-Brown & Duguid, 1991, p. 48)

Learning in the workplace, then, is best understood as learning how to behave as a community member.

Integrating knowledge into practice is also critical in instances where discussion was not sufficient to create a shared mental model. Sometimes organizational members emphasize cognition and getting everyone "on the same page," but there may be too many disparate interpretations of the problem to assume that discussion will produce shared understanding. Moreover, as postmodernists such as Derrida (1976) note, language is indeterminate, word meanings are in flux, and the same piece of information may conjure multiple divergent interpretations. Group members, therefore, may need to take actions together in order to discover what they think and believe collectively. As Crossan et al. (1999) note, "shared understanding may not evolve unless shared action or experimentation is attempted . . . leading with action, rather than bluntly focusing on cognition, may provide a different migration path to shared understanding" (p. 533).

The fourth process in Crossan et al.'s model is **institutionalizing**, whereby learned behaviors are embedded into the routines of the organization. Organizations develop an infrastructure to implement more widely group practices that are deemed effective and potentially beneficial to other organizational units. The danger, here, is that institutionalized learning may obstruct the other forms of learning. Referring to March's (1991) framework, the organization may emphasize exploiting what has already been learned rather than exploring for new things to learn. Learning that has become institutionalized, therefore, may inhibit intuition and subsequent processes of interpretation and integration unless steps are taken to continually promote exploration for new ideas.

Crossan et al. (1999) suggest that organizations with a high degree of institutionalized learning should engage in periods of "creative destruction" in which organizational members set aside the current organizational order and "enact variations that allow intuitive insights and actions to surface and be pursued" (p. 533). Currently successful practices are actively critiqued and prevailing thought patterns are suspended as organizational members envision alternative goals, structures, and work processes.

Seely-Brown and Dugid (1991) also offer recommendations for creating organizational designs that permit flexibility for pursuing new insights, but also ensure connectivity for linking groups so that all members can benefit from learning that occurs anywhere in the organization. They describe an organizational architecture that links together the multiple communities of practice that exist within an organization. "This architecture should preserve and enhance the healthy autonomy of communities [of practice], while simultaneously building an interconnectedness through which to disseminate the results of separate communities' experiments" (p. 54). In this scenario, organizational members need to abandon the notion that information is to be hoarded and controlled and instead seek open exchanges that make data and information widely available.

Crossan et al.'s (1999) model is presented in Figure 6.4. We can see how the total model works by reinterpreting a case presented by Kim (1993). The case study described a product design team that added so many expensive features to a product that managers became concerned that its cost would exceed what customers would be willing to pay. The manager alerted team members that they were falling victim to the "tragedy of the commons" phenomenon (Harden, 1968), whereby individuals pursue actions that are beneficial to themselves but that deplete common resources and result in worse

FIGURE 6.4
Linkages Among Individual, Group, and Organizational Learning

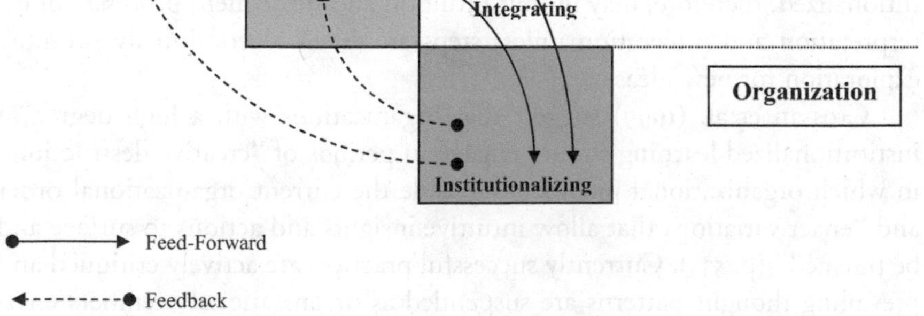

Adapted from Crossan et al. (1999).

conditions for everyone. If each member of the design team added his or her favorite feature to the product, then individual satisfaction may be high, but the team may ultimately design a product that is so expensive that no customer would purchase it—an outcome that obviously would jeopardize the jobs of all members of the design team. When team members saw that their behaviors conformed to the tragedy of the commons metaphor, "they realized that the problem could not be solved at the individual level; only a collective governing body or an individual with the authority to impose constraints on all the teams could resolve the situation" (Kim, 1993, p. 48). The tragedy of the commons metaphor helped team members define the problem and reorganize their work behaviors to solve it. The solution was to appoint a project manager with wide authority over all teams involved in product development. The project manager would ensure that design teams adhere to the pricing model for each new product. This solution was subsequently adopted by the entire organization. Hence, a manager's *intuitive insight* was *interpreted* by team members, *integrated* into their practices, and eventually *institutionalized* by the organization.

The process is actually less linear than the model appears. Crossan et al. (1999) note that "as one moves from the individual level of intuiting/interpreting through group integrating to organizational institutionalizing, the process of learning is less fluid and incremental and becomes more staccato and disjointed" (p. 530). Rather than move in a linear progression from intuition to interpretation, integration, and institutionalization, learning may cycle back to previous stages. For example, collective actions that integrate learning into group practices may generate feedback that changes the group's interpretation of the problem. Thus, the model includes both feed-forward and feedback processes that reveal the dynamic, interactive effects among the four learning levels.

The Crossan et al. model explains how organizations learn, but it does not explain what they learn. What types of intuition will generate shared mental models? Which interpretations are likely to be integrated into group practice? What kinds of group knowledge are most often institutionalized by the organization? As Crossan et al. (1999) note, "all intuitive insights should not, and cannot, be immediately interpreted, integrated, and institutionalized. What enables the organization to 'separate the wheat from the chaff'— the good from the bad—as ideas and practices develop and are refined over time?" (p. 535). Crossan et al. suggest that the strategic context of the organization—its environment and its modes for dealing with it—helps frame which insights are relevant and worthy of being institutionalized. But this begs the question of who gets to determine the organization's strategy.

Kim (1993) answers this question more clearly; it is a matter of power and influence. "The strength of the link between individual mental models and shared mental models is a function of the amount of influence exerted by a particular individual or group of individuals. CEOs and upper management groups are influential because of the power inherent in their positions" (p. 45). Similarly, Balbastre and Moreno-Luzón (2003) note that institutionalization is directed by top-level managers. "Institutionalization is the formal process through which the knowledge resulting from interactions among groups, or among groups and individuals, is approved and accepted by top management" (p. 376). This argument, however, raises the concern that influential groups and individuals may prevail over the rest of the organization and assert that learning by top-level management represents lessons that all organizational members must learn (Marsick & Watkins, 1999). In this case, organizational members will lack a conceptual understanding of why they are doing what they are doing. The knowledge will not be embedded in their own community of practice (Seely-Brown & Duguid, 1991). In contrast, Cook and Yanow (1996) offer a framework that suggests that organizational learning occurs through changes in the organizational culture, which may or may not be directed and/or endorsed by top management.

Cultural Conceptualizations of Organizational Learning

Cook and Yanow's (1996) perspective differs from the other theories discussed to this point in the chapter. Positivist theories based on a systems metaphor emphasize information acquisition and processing (Huber, 1991), while some social constructionist theories focus on mental models and cognition (Kim, 1993). Cook and Yanow, however, suggested that culture (rather than cognition) can be seen as the means through which organizations learn. The cultural approach suggests that learning involves "the acquiring, sustaining, or changing of intersubjective meanings through the artifactual vehicles of their expression and transmission and the collective actions of the group" (p. 449). They note:

> Over time and in the course of joint action or practice a group of people creates a set of intersubjective meanings that are expressed in and through their artifacts (objects, language, and acts). Such artifacts include the symbols, metaphors, ceremonies, myths, and so forth with which organizations and groups transmit their values, beliefs, and feelings to new and existing members . . . As new members join the group, each acquires a sense of these meanings through the everyday practices in which the organization's

artifacts are engaged. Through such "artifactual interaction," shared meanings are continually maintained or modified; these are acts that create, sustain, or modify the organization's culture. (p. 440)

In this cultural conceptualization, organizational learning occurs through socialization processes and is manifested in rituals and symbols, rather than in a collective mind, mental model, or memory bank. Weick and Westley (1996) noted that "as culture is explicated, people see more clearly the learning that has already taken place. Once they see past learning more clearly, they are in a better position to retest, modify, and/or reaffirm it" (p. 444).

Management researcher Jay Barney (1986) suggests that organizational culture can be a source of competitive advantage for an organization. Culture represents the unique **collective know-how** of organizational members, which cannot be replicated by competitors. Though organizations may have many common cultural elements, organizational culture in an aggregate sense represents a unique set of values, beliefs, and assumptions (and accompanying artifacts such as rituals and symbols). Culture is what distinguishes the uniqueness of a college or university. The culture of Cornell University, for example, differs significantly from the culture of Harvard, even though both are prestigious Ivy League universities.

Cook and Yanow's study of the flute-making industry reveals the power and uniqueness of an organization's collective know-how. They interviewed workers and managers at three of the finest flute-making companies in the world, and they found that for each of these three organizations, its competitive advantage was based in the collective knowledge of the organization as a whole.

> It is true that each flutemaker knows how to perform his or her individual tasks; but the know-how required to make the flute as a whole resides with the organization, not with the individual flutemaker because only the workshop as a whole can make the flute. This is demonstrated by the fact that when flutemakers have left one of the workshops, the know-how to make the flute has not been lost to the organization . . . Moreover, the organizational know-how entailed in flutemaking at each workshop is, in a significant measure, different from that at the others. Although all three know how to make flutes and all follow similar production operations, each makes its own particular flute, one with a unique, unambiguously recognizable style . . . Further, such organizational know-how is not meaningfully transferable from one shop to the next; it is deeply embedded in the practices of each workshop . . . Over the years, several flutemakers have,

in fact, moved from one company to another, and in every instance they have had to be partially retrained, even to do the same jobs they were doing at the other company. (1996, pp. 443–444)

Thus, Cook and Yanow argue that know-how is unique to an organization and is not transferable to other organizations. Even a wholesale exchange of personnel does not guarantee that the collective know-how of an organization can be transferred to another institution. St. John's College—with campuses in Annapolis, Maryland, and Santa Fe, New Mexico—for example, has a distinctive great books curriculum, which reflects the college's collective know-how regarding teaching. When new faculty members join St. John's, they spend a great deal of time working with other faculty to learn the St. John's way of teaching—even if they have extensive teaching experience elsewhere. The collective know-how must be transmitted through the institution's culture. Moreover, it would be nearly impossible for another college to replicate exactly what the St. John's faculty do in the classroom. Even if a college could replace its entire faculty with teachers from St. John's, it simply could not recreate the same feel of a St. John's education. The history, traditions, and shared experiences that make a St. John's education distinctive simply would not transfer to the new college. In fact, when St. John's expanded to its Santa Fe campus in 1964, its faculty was staffed by transfers from the Annapolis campus. But the unique history and geography of Santa Fe gave that campus a different feel and provided a different experience for students than the Annapolis campus, even though they share the same curriculum and pedagogical approaches.

Developing an understanding of the organization's unique culture can be a first step toward organization-wide learning and change. Hartley's (2003) study of institutional transformation, for example, revealed how three campuses recovered from the brink of financial collapse through rediscovering and **relearning** their institutions' culture. Leaders on each campus were able to communicate a vision for the future that was also grounded in the institution's history and values. Leaders at one campus inspired commitment to the college's founding principles of social justice and access for women and people of color. On another campus, the president rallied faculty around the college's traditional commitment to civic engagement.

To use Cook and Yanow's terminology, each campus identified its collective know-how, which in turn stimulated faculty and staff commitment to a collectively held "web of meaning." The web of meaning reflected the shared history of the college. But as the webs of meaning were further elaborated, new meanings and collective practices were incorporated into the ongoing functioning of the colleges. For example, as the civic engagement focus became more explicit on one campus, meanings associated with the curriculum shifted toward greater emphasis on the liberal arts. And meanings associated with college leadership shifted from aloof and autocratic to participatory and collaborative. The web of meaning provided a linkage to the past but also facilitated a change in the institutions' culture. As Hartley (2003) noted, "These colleges had developed dysfunctional organizational cultures—beliefs and norms that preserved a malignant status quo" (p. 82). When leaders on these campuses triggered cultural learning processes, collective commitments were identified and strengthened, and meanings associated with the old culture (e.g., divide-and-conquer leadership) were discarded.

Cultural theories of organizational learning may be applicable to organizations that utilize a craft-based production technology, rather than mass production (Perrow, 1986). A large university that "batch processes" its undergraduate students in large lecture classes, for example, may not have a distinct pedagogical or curricular know-how. Faculty in such institutions could easily be interchanged with other faculty; little socialization to the teaching role would be necessary. Basically, the thinking would hold that if you have taught one undergraduate student, then you have taught them all. But many colleges and universities are seeking to develop their own **brand identity**, which will distinguish them as a unique institution (Alfred, 2000). A unique brand or institutional identity may serve as a competitive advantage in the recruitment of students and faculty, and it may generate greater feelings of loyalty and attachment to the institution. Thus, a cultural understanding of organizational learning may help college and university leaders identify their institution's unique attributes and brand identity.

To summarize, the cultural approach to understanding organizational learning recognizes the necessity of the learning organization to reflect on the cultural antecedents and contemporary underpinnings of its goals and structure and the relationship of its culture to its constituencies outside of its boundaries. Learning takes place when the organization builds on these understandings to establish anew a stance that rallies its members and provides an identity with which those outside the organization can readily recognize and identify.

Dialectical Perspectives on Cultural Learning

Weick and Westley's (1996) dialectical theory extends the work of Cook and Yanow by providing more specificity regarding how cultural learning occurs. First, however, Weick and Westley argue that organizational learning itself is an oxymoron.

> Organizing and learning are essentially antithetical processes, which means the phrase "organizational learning" qualifies as an oxymoron. To learn is to disorganize and increase variety. To organize is to forget and reduce variety. (p. 440)

Some organizations are particularly good at organizing. Bureaucracies, for example, are "associated with more mechanical division of labor, more rigid chain of command, clearcut distinctions and technical rationality, qualities which are designed to repress or forget confusing or contradictory qualities" (p. 445). Other organizations are well designed for learning. Organic, flexible organizational designs are "particularly good at adapting to changing environments and at innovating in response to environmental demands" (p. 445). These organizations promote creativity and critical thinking. But given their looseness and lack of formal structure, organic organizations may not learn from the creative work of their individual employees. Individual learning may be promoted, but the organization as a whole has few mechanisms to disseminate knowledge. Therefore, elements of both mechanistic and organic organizational design may be necessary to stimulate and disseminate organizational learning.

Brown and Eisenhardt (1997), for example, studied innovation in the computer software industry. The companies that excelled at quickly developing new products were characterized by both well-specified roles and responsibilities *and* extensive autonomy and design freedom. Work autonomy promoted exploration for new product designs, and well-specified roles ensured that the organization was able to exploit a competitive advantage when it identified one in an emerging prototype. Without well-specified roles, the company could not take advantage of the creativity that emerged through autonomy. But without autonomy, new ideas would be unlikely to emerge. The company would likely fall into competency traps by continuing to invest in existing processes without exploring new designs. The successful companies were able to maintain a healthy tension between highly structured work and highly unstructured work. Referring again to March's (1991) theory, Weick and Westley (1996) noted that "the problem of learning should be viewed not as a choice between exploitation at the expense of exploration, or exploration at the expense of exploitation, but rather as an optimal juxtaposition of the two—not through alteration between the two but through the intimate and continuing connection between the two" (p. 445).

By looking closely at the culture of an organization (i.e., its language, material artifacts, and routines), we can better understand the tension between learning and organizing, as well as apprehend how organizations can maintain the dialectical tension between order and disorder that is central to becoming a learning organization. Weick and Westley (1996) identify three mechanisms—humor, small wins, and improvisation—that can help organizations preserve a healthy tension between flexibility and formal structure.

When examining the language of an organization, **humor** promotes organizational learning through a juxtaposition of order and disorder. "On a purely linguistic level, studies of the joke form have indicated that it is precisely designed to name the unnamed, confuse sense with non-sense, and create disorder of our ordered thought systems" (Weick & Westley, 1996, p. 451). Thus, humor can unmask previously hidden contradictions and uncover previously unrecognized connections. An uncomfortable joke about race, for example, may destabilize previously unexamined assumptions about equity in the organization. Moreover, humor is a social process that draws upon previous collective experiences. An inside joke, for example, is only understandable from the perspective of those who belong to the culture of the system that produced the joke; only the members of that system will find it funny. Thus, humor not only destabilizes organizational meanings, but it also reinforces bonds of connection (i.e., shared meanings). In Weick and Westley's framework, humor juxtaposes order and disorder and thus creates the potential for organizational learning.

When examining the artifacts of an organization, Weick and Westley (1996) identified **small wins** as potential learning moments. Small wins are defined as "controllable opportunities of modest size that produce visible and tangible outcomes" (p. 454). They noted that small wins are opportunistic experiments, which occur spontaneously and which are distributed widely across an organization. "Because they are opportunistic, and because opportunities are widely distributed, small wins resemble uncorrelated probes in an evolutionary system. Since they are diverse rather than homogeneous explorations, they are more likely to uncover unanticipated properties of the environment and promote learning" (p. 455).

An academic department chair, for example, may spend hours arguing with her dean in order to get a few extra hundred dollars of travel support for her junior faculty colleagues. On the surface, the effort may seem inefficient. In fact, the cost of the negotiation in terms of the chair's and the dean's time may exceed the amount of new money allocated for travel. But this small win may begin to shift the value system of the college away from "do more with less" toward growth and development. Small wins produce a new way of organizing (i.e., a new organizational order) by generating temporary disorder. The conflict between the dean and the department chair may have created chaos and disruption, but through this disruption, new meanings associated with faculty roles were developed. Weick and Westley

(1996) explained that a small win "becomes an occasion that attracts unexpected allies, deters opponents for reasons that had not been foreseen, uncovers new opportunities, breaches old assumptions, and juxtaposes new symbols with old artifacts to produce new forgetting. Small wins can churn old routines into new learning" (p. 454).

Finally, when examining the routines of an organization's culture, Weick and Westley (1996) argued that **improvisation** provides a venue for learning on the spot. Improvisation can be defined as the act of simultaneously planning and taking action. An improvisational comedy troupe, for example, composes jokes through its real-time interactions with an audience. In organizations, improvisation "is the activity of people who are thrown into the middle of things and play their way out by thinking while doing" (p. 453). Again, improvisation represents the juxtaposition of order and disorder; patterns are identified in the chaos of everyday experience.

Organizational improvisation, like humor and small wins, is a social process, which facilitates a collective learning experience. Improvisation is not defined by a "lone wolf" leader who acts on his or her own impulses. Instead, it represents an interactive "give-and-take" among people and with a particular situation. Weick and Westley's theory is summarized in Table 6.3.

TABLE 6.3
Dialectical Tensions in Organizational Learning

Cultural Construct	Associated Learning Mechanism	Dialectical Process
Language	Humor	Disorder: unmasks contradictions, uncovers hidden connections Order: reinforces shared meanings
Material artifacts	Small wins	Disorder: uncorrelated, opportunistic experiments Order: tangible changes are produced
Routines	Improvisation	Disorder: no opportunity for planning or forethought Order: identifies patterns in chaotic experiences

Based on Weick & Westley (1996).

Cook and Yanow's cultural theory and Weick and Westley's dialectical perspective are limited in that they do not consider the possibility of multiple, competing webs of meaning within a single organization. Weick and Westley (1996), in fact, acknowledged that "organizations have multiple cultures which allow for ongoing comparison and review of what any one culture fails to see" (p. 456). But their theory does not examine how organizations resolve conflicts regarding what ought to be learned collectively. In contrast, the postmodern perspective highlights complexity, fragmentation, and conflict, which may negate organizational learning efforts.

Postmodern Interpretations of Organizational Learning

Postmodernists recognize the disconnectedness of knowledge and note that the transmission of information from the individual to the organization is considered either absurd or mythological. It is no more than a game that is never completed (Hassard, 1996). Organizational life is too fragmented, disjointed, and discontinuous for any generalized insights to be derived as guidance for future action (Bloland, 1995).

This is not to suggest that postmodernists view learning as irrelevant in organizations. In fact, some postmodernists argue that those in power will claim that their positions have enabled them to learn how best to structure and control the organization. Top-level managers, for example, may make claims about what they view to be the important lessons that all members of the organization must learn and incorporate into their practice (Foucault, 1976/1986). People may learn how to leverage the organizational system so that it maintains their status and power, and groups may learn how to gain a larger share of organizational resources through more astute political maneuvers. But at the organizational level, there is no learning; only the structuring of compliance with the directives of the most powerful groups and individuals.

This view of learning, however, need not be nihilistic. Even if organizations as a whole cannot learn, individual organizational members can learn to take more critical stances toward organizational practices and beliefs. Organizations that support various forms of **action research**, for example, are likely to facilitate the type of learning that postmodernists advocate. Teams of practitioners in a college or university can engage an issue or problem through extensive discussion and analysis, considering not only the data, but also the values, beliefs, and actions related to the problem. The research team structure:

> provides the situation and establishes the conditions associated with effective learning, which can bring about important changes in an individual's

beliefs, values, and actions . . . The opportunity for institutional change lies in the possibility that individual participants will transfer their learning to other contexts within the institution, and by doing so, enable others to learn and to change. (Bensimon, Polkinghorne, Bauman, & Vallejo, 2004, p. 113)

This form of consciousness-raising may engender motivation for action. More widespread and inclusive participation in decision making at all levels tends to give confidence to participants that their ideas will be respected. In turn, it makes them more alert to heretofore unrealized problems and encourages them to take action on their own behalf and as facilitators of others' actions. The result is not a new collective understanding or a shared mental map. Instead, these processes engender an ongoing critique of organizational systems, and they destabilize any effort by an individual or group to institutionalize a particular insight as the correct way that the organization should think and act. Instead the goal is to promote diversity of thought and encourage the construction of multiple, varied interpretations of issues, trends, data, and practices. The end result is not to assess the varied interpretations and seek to identify the best one. Instead, what is desired is yet more diversity in thought and action within the organization.

Contingencies Governing the Use of Alternative Learning Models

The topic of organizational learning has received considerable attention in the field of higher education (Boyce, 2003; Dill, 1999; Franklin, Hodgkinson, & Stewart, 1998; Kezar, 2005; Milam, 2001; O'Banion, 1997; Petrides, 2002). And many higher education policies and practices can be understood through cognitive, cultural, and postmodern perspectives on learning. The range of conceptualizations of organizational learning provides significant choice for leaders who seek to stimulate learning processes and outcomes. In this section, we offer a contingency-based framework that leaders can use when deciding how to promote various forms of learning in their organizations. We borrow from Burns and Stalker's (1994) well-tested contingency theory, which is based on two variables: (1) the complexity of the external environment and (2) the rate of change experienced by the organization.

Burns and Stalker suggest that when environmental conditions are complex, organizations need to have highly differentiated structures to deal with the complexity. But when conditions are less complex, a simpler structure with fewer subunits would be more efficient. Applied to organizational learning, we suggest that when complexity is high, then an appropriate learning model will be one that can cope with large amounts of stimuli without succumbing to information overload.

Burns and Stalker also argued that when the rate of change experienced by the organization is low, a more mechanistic, formalized structure will promote greater efficiency and reliability in performance. In stable environments, successful organizations make conscious efforts at systematic data acquisition, analysis, and use for policy development. On the other hand, under different environmental conditions, when organizations must make radical, punctuated, revolutionary change, the learning mode is not necessarily systematic. Hence, we argue that high rates of change necessitate the use of a learning model that is capable of producing nearly instantaneous adjustments in organizational processes and practices.

These two variables—complexity and rate of change—are arrayed in Table 6.4. The juxtaposition of these variables helps us identify appropriate models to facilitate learning under different organizational conditions.

When external conditions are stable and low in complexity, the cognitive model (e.g., single- and double-loop learning) would be appropriate to advance organizational learning. Given stability, the organization could develop elaborate systems of data acquisition and assessment for monitoring performance. Limited complexity would keep the number of measurement indicators to a manageable level, and the organization would not become victim to information overload.

But given more complexity (more stimuli in the environment to attend to), the organization may be unable to employ the cognitive model, which

TABLE 6.4
Effective Organizational Learning Strategies Associated With Differing Environmental Conditions

		Complexity of the External Environment	
		Low	High
Rate of Change in the External Environment	Stable	Cognitive learning models	Cultural learning models
	Unstable	Dialectical learning models	Postmodern learning models

requires extensive monitoring of the external environment. In that case, the organization could rely on a cultural learning model, where it focuses on elaborating its collective know-how through meaningful artifacts and routines. The organization can become more complex internally through greater awareness of its own values and shared commitments. Greater internal complexity can help the organization address the diverse needs of multiple external constituencies. But cultural learning may only be feasible when the environment is relatively stable. Learning based on collective know-how within the organization may be less perceptive of rapidly changing external conditions.

Instead, the dialectical learning model offers several ways for organizations to capitalize on instability. In fact, this model suggests the need to embrace the tension between order and disorder. Learning modes such as improvisation, humor, and small wins enable organizations to learn through healthy tensions. But these modes may not be susceptible to dealing with high levels of complexity. Improvisation, humor, and small wins all constitute relatively finite moments in organizational learning.

Instead, the postmodern learning model, with its emphasis on fragmentation and critique, may be well suited to addressing both instability and high levels of complexity. The goal of learning in this model is not to find an answer or even arrive at a consensus interpretation; rather, the aim is to foster multiple, diverse interpretations. The maintenance of such diversity may be essential to dealing with the complexity and chaos of organizational life.

The Learning Organization

The field of organizational theory increasingly recognizes the critical role that organizational learning plays in creating effective organizations, especially in highly competitive environments. These findings have stimulated a companion field of study on the **learning organization**, which seeks to identify organizational characteristics associated with learning and effectiveness. According to the findings of an empirical study by Kontoghiorghes, Awbrey, and Feurig (2005):

> the following learning organization characteristics were found to be the strongest predictors of rapid change adaptation, quick product or service introduction, and bottom-line organizational performance: open communications and information sharing; risk taking and new idea promotion; and information, facts, time, and resource availability to perform one's job in a professional manner. (p. 185)

These characteristics are most likely to promote the disposition of workers to change quickly and to accept new ideas.

Management consultant Peter Senge (1990) popularized the concept of the learning organization. Building on the work of Chris Argyris and other theorists, Senge developed five "disciplines" to guide organizational learning. A discipline for Senge is "a body of theory and technique that must be studied and mastered to be put into practice. A discipline is a developmental path for acquiring certain skills or competencies" (p. 10). These disciplines are necessary for all workers to master *personally* if the organization as a whole wishes to be a true learning organization.

1. **Personal mastery** is defined as "continually clarifying and deepening our personal vision, of focusing our energies, or developing patience, and of seeing reality objectively" (p. 7); personal mastery produces the individual learning necessary to generate organizational learning.

2. **Mental models** are cognitive maps that guide behavior, often implicitly; "new insights fail to get put into practice because they conflict with deeply held internal images of how the world works, images that limit us to familiar ways of thinking and acting" (p. 174).

3. **Shared vision** is a collectively held desire that fosters commitment toward long-term goals; "they create a sense of commonality that permeates the organization and gives coherence to diverse activities" (p. 206).

4. **Team learning** involves a range of interactive behaviors such as dialogue and discussion; dialogue encourages "the free and creative exploration of complex and subtle" issues, while in discussion "different views are presented and defended and there is a search for the best view to support decisions that must be made at this time" (p. 237). Senge argued that team learning generates greater cognitive capacity than individual managers working alone.

5. **Systems thinking** involves the use of cognitive frameworks that emphasize "seeing interrelationships rather than things, for seeing patterns of change rather than static 'snapshots'" (p. 68).

Senge argues that when organizational members master these five disciplines, their organizations will become more "learningful" and that learning will be guided not just by top-level managers but also by people at multiple levels on the organizational chart. Organizations and the environments in which they exist are simply too complex and dynamic to be led on the basis of the limited knowledge of one individual. Senge (1990) notes that, "It is no longer sufficient to have one person learning for the organization . . . The organizations that will truly excel in the future will be the organizations that discover how to tap people's commitment and capacity to learn at *all* levels in an organization" (p. 4).

Interdisciplinary and cross-functional teams can promote the kind of thinking that Senge identified as critical to the learning organization. Bringing together faculty and staff from across the institution may facilitate systems thinking by encouraging participants to consider issues that extend beyond their home departments. Unfortunately, highly decentralized departmental structures in many colleges and universities may preclude horizontal communication across the organization. Benjamin and Carroll (1998) note that "most higher education institutions and systems evolved decentralized and stovepiped governance structures . . . with little communication between entities at the same level" (p. 100). Recent efforts to promote collaboration between student affairs and academic affairs units, however, may promote greater cognitive complexity and stimulate more organizational learning.

Summary

Institutional knowledge that is stored only in the minds of select individuals is susceptible to the effects of turnover. When people depart the organization, their learning is lost. Instead, organizational learning transcends the learning of individuals; it becomes embedded in the structures, routines, and culture of the organization.

From a systems perspective, organizational learning entails the acquisition, processing, storage, and retrieval of information that is relevant to the goals of the organization. Social constructionists, in contrast, emphasize the interpretive dimensions of organizational learning by focusing on shared mental models and symbolic representations in the organization's culture.

Organizational learning does not necessarily lead to improvement or effective outcomes. Organizational members can fall victim to competency traps and other forms of erroneous learning that stultify organizational development. Moreover, once a novel insight is institutionalized into the everyday practices of the organization, there is a tendency to invest institutional assets into the new practice and not necessarily continue to support ongoing searches for more things to learn. Hence, there is a need for organizational designs that support continuous learning at the individual, group, and organizational levels. Colleges and universities that develop the characteristics of a learning organization are more likely to provide the institutional architecture necessary to support both ongoing exploration and the further development and refinement of what has already been learned.

Review Questions

1. Which of the following examples constitutes organizational learning?
   a. An improvement in students' standardized test scores
   b. Faculty incorporating into their teaching the latest breakthroughs in genetics research
   c. A university revising its promotion and tenure guidelines to reflect new forms of faculty research
   d. All of the above

2. Which of the following organizational conditions is likely to promote organizational learning?
   a. Open communications
   b. Teams and teamwork
   c. Knowledge management systems for organizing data
   d. All of the above

3. Which form of organizational learning entails the adoption of practices deemed successful at peer institutions?
   a. Vicarious learning
   b. Congenital learning
   c. Experiential learning
   d. Superstitious learning

4. Which learning trap occurs when the organization continues to invest in improving its well-tested processes, rather than experiment with new ones?
   a. Competency trap
   b. Familiarity trap
   c. Propinquity trap
   d. Ambiguity of success

5. Double-loop learning differs from single-loop learning in that it:
   a. Utilizes feedback loops
   b. Examines assumptions supporting existing goals and structures and attempts to change them if necessary
   c. Produces behavioral changes among organizational members
   d. Is less likely to generate resistance among organizational members

6. Which of the following exemplifies the cultural conceptualization of organizational learning?

    a. A college that uses feedback to detect and correct errors
    b. A college that maintains a unique organizational identity, which is also flexible enough to accommodate change
    c. A college that adopts the best practices of its peer institutions
    d. All of the above

7. Which learning mechanisms are associated with the dialectical conceptualization of organizational learning?
    a. Collective know-how
    b. Humor, small wins, and improvisation
    c. Congenital, experiential, and vicarious learning
    d. Competency, familiarity, maturity, and propinquity traps

8. Which of the following exemplifies the postmodern perspective on organizational learning?
    a. Promote diverse viewpoints in order to determine the best solution
    b. Promote diverse viewpoints in order to foster yet more variety in thinking
    c. Promote diverse viewpoints as a means to detect errors
    d. Promote diverse viewpoints to avoid competency traps

Case Discussion Questions

Consider again the Outback Community College case described at the beginning of this chapter.

1. Outback Community College invested more money in recruitment in response to consecutive years of enrollment decline. How was this behavior consistent with single-loop learning?
2. Additional resources for recruitment did not improve enrollments; hence, the college reexamined its basic processes and developed a plan to build residence halls. How was this behavior consistent with double-loop learning?
3. The revised residence hall plan aimed to maintain Outback Community College's identity as an open access college but still enable the institution to change to accommodate new demographic and financial conditions. How was this process consistent with cultural conceptualizations of organizational learning?
4. The public protest by faculty and staff could be viewed as a small win. How did this small win facilitate organizational learning?

References

Ahuja, G., & Lampert, C. (2001). Entrepreneurship in the large corporation: A longitudinal study of how established firms create breakthrough inventions. *Strategic Management Journal, 22*(6–7), 521–543.

Alfred, R. (2000). Assessment as a strategic weapon. *Community College Journal, 70*(4), 12–18.

Ancona, D. G., & Caldwell, D. F. (1992). Bridging the boundary: External activity and performance in organizational teams. *Administrative Science Quarterly, 37,* 634–655.

Argyris, C. (1990). *Overcoming organizational defenses: Facilitating organizational learning.* Boston: Allyn and Bacon.

Argyris, C. (1999). *On organizational learning* (2nd ed.). Oxford, England: Blackwell.

Argyris, C., & Schön, D. (1978). *Organizational learning: A theory of action perspective.* Reading, MA: Addison-Wesley.

Arthur, J., & Huntley, C. (2005). Ramping up the organizational learning curve: Assessing the impact of deliberate learning on organizational performance under gainsharing. *Academy of Management Journal, 48*(6), 1159–1170.

Balbastre, F., & Moreno-Luzón, M. (2003). Self-assessment application and learning in organizations: A special reference to the ontological dimension. *Total Quality Management, 14*(3), 367–388.

Bapuji, H., & Crossan, M. (2004). From questions to answers: Reviewing organizational learning research. *Management Learning, 35*(4), 397–417.

Barney, J. (1986). Organizational culture: Can it be a source of sustained competitive advantage? *Academy of Management Review, 11,* 656–665.

Barrett, F. J. (1995). Creating appreciative learning cultures. *Organizational Dynamics, 24*(2), 36–49.

Benjamin, R., & Carroll, S. (1998). The implications of the changed environment for governance in higher education. In W. Tierney (Ed.), *The responsive university: Restructuring for high performance* (pp. 92–119). Baltimore: Johns Hopkins University Press.

Bensimon, E. (2005). Closing the achievement gap in higher education: An organizational learning perspective. In A. Kezar (Ed.), *Organizational learning in higher education: New directions for higher education* (No. 131, pp. 99–111). San Francisco: Jossey-Bass.

Bensimon, E., Polkinghorne, D., Bauman, G., & Vallejo, E. (2004). Doing research that makes a difference. *Journal of Higher Education, 75*(1), 104–126.

Birnbaum, R. (1988). *How colleges work: The cybernetics of academic organization and leadership.* San Francisco: Jossey-Bass.

Blackman, D., Connelly, J., & Henderson, S. (2004). Does double loop learning create reliable knowledge? *Learning Organization, 11*(1), 11–27.

Bloland, H. (1995). Postmodernism and higher education. *Journal of Higher Education, 66*(5), 521–559.

Bokeno, R. M. (2003). The work of Chris Argyris as critical organization practice. *Journal of Organizational Change Management, 16*(6), 633–649.

Bourgeois, L., & Eisenhardt, K. (1988). Strategic decision processes in high velocity environments: Four cases in the microcomputer industry. *Management Science, 34*(7), 816–835.

Boyce, M. (2003). Organizational learning is essential to achieving and sustaining change in higher education. *Innovative Higher Education, 28*(2), 119–136.

Brown, S., & Eisenhardt, K. (1997). The art of continuous change: Linking complexity theory and time-paced evolution in relentlessly shifting organizations. *Administrative Science Quarterly, 42,* 1–34.

Burns, T., & Stalker, G. (1994). *The management of innovation* (3rd ed.). Oxford, England: Oxford University Press.

Carroll, J. S., Rudolph, J. W., & Hatakenaka, S. (2002). Learning from experience in high-hazard organizations. In B. M. Staw & R. M. Kramer (Eds.), *Research in organizational behavior* (pp. 87–187). Amsterdam: Elsevier Science.

Chickering, A. (2003). Reclaiming our soul. *Change, 35*(1), 38–44.

Claxton, C. S., & Murrell, P. H. (1987). *Learning styles: Implications for improving educational practices* (ASHE-ERIC Higher Education Report, No. 4). Washington, DC: ERIC Clearinghouse on Higher Education, George Washington University.

Cook, S., & Yanow, D. (1996). Culture and organizational learning. In M. Cohen & L. Sproull (Eds.), *Organizational learning* (pp. 430–459). Thousand Oaks, CA: Sage.

Crossan, M., Lane, H., & White, R. (1999). An organizational learning framework: From intuition to institution. *Academy of Management Review, 24*(3), 522–537.

Day, G., & Schoemaker, P. (2005). Scanning the periphery. *Harvard Business Review, 83*(11), 135–148.

de Geus, A. P. (1996). Planning as learning. In K. Starkey (Ed.), *How Organizations Learn* (pp. 92–99). London: International Thomson Business Press.

Derrida, J. (1976). *Of grammatology.* Baltimore: Johns Hopkins University Press.

Dill, D. (1999). Academic accountability and university adaptation: The architecture of an academic learning organization. *Higher Education, 38,* 127–154.

Fiol, C., & Lyles, M. (1985). Organizational learning. *Academy of Management Review, 10*(4), 803–813.

Flood, R., & Romm, N. (1996). *Diversity management: Triple loop learning.* Chicester, England: Wiley.

Foucault, M. (1986). Disciplinary power and subjection. In S. Lukes (Ed.), *Power* (pp. 229–242). New York: New York University Press. (Reprinted from M. Foucault, *Power/knowledge: Selected interviews and other writings, 1972–1977,* C. Gordon, Ed., 1976, New York: Random House)

Franklin, P., Hodgkinson, M., & Stewart, J. (1998). Towards universities as learning organizations. *Learning Organization, 5*(5), 228–238.

Harden, G. (1968). The tragedy of the commons. *Science, 162,* 1243–1248.

Hargadon, A. B. (2002). Brokering knowledge: Linking learning and innovation. In

B. M. Staw & R. M. Kramer (Eds.), *Research in Organizational Behavior, Vol. 24* (pp. 41–85). Amsterdam: Elsevier Science.

Hartley, M. (2003). "There is no way without a because": Revitalization of purpose at three liberal arts colleges. *Review of Higher Education, 27*(1), 75–102.

Hassard, J. (1996). Exploring the terrain of modernism and postmodernism in organization theory. In D. M. Boje, R. P. Gephart Jr., & T. J. Thatchenkery (Eds.), *Postmodern management and organization theory* (pp. 45–59). Thousand Oaks, CA: Sage.

Hatch, M. J. (1997). *Organization theory: Modern, symbolic, and postmodern perspectives.* New York: Oxford University Press.

Heraty, N. (2004). Towards an architecture of organization-led learning. *Human Resource Management Review, 14*(4), 449–472.

Herriott, S., Levinthal, D., & March, J. G. (1985). Learning from experience in organizations. *American Economic Review, 75,* 298–302.

Huber, G. (1991). Organizational learning: The contributing processes and the literatures. *Organization Science, 2*(1), 88–115.

Kezar, A. (Ed.). (2005). *Organizational learning in higher education: New directions for higher education* (No. 131). San Francisco: Jossey-Bass.

Kim, D. H. (1993). The link between individual and organizational learning. *Sloan Management Review, 35*(1), 37–50.

Klein, K. J., Dansereau, F., & Hall, R. (1994). Levels issues in theory development, data collection, and analysis. *Academy of Management Review, 19*(2), 195–229.

Klein, K. J., Tosi, H., & Cannella, A. (1999). Multi-level theory building: Benefits, barriers, and new developments. *Academy of Management Review, 24*(2), 243–248.

Kolb, D. A. (1976). Management and the learning process. *California Management Review, 18,* 21–31.

Kolb, D. A. (1984). *Experiential learning as the source of learning and development.* Englewood Cliffs, NJ: Prentice Hall.

Kontoghiorghes, C., Awbrey, S., & Feurig, P. (2005). Examining the relationship between learning organization characteristics and change adaptation, innovation, and organizational performance. *Human Resource Development Quarterly, 16*(2), 185–211.

Levitt, B., & March, J. (1988). Organizational learning. *Annual Review of Sociology, 14,* 319–340.

Lewis, M., & Moultrie, J. (2005). The organizational innovation laboratory. *Creativity and Innovation Management, 14*(1), 73–83.

Lieberman, D. (2005). Beyond faculty development: How centers for teaching and learning can be laboratories for learning. In A. Kezar (Ed.), *Organizational learning in higher education: New directions for higher education* (No. 131, pp. 87–98). San Francisco: Jossey-Bass.

March, J. G. (1991). Exploration and exploitation in organizational learning. *Organization Science, 2,* 71–87.

Marsick, V., & Watkins, K. (1999). Looking again at learning in the learning organization: A tool that can turn into a weapon. *Learning Organization, 6*(5), 207–211.

McGee, J., & Sawyerr, O. (2003). Uncertainty and information search activities: A study of owner-managers of small high-technology manufacturing firms. *Journal of Small Business Management, 41*(4), 385–401.

Milam, J. (2001). *Knowledge management for higher education* (Educational Resources Information Center [ERIC] Document ED464520). Washington, DC: ERIC Clearinghouse on Higher Education.

Morgan, G. (1986). *Images of organization.* Newbury Park, CA: Sage.

Nonaka, I., & Takeuchi, H. (1995). *The knowledge-creating company.* New York: Oxford University Press.

O'Banion, T. (1997). *A learning college for the 21st century.* Phoenix, AZ: Oryx Press.

Perrow, C. (1986). *Complex organizations: A critical essay* (3rd ed.). New York: McGraw-Hill.

Petrides, L. (2002). Organizational learning and the case for knowledge-based systems. In A. Serban & J. Luan (Eds.), *Knowledge management: Building a competitive advantage in higher education: New directions for institutional research* (No. 113, pp. 69–84). San Francisco: Jossey-Bass.

Reagans, R., Argote, L., & Brooks, D. (2005). Individual experience and experience working together: Predicting learning rates from knowing who knows what and knowing how to work together. *Management Science, 51*(6), 869–881.

Riesman, D. (1958). *Constraint and variety in American education.* Lincoln: University of Nebraska Press.

Romme, A. G. L., & van Witteloostuijn, A. (1999). Circular organizing and triple loop learning. *Journal of Organizational Change Management, 12*(5), 439–453.

Roome, N., & Wijen, F. (2006). Stakeholder power and organizational learning in corporate environmental management. *Organization Studies, 27*(2), 235–263.

Rousseau, D. M. (1985). Issues of level in organizational research: Multi-level and cross-level perspectives. *Research in Organizational Behavior, 7,* 1–38.

Seely-Brown, J. S., & Duguid, P. (1991). Organizational learning and communities of practice: Toward a unified view of working, learning, and innovation. *Organizational Science, 2*(1), 40–57.

Senge, P. (1990). *The fifth discipline: The art and practice of the learning organization.* New York: Currency, Doubleday.

Shrivastava, P. (1983). A typology of organizational learning systems. *Journal of Management Studies, 20*(1), 7–28.

Siggelkow, N., & Levinthal, D. (2005). Escaping real (non-benign) competency traps: Linking the dynamics of organizational structure to the dynamics of search. *Strategic Organization, 3*(1), 85–115.

Siggelkow, N., & Rivkin, J. (2005). Speed and search: Designing organizations for turbulence and complexity. *Organization Science, 16*(2), 101–122.

Sitkin, S. B. (1996). Learning through failure: The strategy of small losses. In M. D. Cohen & L. S. Sproull (Eds.), *Organizational learning.* Thousand Oaks, CA: Sage Publications.

Slater, S., & Narver, J. (1995). Market orientation and the learning organization. *Journal of Marketing, 59,* 63–74.

Starbuck, W. H. (1992). Learning by knowledge-intensive firms. *Journal of Management Studies, 29*(6), 713–740.

Watkins, K. E. (2005). What would be different if higher educational institutions were learning organizations? *Advances in Developing Human Resources, 7*(3), 414–421.

Weick, K. (1979). *The social psychology of organizing* (2nd ed.). Reading, MA: Addison-Wesley.

Weick, K. (1995). *Sensemaking in organizations.* Thousand Oaks, CA: Sage.

Weick, K., & Westley, F. (1996). Organizational learning: Affirming an oxymoron. In S. Clegg, C. Hardy, & W. Nord (Eds.), *Handbook of organization studies* (pp. 440–458). Thousand Oaks, CA: Sage.

Yammarino, F., Dionne, S., Chun, J., & Dansereau, F. (2005). Leadership and levels of analysis: A state-of-the-science review. *Leadership Quarterly, 16*(6), 879–919.

7

ORGANIZATIONAL STRATEGY

CONTENTS

Preview   707
Case Context   708
Introduction   711
Strategy and the External Environment   714
The Linear Model of Strategy   723
The Adaptive Model of Strategy   726
The Emergent Model of Strategy   730
The Symbolic Model of Strategy   732
Postmodern Models of Strategy   734
Curriculum as Strategy: Application of the Five Models   736
Heuristics for Choosing a Model of Strategy   738
Summary   741
Review Questions   742
Case Discussion Questions   744
References   745

The authors are most grateful for the critical comments on an early draft of this chapter by James Minor, Michigan State University. The final version, of course, is our own and may or may not reflect the perspective of the reviewer.

Preview

- Three converging trends—competition, lower levels of government funding, and accountability—have increased the importance of strategy for higher education institutions.
- Boundary-spanning personnel occupy key, strategic roles for processing information from the external environment. They also identify and work with external stakeholders who have some degree of involvement in or influence over the institution.
- Organizational strategies are shaped to varying degrees by external and internal coalitions that seek to advance their interests through political behaviors. Different combinations of external and internal coalitions produce power configurations that must be considered when assessing the organization-environment relationship.
- Conceptualizations of organizational strategy can be categorized into one of five models: a linear model that reflects the assumptions of rational decision making, an adaptive model that utilizes principles from systems theory, an emergent model that is based in the social construction of organizations, a symbolic model that reflects the organizational culture, and a postmodern frame that offers a critique of and alternative to positivist and social constructionist theories.
- The linear model of strategy entails an assessment of the internal modes for addressing environmental expectations. The desired outcome is an alignment between organizational behaviors and the institution's mission and goals.
- The adaptive model of strategy posits that organizations are continually engaged in internal adjustments and modifications to address changes in the external environment.
- The emergent model suggests that strategy is revealed through a retrospective assessment of previous organizational behaviors. This type of assessment identifies patterns of behavior, which reflect the historic commitments of the institution rather than its espoused orientations and goals.
- The symbolic model suggests that organizational strategy reflects the values, beliefs, and assumptions of organizational members. Strategies that ignore important aspects of the organizational culture are likely to fail.
- Postmodern perspectives raise critical questions regarding how power and privilege shape organizational strategies. Postmodernism offers an alternative model for strategy development that embraces diversity and dissent.

——————————————— CASE CONTEXT ———————————————

Strategic Planning at Heartland State University

Heartland State University, a large public research institution in the Midwest, withstood the strategic planning fad of the 1980s. The university's president at that time enjoyed telling senior staff that "the strategic plan of this university is not to have a plan." That was his way of reinforcing the idea that each college within the university had autonomy to make its own decisions and pursue its own version of excellence.

By the 1990s, however, the external context had shifted. Heartland State's accrediting body developed new standards that included institution-wide strategic planning and the alignment of resource allocation decisions with those plans. The state legislature was also raising concerns about efficiency and quality. In public hearings, parents complained about students enrolling in far too many large lecture courses, while institutional data revealed that some faculty hardly ever interacted with an undergraduate student.

During an accreditation self-study in 1996, administrators at Heartland State went through the motions of complying with the accrediting body's expectations. They developed an elaborate strategic plan, which was guided by 8 educational goals and 24 objectives. The plan also identified more than 200 indicators that could be used to measure progress toward those objectives across the six colleges of the university.

The accreditation team was impressed with the report, and, during their visit, they were delighted to learn that Heartland State's office of institutional research had already begun collecting data for many of the 200 indicators. "And the institutional research office is going to put all of these data in a binder, and distribute it to the deans on a quarterly basis," proudly declared the vice president for academic affairs. "These goals, objectives, and indicators are going to drive decision making around here."

The 1996 accreditation report praised Heartland State's strategic planning efforts and heralded their administrative team as a model for other large universities seeking to adopt data-based decision making. The report also satisfied legislative committee members who wanted the university to track more consistently faculty productivity data.

Five years later, a group of graduate students from a higher education doctoral program at another university came to Heartland State to interview members of the administrative team that had developed the 1996 strategic plan and assessment system. The students had read about Heartland State's planning process in a recent book on higher education strategy. They selected Heartland State as the site for their own research project on strategic planning. However, when the graduate students arrived on campus, they were disappointed to learn that nearly all of the collegiate deans who had participated in the 1996 self-study had moved on to other institutions. The academic vice presidency had also turned over, and the president had announced his retirement. Only the institutional research director and a few midlevel associate deans remained from that process.

"Oh yes, we have a strategic plan," noted one of the associate deans. "It is on the shelf right behind me. And the institutional research office does a fabulous job with those quarterly data reports. I use them all the time."

"How do you use them?" asked one of the graduate students.

"Well, I, uh—we, we find the data really useful. I mean, we use the numbers to determine whether our programs are meeting their admissions and retention targets. Whether we are hiring enough faculty and advisors in our high enrollment programs. Stuff like that."

"But are the data used to make strategic decisions about the future of the college?" asked another graduate student.

"Well, we use it for decision making all of the time," the associate dean responded. "Like how many faculty to hire, and how many sections to offer for our big lecture courses. But strategic decisions? I am not sure about that."

And neither was the 2006 accreditation site visit team. Ten years after the initial review of Heartland State's strategic planning efforts, another accreditation team produced a very different report. They were highly critical of Heartland State's planning efforts. They noted that, while data were collected, decisions continued to be made on the basis of historical precedent and political criteria (e.g., the colleges that had the most powerful deans received the most resources). More importantly, some of the team members were livid that Heartland State did not follow through on its 1996 strategic planning pledge to emphasize the assessment of undergraduate student learning outcomes. "How can you take seriously eight educational goals, if none of them is assessed?" asked one of the team members.

In anticipation of a negative report, the president gathered a senior administrative task force to address the issue. The new academic vice president was the first to speak. "We need to infuse planning into everything that we do," noted the academic vice president. "At my previous institution, the deans would conduct each year a thorough assessment of their college's strengths and weaknesses. They would also assess the environment. What do employers think of their graduates? What is the market like for new program development? And they would talk with the faculty on an ongoing basis, encouraging them to always make changes. Not wait for the next budget cycle, but if you have a good idea, let's do it now."

Energized by the vice president's presentation, the task force engaged in a six-month process of internal and external assessment. The internal assessment was led by the academic vice president and consisted of 11 subcommittees, which were charged to review data and develop action plans for change. A new research committee was formed to enhance the university's capacity to attract external funding. New student learning assessments were developed, and faculty convened discussions to examine the data. The external assessment included community meetings, an employer survey, and conversations with legislators and other state and local policy makers. New glossy reports were developed to highlight the university's research strengths. Faculty members were provided extensive resources to attend and present at workshops on assessment and student learning. Student affairs staff developed and implemented a range of plans to improve the campus climate.

"I've seen more activity in the past six months than in the past six years," noted the long-time institutional research director. But after six months, people were burned out. One dean resigned in protest. "I spend more time planning than doing," she noted in her resignation letter. Student affairs staff moved on to other issues. Productive research faculty stopped attending university-wide planning meetings, because the meetings took away too much time from their work in the laboratories. And, ultimately, community members and state legislators continued to compile larger and larger lists of issues for the university to address. "I have got to eliminate homelessness, cure AIDS, and fix the public schools—all before lunch," a sarcastic dean joked. "This whole process feels never ending."

Then, on a relatively quiet summer day, the institutional research director began to review all of the undergraduate student outcomes data that his office compiled. Each college had sent him its assessment data at the end of the academic year. "I wanted to see what it looked like in the aggregate," he explained. "No one had done that, which I kind of found strange. I mean, we pressed people for six months, and nobody was reviewing the end result. I guess everyone was too tired at the end of the semester," he added with a laugh.

"After reviewing all of the assessment reports, that is when it hit me," the institutional research director continued. "I noticed that there was a really strong theme across all of them. Nearly every department was assessing something related to applying science to society. Agriculture, engineering, life sciences, education. Everyone wanted their undergraduate students applying their field's science to the needs of society. I guess this should not have been a surprise, since we are a land-grant university, but people were impressed by how extensive the emphasis was and by how strongly it permeated *undergraduate* education, which *was* a surprise to some."

The institutional research director convened a meeting with the deans and several of the more active department chairs. They developed a way to display the "science for society" assessment report in a user-friendly electronic format. The resulting report and Web site were forwarded to the accreditation association as part of the institution's response to the negative aspects of the site visit team's report.

"Well, the accreditation folks were very pleased," noted the institutional research director. "In fact, they called it 'cutting edge' for a large university to have such a coherent undergraduate curriculum. And the best part—at least for the deans and faculty—was that we had already been doing this curriculum for a number of years, even before our big six-month assessment push. Our undergraduate curriculum was stronger than we realized, and I guess thanks to me, we now have a nice slogan—science for society—to describe it."

"The response of the accreditation association was a huge relief," explained one of the department chairs. "It was like a weight had been lifted from our shoulders. The validation was nice. I mean, it was good to know that what we had been doing for a long time was actually valued. But also we got a lot smarter about the whole strategic planning process. Instead of running ourselves ragged trying to respond to every single expectation that's out there, we really used the process to identify the stuff that has been important to us all along, even if we didn't quite realize before how important it was."

"Maybe I shouldn't say this," whispered the institutional research director, "but I think that the strategic planning process was more important than the strategic plan itself. I mean, it brought together people who probably hadn't said more than two words to each other in the past 10 years—not because they were angry with each other, but because this is such a big place. And it was amazing to find so much commonality, so much consistency among these people who hardly ever talk to each other. It was like they had been coordinated all along, and just didn't realize it."

Introduction

S trategy is a critical and controversial construct in organizational theory. Middlemist and Hitt (1988; cf. Hitt, Ireland, & Middlemist, 2005) define strategy in general as "the use and allocation of organizational resources to accomplish long-run objectives" and institutional strategy as "the major plan of action for achieving the long-term objectives of the entire organization (rather than a division)" (p. 433). Strategy promotes a focus on organization-wide objectives rather than departmental or individual priorities, and the emphasis is on long-term goals rather than short-term gain. Beyond these basic foci, however, organizational researchers differ in their assumptions and conceptualizations of strategy. As will become clear in this chapter, there are many questions about the meaning of strategy—who defines it, what it includes and excludes, the purposes it serves, and the latent unintended consequences that sometimes result (Presley & Leslie, 1999).

One conceptualization of strategy stresses the need for internal alignment between organizational processes and long-term performance objectives. In this model, top-level leaders construct a strategic plan consisting of organizational goals, which are linked to specific objectives for each unit in the organization. The units implement plans designed to achieve those objectives, and performance is assessed in order to measure progress toward goal achievement. The intent is to improve performance by aligning activities with specific organizational goals. Chaffee (1985) referred to this process as the **linear model** of strategy; that is, strategy is developed through a sequential process that leads to a rational alignment of behaviors and goals (Chandler, 1962).

A second conceptualization suggests that strategy "provides an important link between the organization and its environment" (Hatch, 1997, p. 123). Strategy can be viewed as the organization's response to a complex and constantly changing external world. This widely held view suggests that strategy is a proactive, rather than passive or reactive, perspective toward the actions needed by the organization in the near and long-term future for continued success. It includes not only a heavy emphasis on learning and on the analytical techniques for understanding and using data, but also on a concern with the modes of action that transform the internal organization into a dynamic force that can deal efficiently and effectively with the challenges of the external environment (Jarzabkowski, 2005; Pettigrew, Thomas, & Whittington, 2002). Chaffee (1985) identified this approach as the **adaptive model.** This model suggests that successful strategy depends in part on the potential of organizations to deviate from extant patterns of behavior, culture, and structure in order to adapt to a changing external environment (Ansoff & Sullivan, 1991; Low & Abrahamson, 1992).

Yet another view of strategy, however, recognizes the increasing difficulties of describing external environments and predicting their futures and instead calls for a more decentralized, temporally relevant organizational reaction. In this model, strategy can only be discerned retrospectively, constituting a record of how the organization responded to various environmental stimuli over a substantial period of time (Mintzberg, Ahlstrand, & Lampel, 1998). In this **emergent model,** strategy is a sensemaking process through which the organization identifies coherent patterns of activity (Mintzberg, 1994a; Mintzberg & Waters, 1985). When utilizing the emergent model, organizational leaders reflect on current and historical patterns of activity. They make sense of these patterns by building an explanation that links the patterns to institutional missions and external expectations. Emergent strategies can reveal how the organization has adjusted to its environment over time (Hardy, Langley, Mintzberg, & Rose, 2003) and how the organization may have modified the environment in which it operates. These adjustments and modifications do not necessarily reflect a planned, intentional response to the environment. Instead, coherent patterns of activity (i.e., strategy) may emerge through trial-and-error learning, historical patterns of interaction, or just plain luck.

Strategy also serves as an important symbol, story, or internal narrative that guides the thinking of organizational leaders and members (Gioia & Thomas, 1996). When the strategic story of an organization is told to internal and external groups, their perceptions of the organization begin to overlap, producing a common understanding of the institution's goals, behaviors, and outcomes (Bormann, 1996; Cragan & Shields, 1992). This idea reflects the **symbolic model** of strategy. It is easy to see, for example, how shared understandings are critical for effective strategy making in higher education. The notion of shared governance, for example, is predicated upon mutual, if unspoken, agreements about institutional meaning, values, goals, and modes of conduct among trustees, administrators, and faculty.

Finally, **postmodern** theorists raise critical questions regarding the formation of strategies (Deetz, 1992; Mumby, 1988). The determination of organizational strengths and weaknesses, they argue, may not be based on a neutral, objective assessment using universally agreed upon criteria. Instead, decisions about strengths, weaknesses, and assessment criteria are undergirded by political values and actions. Valorizing a particular academic program as an institutional strength, for example, may reflect not only supportive data from objective indicators such as test scores and student-faculty ratios. The policies and actions that follow from it may also depend on how powerful the chair of that department is or on how politically connected the alumni of the program are. Therefore, if strategy development is at least in part a political act, then it is important to understand whose interpretation of the environment guides decision making and who is primarily responsible for the development of strategy in a particular organization.

Thus, strategy can:

- provide a rational alignment between group/individual behaviors and organizational goals (linear model);
- enhance knowledge of and responsiveness to external conditions (adaptive model);
- constitute a historical record of previous practices, which helps people make sense of the current state of organizational life (emergent model);
- serve as a story that explains organizational behaviors to internal and external audiences (symbolic model);
- and reflect the balance of power within an organization as well as the relative strength of interest groups (postmodern).

In this chapter, we explain why strategy is a critical concept for college and university leaders. In the first section, we provide the broad contours for understanding strategy as an organization's relationship with the external environment. Systems theory highlights the importance of cross-boundary interactions and the cultivation of key stakeholders in the development of strategy. Then, we explore in more detail the five conceptual models of strategy identified in the introduction: linear, adaptive, emergent, symbolic, and postmodern. We also apply these models to an understanding of curriculum as strategy in colleges and universities. In the final section, we offer a contingency framework for making decisions about which strategy model to apply under different environmental conditions.

Strategy and the External Environment

As we noted earlier, relationships between organizations and their environments are critical to organizational survival and success. All organizations must be continually attentive to changes in their environments (e.g., competitors, government regulations, trends in consumer preferences, etc.). The rapid pace of change, in both the environment for higher education and among the institutions that occupy it, argue for a clear understanding of the variables that must be accounted for in order for institutions to be successful.

Strategy and Higher Education

Three converging sociopolitical and economic trends in higher education suggest the importance of the use of strategy for colleges and universities. First, an increased awareness of the competitiveness of the higher education marketplace has stimulated greater interest and involvement in strategic action on college campuses (Alfred, 2005). Increasing numbers of corporations and for-profit providers now compete with nonprofit colleges and universities. Online education, moreover, has eroded to some degree the boundaries of student choice markets, where students formerly attended institutions that were geographically close to their homes. Second, reductions in government funding for public higher education have led to a clear understanding that institutions cannot be all things to all people. Strategic initiatives are needed to guide more efficient internal resource allocation (Leslie & Fretwell, 1996; Welsh & Nunez, 2005). Third, expectations for accountability to external stakeholders suggest the need to link organizational activities with specific mission-centered goals. The accreditation process, for example, has stimulated strategic change initiatives on several campuses (Martin, Manning, & Ramaley, 2001). Accreditation associations, statewide coordinating boards, private foundations, affiliated religious denominations, and other stakeholders expect that institutional activities will be guided by an overall strategy, which connects the institution to the external publics that it serves.

Richard Alfred, an analyst of the community college sector, suggests that "improving quality is meaningless without knowing what kind of quality is relevant in a turbulent market" (2001, p. 26). Processes of strategy development can help an institution gain a better understanding of its mission and its market. Strategy enables leaders to engage in informed action, rather than merely comply with external directives. College leaders who do not utilize strategy may "become prisoners of external forces and surprises, most of them unpleasant" (Keller, 1983, p. 67).

Identifying Stakeholders

Rather than succumbing blindly to the pressures of external forces, colleges and universities can cultivate relationships with external **stakeholders** who can provide knowledge and resources that are critical to effective institutional performance. Ian Mitroff (1983) has labeled as stakeholders those elements in the environment surrounding the organization that have some reason to care about what happens to it. The reasons vary by type of stakeholder, and it is useful to appreciate similarities and differences among the stakeholders. Hence, careful attention must be paid to identifying stakeholders with historic interests in the institution (e.g., long-standing donors) as well as those that are emerging—such as employers of graduates of the institution. Mitroff observes that there are seven methods for generating a comprehensive list of stakeholders: imperative, positional, reputational, social participation, opinion leadership, demographic, and organizational. Below are brief descriptions of each.

The **imperative** method of identifying stakeholders is based on revealed interest. The method is to find statements made by outsiders regarding the organization (e.g., parents who write letters to the college's president). Through the **positional** method, people are identified who occupy formal roles that relate to the organization. For example, one might look at organizational charts of state government agencies to see who is charged with responsibilities relevant to higher education. The **reputational** method suggests asking knowledgeable or important people to nominate those who may have a stake in the system. An environmental assessor using this method might ask the college president and his or her staff to identify key figures in the local area or in the national policy-making sector who are known to be interested in the institution.

The **social participation** method requires finding people who take active parts in activities related to issues at hand. Certain alumni or retired faculty members, for example, may regularly make themselves available for classroom presentations. By using the **opinion leadership** method, those who shape opinions of other stakeholders are identified. These people may not be part of the formal network of stakeholders, but they consist of those who influence them (e.g., newspaper editors, opinion writers in the *Chronicle of Higher Education*). The **demographic** approach classifies stakeholders by age, gender, race, occupation, or some other category (e.g., 18- to 22-year-olds in a geographic region). Finally, identifying organizations that play key roles with the focal organization (e.g., suppliers, competitors, regulators) is what is meant by the **organizational** method. Many institutions of higher education informally assign staff members to seek out and regularly monitor each of these categories of stakeholder.

External and Internal Coalitions

Henry Mintzberg (1983, 1994b) suggests a somewhat different but partially overlapping approach to describing elements in the environment, preferring to classify stakeholders as **influencers.** These are people or organizations with less than a full-time commitment to the organization—for example, trustees, unions, academic associations, state coordinating boards, and various publics. In contrast to the stakeholder orientation, it is important to view influencers in terms of their *collective* activity and resultant power. Influencers, therefore, act as external coalitions. An **external coalition** is a group of influencers that acts collaboratively to advance a shared agenda. In the case of higher education, that agenda may be directed at the entire institution or may pertain to a particular feature or part of the institution—say, for example, a social cause or a new building.

As institutions grow and develop, **internal coalitions** also form within their boundaries. Mintzberg argues that since both environments and organizations continually evolve, coalitions rise and fall within and across each.

That is, as the environment shifts, different external constituents become allied in order to forward their individual and collective needs. So, too, the internal organization evolves, and components also become related to each other in ways that seem to forward their goals. This combination of external and internal power configurations results in a range of different cross-boundary relationships. Mintzberg suggests that the relationships between those outside and inside the organization fall on a continuum (Table 7.1) from the broad and general public who are only indirectly related to the organization, to more immediately connected agencies that exert irregular but direct and powerful influence over concrete issues.

Mintzberg suggests that different configurations of internal and external groups compete to exert influence over the strategic direction of the organization. Internal influencers include those in top management, middle management, the operating core, administrative staff, support staff, and an intangible institutional ideology (i.e., the organization's dominant belief system). External influencers include a range of individuals and institutions, including potential students, competitor colleges, regulatory agencies, and funding sources such as governments and private foundations.

Both internal and external influencers engage in power struggles within their spheres, with the resulting dominant internal and external configurations then engaging in unique cross-boundary interactions that either solidify or vitiate the power balance. Mintzberg hypothesizes that there are a

TABLE 7.1
Continuum of Influencers

Effects	Form of Influence
General, Indirect, Detached	Social Norms
	Formal Constraints (e.g., state regulatory agencies)
	Pressure Campaigns (e.g., advocates for a living wage for all employees)
	Direct Controls (i.e., a constraint focused only on one organization; e.g., an accreditation association requiring compliance from one college on a specific issue)
Specific, Direct, Focused	Members on boards of directors (in higher education these include boards of trustees and, in the public sector, state coordinating boards)

Adapted from Mintzberg (1979, 1983).

handful of commonly occurring internal/external configurations. We first consider three types of external coalitions: (1) dominated external coalition, (2) divided external coalition, and (3) passive external coalition.

In a **dominated external coalition**, one element in the environment dominates the others and thus controls the interactions between the environment and the organization. One example might be when the governor of a state decides to hire a new leader for the public higher education system with a completely new agenda and gives him or her the power to effect it. The governor (through the actions of the new chief executive for the state system) is in a position to dominate *other* external influencers in the environment and thus, indirectly and directly exercise some power over public colleges and universities.

A **divided external coalition** emerges when power is divided more or less equally among independent influencers (e.g., alumni and state legislators). No single influencer can gain sufficient power over the other external influencers or over the organization.

Finally, a **passive external coalition** is formed when the number of external influencers increases, and power becomes so widely diffused that, in fact, the coalition may be rendered relatively ineffective. The influencers are unable to reach consensus. At that point, the balance of power between the organization and the environment shifts to the organization. A passive external coalition will arise also when the benefits of concerted external power applied to the focal organization redound relatively equally to the benefit of *all* the influencers. The reason is that there is less incentive for any one influencer to expend excessive amounts of energy vis-à-vis the focal organization if there are no incremental benefits apparently forthcoming.

Mintzberg explained how these three coalitions arise under different circumstances. He noted that an external coalition:

> tends to emerge as *dominated* to the extent that the organization experiences some form of dependency in its environment as well as the concentration of its external power either in the hands of a single individual or group (often an owner) or else in an active consensus among its external influencers. The external coalition emerges as *divided* when external power is significant but shared by a limited number of individuals or groups with conflicting goals. And an external coalition tends to emerge as *passive* especially when the external influencers are numerous and dispersed (notably when they can easily exit, are not aroused or driven by normative beliefs, and are not already organized or inclined to be by a "professional organizer"), but also when the external coalition is extremely politicized or overcontrolling, or when the organization is very inconsequential to it or else

strong enough to pacify it by virtue of its leadership, ideology, expertise, or its sheer size [italics added]. (1983, p. 109)

Of equal interest to strategic planners are the modes that external influencers use to exercise their power. Mintzberg suggests that external influencers utilize essentially five modes: **social norms, formal constraints** such as laws, **pressure campaigns, direct interaction,** and **participation internally** (e.g., membership on decision-making bodies such as boards of trustees).

Next, we describe the internal configurations that Mintzberg proposes. Five internal constituencies are displayed in table 7.2.

Depending on the issue, the internal constituency groups form alliances, thus creating internal coalitions (e.g., president-faculty, faculty-administrative staff). Mintzberg labels the internal alliances as **bureaucratic, personalized, ideologic, professional,** and **politicized.** These labels characterize the modes by which the members of the internal coalitions are connected to one another. Imagine, for example, a highly bureaucratic set of interpersonal relationships compared with personal or politicized ones. Each of these internal coalitions has a number of modes of influence available to them (**formal authority, ideology, expertise,** and **politics**). Different internal constituencies are likely to use different modes of influence. The president of a bureaucratic college or university, for example, would be more likely to utilize his or her formal authority as a means of influencing other internal constituencies.

Thus, there are potential alliances outside and inside the organization. How much power do they have? And how do they influence one another? Mintzberg suggests that there are different kinds of *linkages* between each of these different kinds of external coalitions (dominated, divided, and passive) and internal coalitions (bureaucratic, personalized, ideologic, professional, and politicized). There are six primary linkages or combinations among

TABLE 7.2
Internal Constituencies

Internal Constituency	Higher Education Examples
Chief executive officer	College president
Middle management	Vice presidents, deans
Line operators	Faculty
Administrative staff	Supervisors, directors
Support staff	Clerical workers

them and nine less common combinations. The major six are noted in Table 7.3. The linkages are characterized by four different models of intercoalition influence—authority, ideology, expertise, and politics—that describe the complex internal/external relationships that can arise between internal coalitions and external power holders.

This matching of internal and external coalition type represents a helpful diagnostic technique for understanding the organization-environment relationship. With this model, we can predict, for example, the rise of an autocratic power configuration when a personalized internal coalition is matched with a passive external coalition. Imagine a charismatic, if not dogmatic, college president facing an environment whose stakeholders or influencers are widely dispersed. Clearly, we can understand why the president is likely to have his or her way. On the other hand, put that same president in a bureaucratic internal environment where the external environment is dominated by one agency (say the state), and we will find a power configuration like the "instrument" in which the college largely is at the service of the state.

The value of this diagnostic mode to our understanding of strategy is that it illustrates the contingent nature of strategy making. Organizational

TABLE 7.3
Primary Linkages of External and Internal Coalitions and the Resultant Power Relationship

External Coalition	Internal Coalition	Power Configuration
Dominated	Bureaucratic	The Instrument (organization serves the dominant external coalition)
Passive	Bureaucratic	Closed System (control by administrative staff)
Passive	Personalized	Autocracy (control by the chief executive officer)
Passive	Ideologized	Missionary (control by ideology)
Passive	Professional	Meritocracy (control by experts)
Divided	Politicized	Political Arena (control through conflict)

Adapted from Mintzberg (1983).

leaders are bound in varying degrees by external and internal conditions and, equally important, by the fit or lack of fit between the two (Hitt, Ireland, & Hoskisson, 2001).

Boundary-Spanning Personnel

In most organizations, boundary-spanning personnel are responsible for a range of cross-boundary relationships between the organization and its external stakeholders. Different persons in the organization have jurisdiction over the stance of the organization vis-à-vis relevant actors and coalitions in the environment. Some of the responsibilities of boundary-spanning personnel include:

1. Input acquisition: How will students be recruited to the institution; under what conditions will they be admitted?
2. Resource acquisition: How will funds be secured?
3. Information acquisition: What changes are taking place in society that may affect the institution?
4. Product or service dispensing: What happens to students after graduation? How are they dispersed throughout society? Is this in accordance with institutional expectations?
5. Information dispensing: Who will manage the image of the institution? Who will engage in public relations activities?

Boundary-spanning activities usually take place at the system input and system output ends of organizational activity. Evan's (1972) organizational set theory (Figure 7.1), for example, suggests that to improve the effectiveness of boundary spanning, the following relationships should hold:

FIGURE 7.1
Evan's Organizational Set Theory

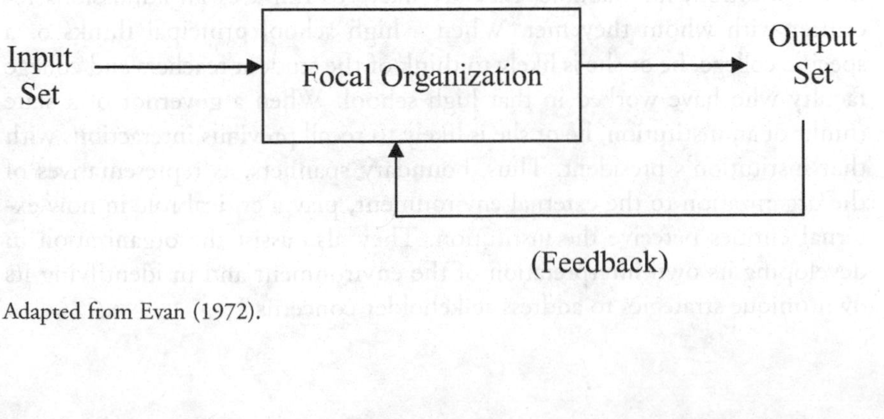

Adapted from Evan (1972).

1. The bigger the organization's input set, the larger the number of boundary personnel.
2. The more diverse the input set, the more differentiated the boundary personnel must be.
3. The more diverse the output set, the more differentiated the boundary personnel.
4. The more turbulent the environment, the more differentiated the boundary personnel.

Thus, organizations operating in complex environments need many boundary spanners who collectively possess a wide range of skills and expertise. Boundary-spanning activities address two important functions for organizations: information processing and external representation. In their information-processing role, boundary spanners help the organization monitor the environment. Organizations rely on boundary spanners to provide the information necessary to make sense of a complex external world. Organizations that continually monitor events in their environments are more sensitive to external feedback and can develop appropriate strategies in a timely way. Hence, the creation of organizational strategy will depend on the interpretations and sensemaking of the boundary spanners, as well as those within the organization (e.g., executive staff members) whose responsibility it is to create a coherent strategy from the disparate impressions of the boundary spanners.

Organizational strategy, therefore, depends importantly on the knowledge and skills of boundary spanners who can assess environmental trends and interpret and explain the implications of those trends for the organization. Interpretation and impression making, however, flow in *both* directions across the organizational boundary. Boundary spanners also help shape how external constituents view the organization. As representatives of the organization, boundary spanners represent the "public face" of the organization. They personify the institution. When prospective students think of a particular institution, for example, they are likely to think of an admissions recruiter with whom they met. When a high school principal thinks of a specific college, he or she is likely to think of the student teachers and college faculty who have worked in that high school. When a governor of a state thinks of an institution, he or she is likely to recall previous interactions with that institution's president. Thus, boundary spanners, as representatives of the organization to the external environment, play a critical role in how external entities perceive the institution. They also assist the organization in developing its own interpretation of the environment and in identifying its own unique strategies to address stakeholder concerns.

An understanding of the external environment is a critical piece in the puzzle of organizational strategy. In fact, we argue that different models of strategy will be more or less appropriate depending on the characteristics of the environment, on the internal power configurations, and on the relations between external and internal groups. In the following sections, we delineate five models of strategy and then offer a contingency framework, which can be used to select a model that is appropriate for a given set of environmental conditions.

The Linear Model of Strategy

Alfred Chandler (1962), then a management professor at the Massachusetts Institute of Technology (MIT), was among the first to conceptualize organizational strategy and its implications for leadership. Chandler articulated a version of strategy that was long-term in its focus and directed by upper management. From this perspective, strategic decisions by top-level managers shape the structure of the organization. In Chandler's words, "structure follows strategy" (p. 14). Chandler's archival and case study research on large corporations such as Standard Oil and General Motors revealed that strategic decisions—for example, to expand into new product lines or into new geographical areas—necessitate the development of new structural forms. Moreover, different types of strategic decisions lead to the adoption of different types of structures.

> The decision to expand into new types of functions called for the building of a central office and a multidepartmental structure, while the developing of new lines or products or continued growth on a national or international scale brought the formation of the multidivisional structure with a general office to administer the different divisions. (p. 14)

In this model, strategy is a planned, intentional effort that seeks to align internal organizational structures with a set of goals and performance objectives. The assumption is that aligning structures with goals will result in higher levels of efficiency. Organizational members would be less likely to drift toward unnecessary activities and more likely to concentrate on those actions that contribute to the overall effectiveness of the organization. Moreover, this process is rational, because strategic decisions are made on the basis of data, goals, and plans, rather than nonrational criteria such as feelings, intuition, or tradition. This process is also linear, because strategy proceeds in a stepwise fashion from analysis to planning to implementation. Strategy development follows a linear process of identifying goals, gathering data, assessing alternatives, and making decisions that are most likely to achieve desired results.

When this rational, linear model is employed, top management develops the strategy, though preferably with input from lower levels of the organization's hierarchy. That input from below can improve capacity for decision making, since the members of the organization occupying lower rungs in the hierarchy, unlike the top managers, will have direct experience with the problems being addressed. Moreover, these personnel will likely have responsibility for implementing the strategy. Their participation in developing the strategy may increase the likelihood that they will be committed to the strategy, knowledgeable of the intent behind the strategy, and thus better able to make effective adjustments as they implement the strategy.

Even though lower level personnel play a critical role in the linear model, the authority to develop strategy is vested in the top management. Lower level employees may be given some discretion in terms of implementation tactics, but the actual strategy is set by those at the top of the organizational chart (Chandler, 1962). The assumption is that top management is free from conflict of interest and therefore can objectively assess what is in the best interest for the organization as a whole. Henry Rosovsky (1990), a former dean at Harvard, suggested that faculty members should not determine institutional strategy. He argued that it would be difficult for faculty to transcend their departmental loyalties and do what is best for the institution as a whole. The tendency would be to protect the department in which the faculty member is based. Though faculty should have a voice in strategy development and should have autonomy to make adjustments during implementation, Rosovsky argued that ultimately top-level administrators should set institutional strategy.

Chandler's linear model continues to have a significant impact on how researchers study strategy. Many current authors have retained the linear model's primary orientation toward internal organizational alignment. Australian organizational theorist Lex Donaldson (2000), for example, argued that internal structures need to be aligned with the core strategy of the organization in order to ensure high levels of effectiveness. In studies of Japanese manufacturing firms, Donaldson found that strategy determines the size of the organization, the degree of innovation in organizational processes, the amount of diversification of product lines, and the geographical extent of the organization's market. Size, innovation, diversification, and geography, in turn, determine the tasks that must be carried out for the organization to succeed. These task requirements determine the appropriate structure of the organization. If structure and strategy are out of alignment (e.g., a strategic emphasis on innovation, but a bureaucratic structure that promotes conformity), then the organization is likely to be ineffective.

Despite the practical utility of the linear model, it has received criticism. The linear model assumes that top-level managers have significant control over the organization, but this may be the case only in tightly coupled, bureaucratic organizations. Loosely-coupled colleges and universities, where faculty and staff are often given significant autonomy in their areas of expertise, may not be well suited to linear forms of strategy. College and university structures may not be easily molded and shaped to align with a strategy developed by senior administrators. Autonomy of the academic disciplines, shared governance, and highly departmentalized structures make top-down strategy development difficult (Del Favero, 2003; Kezar, 2004; Schuster, Smith, Corak, & Yamada, 1994). These structural arrangements may preclude the development of certain types of strategies. Thus, the existing structure of an institution restricts the range of strategies that can develop. Chandler (1962), of course, argued that structure is determined by strategy, but critics of the linear model note that strategy is also shaped by the existing structure of the organization.

The linear model also assumes that the environment is relatively predictable and stable. Strategy development in this model unfolds sequentially over time; goals are developed, options are assessed, decisions are made, and plans are implemented. But there may be a significant time lag between when a strategic decision is made and when structural changes are actually implemented. In the meantime, the environment is assumed to remain stable; otherwise, the strategic decision may no longer reflect the realities of the environment. Mintzberg (1994a), however, noted that the fallacy of linear strategy is that it assumes that "the world is supposed to hold still while a plan is being developed and then stay on the predicted course while that plan is being implemented" (p. 110). For many organizations, the environment is too turbulent to assume that conditions will remain constant long enough for a strategic plan to be implemented successfully. Thus, it may be unwise to design strategies and structures around longitudinal projections such as 5-year or 10-year enrollment plans (Cutright, 2001).

Finally, critics suggest that the linear model promotes excessive caution (Keller, 1983). Actions will not be taken until sufficient data can justify the new course of action. Structures must be aligned with new strategies before implementation can be successful. These assumptions can reinforce preferences for the status quo, lead to risk aversion among organizational leaders, and diminish organizational members' proclivities toward innovation and change (Bensimon, 2004).

By the mid-1970s, the linear model had begun to lose favor with organizational theorists and management scholars (Chaffee, 1985). The impact of systems theory had taken hold and conceptualizations of strategy shifted to an adaptive model.

The Adaptive Model of Strategy

Building on the biological metaphor of systems theory, the adaptive model suggests that organizations are constantly assessing their external environments and internal conditions. Much like a cybernetic feedback loop in systems theory, organizations are continually engaged in adjustments and modifications to address more effectively environmental expectations and to capitalize more frequently on environmental opportunities. Unlike the linear model where strategy unfolds gradually, the adaptive model views institutions as living organisms capable of making multiple, simultaneous adjustments in processes, practices, and policies. George Keller (1983) was an early advocate for the adaptive model. Keller stated that the goal of strategy is "not to prod the contemporary university to behave more like a business, but to nudge it to behave more like an organization. Or better, to get it to behave like an organism that must feed itself, change, and adapt to its environment" (p. 174).

Adaptive strategy can make an organization more agile—better able to shift processes and practices to capitalize on changes in the external environment. Organizations that are better able to adapt to their environments are said to have a **competitive advantage** over other organizations in the same field or industry (Day & Schoemaker, 2005; Porter, 1985). Colleges and universities maintain their competitive advantage by constantly scanning the environment, looking for practices to borrow, markets to enter, and new ideas to implement. Thus, the adaptive model of strategy promotes extensive interaction with the external environment and constant recalibration of organizational processes. In the adaptive model, environmental analysis and organizational adaptation are concurrent, rather than sequential processes. Organizations that apply this model are constantly making changes based on new information, rather than waiting for a new planning cycle to commence. Therefore, the time lag inherent in the linear model (i.e., the hiatus between planning and implementation) does not exist in the adaptive conceptualization of strategy.

A key feature of the adaptive model is its ability to help organizational members deal with the complexity of the external environment by reducing uncertainty. Milliken (1990) suggests that there are three types of uncertainty about the external environment, each of which evokes a different kind of

managerial strategy to minimize perceived risks. These types are described in
the following list:

1. **State uncertainty:** perceived uncertainty about the future general state
    of the environment; for example, how turbulent, how competitive
2. **Effect uncertainty:** perceived uncertainty concerning the impact on
    the institution of more specific events; for example, a shift in the po-
    litical party in power in the governor's office
3. **Response uncertainty:** perceived uncertainty with respect to what re-
    sponse options are possible for the organization; that is, what re-
    sources at the organizational level are available and can be marshaled

Organizational leaders tend to take different actions depending on
which uncertainty they wish to address. In the case of state uncertainty, the
approach to risk reduction will often be to try to obtain more information
from the environment. Regular scanning of the environment is one means of
discovering what kinds of information exist and in what form. But tentative
conclusions about future states often do not suggest immediate strategic responses. In fact, such information may produce other forms of uncertainty.
More extensive information about the external environment may reveal new
complexities that cannot be controlled by the organization. Thus, additional
uncertainty reduction strategies are needed. In these cases, envisioning different scenarios and assigning probabilities to them can reduce anxiety about
the future. Organizational members can identify the range of possible events
or outcomes that can occur in the external environment, assign a probability
to each scenario, and then develop multifaceted strategies that can be employed under different conditions. In this way, state uncertainty is reduced,
because organizational members have considered a range of possible environmental conditions, put limits on the range of possibilities (determining, for
example, that some events are much less likely to occur than others), and
developed multiple repertoires that they can employ if different scenarios
come to fruition. Thus, the organization will be prepared for a range of alternative futures and will have anticipated how to respond under different
scenarios.

Leaders addressing effect uncertainty attempt to find appropriate cross-
boundary response strategies that reduce the organization's susceptibility to
perceived environmental determinism. They may engage, for example, in diversification strategies so as to minimize the risk of total failure from having
"all the eggs in one basket." Colleges, for example, may offer a more diverse
curriculum so that shifts in demand by students for one particular area will

not have an overwhelming influence on the college as a whole. This strategy also recognizes the dangers of relying on stable resource relationships that leave organizations vulnerable when a key provider becomes unreliable. A college that depends on a stable set of feeder high schools to supply an adequate enrollment base, for example, may be caught flat-footed if those high schools begin to send their students to other institutions. In contrast, if the college establishes diversified (though dependable) sources of students—for example, through out-of-state recruiting and articulation agreements for community college transfer—then it will be less susceptible to wild fluctuations in enrollment.

When confronted with response uncertainty, leaders who are unsure about response options may adopt a safe approach, borrowing observable, demonstrably successful strategies from other organizations. In this case, organizational leaders adopt a "wait and see" approach. They delay innovative activity until the uncertainty diminishes, wait until other organizations respond to similar circumstances, and then adopt those practices that proved to be successful. This approach, however, is reactive rather than strategic. It does not capitalize on the organization's unique capabilities and environmental opportunities. In contrast, strategy theorists have recommended adaptive approaches that rely on assessments of the organization's distinctive strengths and capacities for change and ongoing development.

SWOT Analysis: Practical Application of the Adaptive Model

George Keller (1983) was among the first to apply the adaptive model to colleges and universities. Keller argued that higher education strategists should identify opportunities and threats in the environment and then consider how the institution's strengths and weaknesses relate to those conditions. This is known as SWOT analysis (SWOT is an acronym for strengths, weaknesses, opportunities, and threats). SWOT analysis encourages organizational leaders to ask questions such as the following: Are the competencies of the organization congruent with conditions in the environment? Does the college have unique strengths in areas of developing need? Do current academic programs fit the needs of the community or region?

Keller's SWOT analysis consists of an internal appraisal and an external appraisal (see Table 7.4). College leaders conducting an internal appraisal assess the institution's traditions, values, and aspirations for the future, as well as current academic and financial strengths and weaknesses. The external appraisal seeks to identify opportunities and threats in the environment through the analysis of social and demographic trends, market preferences, and the activities of competing institutions.

Based on the internal and external appraisals, organizational leaders

TABLE 7.4
Keller's Strategic Analysis Framework

Internal Appraisal	External Appraisal
• Institutional history, traditions, values, and aspirations for the future • Academic and financial strengths and weaknesses • Abilities and priorities of institutional leadership	• Environmental trends: sociocultural and demographic shifts • Market preferences • Activities of competing institutions

Adapted from Keller (1983).

match opportunities found in the environment to organizational strengths (e.g., matching a strength in genetics research to grant opportunities offered by the federal government and private foundations). Hatch (1997) notes that if the appraisals are conducted "in relation to the organization's competitors, the analysis will typically reveal the organization's core competencies—the particular strengths that give the organization its competitive edge in the environment (e.g., outstanding service, product design, brand or organizational image, cost effectiveness, market responsiveness, technical innovation)" (p. 108). **Core competencies** define what the organization does well, perhaps what it does better than any other institution. Michael Porter (1985, 1996), for example, identified three basic strategies that organizations can use to achieve competitive advantage.

1. **Overall cost leadership:** the ability to provide quality at a lower cost than competitors; this tends to be a core competency of community colleges
2. **Differentiation:** the organization provides a distinctive product or service that is of value to potential consumers; many colleges and universities develop core competencies based on differentiation by institutional type (e.g., liberal arts colleges, research universities)
3. **Market focus:** the organization furnishes a specific product or service that addresses the needs of a particular market segment; specialized institutions such as military academies, fine arts conservatories, and religious seminaries claim core competencies in this area

Criticisms of the Adaptive Model

The adaptive model avoids some of the pitfalls of the linear model. Unlike the linear model, the adaptive model fully engages many participants in the development of strategy—not just top-level managers and the relative few whom they consult. Keller (1983) argues that strategy should not be the "personal vision of the president or board of trustees" (p. 141). Moreover, the adaptive model avoids the decision lag inherent in the linear model, where environmental scanning and organizational adaptation are separated temporally by a period of time for planning. Instead, scanning and adapting occur almost simultaneously in the adaptive model.

Critics, however, have raised concerns that the adaptive model does not reflect the messiness and unruliness of organizational strategy (Abrahamson, 2002). Colleges and universities have been described as organized anarchies (Cohen & March, 1974) where decisions are produced by elaborate governance systems that are relatively unguided by anyone in particular. In fact, linkages among problems, solutions, and decision-making opportunities may be random occurrences, rather than intentional strategic activities (Cohen, March, & Olsen, 1972; Weick, 1976). Strategy, in this view, may *evolve* rather than be developed through intentional deliberative processes. It will be the result of political behavior, unplanned experimentation, and after-the-fact sensemaking, which attributes intentions to previous behaviors even if those behaviors were not taken with that specific intention in mind.

The Emergent Model of Strategy

The emergent model reverses the traditional think-act planning cycle found in both the linear and adaptive models. Instead of viewing strategy as a process of gathering together strategists to think about what the next action should be, the emergent model suggests that individuals take actions and *then* reflect on what those actions mean for the organization (Mintzberg, 1994a). Organizational members take actions, assign meaning to those actions, and those meanings may be considered strategic. In this way, strategy emerges from action.

Under the assumptions of the emergent model, the role of the organizational strategist is not to develop specific courses of action based on predictions about the future; instead they seek to identify patterns in the chaos and complexity of organizational life (Cutright, 2001; Peters, 1987). The strategist reviews previous organizational activities, perhaps studying the entire history of the college, and looks for patterns, connections, and common threads that can link together seemingly disparate activities (Hardy et al., 2003). These patterns, once identified, can describe the organization's strategy (Balogun & Johnson, 2005; Carr, Durant, & Downs, 2004).

An institutional team preparing for an accreditation visit, for example, may analyze activities over the previous 10 years and identify an emerging trend toward online learning. This trend may then be explained as a strategic action related to the college's mission of extending access to under-served populations, even though there never was a deliberate, intentional plan to extend access to these populations through online courses. In the emergent model, the meaning and dimensions of strategy become clear when people analyze and interpret prior activities.

In this way, organizational leaders can reinterpret ongoing activities as new solutions to emerging problems. In Leslie and Fretwell's (1996) study of college and university responses to difficult economic conditions, they found that aquaculture and marine science programs at one research university were reinterpreted by organizational leaders as strategic responses to local economic development needs. The academic programs existed *before* the identification of the economic development strategy. In this case, the institution reinterpreted the strategic meaning of programs that it already had in place.

The emergent model, by de-emphasizing the role of centralized planning, enables a broad range of organizational behaviors to inform the institution's strategy. Ideas and innovations can percolate up from the grassroots of the organization and become recognized as an important part of the overall strategy. As Mintzberg (1994b) noted, strategies can "grow like weeds in a garden" (p. 287). They can spring up anywhere in the organization. In the emergent model, the role of organizational leaders is to "recognize the initiatives already being undertaken by many units, to support them, and to seed strategic efforts elsewhere through selective and gentle persuasion" (Rhoades, 2000, p. 60).

This is not to suggest that strategy development is an "anything goes" process or that the organization's strategy is simply the compilation of multiple localized strategies. Not every localized action is interpreted as strategic. Grassroots activities need to be recognized at the organizational level before they can become part of the institution's strategy. The innovative activity of a single department, for example, may be identified as part of a larger pattern or trend within the institution. A chemistry department, for instance, may tout in its annual report an emphasis on involving undergraduate students in faculty research projects. Other department chairs may then read the report and note examples of similar undergraduate research initiatives in their own units. After meeting with these department chairs, an academic dean may recognize that undergraduate research is an emerging trend in the college's programs and perhaps even connect that trend to data that show that students in the college achieve high acceptance rates when they apply to graduate schools. Thus, undergraduate involvement in research becomes identified—perhaps eventually by all faculty and administrators—as an important strategy for promoting student success. In this case, the chemistry department's actions became linked to a collective activity that pervades the behavior of the entire organization (Mintzberg, 1994b).

The emergent model emphasizes the creativity and innovative thinking of organizational members. Rather than viewing strategy as a sequential, machine-like process, or as an ongoing effort to align the organization with an unpredictable environment, the emergent model focuses on human agency and the ability of organizational members to shape their futures. As Peterson (1997) notes, while the future may not be predictable, it is malleable. Organizational members can shape new alternative futures through experimentation and consistent effort toward long-term commitments.

But how do colleges and universities identify their shared commitments? And how do organizations sort out multiple competing patterns that vie for designation as organizational strategy? Consider the college that identified undergraduate research as a key strategy. Perhaps this was at the expense of devoting more attention and resources toward developmental coursework and academic skill building for underprepared students. What explains why one pattern was recognized as strategic while an equally viable pattern was denied such recognition? The emergent model does not provide answers to these questions. It does not address the cultural and political factors that affect strategy development. These factors are examined in the next two strategy models discussed in this chapter—the symbolic and postmodern approaches.

The Symbolic Model of Strategy

Strategy can be viewed as an important symbol that represents the organization's culture (Hardy, Palmer, & Phillips, 2000). The values, beliefs, and assumptions collectively held by organizational members can have a significant effect on the types of strategy that emerge (Hatch & Schultz, 2003; Melewar, Karaosmanoglu, & Paterson, 2005). Values that favor social justice and equity may support an open enrollment strategy of a community college. Beliefs in the efficacy of community-based learning may shape a college's pedagogical strategy. Assumptions about appropriate forms of research are likely to guide a university's academic strategy. In contrast, a strategy that ignores important aspects of the institution's culture is likely to fail (Chaffee & Jacobson, 1997; Rhoades, 2000). An academic strategy that favors interdisciplinary courses and community-based research is unlikely to succeed if disciplinary ties are strong and faculty members express preferences for more traditional forms of scholarship. If faculty members assume that teaching should be organized according to the conventions of academic disciplines and believe that the best science occurs in the laboratory rather than in community settings, then even large amounts of resources may not ensure the success of this strategy. Thus, strategies need to be consistent with the culture of the organization (Kezar & Eckel, 2002).

In addition, the strategy development process can help organizational members come to understand more thoroughly the culture of the organization in which they work. Strategy development can be viewed as a learning process through which organizational members begin to focus attention on what they collectively view as important (Weick, 1995). Tierney (1992), for example, emphasizes the importance of dialogue and the need to convene institutional conversations on mission and purpose. Through these conversations, participants can identify shared commitments that guide their work together as a community (Dee, 2006). These commitments ensure that behaviors across the organization are aligned with systemic interdependencies rather than idiosyncratic preferences. If, for example, faculty members identify a shared commitment toward improving access for low-income students, then individual academic departments will likely take income level into consideration when making admissions decisions. The shared commitment reflects the values of a professional community and guides the behavior of the members of that community. Shared commitments can be recognized as organizational strategies, when people become aware of the impact that these commitments have on their behavior.

The symbolic model of strategy "is based on a social contract, instead of an organismic or biological view of the organization" (Chaffee, 1985, p. 93). Rather than engage in constant adjustments to an external environment (as in the adaptive model), organizational members construct a social contract, consisting of their shared commitments. Cutright (2001) refers to this process as the distillation of the institution's key values and purposes. Once these shared commitments and values have been identified, they "allow the actors within the system to make decisions consistent with the organization's collective identity, purposes, and goals, and to make decisions about the deployment of finite resources" (p. 63). Gioia and Thomas (1996), for example, found that a university's shared commitment to becoming a "top ten" research university strongly guided strategic decision making in that institution. The top ten image served as an important symbol that influenced how institutional leaders perceived key issues—both internal and external to the university. Thus, rather than having internal and external appraisals shape the strategy (as in the adaptive model), the organization's strategy shaped how leaders viewed both the organization and its environment.

The symbolic model suggests that when strategies are developed in ways that are consistent with the culture of the organization, they are more likely to be successful. However, what are the implications of developing strategy in an organization that has an oppressive culture, where diversity is suppressed and alternative viewpoints are minimized? Do we want strategies to be effective if they represent oppressive value systems? Simply developing strategies that are consistent with an organization's culture is no guarantee that colleges and universities will promote equitable outcomes and just treatment for all. These issues are examined in the postmodern perspective on strategy.

Postmodern Models of Strategy

Postmodern theorists view all models of strategy with some degree of skepticism (Deetz, 1992), largely because of their epistemological assumptions and distrust of rationalist models that claim that the past is or can be a reliable predictor of the future. Many postmodernists view statements of strategy as a metanarrative that falsely asserts a commensurability among the organizational elements that are used to guide and plan for the organization (Lyotard, 1979/1984).

In addition, postmodernists note that organizational strategies largely reflect the desires of top management, frequently to the neglect of other organizational constituents; in fact, this is an explicit component of the linear model. Thus, organizational strategies may merely reproduce conditions that favor the status quo. (This perspective assumes, of course, that top management would be unlikely to engage in strategies that run counter to their prevailing view of the organization.) The result often is a hierarchical, stratified organization where top management determines strategies that are implemented by lower level employees.

Postmodern theorists raise important questions regarding the formation of strategies (Bloland, 2005; Gordon & Grant, 2005; Grandy & Mills, 2004). Who participates in their creation? Whose interpretation of the environment guides decision making? Are there ways for dissenting voices to inform strategy development? The determination of organizational strategy, postmodernists argue, is not a neutral, objective assessment based on clear criteria. Postmodern theorists indicate the need for surfacing institutional values and raising questions regarding whom those values privilege.

Some leaders have responded to these critiques by including lower level employees in the strategy development process. But postmodernists suggest that participation from lower level employees is hardly on equal footing with that of the top managers. The voices of lower level employees may be acknowledged only when they echo those of top management. Lower level employees may contribute new ideas to improve implementation, but seldom do they have much power in setting the general course—the strategy—of the organization.

How can strategy development become inclusive of multiple voices, even those that offer dissenting opinions? Postmodern theorists emphasize the need to conceptualize diversity as an important value in institutional strategy making. The type of diversity that postmodernists refer to is not the diversity of representation (e.g., having a certain number of faculty of color on the planning committee or enrolling a target number of students of color) or the diversity of locating similarities across differences (e.g., promoting unity or celebrating community). Instead, postmodernists emphasize the differences, conflict, and tension inherent in diverse societies. Tierney (1992), for example, argued for the creation of decision-making systems that allow differences "to be visible and viable" (p. 17). Providing venues for faculty, staff, and administrators to express their differences may be a critical step toward having organizational strategy informed by a wider variety of perspectives. The goal of such venues is not to choose the most valid or best perspective among competing options; this would only inflame tensions among diverse interests. Nor is the goal to arrive at a compromise that partially satisfies the competing parties. Compromise aims for a lowest common denominator of agreement, which may not withstand the turbulence brought on by future conflict. Instead, higher education leaders can aim for an integration of diverse perspectives, in which "the desires of all sides have been met and skillfully combined" (Cutright, 2001, pp. 65–66). Rather than forcing a choice between options, this integrative approach weaves together insights from multiple standpoints.

Estela Bensimon's (2004) Diversity Scorecard Project offers an example of how diverse perspectives can inform new strategies for promoting access and equity. Each institution participating in the project was required to form a team of administrators, institutional researchers, and faculty to examine data related to student performance. Results were disaggregated for different racial and ethnic groups. On some campuses, the data analyses were superficial, and participants looked for quick solutions or claimed that more data were needed before any action could be taken. But on other campuses, conflicting perspectives were expressed, assumptions about students of color were opened for discussion, and integrative solutions were constructed. At one campus, for example, some participants noted that Latino students had the highest graduation rate among any student group in the college, but other team members challenged that view with data that showed Latino students earning lower GPAs and majoring in fields that tended to result in lower paying jobs. As a result of these difficult conversations, the team members felt empowered to become change agents and take action to address inequitable educational outcomes.

Curriculum as Strategy: Application of the Five Models

To this point, we have reviewed five models of organizational strategy; two from the positivist perspective (linear and adaptive), two from the social constructionist perspective (emergent and symbolic), and the last using a postmodern conceptualization. In this section, we employ each of these models in an analysis of a key strategic issue in colleges and universities—the curriculum—and present a contingency framework that leaders can use to make decisions regarding when to use each of the strategy models.

Kushner (1999) argued that a college's curriculum can be viewed as an indicator of the strategic direction of the institution. Curriculum is strategic, because it affects nearly every policy area within a college or university, including decisions about internal structure (e.g., how academic departments will be organized, how faculty positions will be allocated) and decisions about external relations (e.g., how programs will be marketed, which students will be recruited). Curricular choices, in fact, may be viewed as efforts to align internal structures and preferences with external markets. The decision to create a criminal justice program, for example, may reflect both faculty research interests in criminology as well as growing student interest in careers in this field. Faculty and administrators are likely to conduct, formally or informally, an assessment of both internal capabilities and external demand prior to creating the new program. Once the program has been implemented, subsequent decisions regarding internal resource allocation, marketing, and recruitment will need to be realigned to reflect the new curricular strategy; thus, following the rationality inherent in the linear model.

Curricular decisions may also reflect the adaptive model's emphasis on continuous environmental scanning and ongoing organizational change. In this model, strategy formation is not bound by a particular time frame or formal process such as a five-year strategic plan. Instead, the organization is constantly responding to its environment and engaging in a multitude of strategic actions. A quick scan of an institution's Web site, for example, may reveal a range of new online programs, corporate training initiatives, and professional development workshops. Decisions to create these offerings may have been made quickly—almost reflexively—at an institution that excels at responding to external markets. This spontaneous, adaptive process may be necessary when institutions seek to shape curricula in ways that differ from tradition (Kushner, 1999).

But curriculum also embodies strategy as an emergent phenomenon, which reflects the institution's unique history, culture, and market niche (Chaffee & Tierney, 1988; Mintzberg, 1988). The curricular strategies of liberal arts colleges—small classes with interactive pedagogies that focus on general knowledge rather than practical techniques—are a reflection of their historical evolution and the values of arts and sciences faculty. Kushner (1999) found that when liberal arts colleges began to add more practically focused programs such as business, they tended to construct those programs in ways that were consistent with their current academic strategy. Rather than engage in a deliberate process to reshape strategy, the extant traditions and values of the college shaped the strategy that emerged. The business programs were viewed not as professional programs per se; instead, faculty and staff characterized the programs as consistent with the liberal arts educational tradition.

Both adaptive and emergent strategies can be viewed in the curricula of community colleges, which have long emphasized both transfer-oriented academic programs and professional degrees that lead directly to employment. The relative emphasis on transfer or professional programs often reflects the history of the college, the market being served, and the preferences and interests of the faculty. A community college located in an industrial area may be more likely to develop technical programs and hire faculty in professional fields such as engineering. A community college founded near large urban high schools, however, may emphasize the transfer function and hire liberal arts faculty who continue to make decisions that reinforce the primacy of transfer-oriented curricula. Thus, historical and market forces over time shape the strategy of the college. However, community college administrators have also engaged in planned, deliberate strategies to capitalize on emerging educational markets, such as corporate training and community education courses. The overall strategy of a community college may, therefore, be understood both retrospectively through an analysis of historical trends, as well as through an examination of forward-looking plans for future growth and development.

In addition to reflecting elements of both the adaptive and emergent forms of strategy, curriculum also serves as an important strategic symbol for the institution. The curriculum carries symbolic importance for defining the institution's identity, as well as for forming the contours of the external image that it projects to the outside world. For example, the public knows what a liberal arts college stands for based on the curricular image that is projected by these institutions. Internally, that image shapes how students and faculty think about their roles within those institutions (Gioia & Thomas, 1996). The liberal arts image, for example, can shape student and faculty identities. Faculty may proudly proclaim that they work at a liberal arts institution; the liberal arts image shapes a faculty member's own professional identity. Similarly, a student may be proud to identify herself as a community college transfer student, if community colleges have a positive image in her state; or she may be hesitant to identify herself as a transfer student if those institutions have a poor public image. Curriculum, therefore, presents an important symbolic image of the organization, which shapes public perceptions and affects internal identifications and behaviors.

Finally, from a postmodern perspective, curriculum represents an arena for conflict and contest regarding the strategic direction of the institution. So-called curriculum wars over what constitutes the literary canon, for example, reflect ongoing debates and tensions within the academy. The development of ethnic and gender studies programs can be viewed as curricular responses to the diversity of perspectives found in the postmodern era. These types of curricular decisions are likely to have significant strategic impacts on a range of institutional functions, including faculty hiring practices and student recruitment emphases, which in turn may lead to greater openness and empowerment, or toward reinforcement of existing power differences. Consider, for example, two community colleges. One college focuses its composition courses almost exclusively on appropriate grammar and syntax. Another college reforms its composition curriculum to accommodate the needs of English language learners. The first college reinforces barriers that may limit college success for recent immigrants, while the second college strives for greater openness and access for traditionally less powerful groups. The postmodern perspective emphasizes the role of power differences in shaping the strategy for the institution. Extensive policy changes may be necessary to disrupt strategies that favor existing power disparities.

Heuristics for Choosing a Model of Strategy

Following systems theory, we argue that the choice of an appropriate strategy model should consider conditions in the external environment. Positivists and social constructionists would likely disagree on whether the organization's environment consists of measurable phenomena or is enacted through the perceptions and interpretations of organizational members. However, regardless of whether the environment is understood as an objective or subjective phenomenon, organizational members' understandings of the environment should guide the selection of strategy models. When a strategy model is well suited to environmental conditions, it is likely to contribute to overall organizational effectiveness (Donaldson, 2001; Nadler & Tushman, 1988).

To characterize the external environment, we consider two variables that are likely to explain a great deal of variation in the environments in which colleges and universities operate: environmental determinism and perceived organizational choice. The first variable is the extent to which the organization is controlled by the external environment. Organizations in the "high determinism" category experience significant external control through, for example, government regulation or an excessive dependence on a limited number of resource suppliers. A public university, for example, may have many of its policies mandated by a state board of higher education and may depend on a limited geographic area for its student enrollments. Such a university operates in a highly deterministic environment. In contrast, other institutions have few external constraints. Colleges and universities in the "low determinism" category are relatively free from pressures to conform to external expectations.

The second variable relates to the extent to which organizational members perceive that they have choices regarding how to respond to the external environment. This variable relates to the agency of organizational members. To what extent do they believe that they are able and capable of charting their own course for the future? To what extent do they believe that factors beyond their control determine the fate of the organization? In the first instance, the organization is characterized by "high perceived choice" (i.e., a high level of agency). In the second instance, organizational members would report "low perceived choice" (i.e., a low level of agency).

By juxtaposing determinism and perceived choice, we can identify four distinctive organization-environment relationships. In Table 7.5, the alternative models of organization-environment relationships are matched with what would appear to be appropriate models of organizational strategy.

The linear model of strategy would be appropriate when the organization is largely externally controlled and has little perceived choice in terms of how it responds (quadrant four). The alignment of structure and strategy—a key principle of the linear model—would appear rational to external actors and would likely address their expectations for efficient allocation of resources to mission-related topics (e.g., a state board of higher education expecting a community college to have a rational plan for allocating resources to programs that are most central to its mission).

The adaptive model would be appropriate when the organization is highly dependent on the environment but also perceives that it has choice (agency) regarding how to respond (quadrant two). The adaptive model would allow the organization to be highly responsive to external expectations

TABLE 7.5
Organizational-Environment Conditions and Strategy Models

		Environmental Determinism (degree of control environment has over organization)	
		Low Determinism	High Determinism
Perceived Strategic Choice (organization's perceived degree of freedom to control environment)	Perceived High Choice	*Quadrant One* Emergent and symbolic models of strategy	*Quadrant Two* Adaptive model of strategy
	Perceived Low Choice	*Quadrant Three* Nonstrategy (Consider the postmodern model as well as attempt to promote organizational learning)	*Quadrant Four* Linear model of strategy

Adapted from Hrebiniak and Joyce (1985); Carlson (1965); and Daft and Weick (1984).

and would adjust to changing needs on an ongoing basis, based on information gathered by boundary-spanning personnel. Unlike the linear model, however, organizational strategists would have significant choice regarding the specific responses that they develop. In other words, the organization would be responsive to external expectations, but organizational leaders would have the flexibility to develop their own unique responses (in contrast to formal policy mandates from an external authority, which diminish levels of perceived choice).

Both the emergent and symbolic models would be appropriate when the organization is less externally controlled and when leaders perceive that they have choices (agency) regarding the strategic options that they can pursue (quadrant one). Under these conditions, the organization can actually enact its own environment (Weick, 1979) and develop creative, innovative strategies that reflect the shared values and commitments of organizational members. Strategy in this case is focused more strongly on internal dimensions of the organization, such as sensemaking (emergent model) and culture (symbolic model).

The low determinism, low perceived choice quadrant (number three) does not encourage strategic organizational behavior. Under these conditions, changes occur through random transformation or by chance. There is no active effort to determine an overall direction for the institution. The organization is not significantly externally controlled, yet organizational members believe that they have low levels of choice. Why is that the case?

Are sunk costs and preferences for the status quo preventing the organization from taking a more strategic posture? By definition, the members of this organization presently feel that they have no agency—no energy to drive change. In this case, the organization is moribund and probably powerless. How could organizational leaders reverse these conditions?

One approach would be to engage the organization in a series of activities and processes that promote organizational learning. In the previous chapter, we defined organizational learning as an interactive process that creates and recreates a shared knowledge base that guides behavior and shapes meaning and experience. Processes associated with organizational learning—such as organization-wide self-studies and environmental scanning—may help organizational members identify their shared values and collective competencies. Such knowledge may imbue them (and their stakeholders) with a sense that they can, in fact, be proactive and make a valuable contribution to setting the future direction of the organization. We also suggest that leaders can consider the implications of the postmodern critique of organizational strategy and critically examine the basic assumptions of their organization. Following postmodern perspectives, leaders could attempt to have more diverse perspectives inform strategy development and perhaps even encourage the expression of conflict and dissent.

Summary

No omnibus conceptualization of strategy fits the complexity and nuances of the problems facing colleges and universities. A naïve view of strategy suggests that it is possible, indeed imperative, to set goals, identify the means to achieve them, establish timetables, monitor progress, and utilize feedback. This conceptualization assumes that the issues in contemporary college and university organizational life can be apprehended through rationality and logic and that, from the conclusions of this appraisal, the future can be predicted and planned for with some certainty. The view of some researchers mirrors this perspective. But a widely held contrary perspective is that strategy can only be viewed retrospectively—constituting a record of how the organization responded historically and especially over the recent past to various environmental stimuli. This is not to suggest that "muddling through" will always be successful. Indeed, it indicates that a contingency model needs to be adopted, as this will permit strategic responses that properly match environmental circumstances.

Some other summary observations can be made:

1. We can look at organizations and characterize their relationships to their environments in terms of strategy.

2. Most organizations have relationships with other organizations. One way of thinking about other organizations is to divide them into input and output sets. As Evan notes, each one must be dealt with somewhat differently.
3. Boundary spanners are most effective when there are matches between the characteristics of the external environment and the skills of the boundary personnel.
4. Who does the environmental scanning can distort the appraisal of the environment, as power seekers may pretend to see the environment in ways that increase or reinforce their power.

Review Questions

1. Based on Evan's organizational set theory, which of the following organizations would have the greatest need for highly differentiated boundary-spanning personnel?
    a. A small religious seminary
    b. A large technical institute serving the specific fields of engineering and health sciences
    c. A comprehensive state university that serves a wide range of student ability levels and prepares students for a variety of careers
    d. A military academy

2. The linear strategy model promotes efficient organizational outcomes because it:
    a. Aligns organizational structures and actions with espoused organizational goals
    b. Allows lower level personnel to play the primary role in strategy development
    c. Is consistent with the loosely coupled structure of most colleges and universities
    d. Assumes that the environment is predictable and stable

3. Based on a new state law, leaders at a public university know that the institution will not be permitted to offer remedial/developmental courses next year (only community colleges will be allowed to do so). But university leaders are not certain how they will go about serving their academically underprepared students. What type of uncertainty is the university experiencing, and what strategic actions may be necessary to address this uncertainty?

    a. Collect more information to deal with state uncertainty

    b. Diversify the resource base to address effect uncertainty

    c. Borrow successful strategies from other institutions in order to address response uncertainty

4. Which of the following is *not* a component of the adaptive strategy model?

    a. Internal and external appraisals occur on an ongoing basis

    b. The organization's core competencies are identified

    c. Seeks a fit between environmental opportunities and organizational strengths

    d. Enables the institution to become the overall cost leader in its market

5. Which of the following is *not* a component of the emergent strategy model?

    a. Studying the history and culture of the college

    b. Reflecting on previous organizational activities and identifying patterns and connections across those activities

    c. Focusing on ideas and innovations at the grassroots level of the organization

    d. Aligning college structures and programs with the mission statement

6. According to the symbolic model, strategy is:

    a. A social contract among organizational members

    b. A distillation of the college's values and purposes

    c. A motivating image for the future

    d. All of the above

7. Which of the following colleges can be said to have utilized a postmodern approach to strategy?

    a. The college has strong consensus around a set of clear goals and allocates resources accordingly

    b. The college's strategic-planning committee has an exceptionally diverse membership, all of whom share a strong value for liberal education

    c. The college has created venues for conflict and dissent to be voiced in order to seek new, integrative solutions

    d. The college values compromise and seeks to avoid conflict

8. A state college is subject to extensive external regulation, and, given limited resources and high levels of staff and faculty turnover, the college

leadership believes that it has few choices regarding how to respond to its environment. Which strategy model would be most appropriate for this institution?

a. Linear
b. Adaptive
c. Emergent and/or symbolic
d. Postmodern

9. A public university in another state is subject to a similar degree of external regulation, but it has an energetic leadership team that believes that it can make effective choices regarding how to guide the university through turbulent times. Which strategy model would be most appropriate for this institution?

a. Linear
b. Adaptive
c. Emergent and/or symbolic
d. Postmodern

Case Discussion Questions

Consider the Heartland State University case presented at the beginning of this chapter.

1. How did the external pressures of the 1990s lead to a linear model of strategy at Heartland State? What elements of linear strategy were evident in the planning document that Heartland State produced in response to those external pressures?

2. The graduate student researchers did not find much activity on campus that related to the original strategic plan. Why not? How might the limitations of linear strategy explain this lack of activity?

3. In anticipation of a negative accreditation report, the academic vice president instituted a second wave of strategic planning. How did this version of strategy differ from the first wave? To what extent were this vice president's ideas about strategy consistent with the adaptive model?

4. Following an exhausting six-month assessment push, almost by accident, university leaders identified "science for society" as a key strategy in undergraduate education. To what extent can this process be characterized as emergent strategy?

5. Consider the symbolic power of strategy at three points in the case: (a) the president in the 1980s telling senior administrators that the

university's strategy was to not have a plan, (b) the associate dean keeping the original strategic planning document on a shelf near his desk, and (c) the validation that the department chair felt when the university's undergraduate curriculum was viewed favorably by the accreditation agency. What values regarding strategy were communicated in each of these three instances?

6. Would postmodern theorists be concerned about the commonality and consistency that the institutional research director noted regarding the thinking of so many academic leaders on campus? If so, why?

References

Abrahamson, E. (2002). Disorganization theory and disorganizational behavior: Toward an etiology of messes. *Research in Organizational Behavior, 24,* 139–180.

Alfred, R. (2001). Strategic thinking: The untapped resource for leaders. *Community College Journal, 71*(3), 24–28.

Alfred, R. (2005). *Managing the big picture in colleges and universities: From tactics to strategy.* Westport, CT: Praeger.

Ansoff, H. I., & Sullivan, P. A. (1991). Strategic responses to environmental turbulence. In R. H. Kilmann, I. Kilmann, & Associates (Eds.), *Making organizations competitive: Enhancing networks and relationships across traditional boundaries.* San Francisco: Jossey-Bass.

Balogun, J., & Johnson, G. (2005). From intended strategies to unintended outcomes: The impact of change recipient sensemaking. *Organization Studies, 26*(11), 1573–1601.

Bensimon, E. (2004). The diversity scorecard: A learning approach to institutional change. *Change, 36*(1), 45–52.

Bloland, H. (2005). Whatever happened to postmodernism in higher education?: No requiem in the new millennium. *Journal of Higher Education, 76*(2), 121–150.

Bormann, E. (1996). Symbolic convergence theory and communication in group decision making. In R. Hirokawa & M. S. Poole (Eds.), *Communication and group decision making* (2nd ed., pp. 81–113). Thousand Oaks, CA: Sage.

Carlson, O. (1965). *Adoption of educational innovations.* Eugene: Center for the Advanced Study of Educational Administration, University of Oregon.

Carr, A., Durant, R., & Downs, A. (2004). Emergent strategy development, abduction, and pragmatism: New lessons for corporations. *Human Systems Management, 23*(2), 79–91.

Chaffee, E. (1985). Three models of strategy. *Academy of Management Review, 10*(1), 89–98.

Chaffee, E., & Jacobson, S. (1997). Creating and changing institutional cultures. In M. Peterson, D. Dill, & L. Mets (Eds.), *Planning and management for a changing environment: A handbook on redesigning postsecondary institutions* (pp. 230–245). San Francisco: Jossey-Bass.

Chaffee, E., & Tierney, W. (1988). *Collegiate culture and leadership strategies.* New York: Macmillan.

Chandler, A. (1962). *Strategy and structure: Chapters in the history of the American industrial enterprise.* Cambridge, MA: MIT Press.

Cohen, M., & March, J. (1974). *Leadership and ambiguity: The American college president.* Boston: Harvard Business School Press.

Cohen, M., March, J., & Olsen, J. (1972). A garbage can model of organizational choice. *Administrative Science Quarterly, 17*(1), 1–25.

Cragan, J., & Shields, D. (1992). The use of symbolic convergence theory in corporate strategic planning: A case study. *Journal of Applied Communication Research, 20,* 199–218.

Cutright, M. (Ed.). (2001). *Chaos theory and higher education: Leadership, planning, and policy.* New York: Peter Lang Publishing.

Daft, R. L., & Weick, K. E. (1984). Toward a model of organizations as interpretation systems. *Academy of Management Review, 9*(2), 284–295.

Day, G., & Schoemaker, P. (2005). Scanning the periphery. *Harvard Business Review, 83*(11), 135–148.

Dee, J. (2006). Institutional autonomy and state-level accountability: Loosely-coupled governance and the public good. In W. Tierney (Ed.), *Governance and the public good* (pp. 135–155). Albany: State University of New York Press.

Deetz, S. (1992). *Democracy in an age of corporate colonization: Developments in communication and the politics of everyday life.* Albany: State University of New York Press.

Del Favero, M. (2003). Faculty-administrator relationships as integral to high performing governance systems: New frameworks for study. *American Behavioral Scientist, 46*(6), 901–922.

Donaldson, L. (2000). Design structure to fit strategy. In E. Locke (Ed.), *Blackwell handbook of principles of organizational behavior* (pp. 291–303). Oxford, England: Blackwell Publishers.

Donaldson, L. (2001). *The contingency theory of organizations.* Thousand Oaks, CA: Sage Publications.

Evan, W. (1972). An organization-set model of interorganizational relations. In M. F. Tuite, M. Radnor, & R. K. Chisholm (Eds.), *Interorganizational decision making* (pp. 181–200). Chicago: Aldine-Atherton Publishing.

Gioia, D., & Thomas, J. (1996). Identity, image, and issue interpretation: Sensemaking during strategic change in academia. *Administrative Science Quarterly, 41*(3), 370–403.

Gordon, R., & Grant, D. (2005). Knowledge management or management of knowledge? Why people interested in knowledge management need to consider Foucault and the construct of power. *TAMARA: Journal of Critical Postmodern Organization Science, 3*(2), 27–38.

Grandy, G., & Mills, A. (2004). Strategy as simulacra? A radical reflexive look at the discipline and practice of strategy. *Journal of Management Studies, 41*(7), 1153–1170.

Hardy, C., Langley, A., Mintzberg, H., & Rose, J. (2003). Strategy formation in the university setting. In J. L. Bess (Ed.), *College and university organization: Insights from the behavioral sciences* (pp. 169–210). Amherst, MA: I & I Occasional Press.

Hardy, C., Palmer, I., & Phillips, N. (2000). Discourse as a strategic resource. *Human Relations, 53*(9), 1227–1248.

Hatch, M. (1997). *Organization theory: Modern, symbolic, and postmodern perspectives.* New York: Oxford University Press.

Hatch, M., & Schultz, M. (2003). Bringing the corporation into corporate branding. *European Journal of Marketing, 37*(7–8), 1041–1064.

Hitt, M. A., Ireland, R. D., & Hoskisson, R. E. (2001). *Strategic management, competitiveness and globalization* (4th ed.). Cincinnati, OH: South-Western College Publishing.

Hitt, M. A., Ireland. R. D., & Middlemist, R. D. (2005). *Organizational behavior.* Hoboken, NJ: Wiley.

Hrebiniak, L. G., & Joyce, W. F. (1985). Organizational adaptation: Strategic choice and environmental determinism. *Administrative Science Quarterly, 30,* 336–349.

Jarzabkowski, P. (2005). *Strategy as practice: An activity-based approach.* Thousand Oaks, CA: Sage.

Keller, G. (1983). *Academic strategy: The management revolution in higher education.* Baltimore: Johns Hopkins University Press.

Kezar, A. (2004). What is more important to effective governance: Relationships, trust, and leadership, or structures and formal processes? In W. Tierney & V. Lechuga (Eds.), *Restructuring shared governance in higher education: New directions for higher education* (No. 127, pp. 35–46). San Francisco: Jossey-Bass.

Kezar, A., & Eckel, P. (2002). The effects of institutional culture on change strategies in higher education: Universal principles or culturally responsive concepts. *Journal of Higher Education, 73*(4), 443–460.

Kushner, R. (1999). Curriculum as strategy: The scope and organization of business education in liberal arts colleges. *Journal of Higher Education, 70*(4), 413–440.

Leslie, D., & Fretwell, E. (1996). *Wise moves in hard times: Creating and managing resilient colleges and universities.* San Francisco: Jossey-Bass.

Low, M. B., & Abrahamson, E. (1992, August). *Movements, bandwagons, and ventures: Density dependence and the entrepreneurial process.* Paper presented at the annual meeting of the Academy of Management, Las Vegas, NV.

Lyotard, J.-F. (1979/1984). *The postmodern condition: A report on knowledge* (G. Bennington & B. Massumi, Trans.). In W. Godzich & J. Schulte-Sasse (Series Eds.), *Theory and history of literature, Vol. 10.* Minneapolis: University of Minnesota Press.

Martin, R., Manning, K., & Ramaley, J. (2001). The self-study as a chariot for strategic change. In J. Ratcliff, E. Lubinescu, & M. Gaffney (Eds.), *How accreditation influences assessment: New directions for higher education* (No. 113, pp. 95–115). San Francisco: Jossey-Bass.

Melewar, T., Karaosmanoglu, E., & Paterson, D. (2005). Corporate identity: Concept, components, and contribution. *Journal of General Management, 31*(1), 59–81.

Middlemist, R. D., & Hitt, M. A. (1988). *Organizational behavior: Managerial strategies for performance.* St. Paul, MN: West Publishing Company.

Milliken, F. J. (1990). Perceiving and interpreting environmental change: An examination of college administrators' interpretation of changing demographics. *Academy of Management Journal, 33*(1), 42–63.

Mintzberg, H. (1979). *The structuring of organizations.* Englewood Cliffs, NJ: Prentice-Hall.

Mintzberg, H. (1983). *Power in and around organizations.* Englewood Cliffs, NJ: Prentice-Hall.

Mintzberg, H. (1988). Opening up the definition of strategy. In J. Quinn, H. Mintzberg, & R. James (Eds.), *The strategy process: Concepts, contexts, and cases.* Englewood Cliffs, NJ: Prentice-Hall.

Mintzberg, H. (1994a). The fall and rise of strategic planning. *Harvard Business Review, 72*(1), 107–114.

Mintzberg, H. (1994b). *The rise and fall of strategic planning: Preconceiving roles for planning, plans, and planners.* New York: Free Press.

Mintzberg, H., Ahlstrand, B., & Lampel, J. (1998). *Strategy safari: A guided tour through the wilds of strategic management.* New York: The Free Press.

Mintzberg, H., & Waters, J. A. (1985). Of strategies, deliberate and emergent. *Strategic Management Journal, 6*(3), 257–272.

Mitroff, I. (1983). *Stakeholders of the organizational mind.* San Francisco: Jossey-Bass.

Mumby, D. (1988). *Communication and power in organizations: Discourse, ideology, and domination.* Norwood, NJ: Ablex.

Nadler, D. A., & Tushman, M. L. (1988). *Strategic organizational design: Concepts, tools, and processes.* New York: Harper Collins.

Peters, T. J. (1987). *Thriving on chaos: Handbook for a management revolution.* New York: Knopf.

Peterson, M. (1997). Using contextual planning to transform institutions. In M. Peterson, D. Dill, & L. Mets (Eds.), *Planning and management for a changing environment: A handbook on redesigning postsecondary institutions* (pp. 127–157). San Francisco: Jossey-Bass.

Pettigrew, A., Thomas, H., & Whittington, R. (2002). Strategic management: The strengths and limitations of a field. In A. Pettigrew, H. Thomas, & R. Whittington (Eds.), *Handbook of strategy and management* (pp. 3–30). Thousand Oaks, CA: Sage Publications.

Porter, M. E. (1985). *Competitive advantage: Creating and sustaining superior performance.* New York: Free Press.

Porter, M. E. (1996). What is strategy? *Harvard Business Review, 74*(6), 43–59.

Presley, J. B., & Leslie, D. W. (1999). Understanding strategy: An assessment of theory and practice. In J. C. Smart (Ed.), *Higher education: Handbook of theory and research, vol. XIV* (pp. 201–239). New York: Agathon Press.

Rhoades, G. (2000). Who's doing it right? Strategic activity in public research universities. *Review of Higher Education, 24*(1), 41–66.

Rosovsky, H. (1990). *The university: An owner's manual.* New York: W. W. Norton.

Schuster, J., Smith, D., Corak, K., & Yamada, M. (1994). *Strategic academic governance: How to make big decisions better.* Phoenix, AZ.: Oryx.

Tierney, W. (1992). Cultural leadership and the search for community. *Liberal Education, 78*(5), 16–21.

Weick, K. (1976). Educational organizations as loosely coupled systems. *Administrative Science Quarterly, 21,* 1–19.

Weick, K. (1979). *The social psychology of organizing* (2nd ed.). Reading, MA: Addison-Wesley.

Weick, K. (1995). *Sensemaking in organizations.* Thousand Oaks, CA: Sage.

Welsh, J., & Nunez, W. (2005). Faculty and administrative support for strategic planning: A comparison of two- and four-year institutions. *Community College Review, 32*(4), 20–39.

8

ORGANIZATIONAL GOALS, EFFECTIVENESS, AND EFFICIENCY

CONTENTS

Preview	751
Case Context	752
Introduction	755
Conceptualizations of Effectiveness and Efficiency	755
Model 1: The Goal Model	758
Model 2: The System Resource Model	764
Model 3: The Internal Process Model	765
Model 4: Strategic Constituencies Model	766
Model 5: Phase Models	767
Model 6: Fit Models	767
Model 7: Competing Values Model	770
Model 8: Quality Model	772
Model 9: Other Models of Effectiveness	772
The Social Construction Model of Organizational Effectiveness	774
Postmodern Perspectives on Effectiveness	777
Organizational Efficiency	779
Summary	781
Review Questions	781
Case Discussion Questions	783
References	784

The authors are most grateful for the critical comments on an early draft of this chapter by Barbara Sporn, Vienna University. The final version, of course, is our own and may or may not reflect the perspective of the reviewer.

Preview

- Effectiveness and efficiency are highly salient in the changing world of increased accountability in higher education.
- Both effectiveness and efficiency are complex concepts that must be unpacked to discover the variety of their meanings.
- There are many models of effectiveness, not all of which are necessarily consistent with one another.
- The goal model of effectiveness is the most common one in institutions of higher education, partly because of its intuitive sensibility, especially when goals are or can be made clear and unambiguous.
- From a political perspective, goals are the negotiated creations of organizational coalitions.
- Goals can legitimize the organization both to internal groups and external constituencies.
- From a system resource perspective, an organization can be said to be effective if it continues to attract sufficient resources over a long period of time.
- An organization can also be said to be effective if its internal state is in equilibrium, especially if human resources are disposed to be cooperative.
- Organizations may be considered effective if their external stakeholders are satisfied.
- Effectiveness criteria differ as organizations go through different life cycle changes.
- If all of the components of an organization fit well together, the organization can be said to be effective.
- Some colleges and universities have adopted a quality model of effectiveness, which identifies and assesses critical success indicators.
- Effectiveness can be conceptualized as a social construction; assessments of effectiveness focus attention on organizational sensemaking and shared commitments.
- Postmodernists note that organizations contain multiple competing narratives that provide different pictures of effectiveness. The selection of only one of these pictures presents a limited and biased view. Postmodernists, therefore, conceive of organizational effectiveness as the successful integration of disparate views of effectiveness from the perspectives of different constituents.
- Efficiency can be defined as an input-output ratio where output is maximized relative to input. State systems of higher education have devised a range of efficiency measures for public colleges and universities.

———————————————— CASE CONTEXT ————————————————

Accreditation at Owens College

The accreditation steering committee at Owens College gathered for its first meeting to prepare for the self-study process. Some of the senior faculty members who had participated in Owens College's previous accreditation review, now nearly eight years ago, were standing near the table where refreshments had been set out for the committee members.

"I think we had better sandwiches the last time that we did this," joked the chair of the chemistry department.

"And better coffee, too," noted the chair of women's studies. "Everyone knows that caffeine is an essential element to any self-study."

"Well, it's not just the coffee and sandwiches that are going to be different this time," interjected the president, who had somehow made his way to the table without getting noticed. "This time around, the accreditation association has new effectiveness criteria, and we will be one of the first institutions to go through under the new system."

"Effectiveness criteria," huffed a faculty member from psychology. "Who the hell are they to tell us whether we are effective or not? We are one of the best liberal arts colleges in the nation. Students come here from all over the world to work with our faculty. And faculty would practically kill to teach here. Did you know that I received nearly 250 applications for one assistant professorship last year? I don't know about you, but I am inclined just to give the accreditation folks the data that they want, and then we can be on our own merry way."

"I'm afraid it is not going to be that simple this time," noted the president. "We need to show that our goals are linked to our strategic plan, that we are measuring our goals, and that the data are being used to inform our decisions about programs and curriculum."

One of the faculty members began to laugh. "I am serious, here," declared the president. "And quite frankly, this whole process could actually be useful for us. We need to guard against complacency. Just because we always have a steady stream of applicants with high SATs does not mean that it will be that way in perpetuity. And yes, everything seems to be running fine. The endowment is growing. Faculty want to work here. Students want to learn here. And that's great. But when was the last time that we did anything that really caught people's attention? When was the last time that we did something that made people stand up and take notice? I was at a chamber of commerce meeting last week, and the president of Urban

University was there; she was talking about all of the work that they were doing with the local schools and the hospitals and economic development. And the audience was enthralled."

"We have nothing to worry about from Urban University," the physics chair noted. "That place is a mess. The faculty just voted 'no confidence' in the provost. Their whole governance process is in shambles, and the pay there is lousy."

"And their tuition is about one-third of ours, and that go-getter president of theirs just lined up three new endowed professorships," responded the president. "They are in the newspapers nearly every week with something new. And unfortunately, 'Owens College gets students with high SATs' is not newsworthy these days."

"You keep mentioning SATs," noted the women's studies chair. "And that is actually something that I wanted to talk about today. I am a little tired of having the average SAT scores be the only way that we talk about student quality. Our students bring a lot of qualities to the college, and test scores are only one of them."

At that point, the president convened the entire committee and made a few announcements regarding the new accreditation standards and the timeline for the self-study.

"Well, let's get right into discussing our effectiveness criteria," the president declared. "Right now, we have a very limited set of performance indicators that we include in the annual report to the trustees. These are things like entering class SAT scores, graduation rates, number of students who go on to graduate school, number of faculty publications, endowment growth, and the like. But none of these things are a direct measure of our core business, so to speak, and that core business is teaching and learning. How do we know what and how much our students are learning?"

"Well, I take issue with your assumptions," argued the psychology professor. "Our mission as a liberal arts college cannot be measured in any quantifiable way. You simply cannot reduce a liberal arts education to a quantifiable score."

"Yet we use quantifiable scores as the primary basis for admissions," noted the women's studies chair. "Did you know that the campus is less diverse now than it was during our last self-study? Our single-minded obsession with having the highest SATs in our peer group of institutions is narrowing the campus to a group of well-to-do white kids."

"Now wait a minute." The institutional research director felt compelled to speak. "We have increased financial aid significantly in the past few years. We now meet the full financial need of every single student we admit."

"Well, that's much easier to do when you admit so few of them with need," responded the women's studies chair. "And the financial aid increases have barely kept pace with our tuition increases. In fact, we now have fewer low-income students and fewer students of color than 10 years ago."

"But the picture is not that simple," noted the vice president for academic affairs. "Our African American and Latino students have exceptionally high graduation rates. In fact, our Latino students have the highest graduation rates in the entire college."

"OK, but what are their GPAs? What are they majoring in? Are they going on to graduate school?" asked the women's studies chair.

"I don't know," mumbled the vice president.

"I have to agree with her," noted a faculty member from the history department. "Our reputation in the community is really elitist. I was just talking with one of our alumnae, and she's now a very successful lawyer. Just made partner. Financially, very well-to-do. And I asked her if she would want her children—she just had twins—to attend Owens College. And she kind of laughed and said she wasn't sure. She said that she wants her kids to go to a school where they will interact with people from diverse cultures and where they will develop an appreciation for the environment and for public service. And she wasn't sure if we were that kind of place."

After a bit more discussion, the president summarized the conversation by highlighting the need to address three issues: (1) how to develop measures of student learning in the context of a liberal arts curriculum; (2) how to disaggregate existing student performance data by race, ethnicity, and gender to determine whether the college is promoting equitable educational outcomes; and (3) how to focus the college on the perceptions and needs of the external environment, including the local community in which the college is located. The members formed task forces around each of these issues and agreed to report back at the next meeting.

After the committee members left the room, the academic vice president turned to the president and asked, "Well, what do you think?"

"At least they're not complaining about the sandwiches any more," laughed the president. "Now they are arguing, challenging each other, critically examining the goals of the college. Let's see what these task forces do, but I am optimistic that this process will not only bring about reaccreditation, but also revitalize the campus."

Introduction

Of all the topics in this book, effectiveness and efficiency create the greatest problems conceptually. They virtually defy the adoption of any single theoretical approach that fits the unique nature of higher education. In part, this is because higher education has so many constituencies, both internal and external, each with its own notions of what an effective college or university is (Herman & Renz, 2004; Lenning, Lee, Micek, & Service, 1976). Students, for example, often view college instrumentally—what kind of a job will it train or educate me to do? and, how much income will that job generate? Parents may ask, was the college effective in preparing my child to live a good life after college? Faculty ask how well the institution provided them with the resources necessary to do their work. Among many other criteria, administrators evaluate the degree to which goals set by them and trustees have been achieved, the financial well-being of the institution, and the relative status of the institution compared to similar others. Community members want to know how the college's presence has enhanced economic and cultural quality of life. Many other constituencies also have their own definitions of effectiveness.

Complicating the issue is that even within these constituencies there is little agreement about what the terms mean. What, after all, is the nature of the "good life" after graduation that institutions are being held accountable for? And to what extent can colleges and universities be held responsible for the remainder of a person's life? In addition, some question whether efficiency and effectiveness constitute proper ends of higher education organizations. According to some, there is an undue emphasis on results—usually viewed comparatively—at the expense of the process (Judd, 1987). Perhaps a successful college or university is one that engages in educational processes that are equitable, meaningful to participants, and satisfying, regardless of the ultimate results or impact.

Conceptualizations of Effectiveness and Efficiency

Over the course of this book, we have studied a variety of tools for understanding organizations, predicting the effects of policy, and intervening in organizations. We have had to make some rather slippery assumptions, however, about the goals of administrative action—for example, improvements in effectiveness and efficiency. In earlier chapters, effectiveness and efficiency have been loosely defined, dependent variables in a number of theories that we have discussed. So in this chapter, we will be more specific about the meanings and definitions of these terms in organizations.

Effectiveness and efficiency are often in a zero-sum relationship. If the organization stresses efficiency too much, it may ignore important outside changes requiring adaptation of internal structures and processes; if it becomes too focused on effectiveness (paying too much attention to meeting external needs), it may become less efficient as subunits change too frequently to allow sustained, predictable relations among them.

An undergraduate college, for example, may see that its graduates are not being admitted into graduate schools or are not securing jobs that the college feels they ought to. The failure is then noted by the public—parents, students, and public funding agencies. The result is often an increasing reluctance to continue to provide resources to the institution. In some sense, as a nonprofit organization, the college or university suffers from a low return on investment. While in the profit-making sector, organizations and their potential (and real) investors can, and do, calculate in relation to comparable organizations the degree to which assets are producing profits. In higher education, profits are essentially the long-term good will of the institution. Good will can be thought of as the residual, intangible result of the effectiveness of the organization over a long period of time. Concomitantly, internally, the college may observe that its workers seem not to be exerting sufficient effort or are unwilling or unable to collaborate in unified action toward organizational goals. From the perspective of internal efficiency, the college has failed.

The pressures for change, therefore, come from both outside and inside. Leaders seeking to adapt the organization to outside pressures understand that present cross-boundary activities are neither maximizing goals nor permitting the flow of continued, dependable inputs. Leaders seeking to adapt the organization to inside pressures, on the other hand, understand that present internal activities are not maximizing the goals of subunits (e.g., admissions or student services). In both cases, the need for some kind of structural reorganization is recognized with a corresponding shift in resources. Each of these imbalances calls for a change in the resources dedicated to various subsystems (internal or cross-boundary), thus suggesting new work processes, new ways of interacting with the external environment, or new linkages among the units within the organization.

If an organization perceives a gap between what it is and what it should be, it must first have some ideal notion of what "ought to be" in order to address that gap. What ought to be is some person or group's ideal conceptualization of an efficient and effective organization. So, it is important to have some conceptual tools for understanding different ways of thinking about efficiency and effectiveness. Then (and only then) we can consider the means to change from the present to the desired state.

To begin, we consider some definitions. Daft approaches effectiveness from the perspective of goal achievement. He suggests that:

> Organizational effectiveness is the degree to which an organization realizes its goals. Effectiveness is a broad concept. It implicitly takes into consideration a range of variables at both the organizational and departmental levels. Effectiveness evaluates the extent to which multiple goals—whether official or operative—are attained. (Daft, 1995, p. 53)

Daft defines efficiency as follows:

> Efficiency is a more limited concept that pertains to the internal workings of the organization. Organizational efficiency is the amount of resources used to produce a unit of output. It can be measured as the ratio of inputs to outputs. (Daft, 1995, p. 53)

Katz and Kahn (1978) combine these two measures, suggesting that both internal efficiency and external effectiveness are defined by returns to the organization from economic, technical, and political efforts. According to Cameron and Whetten (1983; see also Van de Ven & Ferry, 1980), however, the matter is much more complicated. A number of critical questions must be addressed when considering effectiveness models: (1) Whose perspective should dominate the assessment of organizational effectiveness? (e.g., organizational members such as executive officers, external resource providers such as the state, or dominant internal coalitions such as the more powerful departments); (2) Which domain of activity is the focus of the evaluation? (e.g., teaching, research, or public service); (3) What is the appropriate level of analysis? (e.g., macro-organizational level, the institution as a whole, or organizational subunits and individuals); (4) To what use will the results of the effectiveness evaluation be put? (e.g., consider the differences between a purpose such as personnel reviews versus accreditation); (5) What should be the appropriate time frame—long-term or short-term—and who should set the parameters of the time frame?; (6) What are the appropriate types and sources of data? (e.g., organizational records, perceptual measures, or qualitative data collected by institutional researchers); and (7) What is the standard or benchmark against which effectiveness is to be assessed? (e.g., is the organization being compared to other organizations or to itself over several periods of time?)

Moreover, efficiency involves more than the omnibus ratio of inputs to outputs. As Kilmann and McKelvey (1975) report, efficiency must take into account the perspective of the observer, especially his or her psychological disposition and understanding of organizational priorities. Different kinds of data are required depending on the information needs of each manager or leader (Rockart, 1979).

To answer these questions, many conceptual models have been developed (e.g., Lewin & Minton, 1986; Lysons, 1993; Lysons & Hatherly, 1996; Ostroff & Schmitt, 1993). Nine of the most important models are noted in Table 8.1, with parallels where possible to the four functional prerequisites of Talcott Parsons introduced in earlier chapters. We consider each of these models in some detail.

Model 1: The Goal Model

Goals can be defined as "a desired state of affairs which the organization attempts to realize" and a "future state of affairs which the organization as a collectivity is trying to bring about" (Etzioni, 1964, p. 6). The idea of a goal as a concept borrows from traditional ideas in Western societies that advance the importance of progress, rationality, and satisfaction from achievement. Most organizations do appear to be striving to reach a level of achievement that its members—or at least some of its members—identify with and would claim as a legitimate objective. Indeed, much of modern day management

TABLE 8.1
Effectiveness Models and Their Relationship to
Parsons's Functional Prerequisites

Model	*Parsons's Prerequisite* (where applicable)
1. Goal model	Adaptation
2. System resource model	Adaptation
3. Internal process model	Integration, Latency
4. Strategic constituencies (stakeholders) model	Goal Attainment
5. Phase models	
6. Fit or congruence models	Goal Attainment
7. Competing values model	
8. Quality model	
9. Other models such as gross malfunctioning analysis and revelatory analysis	

assumes that goals are in place and that executives work toward setting up methods to achieve them.

Under the goal model, an organization is effective if it accomplishes its goals over the long term. Effectiveness is measured by the degree to which the organization attains identified output targets. In higher education, benchmarking (Alstete, 1995; Barak & Kniker, 2002; Layzell, 1999; Smart, Elton, & Martin, 1980), performance funding (Banta, 1993), institutional and professional expectations (Betz, Cunliff, & Guinn, 2003), and many evaluation service instruments (such as those of the National Center for Higher Education Management Systems and the Council for the Advancement of Standards in Higher Education) all embody the goal model of effectiveness.

Most researchers and practitioners suggest that the achievement of goals must be understood not in terms of some ideal for all organizations but instead viewed realistically in terms of the constraints on goal achievement that may limit a particular organization (Cyert & March, 1963; Steers, 1977). That is, organizational effectiveness should be judged in terms of what the organization's members can be expected to do, not in terms of unrealistic hope (Richman & Farmer, 1974).

Here we also make an important distinction between **official goals** and **operational goals** (Perrow, 1961). Official goals are sometimes called the mission of the organization, which is a somewhat more grandiose statement of the organization's purported vision of the present and future, capturing both ambiguously and succinctly not only the desired future direction for the organization but also its central values as they are related to those of the external society it serves. Official goals may reflect the organization's public relations spin, but their importance should not be downgraded. They serve several useful functions. First, they identify the organization to outside publics. In this way, they serve an image-making function. Second, official goals provide a source of identification for organizational members. This affective/emotional attachment to the organization and its goals (and achievements) provides the basis of continuing motivation to work conscientiously toward the goals, and it may strengthen commitment to remain with the organization.

Operational goals, in contrast, are usually cast in more concrete terms of measurable outcomes. They can include both output goals and process goals (Educational Testing Service [ETS], 1973). For example, "the university should produce 350 graduates in academic year 2009–2010" versus "the university should develop a new curriculum in forensic anthropology next year." The former is an output goal; the latter a process goal. Operational goals typically are stated for each of the functional subsystems of an organization. For a university, these might include teaching assignments, publishing expectations, share of student market, admissions criteria such as SAT scores, employee turnover rates, and student graduation rates.

Operational goals designate the work that is required of organizational members, rather than what the organization aspires to do. These goals serve to reduce uncertainty for workers by substituting explicit organizational directives for individual discretion and by providing a specific basis for evaluation of performance. When provided a clear operational goal, organizational members can easily determine when they have been effective. Moreover, the delineation of operational goals protects organizational members from being held accountable to arbitrary standards. Highly specific goals, however, can constrain professional autonomy and limit innovation and creativity. Effectiveness in higher education, therefore, is often contingent on the proper *balance* between the strength of formal operational goals and the individual autonomy of discretionary action. In the following sections, we consider more fully the benefits and limitations of the goal model of organizational effectiveness.

Benefits of Organizational Goals

Goals help pave the way for interactions both within and across organizational boundaries. "People tend to react to organizations *as if* they were going somewhere" (Porter, Lawler, & Hackman, 1975, p. 78). Knowing what an organization intends to do—seeing the definition of its products or services—permits organizational members to elect alternative modes of interaction, ranging from noninvolvement, to occasional contact, to total commitment. Goals also legitimize the organization to outside constituencies. "An organization whose goals are deemed legitimate enjoys a greatly enhanced ability to obtain resources and other support from its environment" (Bedeian & Zammuto, 1991, p. 31).

Within the organization, goals provide general guidelines for action that allow further elaboration of objectives that follow from them. Organizations with a clear sense of goals also provide workers with limitations about what kinds of endeavors are legitimate. The goals define the outer limits of action, constraining workers from deviating so greatly that collective action is made difficult (Dutton, Dukerich, & Harquail, 1994).

Finally, goals offer directions for organizational design. When organizations begin with the definition of the desired end product or service, they provide workers with targets for the ultimate use of the outputs, with systematic design parameters for the transformation processes, and with directions for utilizing the required inputs. Goals also provide standards for evaluation of performance. In the absence of goals, the organization often has difficulty ascertaining the degree of its success and developing a basis for rewarding employees for their contributions.

Goals are sometimes intentionally made nebulous, however. Vague goals may permit a wider range of interpretation and thus allow employees with different agendas to work together without conflict. The downside of such a policy is that the freedom of interpretation permitted to organizational members may result in their working at cross-purposes. Organizations with vague goals, therefore, need highly elaborated coordination systems in order to ensure effective performance.

Setting Goals

Organizations are not completely free to set their own goals. That is, most organizations are constrained by their environments to conform to the goals expected by external constituencies and by the adaptations of their competitors to those constituencies. Thus, in higher education, most universities tend to (or try to) set goals quite similar to those of the most prestigious universities (Riesman, 1958) or seek to adopt the practices of institutions deemed best within a particular institutional type. Occasionally, however, some institutions are able to identify themselves as different but better. They define themselves as unique and as deserving the public's attention, even though they do not conform to the traditional models of success.

Goals are set in different ways in different kinds of colleges and universities. Generally, the dominant coalition (Cyert & March, 1963) can sway the organization toward its perspective (Gioia & Thomas, 1996). In community colleges, for example, the administration usually dominates, and its goals generally become operative (Smart & Hamm, 1993). Goals change over time, however, as different constituencies gain and lose power. Charles Perrow (1963) observed the history of a general hospital and found that goals shifted with the changes in the strength of the bargaining positions of administrators, trustees, and doctors.

Goals are generated when individuals come together and recognize some common purpose or objective that can best be attended to by collective action. However, not all individuals who join a group or organization are equally committed to the goals. Indeed, some authors suggest that goals are the creation of organizational coalitions whose members band together to maximize their own—not the organization's—aims. Goals then become negotiated end states that are ultimately determined by power in a politically dominated system, rather than through rational decision making in a bureaucratic organization (Cyert & March, 1963). To the extent that colleges and universities are political entities comprising diverse groups of individuals, the goals of the most powerful coalition in the organization usually determine the operative goals for the entire organization.

How different subsystems in the organization perceive goals and how they attempt to carry out goals may vary considerably. While goals of organizations can be openly stated in official charters, policy manuals, and chief executive officer promulgations, they are still subject to alternative interpretations. Indeed, each subsystem is likely to place its own emphasis on that part of the goal that benefits it the most. Furthermore, as March and Olsen (1976) and postmodernists suggest, colleges and universities may resemble (or act as if they are) organized anarchies—in which case the allocation of attention to one or another goal or set of goals becomes problematic.

Goal Succession

Goals of organizations are rarely constant over long periods of time. Adaptation to changes in the requirements of the external environment for different or new products and services requires shifts in goals. The process of goal succession is different for different kinds of organizations, depending on their sensitivity to the environment and the sources of resistance to change within the organization. In higher education, some goals are quite stable, since colleges and universities continue to serve essential social and economic needs, while other economic and legal exigencies place demands on institutions for short-run adaptability and necessitate the adoption of new goals and sometimes the shedding of old ones.

Goal Displacement

A different kind of change occurs when goals are displaced. When an organization substitutes for its legitimate goals other goals for which it was not established and to which resources are diverted, the original goal is said to have been displaced. Research goals, for example, may displace the teaching goals upon which many institutions were founded. Thus, a liberal arts college with a traditional emphasis on undergraduate teaching may see the teaching goal displaced by a focus on bringing in more research grants. Further, in many organizations, institutional *output* goals are replaced by *process* goals. This is especially true in organizations like colleges and universities where outputs are less tangible. In the absence of consensus on what institutional goals mean, members tend to focus on more available, apparently more meaningful, or at least achievable objectives. There is, in other words, a means-ends inversion. Student affairs staff, for example, may find it easier to concentrate on ensuring students' conformity to rules rather than maximizing student growth and development.

Further, goals are displaced because of a perceived need by organizational members to measure achievement. Enhanced importance is attached to achieving numbers that appear to have value to supervisors and external evaluators (Daft, 2001). An academic department whose funding for faculty lines depends on its enrollment may lower its admissions standards or its grading standards in order to assure a continuity of inputs and a reduced dropout rate—but at a cost of achieving its stated mission.

Organizations tend also to suboptimize. Narrow goals that are relevant to subunit or departmental objectives rather than total institutional aims are easier to pursue and are perceived as having a higher payoff to the subunit or department (Etzioni, 1964; Mintzberg, 1979). Suppose also that an organization has multiple goals, some of which may be in conflict or not all of which are achieved. Resources addressed to these conflicting goals must be adjudicated judiciously and equitably.

Goal Ambiguity

The goal approach is also problematic when goals in organizations are intangible and outputs are difficult to measure, especially in the short run. When, for example, do students benefit—upon graduation or later in life? When should their achievements be measured and how can they be traced back to the benefits of attending a particular institution? Similarly, can the effects of research findings be measured when their benefits may not be revealed for several decades?

Most official organizational goals are abstract—sometimes intentionally so, in order to accommodate a broad range of perspectives. This is particularly true in higher education, where academic freedom demands a tolerance of a variety of perspectives. Some would argue that the abstract nature of institutional goals allows too much freedom, indeed, laxity among workers who cannot be held strictly accountable. Further, organizational design and decision making is made difficult when goals are abstract (Lutz, 1982). Others would argue equally vociferously that the abstractness and accompanying academic freedom permits a wider range of viewpoints and promotes creativity and innovation (Tierney, 1992).

As noted earlier, it seems reasonable that goals be considered in the determination of an organization's effectiveness. However, goal setting, goal succession, goal displacement, and goal ambiguity generate key questions that need to be addressed when we consider how goals are conceived in higher education and how organizational members at different levels utilize them in their work. We turn now to the second approach to understanding organizational effectiveness.

Model 2: The System Resource Model

The system resource approach was originally developed in the 1950s and refined by many, especially Yuchtman and Seashore (1967). The basic principle of this approach to effectiveness is ecological: What counts is survival. Goals and goal accomplishment are less relevant than the capacities for resource acquisition and system maintenance. Thus, virtually the only way to tell if an organization is successful is if it continues to attract resources over a long period of time. Ongoing competitive advantage, according to this theory, is what counts as effectiveness. The long-standing rankings of the Ivy League institutions, for example, testify to their continued ability to attract funds to support their missions.

The focus of the system resource model is on the continuous bargaining relationship that organizations have with their environments (Pfeffer, 1977). The Japanese *keiretsu* system is an example. In that system, long-term, stable relationships between an organization and its suppliers are developed over time. The relationships ensure continuation of the supply of critical resources. In the case of higher education, colleges that are able over many years to continue to attract applications from students through established feeder high schools are said by some observers to be effective, regardless of the actual quality of the education delivered.

Table 8.2 lists alternative types of colleges and universities, not all of which could be said to be effective in the goal sense, but which, nevertheless, might be effective in the system resource sense. The criteria used are reputation, size of budget, and value added to students.

In the system resource approach, then, sustained inputs replace outputs as the primary criterion of effectiveness. There are, however, several problems with this approach:

1. Difficulty of operationalization (Sowa, Selden, & Sandfort, 2004). How should optimum procurement of external resources be characterized? Could the institution do better? At what cost? Are minimum or maximum inputs a sign of success? Could the college have built a *better* reputation and thus received more income?

2. Selection of appropriate resources. Which resources should be identified as constituting evidence of effectiveness? Funds (e.g., gifts and endowments)? Personnel (e.g., faculty with reputations)? Institutional reputation? Are all inputs equal?

3. Efficiency of allocation. Have the resources been efficiently distributed internally? Simply acquiring resources does not say anything about how well they are used.

TABLE 8.2
Categories of Colleges With Varying Combinations of Reputation,
Financial Health and Value Added to Students

Institutional Category	Indices of Effectiveness		
	Reputation	Financial Health	Value Added to Students
Winners	High	High	High
Coasters	High	High	Low
Efficients	High	Low	High
Showboats	High	Low	Low
Laid Backs	Low	High	High
Wizards	Low	Low	High
Cheaters	Low	High	Low
Losers	Low	Low	Low

Adapted from Bess and Shearer (1994).

Model 3: The Internal Process Model

In contrast, the third effectiveness model—the internal process model—focuses on the inner workings of an organization that the system resource model neglects. The focus in this model is on the integration of personnel (Kahn, 1974; Murphy & Cooper, 2000; Zaleznik, Christensen, & Roethlisberger, 1958). Here, a university or college would be effective if there is an absence of internal strain and if there is a highly cooperative system in place. In effective organizations of this type, there is much trust among organizational members and much honest communication in all directions. It is not, however, a "country club" organization where good social relationships take precedence over task accomplishments. Rather, the comity of internal relations is accompanied by the desire for and effort expended toward the achievement of organizational outcomes. In contrast, an educational organization might be said to be *ineffective* if over a period of time it is clear that people are unable to reach agreement about how to achieve the agreed upon aims of the organization. A college in constant internal turmoil would not be considered effective even if it continued to graduate students for many years. Certain kinds or levels of conflict over time may lead to deterioration in the internal processes of the organization and to a decline in the quality of organizational life.

A problem with this approach, however, arises when one examines the assumptions of the structure of the organization. As we observed in studying Gamson's (1968) political model (see chapter 3), when organizations are conceived as polities, conflict is inevitable, and certain kinds of conflict are even functional. Thus, institutions can be effective even if internal processes are not smooth, provided that the turbulence is functional in the long run.

Model 4: Strategic Constituencies Model

Sometimes called the "multiple constituency" model or the "stakeholders" model (Connolly, Conlon, & Deutsch, 1980; Kilmann & Herden, 1976), this model examines effectiveness from the perspective of the members of the external environment. Since the organization is part of a larger system in which it plays a role, it can be considered effective to the extent that it satisfies the goals of its primary *external* stakeholders. An indicator of effectiveness in this model is the expression of satisfaction. For example, do the parents, community residents, graduate schools, employers of graduates, and government regulators all report being satisfied with the performance of a particular college or university? For community colleges, such stakeholders are key players in the definition of institutional effectiveness (Alfred, Ewell, Hudgins, & McClenney, 1999), given the importance of local taxes as a source of funding.

This model, as with the others, has several shortcomings:

1. Provides no guidance regarding the validity of alternative perspectives expressed by different stakeholders. Constituents may have different value perspectives on the institution's goals. Are they all valid and of equal worth? Or, are the parties merely self-interested; that is, concerned only with advancing their own causes even at the expense of others? Which claims are more important in the measurement of overall effectiveness? Must they all be equally satisfied? How should they be integrated?

2. Does not account for partially achieved goals. Constituents may have competing goals for the organization. Suppose some are fully achieved, and some only partially. For example, the success of a women's basketball team may make both the team members and many alumni and alumnae quite happy (satisfied), but other stakeholders might say that the effectiveness of the institution should not be judged on the basis of the success of its athletics programs. Athletic success only partially achieves the goals of the institution.

3. Ignores the satisfactions of organizational members. Calculating only

the satisfaction of *external* constituents may result in the exploitation of employees. The needs, goals, and aspirations of organizational members are subordinated in this model to the priorities of external groups.

Model 5: Phase Models

Over different phases of an organization's development, it must deal (sometimes sequentially, sometimes simultaneously) with pressing problems *across* its boundaries as well as *within* its boundaries. It also goes through phases of addressing issues of individual motivation, as well as larger scale structural design factors. More colloquially, organizations balance task and people needs and instrumental, long-term considerations with more immediately consummatory requisites (Cyert & March, 1963; March & Simon, 1958; Quinn & Cameron, 1983).

An effective organization under the phase model is attentive to the needs of the current phase and will anticipate the next, taking steps internally and externally to be ready to modify organizational behavior. Some colleges and universities in a building (expansionary) phase may ignore or choose to neglect some internal conditions and focus instead on marketing a new image for the institution. Other more established institutions may be judged effective when their methods and procedures of operation have been made highly efficient. This model emphasizes the need for organizational leaders to assess the priorities that are and should be attached to different phases of organizational development and to identify transition states between the phases.

Model 6: Fit Models

Two submodels fall in the category called **fit.** The first submodel claims that there is a need for integrative consistency across the components of organizations. The more consistent the components are with one another, the more effective the organization will be. Nadler and Tushman (1977), for example, propose a model that comprises three components: inputs (environment, resources, past managerial behavior), within-boundary conditions (individual, task, informal organization, organizational arrangements), and outputs (individual, group, and system). As Nadler and Tushman (1977) note, "Between each pair of inputs there exists a degree of consistency or inconsistency," or fit. They define fit as:

> The degree to which the needs, demands, goals, objectives, and structures of one component are consistent with the needs, demands, goals, objectives, and structures of another component. (p. 93)

Their hypothesis:

> Other things being equal, the greater the total degree of consistency or fit
> between the various components, the more effective will be organizational
> behavior at multiple levels. Effective organizational behavior is defined as
> behavior which leads to higher levels of goal attainment, utilization of re-
> sources, and adaptation. (pp. 93–94)

Thus, effectiveness for Nadler and Tushman involves matching components
to one another. In the case of higher education, to examine an institution's
effectiveness using this model, we can evaluate such fits as may exist between
stakeholders and boundary personnel, group norms and organizational goals,
organizational design and the tasks (roles) that faculty and staff must perform, and preferred satisfactions of organizational members and institutional
reward systems.

The second submodel in the fit or congruence group suggests that not
all organizations can be evaluated using the same criteria of effectiveness.
Certain effectiveness criteria are more appropriate for some kinds of organizations than others. The criteria of effectiveness for different institutional
types are not the same. Both internal and external evaluators of effectiveness
in a community college, for example, might apply quite different standards
than would those in a research university.

This conclusion raises the question of whether it is fair and reasonable
to demand of colleges and universities that they perform effectively in the
same ways as, say, organizations in the corporate sector? Or as hospitals? Or
even as the so-called best educational institutions in the field? In fact, some
useful research findings have been published on this subject. In 1981, Cameron selected for his research three distinctive types of organizational cultures
commonly identified in the literature—a collegial culture (that emphasizes
trust, communication, and professionalism), a market culture (that focuses
on exploiting economic opportunities), and an adhocracy culture (where
there is much ad hoc decision making). He then sought to determine if those
cultures were correlated with different domains of organizational effectiveness in higher education (Cameron, 1981; Cameron & Whetten, 1983). In an
earlier study (Cameron, 1978), Cameron found nine distinctive areas that
administrators believed were indicative of an effective institution of higher
education. These were later conceptually collapsed into four domains:

- Academic domain: student academic development, quality of faculty,
  and ability to acquire resources
- Morale domain: student, faculty, and administrator satisfaction

- External adaptation domain: comprising student career development, among other variables
- Extracurricular domain: including students' personal, nonacademic development outside of the formal curriculum

In Table 8.3 is a juxtaposition of nine measures of effectiveness of colleges and universities, their associated domains, and the organizational culture with which the effectiveness domains were most closely related. Student educational satisfaction, for example, is part of the morale dimension and is most commonly found in an organizational culture with collegial characteristics. On the other hand, system openness and community interaction are more likely to take place in an organization with an adhocracy culture.

The data suggest that different types of organizational cultures can maximize different domains of effectiveness in colleges and universities. To be effective in each of the nine domains, organizations may need to have cultures that reflect elements from all three types: collegial, market, and adhocracy. Different parts of the organization can be organized in different forms,

TABLE 8.3
Highest Scoring Culture on Different Dimensions of Organizational Effectiveness

Effectiveness Dimension	Domain	Cultural Type Scoring Highest
1. Student educational satisfaction	Morale	Collegial
2. Student academic development	Academic	Adhocracy
3. Student career development	External adaptation	Adhocracy
4. Student personal development	Morale	Collegial
5. Faculty and administrator employment satisfaction	Morale	Collegial
6. Professional development	Academic	Adhocracy
7. System openness and community interaction	External adaptation	Adhocracy
8. Ability to acquire resources	Academic	Market
9. Organizational health	Morale	Collegial

Adapted from Cameron (1981).

thus supporting cultural variation within the college or university. Some units may be characterized by elements of the collegial culture, while others emphasize market or adhocracy characteristics. Some evidence suggests that such a division of organizational culture within institutions of higher education commonly takes place—for example, between administrative and faculty cultures, between student affairs and academic affairs cultures, and among the different cultures of the academic disciplines (Hellawell & Hancock, 2001; Kramer & Berman, 1998; Kuh & Whitt, 1988; Lee, 2004).

Overall organizational effectiveness may to some extent be a function of the degree to which the organization is able to accommodate and reconcile differences among multiple organizational cultures. In some institutions, however, it may not be possible to support simultaneously all of the cultural dimensions that underlie each of the nine effectiveness indicators. As Cameron points out, organizational effectiveness is a multidimensional construct, thus requiring an understanding by leaders of the priorities of the institution, especially as the organization moves through different phases. For example, it may be necessary to emphasize certain aspects of a market culture when the resource acquisition dimension of effectiveness needs to be improved and provide less attention to the other effectiveness domains. Thus, some compromise in *overall* organizational effectiveness may be necessary, depending on the priorities of a particular phase of organizational development.

Model 7: Competing Values Model

This model takes into account all of the above models and recognizes that organizations need to attend to different conditions and demands at different times, yet not neglect any for too long a period. To be effective, organizations must maintain internal efficiency as well as perform a function in the external environment in which they are immersed. That is, they must address the conditions of the environment as well as internal issues. Colleges and universities, for example, must be simultaneously concerned with changing external demands and internal group dynamics. Maintaining a stable, unchanging faculty, for example, will not be functional if the needs of incoming students are changing and thus require different curricula and perhaps new faculty skills. On the other hand, too many changes in the faculty will make for difficult interpersonal and interdepartmental relations.

More formally, the competing values model holds that all organizations must achieve four goals: economic efficiency, internal integration and coordination, adaptation and responsiveness to the external environment, and utilization of human capital (Quinn, 1981; Quinn & Rohrbaugh, 1983). The objective is to achieve these simultaneously. However, since the four goals are in competition for limited physical, financial, and human resources, it is impossible to achieve that objective. As a consequence, organizations are forced to prioritize these goals and engage in trade-offs among competing priorities. Underlying the competing goals are four models of effectiveness, which are displayed in Table 8.4.

The **human relations model** focuses on developing human resources and sustaining high morale within the organization. In the **open systems model**, on the other hand, the focus is external. Organizational members focus on growth and adaptability to changes in the outside environment. The **internal process model** is focused internally, and the orientation is toward control

TABLE 8.4
Four Models of Effectiveness Values

		FOCUS	
		Internal	*External*
STRUCTURE	Flexibility	**Human Relations Model** Goal values: utilization of human capital, human resource development Subgoals: cohesion, morale, training	**Open Systems Model** Goal values: adaptability and responsiveness to external environment, growth, resource acquisition Subgoals: flexibility, readiness, external evaluation
	Control	**Internal Process Model** Goal values: internal integration and coordination, stability, equilibrium Subgoals: information management, communication	**Rational Goal Model** Goal values: economic efficiency, productivity, profit Subgoals: planning, goal setting

Adapted from Daft (1995).

and stability, especially through information management. The last model, the **rational goal model,** focuses on the outside and attempts to control the organization's relationship with external constituencies through planning and goal setting.

Attention to each of these concerns may require successive or, on occasion, simultaneous use of all four models of organizational effectiveness. An open systems approach, for example, may be needed to focus the organization on achievable short-run objectives (e.g., establishing a market niche in the external environment). A rational goal approach can focus on securing with some certainty high-quality system inputs—for example, students and research grants. Extra attention to human relations may be needed on a campus that is demoralized by budget cuts, while in other circumstances the goal of a campus may be to create integrated systems and the feeling of stability and predictability—the focus of the internal process model.

Model 8: Quality Model

Cameron and Whetten (1996) suggest that in recent years there has been a noticeable shift away from effectiveness models and toward the consideration of quality. Gradually, colleges and universities have come to recognize some of the innovations in the profit-making field (e.g., the Baldrige National Quality Program and the European Foundation for Quality Management) that take into account different dimensions of organizational activity (Hertz, 2005; Peterson & Cameron, 1994). Practices associated with total quality management (Choppin, 1991; Dale, Wu, Zairi, Williams, & Van der Wiele, 2001; Rahman, 2004) have influenced the choice of data used to evaluate organizational success. Among many colleges and universities that have institutionalized total quality management are Northwest Missouri State University (Thomson, 2005) and the University of Hawaii at Hilo, which has developed a program of critical success factors that includes a variety of qualitative and quantitative measures (University of Hawaii at Hilo, 2004). Powell (1995), however, found that total quality management features were not generally effective. Rather, he notes that "certain tacit, behavioral, imperfectly imitable features—such as open culture, employee empowerment, and executive commitment—can produce" competitive advantage (p. 15). On the other hand, the accreditation movement has led to much more sophisticated modes of evaluation of college and university effectiveness, particularly in quantitative measures.

Model 9: Other Models of Effectiveness

Most of the models above project a rational, comprehensible, and somewhat predictable set of criteria for evaluating the effectiveness of organizations such as colleges and universities. Other approaches, perhaps equally valid, offer different criteria. Weick (1977), for example, offers irreverent, but nonetheless valid, alternative effectiveness criteria, including organizational "abilities" to be garrulous, clumsy, superstitious, hypocritical, monstrous, and grouchy. Each of these directs the analyst to quite different organizational phenomena than the standard effectiveness variables that have appeared throughout this chapter. It is probably not the case that Weick means to assert that the above criteria should replace the more traditional measures, but that they should augment them.

Another irreverent look at effectiveness comes from the work of Charles Perrow (1977), who suggests that organizational analysts should more properly address themselves to the criteria of *ineffectiveness* through two approaches that he calls **gross malfunctioning analysis** and **revelatory analysis.** Most of the theories described above are concerned with identifying variables that discriminate between the so-called best organizations and the so-called next best. Perrow suggests that it would be much more fruitful for entire fields of applied organizational analysis (e.g., studies of higher education organizations) if we compared failing institutions with successful ones through gross malfunctioning analysis. In other fields, few social scientists want to study, for example, why a railroad is poorly run, why a prison is dehumanizing, why a hospital swindles patients, or why a government agency is dishonest. In higher education, we tend to want to understand why our model institutions are so good and to use those findings to improve the middle-of-the-road ones. Better, says Perrow, to pull ourselves up by our bootstraps.

Through revelatory analysis, Perrow suggests that we try to find out more about the ways that organizations are used by various constituent groups. Perrow notes that the domain of employee satisfaction contributes heavily in effectiveness studies, but satisfaction is usually defined as people finding gratification in doing what the organization wants them to do. Instead, he says, we should use questions such as the following to determine effectiveness:

> Do you find this a good place to have pleasant chats with others about things that interest you? Can you daydream or relax without being bothered? Can you use the organization's facilities for your own personal needs (the telephone, typists, office supplies, machine shop, personnel department, travel facilities)? Could you get a friend or relative a job here? Can you control your work so that when you are not in the mood you do not have to work too hard? Can you hide your mistakes and advertise your successes? Can you make use of tediously acquired skills and knowledge so that you have some bargaining edge with co-workers or superiors, or some sense that what you are doing is meaningful because you have had to learn how to do it and control it somewhat? Do you pick up any interesting

tidbits about the world working here, or can you be interesting at social gatherings because of what you do here or learn here? Can you expect to have a job here as long as you need it? (Perrow, 1977, p. 102)

This set of questions is obviously controversial—and meant to be. The state of the art or science of evaluating effectiveness is itself controversial, and irreverent questions may be needed to provoke new perspectives and new thinking.

The Social Construction Model of Organizational Effectiveness

Just as Perrow's irreverent questions provoke new thinking on effectiveness, the social construction perspective offers an alternative to conceptualizations that suggest that effectiveness can be determined by assessing the quality of organizational outcomes. In contrast, social constructionists argue that effectiveness deals with values and preferences that cannot be measured objectively (Scott, 1998). Social constructionists emphasize the importance of perceptual measures rather than written records for demonstrating effectiveness (Cameron, 1978). This is not to suggest that quantitative data are unimportant. Instead, the social construction of data—that is, what the data mean to different people—shapes how the organization constructs its own interpretation of effectiveness (Bensimon, Polkinghorne, Bauman, & Vallejo, 2004). For example, Anna Neumann (1995) examined how colleges interpret their financial conditions. In one case, college leaders constructed an interpretation of resources that inspired confidence in the future, even though objective measures showed severe financial constraints. In another setting, faculty and staff displayed high levels of anxiety and concern regarding resources, even though the financial data indicated relative health. Neumann concluded that the social construction of data had more impact on assessments of financial health than did the objective financial records.

Effectiveness and Sensemaking

The assessment of effectiveness can be viewed as a sensemaking process that helps the organization focus attention on what its members collectively view as important. Sensemaking involves the development of cognitive frames of reference to understand and interpret experience (Weick, 1995). The ambiguity and complexity of organizational life, for example, is made more sensible through the construction of frames (or mental maps) that guide interpretation and action. Subsequent actions, in turn, allow people to test and redefine their frames of reference.

The act of assessment forces organizational members to reflect on their actions and to construct a rationale that justifies those actions. Weick (1995) notes that when people become committed to an action, "sensemaking becomes focused on a search for explanations that justify the action" (p. 174). Thus, organizational members may use assessments of effectiveness as a means to justify the actions to which they are committed. In other words, effectiveness is not necessarily related to measuring how well the organization does something; instead, the assessment process helps organizational members identify their commitments and construct compelling rationales that support related actions. The assessment of effectiveness, therefore, can be viewed as a process that focuses sensemaking on actions that organizational members believe are worth taking.

Some social constructionists of effectiveness, however, may uncritically justify actions and commitments that are self-serving or resistant to change. So how can organizations keep the assessment of effectiveness from becoming self-congratulatory or status quo endorsing? First, organizational leaders can ensure that the assessment of effectiveness occurs through open communication, which allows multiple actors (e.g., faculty, staff, and students) to have a role in the identification of organizational commitments. Open communication enables multiple interpretations to shape the social construction of effectiveness.

A common tendency in higher education organizations, however, is to attempt to reconcile multiple interpretations through the collection of more data. Bensimon (2004) notes that administrators often attempt to collect additional data to reduce uncertainty, rather than utilize the data that are currently available. Such tendencies may further frustrate decision makers, rather than help them identify shared commitments. As Weick (1995) notes:

> the same events mean different things to different people, and more information will not help them. What will help them is a setting where they can argue, using rich data pulled from a variety of media, to construct fresh frameworks of action-outcome linkages that include their multiple interpretations. The variety of data needed to pull off this difficult task are most available in variants of the face to face meeting. (p. 186)

Meetings and forums that promote open communication are more likely to generate critical reflection on organizational effectiveness. Additional data collection, in contrast, may delay or forestall efforts to make sense of organizational effectiveness. Data collection may displace sensemaking opportunities, when people spend more time collecting data than discussing the implications of their findings.

Having too little data, however, is just as problematic as having too much. The assessment of effectiveness may conclude prematurely, because confirmatory data were easy to find (Weick, 1995). Meanwhile, data that may point to a different conclusion remain unexamined. Organizations that utilize too few data in their assessments of effectiveness are subject to groupthink and other limitations on sensemaking. Deliberately searching for disconfirming data, therefore, is a second way to ensure that the social construction of effectiveness does not devolve into a self-serving process. A group member, for example, could play the role of devil's advocate and pose critical questions that challenge others to examine their assumptions about what constitutes organizational effectiveness.

Limitations of the Social Constructionist Perspective on Effectiveness

An important limitation of the social constructionist perspective on effectiveness is that it tends to underestimate the power that the external environment has over organizations (Pfeffer & Salancik, 1978). The political and economic context of higher education has significant influence over the extent to which colleges and universities are perceived as effective. State policy mandates, local government regulations, and competitive markets for students and faculty constrain the extent to which internally derived social constructions of effectiveness may be accepted as legitimate by external actors. An entrepreneurial community college, for example, may construct a definition of effectiveness that is centered on adaptability and responsive academic programs, but may encounter resistance from state policy makers who conceptualize effectiveness in terms of headcount enrollments. Some colleges and universities, especially public institutions, are subject to extensive external controls and have relatively less discretion regarding the ways in which they can shape assessments of effectiveness.

Some theorists, however, argue that both the market and the policy environment are social constructions (Fligstein, 1990). The market is shaped not only by external demand but also by marketing and publicity that emanate directly from the organization. Similarly, the relationship between state governments and public institutions is socially constructed through repeated interactions between state policy makers and college leaders (Dee, 2006). Moreover, institutions often have a range of discretion in terms of how they respond to state policies (Mills, 1998). Seldom do state higher education policies enact a strict statute framework that dictates organizational behavior. More often, institutions are allowed to craft their own practices and responses to legislative priorities. Thus, some institutions may have more latitude in shaping external perceptions of effectiveness than their leaders realize.

Postmodern Perspectives on Effectiveness

As we have noted in earlier chapters, postmodernism is an amalgam of epistemological and ideological positions that reflects the alleged logical impossibility of making predictions based on positivist assumptions about reality—such as the notion that reality is an objective phenomenon and that generalized principles can guide future action. In addition to serving as a critique of positivism, postmodern thought also embodies the recent sociocultural evolution of organizational life and recognizes the semiotic limitations of trying to describe it. These notions raise important questions about what effectiveness can mean in colleges and universities and whether it can and should be measured. Further, because postmodernists (at least some postmodernists) believe that data-based evaluation in the positivist mode leads to ethically questionable institutional policies, it is important to explore the meaning of effectiveness from this perspective.

Lincoln and Denzin (1994) note that organizations are characterized by **polyvocality**; that is, the presence of many stories, tales, and dramas that explain organizational life. Given multiple voices and perspectives, postmodernists argue that there is no single voice—no metanarrative—that speaks for the entire organization (Clegg & Hardy, 1996). Hence, the construction of a metanarrative to explain the effectiveness of an organization is illusory. The search for the most accurate measures of effectiveness is moot, because the very phenomenon being assessed may not exist as a unitary construct. Instead, organizations have multiple **competing narratives** that provide different pictures of effectiveness.

In this context, summative conclusions about effectiveness privilege one competing narrative over the others that exist in the organization. One narrative becomes *the* definitive statement on the performance of the organization. These types of summative conclusions deny the presence of polyvocality; they impose a single voice to speak for the organization. The single voice often attempts to provide clarity, offer feedback on performance, and guide the way toward improved practice. However, if organizational life is indeed fragmented and polyvocal, as postmodernists suggest, then such assessments are suspect and may in fact reflect the political motivations of individuals and groups (Alvesson & Deetz, 2000).

Assessments of effectiveness are subject to political motivations that reveal themselves through account giving and other forms of information sharing. When organizational members provide data for assessments of effectiveness, they may attempt to privilege certain interpretations and suppress alternative points of view. Consider, for example, a manager who only forwards data that reflect well upon his department, or the supervisor who twists a performance review to justify the firing of a staff member. Assessments of effectiveness reflect "the struggle for the justification and dominance of particular values, points of view and interests" (Buchanan, 2003, p. 17).

Some researchers have portrayed polyvocality as the struggle between the competing interests of management (often allied with corporate shareholders and/or governmental regulators) and lower level employees (Braverman, 1974; Dawson, 1994). In higher education organizations, this is sometimes viewed as a struggle between administrators who emphasize efficiency and accountability, and faculty members who emphasize self-regulation for ensuring effectiveness. Postmodernists, however, note that polyvocality is actually much more complex than a struggle between two groups with different preferences for effectiveness criteria. They argue that organizational members at all hierarchical levels "position themselves as sponsors, victims, survivors, spectators, or drivers" (Buchanan, 2003, p. 16). The positions that people assume cannot be predicted on the basis of their hierarchical location within the organization. A top-level manager, for example, may position himself as a victim when explaining the effectiveness of his unit to the college president or board of trustees. Competing narratives, therefore, are not simply the result of structural differentiation; instead, they reflect a range of cross-cutting issues and identities of organizational members who cannot be reliably categorized into definable interest groups such as labor versus management or faculty versus administrators (Martin, 1992). Hence, the assessment of effectiveness is constrained not only by *competing interests* (positivists admit as much), but also by *competing narratives* that reflect the fragmentation and indeterminacy of organizational life.

Postmodern perspectives, however, need not lead to nihilistic conclusions that "anything goes" and that there is nothing that can be done to improve organizational performance. Instead, assessments of effectiveness can be framed as opportunities for surfacing and discussing the multiple narratives of the organization. As Buchanan (2003) notes, the challenge "is to present competing narratives as opportunities for learning and innovation, not to elicit judgment" (p. 19). Through discussions of competing narratives, organizational members can identify the values and assumptions that underlie different interpretations of effectiveness. The values and assumptions can then be examined and critiqued by a broad range of organizational members—for example, students, faculty, and administrators.

Some postmodernists suggest the need for **deconstructing** dominant organizational assumptions and the practices that follow from them, which are seldom questioned in day-to-day organizational life but can be surfaced through assessments of effectiveness. Martin (1992) suggests that organizations can "examine different kinds of effectiveness, perhaps using the criterion, 'Who benefits?': top and middle managers, shareholders, lower-ranking employees, or various demographic groups?" (p. 191). Estela Bensimon's (2004) Diversity Scorecard Project is another example of how higher education leaders can deconstruct their assumptions about organizational effectiveness. Bensimon et al. (2004) conceptualized effectiveness as the institution's ability to yield equitable educational outcomes. They argue that standard outcome and process measures, such as retention and graduation rates, provide an insufficient picture of effectiveness. A high graduation rate, for example, may not reflect equitable outcomes if students of color enter lower paying jobs or have more difficulty gaining admission to graduate schools. Instead, Bensimon et al. (2004) challenge higher education leaders to disaggregate their data by race and ethnicity in order to determine if institutions are promoting the success of diverse students.

The value of the introduction of postmodernism into the discourse of organizational effectiveness is a pragmatic one. As John Dewey frequently observed, truth is what works. Hence, the value of postmodernism is in its guide to better practice, even if it does not conform to positivist assumptions about prediction and control.

Organizational Efficiency

Colleges and universities are frequently under the gun to become more efficient, since the expenses of conducting research and teaching have been increasing—in some institutions faster than the rate of increase in revenues. One definition of efficiency is the degree to which a transformation process consumes resources—especially time and money (Roberts, 1994). Traditionally, efficiency measures use a ratio-based mode of analysis. The lower the ratio of inputs (usually expressed as a monetary figure) to outputs as compared with other similar units being evaluated, the more efficient the unit.

There is a long history of research on and practice of efficiency improvement in the United States (and more recently in other countries, Casu & Thanassoulis, 2006). The efficiency movement was highly salient during the Progressive Era (ca. 1890–1932), when society as a whole was concerned with excessive waste and inefficiency (Haber, 1964). In the early part of the 20th century in the United States, industries began to take up the theories and recommendations of Frederick Taylor for scientific management (Kanigel,

1997; Taylor, 1914)—a system of precise and scientific study of individual worker action intended to reduce wasted motion. Attempts of industrial firms to become more efficient were informed by economists who examined methods to reduce costs associated with given levels of output (Weiermair & Perlman, 1990). Causes of inefficiency lie frequently in miscalculations of the amount of labor and capital needed per unit of output, on the overproduction of units of output required for the market, and on lack of worker motivation to utilize resources.

As a result of new accountability expectations, most colleges and universities are engaged in much more assiduous efforts to plan and budget carefully so that expenditures are in line with available funds and with institutional goals. Program planning and budgeting (Katzenbach, 1968) and management information systems have been developed to provide more accurate data on budgeting and productivity (Baker, 2005; Tricker & Boland, 1982) especially through the creation of performance indicators and accountability indexes (Ruppert, 1994). National agencies have produced new measures that track expenditures in different categories. These include the National Center for Higher Education Management Systems, the National Association of College and University Business Officers, the Education Commission of the States, the Southern Regional Education Board, and the American Association of Community Colleges. In addition, policy makers have expressed interest in calculating the degree to which funds expended by institutions have, indeed, produced desired results. Performance funding programs at the state level are now virtually universal (Banta, Rudolph, Van Dyke, & Fisher, 1996; Borden & Banta, 1994; Burke, Minassians, & Yang, 2002). Tennessee has been at the forefront of this movement (Bogue & Brown, 1982) as has Texas (Texas State Higher Education Coordinating Board, 2003). Community colleges have made significant advances in making their systems more sophisticated (Dougherty, Kim, & Hong, 2002). Here are some typical measures of efficiency in higher education, usually measured over time (Thomas, 1996):

- instructional cost per student credit hour by course level and field of study
- department salaries per course and/or by student enrolled
- average faculty salary per graduating senior
- annual physical plant cost per department
- donation income per current enrolled student and/or by number of alumni

Still, at all levels, there are missing links in the performance reporting chain (Burke & Minassians, 2002) and there are many questions as to whether systems designed to measure efficiency work, and, equally important, whether they make any difference in organizational outcomes (Burke, 2001; Gray & Banta, 1997). In higher education, several complications arise. Both input and output variables can be defined differently by governmental and institutional evaluators. Further, the time dimension is critical. Some dimensions of efficiency may not be detectable over limited time horizons.

Summary

In this age of increased accountability in higher education, far more attention is being paid to evaluation at all levels of colleges and universities. Trustees and presidents find themselves having to answer more completely and quickly to state agencies, accreditation associations, students, parents, and the local community. Each of these stakeholders may have a somewhat different view about what constitutes an effective college or university. So also do the organizational members themselves have divergent perspectives on organizational performance. Further complicating the assessment of effectiveness is the issue of the time frame for drawing conclusions about how well a college or university is doing. Choices driven by short-term forces may induce the adoption of policies and practices that in the long run may work to the detriment of the institution.

Thus, the conceptualization and measurement of effectiveness and efficiency constitute significant challenges for organizational leaders. To understand how different criteria are being utilized in evaluating effectiveness and efficiency in higher education, the literature provides useful models. However, no single model accurately describes the conditions in an institution. Instead, using multiple models provides a richer understanding of organizational outcomes. It would seem incontrovertible, therefore, that open discussions of criteria for effectiveness and efficiency must be an ongoing and continual priority of all colleges and universities.

Review Questions

1. A college president wishes to decide whether to use a goal approach or a system resource approach to assess his institution's effectiveness. He sees that the two modes differ in which of the following way(s):
   a. The period over which the evaluation is measured
   b. The people doing the evaluation
   c. The unit of analysis

   d. All of the above
   e. None of the above

2. The *U.S. News and World Report* rankings of schools and colleges is an operational measure of the system resource model of effectiveness. True or false?
   a. True
   b. False

3. A college president is concerned with maximizing the personal development of students. Which of the following organizational types in the Cameron model will be likely to be effective?
   a. Collegial
   b. Adhocracy
   c. Market

4. Which of the following models of effectiveness best describes the policy of the chair of a chemistry department in her attempts to balance the demands of the faculty and staff for personal growth and development with the demands of a dean of the College of Arts and Sciences for greater publication output?
   a. System resource model
   b. Internal process model
   c. Strategic constituencies model
   d. Phase models
   e. Fit or congruence models
   f. Competing values model

5. For 40 years, a single liberal arts college in a thinly populated state has served a constituency that has few choices of postsecondary education. Which of the models of effectiveness can best be used to evaluate its effectiveness?
   a. System resource model
   b. Internal process model
   c. Strategic constituencies model
   d. Phase models
   e. Fit or congruence models
   f. Competing values model

6. Which of the following is a characteristic of the social construction perspective on organizational effectiveness?

a. The assessment of effectiveness focuses attention on actions that organizational members believe are worth taking
b. The assessment of effectiveness entails making sense of actions and constructing plausible rationales that justify those actions
c. Meetings and forums, rather than more data collection, will help the organization determine its level of effectiveness
d. All of the above

Case Discussion Questions

Consider the Owens College case presented at the beginning of this chapter.

1. The new accreditation standards operate under the assumptions associated with the goal model of effectiveness. In what ways may this new emphasis be a challenge for Owens College? In what ways may the college benefit from paying more attention to goals?
2. The president noted that none of the college's current performance indicators provide a direct measure of the official goal of the college, which is to provide a liberal arts education. How might the college go about developing operational goals to assess its performance on liberal arts learning outcomes?
3. When considering the system resource model, Owens College would be viewed as effective; it receives a steady flow of highly academically qualified students and obtains significant endowment growth each year. But how may the limitations of the system resource model provide an inflated sense of effectiveness at Owens College?
4. Apply the internal process model to assess the effectiveness of Owens College and Urban University. Which institution appears more effective? Then, apply the strategic constituencies model to both institutions. How do the two institutions compare?
5. Consider the competing values model. Was there a shift during the steering committee meeting regarding the relative focus on internal dynamics versus external demands, or in the emphasis on stability/control versus flexibility/change? Plot this movement in the quadrants of Table 8.4. Based on this shift, which effectiveness criteria may gain prominence in the self-study as it unfolds?
6. Describe the steering committee meeting in terms of sensemaking. In what ways did the meeting help the committee members begin to focus collectively on their shared commitments?

References

Alfred, R., Ewell, P., Hudgins, J., & McClenney, K. (1999). *Core indicators of effectiveness for community colleges.* Washington, DC: Community College Press, American Association of Community Colleges.

Alstete, J. W. (1995). *Benchmarking in higher education: Adapting best practices to improve quality* (ASHE-ERIC Higher Education Report, No. 5). Washington, DC: George Washington University, Graduate School of Education and Human Development.

Alvesson, M., & Deetz, S. (2000). *Doing critical management research.* Thousand Oaks, CA: Sage.

Baker, E. L. (2005). *Improving accountability models by using technology-enabled knowledge systems (TEKS)* (Research/Technical Report, No. 143). Los Angeles: National Center for Research on Evaluation, Standards, and Student Testing, Center for the Study of Evaluation, University of California Los Angeles.

Banta, T. (1993). *Making a difference: Outcomes of a decade of assessment in higher education.* San Francisco: Jossey-Bass.

Banta, T., Rudolph, L., Van Dyke, J., & Fisher, H. (1996). Performance funding comes of age in Tennessee. *Journal of Higher Education, 67*(1), 23–45.

Barak, R., & Kniker, C. (2002). Benchmarking by state higher education boards. In *New directions for higher education* (No. 118, pp. 93–102). San Francisco: Jossey-Bass.

Bedeian, A. G., & Zammuto, R. F. (1991). *Organizations: Theory and design.* Chicago: Dryden Press.

Bensimon, E. (2004). The diversity scorecard: A learning approach to institutional change. *Change, 36*(1), 45–52.

Bensimon, E., Polkinghorne, D., Bauman, G., & Vallejo, E. (2004). Doing research that makes a difference. *Journal of Higher Education, 75*(1), 104–126.

Bess, J. L., & Shearer, R. E. (1994, April). *College image and finances: Are they related to how much students learn?* (ERIC Document No. ED372670). Paper presented at the annual meeting of the American Educational Research Association, New Orleans, LA.

Betz, D., Cunliff, E., & Guinn, D. (2003). Alternative road to "paradise": Growing toward AQIP. In S. E. Van Kollenburg (Ed.), *Organizational effectiveness and future directions, Vol. 2.* Chicago: The Higher Learning Commission of the North Central Association of Colleges and Schools.

Bogue, E., & Brown, W. (1982). Performance incentives for state colleges. *Harvard Business Review, 60*(6), 123–128.

Borden, V. M. H., & Banta, T. W. (Eds.). (1994). Using performance indicators to guide strategic decision making. In *New directions for institutional research* [Special Issue] (No. 82). San Francisco: Jossey-Bass.

Braverman, H. (1974). *Labor and monopoly capital: The degradation of work in the twentieth century.* New York: Monthly Review Press.

Buchanan, D. (2003). Getting the story straight: Illusions and delusions in the organizational change process. *TAMARA: Journal of Critical Postmodern Organization
Science,* 2(4), 7–21.

Burke, J. C. (2001). *Accountability, reporting, and performance: Why haven't they
made more difference?* Keynote address presented at the 39th Annual Conference
of the Research and Planning Group for California Community Colleges, Lake
Arrowhead, CA.

Burke, J. C., & Minassians, H. P. (2002). Reporting higher education results: Missing links in the performance chain. In *New directions for institutional research*
(No. 116). San Francisco: Jossey-Bass.

Burke, J. C., Minassians, H. P., & Yang, P. (2002). State performance reporting
indicators: What do they indicate? *Planning for Higher Education, 31,* 15–29.

Cameron, K. S. (1978). Measuring organizational effectiveness in institutions of
higher education. *Administrative Science Quarterly, 23*(4), 604–632.

Cameron, K. S. (1981). Domains of organizational effectiveness in colleges and universities. *Academy of Management Journal, 24*(1), 25–47.

Cameron, K. S., & Whetten, D. A. (1983). Some conclusions about organizational
effectiveness. In K. S. Cameron & D. A. Whetten (Eds.), *Organizational effectiveness: A comparison of multiple models* (pp. 261–277). New York: Academic Press.

Cameron, K. S., & Whetten, D. A. (1996). Organizational effectiveness and quality:
The second generation. In J. C. Smart (Ed.), *Higher education: Handbook of theory and research, Vol. XI.* New York: Agathon Press.

Casu, B., & Thanassoulis, E. (2006). Evaluating cost efficiency in central administrative services in UK universities. *Omega, 34*(5), 417–426.

Choppin, J. (1991). *Quality through people: A blueprint for proactive total quality management.* San Diego: Pfeiffer & Company.

Clegg, S., & Hardy, C. (1996). Organizations, organization, and organizing. In
S. Clegg, C. Hardy, & W. Nord (Eds.), *Handbook of organization studies*
(pp. 1–28). Thousand Oaks, CA: Sage.

Connolly, T., Conlon, E., & Deutsch, S. (1980). Organizational effectiveness: A
multiple-constituency approach. *Academy of Management Review, 5*(2), 211–217.

Cyert, R. M., & March, J. B. (1963). *A behavioral theory of the firm.* Englewood
Cliffs, NJ: Prentice-Hall.

Daft, R. L. (1995). *Organization theory and design* (5th ed.). Minneapolis/St. Paul,
MN: West Publishing Company.

Daft, R. L. (2001). *Organization theory and design* (7th ed.). Cincinnati, OH: South-
Western College Publishing.

Dale, B. G., Wu, P. Y., Zairi, M., Williams, A. R. T., & Van der Wiele, T. (2001).
Total quality management and theory: An exploratory study of contribution.
Total Quality Management, 12(4), 439–449.

Dawson, P. (1994). *Organizational change: A processual approach.* London: Paul
Chapman Publishing.

Dee, J. (2006). Institutional autonomy and state-level accountability: Loosely-coupled governance and the public good. In W. Tierney (Ed.), *Governance and the public good* (pp. 133–155). Albany: State University of New York Press.

Dougherty, K. J., Kim, J. E., & Hong, E. (2002, April). *Performance accountability and community colleges: Forms, impacts, and problems.* Paper presented at the annual meeting of the American Educational Research Association, New Orleans, LA.

Dutton, J. E., Dukerich, J. M., & Harquail, C. V. (1994). Organizational images and member identification. *Administrative Science Quarterly, 39,* 239–263.

Educational Testing Service. (1973). *The institutional goals inventory.* Princeton, NJ: Educational Testing Service.

Etzioni, A. (1964). *Modern organizations.* Englewood Cliffs, NJ: Prentice-Hall.

Fligstein, N. (1990). *The transformation of corporate control.* Cambridge, MA: Harvard University Press.

Gamson, W. A. (1968). *Power and discontent.* Homewood, IL: Dorsey Press.

Gioia, D. A., & Thomas, J. B. (1996). Identity, image, and issue interpretation: Sensemaking during strategic change in academia. *Administrative Science Quarterly, 41*(3), 370–403.

Gray, P. J., & Banta, T. W. (Eds.). (1997). *The campus-level impact of assessment: Progress, problems, and possibilities.* San Francisco: Jossey-Bass.

Haber, S. (1964). *Efficiency and uplift: Scientific management in the Progressive Era, 1890–1920.* Chicago: University of Chicago Press.

Hellawell, D., & Hancock, N. (2001). A case study of the changing role of the academic middle manager in higher education: Between hierarchical control and collegiality? *Research Papers in Education, 16*(2), 183–197.

Herman, R. D., & Renz, D. O. (2004). Doing things right: Effectiveness in local nonprofit organizations, a panel study. *Public Administration Review, 64*(6), 694–703.

Hertz, H. S. (2005). *Education criteria for performance excellence.* Gaithersburg, MD: Baldrige National Quality Program.

Judd, C. M. (1987). Combining process and outcome evaluation. In. M. M. Mark & R. L. Shotland (Eds.), *Multiple methods in program evaluation: New perspectives for program evaluation* (No. 35, pp. 23–41). San Francisco: Jossey-Bass.

Kahn, R. L. (1974). The work module: A proposal for the humanization of work. In J. O'Toole (Ed.), *Work and the quality of life: Resource papers for work in America* (pp. 199–226). Cambridge, MA: MIT Press.

Kanigel, R. (1997). *The one best way: Frederick Winslow Taylor and the enigma of efficiency.* New York: Penguin.

Katz, D., & Kahn, R. L. (1978). *The social psychology of organizations* (2nd ed.). New York: Wiley.

Katzenbach, E. L. (1968). *Planning programming budgeting systems: PPBS and education.* Cambridge, MA: New England School Development Council.

Kilmann, R. H., & Herden, R. P. (1976). Toward a systemic methodology for evaluating the impact of interventions on organizational effectiveness. *Academy of Management Review, 1*(3), 87–98.

Kilmann, R. H., & McKelvey, B. (1975). The MAPS route to better organization design. *California Management Review, 17*(3), 23–31.

Kramer, M. W., & Berman, J. E. (1998, November). *Stories of integration, differentiation, and fragmentation: One university's culture.* Paper presented at the annual meeting of the National Communication Association, New York.

Kuh, G. D., & Whitt, E. J. (1988). *The invisible tapestry: Culture in American colleges and universities* (ASHE-ERIC Higher Education Report, No. 1). Washington, DC: Association for the Study of Higher Education.

Layzell, T. (1999). Linking performance to funding outcomes at the state level for public institutions of higher education: Past, present and future. *Research in Higher Education, 40*(2), 233–246.

Lee, J. (2004). Comparing institutional relationships with academic departments: A study of five academic fields. *Research in Higher Education, 45*(6), 603–624.

Lenning, O., Lee, Y. S., Micek, S. S., & Service, A. L. (1976). *A structure for the outcomes of postsecondary education.* Boulder, CO: National Center for Higher Education Management Systems.

Lewin, A. Y., & Minton, J. W. (1986). Determining organizational effectiveness: Another look and an agenda for research. *Management Science, 32*(5), 514–553.

Lincoln, Y., & Denzin, N. (1994). The fifth moment. In N. Denzin & Y. Lincoln (Eds.), *Handbook of qualitative research* (pp. 575–586). Thousand Oaks, CA: Sage.

Lutz, F. (1982). Tightening up loose coupling in organizations of higher education. *Administrative Science Quarterly, 27,* 653–669.

Lysons, A. (1993). The typology of organizational-effectiveness in Australian higher education. *Research in Higher Education, 34*(4), 465–488.

Lysons, A., & Hatherly, D. (1996). Predicting a taxonomy of organizational effectiveness in U.K. higher educational institutions. *Higher Education, 32*(1), 23–39.

March, J. G., & Olsen, J. P. (1976). *Ambiguity and choice in organizations.* Bergen, Norway: Universitetsforlaget.

March, J. G., & Simon, H. A. (1958). *Organizations.* New York: Wiley.

Martin, J. (1992). *Cultures in organizations: Three perspectives.* New York: Oxford University Press.

Mills, M. (1998). From coordinating board to campus: Implementation of a policy mandate on remedial education. *Journal of Higher Education, 69*(6), 672–697.

Mintzberg, H. (1979). *The structuring of organizations: A synthesis of the research.* Englewood Cliffs, NJ: Prentice-Hall.

Murphy, L. R., & Cooper, C. L. (2000). *Healthy and productive work: An international perspective.* New York: Taylor & Francis.

Nadler, D. A., & Tushman, M. L. (1977). A diagnostic model for organizational behavior. In J. R. Hackman, E. E. Lawler III & L. W. Porter (Eds.), *Perspectives on behavior in organizations* (pp. 85–98). New York: McGraw-Hill.

Neumann, A. (1995). On the making of hard times and good times: The social construction of resource stress. *Journal of Higher Education, 66*(1), 3–31.

Ostroff, C., & Schmitt, N. (1993). Configurations of organizational effectiveness and efficiency. *Academy of Management Journal, 36*(6), 1345–1361.

Perrow, C. (1961). Goals in complex organizations. *American Sociological Review, 26*(6), 854–865.

Perrow, C. (1963). Goals and power structures: A historical case study. In E. Friedson (Ed.), *The hospital in modern society* (pp. 112–146). New York: Free Press of Glencoe.

Perrow, C. (1977). Three types of effectiveness studies. In P. S. Goodman, J. M. Pennings, & Associates (Eds.), *New perspectives on organizational effectiveness* (pp. 96–105). San Francisco: Jossey-Bass.

Peterson, M., & Cameron, K. S. (1994). *An annotated bibliography of quality in higher education.* Ann Arbor: Center for the Study of Higher and Postsecondary Education, University of Michigan.

Pfeffer, J. (1977). Power and resource allocation in organizations. In B. M. Staw & G. Salancik (Eds.), *New directions in organizational behavior* (pp. 235–265). Chicago: St. Clair Press.

Pfeffer, J., & Salancik, G. (1978). *The external control of organizations: A resource dependence perspective.* New York: Harper & Row.

Porter, L. W., Lawler, E. E., III, & Hackman, J. R. (1975). *Behavior in organizations.* New York: McGraw-Hill.

Powell, T. C. (1995). Total quality management as competitive advantage: A review and empirical study. *Strategic Management Journal, 16*(1), 15–37.

Quinn, R. E. (1981). A competing values approach to organizational effectiveness. *Public Productivity Review, 5,* 122–140.

Quinn, R. E., & Cameron, K. S. (1983). Organizational life cycles and shifting criteria of effectiveness: Some preliminary evidence. *Management Science, 29,* 33–51.

Quinn, R. E., & Rohrbaugh, J. (1983). A spatial model of effectiveness criteria: Toward a competing values approach to organizational analysis. *Management Science, 29,* 363–367.

Rahman, S. (2004). The future of TQM is past. Can TQM be resurrected? *Total Quality Management & Business Excellence, 15*(4), 411–423.

Richman, B. M., & Farmer, R. N. (1974). *Leadership, goals, and power in higher education.* San Francisco: Jossey-Bass.

Riesman, D. (1958). *Constraint and variety in American higher education.* Garden City, NY: Doubleday.

Roberts, L. (1994). *Process reengineering.* Milwaukee, WI: ASQ Quality Press.

Rockart, J. F. (1979). Chief executives define their own data needs. *Harvard Business Review, 57*(2), 81–93.

Ruppert, S. S. (Ed.). (1994). *Charting higher education accountability: A sourcebook on state-level performance indicators.* Boulder, CO: National Center for Higher Education Management Systems.

Scott, W. R. (1998). *Organizations: Rational, natural, and open systems* (4th ed.). Upper Saddle River, NJ: Prentice Hall.

Smart, J. C., Elton, C. F., & Martin, R. O. (1980, April). *Qualitative and conventional indices of benchmark institutions.* Paper presented at the Twentieth Annual Forum of the Association for Institutional Research, Atlanta, GA.

Smart, J. C., & Hamm, R. E. (1993). Organizational effectiveness and mission orientations of two-year colleges. *Research in Higher Education, 34*(4), 489–502.

Sowa, J. E., Selden, S. C., & Sandfort, J. R. (2004). No longer unmeasurable? A multidimensional integrated model of nonprofit organizational effectiveness. *Nonprofit and Voluntary Sector Quarterly, 33*(4), 711–728.

Steers, R. M. (1977). *Organizational effectiveness.* Santa Monica: Goodyear Publishing.

Taylor, F. W. (1914). *The principles of scientific management.* New York: Harper & Brothers.

Texas State Higher Education Coordinating Board. (2003). *Efficiencies at Texas public institutions of higher education, fiscal year 2001–fiscal year 2003.* Austin, TX: Author, Division of Research, Campus Planning and Finance.

Thomas, C. R. (1996). *Taxonomy of administrative activities for colleges and universities* (2nd ed.). Chicago: Consortium for Higher Education Software Services.

Thomson, S. C. (2005). Culture of quality: Northwest Missouri State University's corporate-style goal-setting and number-crunching. *Crosstalk, 13*(2), 9–11.

Tierney, W. (1992). Cultural leadership and the search for community. *Liberal Education, 78*(5), 16–21.

Tricker, R. I., & Boland, R. (1982). *Management information and control systems.* New York: Wiley.

University of Hawaii at Hilo. (2004). *UH Hilo Strategic Plan.* Retrieved February 1, 2007, from www.uhh.hawaii.edu/uhh/strategic/success.php.

Van de Ven, A. H., & Ferry, D. L. (1980). *Measuring and assessing organizations.* New York: John Wiley & Sons.

Weick, K. E. (1977). Re-punctuating the problem. In P. S. Goodman, J. M. Pennings, & Associates (Eds.), *New perspectives on organizational effectiveness* (pp. 193–225). San Francisco: Jossey-Bass.

Weick, K. E. (1995). *Sensemaking in organizations.* Thousand Oaks, CA: Sage.

Weiermair, K., & Perlman, M. (Eds.). (1990). *Studies in economic rationality: X-efficiency examined and extolled.* Ann Arbor: University of Michigan Press.

Yuchtman, E., & Seashore, S. E. (1967). A system resource approach to organizational effectiveness. *American Sociological Review, 32*(6), 891–903.

Zaleznik, A., Christensen, C. R., & Roethlisberger, F. J. (1958). *The motivation, productivity, and satisfaction of workers: A prediction study.* Boston: Harvard University, Division of Research, Graduate School of Business Administration.

9

ORGANIZATIONAL CHANGE IN HIGHER EDUCATION

CONTENTS

Preview   791
Case Context   792
Introduction   794
Defining Change   796
Planned Change Models   798
Emergent Change Framework   808
Synthesis of the Change Models   810
Contingency Framework for Change   813
Postmodern and Critical Perspectives on Change   816
Summary   819
Review Questions   820
Case Discussion Questions   821
References   822

The authors are most grateful for the critical comments on an early draft of this chapter by Jerlando Jackson, University of Wisconsin Madison. The final version, of course, is our own and may or may not reflect the perspective of the reviewer.

Preview

- Complex external environments have heightened the importance of change for higher education organizations, but failure rates for organizational change may be unacceptably high.
- Positivist research seeks to identify organizational variables that objectively identify and define conditions (e.g., goals, structures, values, and people) in an organization that enhance or impede change.
- The planned change model is guided by positivist assumptions and conceptualizes change as an intentional act that is driven by specific goals and plans. Theories related to planned change include diffusion of innovations, sociotechnical theories, and human process theories that include force field analysis.
- The diffusion of innovations framework suggests that new ideas are incorporated into an organization through a sequential process of awareness, persuasion, evaluation, trial, and implementation. New ideas are evaluated in terms of perceived advantage, compatibility, accessibility, divisibility, and communicability.
- Sociotechnical theories emphasize the importance of organizational design in facilitating change. Job enrichment, job enlargement, and job rotation are three practical strategies for modifying organizational designs in order to enhance organizational members' motivation for change.
- Force field analysis displays the relative strength of forces for and forces against change. Processes of unfreezing, changing, and refreezing can foster organization-wide change.
- In contrast to planned change, the emergent change model is based on social constructionist assumptions and suggests that organizational change emerges through multiple, grassroots initiatives.
- The effectiveness of organizational change depends on the development of human resources in organizations. Five contingencies—structure, leadership, culture, resources, and external environment—determine the human resource needs of the organization. The appropriate model for organizational change (e.g., an emphasis on planned change or emergent change) follows from information about these contingencies.
- Postmodernists note that rapid economic, political, and social changes on a global scale have significant effects on colleges and universities; some of these effects may diminish institutional autonomy, but others may promote equity, diversity, and empowerment.
- Critical theory highlights the political dimensions of change and suggests that resistance to change may actually be beneficial to an organization.

———————————————— CASE CONTEXT ————————————————

Curriculum Change at Greenbough Tech

Greenbough Technical University, an historically Black public institution, has strong programs in the natural sciences and engineering fields, as well as a good reputation for having faculty who care deeply about teaching. Administrators in the Provost's Office at Greenbough Tech received a request for proposals from the federal government for a grant to improve college teaching in science and engineering. A group of administrators met to develop a proposal. Given the deadline, however, there was little time to get faculty involved in writing the proposal.

Four months later, the administrators were pleased to announce that Greenbough Tech's proposal had been funded through the national competition. The funds and prestige associated with the grant would give faculty in science and engineering programs significant capacity to change their practices.

However, at department meetings across the university, faculty members raised concerns. Faculty in the chemistry department, for example, were skeptical that the funds would be sufficient to provide enough course release time for faculty to participate in curriculum development. "This stuff takes time," noted the chemistry department chair. "We simply cannot add another task for faculty who already have big teaching loads and major research responsibilities. They have budgeted only one semester of course releases for participating faculty. That's not enough. We would really need to reassign faculty members for at least an entire year in order to do this effectively."

The biology faculty, moreover, were doubtful regarding whether curriculum development would actually count as legitimate faculty work in tenure and promotion reviews. "I sure as hell don't want my junior faculty working on this," the biology chair declared. "And I am not crazy about the senior faculty working on this either. All of us need to be in our labs, doing research. We all care about teaching, but damn it, we have junior faculty who need to get tenure. And all of our faculty need to publish."

Initially, administrators were angered by the faculty responses and viewed their comments as a sign of resistance to change. "Here we are coming in with bags of money, and they still don't want to do anything different," complained the provost. But after a few days, the provost met with the department chairs to discuss their ideas for curriculum change. And she started the meeting in an interesting way.

"OK, let's forget about this grant for a minute," she explained. "And just tell me what your faculty are already doing in their classrooms." The department chairs welcomed this discussion and spent the next hour sharing with the provost all that their faculty were doing to update syllabi, experiment with new pedagogical practices, and engage both graduate and undergraduate students in their research projects.

"All of this is quite exciting," noted the provost. "Actually, the parameters of the grant give us quite a bit of flexibility regarding the activities themselves. So let's revise the activities. Let's use the course release funds for updating syllabi. Let's shift the focus of our summer workshops to concentrate instead on new pedagogical practices, especially the innovative stuff that you are doing to promote collaborative learning in large lecture classes. And let's use those travel funds to promote undergraduate research with faculty."

"I like this idea," replied the chemistry chair, "because it keeps the same goals, outcomes, and indicators as the original grant proposal, but the activities will actually be designed to provide more support for the things that we are doing already."

"But what about the issue regarding tenure and promotion criteria?" asked the biology chair.

"Well, we already have a policy on the books that allows a faculty member to specialize in applied research. We can add curriculum development to the list of examples of applied scholarship," explained the provost, who continued to note that this policy change would be consistent with Ernest Boyer's (1990) conceptualization of faculty research, which includes the scholarship of discovery (empirical research), the scholarship of integration (interdisciplinary synthesis), the scholarship of service (applied research to serve the public), and the scholarship of teaching and learning (inquiry into pedagogy, curriculum, and learning modes).

"Let's make that change in policy," replied the provost. "The College of Education is already using curriculum development as a criterion for promotion and tenure, and I think that a few liberal arts departments do, too. At any rate, this policy change has my strong support."

"All right, as soon as the policy changes, I will encourage my faculty to participate," the biology chair responded.

"I see. Trust, but verify," joked the provost.

"Well, no, I trust that you will follow through. But I would just have more confidence going to my faculty after the change is already on the books," explained the biology chair.

"No, I completely understand," the provost noted. "And the good news is that this grant is about to produce its first policy change, which could actually have some long-term implications for teaching and learning on this campus."

Introduction

Higher education leaders encounter an increasingly complex external environment where social, political, and market forces are reshaping the postsecondary landscape (Paul, 2005). Institutions are faced with qualitative and quantitative changes in student populations and in the expanding realms of knowledge that comprise the academic fields and disciplines. Moreover, universities now encounter both competition from and collaboration with the industrial sector, which is in turn making demands for participation in institutional governance decisions about research, curriculum, and admissions (Browning, 2006; Gonzales & Dee, 2004; Slaughter & Rhoades, 2004).

In recent years, some observers have criticized higher education as slow to respond to feedback about the changing composition and nature of the external environment. Whether these authors are concerned about responsiveness to the needs of students, industry, or the public good, they are united in their assessment that higher education institutions are fundamentally inward looking and tend to preserve the status quo (Braskamp & Wergin, 1998; Keller, 1983; Tierney, 1992). Other observers have commented on higher education's tendency to downplay internal feedback mechanisms. Opportunities for change are diminished when upper level administrators do not respond to feedback from faculty, staff, and midlevel managers who have specific, practical knowledge that could improve organizational performance. The creative talents of organizational members may be squandered where voices for change are marginalized by institutional and departmental norms that preserve hierarchical distinctions and that centralize power and authority among those who would block change (Kezar, 2002).

While individual units and departments may regularly scan their environments informally to observe changes that may affect their operations, the college or university as a whole often fails to develop a forward looking agenda for long-term concerted action at the institutional level. Instead, institutions tend to make incremental changes that do not involve major disruptions in processes or internal structures. Faculty, staff, and administrators simply take on additional roles and drop others.

Over time, incremental changes and increments in workload place unmanageable burdens on personnel and call for more fundamental changes to core processes and operating procedures (Romanelli & Tushman, 1994; Simsek & Louis, 1994). In the shifting environment for higher education, colleges and universities are beginning to recognize the need for new modes of adaptation and change. Wise strategies for change may determine, to a large extent, the degree to which colleges and universities experience success in turbulent environments. In some cases, organizational survival itself may depend on whether an institution can accurately appraise its own strengths and weaknesses in light of external conditions, appreciate the modes of change that are necessary, and change course and chart a new direction for the future (Hartley, 2003).

The importance of change, however, may be equaled by the difficulty of achieving it (Burnes, 2004a, 2004b). Despite prodigious efforts and even adequate financial support, organizational change may remain elusive. Eckel and colleagues (Eckel, Hill, & Green, 1998; Eckel & Kezar, 2003), for example, examined 26 change initiatives, which were funded by the Kellogg Foundation and guided by the American Council on Education (ACE). The ACE projects were designed to promote organizational change that was deep and pervasive. Eckel's research revealed that few of these initiatives actually yielded anything close to the transformative effects for which the grant recipients hoped. At the conclusion of the ACE project, only 6 of the 26 institutions were found to be successfully transforming (Eckel & Kezar, 2003), and a subsequent study four years after the completion of the project (Ventimiglia, 2005) found that only three of those institutions could be considered successfully transforming.

How and why higher education institutions change is the subject of this chapter. Understanding the dynamics of the change process permits more insight into the procedures needed to facilitate change and the leadership required to put them into place. In this chapter, we explore two models that derive from different definitions: planned change and emergent change. The planned change model includes innovation adoption, sociotechnical, and human processual theories of change. In contrast, sensemaking and improvisation are important concepts in the emergent model. Rather than promote one model over the other, we suggest that higher education leaders need to become skilled in the application of both planned and emergent change. We offer a diagnostic framework that organizational leaders can use in determining when to employ each model. Finally, we conclude the chapter by exploring critical theory and postmodern perspectives, which serve as important cautions against moving forward without considering the ethical dimensions of change.

Defining Change

Change can be defined as an alteration in the structures, processes, and/or behaviors in a system (Zaltman & Duncan, 1977) or as the introduction of something new to an organization. In the latter case, this type of change is called an innovation; that is, the adoption of an idea, behavior, or process that is new to the organization (Damanpour & Evan, 1984).

Some changes are **transformational** and produce a major overhaul of the organization's structure and strategy. Attempts by some community colleges to add four-year programs to their degree offerings, for example, represent transformational changes in the traditional missions of these institutions. Other changes in higher education are **incremental** and result in less dramatic effects; though, over the long term, incremental changes may set the organization on an entirely new path. A faculty shortage brought on by an unanticipated wave of retirements, for example, may incrementally lead to the use of more adjunct faculty in courses for first-year students.

Keller (1983) notes that when higher education institutions change, they often do so incrementally; that is, they are adaptive but in an unplanned way. Muddling through with bit-by-bit changes to the organization can avoid significant conflict and, over time, yield a trajectory toward institutional improvement (Lindblom, 1959). Keller, however, argues that incremental changes in higher education organizations are unlikely to address effectively the needs of society. Incremental change is not guided by a unifying vision; adaptations, consequently, are often haphazard, inefficient, and not necessarily responsive to institutional goals. Moreover, incremental change in higher education has often taken the form of adding more functions to the roles of the same personnel (e.g., adding community outreach and extension functions to the roles of faculty members or adding service-learning functions to the roles of student affairs staff). These increments in workload can place unmanageable burdens on faculty, administrators, and staff.

According to Van de Ven (1986), there are four central problems in the management of change:

1. A **human problem** of managing attention. When a college is successful, most organizational members are engaged in maintaining or enhancing success by improving the efficiency of the system. They are focused on achieving current goals and have little time for examining or developing new ideas, and often they do not.

2. A **process problem** in managing new ideas. Most organizational

changes require concerted, collaborative action. While it may be possible to gain the attention of some individuals or groups of individuals, it is more difficult to mold whole organizations that often comprise competing interest groups or coalitions.

3. A **structural problem** of managing part-whole relationships. It is difficult for isolated units to embrace an organization-wide innovation when changes in their unit must also be linked to other changes across the organization. A significant change in undergraduate general education requirements, for example, is a case in point, as each affected department must see its contribution to the curriculum for the whole institution. Instead, frequently, they see only the local impact of the change on their own unit, which may appear initially to be more disruptive than beneficial.

4. A **strategic problem** of institutional leadership. The "business as usual" syndrome is difficult to overcome. Colleges and universities may adopt a "sunk cost" mentality, whereby investments in existing technologies preclude consideration of new expenditures toward innovation (Seymour, 1988). As a result, organizations must be cultivated to remain receptive to ideas from the outside. Under the right circumstances, there can be considerable willingness to explore new ways of achieving goals.

In order to address these challenges, organizational researchers have developed theories and models to guide the change process. The **planned change** framework, for example, is conceptualized as an intentional effort to improve organizational processes through the implementation of new ideas based on scientific knowledge (Bennis, Benne, & Chin, 1961). In colleges and universities, the knowledge may be based on institutional research, accreditation self-studies, or program reviews (Martin, Manning, & Ramaley, 2001). Research and practice in higher education have been located primarily in the planned change tradition. The ACE initiatives studied by Eckel et al. (1998), for example, were intentional efforts developed by senior administrators at each institution, and the initiatives ranged from infusing technology into the classroom to revising promotion and tenure guidelines.

On the other hand, in decentralized, loosely coupled systems (Orton & Weick, 1990) organizational change is more likely to emerge through the interaction of multiple, localized adaptations (Spender & Grinyer, 1995). Within any college or university, multiple reforms are occurring on an ongoing basis, as faculty and staff develop localized responses to practice-based challenges. These local adaptations do not deliberately seek to change the entire organization, but over time they can be mapped to reveal the direction of change in the organization (Hardy, Langley, Mintzberg, & Rose, 2003).

This notion of **emergent change** (decentralized local adaptation) differs from the slow incrementalism criticized by Keller (1983) and others. Critics of incrementalism argue that higher education institutions cannot afford to wait years for new strategies to be identified; change is needed immediately. In all likelihood, however, emergent change has been occurring in most institutions for many years in response to changes in student characteristics, new research opportunities, and other external stimuli. These decentralized, grassroots changes may in turn have cumulative effects on the organization as a whole. Poindexter (2003), for example, notes that the cumulative and interactive effects of multiple pedagogical reforms such as service learning, collaborative learning, and student-centered learning can change the teaching and learning culture of an entire institution. Creative leaders can identify unifying patterns and themes in the organization's dispersed grassroots initiatives and then provide the recognition and support necessary to carry those changes to the entire institution.

In the following sections, we explore both planned and emergent models of change. Specifically, we examine three frameworks for understanding how organizations plan for change: (1) adoption of innovations, (2) sociotechnical perspectives, and (3) human processual theories. Then, we consider how organizational change emerges from the multiple, grassroots initiatives that occur quite frequently in loosely coupled organizations. We contrast the top-down perspectives of the planned change model with the bottom-up emphasis of emergent change, and we offer a contingency framework for employing both models under different organizational conditions.

Planned Change Models

Planned change models are based with frequency in systems theory assumptions and frameworks. Systems theory in the positivist tradition, however, appears to focus on stability rather than change. The presumption is that systems such as organizations are self-regulating and seek to maintain a state of equilibrium. In other words, equilibrium appears as the typical condition with pressures for change considered temporary aberrations until the system can return to a steady state (Katz & Kahn, 1978).

An intriguing question, then, is how significant change can occur if the system has a natural tendency to return to its original, steady state? One answer from some organizational sociologists is to turn the model on its head and suggest that change should be concerned as the normal state of the system with equilibrium or stasis the aberration (Luhmann, 1995). This perspective suggests that change is dynamic, ongoing, and evolving; the organization is constantly changing—in contrast to viewing change as a periodic remedy to address problems that occasionally present themselves.

If we assume that organizations are constantly changing, then equilibrating forces such as standard operating procedures and long-standing traditions may act as inhibitors to ongoing change and development. It is, therefore, important for higher education leaders to understand whether leadership means bringing an organization (especially a successful one that may seem to have gone astray) back into equilibrium or pressing an organization toward continuous change. A sensible and perhaps more realistic approach is to aim toward an optimum balance between the two.

The ability to maintain an effective balance between stability and change may depend on the utilization of two feedback sources that exist in all organizations, though the feedback modes do not always operate effectively. The first source is information about change in the environment, indicating a need to be adaptive across organizational boundaries in order to survive, compete, and be successful. The second feedback source is internal. Adaptive organizations develop internal feedback loops through processes such as assessment and program evaluation, which highlight needs for improvement and change.

External feedback, when detected by boundary-spanning organizational members, can be an important impetus toward change. These external data sources include changes in student populations, ecological changes (competition), public policy changes, resource availability, and the pace and complexity of changes in the broader culture and society. On the inside of the organization, forces toward change include dissatisfaction with organizational performance and changes in the characteristics of organizational members.

The mere perception of the need for change, however, does not guarantee that change will occur. In successfully changing organizations, antientropic forces (i.e., forces against the dissolution of energy in the organization) are mobilized to take action. Leaders and decision makers emerge to focus energy in structures and activities charged expressly with the function or responsibility for managing change. This is the very essence of planned change. As Levy (1986) notes, planned change "originates with a decision by the system to deliberately improve its functioning" (p. 6).

Again, feedback from outside and inside the organization is critical in planning for change. Theories that pertain to the adoption of innovations explain how organizations use external feedback for change. The sociotechnical and human processual theories, in contrast, offer frameworks for understanding internal feedback.

Adoption of Innovations

External forces for change can be examined through the diffusion of innovations framework. Researchers who utilize the diffusion framework identify an innovation and track its adoption across organizations over time. Mort (1946), in a study of public school innovation, found that initially only a few schools would adopt an innovation (early adopters), then a large majority would implement the idea, and finally, a small group of late adopting schools would innovate.

Everett Rogers (1962; Rogers & Shoemaker, 1971) developed a model that depicts five stages through which organizations adopt an innovation: (1) awareness, (2) persuasion, (3) evaluation, (4) trial, and (5) implementation. **Awareness** begins with some type of environmental scanning, formal or informal, at some level of the organization. "Did you hear what one of our peer institutions is doing with its undergraduate curriculum?" a faculty member might muse aloud to her colleagues. This type of informal assessment or a more elaborate market analysis may trigger a desire to adopt an innovation. In the second stage, **persuasion**, a change agent (perhaps the faculty member or her department chair, in the example above) begins to advocate on behalf of adopting the innovation. Potential adopters (e.g., colleagues in that department and across the campus) then **evaluate** the potential innovation as favorable or not depending on several criteria:

1. Perceived advantage: the extent to which potential adopters view the innovation as an improvement over previous practices
2. Compatibility: the extent to which potential adopters perceive the innovation as consistent with existing values and past experiences
3. Accessibility: the ease with which the innovation can be understood
4. Divisibility: the degree to which the innovation can be tried on a limited or incremental basis
5. Communicability: the degree to which the innovation can be easily described and visualized

For example, an apparent improvement in the undergraduate curriculum at another institution may be seen by some as better than what exists at the present institution (perceived advantage), but not as significantly different from current patterns (compatibility). If the new curriculum can be easily understood by the current faculty (accessibility), tested on a limited basis (divisibility), and easily described (communicability) to nonexperts (e.g., trustees and prospective students), then there is a good likelihood that it will be adopted. After a **trial** period in a particular department, the innovation may then be **implemented** college-wide.

Van de Ven (1986) developed a modification of the Rogers model that is less linear. He added such process elements as *gestating events, shocking events, proliferating events, setback events, learning events,* and *shifting innovation characteristics* such as novelty and size. Each of these either speeds up, impedes, or merges the stages in the sequence of the adoption process. Change agents—that is, people in the organization who take active steps to promote change—can watch for these elements and use them to advance change efforts. As Van de Ven notes, however, one of the key challenges of managing change is to get people within the organization to appreciate and attend to new ideas and opportunities. Therefore, change agents need to be knowledgeable of both external conditions and internal dynamics.

Sociotechnical Theories

In addition to exploring how external ideas diffuse into organizations, research on planned change examines how internal organizational design characteristics may foster or impede change. Sociotechnical theories test relationships between existing and hypothetical characteristics of organizational design and their effects on desired outcomes. The organizational design characteristics are typically described in terms of mechanistic and organic dimensions (Burns & Stalker, 1994). Organic organizational designs usually lead to loosely coupled linkages among units and departments. Under these conditions localized, departmental innovation may take place more readily, but organization-level changes may require more mechanistic designs that specify clear connections among the multifaceted units of a college or university (e.g., specific linkages among academic departments for general education reform or linkages between academic affairs and student affairs divisions to promote service learning).

Centralization is another organizational design variable that affects the change process. Organizations can be classified on a continuum from highly centralized (where just a few people have the authority to make decisions) to highly decentralized (where decision-making authority is dispersed widely among many organizational members). When organizations are decentralized, localized changes occur more readily, while large-scale changes are more difficult. Under decentralized conditions, no authority from the top is required to engage in change, but there are many different subunits to change before the organization as a whole can be said to have changed. If the central administration of a university wanted to make an institution-wide change, it would have to work through every department. But each department could make local changes without having to clear those decisions through central administration. However, when the organization is centralized, large-scale changes can be accomplished by fiat. Significant changes in the organization can be declared by central command, but small changes become harder to implement locally, since they must be approved at many levels in the bureaucratic structure (Damanpour, 1996). Table 9.1 summarizes the effects of organizational design characteristics on the change process.

Sociotechnical theories offer practical recommendations for redesigning organizations to improve prospects for successful organizational change. The central unit of change is the nature of the tasks performed, restructuring them to increase organizational members' motivation for change. Job redesign programs, for example, encompass a variety of specific techniques, including job enrichment, job enlargement, and job rotation.

Job enrichment is derived from theories of work motivation (Herzberg, Mausner, & Snyderman, 1959), which suggest that motivators can be built into work. These motivators include opportunities for achievement, recognition, responsibility, advancement, task capability, and knowledge growth. From this perspective, tasks from a *vertical* slice of the organization are brought together into a single job to increase the level of challenge of the job. Here, the role occupant not only interacts up and down the organizational hierarchy but also absorbs some of the responsibilities from higher levels. Thus, the job becomes enriched. The assumption is that by providing organizational members with tasks that offer greater challenge, intrinsic motivation for change will be enhanced.

Job enlargement consolidates tasks from a *horizontal* slice of the work unit to provide greater task variety and a stronger sense of responsibility for the whole task. For example, instead of having a clerk in the admissions office work exclusively with sorting incoming applications, the clerk can be given an enlarged role that includes more task variety—not just sorting applications but also organizing campus tours for prospective students. By building into the job greater variety, discretion, feedback, and responsibility for the whole task, motivation for change will likely improve (Hackman & Oldham, 1980).

It is important to express a caveat at this point. Depending on the technology of the job, enlargement may not always work. A job with high demands for interdependence, for example, often causes great stress when too many different tasks are added. A person scheduling space for meetings in an overbooked student activities center, for example, may have problems handling additional tasks. In addition, sometimes combining many boring jobs into one just makes one giant boring job!

Job rotation is another task-based mode for fostering change. With job rotation, organizational members not only gain skills in different tasks, but they expand their range of social connections throughout the organization and thus increase their commitment to the organization as a whole, rather

TABLE 9.1
Effects of Organizational Design on the Change Process

Organizational Design Characteristic	Effects on Organizational Change
Organic/mechanistic structure	The looseness of structure or the coupling among units affects the internal diffusion rate. Loose coupling usually leads to weak linkages that allow local innovation to take place more readily. Tighter coupling may permit more rapid implementation of organization-wide change, but it may also yield more resistance from organizational members.
Centralized versus decentralized	When the organization is decentralized, small changes take place more easily, while large-scale changes are more difficult to implement. When the organization is centralized, large-scale change can often be accomplished by administrative fiat. Significant changes in structure can be declared by central authority. But small changes desired by central administrators are harder to implement locally, since they must be cleared first with lower levels. There is more resistance to large change in decentralized organizations. There is more resistance to small change in centralized organizations.
Governance and decision making	Shared power and the activities of special interest groups make change difficult, except under unusual conditions (e.g., small size, narrow goals).
Structural interdependence	The interdependence of units impedes change. A change in unit X may have (often unknown) implications for a change in unit Y.
Personnel	Organizational members who have been in their positions longer have more vested interests and more resistance to change. On the other hand, long-standing employees may have strong commitments to seeing the organization succeed. The less frequent the turnover in personnel, the fewer new ideas that can be brought in by newly hired employees.

(continued)

TABLE 9.1 (Continued)

Organizational Design Characteristic	Effects on Organizational Change
Reward systems	The more the reward system focuses on satisfying lower order needs instead of opportunities for growth and development, the less receptivity to change.
Organizational climate	A risk-averse climate can inhibit change.
	Organizations that avoid or suppress conflict tend to be more resistant to change.
	Organizations that experience excessive conflict are also resistant to change.
	Organizational climates that are evaluative with punitive consequences for failure are likely to be more resistant to change than those in which data collected in the course of evaluation and assessment are fed back to workers for their own use in improvement.
	Organizations that demand explicit rational justification for all changes are less likely to be receptive to new ideas than other organizations where the level of trust permits more tolerance of ideas that are in formative stages.
	Strong traditions can cause passivity, ritualism, and ultimately resistance to change.

than only to the one unit to which they might have been otherwise assigned. Furthermore, the multiskilled generalist capacities of organizational members participating in such programs result in more and better ideas for change than are typically forthcoming from narrow specialists. The downside of such a practice, however, is that just when workers become highly skilled at one task, they are transferred to another. Training and retraining costs, therefore, must be balanced against the gains in general skills and wider organizational commitment.

Sociotechnical theories suggest that it is more effective first to change the structure of the organization and then allow changes in organizational members' attitudes to follow. The assumption is that structural redesign can enhance individuals' propensities toward change. In contrast, human processual theories focus on the need to change people first, before organization-wide change can occur.

Human Processual Theories (Lewin)

Psychologist Kurt Lewin (1951) was one of the first to develop an approach for analyzing the forces for and against change. His *force field* analysis recognized that resistance to change can be overcome when people understand and contrast the forces that may be leading them to resist (restraining forces) and the forces inducing them to change (driving forces). Consider, for example, a college that proposes to change a compensation system for faculty from stepped annual raises to a merit-based system. Figure 9.1 displays vectors that indicate the relative strength of the forces for and against change. At first, there may be an equilibrium between the forces for and the forces against change. In order to implement the change, one or more of the forces for change must be increased or one or more of the forces against change must be reduced, or some combination of the two.

The use of force field analysis—a pictorial representation of the pressures promoting and impeding change—helps change agents diagnose more realistically and specifically the forces that are involved and their relative strength (Couger, Higgins, & McIntyre, 1993). Portraying the forces on a diagram further permits a decision about which forces are susceptible to change and to what degree they are changeable. Sometimes combinations of changes in both forces for and forces against can be arranged strategically to effect the desired change.

Lewin also developed a mechanism for managing the process of change. It involves three steps: unfreezing, changing, and refreezing. **Unfreezing,** the first step, requires the presentation of data to organizational members that disconfirms their current conceptions of what constitutes effective performance. The premise is that everyone wants to achieve a sense of competence and self-efficacy, but each person's equilibrium must be disturbed (but not destroyed) so that the person is compelled to seek change. By conveying information that shows people that they may not be performing as effectively as they believe, people are encouraged and led in nonthreatening ways to take stock of themselves and become open to new ideas and approaches. For example, if a faculty member who thinks he is highly effective is presented with evidence that he is not (e.g., poor teaching evaluations from students), then he may become open to different ways of behaving that will lead to greater success. Realistically, however, because knowledge of failure can be threatening, the first reaction of people to disconfirming evidence of their assumed success is often the rejection of the validity and reliability of the

FIGURE 9.1
A Force Field Analysis of a Change in a College From Stepped Raises to Merit-Based Raises

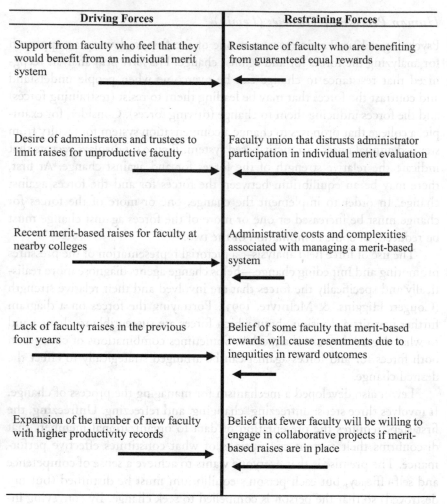

Driving Forces	Restraining Forces
Support from faculty who feel that they would benefit from an individual merit system	Resistance of faculty who are benefiting from guaranteed equal rewards
Desire of administrators and trustees to limit raises for unproductive faculty	Faculty union that distrusts administrator participation in individual merit evaluation
Recent merit-based raises for faculty at nearby colleges	Administrative costs and complexities associated with managing a merit-based system
Lack of faculty raises in the previous four years	Belief of some faculty that merit-based rewards will cause resentments due to inequities in reward outcomes
Expansion of the number of new faculty with higher productivity records	Belief that fewer faculty will be willing to engage in collaborative projects if merit-based raises are in place

Note: Length of arrow represents strength of force.

data. Disbelieving the evidence preserves the ego. It is critical, therefore, that the sources of information be credible, making it difficult for organizational members to dismiss them.

The second stage, **changing**, necessitates a shift in the way people think about themselves—showing them that new behaviors in new contexts can result in enhanced self-efficacy and high levels of satisfaction. This is, however, an especially difficult process. Often an effective method is to involve someone from outside the organization whom organizational members trust. Negotiating through informal leaders is also useful. Another way is to involve organizational members in the planning of the change so that they will feel ownership toward it and be committed to it.

The third stage, **refreezing,** suggests that unless organizational members are frozen into their new attitudes, values, and work patterns, they will revert back to the old ones in the absence of reinforcement. So refreezing includes the stabilization of the organization in its new structural framework, which may include new job roles, new reward systems, and changes in leadership style. Refreezing also refers to the process of integrating new beliefs, attitudes, and values that support the changed behavior patterns and relationships. In other words, the changed behavior must be supported by the culture of the institution. A shift in faculty attitudes toward the importance of teaching, for example, will not persist if the culture of the institution does not contain values that overlap with the faculty members' new orientation.

To summarize, Lewin's framework is based in an assumption of individual psychological resistance to change. Lewin's model emphasizes the need to unfreeze workers by providing information that disconfirms the individual's sense of self and that induces guilt and anxiety, which in turn fosters a change in behavior (Burnes, 2004a). Lewin's model, however, has been criticized as control-oriented, top-down, and overly simplistic. Kanter, Stein, and Jick (1992), for example, argued that Lewin's approach was too static and linear and did not reflect the multidirectional nature of organizational change. Instead of focusing on how a single leader can force change, Kanter and her colleagues developed a model to track the evolution of change at multiple organizational levels. The three components of the Kanter model include:

1. Macroevolutionary forces for change
2. Microevolutionary forces for change
3. Political forces for change

At the **macro level,** other organizations elicit changes in the focal organization. Colleges and universities may change in response to changes in the population of institutions to which the college or university belongs (DiMaggio & Powell, 1983). For example, when Harvard and Princeton began to offer large grants to low-income students, other Ivy League institutions revisited their financial aid practices. Pressures toward mimetic conformity, competition for scarce resources, and the regulatory environment in which the institution operates all contribute momentum toward change.

At the **micro level**, organizational age, size, growth, and decline set the context for change and encourage certain types of changes to occur. The challenges of change for a new start-up college are much different than those experienced by a well-established institution. Large, decentralized universities have coordination and communication issues that differ significantly from small liberal arts colleges. Finally, **political forces** for change emanate from power struggles among individuals and interest groups. Change and resistance reflect the ebb and flow of power within the organization. Moreover, any change that is adopted by the organization is likely to have a residual effect on the power balance within the organization—giving more power to certain groups and/or depriving others of the opportunity to influence the direction of the organization.

The Kanter et al. (1992) model is useful in that it facilitates a multilevel analysis of organizational change that moves beyond top-down perspectives, which focus on formal leaders and large-scale initiatives. However, as Hatch (1997) notes, the Kanter, Stein, and Jick model conceptualizes the individual as a rather passive respondent to broader organizational and political forces. The model does not recognize, for example, the ability of individuals to transcend the current political context and effect practical changes in their everyday work life.

An alternative perspective is to consider the individual not as a passive pawn in management's change agenda but as an agent both cognitively and psychologically capable of initiating and carrying out change. In the following section, we discuss models of emergent change that focus on grassroots initiatives undertaken by individuals and groups at multiple levels of the organization. Rather than beginning with an assumption that individuals resist change, the emergent model assumes that people desire to make consequential changes in their work roles and relationships.

Emergent Change Framework

The basic assumption of the emergent model is that people throughout the organization make frequent changes in their everyday work practices in response to local conditions. Faculty members, admissions counselors, financial analysts, and institutional researchers make constant adjustments in their daily interactions with other organizational members and with external clients and stakeholders. Sometimes these local-level changes become recognized by top-level administrators who then provide substantial support to expand and institutionalize the efforts. Major pedagogical innovations such as service learning, for example, emerged through local faculty initiative and have since been incorporated on a large scale at many institutions. Similarly, an institution-wide collaboration between student affairs and academic affairs units may have begun as a small project involving only a few faculty and staff members. In these examples, the benefits of change may be demonstrated on a small, localized scale and then distributed more widely throughout the entire organization.

The emergent model recognizes the substantial potential for creativity and innovation possessed by people at all levels of the organization. Organizational leaders may neglect an important source of change if they do not attend to the effects of local-level initiatives. Devoting the organization's resources entirely to large-scale initiatives may, in fact, reduce the likelihood for change. Leslie (1996), for example, argued that formal governance structures and strategic plans are generally not the locus of organizational change in higher education. Instead, organizational change is more likely to emerge from "street-level" decisions made by faculty and staff "in the trenches." Research on corporate entrepreneurship (Stopford & Baden-Fuller, 1994) also supports the notion that organizations change from the bottom-up through small experiments.

The bottom-up focus of the emergent model does not imply that leaders are irrelevant to the change process. Instead, the role of leadership shifts from directing and controlling change to facilitating creativity and experimentation among others. Rather than articulate an agenda for change and attempt to persuade or coerce others to "buy in" to that agenda, organizational leaders can pay attention to local-level changes, make sense of the patterns that emerge from those changes, and then articulate a vision that reflects common strengths across multiple adaptations. From this perspective, a critical skill in the leadership of change is the ability to skillfully craft an institutional vision that reflects the multiple, localized changes occurring in a college or university on an ongoing basis (Albert & Whetten, 1985; Dutton & Dukerich, 1991; Gioia & Thomas, 1996).

The challenge, however, is to identify emergent patterns and trends across a wide range of decentralized initiatives, while recognizing that not all local-level changes can or should become institutionalized. Limited resources, for example, preclude the ability to support more fully all localized initiatives. Even when resources are plentiful, if the institution invests in too many changes, then its mission will become less focused and it will fail to invest more heavily in areas that have greater potential for excellence (Balderston, 1995). In order to avoid overextension and mission drift, organizational leaders can construct a compelling organizational identity that unifies individual and group efforts around a common set of values, commitments, and priorities. Shared values and commitments can keep local-level change focused on broader organizational priorities, rather than drifting toward idiosyncratic goals. In order to sustain localized innovation and creativity, however, organizational leaders cannot impose conformity to a predetermined set of goals and objectives. The shared vision for the future must be flexible enough to permit the experimentation and risk taking necessary for new patterns of growth and development to emerge.

The emergent perspective on change suggests that higher education leaders need to examine the ongoing grassroots efforts of faculty and staff to adapt locally to changes that they detect in the microenvironments in which they operate. A focus on individuals and small groups as the locus of change, moreover, suggests the importance of recent conceptualizations for promoting creativity and **improvisation**—that is, the act of simultaneously initiating and implementing change (Brown & Eisenhardt, 1997). Faculty members, for example, improvise when they adapt instructional methods and techniques to meet the needs of students more effectively. They can utilize techniques such as fast feedback to assess student learning needs and to identify discrepancies between lesson objectives and learning outcomes (Roberts, 1995). The pace, method, and/or style of instruction may be modified, in turn, to reflect students' preferred ways of learning.

Faculty members in this setting may not rely on established course syllabi and traditional pedagogical practices. Instead, they continually redesign their courses to reflect the range of educational goals and academic abilities of their students. Improvisation in this context requires extensive communication and coordination among colleagues, as well as flexibility in work-related behaviors (Bastien & Hostager, 1988). Open communication is needed to facilitate the development of feedback channels, which enable faculty members to coordinate and mutually adjust their behavioral repertories and professional interactions. Improvisational activity may also require flexible work processes and procedures, which enhance individual capacities to adapt to the rapid pace of change in the institutional environment. Many colleges and universities, however, lack the horizontal communication structures necessary to support improvisational change; instead, structural differentiation and rigid boundaries between academic disciplines preclude creative exchanges of ideas and practices (Benjamin & Carroll, 1998).

Synthesis of the Change Models

Debates between proponents of planned change and advocates of emergent change characterize recent trends in the study of organizational change

(Burnes, 2004b). Top-down, centralized structures employ a planning approach to facilitating change. Bottom-up, decentralized structures promote grassroots, emergent change. The planned change approach is typically employed when the prominent organizational concern is being responsive to the external environment and when resources and time are limited. The emergent change model is employed more frequently when the focus is on innovation and creativity and when there is a culture of trust in the organization.

Many additional considerations are associated with planned versus emergent change. In the first instance, the ambitious goals of planned, institution-wide change are often formulated by change agents with vision. But the execution of the change over time is carried out by others at different levels of the organization who may not share the same vision or ambition. Over time, therefore, large-scale change tends to get watered down and loses energy. Major change initiatives tend to be transitory (Hardy et al., 2003), especially if faculty and staff are not involved in their development.

The emergent change model, on the other hand, may ignore powerful political movements toward hierarchical authority and control over higher education. Some institutions—especially public colleges and universities—experience significant external control in the form of accountability mandates from state government. Even private institutions now encounter a more intrusive external environment, as accreditation associations and professional licensure boards (such as those for nursing, education, and social work) exert more power over institutional decision making. Under these conditions, local-level change may be constrained significantly. Moreover, some changes can only be carried out through big initiatives that destabilize the organization and elicit fundamental changes in operations—sometimes called *frame-bending change* (Nadler & Tushman, 1989).

Local-level change, by definition, is fragmented and disconnected. For a unified organizational vision to arise and be a significant planning tool and source of motivation for workers, a leader or leadership group must be able to make critical and oftentimes difficult decisions about which parts of the bottom-up initiatives can and should be adopted institution-wide. Moreover, the communication and institutionalization of a consistent, unified vision, though its parts are generated from the bottom, can best be managed from the top—taking care, of course, not to claim ownership or close opportunities for additional changes in the future. Thus, organizational leaders at the top have responsibilities for organizing the multiple visions that have emerged so that they can be unified into a total plan for action. Also, leaders must link the separate, local-level changes together in a way that captures the imagination of organizational members and allows them to identify the vision as their own (rather than view the vision as being imposed upon them).

As higher education leaders encounter trends toward more managerial accountability (leading to higher levels of centralization) and toward the creation of more decentralized units within higher education institutions, they will likely need frameworks for organizational change that reflect both top-down and bottom-up perspectives. These change frameworks are displayed in Table 9.2.

In a longitudinal study of organizational change in the profit-making sector, Burnes (2004b) found that innovative organizations utilized both planned (centralized) and emergent (decentralized) approaches to change. Rather than viewing these approaches as competing perspectives, Burnes found that they were complementary. Other research by Brown and Eisenhardt (1997) in the computer software industry found that innovative firms were characterized by both clear lines of authority and extensive autonomy and design freedom. This study showed that successful organizational change may require both centralized and decentralized approaches. As Brown and Eisenhardt (1997) noted, "This combination is neither so rigid as to control the process nor so chaotic that the process falls apart" (p. 3). These studies suggest that higher education leaders should avoid searching for the "one best way" to enact organizational change. Instead, they need to seek complementary approaches that are well suited to guiding change in the context of paradoxical trends toward both greater centralization (planned change) and more decentralization (emergent change).

The research literature in higher education, however, does not provide clear guidance regarding when to use these different models of change. Primarily the research focuses on centralized, planned change initiatives (e.g., Eckel et al., 1998; Kezar & Eckel, 2002a, 2002b). Given the growing complexity of higher education institutions and the mounting expectations for external accountability, college and university leaders need to become skilled

TABLE 9.2
Frameworks for Planned and Emergent Change

	Externally Driven	*Internally Driven*
Planned	• Policy mandates • Government regulations	• Strategic planning
Emergent	• Social and cultural trends	• Grassroots initiatives

in employing multiple models of change. In the following section, we attempt to identify some of the contingencies that may differentiate opportunities for effectively using planned and emergent models for change.

Contingency Framework for Change

Which combination of change models is actually of most benefit to an organization depends on several contingencies, the primary one being the maximization of human resource development. The underlying assumption is that if organizations wish to improve their effectiveness, then they need to develop more fully their human resources (i.e., the skills and capabilities of personnel). The more that a change model leads to increases in human resource development, the more effective the organization will be. Thus, human resource development is an intervening variable in the movement of organizations from less effective to more effective.

We have identified five additional contingencies that must be considered when choosing a change model that will improve human resource development. These are:

1. **The structure for action.** Are organizational behaviors carried out in a sequential and linear order, or are behaviors permitted to take place simultaneously in overlapping time frames? Planned change initiatives are likely to strengthen the skills and capacities of personnel who work in tightly linked, interdependent structures. A highly coordinated approach to change helps organizational members address the complexities of interdependent tasks with many interlocking steps and stages. In contrast, when workers are engaged in multiple projects at different stages of development, planned change initiatives would likely stifle their efforts to work simultaneously on different tasks. Planned change would force workers to direct their attention to specific tasks and process stages, rather than work on multiple tasks at different stages. Under these conditions, the emergent change model would be more appropriate, because it allows organizational members to develop capacities for engaging in multiple, simultaneous projects.

2. **Leadership capacities at all levels.** Is wisdom about the need for and nature of organizational change lodged exclusively at the top of the organization, or is such knowledge widely dispersed? Instituting change from the top (planned change) will likely be ineffective if top-level executives are inept. Similarly, grassroots emergent change will

not be effective if organizational members at all levels do not have sufficient training and knowledge in their areas of specialization.

3. **The culture of trust**. Change models will have different effects on human resource development in a culture in which openness and honesty of communication are the norm. In a system in which there is distrust, it is unlikely that collaborative change from the bottom-up will be effective. Rather, imposed change from the top can, in the short run, result in immediate changes in human resource development, as personnel are assigned to positions where their capacities can be utilized more effectively.

4. **Financial slack**. When resources are ample, organizations can support multiple grassroots initiatives without the pressure of needing any of them to pay off immediately. Slack resources allow an organization to take risks with innovative practices and permit organizational members to experiment with changes at the subunit level. Moreover, resources are sufficient to support the training and development that might be necessary for faculty and staff to engage in local-level change. In contrast, where financial resources are limited, planned change efforts can direct resources toward those avenues that are most likely to yield success for the organization. Planned change efforts are also more likely to attract additional resources from the environment, because the organization provides a specific focus for external entities to support. In contrast, it may be more difficult to secure funding for the more amorphous goal of stimulating yet unspecified grassroots changes.

5. **External environment constraints and opportunities**. Organizations that depend on a limited number of suppliers of inputs (e.g., colleges than rely on a stable set of feeder high schools for student enrollments) will likely be more successful with planned change initiatives that give boundary-spanning personnel clear guidance regarding how to interact with external constituents. In contrast, when the organization's set of suppliers is large and diverse, emergent change models allow boundary spanners to craft their own responses to unique opportunities in the environment.

An analysis of these contingencies will identify the combination of change models that is likely to stimulate higher levels of human resource development and in turn higher levels of organizational effectiveness (see Figure 9.2). It is certainly possible that some of the contingencies will point toward the use of a planned change model, while other contingencies

FIGURE 9.2
Contingencies in Change Strategies

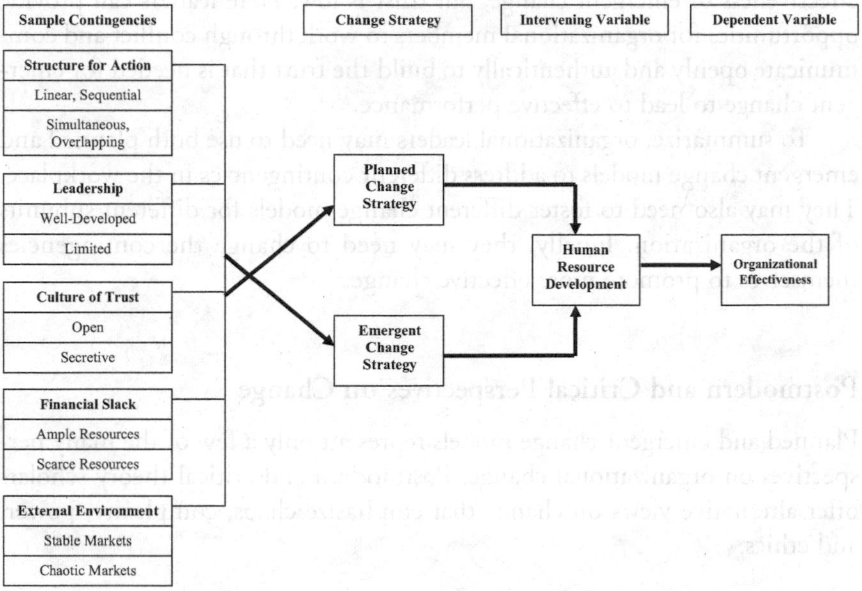

Sample Contingencies		Change Strategy	Intervening Variable	Dependent Variable

Structure for Action
- Linear, Sequential
- Simultaneous, Overlapping

Leadership
- Well-Developed
- Limited

Culture of Trust
- Open
- Secretive

Financial Slack
- Ample Resources
- Scarce Resources

External Environment
- Stable Markets
- Chaotic Markets

Planned Change Strategy

Emergent Change Strategy

Human Resource Development

Organizational Effectiveness

Note: Based on an assessment of all contingencies, organizational leaders select a change strategy that will maximize human resource development and, in turn, promote organizational effectiveness.

suggest the use of an emergent model. Thus, a combination of models may be necessary.

Consider an organization where the structure for action comprises simultaneous, overlapping projects. Leadership capacities are well developed throughout the organization, trust is high, and the external environment is highly differentiated. Resources, however, are limited. In this scenario, leaders may use a planned change model to attract external funding around a specific change agenda. The infusion of new resources also frees capacity for workers to engage in innovative decentralized projects (i.e., the emergent change model) that attempt to capitalize on multiple initiatives directed toward a range of external constituents.

Similarly, consider an organization where the actions of workers in one department are tightly linked, but the tasks of others in a different subunit are more flexible with overlapping time frames. Planned change initiatives may be more effective for the first department, while emergent change can be promoted in the second unit.

In addition to using multiple change models, leaders can work to change the contingencies themselves. Consider an organization (or department or other subunit) where four of the five contingencies are pointing toward the effectiveness of emergent change, but trust is low. Here leaders can provide opportunities for organizational members to work through conflict and communicate openly and authentically to build the trust that is needed for emergent change to lead to effective performance.

To summarize, organizational leaders may need to use both planned and emergent change models to address different contingencies in the workplace. They may also need to foster different change models for different subunits of the organization. Finally, they may need to change the contingencies themselves to promote more effective change.

Postmodern and Critical Perspectives on Change

Planned and emergent change models represent only a few of the many perspectives on organizational change. Postmodern and critical theory scholars offer alternative views on change that emphasize chaos, complexity, power, and ethics.

Postmodernism and Change

Postmodernists argue that large-scale social, cultural, economic, and political changes have had significant effects on colleges and universities (Bloland, 1995, 2005). Globalization, the rise of multinational corporations, and the rapid advance of communications technology have engendered significant flux and indeterminacy in social relations and organizational life. In particular, organizational systems are becoming more random with parts less obviously connected. The result is a declining ability to predict which interventions and changes are likely to be successful in any organization. External turbulence and uncertainty, for example, may vitiate the assumptions of planned change models that rely on accurate scanning of the environment in order to determine which innovations are suitable for adoption by the organization. Environmental scans may be subject to so much error and misinterpretation as to render them nearly useless. Similarly, internal fragmentation within the organization may nullify efforts to identify emergent changes; organizations may be characterized by so much dissensus and indeterminacy that coherent patterns and themes cannot be constructed. Moreover, if such patterns were identified under fragmented conditions, then the themes would merely reflect the power positions of those articulating the themes, rather than some true or authentic interpretation of the organization (Buchanan, 2003).

Postmodernists also challenge the notion that change represents progress. Instead, change may simply reflect the ability of one interest group to subordinate others, and it may be associated as much with oppression and damage as with progress and advancement (Bloland, 1995). More optimistic readings of postmodernism, however, suggest that macrolevel changes have created a more open society, which presents an opportunity for reorganizing colleges and universities so that they promote equity, diversity, and empowerment (Hirschhorn, 1997; Tierney, 1992). Similar arguments and tensions are present in critical theory.

Critical Theory and Change

Critical theory calls into question the tendency to stigmatize resistance to change. Critical theorists view change primarily as a political struggle. More powerful interests compel those less powerful to change, or changes desired by less powerful groups are suppressed by the more powerful (Lukes, 2005). One implication of this perspective is that organizational leaders ought not to dismiss resistance as intransigence or a lack of commitment to the organization. On the contrary, resistance itself is a form of change that can have productive benefits for the organization (Baez, 2000).

Critical theory raises a second important question regarding assumptions about organizational change. Many (but certainly not all) studies of organizational change are motivated by managerial concerns about slow response times and lack of responsiveness to the external environment. The research on change in higher education has a distinctly managerial perspective that may privilege the voices of college presidents and other top administrators, and this perspective may underestimate or silence the perspectives of mid-level administrators, faculty, and students (Kezar, 2000). The overarching emphasis of this research is to determine how to get people to change their behavior in ways deemed appropriate by top-level management, rather than how organizational leaders can support grassroots change initiated by people in the trenches. As Fiol (2003) points out, most researchers have focused on how to squeeze more innovation out of organizations (and the people in them) without taking into account the need for continuous accumulation of new knowledge.

Critical theory, instead, locates actors within structures that both constrain activity and provide opportunities for change (Baez, 2000). British sociologist Anthony Giddens (1984) argues that people enact structures in their daily organizational activities and that these activities are mediated through the structural context that organizational members have created over time. As an example, if previous patterns of interaction have created a mechanistic, hierarchical structure, then current and future patterns of interaction will likely replicate these structural arrangements unless the behavioral patterns of organizational members are changed. Different theoretical perspectives offer divergent approaches for explaining these behavioral changes. The Lewinian approach suggests that a top-level leader can break these patterns by challenging and then changing the psychological orientations of individuals. Critical theory, in contrast, focuses on the ability of individuals to reconstruct power relations within organizations. The focus is on activism from the grassroots up, rather than persuasion from the top down.

Thus, the implications of critical theory are consistent with the emergent model of change, although critical theorists remain suspicious of change models that allegedly enhance grassroots innovation. They question whether workers truly have autonomy to make decisions that deviate from the status quo (Mumby, 2005). What would occur if a self-managed team were to deviate substantially from the wishes of upper level management? Critical theorists argue that although new organizational forms and processes have invited more participation, the underlying ideology has not changed. Self-managed teams and other forms of workplace participation simply carry out managerial directives through less coercive means (Deetz, 1992).

Critical theorists argue that a new ideology of organizational leadership is necessary in order to enact a more humanistic approach to change. The field of organizational development (OD) offers an alternative set of values and assumptions that can replace power- and control-centered ideologies. Proponents of OD (French & Bell, 1995; Gellerman, Frankel, & Ladenson, 1990) believe that organizations should:

- promote the development of human potential and empowerment to the fullest extent possible
- respect the dignity and inherent worth of each individual
- be flexible and encourage learning, growth, and transformation
- provide widespread meaningful participation in decision making
- embody honesty, openness, and trust

Practices associated with these values include facilitating open communication, collaborative problem solving, and continuous learning. Cynics may counter that OD adherents are naïve and hold romantic notions that organizations can be all things to all people; hard choices must be made, priorities must be adhered to, and not everyone is going to be happy. Critical theorists and OD authors, however, do not deny that organizations have limited resources and must be responsive to pressures from external actors who may not share such humanistic values (e.g., an impatient trustee or a demanding state legislator). But where organizations do have discretion in the choices that they make, these theorists offer alternative assumptions that emphasize openness, fairness, and ethical treatment—rather than control, environmental exploitation, and the maximization of employee effort relative to cost (Wooten & White, 1999).

Summary

Higher education organizations change in many ways—in inputs (e.g., applicants), outcomes (e.g., types of graduates), processes (e.g., new pedagogical approaches), organizational design (e.g., shifts from single discipline departments to interdisciplinary institutes), culture, and leadership. Change also occurs on multiple system levels. Macrolevel changes in the college's environment, such as state and federal policies and social and economic trends, often have a direct and immediate effect on the organization. At the microlevel, departments within the college or faculty and staff within those departments may engage in changes that eventually have a substantial impact on the organization as a whole.

In this chapter, we offered two different perspectives on change:

- change is elusive and difficult to initiate and manage, and
- change is always occurring at all levels of the organization.

At first glance, these perspectives appear contradictory (change is difficult to initiate, but it is always occurring). Both of these perspectives, however, may represent the realities of organizational change (Burnes, 2004b). Organizations routinely engage their members in the difficult task of revamping policies, practices, and procedures. In addition, individuals and groups in their localized practice are continuously adapting to new conditions and emergent environmental trends; over time, these localized adaptations can have significant effects on the entire organization.

Leaders may need to move back and forth between planned change and emergent change in order to address the needs for both coordinated action and inventive adaptation. Planned change can set in place structures that solidify the systemic interdependencies necessary for implementing complex reforms. These structures may be essential when organizational change involves sequential, interdependent reforms. Support for emergent change, in contrast, allows organizational members to operate outside the constraints of formal structure and make localized changes that respond to unique environmental and contextual dimensions of work. These localized adaptations can yield inventive new ideas, which may be beneficial to the entire organization.

Thus a key challenge for organizational leaders is preserving the paradoxical tension between planned change and emergent change. Leaders, therefore, need to develop complementary skill sets: the ability to plan and implement change as well as capacities for vision and sensemaking and a willingness to support grassroots initiatives that may lead to new frameworks for organizing the institution.

Review Questions

1. Which of the following characteristics of a pedagogical innovation enhance the likelihood that a college will adopt it?
   a. The new pedagogy is consistent with the current values and practices of the faculty
   b. The new pedagogy would require little additional training or preparation to implement
   c. The new pedagogy can be implemented incrementally in specific courses without the need for wholesale changes in the current curriculum
   d. All of the above

2. Based on Lewin's force field analysis, how can a change agent enhance the likelihood that an organizational change will be implemented?
   a. Increase forces for change
   b. Decrease forces against change
   c. Some combination of A and B
   d. All of the above

3. Why is refreezing important after a change occurs?
   a. To stabilize new roles, rewards, and leadership to support the change
   b. To integrate new beliefs and values into the culture of the organization
   c. Both A and B
   d. Neither A nor B

4. Planned change is characterized as:
   a. An intentional effort to improve organizational processes through the implementation of new ideas based on scientific knowledge
   b. The recognition and widespread promotion of grassroots change initiatives
   c. Both A and B
   d. Neither A nor B

5. How do the planned and emergent models of change differ?
   a. In the planned model, change is a single initiative; in the emergent model, change is multiple
   b. In the planned model, change is implemented in a centralized structure; in the emergent model, change is decentralized
   c. The planned model focuses on responsiveness and rationality; the emergent model focuses on organizational identity and improvisation
   d. All of the above

6. Which of the following contingencies would support the use of a planned change model?
   a. The organization is significantly externally controlled by a few dominant suppliers
   b. The organization has no financial slack
   c. The organization is characterized by a high level of distrust
   d. All of the above

7. Postmodern perspectives on change note that:
   a. Change may not necessarily reflect progress
   b. External turbulence may nullify planned change models that rely on environmental scanning
   c. Internal fragmentation may thwart efforts to identify changes that emerge within the organization
   d. All of the above

Case Discussion Questions

Consider again the Greenbough Tech case presented at the beginning of this chapter.

1. Conduct a force field analysis of the curriculum change grant. What were the forces for and forces against change? Display the relative strength of these forces. Did academic administrators take any actions to either increase the strength of the forces for change or reduce the strength of the forces against change?
2. In what ways did the administration's grant proposal development process reflect aspects of the planned change model?
3. How did the provost's response to faculty resistance employ the emergent change model?
4. Consider the structure, leadership, culture, resources, and external environment regarding the curriculum change grant. Given these

contingencies, does a planned change model or an emergent change model seem more likely to yield successful outcomes?

References

Albert, S., & Whetten, D. (1985). Organizational identity. In L. Cummings & B. Staw (Eds.), *Research in organizational behavior, Vol. 7* (pp. 263–295). Greenwich, CT: JAI Press.

Baez, B. (2000). Race-related service and faculty of color: Conceptualizing critical agency in academe. *Higher Education, 39,* 363–391.

Balderston, F. (1995). *Managing today's university* (2nd ed.). San Francisco: Jossey-Bass.

Bastien, D., & Hostager, T. (1988). Jazz as a process of organizational innovation. *Communication Research, 15,* 582–602.

Benjamin, R., & Carroll, S. (1998). The implications of the changed environment for governance in higher education. In W. Tierney (Ed.), *The responsive university: Restructuring for high performance* (pp. 92–119). Baltimore: Johns Hopkins University Press.

Bennis, W., Benne, K., & Chin, R. (1961). *The planning of change: Readings in the applied behavioral sciences.* New York: Holt, Rinehart, & Winston.

Bloland, H. (1995). Postmodernism and higher education. *Journal of Higher Education, 66*(5), 521–559.

Bloland, H. (2005). Whatever happened to postmodernism in higher education?: No requiem in the new millennium. *Journal of Higher Education, 76*(2), 121–150.

Boyer, E. (1990). *Scholarship reconsidered: Priorities of the professoriate.* Princeton, NJ: The Carnegie Foundation for the Advancement of Teaching.

Braskamp, L., & Wergin, J. (1998). Forming new social partnerships. In W. Tierney (Ed.), *The responsive university: Restructuring for high performance* (pp. 62–91). Baltimore: Johns Hopkins University Press.

Brown, S., & Eisenhardt, K. (1997). The art of continuous change: Linking complexity theory and time-paced evolution in relentlessly shifting organizations. *Administrative Science Quarterly, 42,* 1–34.

Browning, L. (2006, August 29). BMW's custom-made university. *New York Times,* pp. C1, C6.

Buchanan, D. (2003). Getting the story straight: Illusions and delusions in the organizational change process. *TAMARA: Journal of Critical Postmodern Organization Science, 2*(4), 7–21.

Burnes, B. (2004a). Kurt Lewin and the planned approach to change: A re-appraisal. *Journal of Management Studies, 41*(6), 977–1002.

Burnes, B. (2004b). Emergent change and planned change: Competitors or allies? The case of XYZ construction. *International Journal of Operations and Production Management, 24*(9–10), 886–902.

Burns, T., & Stalker, G. (1994). *The management of innovation* (3rd ed.). Oxford, England: Oxford University Press.

Couger, J., Higgins, L., & McIntyre, S. (1993). (Un)structured creativity in information systems organizations. *MIS Quarterly, 17*(4), 375–397.

Damanpour, F. (1996). Organizational complexity and innovation: Developing and testing multiple contingency models. *Management Science, 42,* 693–716.

Damanpour, F., & Evan, W. (1984). Organizational innovation and performance: The problem of organizational lag. *Administrative Science Quarterly, 29,* 392–409.

Deetz, S. (1992). *Democracy in an age of corporate colonization: Developments in communication and the politics of everyday life.* Albany: State University of New York Press.

DiMaggio, P., & Powell, W. (1983). The iron cage revisited: Institutional isomorphism and collective rationality in organizational fields. *American Sociological Review, 48,* 147–160.

Dutton, J., & Dukerich, J. (1991). Keeping an eye on the mirror: The role of image and identity in organizational adaptation. *Academy of Management Journal, 34,* 517–554.

Eckel, P., Hill, B., & Green, M. (1998). *En route to transformation.* Washington, DC: American Council on Education.

Eckel, P., & Kezar, A. (2003). *Taking the reins: Institutional transformation in higher education.* Westport, CT: Praeger.

Fiol, C. M. (2003). Designing knowledge work for competitiveness: About pipelines and rivers. In S. E. Jackson, M. A. Hitt, & A. S. DeNisi (Eds.), *Managing knowledge for sustained competitive advantage: Designing strategies for effective human resource management.* San Francisco: Jossey-Bass.

French, W. L., & Bell, C. H. (1995). *Organizational development: Behavioral science interventions for organizational improvement* (5th ed.). Englewood Cliffs, NJ: Prentice-Hall.

Gellerman, W., Frankel, M., & Ladenson, R. (1990). *Values and ethics in organizational and human systems development: Responding to dilemmas in professional life.* San Francisco: Jossey-Bass.

Giddens, A. (1984). *The constitution of society.* Berkeley: University of California Press.

Gioia, D., & Thomas, J. (1996). Identity, image, and issue interpretation: Sensemaking during strategic change in academia. *Administrative Science Quarterly, 41*(3), 370–403.

Gonzales, R., & Dee, J. (2004, November). *Corporate partnerships in graduate education: Faculty roles, academic policy, and institutional strategy.* Paper presented at the annual meeting of the Association for the Study of Higher Education, Kansas City, MO.

Hackman, J. R., & Oldham, G. R. (1980). *Work redesign.* Reading, MA: Addison-Wesley.

Hardy, C., Langley, A., Mintzberg, H., & Rose, J. (2003). Strategy formation in the university setting. In J. L. Bess (Ed.), *College and university organization: Insights from the behavioral sciences* (pp. 169–210). Amherst, MA: I & I Occasional Press.

Hartley, M. (2003). "There is no way without a because": Revitalization of purpose at three liberal arts colleges. *Review of Higher Education, 27*(1), 75–102.

Hatch, M. J. (1997). *Organization theory: Modern, symbolic, and postmodern perspectives.* New York: Oxford University Press.

Herzberg, F., Mausner, B., & Snyderman, B. (1959). *The motivation to work.* New York: John Wiley and Sons.

Hirschhorn, L. (1997). *Reworking authority: Leading and following in a postmodern organization.* Cambridge, MA: MIT Press.

Kanter, R., Stein, B., & Jick, T. (1992). *The challenge of organizational change: How companies experience it and leaders guide it.* New York: The Free Press.

Katz, D., & Kahn, R. L. (1978). *The social psychology of organizations* (2nd ed.). New York: Wiley.

Keller, G. (1983). *Academic strategy: The management revolution in higher education.* Baltimore: Johns Hopkins University Press.

Kezar, A. (2000). Pluralistic leadership: Incorporating diverse voices. *Journal of Higher Education, 71*(6), 722–743.

Kezar, A. (2002). Reconstructing exclusive and static images of leadership: An application of positionality theory. *The Journal of Leadership Studies, 3*(3), 94–109.

Kezar, A., & Eckel, P. (2002a). The effects of institutional culture on change strategies in higher education: Universal principles or culturally responsive concepts. *Journal of Higher Education, 73*(4), 443–460.

Kezar, A., & Eckel, P. (2002b). Examining the institutional transformation process: The importance of sensemaking, inter-related strategies, and balance. *Research in Higher Education, 43*(4), 295–328.

Leslie, D. (1996). Strategic governance: The wrong questions? *Review of Higher Education, 20*(1), 101–112.

Levy, A. (1986). Second-order planned change: Definition and conceptualization. *Organizational Dynamics, 15*(1), 5–23.

Lewin, K. (1951). *Field theory in social science.* New York: Harper & Row.

Lindblom, C. (1959). The science of muddling through. *Public Administration Review, 19,* 78–88.

Luhmann, N. (1995). *Social systems.* Palo Alto, CA: Stanford University Press.

Lukes, S. (2005). *Power: A radical view* (2nd ed.). New York: Palgrave Macmillan.

Martin, R., Manning, K., & Ramaley, J. (2001). The self-study as a chariot for strategic change. In J. Ratcliff, E. Lubinescu, & M. Gaffney (Eds.), *How accreditation influences assessment: New directions for higher education* (No. 113, pp. 95–115). San Francisco: Jossey-Bass.

Mort, P. (1946). *Principles of school administration.* New York: McGraw-Hill.

Mumby, D. (2005). Theorizing resistance in organizational studies: A dialectical approach. *Management Communication Quarterly, 19*(1), 19–44.

Nadler, D., & Tushman, M. (1989). Organizational frame bending: Principles for managing reorientation. *Academy of Management Executive, 3*(3), 194–204.

Orton, J., & Weick, K. (1990). Loosely coupled systems: A reconceptualization. *Academy of Management Review, 15*(2), 203–223.

Paul, D. A. (2005). Higher education in competitive markets: Literature on organizational decline and turnaround. *JGE: The Journal of General Education, 54*(2), 106–138.

Poindexter, S. (2003). The case for holistic learning. *Change, 35*(1), 24–30.

Roberts, H. (1995). *Academic initiatives in total quality for higher education.* Milwaukee, WI: ASQC Quality Press.

Rogers, E. (1962). *Diffusion of innovations* (1st ed.). New York: The Free Press.

Rogers, E., & Shoemaker, F. (1971). *Communication of innovations: A cross-cultural approach.* New York: The Free Press.

Romanelli, E., & Tushman, M. (1994). Organizational transformation as punctuated equilibrium: An empirical test. *Academy of Management Journal, 37*(5), 1141–1166.

Seymour, D. (1988). *Developing academic programs: The climate for innovation* (ASHE-ERIC Higher Education Report, No. 3). Washington, DC: Association for the Study of Higher Education.

Simsek, H., & Louis, K. S. (1994). Organizational change as paradigm shift. *Journal of Higher Education, 65*(6), 670–695.

Slaughter, S., & Rhoades, G. (2004). *Academic capitalism and the new economy: Markets, state, and higher education.* Baltimore: Johns Hopkins University Press.

Spender, J.-C., & Grinyer, P. (1995). Organizational renewal: Top management's role in a loosely coupled system. *Human Relations, 48*(8), 909–926.

Stopford, J., & Baden-Fuller, C. (1994). Creating corporate entrepreneurship. *Strategic Management Journal, 15*(7), 521–536.

Tierney, W. (1992). Cultural leadership and the search for community. *Liberal Education, 78*(5), 16–21.

Van de Ven, A. H. (1986). Central problems in the management of innovation. *Management Science, 32*(5), 590–607.

Ventimiglia, L. (2005). *Collective leadership: Faculty and administrators transforming higher education.* Unpublished doctoral dissertation, University of Massachusetts, Boston.

Wooten, K., & White, L. (1999). Linking OD's philosophy with justice theory: Postmodern implications. *Journal of Organizational Change Management, 12*(1), 7–20.

Zaltman, G., & Duncan, R. (1977). *Strategies for planned change.* New York: John Wiley.

IO

LEADERSHIP

CONTENTS

Preview	827
Case Context	828
Introduction	829
Defining Leadership	830
A History of the Study of Leadership	835
Idiographic Leadership Theories	838
Nomothetic Approaches to Understanding Leadership	843
Behaviorist Theories of Leadership	847
Interactive Theories of Leadership	852
Matching Traits, Contingencies, and Behaviors for Effective Leadership	854
Other Approaches to Leadership	864
Social Construction and Leadership	866
Summary	875
Review Questions	875
Case Discussion Questions	876
References	877

The authors are most grateful for the critical comments on an early draft of this chapter by Judith Glazer-Raymo, Teachers College, Columbia University. The final version, of course, is our own and may or may not reflect the perspective of the reviewer.

Preview

- Leadership can be described as an influence process, as the facilitation of the achievement of desirable organizational outcomes, as the fulfillment of group members' psychological needs, as an inherent characteristic of a person, and as an exchange process.
- Leaders and followers are reciprocal parts of a leadership role that must be played in all organizations. There are no leaders without followers.
- Leadership takes place continually at all levels in an organization, sometimes politically and charismatically, sometimes bureaucratically, sometimes at a distance, or at times face-to-face.
- Trait theory explains leader effectiveness in terms of the personality characteristics of great leaders.
- Transactional leaders recognize what subordinates want from their workplaces and attempt to see that they receive it, if performance warrants it; transformational leaders instead induce workers to transcend their own self-interests for the sake of the team or organization.
- Cultural determinist theories attribute effective leadership to conditions in the environment that constrain leaders to act in predetermined directions.
- Many organizational conditions abet or constrain leaders in their tasks. These substitutes for leadership must be recognized if leadership is to be effective.
- Leadership can be studied from the perspective of the behaviors that leaders engage in under varying organizational and environmental conditions.
- Situational views of leadership suggest that the characteristics of followers—such as their maturity levels—must be taken into account in leader behavior.
- Path-goal theory argues that effective leaders are those who can assist workers in understanding how achievement of organizational objectives provides them with desirable rewards.
- In leader-member exchange theory, leaders and subordinates evolve through a series of relationships that results, if effective, in networks of collaboration between not only leaders and followers but also among followers and in relationships between followers close to the leader and those more distant.
- Leader-match theory suggests that a leader's style is relatively intransigent so that if it does not fit the circumstances, then the circumstances, not the leader, must change.
- Social constructionist perspectives on leadership emphasize the importance of organizational culture, images, and symbols. Processes of sensemaking and reframing illustrate how organizational members construct leadership in particular contexts.

> • Feminist theories of leadership raise important questions regarding patriarchy; specifically, gendered relationships in organizations may be socially constructed in ways that subordinate women. Organizational leaders are advised to examine power relationships and create structures that affirm the contributions of both women and men.

CASE CONTEXT

The New Dean at East Harbor College

Janet Torres was savoring one of the final weekends of the summer. She knew that beginning on Monday, her professional life would change dramatically. She had recently been appointed dean of arts and sciences at East Harbor College, a small liberal arts institution in the Northeast. She would become the first woman to serve as arts and sciences dean in the college's history.

Based on her interview, Dean Torres knew that she would have a bit of a honeymoon period. The previous dean had not been well liked. Some of the department chairs described him as a taskmaster who had no sense of compassion for students or faculty. "He was driven by budgets and outcomes," reported one chair. "That was all he cared about."

Most of the department chairs had been in their roles for several years and were highly committed to the goals of East Harbor College, but they chafed under the watchful eye of the previous dean. "We did not need to be told what to do," said the chair of chemistry. "We needed someone with an intellectual vision, and he wasn't it."

Dean Torres spent the summer meeting informally with the department chairs. She found them to be knowledgeable, congenial, and willing to try new things. But the chairs lamented the fact that they seldom got together as a group and found that the department chair role was quite isolating. Another issue that emerged through her conversations was assessment and academic quality. The chairs indicated that their programs were all of high quality (who would admit otherwise?), but they were not convinced that the existing assessment plan would adequately demonstrate their achievements. Whereas the chairs could talk at length and with excitement about the projects in which their faculty and students were engaged, they spoke with less clarity about desired and actual outcomes.

Dean Torres also spent the summer assessing her leadership style and preferences. Through a professional development workshop for new deans, she received feedback on her communication skills (strong) and interpersonal abilities (more focused on tasks than relationships). When asked to reflect on her limitations, Dean Torres noted, "I am not good about maintaining distance. I am not a micromanager, but I don't like to feel disconnected from the work that people are doing. I don't want to be sitting up in my office not interacting with people. I want to talk with the chairs and the faculty nearly every day that I am there."

When asked about her leadership style, she described it as collaborative. Dean Torres explained, "I try to involve people in decision making. I spend a lot of time building consensus and trust, and showing that I am trustworthy. I do that by making sure that I follow up on all of the commitments that I make. I don't leave people hanging." Regarding risk taking, Dean Torres told her workshop coordinator, "Yeah, I will bet on a long shot. Sometimes they pay off big."

Before arriving on campus, Dean Torres reviewed the college's course catalogs, marketing brochures, and departmental reports. Initially, the amount of data appeared overwhelming. "There is just so much information to digest," she thought at one point. But then she realized that she was missing the forest for the trees. She decided to pay less attention to the specifics, and instead she attempted to identify key themes and connections across the documents. "I was trained in qualitative methods," she told her husband one evening. "Just because I became an administrator doesn't mean that I can't use those skills anymore."

Through this analysis, she identified three key themes: (1) liberal education for civic engagement, (2) connecting in-class learning to extracurricular experiences, and (3) active pedagogical approaches that put students in real world settings. She decided to focus on these themes during her year-opening address to the arts and sciences faculty. "I want to see if these themes resonate with faculty, or if I am totally off base," she said to a colleague at her former institution. "I have been trying to learn as much as I can. The first test comes in September."

Introduction

In the 1800s in the United States, when much smaller colleges and universities prevailed, it was possible for one person to exercise profound influence over internal academic affairs and external relations. Nicholas Murray Butler (Columbia), Andrew Dickson White (Cornell), William Rainey Harper (University of Chicago), and Daniel Coit Gilman (Johns Hopkins) could and did significantly change the course of education on their campuses. Today, such personal influence may not be possible. As Clark Kerr (1963) reported some years ago, though later recanted somewhat (Kerr,

2001), college presidents may now act more as mediators of conflict, both internally and across boundaries, rather than as initiators of change. Regardless of whether college leaders at the top today can exercise significant leverage for institutional change, the very belief that they are so empowered carries significant weight among internal and external constituents who look to those in authority for guidance, initiative, and direction. Praise or blame for organizational outcomes falls regularly on the shoulders of those titularly in charge.

In all organizations, including and perhaps especially higher education institutions, leadership takes place not only at the top but throughout the organization. Thus, deans, department chairs, program directors, committee heads, and faculty have formal responsibility for leadership, but leadership is often also assumed by those without formal leadership titles. Further, informal leadership in small group settings is often a more potent power than formal leadership. Increasingly, leadership in and by teams has come to be seen as having high potential for addressing the diverse needs of all institutions (Hackman, 1990; Hinds & Kiesler, 2002) and especially of colleges and universities (Bensimon & Neumann, 1993).

Issues of leadership in colleges and universities are extremely complex because of the unusual confluence of bureaucratic organization and polity (shared governance) and the concomitant need for leaders to be effective in both contexts. Further, because of the increasing importance of fund-raising in both private and public institutions, cross-boundary leadership—that is, institutional leadership in the external environment—must also be carried out and effectively synchronized with internal conditions (Ouchi, 1980). Leadership is additionally complicated by the loose coupling (Weick, 1976) that characterizes organizations of higher learning. That is, although leader initiatives may ramify throughout the organization, the direct effects of those actions may not be easily discernable.

In this chapter, we provide an overview of the large number of definitions and conceptualizations of leadership. We then examine theories that pertain to the personal characteristics and traits of leaders, the external conditions and constraints on leadership, the interaction of personal and environmental characteristics, and the complex relationships between leaders and followers. We conclude with social constructionist and feminist perspectives that extend conceptualizations of leadership to include collaborative and nonhierarchical forms.

Defining Leadership

In the popular press, there are articles about leadership almost daily, and there has been an enormous amount published in the academic literature.

Most organizational members admire, ignore, or suffer (sometimes all three!) incumbents in leadership positions. Few are unaware of the impact of leadership on their lives and most have opinions about how better leaders can be identified and how leadership can best be exercised.

Given so many opinions, what should be the definition of leadership? Many approaches are available in the literature (Fincher, 2003; Hunt, 2004; Smith & Hughey, 2006). Some place the origin of leadership on the idiographic side (e.g., personal traits and dispositions); others on the nomothetic side (including external environment and internal organizational culture); still others in between these two sides. In this chapter, our approach follows Lewin's (1938) social systems model presented in chapter 1; namely, $B = f(P,E)$—that is, leadership behavior is a function of *both* person and environment. Hence, the discussion in this chapter will consider theories emphasizing one or more of these terms and/or the interaction of them in leadership situations.

We begin with a consideration of some representative definitions of leadership. They fall into five classes: (1) leadership as an intentional activity initiated by an influential person, (2) leadership as a process aimed toward organizational objectives, (3) leadership as a fulfillment of individual needs, (4) leadership as a characteristic of a person, and (5) leadership as an exchange process.

1. Leadership as an **influence process:**
   a. "Leadership is the process by which one individual consistently exerts more influence than others in the carrying out of group functions" (Katz, 1973, p. 204). That is, leadership is one of a set of functions that must be carried out by the group. Others, for example, are task accomplishment, communication, and resource distribution.
   b. Leadership is "an interaction between members of a group. Leaders are agents of change, persons whose acts affect other people more than other people's acts affect them . . . Leadership occurs when one group member modifies the motivation or competencies of others in the group" (Bass, 1990, pp. 19–20). Bass also sees the role of leaders as inducing followers to adopt the leader's vision of the future of the organization and to accept personal responsibility for helping to carry out that vision.
2. Leadership as the facilitation of the achievement of **desired organizational outcomes.** Leadership is the performance of actions that help the group achieve preferred outcomes. It is the recognition by the

leader of desired outcomes and the facilitation of individuals and groups in the achievement of those outcomes (Stogdill, 1974).

3. Leadership as the fulfillment of group members' **psychological needs.** Leadership is the capacity to act as an internal ego ideal to individuals in groups (Hill, 1984; Maccoby, 1981). The leader best manifests the dreams and aspirations of organizational members; hence, they are willing to follow.

4. Leadership as a **characteristic of a person.** Leaders may be invested with personal qualities—for example, charisma—that induce followers to accept the legitimacy of their behavior and values (Conger, 1989).

5. Leadership as an **exchange process:**
   a. Leaders engage in exchanges with followers who by virtue of the special nature of the exchange contribute both leader and follower behaviors (Graen, 1976; Graen & Ulh-Bien, 1995; Hollander & Offermann, 1990; Wayne, Short, & Liden, 1997).
   b. Influence is synonymous with leadership only when the word "intended" precedes it. That is, if someone does not mean to (is not motivated to), it is not leadership (Zaleznik & Moment, 1964).

We will pursue in some detail each of these approaches to the conceptualization of leadership. At the end, we will see that each has validity but that no single definition adequately describes the entire mysterious process, especially as the context and contingencies differ.

Leaders and Followers

It almost goes without saying that there is no leadership without followers. Leaders and followers are collaborators. As Gibb (1954) notes:

> Probably the most important thing to be said about the concept of followers is that they, too, fulfill active roles. They are not to be thought of as an aggregation minus the leaders. It is part of the intention of the group concept to imply that all members actively interact in the course of movement in a common direction.
>
> The concepts of leading and following define each other. There can be no leading without following, and, of course, no following without leading. (p. 915)

A dean, for example, does not lead without faculty who support or resist him or her. No amount of public speaking, planning, threatening, or cajoling can be called acts of leadership unless followers, out of desire or fear, take action as a result of it.

It is not the case, however, that every follower must follow the leader for the leader to be exercising leadership. Almost inevitably, there will be dissidents.

> Not all members of any given group will, at any particular time and with a particular leadership, be followers, but all members will at some times, under some conditions, be followers or they will forfeit their membership. (Gibb, 1954)

That is, organizational members cannot resist leadership indefinitely or they will no longer technically or practically be part of a follower group. If a faculty member declines always to be influenced by a department chair, for all practical purposes he or she is no longer a member of the group being led by the chair. The recalcitrant faculty member may be dismissed, or he or she may be permitted to act independently from the group. In both cases, the faculty member has forfeited his or her membership in the group.

The Locus of Leadership

As noted above, leadership takes place at many levels in an organization (Dansereau & Yammarino, 1998). The level at which leadership is exercised depends, in part, on the organizational design and culture—for example, the formal decision-making structure and the informal norms. There are, of course, overlaps in design and culture across organizational levels and, correspondingly, at least some common characteristics. For example, politics takes place not only at the macro-organizational level but also in small groups, while small group behavior occurs in larger political settings (e.g., presidential cabinets and faculty senates), and both politics and small groups operate in all organizations.

What kinds of leadership work best seem to depend in some measure on the distance between the leader and the followers (Collinson, 2005; Kiesler & Cummings, 2002). Initial work on this subject was begun (and later carried on) by Robert House (1977). Important contributions followed from Waldman and Yammarino (1999), Antonakis and Atwater (2002), and many others. The interest continues. A recent *Wall Street Journal* article (Sandberg, 2005) discusses the efforts of some major firms to situate executive officers' desks in close physical proximity to their subordinates. In a study of research and development leadership in Japan (Bess, 1995), the leadership setting was circumscribed by the placement of desks in a small department in which the formal leader had daily face-to-face contact with subordinates. The leadership dynamics in that situation were quite different from those in more distant leadership environments.

Leader-follower distance is reflected in frequency of contact—the more distant, that is, the more intervening levels of hierarchy, the less frequent the contact. When contact is infrequent, some forms of leadership tend to be more effective than others. Leaders with charisma, for example, may be more effective in situations where leaders and followers are at a distance. Historically, charisma has been viewed as a mystical aura, a set of behaviors, a cluster of traits, or a divine gift (Conger et al., 1988).

When contact is more frequent, different forms of leadership may be necessary. Leaders who work in close proximity to followers may develop extensive knowledge of the followers' needs (Hersey & Blanchard, 1977), as well as a thorough understanding of the task and social environments in which they work (Blake & McCanse, 1991). Rather than rely on charisma, leaders can utilize knowledge of followers and knowledge of the work environment to make decisions that enhance the effectiveness of both the followers and the overall organization.

Thus, the nature of the collectivity or setting must be considered in understanding leadership. Within large organizations, formal leadership may be at a distance. In a large university, faculty and staff may seldom interact with the president. Within small organizations, however, leaders and followers may be in close proximity. The president of a small college, for example, could engage in frequent communication with nearly every faculty and staff member. The very conceptualization of the organizational character of an institution, therefore, to some extent sets the parameters for leadership.

In addition to recognizing differences in leadership based on proximity, it is important to note how leadership is applied in at least three functional domains (Parsons, 1951).

1. Technical/production level—decisions about the tasks to be performed; for example, what and how to teach
2. Managerial level—decisions about control of people and processes; for example, eliminating overlapping decision-making jurisdictions
3. Institutional level—decisions about the social system (its cultural norms and motivational conditions); for example, setting goals and engendering commitment from faculty and staff

To these, we add a fourth: institution-environment–level decisions about the strategic placement and maintenance of an institution among its suppliers and purchasers of its products. These are cross-boundary decisions.

To summarize, leadership takes place continually at all levels within an organization and across its boundaries. It occurs sometimes politically and charismatically, sometimes bureaucratically, sometimes at a distance, or at times face-to-face. At certain times, it is exercised by those in formal positions of leadership. On other occasions, leadership emanates from informal sources throughout the organization. And it covers a range of requisite organizational decisions.

A History of the Study of Leadership

As an orienting framework to understand the history of the study of leadership, we present the work of Jeffrey Barrow (1977) who parsimoniously identified the elements in each of the concepts in the social systems model: personal characteristics or traits (P), environmental factors (E), and leader behavior (B). Barrow does not offer hypotheses connecting the elements in each dimension, nor does he relate the elements to the concept of organizational effectiveness. Nevertheless, the model (Figure 10.1) is useful as a beginning guide for exploring the leadership literature.

Note that the vertical dimension in the Barrow conceptualization is the **idiographic** dimension, including traits, personality, skills, and self-orientation. The horizontal axis is the type of leader **behavior,** while the third, lateral axis is the **nomothetic** or situational dimension, labeled "environmental factors." These factors include a wide range of conditions in the organization—for example, organizational norms and values, task and technology characteristics, subordinate characteristics and behavior, and organizational and group characteristics (e.g., group dynamics, organizational design, the nature of the external environment, and leader position power).

When we connect Barrow's conceptualization of leadership to the social systems framework that guides this book, we find first a focus on the idiographic side *(P)*—on personal characteristics and traits. Then, interest shifts to the nomothetic side *(E)*—to understanding the environments or particular contexts in which certain kinds of leadership are more effective than others. Another strand picks up the third component of social systems theory, observed behavior *(B),* by examining the actual behaviors of leaders. Finally, we can explore interactions between personal characteristics *(P)* and environmental contingencies *(E),* as well as consider how leadership affects overall organizational effectiveness. We briefly expand on these approaches.

  1. **Idiographic.** Trait theory, for example, views leadership as a characteristic of a person. It seeks to identify the personal qualities (physical, attitudinal) of leaders. Are they, for example, taller? Braver? More caring? Trait theory examines the kinds of personal characteristics that inhere in the incumbents in different organizational positions— for example, college presidents or deans (Padilla, 2005). Similarly,

FIGURE 10.1*
Leadership Framework

Nomothetic Dimension
- external stability versus turbulence
- organizational design and authority
  structure
- group characteristics, social norms
- task characteristics and technology
- organizational philosophy and norms
- subordinate characteristics

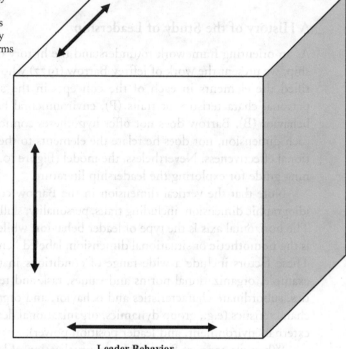

Idiographic Dimension
- physical features
- person versus task
  orientation
- personality
- task experience

Leader Behavior
- initiating structure
- consideration

*Adapted from Barrow (1977).

theories of transactional and transformational leadership consider the values and objectives of leaders in terms of the behaviors and attitudes that leaders wish to engender among followers.

2. **Nomothetic.** Deterministic leadership theories, for example, look to the cultural and situational conditions that induce persons in leadership positions to behave in predictable ways. Some nomothetic theories of leadership, furthermore, conceive of characteristics of the organization that relieve leaders of some of their roles (i.e., features that substitute for leader behavior) or other organizational conditions that augment their leadership.

3. **Leadership as a set of behaviors.** Certain acts can be said to be leadership according to behavioral theories. When a person does something to influence a group or organization to which he or she belongs, leadership can be said to have been exercised. The modes by which that influence is exercised are closely examined in this conceptualization of leadership.

4. **Leadership as interaction.** Researchers using this school of thought believe that leadership results from the interaction of person and environment *(P,E)*—of the individual and the situation. The focus is on behavior, just as in list item number 3 above, except in this case the concern is with the explanation of the behavior, rather than simply identifying the behavior itself.

5. **Leadership effectiveness.** This approach is a product of groups of individuals interacting among themselves and with the situation to produce some desired change or to sustain the status quo.

These five strands of leadership research have received different amounts of attention over the years. Rost (1991) and others have suggested the following rough time line describing the relative emphases: leader traits (1930s and 1940s), cultural and situational determinism (1930s and 1940s), behavioral theories (1950s and 1960s), interaction/contingency theories (1970s), and organizational excellence/effectiveness theories (1980s and 1990s).

Rost summarizes his integration of the theories as follows:

> Leadership produces excellent organizations because leaders are great executives who have certain traits (high energy, trustworthiness, charismatic persona, visionary purpose, honest communication, obsession with goals) that help them choose the correct behaviors (challenge the process, model the way, manage by walking around, position the organization, manipulate the culture, encourage the heart, empower collaborators, and stick to the knitting) so that they do the right thing in key situations (mergers, international economic competition, lower productivity, consumer dissatisfaction, volatile times), by facilitating the work group democratically and forcefully. (pp. 18–19)

It should be noted that Rost's definition attributes a great deal of the success of leaders to their initiative and agency—a potentially dangerous conceptualization that Murphy (2000) warns may raise unrealistic expectations of the performance of leaders.

We now turn to an exploration of the particular theories in depth. We examine the theories roughly in the order suggested by Rost's time line of the evolution of leadership theory. However, it is important to keep in mind that although a particular theory may be associated initially with a specific time period, all of these leadership theories continue to influence the research and practice of leadership. Trait theory, for example, was ascendant in the 1930s and 1940s but retains its impact today in more recent conceptualizations of charisma and emotional intelligence.

Idiographic Leadership Theories

Idiographic theories focus on leader traits, leadership styles, and the values and philosophies of leadership. Scholars have developed an extensive body of research on leader traits, but no uniform set of traits predicts effective leadership. Moreover, trait theories are somewhat controversial because they suggest that some people (those with the appropriate traits) are destined for leadership, while others are not. This perspective may be viewed as exclusionary of certain types of leaders.

Major perspectives on leadership style include transactional and transformational. Transactional leaders aim to improve organizational morale and worker motivation by providing rewards and recognition for effective performance. They try to make the current system work better, rather than attempt to reinvent key processes or change traditional practices. Transformational leaders, in contrast, encourage workers to move beyond self-interest and seek to satisfy higher order needs for self-actualization. As a result, leaders and followers become change agents who work to reform the system (rather than simply attempt to make the current system work better).

The idiographic perspective also examines leaders' values and philosophies. Do leaders, for example, believe that workers need to be cajoled, coaxed, and sometimes pushed to perform better? Or do they believe that people have intrinsic drives for work and achievement? These different philosophies shape how leadership is exercised in organizational settings.

Trait Theory

According to this approach, the history of social and organizational change is really the history of particular individuals—especially at the nation-state level. For example, the historian Thomas Carlyle (1841) wrote that political leaders seem to be persons endowed with unique qualities that capture the imagination of the masses. In *English Men of Science,* Galton (1875) similarly tried to explain leadership on the basis of inheritance.

At the organizational and small group level, many studies have attempted to find the personality traits and motivational factors that interact to determine the job success of managers. Hundreds of studies were conducted during the 1920s and 1930s. Both leaders and nonleaders were compared on all types of personality and intelligence scales to determine differences among them. Some typical traits studied (Stogdill, 1948) include: (1) **physical characteristics:** activity, energy, age, appearance, height, weight; (2) **social background and socioeconomic status:** education, social status, mobility; (3) **intellectual skills and ability:** intelligence, judgment, decisiveness, knowledge, fluency of speech; (4) **personality:** adaptability, adjustment/ normality, aggressiveness, assertiveness, alertness, ascendance/dominance, emotional balance, enthusiasm, extroversion, self-confidence; (5) **task-related characteristics:** achievement drive, desire to excel, task orientation; and (6) **social characteristics:** ability to enlist cooperation, cooperativeness, nurturance, popularity, and tact.

Bird (1940) examined a variety of studies that included 79 different traits. He found that at least 50 of the 79 were mentioned in only one empirical study—that is, were appropriate only to that situation. "Only four of the traits (extroverted, humor, intelligent, and initiative) appeared in five or more studies" (Stogdill, 1974, p. 72). In 1971, social scientist Edward Ghiselli, summarized the prior research on this subject, conducted additional studies and produced a shorter, presumably more adequate explanatory set of leadership components comprising intelligence, initiative, supervisory ability, self-assurance, and occupational level (i.e., the perceived degree to which a person sees himself or herself as belonging to high or low socioeconomic status) (Ghiselli, 1971).

But are all of these traits necessary with the same levels of intensity for all situations and at all levels of the organization? Or are certain traits more important under different conditions? Finding answers to these questions continues to occupy leadership researchers. By 1974, despite hundreds of empirical studies, Stogdill noted that there was still no firm agreement on which traits are absolutely necessary no matter what the situation. Locke and his associates (Kirkpatrick & Locke, 1991) reported the following traits as significantly related to leadership effectiveness: energy level and stress tolerance, self-confidence, internal locus of control, emotional maturity, integrity, power motivation, achievement orientation, and need for affiliation.

McClelland and Boyatzis (1982) identified another smaller number of traits as essential: (1) desire to be influential, power motivation; (2) social skills; (3) task orientation—for example, initiative and emphasis on achieving goals; and (4) self-confidence. Still other research suggests that intelligence, extroversion, and achievement motivation are related to leadership, though it is not clear how these traits are related to leadership performance and to training for that performance (Mumford, Zaccaro, Johnson, Diana, Gilbert, & Threlfall, 2000). Recently, emotional intelligence has been added as a characteristic that can predict leadership effectiveness. Emotional intelligence is a mode of monitoring and discriminating among a person's feelings and emotions and those of others as a means for providing better leadership (Goleman, 1995, 1998; Goleman, Boyatzis, & McKee, 2002). The traits of emotional intelligence comprise self-awareness, self-regulation, motivation, empathy, and social skill. Sensitivity to these characteristics could make leaders more effective in their behaviors (George, 2000).

The underlying rationale of all these trait studies is that if social scientists were able to obtain an individual's scores on each of these measures, it might be possible to predict how well a person would perform as a leader. Moreover, organizations could recruit and promote on the basis of their scores on these dimensions. Even if job candidates do not take psychological tests, employers could (and probably now do) qualitatively assess prospective employees on these traits and make hiring judgments.

What can we conclude from these many studies? There is very little predictive validity from any one trait. Perhaps energy and stamina help. Perhaps better education and having a family with a high socioeconomic status predisposes some people to believe that they either are capable of leadership and/or deserve to be in capacities where leadership is exercised (Bourdieu, 1986; Cohen & Prusak, 2001). But traits alone do not explain leadership effectiveness.

Transformational and Transactional Leadership

A second conceptualization in the ideographic orientation comes in the form of transformational versus transactional leadership. In recent years, researchers have identified yet another alleged paradigm shift in the conceptualization of leadership (Bass, 1990). The transition has been described as a movement away from transactional leadership to transformational leadership (Bennis & Nanus, 1985; Hunt, 1991; Piccolo & Colquitt, 2006). **Transactional leaders** recognize what subordinates want from their work environments and attempt to ensure they receive it, if performance warrants it. That is, there is a genuine exchange of promises and rewards for effort. As James McGregor Burns (1978; cf. Avolio & Bass, 1988) notes, in transactional leadership, leaders approach followers with an eye to exchanging one thing for another: jobs for votes, or subsidies for campaign contributions. Such transactions comprise the bulk of the relationships among leaders and followers, especially in groups, legislatures, and political parties. In organizational settings, transactional leadership involves the development of a reward system that recognizes excellent performance. Employees are willing to extend extra effort toward organizational goals, because they know that leaders will reciprocate with valued rewards such as bonuses, pay raises, and promotions. In many ways, transactional leaders fulfill the roles typically associated with management, rather than leadership. Bennis and Nanus (1985), for example, suggest that "managers are people who do things right and leaders are people who do the right thing" (p. 21).

Transformational leaders, on the other hand, lead "by raising our level of awareness, our level of consciousness about the importance and value of designated outcomes, and ways of reaching them" (Burns, 1978, p. 20). These leaders encourage workers to transcend their own self-interests for the sake of the team, organization, or larger society. Transformational leadership, while more complex, can also be more potent. The transforming leader looks for unique potential motivators among followers, seeks to satisfy higher order needs, and engages the full person of the follower (rather than simply viewing the follower as an instrument for completing tasks). The result is a mutual relationship between leaders and followers that may over time convert followers into leaders and may convert leaders into agents for change.

According to Bass (1985), transformational leadership has four key dimensions: (1) charisma, which results in respect, trust, and confidence; (2) inspiration, enabling the communication of a vision; (3) capacity for intellectual stimulation; and (4) consideration for individual needs. These traits, then, are charisma, communication ability, intelligence, and interpersonal skills.

Translating traits into transformational leadership behavior, however, is more difficult. Bennis and Nanus (1985) suggest the following transformational leadership behaviors:

1. Focus attention by providing a vision
2. Make meaning through communication
3. Establish trust
4. Demonstrate positive self-regard and concentrate on winning, instead of not losing
5. Accept people as they are
6. Approach relationships and problems in terms of the present, not the past
7. Treat close staff with dignity
8. Trust others despite risk
9. Don't wait for approval

Transformational leadership has received considerable attention in the literature of higher education (Cameron & Ulrich, 1986), and has informed several studies of how colleges and universities engage in organizational change (Eckel & Kezar, 2003).

Leader Philosophy, Values, and Assumptions

A third approach in the tradition of idiographic understandings of leadership lies in the area of leader philosophy and values. Selznick (1957) suggests that leaders institutionalize values by embedding them in the organization's goals and objectives. In so doing, organizational members come to see the values of the leader as forwarding the aims of the institution as well as their own. These values, however, must fit with the culture of the organization. A college president with a dictatorial style may attempt to promulgate his or her values, but it is rare that such a style will fit most colleges or universities, thus these values will not be able to be institutionalized. The effectiveness of the institution, consequently, will be vitiated by this lack of fit. This is not to suggest that leaders cannot influence the culture of an organization; it is just that a congruence of leader values and institutional culture makes leadership initiatives more palatable to organizational members.

Perhaps the most well-known of the organizational theorists who have considered leadership philosophy is Douglas McGregor. His book, *The Human Side of Enterprise* (1960), remains a classic. McGregor developed the idea that there are two essential sets of assumptions about human nature that influence leader beliefs about the motivation of workers in organizations. For want of a better name, he called them *theory X* and *theory Y*. Theory X adherents assume that all human beings are predisposed to be lazy, desire security, and avoid responsibility. Theory Y believers, on the contrary, hold that most people are naturally energetic and are capable of and desire responsibility, self-direction, and self-control. Hard work is viewed as natural as play or relaxation. A college president, dean, or department chair holding one or the other of these two values will exercise leadership quite differently. If, however, the norms and values of the organizational culture in which those philosophies and associated behaviors are manifested reflect contrary assumptions, then it is likely that leadership effectiveness will be diminished.

Charismatic Leadership

Charisma is another trait that has been deemed central to leadership effectiveness, and it has become a focal point for a number of recent theories. Charismatic leadership has been defined as an interaction between leaders and followers that results in (1) making the followers' self-esteem contingent on the vision and mission articulated by the leader, (2) strong internalization of the leader's values and goals by the followers, (3) strong personal or moral (as opposed to calculative) commitment to these values and goals, and (4) a willingness on the part of followers to transcend their self-interests for the sake of collective interests (e.g., the team or organization) (House & Shamir, 1993).

Leaders with charisma are said to be endowed with a quality of personality and a set of behaviors that induce followers to endorse the leader's wisdom, power, and influence (House, 1999). Subordinates come to trust leaders with charisma, and such trust has been found to be associated with organizational citizenship behavior, satisfaction with leaders, and the intent to stay at their institutions (Avolio, Gardner, Walumbwa, Luthans, & May, 2004). Charismatic leadership has been found to be strongly related to subordinates' positive attitudes toward their work (de Hoogh, et al., 2005). In short, charismatic leaders appear to be able to produce higher morale than other kinds of leaders.

Charismatic leadership will usually be more effective when the distance between leader and subordinates is greater, because when the leader is out of sight for relatively long periods of time, workers base their judgments on fleeting images of leaders—especially ones that are admired (Kiesler & Cummings, 2002). The creation of charisma in political leaders via television, for example, relies on these transitory images (although current news saturation practices may be undermining this principle). Under conditions of distant leadership, in other words, followers have less information on which to base their judgments of the skills, talents, and wisdom of leaders. More frequent contact reduces charisma and requires more demonstrable reasons for leadership position—that is, providing more justification for following. The relatively infrequent visits of a college president to academic departments, for example, may render an image that convinces the faculty members that the president is on the right track in leading the institution. On the other hand, such distant leadership may engender a lack of belief in the leader's ability to ascertain and be in touch with the followers' needs and priorities. Ambiguity of image combined with ambiguity of policy may result not in charismatic effects but in doubt and skepticism as to the leader's ability.

Nomothetic Approaches to Understanding Leadership

We now turn to the second dimension in Barrow's model—the nomothetic. In this section, we discuss three conceptualizations of leadership that are largely externally determined. These theories suggest that the situation plays a critical influence in facilitating the emergence of persons suitable for leadership responsibility. Such situational conditions include:

1. **External stability versus turbulence.** Conditions outside the organization may determine which leadership behaviors are effective. Different leader traits and behaviors are needed to match external situations. Thus, different types of leaders are needed when the environment is uncertain versus certain, or when resources are plentiful versus scarce. Some leaders are good at managing turbulent external circumstances (e.g., budget cuts in a state university system); others are better at managing difficult internal crises.

2. **Organizational design/authority structure.** Organic compared with mechanistic designs call for different kinds of leaders. In flexible, organic organizations, leadership is expressed through information gathering from different constituencies and the development of structures for decisions to be made conjointly by lower level and upper level participants. In more formalized, mechanistic organizations, occupants of upper level positions are likely to make unilateral decisions.

3. **Group characteristics and social norms.** These conditions must be accounted for by leaders who seek to understand the ways in which the informal organization affects the behaviors of workers who are also attempting to fit into the more formal, prescribed roles to which they are assigned. These social dynamics are especially complex in small work groups and teams.

4. **Task characteristics.** The fourth variable on Barrow's nomothetic dimension takes into account the repetitiveness, danger, complexity, creativity, difficulty, structure, standardization, and solution multiplicity of work tasks in organizations. Consider the alternative leadership stances required in machine-dominated versus professional work—for example, an office of information technology compared to an academic department. Here, the differences in organizational design and culture between these two units will call for different leadership styles.

   Consider in addition that as an organization or subunit moves from one task to another, the situational demands alter in such a way that different forms of leadership are required. Different degrees of participation by members with special skills or expertise must be taken into account in a complex interaction. Therefore, in rapidly changing organizations, the *authority of the situation* (Follett, 1924) often dominates. That is, regardless of formal role or status, what helps to legitimate any person's true leadership responsibility and behavior is the possession of requisite skills for the particular situational demands at the time (Calas & Smircich, 1996).

5. **Organizational philosophy and norms.** Imagine how the organizational histories, values, and folklore of different colleges and universities emerge to guide the structure and leadership behavior in these institutions (Clark, 1972; Peterson & Spencer, 1990). These contingencies are related strongly to the organization's culture and may be understood more thoroughly through an examination of social constructionist perspectives on leadership, which we will address later in this chapter.

6. **Subordinate characteristics.** This is the final variable along the environmental axis in Barrow's conceptualization. Leaders must consider organizational members' expectations, socialization, education, experience, and work environment preferences. All of these factors influence the ways in which leaders must interact with followers.

We now examine theories that emphasize one or more of the six nomothetic leadership variables. Specifically, we examine perspectives on group characteristics and social norms, cultural determinism, and substitutes for leadership.

Group Characteristics and Social Norms

A prominent theory on the nomothetic axis in the Barrow framework is **small group theory.** In the late 1930s, Lippitt and White at the University of Iowa, under the guidance of Kurt Lewin, explored differences among three leadership styles—democratic, laissez-faire, and autocratic (Lewin, Lippitt, & White, 1939). This research constituted one of the more systematic explorations of group phenomena by social scientists using experimental methods. One of their most significant findings was that leaving groups to themselves without leaders (a laissez-faire style) was not as effective as providing some leadership, particularly in a democratic (participatory) mode. Workers need and appreciate some leadership. Though the sample was limited and somewhat artificial and the experiment only brief, the findings were immediately seen as consequential, especially when coming from respected researchers. Later researchers (Pelz & Andrews, 1976) found, too, that total freedom from control for research workers resulted in less output and lower quality—an important lesson for those who would grant complete autonomy to organizational workers. Some type of control structure may be necessary to ensure high performance, even among technical and professional workers. In their study of computer software firms, Brown and Eisenhardt (1997) found that neither complete autonomy nor extensive oversight resulted in high levels of product innovation. The most effective companies had leaders who provided both structural guidance and operational flexibility.

Cultural Determinism

In Daniel Katz's (1973) conceptualization, "leaders . . . are produced by historical force and are constrained in their roles by ongoing social processes . . . It is the situation, not the actor, that determines the outcome" (p. 208). As Admiral W. F. Halsey purportedly claimed, "There are no great men. There are only great challenges which ordinary men are forced by circumstances to meet."

Here are some examples:

1. Despite vociferous declarations about not wanting to interact with Communist countries, Richard Nixon was forced to normalize relations with China. He became a more effective leader in some eyes because of this initiative.
2. Charles W. Elliot, president of Harvard for most of the post-Bellum period (1869–1909), instituted a free elective system for students at Harvard. Trait theorists might say this decision can be attributed to his unique leadership abilities, but determinists would say it was because the circumstances of the industrial revolution and the needs of the college forced him to open up the curriculum.

Substitutes for Leadership

Another theory in the nomothetic tradition pertains to substitutes for leadership, presented by Kerr and Jermier (1978). In some organizations, characteristics of subordinates, tasks, or the organization itself substitute for leadership (Howell, Dorfman, & Kerr, 1986; Kerr & Jermier, 1978) and either inhibit or facilitate the leaders' efforts, depending on how they are used (see Table 10.1). Some substitutes affect instrumental leadership, which entails directive behaviors associated with planning and controlling, while other substitutes impact supportive leadership, which focuses on the well-being and satisfaction of subordinates. Considerable research on the validity of these concepts has usually drawn the conclusion that organizational effectiveness is enhanced by a combination of leadership and leadership substitutes (Minor, 2005).

Jeff Van Gundy, basketball coach (New York Knickerbockers, then Houston Rockets), recognized his limitations as a formal leader and saw cohesive work groups as an important way to augment his leadership. He worried that, though peer pressure in his teams was substantial, it frequently was not sufficient to generate high-quality performance in each player. Moreover, as a formal leader, by definition, he was not part of the peer group of players, and his efforts, like those of any formal leader, could be perceived

TABLE 10.1
Substitutes for Leadership

Leadership Substitutes	*Impact on Leadership*
Subordinate Characteristics	
• experience, ability, and training	• augments instrumental leadership
• professional orientation • capacity for self-management	• augments instrumental and supportive leadership
• indifference toward organizational rewards	• neutralizes instrumental and supportive leadership
Task Characteristics	
• structured and routine tasks	• augments instrumental leadership
• feedback within the task	• substitutes for instrumental leadership
• intrinsically satisfying task	• substitutes for supportive leadership
Organizational Characteristics	
• cohesive work groups	• augments instrumental and supportive leadership
• low position power of leader	• neutralizes instrumental and supportive leadership
• formalization	• substitutes for instrumental leadership
• organizational inflexibility	• neutralizes instrumental leadership
• leader physically isolated from subordinates	• neutralizes instrumental and supportive leadership

Adapted from Kerr and Jermier (1978).

as intrusive and disruptive of the norms, values, and informal status hierarchies developed among the members. Van Gundy tried, nevertheless, to instill in the team and in each individual a hard work ethic and intolerance of poor performance by other team members.

Behaviorist Theories of Leadership

By the late 1940s, researchers recognized a need for a more intensive investigation of the nature of leadership, particularly in organizations in a rapidly expanding postwar economy. During this period, there was an important shift from the narrow concepts of both idiographic and nomothetic—that is, from viewing leadership as a largely personal quality inhering within an individual, or conceptualizing leadership as mostly situationally determined—to the study of leadership as behavior. At this time, studies began to be concerned with what leaders do, rather than with what qualities exist in them or in the situations in which they lead.

As behavioral studies of leadership became more academically respectable, especially in the light of social science interest in practical business applications, researchers began to examine leaders in organizational settings. There were four major research thrusts: Ohio State, Michigan's Survey Research Center, Harvard, and Michigan again.

The Ohio State Leadership Studies

Out of the depression of the 1930s came a belief, especially among social psychologists studying groups (following the work of Lewin, Lippit, and White), that democracy and democratic leadership were both necessary and more effective than other approaches. Interest turned to how effective leaders actually behaved (observed behavior in the social systems model). Beginning in 1946, a 10-year program of studies was undertaken at Ohio State University to discover and categorize the dimensions of leader behavior in formal organizations. Leadership was defined as the behavior of an individual while involved in directing group activities (Hemphill & Coons, 1957). The major data collection technique was survey research. The Ohio State researchers found two basic characteristics of leadership (Korman, 1966):

1. Initiating structure—which "reflects the extent to which an individual is likely to define and structure his role and those of his subordinates toward goal attainment. A high score on this dimension characterizes individuals who play a more active role in directing group activities through planning, communicating information, scheduling, trying out new ideas" (Korman, 1966, p. 349).

2. Consideration—which "reflects the extent to which an individual is likely to have job relationships characterized by mutual trust, respect for subordinates' ideas, and consideration of their feelings. A high score is indicative of a climate of good rapport and two-way communication. A low score indicates the supervisor is likely to be more impersonal in his relations with group members" (Korman, 1966, pp. 349–350).

This model is presented in Table 10.2.

The model shows that a leader could engage in both kinds of behavior, one but not the other, neither, or perhaps some degree of each. There is still

TABLE 10.2
Ohio State Leadership Model

		Initiating Structure	
		Low	High
Consideration	High	High consideration Low initiating structure	High consideration High initiating structure
	Low	Low consideration Low initiating structure	Low consideration High initiating structure

Adapted from Hemphill & Coons (1957).

disagreement today on which combination is most effective. Is it low-profile, laissez-faire? Half and half? Strong on both? Further, what is meant by *effectiveness*? Is it more productivity? More worker satisfaction? In the short run or the long run? For all kinds of outcomes?

The Ohio State researchers initially believed that a moderate balance of each of the dimensions would work best. That is, too much initiating structure or too much consideration, even at maximum strength, would not be effective. This approach to understanding leadership still has strong adherents today, despite some empirical evidence showing its limitations (Judge, Piccolo, & Ilies, 2004).

Survey Research Center, University of Michigan

A short time later, similar efforts were begun at the Survey Research Center at the University of Michigan (Kahn & Katz, 1960). This time, interview methods were used. The results, however, were very much like those at Ohio State. Though the labels were different, the categories were similar: (1) employee orientation—concern with group maintenance and (2) production orientation—concern with group achievement.

As researchers continued their testing of the Ohio State and Michigan models, they began to understand that a serious limitation of the behavioral approach was in ignoring situational contingencies, which could have an impact on the effectiveness of any leadership behavior. Sometimes initiating structure is better; sometimes consideration. For example, when the task is boring, consideration is more important in assuring high productivity.

To address these limitations, Blake and Mouton (1964) developed the grid system, which became a popular modification of the Ohio State approach. One objective of this research program was to demonstrate how leadership can be related to the long-run development of the organization by focusing on the more integrative dimensions, which hypothetically lead to both organizational effectiveness and worker fulfillment. Once again, the methodological approach was to consider the dimensions of *concern for people* and *concern for tasks*. In Figure 10.2, the Blake and Mouton leadership theory is depicted.

Note in the model that the interaction of the horizontal and vertical dimensions is crucial. That is, the 9 in 1,9 is not the same as the 9 in 9,9. In 1,9, the leader wants workers to be happy. In 9,9, the leader wants workers to be involved in their work and striving with enthusiasm to achieve organizational goals. The grid's organizational development approach assesses initial leadership predispositions, then assists the leader in moving toward a 9,9 position by developing both interpersonal and production skills. For Blake and Mouton, there is no necessary conflict between the two skill sets. In describing their grid, they say:

> The 9, 9 managerial theory links individual effort to organizational purpose(s) through goal setting. When this way of managing has become a way of life, an individual is not only working for the corporation, he is also working for himself. Individual and organizational purposes have come together. (Blake & Mouton, 1978, p. 101)

Harvard University

Around this same time, still another group of studies was conducted at Harvard University by Robert Bales (Bales & Slater, 1955). This time, the research setting was small groups. Bales analyzed small group processes and leadership dynamics. Again, the same two fundamental dimensions appeared—socioemotional and task-oriented factors in leadership behaviors.

University of Michigan

A somewhat expanded set of leadership dimensions was produced at Michigan by Bowers and Seashore (1966), who developed a *four-factor* theory, which suggested that there were four leadership dimensions, again quite similar to the Ohio State model. The first two resemble consideration in the latter model:

1. **Supportive behaviors**—these behaviors enhance the worker's image or sense of personal self-worth.
2. **Interaction facilitation**—such leader behavior encourages good personal working relationships among employees.

FIGURE 10.2
The Managerial Grid

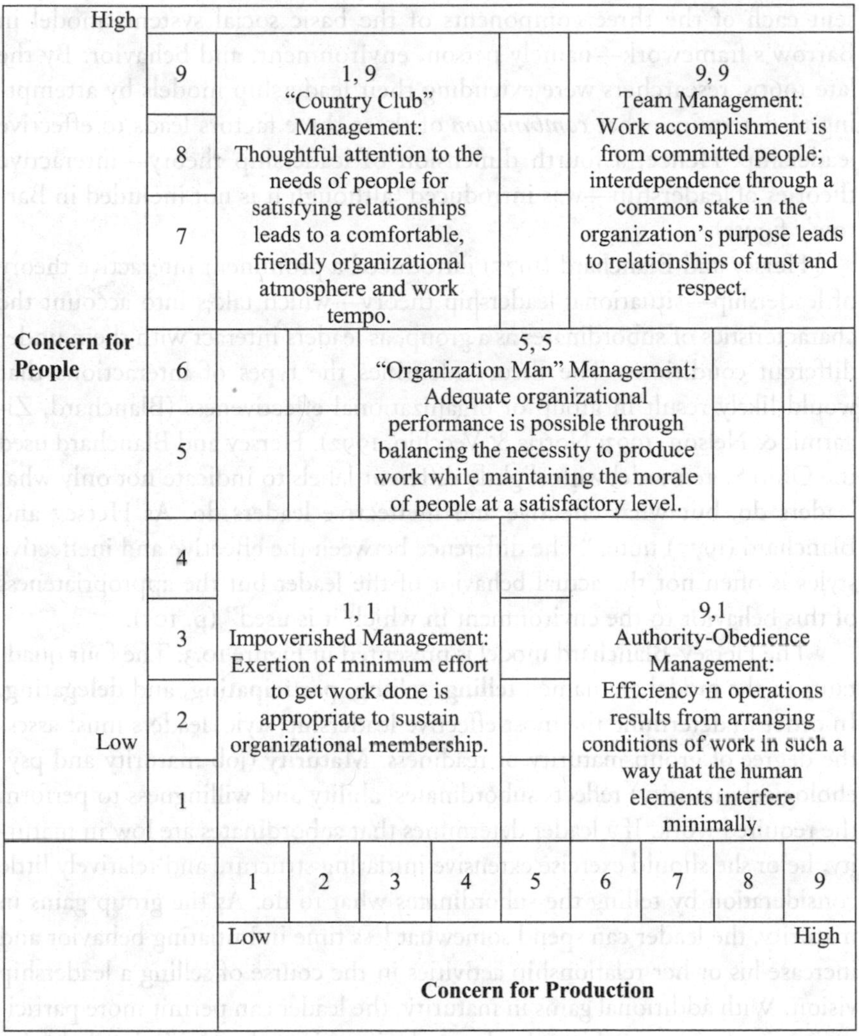

High						
	9	1, 9 "Country Club" Management:		9, 9 Team Management:		
	8	Thoughtful attention to the needs of people for		Work accomplishment is from committed people; interdependence through a		
	7	satisfying relationships leads to a comfortable, friendly organizational atmosphere and work tempo.		common stake in the organization's purpose leads to relationships of trust and respect.		
Concern for People	6	5, 5 "Organization Man" Management: Adequate organizational				
	5	performance is possible through balancing the necessity to produce work while maintaining the morale of people at a satisfactory level.				
	4					
	3	1, 1 Impoverished Management:		9,1 Authority-Obedience Management:		
	2	Exertion of minimum effort to get work done is appropriate to sustain		Efficiency in operations results from arranging conditions of work in such a		
Low	1	organizational membership.		way that the human elements interfere minimally.		
	1 2 3 4 5 6 7 8 9					
	Low				High	
	Concern for Production					

Adapted from Blake and McCanse (1991).

The next two are like initiating structure in the Ohio State model:

3. **Goal emphasis**—these activities facilitate the meeting of a group's goal or achieving its standard of excellence.

4. **Work facilitation**—this includes the planning, scheduling, and coordinating of group task achievement.

Interactive Theories of Leadership

Thus far, we have considered theories of leadership that separately represent each of the three components of the basic social systems model in Barrow's framework—namely person, environment, and behavior. By the late 1960s, researchers were extending their leadership models by attempting to determine what *combination* of these three factors leads to effective leadership. Hence, a fourth dimension of leadership theory—interactive theories of leadership—was introduced (although it is not included in Barrow's figure).

Hersey and Blanchard (1977) introduced a prominent interactive theory of leadership—situational leadership theory—which takes into account the characteristics of subordinates as a group, as leaders interact with them under different conditions. The theory identifies the types of interactions that would likely result in group or organizational effectiveness (Blanchard, Zigarmi, & Nelson, 1993; Norris & Vecchio, 1992). Hersey and Blanchard used the Ohio State model with slightly different labels to indicate not only what leaders do, but what effective and ineffective leaders do. As Hersey and Blanchard (1977) note, "The difference between the effective and ineffective styles is often not the actual behavior of the leader but the appropriateness of this behavior to the environment in which it is used" (p. 105).

The Hersey-Blanchard model is presented in Figure 10.3. The four quadrants in the model are named **telling, selling, participating,** and **delegating**. In order to determine the most effective leadership style, leaders must assess the degree of group maturity or readiness. **Maturity** (job maturity and psychological maturity) reflects subordinates' ability and willingness to perform the required work. If a leader determines that subordinates are low in maturity, he or she should exercise extensive initiating structure and relatively little consideration by telling the subordinates what to do. As the group gains in maturity, the leader can spend somewhat less time in initiating behavior and increase his or her relationship activities in the course of selling a leadership vision. With additional gains in maturity, the leader can permit more participation in decision making, further reducing his or her initiating behavior while slowly reducing consideration. With a fully developed, mature subordinate group, the leader can delegate most decision making, freeing the leader from engaging in unnecessary supervision. In short, the subordinates are capable of and desire to direct themselves.

It should be noted that the model's simplicity makes it easy to use, but there are a number of difficulties that can arise, some of them methodological (Lueder, 1985). Frequently, for example, there is no uniform level of

FIGURE 10.3

Situational Leadership: Graphing Leadership Behavior and Follower Maturity

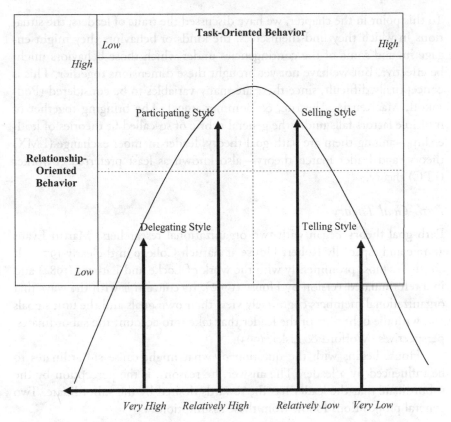

Adapted from Hersey and Blanchard (1977).

maturity or readiness among all members of a group. Hence, leaders cannot treat the group uniformly. Moreover, the model does not explain when and how subordinates become mature. Dvir and Shamir (2003) suggest that initial developmental level and the distance of the followers from the leader determine the effectiveness of the leader (especially a transformational leader) in assisting in the development of maturity. The remoteness of leadership across different levels in an organization (e.g., from college president to academic department chair) makes it difficult for the more distant leader to be sensitive enough to the needs of workers to facilitate their development toward maturity.

Matching Traits, Contingencies, and Behaviors for Effective Leadership

To this point in the chapter, we have discussed the traits of leaders, the situations in which they find themselves, the kinds of behaviors they might engage in, and some of the contingencies under which those behaviors might be effective. But we have not yet brought these dimensions together. This is conceptually difficult, since there are many variables to be considered (Podsokoff, MacKenzie, Ahearne, & Bommer, 1995). The bringing together of multiple factors falls under the general rubric of so-called fit theories of leadership—among them are path-goal theory, leader-member exchange (LMX) theory, and leader match theory—also known as least preferred coworker (LPC) theory.

Path-Goal Theory

Path-goal theory began with two organizational researchers, Martin Evans at Yale and especially Robert House at Baruch College in the early 1970s. It continues most prominently with the work of Locke and Latham (1984) and in a reformulated version by House (1996). Its concern is with the ways that organizational members cognitively view their own goals and the unit's goals and with the behaviors of the leader that take into account the subordinates' perspectives (Wofford & Liska, 1993).

House begins with the question of what might cause subordinates to be influenced by a leader. The answer, he reasons, is the perception by the subordinate that the leader has the rewards desired by the subordinate. Two general propositions follow from these assumptions:

1. The motivational functions of the leader involve making salient the payoffs to subordinates for accomplishing the goals of the organization and of clarifying the paths to making those payoffs realistic (House, 1971).
2. The leader will be an effective motivator of his or her subordinates if the leader makes clear that the subordinates' own needs will be satisfied by accomplishing the goals of the organization and if the leader provides coaching, advice, support, and rewards for effective performance (House & Mitchell, 1974). Subordinates, in other words, must believe that their own effective behavior is the determinant of leader support, and they must believe that that support is forthcoming.

Thus, the key to effective path-goal leadership is to help the subordinate become aware of desirable organizational objectives and to show him or her that by achieving those objectives, the desired rewards will be forthcoming. A department chair dealing with a temporarily unmotivated faculty member, for example, can help that faculty member understand departmental goals and recognize that goal-related behavior will, indeed, be beneficial to that faculty member, as well as to the department as a whole.

Further, the subordinate must perceive that the leader has the key to opening the path to achieving the desired ends. The department chair who promises, but cannot deliver will not be seen as effective and will not, in fact, be effective. A leader, therefore, helps to clarify the path to the desired goals. Hence, path-goal theory.

How can a leader accomplish this clarification? House indicates that leaders must assess two of the basic contingencies that we have already discussed: the nature of the subordinates and the nature of the tasks to be completed. Different subordinates respond to different kinds of leadership. And different tasks call for different leader behaviors.

By subordinate characteristics, House essentially means personality characteristics. So, in an extreme example, a masochist may really want to be ordered around by the organization's leaders, while autonomy-seeking subordinates may want not to be told anything and insecure types may want more reinforcement. Note that this contingency is not a group contingency (as in Hersey and Blanchard's theory), but an individual contingency reflecting the dyadic nature of the relationship between a leader and a subordinate. More concretely, here are the subordinate personality characteristics on which House believes leaders should concentrate. House initially suggested three, but subsequent researchers have added others.

1. Authoritarianism—the degree to which people accept external authority. For example, in different cultures or in different social class settings, authority is perceived differently.
2. Locus of control—the degree to which workers believe that their work and lives are under their own control versus those who believe that rewards are beyond their own control. For instance, if a faculty member believes that if she works hard, she will get the rewards she desires, regardless of situational contingencies, she has an internal locus of control. Note that this is not the same as the belief that if she works hard, rewards will be forthcoming. It is a more general personality disposition, not a reasoned expectation based on experience in the organization. The point is that even if a subordinate believes the leader has control over rewards that are important to her, she probably will not work hard if her personality does not dispose her generally to feel that hard work pays off.

3. Abilities—the degree to which workers believe that they have the necessary abilities to perform the desired tasks.
4. Need for achievement—the degree to which people desire to succeed.
5. Need for affiliation—the degree to which people need to feel that they belong.

Depending on where workers fall within these five dimensions, they will be more or less responsive to different kinds of leader behaviors. But the choice of effective leader behaviors also depends on the situation. In addition to subordinate characteristics, House wants us to look at the following organizational characteristics.

1. The nature of the task performed by the subordinates. Is it routine or ad hoc?
2. The formal authority system in the organization. Does control over behavior stem from a strong, formal hierarchical system?
3. The primary work group. How strong are the norms in the work unit?

To summarize, there are two types of contingencies that the leader must consider when deciding on what kind of behavior will convince subordinates to adopt organizational goals and to work toward them: the characteristics of the subordinates and the nature of the task. Next, we identify the alternative kinds of leader behavior and then match those behaviors to the contingencies.

Types of Leadership in Path-Goal Theory

There are four kinds of leader behaviors in path-goal theory. Three of them—1, 3, and 4—borrow from Ohio State's consideration and initiating structure; one of them—2—adopts the Hersey and Blanchard notion of participation.

1. **Supportive leadership**—giving consideration to the needs of subordinates, displaying concern for their well-being, status, and comfort, and creating a friendly and pleasant climate. Being friendly, approachable, and concerned with pleasant interpersonal relationships. Basically, this is *consideration* from the Ohio State model.
2. **Participative leadership**—sharing of information, power, and influence between supervisors and subordinates. In other words, a consultative leadership style.
3. **Instrumental leadership** (directive behavior)—planning, organizing,

controlling, and coordinating of subordinate activities (like initiating structure in the Ohio State model).

4. **Achievement-oriented leadership** (directive behavior)—setting challenging goals, expecting subordinates to perform at high levels, seeking improvement in performance, expecting subordinates to be successful. This behavior emphasizes excellence and shows confidence in the subordinate's ability to achieve it.

The key question for practice is, When should each of these be used? How should characteristics and leadership style be mixed and matched? In Table 10.3, we provide some examples (but certainly not all that can be generated from path-goal theory).

Path-goal theory is obviously complicated, with many contingencies. Is the theory practical? To put together all of these contingencies, it would be necessary to develop working heuristics of the following type:

> "When the task is clear and the subordinates are not ego-involved in the work, participative leadership will contribute to satisfaction and performance only for highly independent, non-authoritarian subordinates."

Quite obviously, this theory is too cumbersome to use in a practical, immediate sense. It is probable, however, that with training, leaders can develop a set of responses that are intuitively in line with these prescriptions. The theory, therefore, can best be used as a heuristic device to analyze problems of leadership when current practices seem ineffective.

Management by Objectives

A more practical interpretation of path-goal theory is called management by objectives. Using this approach, a manager establishes a contract with the subordinate whereby they both agree on a reasonable set of objectives for a given time period. Then it is the responsibility of the manager to facilitate the subordinate's achievement of the agreed-upon objectives. The approach directs attention to goals that are workable and establishes a collaborative relationship between managers and subordinates. There are, however, a number of possible negative consequences. For one thing, subordinates may limit themselves to the achievement of specified goals and may not deviate from them, even when doing so is organizationally desirable. Moreover, interactions between leaders and subordinates become transactional and rarely involve subordinates in the consideration of goals and procedures that transcend the immediate work tasks (as in transformational leadership). It should be noted that the increasing use of contract systems for faculty (rather than

TABLE 10.3
Contingencies in Path-Goal Leadership Theory

Contingencies	Appropriate Leadership Style
• When subordinate characteristics reveal a high need for affiliation	• Supportive leadership
• When task characteristics show that work is frustrating and/or dissatisfying	• Supportive leadership
• When subordinate characteristics reveal that subordinates are not ego-involved in the work and have an internal locus of control	• Participative leadership
• When tasks are perceived as challenging but ambiguous	• Participative leadership
• When subordinate characteristics show that subordinates prefer to be told what to do, have a low sense of their own task abilities, and have an external locus of control	• Instrumental leadership
• When tasks are perceived as ambiguous and organizational policies and procedures are unclear or conflicting (When things are clearer, on the other hand, such initiation will be seen as interference.)	• Instrumental leadership
• When subordinate characteristics show a high need for achievement	• Achievement-oriented leadership
• When tasks are perceived as ambiguous and non-routine (In this case, achievement-oriented leadership will induce subordinates to raise their standards and increase their confidence in their ability to meet goals.)	• Achievement-oriented leadership

tenure) reflects the management-by-objectives approach and manifests these same limitations (Bess, 1998).

Leader-Member Exchange (LMX)

The **LMX model** gives considerable attention to the interpersonal relationships among leaders and followers. In its earlier conceptualization as *vertical dyad linkage* by Graen and others (Duchon, Green, & Taber, 1986; Graen, 1976), the theory suggested that effective leader behavior requires particularistic (rather than universalistic) attention to each individual. With some superior-subordinate dyadic relationships, close personal ties can develop, while with others more distant relations may be more effective.

One result of this phenomenon is the emergence of a core group of subordinates whose relationships with the supervisor and with each other are warm and trusting and the rise of a second group who are largely excluded from important decision-making processes. The larger the in-group, the more the alienation of the out-group. Whether this results in more effective leader behavior is not clear (Liden, Wayne, & Stilwell, 1993). Excluded group members may not be incompetent low performers and may be in the out-group for reasons unrelated to work (e.g., personality clashes).

The theory has in recent years received considerable attention, with a number of critical commentaries relating it to other issues of leadership and organizational culture (Scandura, 1999). Newer revisions of LMX (Schriescheim, Castro, & Gogliser, 1999) say that there are four stages in the evolution of relationships between leaders and subordinates. In the first stage, the relationship is a vertical dyadic one in which the leader develops differentiated kinds of rapport and interactions with different subordinates. The second stage recognizes relationships not only between the leader and the subordinate but among subordinates in their relationships with leaders. In the third stage, leaders and subordinates develop collaborative partnerships in which leadership is shared. In the final stage, both leaders and followers become connected dyadically within a wider follower net, outside of the initial circle of subordinates.

Leader Match Theory

We move now to the third of the so-called fit theories—the **leader-match theory** of Fred Fiedler (Fiedler, Chemers, & Mahar, 1976), also known as the least preferred coworker (LPC) theory. This approach comprises a more limited set of contingencies and a more exact prescription of what kind of leadership behavior is called for under different conditions. Recall that Hersey and Blanchard (1977) and others added various contingencies into the equation of leadership effectiveness. For example, they hypothesize that different leadership behaviors are more effective when matched to different degrees of subordinate maturity. Fiedler, too, is concerned with effectiveness. His theory, however, returns to trait theory in combination with other contingencies. He suggests that leader behavior is partly a function of leader personality. When leader personality and associated behaviors fit with key organizational design features and with informal relationships between the leader and the followers, the leader's behavior will be effective.

Thus, Fiedler provides a synthesis of idiographic and nomothetic variables as an explanation of the conditions associated with effective leader behavior. Four measurable variables interact in Fiedler's theory to determine effectiveness:

1. Idiographic—leader personality
2. Nomothetic
    a. Leader position power (authority structure)
    b. Task structure (organizational design)
    c. Leader-member relations (power/trust/informal relations)

This last variable (2c) is the most important in Fiedler's theory. We discuss each of these four variables in greater detail below.

1. *Leader personality.* In Fiedler's view, personality is a cluster of traits that produce dispositions to behave in unique ways. The two dimensions of Fiedler's personality measure are task orientation versus people orientation. A leader's personality is measured through his or her scores on the LPC scale. Fiedler defines LPC as the leader's opinion of or esteem for the one particular worker in his or her organization with whom the leader has been able to work the *least* well or with whom the leader would *least like to work*. This person can be someone with whom the leader is presently working or with whom he or she has worked in the past. It can be a peer, subordinate, or supervisor. The LPC scale contains 18 to 21 adjective responses scored on a scale of 1 to 8. A sample of the items in the scale is given in Table 10.4. The personality type is determined by summing the scores. A low LPC leader describes his or her least preferred coworker in unfavorable terms; a high LPC leader, in favorable terms. The LPC scores reveal different kinds of satisfactions sought by leaders.

    A low LPC leader is likely to be more satisfied by successful task performance, while a high LPC leader is more likely to be satisfied by successful interpersonal relations. To borrow loosely some terms from

TABLE 10.4
Sample Items in Fiedler's LPC Scale

Agreeable									Disagreeable
	8	7	6	5	4	3	2	1	
Open-minded									Closed-minded
	8	7	6	5	4	3	2	1	
Courteous									Rude
	8	7	6	5	4	3	2	1	
Calm									Agitated
	8	7	6	5	4	3	2	1	
Fascinating									Dull
	8	7	6	5	4	3	2	1	

theories described earlier in this chapter, low LPCs are essentially task oriented, while high LPCs are basically relationship oriented. That is, if a leader is able to describe his or her *least* preferred coworker in relatively positive ways, that leader is considered by Fiedler to be a people person—at least as compared with another leader who is less favorably disposed toward the least preferred coworker.

We now consider the situational side. Fiedler identifies three dimensions that determine the degree of control a leader has in a particular situation.

2a. *Position power.* The degree to which the position itself (e.g., director, dean, department chair) enables the leader to get his or her group members to comply with and accept his or her direction and leadership. It is the power or authority delegated by the formal organization to the leader, regardless of the leader's willingness or ability to use it.

2b. *Task structure.* The degree to which task performance can be programmed. It is the extent to which task requirements are clearly specified (e.g., routine assembly line work) versus ambiguous and undefined (as in creative research).

2c. *Leader-member relations.* The affective relations between a leader and group members—the acceptance that can be obtained and the loyalty that can be engendered through leader-member interactions. According to Fiedler, a leader who describes his or her work group favorably feels well accepted by group members and sees the group as low in tension.

Together, these three factors determine the degree of favorableness of the situation to the leader (i.e., most favorable when there are good relations, high task structure, and high position power). The key to Fiedler's leadership theory concerns the match between the nomothetic (situational favorableness) and the idiographic (LPC orientation). Certain combinations result in poor leadership behavior; others result in effective leadership. More specifically, when the leader is task oriented (low LPC score), he or she will be more effective when the situation is either highly favorable or highly unfavorable. On the other hand, when the leader is relationship oriented (high LPC score), the leader will be more effective when the situation is moderately favorable. These relationships are illustrated in Tables 10.5 and 10.6.

In some situations, leader behavior will be positively correlated with measures of effectiveness; in others, it will be negatively correlated. Fiedler found, for example, that a high LPC leader in a situation with high control (high favorableness) will behave poorly because he or she will become aloof, autocratic, and self-centered. That is, with things going so well, relationship-oriented leaders cannot use the personality dispositions that are natural to them and revert to other behaviors. Similar results occur under other mismatched conditions.

Fiedler's theory makes an important assumption about leadership style that distinguishes it from most of the others. Previous research on leadership (and conventional wisdom) suggests that good leaders can and do adapt to the situation or context (Hogg, 2001). Good leaders see what is required (e.g., in the Ohio State model, consideration or initiating structure; in Hersey and Blanchard's model, address levels of subordinate maturity) and make the necessary adjustments in their behavior. Fiedler, however, says this adaptability is unrealistic. Leader personality is a genetic characteristic from which individuals cannot escape. They are stuck with their basic personalities and traits. High-LPC or low-LPC leaders are permanently disposed to behave in certain ways and seek satisfactions from that behavior. Persons who find themselves in incompatible situations, Fiedler notes, must either **change the situation** or **change jobs.** For example, if the leader is in a position of low situational favorableness, the theory says a low-LPC, task-oriented person will be effective. A high-LPC, relationship-oriented person in that situation, therefore, would have to modify the *situation* to make it more favorable. Suppose, however, that the leader has no position power, the tasks are largely unprogrammable, and the followers are idiosyncratic, irascible persons. Given those conditions, the best option for the high-LPC person is to move to another job. He or she has no way to become effective, as none of the variables are controllable.

Fiedler's theory, as the others, is not without critics (Jago & Ragan,

TABLE 10.5
Summary of Leadership Style, Behavior, and Performance in Varying Situations

Leader Type	Situational Control		
	High Control	*Moderate Control*	*Low Control*
High LPC	*Behavior* Somewhat autocratic, aloof, and self-centered. Seemingly concerned with tasks. High LPC leaders in complete control will not be compelled to use their people-oriented skills.	*Behavior* Considerate, open, and participative. Highly considerate leaders will focus on the needs of their subordinates.	*Behavior* Anxious, tentative, overly concerned with personal relations. High LPC leaders will become too nervous about what is happening in their group and will devote too much attention to interpersonal and group relations.
	Performance Poor	*Performance* Good	*Performance* Poor
Low LPC	*Behavior* Considerate and supportive. Task-oriented leaders in favorable conditions will not have to worry about people, so they will be able to concern themselves with task performance.	*Behavior* Tense and task focused. In situations requiring attention to people, task-oriented leaders will not be able to deal with the needs of those people.	*Behavior* Directive, task focused, serious. When the situation is decidedly unfavorable, task-oriented leaders will not be distracted by people problems, and, at least in the short run, will be able to direct people to task accomplishment.
	Performance Good	*Performance* Poor	*Performance* Relatively good

Adapted from Fiedler (1972).

TABLE 10.6
Recommended Leader Behaviors for Various Situations

Situations	1	2	3	4	5	6	7	8
Leader-Member Relations	Good	Good	Good	Good	Poor	Poor	Poor	Poor
Task Structure	High	High	Low	Low	High	High	Low	Low
Leader Position Power	Strong	Weak	Strong	Weak	Strong	Weak	Strong	Weak
Effective Leadership Performance	Task oriented	Task oriented	Task oriented	Person oriented	Person oriented	Person oriented	Person oriented	Task oriented
Situation Favorableness for the Leader	Most favorable is #1	←					→	Least favorable is #8

Adapted from Fiedler (1972).

1986; Kabanoff, 1981). It is alleged to be empirically driven, rather than having a logical, theoretical base. Its validity also has been questioned, particularly for situations where situation favorableness is neither extremely high nor low. Finally, it is important to point out that neither high- nor low-LPC leadership is necessarily good or bad in and of itself. Leaders with different styles perform well or poorly, depending on the situation.

Other Approaches to Leadership

Other leadership theories focus on organizational characteristics, rather than those of the leaders and followers themselves. One set of theories examines how different leadership styles are needed for success under different phases of organizational development. A second group of theories examines leader succession—specifically, the effects of one leader leaving and another arriving.

Stages/Phases in Organizations and the Demands for Leadership

All organizations proceed through stages of expansion and consolidation with varying levels of emphases on effectiveness versus efficiency (Cameron & Whetten, 1984, 1988; Parsons & Bales, 1955). As might be expected, different kinds of leaders are required for each of these phases. Steve Jobs's leadership style at Apple Computer was exemplary during its small, inventive, expansionist phase, but it took another kind of leader to manage the company during its bureaucratization phase and still another (Steve Jobs, again) to renew the company thereafter (Kozlowski, Gully, McHugh, Salas, & Cannon-Bowers, 1996).

Different kinds of leaders and different leadership behaviors are required at different times in the organization's development—decline, steady state, or expansion (Whetten & Cameron, 2005). Compare, for example, leaders needed during periods of downsizing versus stability or growth.

At least five major phases of organizational development demand different kinds of leadership. The stages are: (1) taking hold, (2) immersion, (3) reshaping, (4) consolidation, and (5) refinement (Gabarro, 1987). The first extends through the first six months of the appointment to the leadership position. The focus is on learning how the organization operates and what its goals and priorities are. In the immersion stage, the leader becomes more involved at a deeper level than the earlier orientation stage. During reshaping, which typically lasts approximately three to six months, the leader embarks on significant structural changes. This period is followed by consolidation of the changes already made. According to Gabarro, this takes three to nine months. It involves new kinds of learning, particularly on the effects of the changes already made. The final stage of refinement requires largely the securing of the changes and their incremental improvement, with few additional important changes.

Leader Succession

Most colleges and universities spend a great deal of time and organizational energy in recruiting and hiring new leaders. Unfortunately, the transitional processes are then left almost entirely to the new incumbent, frequently with awkward and adverse effects (Rowe, Cannella, Rankin, & Gorman, 2005). Fortunately, there is a growing body of theoretical and practical literature that informs the leadership transition process (Fulmer & Conger, 2004).

The early contributions of Oscar Grusky (1960, 1963) on the effects of leader succession on organizational performance introduced systematic research on the transitional effects of one leader's leaving and another arriving. The process of changing from one leader to the next may be disruptive and destabilizing, since the new leader may initiate new policies and procedures as well as shifts in organizational design and personnel. As Kesner and Sebora (1994) note, "speculation often runs high after a succession event, and it is not uncommon for succession to trigger other dramatic changes" (p. 329) such as the turnover of additional top-level administrators and major shifts in the strategy of the organization.

Leader succession can contribute to organizational renewal through the infusion of new ideas from the top, but it can also be viewed as symptomatic of a vicious cycle where frequent turnover results in a downward spiral toward poor performance. Researchers have attempted to identify the factors that differentiate successful from unsuccessful transitions. The answer depends, in part, on the characteristics of the new leader coming into the organization as well as the conditions within the organization itself. Studies have shown that leader succession produces different outcomes depending on whether the new leader is an outsider or someone promoted from within. New leaders coming from outside the organization tend to produce higher levels of organizational change (Brady & Helmich, 1982; Chung, Lubatkin, Rogers, & Owers, 1987), while promotion from within typically generates more continuity and stability. Moreover, hiring leaders from similar types of institutions produces a similar effect. In a study of college presidents, Birnbaum (1971) found that successors who had been socialized and trained in similar types of institutions were able to promote greater organizational stability than presidents who came from quite different professional backgrounds. Thus, if organizational conditions warrant significant change, an outside leader may stimulate higher levels of effectiveness; however, if continuity and stability are needed, then an internal successor may reduce anxiety about the future and lead to better performance. Again, matching leader characteristics to organizational conditions can be a successful approach for promoting effective leadership successions.

Social Construction and Leadership

To this point in the chapter, we have examined leadership theories that are based in positivist assumptions about organizational reality. Positivist theories attempt to identify contingencies in the leadership context (individual, organizational, or situational) that predict which types of leadership behavior (task or relationship oriented) are likely to yield higher levels of organizational effectiveness. The social construction paradigm offers an array of additional concepts that leaders can consider. Social constructionists emphasize the importance of understanding organizational culture and being aware of the leader's role in the sensemaking process (Tierney, 1988; Weick, 1995). From this vantage point, leaders recognize that organizational members develop multiple interpretations of reality and can have very different perspectives on internal working conditions and external forces affecting the organization. Given diverse views and perspectives, leaders are challenged to find innovative ways to promote collective action toward common goals.

Therefore, the ability to foster collaborative leadership has become increasingly important (Bensimon & Neumann, 1993; Kezar, 2000).

Organizational Culture and Symbolic Leadership

Social constructionists assert that there is no single interpretation of the organization, its environment, or its leadership that is uniformly embraced by all organizational members (Berger & Luckmann, 1966; Weick, 1979). Mission statements, marketing studies, and presidential speeches are interpreted differently by faculty, staff, and students. Even when the words and data in speeches and reports remain consistent over time, different organizational members assign different meanings and interpretations to those words and numbers. The announcement of a new merit-based scholarship program, for example, may be greeted with excitement from those who interpret the announcement as a confirmation of the college's attempt to become an academically excellent institution, but it also may be greeted with skepticism from those who believe that the program will siphon money away from financial aid for economically disadvantaged students.

So how are leaders to proceed, knowing that their goals, plans, and initiatives are likely to be interpreted in very different ways by organizational members? How can a leader provide direction for an institution if everyone interprets things differently? Social constructionists suggest that a first step for organizational leaders is to begin to view the organization not as a rational machine, but as theater, improvisation, or a jazz combo, where leaders are actors and musicians who capture attention, set a tone, and frame experience for others (Bastien & Hostager, 1988). The focus shifts from controlling behavior to providing new frames of reference for interpreting experiences in the organization.

This emphasis on interpretation is not to suggest that leaders should attempt to manipulate people into doing what they want or that style is more important than substance. Instead, social constructionists emphasize the importance of images, symbols, rituals, and stories in the leadership process (Tierney, 1988). These elements of the organization's culture have a significant influence over how people make sense of their experiences and how they understand the goals and purposes of the organization. A ribbon-cutting ceremony for a new student center, for example, may convey a sense of optimism and a renewed spirit of community. Colleges affiliated with a religious denomination may use symbols such as the Christian cross to promote identification with the teachings of the particular faith tradition. Graduation ceremonies, alumni magazines, college logos, and athletics teams are all important cultural artifacts, and each affects how different constituents think about the organization and their role in it.

Leaders can use symbols and other cultural artifacts to shape an image of the organization. Images can inspire commitment and high-level performance when they provide a vision for the future and reflect the organization's history and traditions. Hartley's (2003) analysis of three struggling liberal arts colleges, for example, found that leaders were able to reinvigorate these campuses by challenging faculty and staff to reclaim their heritage. The president of one campus galvanized the faculty around the college's traditional commitment to civic education. On another campus, leaders rallied faculty and staff around the college's founding principles of social justice and access for women and people of color. These images were compelling because they connected with faculty and staff members' values and personal commitments; the images were also forward looking in that they inspired people to act in the interest of a common vision. These examples illustrate how leaders can draw upon organizational culture and history to craft compelling images that inspire commitment and motivation for action and change.

Leaders themselves are important symbols of the organization to whom people turn during periods of uncertainty. As Bolman and Deal (2003) note, "in the face of widespread uncertainty and ambiguity, people create symbols to resolve confusion, increase predictability, find direction, and anchor hope and faith" (p. 242). Organizational members often turn to formal and informal leaders to help them make sense of what is going on. A leader's actions, therefore, are important not only for the tangible outcomes of the behavior (e.g., the creation of a new program), but also for the meanings that organizational members assign to those behaviors. In Neumann's research (1995), college presidents had a significant impact on how faculty and staff interpreted the financial health of the institution. In one case (Industrial College, a pseudonym) the president communicated a confident vision for the future of the institution, in spite of a difficult resource context. In another case (Arcadia College, another pseudonym), the president's actions created higher levels of anxiety about resources, even though objective data showed the college to be on sounding financial footing.

> The faculty at Industrial College had become hopeful and optimistic—about their college, themselves, and their leadership—not because the college's financial fortunes had improved, but because through their new president, they seemed to find new (and renewed) meaning in their work together. The pattern was just the opposite at Arcadia, where the faculty's sense of comfort fell, not in relation to any objectively measured resource change, but because something had changed in the relationship between the president and the campus. (pp. 21–22)

In both cases, the college president influenced how people interpreted the financial situation of the institution. The meanings that faculty and staff assigned to the president's behaviors were more important than objective financial data in determining how people felt about the budget. Anxiety was produced in one case where the financial data actually indicated stability, while confidence was engendered in another institution where the financial picture was considerably less rosy.

The presidents of these two colleges had a significant effect on how other organizational members made sense of the financial complexities of the institution. In order to deal with the complexities and ambiguities of daily life, people construct frames of reference into which they organize information from their external environments (Weick, 1995). These **mental models** help people make sense of their experiences in the organization. The actions of leaders can draw attention to issues and shape how others interpret organizational events and experiences. By focusing attention on opportunities for resource growth, a college president, for example, can shape positive frames of reference even when the college's financial condition is tenuous. Thus, leaders can affect the sensemaking process for the entire organization. As Neumann (1995) notes, however, leaders' influence over the sensemaking process may have negative consequences, intended or not. History is replete with examples of devious leaders who manipulated public opinion toward immoral acts with catastrophic consequences. At an organizational level, the rhetoric of leaders may cause some members of the organization to feel that their contributions are less valued or unimportant. Even well-intentioned leaders may generate dysfunctional frames of reference. An academic vice president who continually draws attention to acquiring research grants, for example, may generate demoralization among faculty who do not bring in grants and instead focus on teaching.

Collaborative Leadership

Social constructionists also emphasize that leadership is a process, rather than a particular person or role in the organization (e.g., only college presidents and vice presidents are leaders). Leadership can be viewed as a process that is socially and culturally constructed by people at all levels of the organization (Rost, 1991). As such, leadership can emanate from any location in the organization (Ogawa & Bossert, 1995). In fact, collaborative approaches to leadership are gaining prominence and have demonstrated significant benefits toward organizational effectiveness, especially under conditions of ambiguity and change (Denis, Langley, & Cazale, 1996; Katzenbach & Smith, 1993).

Collaborative leadership is defined as a mutual influence process where the boundaries between leaders and followers are fluid and flexible (Evans & Wolf, 2005; Rost, 1991). Decisions are made through group processes such as consensus where people from multiple levels of the organization have an ability to influence both the process and the outcomes of decision making. In this way, leadership is not exercised by a single person; instead, it emerges through the interactions and communications of multiple workers.

Collaborative leadership is not about getting people to "buy in" to a goal established by top-level, formal leaders; instead it is about engaging in an open process of collective discovery where people can create a shared vision and identify commitments to guide their work together. This type of leadership often requires a redistribution of power within the organization (Ferren & Stanton, 2004). As new ideas and challenges emerge, authority relationships can be rearranged to reflect the unique expertise and experiences of organizational members. This idea dates back to the writings of Mary Parker Follett (1924) who suggested that leadership ought to reside with those who have the most expertise required by the demands of the situation. When new situations and circumstances emerge, different people within the group can assume new roles in the leadership process, regardless of their formal titles or position within the organization. For example, in an academic department, adjunct faculty who teach introductory courses could exercise significant influence regarding decisions about curricular choices for first-year students; a department chair may defer to their judgment regarding appropriate learning outcomes. In this way, individuals who are typically less powerful in the formal leadership structure can influence the direction of the unit or department.

Collaborative leadership is most frequently conceptualized at the organizational subunit level, such as a team, committee, or academic department (Eckel, 1998). But entire organizations can be led collaboratively when hierarchical structures are flattened and decisions are made by groups, rather than individuals (Bensimon & Neumann, 1993; Kezar, Carducci, & Contreras-McGavin, 2006).

Research has demonstrated that collaborative leadership can contribute to significant organizational improvements. Collaborative leadership strengthens employee involvement in the organization. Workers are no longer passive cogs in a machine, taking orders from above; instead, they are actively engaged in setting collective goals and structuring their own work roles. This type of participation in the leadership of the organization may be viewed as a prerequisite for high levels of commitment and motivation, especially among *knowledge workers* who desire autonomy, interdependence, and opportunities for team development (Janz, Colquitt, & Noe, 1997; Mohrman, Cohen, & Mohrman, 1995).

On the other hand, collaborative leadership presents a series of challenges that include building trust, establishing accountability, developing communication skills, and supporting opportunities for professional development (Katzenbach & Smith, 1993; Kirkman & Rosen, 1999). Efforts to forge team- or group-based approaches to leadership often fail in organizations with low trust and in contexts where organizational members are not accountable to each other. Moreover, when organizational members lack the skills needed for group problem solving and collective action, collaborative leadership may be destined to fail. Thus, in order to make an authentic commitment to collaborative leadership, organizations need to invest significantly in team building and skill development.

Sex and Gender Issues in Leadership

Increasingly in recent years, researchers and practitioners have come to recognize the differences in interaction styles, behaviors, and preferences of both leaders and followers of different sexes (Eagly & Johnson, 1990). Offermann and Beil (1992), for example, found that women leaders "perceived more support from their institutions and attached more importance to contributing to their community and becoming an authority in their field" (p. 37) than male leaders. Women leaders, however, were significantly less likely to find satisfactions in competing for high achievements than were male leaders.

Some studies of brain physiology suggest that sex differences may, in part, be hard wired into our cognitive makeup. Baron-Cohen (2003), for example, used neurological and case study data to argue that the female brain is predisposed toward empathy and the male brain is driven to understand systems. Put simply, women empathize and men systematize. Women may more readily and more accurately identify the emotional states of others and respond appropriately. Men, on the other hand, may have tendencies toward identifying principles that explain how systems work, and they use those principles to predict and control the behavior of others. To extend Baron-Cohen's argument to organizational leadership, the male brain may be wired for positivist leadership; specifically, seeking to identify patterns and predict the outcomes of various interventions into the system. And the female brain may be wired for socially constructed leadership, given stronger drives for understanding the unique circumstances of individuals and the social dimensions of organizational life.

As an example of social constructionist leadership, Helgesen (1990) notes that successful female leaders may develop innovative organizational structures that promote high levels of participation and empowerment. Rather than organizing work on the basis of hierarchy, the women leaders that Helgesen studied designed *webs of inclusion* where information sharing was encouraged. Whereas a hierarchy funnels information and directives through a chain of command, a web of inclusion provides more points of contact among workers. These connection points in the web facilitate information flow and stimulate creative dialogue among employees who under conditions of hierarchy may not have had a chance to learn from each other. In this way, women's leadership also has much in common with postmodern perspectives that emphasize the following:

- personal relationships over hierarchical ones
- empowerment rather than control and obedience
- autonomy rather than formalized roles and rules
- a culture of openness and trust (Hirschhorn, 1997)

It is, however, important to keep in mind that an emphasis on sex differences can lead to stereotyping when these differences become rigidified in organizational role expectations. Many studies of sex differences are based on statistical averages; an individual man or woman may have strong tendencies toward either empathizing or systematizing, and all people can learn both sets of skills. In fact, psychologists and psychiatrists continue to debate the extent to which sex differences are based in biology or are socially constructed and learned through the expectations that society sets for so-called appropriate male and female behaviors. Are sex-based leadership differences caused by brain physiology, or are they the result of how men and women are socialized at home, school, and work? Even if we agree with Baron-Cohen's (2003) analysis that brain physiology accounts for behavioral differences between men and women, we still must consider the social and cultural forces that reproduce and reinforce those differences over time.

To differentiate between biological and sociocultural perspectives, researchers make a distinction between sex and gender. Sex refers to biological characteristics and physiological differences such as those noted by Baron-Cohen. Gender, on the other hand, refers to the social roles that males and females occupy. Gender is socially constructed through socialization processes that communicate role expectations for males and females in various social settings, including work organizations (Powell & Graves, 2003). The study of gender is central to the work of feminist theorists.

Feminist theorists have generated numerous scholarly writings and research studies that illuminate the social and cultural forces that produce and reproduce gender differences. Rosabeth Moss Kanter (1977) was among the first to analyze gender and power in organizations. Kanter argued that women often have less power in organizations because they are not well represented in formal leadership positions. This unfavorable ratio is the result of historical and structural factors, including traditional notions of *separate spheres* of influence for men and women (Kerber, 1975). Women traditionally had influence over the home and family, while men were leaders in the worlds of work, religion, and politics. During the colonial period in the United States, for example, women were prohibited from entering into contracts or appearing in court. The Industrial Revolution, according to some historians, actually rigidified these separate spheres. As men shifted from farm to factory labor, they began to bring more outside money into the home; thus, the value of men's work became linked to the monetary economy, while women's work in the home was not remunerated and hence became less valued (Powell & Graves, 2003).

These historical divisions contributed to a system of **patriarchy**, which is defined as an ideology that promotes the subordination of women (Lorber, 1994). Under conditions of patriarchy, interpersonal relationships between men and women are characterized by unequal distributions of power. Patriarchal relations, in turn, become embedded in social systems, including government agencies, religious institutions, work organizations, and educational institutions (Glazer-Raymo, 1999). These social systems continually reproduce power disparities that disadvantage women. When patriarchal male leaders control the hiring and promotion process, they may select personnel who endorse and promote patriarchal values, including women who implicitly agree not to disrupt the traditional gender roles of the organization. Hence, women who accept gender-typical roles and enact gender-typical behaviors (e.g., a female faculty member who is caring and nurturing of students) are likely to be valued by organizational leaders, while women who attempt to disrupt patriarchal structures tend to be viewed negatively (Tierney & Bensimon, 1996).

Betty Friedan (1963) was one of the first to critique systems of patriarchy. In particular, she criticized functionalist sociologists such as Talcott Parsons for promoting the notion of separate spheres of influence for men and women. Parsons argued that women fulfill internal functions such as caregiving and ensuring family cohesion, while men fulfill external functions such as providing income. The feminine role, according to Parsons, was expressive, and the masculine role was instrumental (Parsons & Bales, 1955). This gender-based separation of roles was said to promote family stability. In contrast, Friedan argued that many women felt trapped by these rigid roles. Parsonian functionalism promoted a status quo that reinforced patriarchy and left women in a perpetually subservient position in the monetary economy.

Though Friedan was later criticized for overlooking the concerns of working-class women and women of color (she focused mainly on white, middle-class, suburban women), her analysis highlighted how patriarchal structures pressure women to conform in order to survive. These pressures can have negative cumulative effects on women who aspire to organizational leadership positions. Women leaders may feel compelled to behave like men (i.e., appear tough and aggressive) in order to be accepted in the organization and to enhance prospects for promotion. These efforts to *pass* in a male-dominated organization are likely to take a psychological toll on women leaders. For example, think of the psychological violence embedded in the image of breaking through the glass ceiling. (The glass ceiling refers to a metaphorical discriminatory barrier to the advancement of women and minorities in organizations.) Implicit in this notion is that women must do damage to the organization and to themselves if they are to achieve top-level leadership positions. Reciniello (1996) refers metaphorically to "body parts . . . poking through" the glass ceilings of male-dominated industries (p. 6).

What do feminist theorists recommend to alleviate these circumstances? The first step is to recognize that all organizations are gendered organizations (Acker, 1990). Feminist theorists argue that organizational leadership needs to be examined through the lens of gender, and they suggest that organizational leaders and researchers need to pay particular attention to power differentials between men and women.

A second key idea from feminist theory is that organizational leaders do not need to consider patriarchy as a static organizational condition; they can take steps to reduce power disparities. It is important to keep in mind that gender itself is a neutral term that encompasses both positive and negative interactions between men and women (Lorber, 1994). Leaders can take steps to identify gender differences and improve organizational conditions for both men and women.

Tierney and Bensimon (1996), for example, note the importance of creating women-affirming structures and promoting organizational cultures that are responsive to gender differences. Family leave policies and the creation of women's studies programs are two examples of structures that embody responsiveness to gender differences. The aim is not to break down gender differences, but to acknowledge them and create new structures that do not replicate patriarchy.

Women-affirming structures, in fact, often have benefits that redound to men as well. Men may choose to avail themselves of family leave time and may benefit from discussions of feminist pedagogy that emerge from women's studies programs. The converse may also be true; men may pay a price when organizations are based on models that maintain patriarchy and enforce subservience, which can be disempowering for both men and women. Hence, both men and women may benefit from the application of feminist approaches to leadership.

Summary

In this chapter, we discussed many different models of leadership, not all of which apply equally well to institutions of higher education (Kezar, 1996). Universally applicable, however, is the approach of Philip Selznick (1957) who notes that leadership takes place when "choice affects the basic character of the enterprise and involves the molding of the social character of the enterprise" (p. 139). Leadership is the management of institutional integrity once it is infused with value. It is the institutional embodiment of purpose.

Increasingly, people are recognizing that no single leader has all of the capabilities necessary to provide the multiple functions of organizational leadership. Many organizational members share leadership roles, but the playing of these roles is commonly informal and understated, rather than ostentatiously manifested. Though responsibility for realms of goal attainment is formally delegated, it is usually the case that decisions are discussed in groups and committees at all levels—highest and delegated—prior to final action. In these groups, different persons can play key complementary roles. This is particularly true as organizations like colleges and universities become even more loosely coupled and new forms of temporary teams are developed for purposes of teaching, research, and public service.

Review Questions

1. A small set of personality traits will almost always be found in effective leaders, regardless of the situation.
   a. True
   b. False

2. The highly talented faculty in a mathematics department have set high goals for themselves and have exhibited strong motivation to achieve them. According to Hersey and Blanchard, their department chair should employ which of the following leadership styles?
   a. Telling
   b. Selling
   c. Participating
   d. Delegating

3. Which of the following is *not* true concerning LPC?
   a. It is a measure of behavioral preferences
   b. LPC orientation prevents leaders from seeing the need to act according to the contingencies of the situation

   c. A high-LPC leader has as an important goal the desire to have positive interpersonal relationships with others

   d. A low-LPC leader has high group achievement as an important goal

4. Fiedler feels that the most favorable position for a low-LPC leader is when:

   a. Group atmosphere is high, the task is unstructured, and leader position power is weak

   b. Group atmosphere is poor, the task is structured, and leader position power is strong

   c. Group atmosphere is high, the task is structured, and leader position power is strong

   d. Group atmosphere is poor, the task is structured, and leader position power is weak

5. Which of the following is *not* associated with collaborative leadership?

   a. Creating fluid, flexible boundaries between leaders and followers

   b. Building consensus

   c. Achieving "buy in" from organizational members

   d. Redistributing power within the organization

6. Which of the following most accurately describes symbolic leadership?

   a. Framing experience for self and others

   b. Emphasizing style over substance

   c. Diverting attention away from objective data

   d. Finding substitutes for leadership

7. Which of the following is most closely associated with a feminist perspective on organizations?

   a. Differences between men and women are determined biologically

   b. Women fulfill internal functions that promote family cohesion

   c. Patriarchal organizations produce and reproduce power disparities

   d. None of the above

Case Discussion Questions

Consider the East Harbor College case presented at the beginning of this chapter.

   1. Why was the previous dean resented by the department chairs? Consider Hersey and Blanchard's situational leadership model. Was the

previous dean's leadership behavior misaligned with the needs of the chairs? Which leadership model would you recommend for new Dean Torres?

2. Dean Torres's conversations with department chairs revealed two concerns: lack of collegial relationships and uncertainty about assessment. Use path-goal theory to analyze the needs of the chairs and recommend a leadership approach that would most likely be effective. Keep in mind that different types of leadership may be necessary to address different types of needs.

3. Consider Dean Torres's leadership style and assess her potential for transformational versus transactional leadership. Which dimensions of her personal style lend themselves to either of these forms of leadership?

4. Use Fiedler's least preferred coworker (LPC) theory to assess whether Dean Torres's leadership behavior is likely to be a good fit for the current organizational situation. First, recall that the relationship between Dean Torres and the department chairs has been described as a honeymoon period. Second, recall the ambiguity that the chairs expressed regarding assessment and how student learning outcomes were not clearly structured. Third, understand that the new dean has relatively strong position power and that the overall situation is moderately favorable (i.e., people are initially favorably disposed to the new dean but lack of clear learning outcomes and lingering resentment related to the previous dean make the situation less than ideal). Is Dean Torres's leadership style a good fit for the current situation or should she seek to change the situation?

5. Describe how Dean Torres has engaged in sensemaking. What frame of reference is she developing? How will she know if she has constructed a compelling future image for the college?

6. Dean Torres is aware that she is the first woman in this role in East Harbor College's history. Are there elements of feminist theory that could assist the dean in understanding the gendered context of leadership at East Harbor College? Are there feminist leadership practices that could be implemented to meet the needs of the arts and sciences division and its department chairs?

References

Acker, J. (1990). Hierarchies, jobs, bodies: A theory of gendered organizations. *Gender and Society, 4*(2), 139–158.

Antonakis, J., & Atwater, L. (2002). Leader distance: A review and a proposed theory. *Leadership Quarterly, 13*(6), 673–704.

Avolio, B. J., & Bass, B. M. (1988). Transformational leadership: Charisma and beyond. In J. G. Hunt, B. R. Baliga, H. P. Dachler, & C. A. Schriesheim (Eds.), *Emerging leadership vistas* (pp. 267–308). Lexington, MA: Lexington Books.

Avolio, B. J., Gardner, W. L., Walumbwa, F. O., Luthans, F., & May, D. R. (2004). Unlocking the mask: A look at the process by which authentic leaders impact follower attitudes and behaviors. *The Leadership Quarterly, 15*(6), 801–823.

Bales, R. F., & Slater, P. E. (1955). Differentiation in small decision-making groups. In T. Parsons (Ed.), *Family, socialization, and interaction processes.* Glencoe, IL: Free Press.

Baron-Cohen, S. (2003). *The essential difference: The truth about the male and female brain.* New York: Perseus Books.

Barrow, J. (1977). The variables of leadership: A review and conceptual framework. *Academy of Management Review, 2*(2), 231–251.

Bass, B. M. (1985). *Leadership and performance beyond expectations.* New York: Free Press.

Bass, B. M. (1990). *Handbook of leadership: Bass and Stogdill's handbook of leadership: Theory, research, and managerial applications.* New York: Free Press.

Bastien, D., & Hostager, T. (1988). Jazz as a process of organizational innovation. *Communication Research, 15,* 582–602.

Bennis, W., & Nanus, B. (1985). *Leaders: The strategies for taking charge.* New York: Harper Collins.

Bensimon, E. M., & Neumann, A. (1993). *Redesigning collegiate leadership: Teams and teamwork in higher education.* Baltimore: Johns Hopkins University Press.

Berger, P., & Luckmann, T. (1966). *The social construction of reality: A treatise in the sociology of knowledge.* Garden City, NY: Doubleday.

Bess, J. L. (1995). *Creative R & D leadership: Insights from Japan.* Westport, CT: Quorum Books.

Bess, J. L. (1998). Contract systems, bureaucracies, and faculty motivation: The probable effects of a non-tenure policy. *Journal of Higher Education, 69*(1), 1–22.

Bird, C. (1940). *Social psychology.* New York: Appleton-Century Co.

Birnbaum, R. (1971). Presidential succession: An inter-institutional analysis. *Educational Record, 52*(2), 133–145.

Blake, R. R., & McCanse, A. A. (1991). *Leadership dilemmas: Grid solutions.* Houston, TX: Gulf Publishing.

Blake, R. R., & Mouton, J. S. (1964). *The managerial grid: Key orientations for achieving production through people.* Houston, TX: Gulf Publishing.

Blake, R. R., & Mouton, J. S. (1978). *Making experience work: The grid approach to critique.* New York: McGraw-Hill.

Blanchard, K. H., Zigarmi, D., & Nelson, R. B. (1993). Situational leadership after 25 years: A retrospective. *Journal of Leadership Studies, 1,* 21–36.

Bolman, L., & Deal, T. (2003). *Reframing organizations: Artistry, choice, and leadership* (3rd ed.). San Francisco: Jossey-Bass.

Bourdieu, P. (1986). The forms of capital. In J. G. Richardson (Ed.), *Handbook of theory and research for the sociology of education* (pp. 241–258). New York: Greenwood Press.

Bowers, D. G., & Seashore, S. E. (1966). Predicting organizational effectiveness with a four-factor theory of leadership. *Administrative Science Quarterly, 11*(2), 238–263.

Brady, G., & Helmich, D. (1982). The hospital administrator and organizational change: Do we recruit from the outside? *Hospital and Health Services Administration, 27*, 53–62.

Brown, S., & Eisenhardt, K. (1997). The art of continuous change: Linking complexity theory and time-paced evolution in relentlessly shifting organizations. *Administrative Science Quarterly, 42*, 1–34.

Burns, J. M. (1978). *Leadership.* New York: Harper & Row.

Calas, M. B., & Smircich, L. (1996). Not ahead of her time: Reflections on Mary Parker Follett as prophet of management. *Organization, 3*(1), 147–152.

Cameron, K. S., & Ulrich, D. O. (1986). Transformational leadership in colleges and universities. In J. C. Smart (Ed.), *Higher education: Handbook of theory and research, Vol. 2* (pp. 1–42). New York: Agathon Press.

Cameron, K. S., & Whetten, D. A. (1984). Models of the organizational life cycle: Applications to higher education. In J. L. Bess (Ed.), *College and university organization: Insights from the behavioral sciences.* New York: New York University Press.

Cameron, K. S., & Whetten, D. A. (1988). Models of the organizational life cycle: Applications to higher education. In K. S. Cameron & R. I. Sutton (Eds.), *Readings in organizational decline: Frameworks, research, and prescriptions.* New York: Ballinger Publishing Company, Harper & Row Publishers.

Carlyle, T. (1841). *On heroes, hero-worship, and the heroic in history.* London: James Fraser.

Chung, K., Lubatkin, M., Rogers, R., & Owers, J. (1987). Do insiders make better CEOs than outsiders? *Academy of Management Executive, 1*, 323–329.

Clark, B. R. (1972). Organizational saga in higher education. *Administrative Science Quarterly, 17*(2), 178–184.

Cohen, D., & Prusak, L. (2001). *In good company: How social capital makes organizations work.* Boston: Harvard Business School Press.

Collinson, D. L. (2005). Questions of distance. *Leadership, 1*(2), 235–250.

Conger, J. A. (1989). *The charismatic leader: Behind the mystique of exceptional leadership.* San Francisco: Jossey-Bass.

Conger, J. A., Kanungo, R. N., & Associates (1988). *Charismatic leadership: The elusive factor in organizational effectiveness.* San Francisco: Jossey-Bass.

Dansereau, F., & Yammarino, F. J. (Eds.). (1998). *Leadership: The multiple-level approaches, contemporary and alternative.* Stamford, CT: JAI Press.

de Hoogh, A., den Hartog, D. N., Koopman, P. L., Thierry, H., van den Berg, P. T., van der Weide, J. G., & Wilderom, C. (2005). Leader motives, charismatic leadership, and subordinates' work attitude in the profit and voluntary sector. *The Leadership Quarterly, 16*(1), 17–38.

Denis, J.-L., Langley, A., & Cazale, L. (1996). Leadership and strategic change under ambiguity. *Organization Studies, 17*(4), 673–699.

Duchon, D., Green, S. G., & Taber, T. D. (1986). Vertical dyad linkage: A longitudinal assessment of antecedents, measures, and consequences. *Journal of Applied Psychology, 71,* 56–60.

Dvir, T., & Shamir, B. (2003). Follower developmental characteristics as predicting transformational leadership: A longitudinal field study. *The Leadership Quarterly, 14*(3), 327–344.

Eagly, A. H., & Johnson, B. T. (1990). Gender and leadership style: A meta-analysis. *Psychological Bulletin, 108*(2), 233–256.

Eckel, P. (1998). Thinking differently about academic departments: The academic department as a team. *New Directions for Institutional Research, 25*(4), 27–38.

Eckel, P., & Kezar, A. (2003). *Taking the reins: Institutional transformation in higher education.* Westport, CT: Praeger.

Evans, P., & Wolf, B. (2005). Collaboration rules. *Harvard Business Review 83*(7/8), 96–104.

Ferren, A. S., & Stanton, W. W. (2004). *Leadership through collaboration: The role of the chief academic officer.* Westport, CT: Praeger Publishers.

Fiedler, F. E. (1972). The effects of leadership training and experience: A contingency model interpretation. *Administrative Science Quarterly, 17*(4), 453–470.

Fiedler, F. E., Chemers, M. M., & Mahar, L. (1976). *Improving leadership effectiveness: The leader match concept.* New York: Wiley.

Fincher, C. (2003). *Administrative leadership in academic governance and management.* Lanham, MD: University Press of America.

Follet, M. P. (1924). *Creative experience.* New York: Longman.

Friedan, B. (1963). *The feminine mystique.* New York: Norton.

Fulmer, R. M., & Conger, J. A. (2004). *Growing your company's leaders: How great organizations use succession management to sustain competitive advantage.* New York: AMACOM.

Gabarro, J. (1987). *The dynamics of taking charge.* Boston: Harvard Business School Press.

Galton, F. (1875). *English men of science: Their nature and nurture.* New York: D. Appleton.

George, J. M. (2000). Emotions and leadership: The role of emotional intelligence. *Human Relations, 53*(8), 1027–1055.

Ghiselli, E. E. (1971). *Explorations in managerial talent.* Pacific Palisades, CA: Goodyear Publishing.

Gibb, C. A. (1954). Leadership. In G. Lindzey (Ed.), *Handbook of social psychology, Vol. 2* (pp. 877–920). Cambridge, MA: Addison-Wesley.

Glazer-Raymo, J. (1999). *Shattering the myths: Women in academe.* Baltimore: Johns Hopkins University Press.

Goleman, D. (1995). *Emotional intelligence.* New York: Bantam Books.

Goleman, D. (1998). What makes a leader? *Harvard Business Review, 76*(6), 93–102.

Goleman, D., Boyatzis, R., & McKee, A. (2002). *Primal leadership: Realizing the power of emotional intelligence.* Boston: Harvard Business School Press.

Graen, G. (1976). Role-making processes within complex organizations. In M. D. Dunnette (Ed.), *Handbook of industrial and organizational psychology* (pp. 1210–1259). Chicago: Rand McNally.

Graen, G., & Ulh-Bien, M. (1995). Relationship-based approach to leadership: Development of leader-member exchange (LMX) theory of leadership over 25 years, applying a multi-level, multi-domain perspective. *Leadership Quarterly, 6*(2), 219–247.

Grusky, O. (1960). Administrative succession in formal organizations. *Social Forces, 2,* 105–115.

Grusky, O. (1963). Managerial succession and organizational effectiveness. *The American Journal of Sociology, 68,* 47–54.

Hackman, J. R. (Ed.). (1990). *Groups that work (and those that don't): Creating conditions for effective teamwork.* San Francisco: Jossey-Bass.

Hartley, M. (2003). "There is no way without a because": Revitalization of purpose at three liberal arts colleges. *Review of Higher Education, 27*(1), 75–102.

Helgesen, S. (1990). *The female advantage: Women's ways of leadership.* New York: Doubleday.

Hemphill, J. K., & Coons, A. (1957). Development of the leader behavior description questionnaire. In R. Stogdill & A. Coons (Eds.), *Leader behavior: Its description and measurement.* Columbus: The Ohio State University Press.

Hersey, P., & Blanchard, K. H. (1977). *Management of organizational behavior: Utilizing human resources* (3rd ed.). Englewood Cliffs, NJ: Prentice-Hall.

Hill, M. A. (1984). The law of the father: Leadership and symbolic authority in psychoanalysis. In B. Kellerman (Ed.), *Leadership: Multidisciplinary perspectives* (23–38). Englewood Cliffs, NJ: Prentice-Hall.

Hinds, P., & Kiesler, S. (Eds.). (2002). *Distributed work.* Cambridge, MA: MIT Press.

Hirschhorn, L. (1997). *Reworking authority: Leading and following in a post-modern organization.* Cambridge, MA: MIT Press.

Hogg, M. A. (2001). A social identity theory of leadership. *Personality and Social Psychology Review, 5*(3), 184–200.

Hollander, E. P., & Offermann, L. R. (1990). Power and leadership in organizations: Relationships in transition. *American Psychologist, 45*(2), 179–189.

House, R. J. (1971). A path-goal theory of leadership effectiveness. *Administrative Science Quarterly, 16*(3), 321–338.

House, R. J. (1977). A 1976 theory of charismatic leadership. In J. G. Hunt & L. L. Larson (Eds.), *Leadership: The cutting edge* (pp. 189–207). Carbondale: Southern Illinois University Press.

House, R. J. (1996). Path-goal theory of leadership: Lessons, legacy, and a reformulated theory. *Leadership Quarterly, 7* (3), 323–352.

House, R. J. (1999). Weber and neo-charismatic leadership paradigm: A response to Beyer. *The Leadership Quarterly, 10,* 563–574.

House, R. J., & Mitchell, T. R. (1974). Path-goal theory and leadership. *Journal of Contemporary Business, 3,* 81–97.

House, R. J., & Shamir, B. (1993). Toward the integration of transformational, charismatic, and visionary theories. In N. M. Chemers & R. Ayman (Eds.), *Leadership theory and research: Perspectives and directions*. San Diego: Academic Press.

Howell, I. P., Dorfman, P. W., & Kerr, S. (1986). Moderator variables in leadership research. *Academy of Management Review, 11*(1), 88–102.

Hunt, J. G. (1991). *Leadership: A new synthesis*. Newbury Park, CA: Sage.

Hunt, J. G. (2004). What is leadership? In. J. Antonakis, A. T. Cianciolo, & R. J. Sternberg (Eds.), *The nature of leadership* (pp. 19–47). Thousand Oaks, CA: Sage.

Jago, A. G., & Ragan, J. W. (1986). The trouble with leader match is that it doesn't match Fiedler's contingency model. *Journal of Applied Psychology, 71*(4), 555–559.

Janz, B., Colquitt, J., & Noe, R. (1997). Knowledge worker team effectiveness: The role of autonomy, interdependence, team development, and contextual support variables. *Personnel Psychology, 50*(4), 877–904.

Judge, T. A., Piccolo, R. F., & Ilies, R. (2004). The forgotten ones?: The validity of consideration and initiating structure in leadership research. *Journal of Applied Psychology, 89*(1), 36–51.

Kabanoff, B. (1981). A critique of leader match and its implications for leadership research. *Personnel Psychology, 34*(4), 749–764.

Kahn, R. L., & Katz, D. (1960). Leadership in relation to productivity and morale. In D. Cartwright & A. Zander (Eds.), *Group Dynamics: Research and Theory* (2nd ed., pp. 554–571). Evanston, IL: Row, Peterson.

Kanter, R. M. (1977). *Men and women of the corporation*. New York: Basic Books.

Katz, D. (1973). Patterns of leadership. In J. N. Knutson (Ed.), *Handbook of political psychology*. San Francisco: Jossey-Bass.

Katzenbach, J., & Smith, D. (1993). *The wisdom of teams: Creating the high-performance organization*. Boston: Harvard Business School Press.

Kerber, L. (1975). Separate spheres, female world, woman's place: The rhetoric of women's history. *Journal of American History, 75,* 9–37.

Kerr, C. (1963). *The uses of the university*. Cambridge, MA: Harvard University Press.

Kerr, C. (2001). *The uses of the university* (5th ed.). Cambridge, MA: Harvard University Press.

Kerr, S., & Jermier, J. M. (1978). Substitutes for leadership: Their meaning and measurement. *Organizational Behavior and Human Performance, 22,* 375–403.

Kesner, I. F., & Sebora, T. C. (1994). Executive succession: Past, present, and future. *Journal of Management, 20*(2), 327–372.

Kezar, A. (1996, April). *Reconstructing exclusive images: An examination of higher education leadership models*. Paper presented at the annual meeting of the American Educational Research Association, New York.

Kezar, A. (2000). Pluralistic leadership: Incorporating diverse voices. *Journal of Higher Education, 71*(6), 722–743.

Kezar, A., Carducci, R., & Contreras-McGavin, M. (2006). *Rethinking the "L" word in higher education: The revolution of research on leadership*. San Francisco: Jossey-Bass.

Kiesler, S., & Cummings, J. N. (2002). What do we know about proximity and distance in work groups? A legacy of research. In P. Hinds & S. Kiesler (Eds.), *Distributed work.* Cambridge, MA: MIT Press.

Kirkman, B. L., & Rosen, B. (1999). Beyond self-management: Antecedents and consequences of team empowerment. *Academy of Management Journal, 42,* 58–74.

Kirkpatrick, S. A., & Locke, E. (1991). Leadership: Do traits matter? *Academy of Management Executive, 5*(2), 48–60.

Korman, A. K. (1966). Consideration, initiating structure, and organizational criteria: A review. *Personnel Psychology, 19,* 349–361.

Kozlowski, S. W. J., Gully, S. M., McHugh, P. P., Salas, E., & Cannon-Bowers, J. A. (1996). A dynamic theory of leadership and team effectiveness: Developmental and task contingent leader roles. *Research in Personnel and Human Resources Management, 14,* 253–305.

Lewin, K. (1938). *The conceptual representation and measurement of psychological forces.* Durham, NC: Duke University Press.

Lewin, K., Lippitt, R., & White, R. K. (1939). Patterns of aggressive behavior in experimentally created "social climates." *Journal of Social Psychology, 10,* 271–299.

Liden, R. C., Wayne, S. J., & Stilwell, D. (1993). A longitudinal study on the early development of leader-member exchanges. *Journal of Applied Psychology, 78,* 662–674.

Locke, E., & Latham, G. P. (1984). *Goal setting: A motivational technique that works.* Englewood Cliffs, NJ: Prentice-Hall.

Lorber, J. (1994). *Paradoxes of gender.* New Haven, CT: Yale University Press.

Lueder, D. C. (1985). Don't be misled by LEAD. *Journal of Applied Behavioral Science, 21*(2), 143–154.

Maccoby, M. (1981). *The leader: A new face for American management.* New York: Simon & Schuster.

McClelland, D., & Boyatzis, R. E. (1982). Leadership motive pattern and long-term success in management. *Journal of Applied Psychology, 67,* 737–743.

McGregor, D. (1960). *The human side of enterprise.* New York: McGraw-Hill.

Minor, J. B. (Ed.). (2005). *Organizational behavior: Volume 1. Essential theories of motivation and leadership.* Armonk, NY: M. E. Sharpe.

Mohrman, S., Cohen, S., & Mohrman, A. (1995). *Designing team based organizations: New forms for knowledge work.* San Francisco: Jossey Bass.

Mumford, M. D., Zaccaro, S. J., Johnson, J. F., Diana, M., Gilbert, J. A., & Threlfall, K. V. (2000). Patterns of leader characteristics: Implications for performance and development. *Leadership Quarterly, 11*(1), 115–133.

Murphy, J. T. (2000). The unheroic side of leadership: Notes from the swamp. In M. Fullan (Ed.), *The Jossey-Bass reader on educational leadership* (pp. 114–125). San Francisco: Jossey-Bass.

Neumann, A. (1995). On the making of hard times and good times: The social construction of resource stress. *Journal of Higher Education, 66*(1), 3–31.

Norris, W. R., & Vecchio, R. P. (1992). Situational leadership theory: A replication. *Group and Organization Management, 17*(3), 331–342.

Offermann, L. R., & Beil, C. (1992). Achievement styles of women leaders and their peers: Toward an understanding of women and leadership. *Psychology of Women Quarterly, 16*(1), 37–56.

Ogawa, R., & Bossert, S. (1995). Leadership as an organizational quality. *Educational Administration Quarterly, 31*(2), 224–243.

Ouchi, W. G. (1980). Markets, bureaucracies, and clans. *Administrative Science Quarterly, 25*(1), 129–141.

Padilla, A. (2005). *Portraits in leadership: Six extraordinary university presidents.* Westport, CT: ACE/Praeger.

Parsons, T. (1951). *The social system.* Glencoe, IL: The Free Press.

Parsons, T., & Bales, R. F. (1955). *Family socialization and interaction process.* Glencoe, IL: Free Press.

Pelz, D. C., & Andrews, F. M. (1976). *Scientists in organizations* (Rev. Ed.). Ann Arbor: Institute for Social Research, University of Michigan.

Peterson, M., & Spencer, M. (1990). Understanding academic culture and climate. In W. Tierney (Ed.), *Assessing academic climates and cultures* (pp. 3–18). San Francisco: Jossey-Bass.

Piccolo, R. F., & Colquitt, J. A. (2006). Transformational leadership and job behaviors: The mediating role of core job characteristics. *Academy of Management Journal, 49*(2), 327–340.

Podsokoff, P. M., MacKenzie, S. B., Ahearne, M., & Bommer, W. H. (1995). Searching for a needle in the haystack: Trying to identify the illusive moderators of leadership behaviors. *Journal of Management, 21,* 422–470.

Powell, G., & Graves, L. (2003). *Women and men in management.* Thousand Oaks, CA: Sage.

Reciniello, S. (1996, June). *What does psychoanalytic theory and application have to offer the women of workforce 2000?* Paper presented at the annual symposium of the International Society for the Psychoanalytic Study of Organizations, New York.

Rost, J. C. (1991). *Leadership for the twenty-first century.* New York: Simon & Schuster.

Rowe, W. G., Cannella, A. A., Jr., Rankin, D., & Gorman, D. (2005). Leadership succession and organizational performance: Integrating the common-sense, ritual scapegoating, and vicious-circle succession theories. *The Leadership Quarterly, 16*(2), 197–219.

Sandberg, J. (2005, June 22). The CEO in the next cube. *The Wall Street Journal,* pp. B1, B5.

Scandura, T. A. (1999). Rethinking leader-member exchange: An organizational justice perspective. *Leadership Quarterly, 10*(1), 25–40.

Schriescheim, C. A., Castro, S., & Gogliser, C. C. (1999). Leader-member exchange (LMX) research: A comprehensive review of theory, measurement, and data-analytic practices. *Leadership Quarterly, 10,* 63–113.

Selznick, P. (1957). *Leadership in administration.* New York: Harper & Row.

Smith, B. L., & Hughey, A. W. (2006). Leadership in higher education—its evolution and potential: A unique role facing critical challenges. *Industry & Higher Education, 20*(3), 157–163.

Stogdill, R. M. (1948). Personal factors associated with leadership. *Journal of Psychology, 25*, 35–71.

Stogdill, R. M. (1974). *Handbook of leadership: A survey of theory and research.* New York: Free Press.

Tierney, W. (1988). Organizational culture in higher education. *Journal of Higher Education, 59*(1), 2–21.

Tierney, W., & Bensimon, E. (1996). *Promotion and tenure: Community and socialization in academe.* Albany: State University of New York Press.

Waldman, D. A., & Yammarino, F. J. (1999). CEO charismatic leadership: Levels-of-management and levels-of-analysis effects. *Academy of Management Review, 24*(2), 266–285.

Wayne, S., Short, L., & Liden, R. (1997). Perceived organizational support and leader-member exchange: A social perspective. *Academy of Management Journal, 40*(1), 82–111.

Weick, K. (1976). Educational organizations as loosely coupled systems. *Administrative Science Quarterly, 21*, 1–19.

Weick, K. (1979). *The social psychology of organizing* (2nd ed.). Reading, MA: Addison-Wesley.

Weick, K. (1995). *Sensemaking in organizations.* Thousand Oaks, CA: Sage.

Whetten, D., & Cameron, K. S. (2005). *Developing management skills.* Upper Saddle River, NJ: Pearson/Prentice-Hall.

Wofford, J. C., & Liska, L. Z. (1993). Path-goal theories of leadership: A meta-analysis. *Journal of Management, 19*, 857–876.

Zaleznik, A., & Moment, D. (1964). *The dynamics of interpersonal behavior.* New York: Wiley.

II

THE END AND THE BEGINNING: FRESH THOUGHTS ABOUT ORGANIZATIONAL THEORY AND HIGHER EDUCATION

CONTENTS

Purposes of the Book—A Reprise   887
The Complexity of Higher Education   888
Perspectives of and Challenges to the Postmodernist Paradigm   889
The Contributions of Social Constructionist Theory   890
Emerging Organizational Challenges in Higher Education   890
Conclusions   891
References   892

Purposes of the Book—A Reprise

When we proposed to Stylus Publishing a book about the organization and administration of colleges and universities, we noted that our primary purpose was to synthesize as much as possible the extant knowledge from the fields of organizational theory and similar theory from the higher education literature. Our intention was to produce a book that presented and explicated the most relevant organizational theories, classic and contemporary, to both practitioners and researchers. We hoped to be of assistance to current administrators (and those learning to become them) who are struggling to make sense of rapidly changing internal conditions and external environments and to offer a variety of explanations and directions for action. We also endeavored to pose dilemmas in the theories themselves—contradictions raised by competing theories and questions answered inadequately or incompletely by them.

As Jeffrey Pfeffer (1993) observes, the field of organizational theory is more fragmented and diverse than ever and is resistant to a consensus on how organizations work (and/or fail). Such a state of dissensus makes it difficult for leaders to develop reliable policy and for faculty who teach organizational theory to convey to graduate students a unified set of theories on which there is agreement and on which they can rely when out in the field. Our belief is that while many of the features of organizations have remained unchanged for centuries, civilization today presents many new problems that are not answered by age-old theories. Indeed, as we have indicated in our discussion of postmodernism, it is entirely possible that prior notions of consensus were either mistaken or must be supplanted with new perspectives that take into account different epistemological premises that are more relevant to society. We also believe that a multiplex approach to organizational problem solving is more effective than relying on only one theory at a time.

Quite naturally, and thankfully, in the course of doing the research for this book, we discovered many new facets of the field and many heretofore relatively neglected domains. We also became reacquainted with older theories that had fallen into disuse, partly because academia is often more intrigued by the new than the tried and true. We have, in addition, become increasingly aware of the philosophical antecedents of theories themselves and of organizational theory in general. Hence, although the book is predominantly positivist in orientation and content, we have felt it important to present alternative perspectives (multiple paradigms) as cautionary tales to those whose positivism has thus far been pursued without examination, as well as to offer suggestions for possible new venues for thinking for those seeking even deeper understandings.

The Complexity of Higher Education

While all organizations are complicated in their own ways—some more so than others—incontrovertibly colleges and universities are among the most inscrutable. The unique combination of regulation by national, state, local, and institutional bodies and the professional organizations both inside and outside that guide the main production functions of higher education (teaching and research) generate significant challenges for institutions seeking clear-cut rules that can be used to provide efficient guidance for policy and action. Life in college and university organizations also is complicated by the very nature of the missions of these kinds of institutions. Goals and values of education are amorphous, ambiguous, conflicted, and in frequent transition. Institutions fly into the future on hopes that the paths taken are the right ones, buttressed by a devotion to reason and rationality. But hope is by definition not rationally defensible. It is generated by calculations that come as close as possible to accurate prediction of the effects of different variables on others and on the future. There is, nevertheless, an incalculable uncertainty that underlies all decisions. Risk is ever present. To offset risk and its associated anxiety, hope, belief, and even self-deception intrude on individuals' perspectives and on the resolutions that emerge from group decisions. Rational organizational design and intelligent and humanistic leadership become exceedingly difficult under these circumstances.

The reaction of the higher education community in these early years of the 21st century to the perceived need to eliminate or at least reduce risk has been disturbing to many. In addition, the demands for accountability from on high (Burke, 2005) have induced individual institutional leaders to render their organizations even more controlled and regulated, undoubtedly at the expense of individual initiative and creativity (Smyth, 1989; Washburn, 2005). At the same time, the amount of knowledge available for acquisition and use by institutions and individuals has been expanding at ever-increasing rates. Problems of integrating the new with the old are not only becoming more difficult, but are being subjected to greater pressures for rapid solutions to extremely complicated problems. The race to capitalize on academic entrepreneurship has been institutionalized within institutions and individuals as competitive, often commercial, pressures that demand faster outcomes, frequently at the expense of thorough exploration and testing for validity (Slaughter & Leslie, 1997).

The expansion of knowledge has resulted also in an increasing specialization that separates fields and individuals from one another. In each discipline, the very definitions of objectivity and truth have become altered—in part by the stress of incompatible languages (Sokal & Bricmont, 1998). Indeed, the idea of the possibility of objectivity (and its compatriot, rationality) has now been seriously questioned, and alternative views of reality are becoming legitimated (Jameson, 1991). Such a shift in the philosophy and sociology of knowledge has had profound effects on the ways that colleges and universities are organized. Semiotics has entered into our thinking about communication problems in the organization and administration of institutions of higher education. The languages of discourse used throughout higher education institutions are seemingly incommensurable, leading to both structural and cultural fragmentation and certainly adding to the challenges of leadership and administration.

Perspectives of and Challenges to the Postmodernist Paradigm

It has been wisely noted (Dickens & Fontana, 1994) that "postmodernism addresses the same sorts of issues that have fired the sociological imagination since the inception of the discipline in the nineteenth century" (p. 10). The pace of change of society has accelerated since that time, however, making it much more difficult to utilize conceptualizations of society in general and theories in particular that came out of attempts at rational explanations of the relationships of people, institutions, and events to one another. Some observers insist that the change is so fundamental that the discontinuity between past and present renders prediction highly speculative. Rather than view this disjunction as problematic for social scientists, however, some theorists (e.g., Foucault) saw it as liberating, primarily in freeing analysis from global grand theories, which were deemed reductionist. Instead, postmodernists approach the understanding of social systems from a particularistic perspective (Foucault, 1972). Understanding can then be built from the immediate, the substantive, the basic elements that are unique to each situation.

Besides casting doubt on traditional positivist approaches to social science explanation, some proponents of postmodernism have introduced new types of questions about the more fundamental and philosophical underpinnings of thought itself. Whether academics can make sense of themselves and their surroundings, let alone be effective agents in the latter, has threatened to interrupt the evolution of the tightly articulated systems thinking that renders institutions of higher learning visible and understandable in a commonsense mode.

The impact of postmodernist thinking on the conduct of higher education and the planning for its future has in many ways been salubrious. While much of the work of institutions of higher education has proceeded as before, largely in a positivist mode, the challenges from the other paradigms have forced positivists to examine their assumptions and even their behaviors. A potential benefit from the application of postmodern thought is the exposure of the *values* of traditional organizational theories. What is becoming increasingly evident is that many entrenched modernist theories (e.g., bureaucratic theory) are susceptible to abuse by persons who occupy actual, potential, or latent power positions. While Max Weber also warned of such possible misuses of bureaucracy, it is easy to observe how power corrupts the hierarchy of positions by subtly and informally enlarging the domains of responsibility that the formal bureaucracy specifies. The result is often the exploitation of labor. In the term *labor,* we include all members of the academic community—students, faculty, and administrators.

The Contributions of Social Constructionist Theory

Postmodern perspectives offer a cautionary note about the positivist view of organizations based largely on epistemological premises that dissociate the human mind from an alleged external reality. Postmodernism, however, could lead to a dysfunctional solipsistic position that results in a fragmented, disconnected social system. Social constructionist theory, on the other hand, relies on the separateness of perceptions to argue for the need for consensus making through communication. With the expansion of knowledge and the complexity of society, it would appear that individual, isolated decision making, even with the aid of positivist research findings and theories that follow from them, will be less and less reliable. The social constructionist prescription for legitimizing collective improvisation in the interest of finding workable algorithms for organizational action would seem to respond to the continued shifts in information availability and reliability.

Finally, we caution that the baby should not be thrown out with the bathwater. Theories in the positivist tradition have a long history of providing effective guidance to leaders and managers in all organizations, including colleges and universities. As the reader will have noted in all of the chapters, positivist theories are fully explicated. Our hope is that they will be of enormous and durable assistance to practitioners who want to see their institutions become successful.

Emerging Organizational Challenges in Higher Education

We have entered the new millennium with a wealth of experience and knowledge about higher education, but with some worry that it will soon be outdated by the rapidly unfolding changes in aims, structure, function, and personnel within the system. While the worry is legitimate, it does not, of course, mean that all theory must be discarded at once and that we must reinvent our understanding of the field afresh. Colleges and universities constitute a human system in many ways not unlike those that existed thousands of years ago in ancient civilizations. For example, problems of effecting concerted human action, values that unite rather than divide, modes of decision making that are efficient, and strategies of change existed then and continue today. The fundamental manifest aim of an educational system, be it the informal family prior to the establishment of formal schools or the modern, complex institution we call a college or university, remains constant. It is to transform the ways in which people think, believe, and feel about themselves, others, and life itself, and to do so in an organizational context that is meaningful, moral, and fulfilling.

To be sure, there are alternative conceptions about how to define the aims of higher education and about the organizational modes that are most efficient to achieve them. Indeed, another function of higher education is to continually prey on conventional conceptions of society and humanity and to test their predictive validity and strength (Rorty, 1979). Philosophers from Plato to Dewey also urged this critical stance. Colleges and universities, then, both conserve culture and serve as its severe critics.

Conclusions

This book recapitulates some small portion of what is currently known and accepted about the social science of organizations. In this book, we follow Dewey's pragmatic perspective that truth is what works. It does not lie in some abstract realm of permanent reality to be apprehended by solitary study atop some remote hill. Rather, organizational theory becomes true by virtue of its ability to accomplish desired results. If such effects are not forthcoming, then the old theory must be thrown out and replaced with theories that do work.

As we have noted throughout this book, following Lewin, we believe that theory is eminently practical. It provides leaders and administrators with modes of pattern recognition that permit seemingly novel situations to be recognized as not necessarily exceptional and hence more easily navigable. While surely there are many novel and unique situations facing managers, most are not. Having a repertoire of analytical tools to apply to most situations allows an efficient sorting of unique and routine problems. Further, the problems seen as routine can be addressed quickly by means of tried-and-true theories. There is a danger, of course, that truly unusual situations will be overlooked in the press of excessive attempts to fit extant theories to them. And to this danger, organizational leaders must be alert. Certainly in higher education, practical problems abound. College and university decision making is frequently characterized by disjointed incrementalism, which is a reflection of three forces: lack of time, the proclivity to use narrow experience rather than theory, and the inclination to limit risk rather than engage in bold ventures to solve problems.

In some sense, then, theory can be liberating. It can permit organizational leaders to solve well-known problems more quickly and confidently and to spend time and effort in addressing new issues. On the other hand, needless to say, hiding behind theory is neither moral nor fruitful in the long run. Organizational leaders need to recognize that theory can be misused to reduce individual human beings to mere variables to be assessed and then manipulated. Certainly, this book would urge great restraint in this regard. The diversity of human society demands attention to the uniqueness of individuals and to the ways in which they are involved in organizational matters. While there are commonalities across individuals, the development of policies that address those commonalities should not ignore the nonconformists. Indeed, their dissent should constantly be courted as continuing checks on the misuse of theory and as important potential sources of innovation and change.

Colleges and universities are fascinatingly complex—subjects of wonderment that they work at all and of concern that they ought to work better. This domain of educational activity provides services that make life on this planet more fulfilling and satisfying. It deserves continual, dogged scrutiny in order to foster improvement. The use of organizational theory toward that end is and should be a noble enterprise.

References

Burke, J. C. (Ed.). (2005). *Achieving accountability in higher education: Balancing public, academic, and market demands.* San Francisco: Jossey-Bass.

Dickens, D. R., & Fontana, A. (Eds.) (1994). *Postmodernism and social inquiry.* New York: Guilford Press.

Foucault, M. (1972). *The archeology of knowledge.* New York: Random House.

Jameson, F. (1991). *Postmodernism or the cultural logic of late capitalism.* Durham, NC: Duke University Press.

Pfeffer, J. (1993). Barriers to the advance of organizational science: Paradigm development as a dependent variable. *Academy of Management Review, 18*(4), 599–620.

Rorty, R. (1979). *Philosophy and the mirror of nature.* Princeton, NJ: Princeton University Press.

Slaughter, S., & Leslie, L. (1997). *Academic capitalism.* Baltimore: Johns Hopkins University Press.

Smyth, J. (1989). Collegiality as a counter discourse to the intrusion of corporate management into higher education. *Journal of Tertiary Educational Administration, 11*(2), 143–155.

Sokal, A., & Bricmont, J. (1998). *Fashionable nonsense: Postmodern intellectuals' abuse of science.* New York: Picador USA.

Washburn, J. (2005). *University, Inc.: The corporate corruption of American higher education.* New York: Basic Books.

academic affairs, vice president for, 26–27, 27
academic freedom, 3
  tenure and, 34–35
academic institutions, budget making in, 28–29
academic organizations, culture in, 362
academic procession, 672
accommodators, 679
achievement
  leadership and, 857
  need for, 288–289, 856
  themes in, 618
  unequal rewards for, 503
action research, 693–694
activities
  nature of human, 372
  required and emergent, 329
adaptation, 108, 599
  culture and, 373
adaptive subsystems, 100
addressing conflict, modes of, 475
adhocracy culture, 378–379, 379
administration, vice president for, 26
administrative staff officers, roles of, 25–27
adoption of innovations, 800
affect-based decision making, 633
affective conflict, 501
affiliation
  need for, 856
  themes of, 618–619
affirmative action, 131
agency theory, 283, 633
AGIL model, 680
agricultural extension service of land-grant universities, 133
alienation, 556
alliance-building game, 567
allocation
  authority, 212
  resource, 212
  of tasks and responsibilities, 174

alternative dispute resolution (ADR), 511–512
alternative learning models, contingencies governing use of, 694–696
ambients, 291
ambient stimuli, 342
ambiguity
  of language, 470
  role, 265–266
  of success, 667–668
ambiguity-oriented frustration, 505
American Association of Community Colleges (AACC), 134
American Association of University Professors (AAUP), 34, 133
  in protecting academic freedom, 34
American Council on Education (ACE), 134
analysis, 596
  force field, 805
  gross malfunctioning, 773
  organizational
    approaches to, 38–79
  revelatory, 773
  sociometric, of groups, 335–336
  SWOT, 728–729
  tools for, in organizational theory, 11–12
  units of, 53
anarchical culture, 377
anarchies, organized, 634
anomaly, 44
approach-approach conflict, 501
approach-avoidance conflict, 501
appropriation, 227
arbitration, 511
archetypes, 477
architecture, 365
artifacts, 365–369
assimilators, 679
assistant professors, 30
  appointment as, 31–32
assumptions, 370–372
attractors, 160
authoritarianism, 855

authority, 544
    allocation, 212, 214
    charismatic, 203
    downward influence tactics by, 562
    formal, 719
    of situation, 322, 608
    well-defined hierarchy of, 210–212
authorization, 597
autonomy, 9, 304, 609
avoidance-avoidance conflict, 501

Baldrige National Quality Program, 771
behaviorist theories of leadership, 847–851
behaviors
    application of motivation, 282–283
    expected, 112
    observed, 110
beliefs, 369
belonging and social needs, 286
benchmarking, 189, 759
binary distinctions, determining, 70–71
binding decisions, 559
"black box," 102–103, 473
board of trustees, 23
boards of regents, 22–25
"both/and" thinking, 75–76
boundary, 94–96, 472–473
    permeability of, 96–97
    spanners, 95, 155, 479–480, 721–723, 799
brainstorming, intermittent, 604
budget making
    in academic institutions, 28–29
    as game, 567
buffer, 207
bureaucracy, 403–404
    roles as functional positions in, 247–249
    and decision making, 43
    cultures in, 377, 719
    forms of, 200–231
        client or customer, 219
        functional, 215–217
        matrix, 220–222
        product, 217–219
        time or place, 219
    postmodern views on organizational de-
        sign, 228–231
    red tape and, 465

structure, 203–214
    alternative forms of, 212–214
    centralization, 212–214
    decentralization, 212–214
    division of labor, 205–206
    participation, 212–214
    procedural specification, 206–208
    promotion and selection based on
        technical competence, 209–210
    well-defined hierarchy of authority,
        210–212
butterfly effect, 159

calculation-based decision making, 633
career ladder, academic, 29
Carnegie Foundation, 20
carrying capacity, 138
case-based decision mode, 633
Catholic colleges, religious identity of, 156
central concept, criteria for identifying, 420
centrality, workflow, 552–553
centralization, 212–214, 801–802
ceremonies, 368
certainty, 646
chain reaction, 617–618
change, 480, 806–807
    critical theory and, 817–819
    defining, 796–798
    effects of organizational design on process,
        803–804
    emergent, 798
    incremental, 796
    maintaining balance between stability
        and, 799
    mechanism for managing process of,
        805–806
    postmodernism and, 816–817
    problems in management of, 796–797
    transformational, 796
chaos theory, 159–161
charismatic authority, 203, 210
charismatic leadership, 842–843
choice
    decisions based on, 590
    opportunities, 635
    perceived, 135–136
    technological, 366

client forms of structure, 219
climate, organizational, 338, 390–393
closed systems, 95–96, 472, 493
co-acting group, 327
coercion, 565
coercive conformity, 142
coercive formalization, 207
coercive power, 563
    use of, 564
cognitive conflict, 500–501
cohesiveness, 343–344
collaboration, 422
    and leadership style, 869–871
collective action, 224, 422–423
colleges and universities. *See also* higher
        education
    as complex organizations, 2–5
    cultural challenges of, 5
    effectiveness of, 480
    environmental challenges for, 3–4
    features of first, 3
    internal organization of, 21–28
    interpersonal challenges of, 5
    national organization of, 21
    paths to upper-level positions, 209
    role of administrative staff officers, 25–27
    role of executive vice president, 25
    role of the president, 23
    roles and functions of, 20
    structural challenges for, 4
    student participation in decision making,
        35–36
    tenure and academic freedom, 34–35
    transformation processes of, 119
collegial cultures, 376–377, 378, 379
collegiality, strength of, 190
communication
    as key component of interpretation, 682
    patterns in group dynamics, 333
    problems, 503
    in social constructionist perspective, 61
community colleges, 3, 20
    leadership of, 28
    open access missions of, 156
community of practice, 682–683
competency traps, 668, 669
competing narratives, 777

competing values model, 480, 770–771
competitive advantage, 726
competitors, 133
complexity load, 645
complex organizations, colleges and universi-
        ties as, 2–5
compliance conformity, 342
components, system, 100, 473
compromise, organizational decision making
        by, 603–604
computation, organizational decision mak-
        ing by, 602–603
concepts, 466
    defined, 9
    usefulness of, 10
conceptualization, 505–509
    cultural, of organizational learning,
        686–689
    of cultures, 362–364
conceptual models of organizational design,
        170–195
confidence in authorities, 556
conflict, 337, 474–475
    affective, 501
    approach-approach, 501
    approach-avoidance, 501
    avoidance-avoidance, 501
    cognitive, 500–501
    in college and university organizations,
        474
    connotation of, 492
    defined, 492
    goal, 501–502
    in ideology, 497
    as inevitable, 497
    interorganizational, 496
    interpersonal, 495
    interpersonal/intergroup, 501–502
    inter-role, 264–265
    intersender, 262–263
    intragroup, 495–496
    intraorganizational, 496
    intrapersonal, 495, 502
    intrasender, 263
    latent, 498
    versus manifest, 497–498
    malevolent, 475

means, 502
optimum levels of, 499
orientation toward, 510–512
person-role, 262
postmodern perspectives on, 524–526
procedural, 502
as process, 474, 500–501, 503–522
settings in organizations, 495
social constructionist perspectives on,
    522–524
sources of, 496–497
as structure, 474, 500, 501–503
variability of, 502–503
conflict as process
    phase one, frustration, 504–505
    phase two, conceptualization, 505–509
    phase three, behavior, 509
    phase four, interaction, 515–517
    phase five, outcomes, 522
conflict avoidance, 498
conflict in expectations, 250
conflict in organizations, 487–530
    open and closed systems, 493
    unit of analysis, 494–496
conflict management, 337
    gender issues in, 526–527
    integrative and distributive dimensions of,
        513–514
    mixed approaches (structural and process-
        ual) to, 521–522
    process approaches to, 518–521
    rational approaches to, 524
    structural approaches to, 517–518
conflict of interest, 497
conflict of understanding, 497
conflict theory, history of development of,
    498–501
conformity
    coercive, 142
    conditions of, to norms, 341
    mimetic, 142–143
    normative, 143
congenital learning, 670–671
congruence of interests, 514
consensus
    on goals, 602
    on means, 601–602
    organizational decision making by, 603

consortium arrangements, 151
constituent involvement, 320
constrained learning stage, 673–674
constraint perspective, 283
constraints, 558
    formal, 719
constructionism, social, 469
constructive postmodernism, 401–402
consumption society, 67
contextual knowledge, 47
contingencies
    framework for change, 813–816
    governing use of alternative learning mod-
        els, 694–696
contingency theories, 52–53, 138, 145–148, 181,
    481
continuum of trust, 556
contractual relationships, 245
contradictions, 523
convergers, 679
cooperative negotiation, 506–507
co-optation, 559
coordinating board, 22
coordination, 188
    horizontal, 177–178
    mechanisms of, 178
    problem of, as complicated, 205–206
    vertical, 177
core competencies, 729
core technology, 186
cosmopolitan role, 267
counteracting group, 327
counterculture, 384
counterinsurgency game, 567
creative destruction, 683
critical psychological states, 302
critical theory, 62–64
    change and, 817–819
    organizational culture and, 385–386
cross-boundary leadership, 830
cross-boundary power relationships, 550
cross-functional teams, 346, 698
cross-functional units, 217
cultural challenges of colleges and universi-
    ties, 5
cultural conceptualization of organizational
    learning, 686–689

cultural
  determinism, 846
  knowledge, 57
  learning, dialectical perspectives on,
      689–693
  trends, 131
  typologies in higher education, 376–380
  values, 367
  variables, 190
culture(s), 183, 190–191, 392
  in academic organizations, 362
  adaptation and, 373
  adhocracy, 378–379
  anarchical, 377
  bureaucratic, 377
  collegial, 376–377, 378, 379
  conceptualizations of, 362–364
  definitions of, 363
  developmental, 377
  difference and, 388–389
  goal attainment and, 373
  hierarchy, 378
  integration and, 373–374
  latency and, 374–375
  managerial, 377
  market, 378
  negotiating, 377
  organizational, 5
  political, 377
  reasons for studying, 363–364
curricular decisions, 736–737
curriculum
  as strategy, 736–738
customer forms of structure, 219
customers of institutions, 133
customized craft technologies, 188
cybernetic feedback loops, 675

decentralization, 212–214
decision(s)
  choice-based, 590
  classification of
    by organizational function served,
        598–599
    at organizational level, 597
  complexity of, 588
  curricular, 736–737

effectiveness of, 588–589
information utilization and, 643–646
operational, 598
as personality manifestations, 639–643
as role playing, 637–639
rule-based, 590
strategic, 597–598
tactical, 598
as value laden, 589
decisional roles, 637, 638–639
decision avoidance, 592
decision latency, 588
decision making. *See also* organizational deci-
    sion making; individual decision
    making
  bureaucratic forms of, 43
  calculation-based, 633
  categories of, 477–478
  organizational, 475–478
  processes of, 119
  recognition-based, 633
  student participation in, 35–36
  systems as source of potential power, 549
decision modes, 633
decision recognition, 595
decision trees, 647, 649–650
deconstructing, 779
decoupled system, 225
de-differentiation, 230
deductive method of determining meaning,
    10
deep structure, 62
defective pressure cooker syndrome, 498
deficiency needs, 287
demographic approach of identifying stake-
    holders, 716
departmental structural form and model of
    control, 180
department chair, 27
departments
  budget preparation at level of, 28–29
  grouping together of individuals into, 175
dependency reduction, 149–150
dependent variables, 410
  of organizational design, 194
determinism
  environmental, 135
  local, 104

deterministic leadership theories, 836
deterministic model of environments, 136–137
development, vice president for, 26
developmental culture, 377
deviance, 143
diagnosis routine, 595–596
diagram of informal interactions, 335
dialectical learning model, 696
dialectical perspectives on cultural learning, 689–693
dialectical tensions in organizational learning, 692–693
difference, culture and, 388–389
differentiation, 101–102, 473, 503, 729
    in organizational design, 176
differentiation perspective, 362, 389–390
diffuseness of role, 268
discretionary stimuli, 342
disjointed incrementalism, 594
dissatisfactions, 290
disseminator, 638
distribution, norms of, 341
distributive dimension of conflict, 513
disturbance handler, 638–639
divergers, 679
diversity, 74–75
Diversity Scorecard Project, 421–422, 423, 735–736
divided external coalition, 718
division of labor, 205–206, 503
    functional, 215
dominated external coalition, 718
double-loop learning, 674–678
downward influence, 559–562
dualistic ontology, 55–56, 56, 65
duality of structure, 226
dyadic organizing, 258

ecology, 391
economic trends, 131–132
Educational Testing Service, 759
effectiveness, 343–344
    leadership, 837
    measurement of, 759
effect uncertainty, 727
efficiency, organizational, 779–781

either/or scenario, 506
emergent change framework, 798, 808–810
emergent evolution, 402
emergent models, 479, 740
    of strategy, 713, 730–732
emotional subsystem, 335
empire-building game, 567
empowerment, 571–572
enabling formalization, 207
enacting structure, 222–223
enactment, 222
engineering technology, 188
enhancing subculture, 383
Enlightenment, 308
enrollment management, vice president for, 25–26
entrepreneur, 638
entropy, 106–107, 473–474
environment, 98, 182, 473
    organization and, 370–371
    postmodern perspectives on, 158–161
    social construction perspectives on, 152–158
environmental challenges for colleges and universities, 3–4
environmental complexity, 146
environmental determinism, 135
environmental factors, 835
environmental load, 645
environmental niche, 138
environment-behavior, 306–307
epistemology, objectivist, 56–57
equifinality, 104–105, 181, 473
equilibrium, 104
equity theory of motivation, 299–302
ERG theory, 292–294
esteem needs, 286
eucity, 645
European Foundation for Quality Management, 771
evaluation and choice, 597
executive vice president, role of, 25
expanded social systems model, 113
expectancy, 294, 295
expectancy theory, 294–296
expected behaviors, 112
expected utility, 647, 648

experiential learning, 671, 677–680
expertise, 565, 719
expertise game, 567
expert power, 563, 564
exploitive/strategic model, 138
external coalition, 716
external environment, 183–184
    enactment of new, 151–152
    organizational strategy and, 714–723
external linkages, 150–151
external social environment, 110
external stakeholders, 281
extrinsic motivation, 282, 295
extrinsic sources of satisfaction, 290

faculty organization, faculty roles and, 27–28
faculty personnel policies, 21
faculty roles, faculty organization and, 27–28
faculty senate, 176
failure, learning through, 668–669
familiarity trap, 668
fantasy theme, 617–620
feedback, 106, 473, 674
    from job, 304
    mechanisms for, 681
feed-forward processes, 681
feminist theory, 872–874
    in conflict management, 526–527
    motivation and, 307–308
    on organizations, 64–65
    on roles, 260–262
figurehead as interpersonal managerial role,
    637
finance, vice president for, 26
"fit" hypothesis, 117
"fit" models, 767–770
focal person, response of, 257
followers, leaders and, 832–833
force field analysis, 805
formalization, 207
    coercive, 207
    enabling, 207
formal leader behavior, characteristics of, 393
formal organization, 565
    benefits of informal organization to,
        330–332
    chart showing, 101

forming stage of group development, 336
fragmentation viewpoint, 362
frame-bending change, 811
freedom, academic, 3, 34–35
free riding, 342–343
free will, 283–284
frustration
    ambiguity-oriented, 505
    goals-oriented, 505
    kinds of, 504–505
    means-oriented, 505
frustration-regression hypothesis, 292
functional forms, 215–217
functionalist paradigm, 44
functionalist perspective, 105
functional roles, 348
functional task subsystems, 335
function-based departments, 215
functions, utility of identifying, 599–600

gambling metaphor, 477, 646–649
game(s), played by organizational
        participants
    alliance-building, 567
    budgeting, 567
    empire-building, 567
    expertise, 567
    line versus staff, 567
    lording, 567
    rival camps, 567
    sponsorship, 567
    young Turks, 567
game theory, 647
garbage can model, 477, 634–637
gender
    in conflict management, 526–527
    as leadership issue, 871–874
    patriarchal construction of, 65
    studies of, in organizational administra-
        tion, 308
general environment, 131–132
general systems theory (GST), 91, 93–109
gestating events, 801
glass ceiling, 874
globalization, 66
goal attainment, 108, 599
    culture and, 373

goal conflicts, 501–502, 504
goal displacement, 229
goal emphasis, 851
goal model, 758–763
goals, 182–183, 189–190
    ambiguity of, 763
    defined, 758
    displacement of, 762–763
    official, 759
    operational, 759–760
    setting, 761–762
    succession of, 762
goals-oriented frustration, 505
goal theory, 296–299
governance, 119
    faculty participation in, 28
governing boards, 22–25
graduate school, recruitment of students to,
    29–30
grafting, 672
grand theory, 466
    systems theory as, 471–472
gross malfunctioning analysis, 773
group(s), 404–405
    boundaries of, 347
    defined, 326–327
    dynamics of, 332–333
    effectiveness of, 334
    interest, 555
    membership in, 328
    nature of, 465
    norms of, 338–339
    origins of, 328–329
    personal roles in, 333–334
    postmodern perspectives on, 349–350
    quasi, 555–556
    size of, 326
    sociometric analysis of, 335–336
    stages of function and development,
        336–338
    status hierarchy within, 335–336
    study of, 325–329
    subsystems in, 335
    teams, and human relations, 317–350
    teams as, 345–346
    types of, 327
group decision making, individual decision
    making versus, 606–608

group process roles, 348
group structuration, 347
groupthink, 60, 344–345, 465
growth needs, 287

hard sciences, 45
Harvard University on leadership, 850
Hawthorne Studies, 323–324, 325
Hersey-Blanchard model, 852–853
heuristics, 637, 641
    for choosing model of strategy, 738–741
hierarchy
    of needs, 284–288
    of offices, 210
    of prepotency, 288
hierarchy culture, 378
higher education. *See also* colleges and
    universities
    benchmarking in, 759
    changing nature of markets of, 173
    characteristics of United States system of,
        19–20
    complexity of, 888–889
    cultural typologies in, 376–380
    emerging organizational challenges in,
        890–891
    impact of postmodernist thinking on con-
        duct of, 889–890
    number of institutions, 20
    organizational strategy and, 714–715
    paradigm use in, 48–50
    postmodernist implications for, 74–76
    shape of, 400–405
higher needs, 287
homeostasis, 104, 473
horizontal coordination, 177–178
horizontal power, 550
    strategic contingencies theory, 551–554
human activity, nature of, 372
human nature, nature of, 371
human processual theories of change,
    805–808
human relationships, nature of, 372
human relations model, 771
human relations movement, 322–323
    recent developments in, 324–325
human relations theory, 321–325

humor in organizations, 691
hygiene factors in motivation, 290
hypotheses, 410–412
    forms of, 411

identification of patterns in organizational
        theory, 10–11
identity threat, 157
ideologic alliance, 719
ideology, 63, 385, 719
    conflict in, 497
idiographic dimension in social systems the-
        ory, 474, 835
idiographic influences
    proportionate contribution of versus nom-
        othetic influences, 114–116
    strengths of, on behavior, 114–116
idiographic leadership theories, 838–843
immediacy, 553
imperative, technological, 186
imperative method of identifying stakehold-
        ers, 715–716
improvisation, 692, 810
    organizational, 692–693
incommensurability
    methodological, 45
    observational, 45
    semantic, 45
incremental adaptation, 403
incrementalism
    disjointed, 594
    logical, 594
independent variables, 180–181, 410
indeterminate joint outcome space, 507–508
individual decision making, 628–655
    decision trees, 649–650
    garbage can model of, 634–637
    group decision making versus, 606–608
    information utilization and, 643–646
    non-decision making, 650–653
    as personality manifestations, 639–643
    postmodern perspectives on, 653–655
    risk and uncertainty, 646–649
    as role playing, 637–639
individual learning
    linking organizational learning and,
        678–686

nexus between organizational learning
        and, 680–686
individuals as system, 110
inducements, 558
inductive method of establishing meaning, 9
indulgency, 208
industrial psychology, 322
Industrial Revolution, 321
influence process, leadership as, 831–832
influencers, continuum of, 717
informal groups, 328
informal leader, 339
informal organization, 329–345
    benefits of, to formal organization,
        330–332
    defined, 329
information, 132, 477
    accessing preferences for, 477, 640
    distribution of, 666
    interpretation of, 666
    processing preferences for, 477, 640
    roles of, 637, 638
    use of, 643
innovations, adoption of, 800
input/output exchange, 51
inputs, 98–99, 473
    maintenance, 98, 473
    signal, 98–99, 99, 473
input set, 51
inquiry, modes of, 249–250
inspiration, organizational decision making
        by, 604
institutional decision making
    effect of special interest groups, 134
    faculty involvement in, 28
institutional environment, 141–142
institutional identity and image, 155–158
institutionalizing, 683
institutional level of roles, 248
Institutional Research, Office of, 26
institutional review, decision making by,
        590–591
institutional strategy, 711–712
institutional theory, 137, 141–144
instrumentality, 294, 295
instrumental leadership, 856–857
insurgency game, 567

integration, 175, 599, 682
  culture and, 373–374
  in organizational design, 176–178
integration function, 109
integration perspective, 362, 389
integrative conflict management, 520
integrative dimension of conflict, 513–514
intellectual perspective, postmodernism as,
    69–72
intellectual subsystem, 335
intelligent failure, 668–669
interacting group, 327
interaction facilitation, 850
interactionist ways of thinking, 499–500
interactions, 329, 515–517
interactive theories of leadership, 852–853
interdependence, 191–194, 205, 503
  pooled, 192, 327
  reciprocal, 193–194
  sequential, 192–193
interdisciplinary teams, 698
interest groups, 555
interface, 97–98, 473
intermittent brainstorming, 604
internal coalitions, 716–717
internal output, 105
internal process model, 765–766, 771
interorganizational collaborations, 676
interorganizational conflict, 496
interorganizational learning, 672–673
interpersonal challenges of colleges and uni-
    versities, 5
interpersonal conflict, 495, 519
interpersonal interactions, impersonality of,
    208–209
interpersonal/intergroup conflict, 501–502
interpersonal managerial roles, 637–638
interpersonal relationships, 249–250
interpersonal work preference structure, 336
interpretivist paradigm, 44
inter-role conflict, 264–265
intersender conflict, 262–263
intervening variables, 254–257
intragroup conflict, 495–496
intraorganizational conflict, 496
intrapersonal conflict, 495
intrapersonal goal conflict, 501

intrasender conflict, 263
intrinsic motivation, 282
intrinsic rewards, 295
intuition, 681–682
isolates, 338
isomorphism, 142

Japanese *keiretsu* system, 764
job characteristics theory, 302–306
job design, 305–306
job enlargement, 802
job enrichment, 802
job rotation, 518, 802–803
job satisfaction, 9
  problem of diminished, 7
joint outcomes space, 507–508
judicials, 641
jurisdictional ambiguities, 503
just-in-time (JIT) inventory system, 99

keiretsu system, 764
knowledge
  acquisition of, 666
  contextual, 47
  cultural, 57
  expansion of, 888–889
  integrating, into practice, 683
  link between power and, 72–73
  practitioner, 57
  research, 57

land-grant universities, 3, 101
  agricultural extension service of, 133
language
  ambiguity of, 470
  spoken, 367
  written, 367
latency, 109, 599
  culture and, 374–375
latent conflict, 498
latent role, 267
leader-follower distance, 834
leader match theory of, 854, 859
leader-member exchange (LMX) theory, 481,
    854, 859
leader-member relations, 861
leadership, 481, 826–875
  achievement-oriented, 857

behaviorist theories of, 847–851
as characteristic of person, 832
charismatic, 842–843
collaborative, 869–871
contingencies in path-goal theory, 858
defining, 830–835
deterministic theories, 836
effectiveness, 837
as exchange process, 832
followers and, 832–833
Harvard University on, 850
history of study of, 835–838
idiographic theories, 838–843
implication for, using positivist perspective, 53–54
as influence process, 831–832
informal, 339
as interaction, 837
interactive theories of, 852–853
as interpersonal managerial role, 637
leader match theory of, 859
leader-member exchange, 859
leader succession, 865–866
locus of, 833–835
management by objectives theory of, 857, 859
matching traits, contingencies, and behaviors for effective, 854–864
nomothetic approaches to understanding, 843–847
Ohio State studies of, 848–849
organizational culture and symbolic, 867–869
personality and, 860–861
philosophy, values and assumptions of, 842
postmodernist implications for, 76–77
as set of behaviors, 837
sex and gender issues in, 871–874
situational, 852–853
social construction and, 866–871
stages/phases in organizations and demands for, 864–865
substitutes for, 846–847
Survey Research Center, University of Michigan, 849–850
transactional, 481–482, 838, 840–842, 841–842

transformational, 481, 838, 840–841, 840–842
types of, in path-goal theory, 856
University of Michigan on, 850–851
learning
congenital, 670–671
constrained, 673–674
contingencies governing use of alternative models, 694–696
dialectical, 696
dialectical perspectives on cultural, 689–693
double-loop, 674–678
experiential, 671, 677–680
individual, 678–686
interorganizational, 672–673
linkages among individual, group, and organizational, 684–685
single-loop, 674–678
superstitious, 667
through failure, 668–669
trial-and-error, 713
triple-loop, 677
vicarious, 672
learning curve, 671–672
learning events, 801
learning organization, 696–698
least preferred coworker (LPC) theory, 854, 859
legal trends, 131
legitimate power, 563, 564
levels, utility of identifying, 599–600
liaison role as interpersonal managerial role, 638
line and staff personnel, 210
linear model of strategy, 712, 723–726, 739
line versus staff game, 567
line workers, 176
local determinism, 104
local role, 267
locus of control, 855
logical incrementalism, 594
logos, 368
loose coupling theory, 223–226
lording game, 567
lower needs, 287

macro level, 23
  change at, 807–808
maintenance inputs, 98, 473
maintenance subsystems, 100
malevolent conflict, 475
management
  by groping along, 594
  motivation and, 309
  scientific, 322
management by objectives (MBO) theory of, 299, 857, 859
managerial culture, 377
managerial grid, 849–850, 851
managerial level of roles, 248
managerial roles, groups of, 477
managerial subsystems, 100
manifest roles, 267
market culture, 378
market focus, 729
Marxism, 572–573
mass production organizations, 187
mastery themes, 618
matrix design, 27
matrix forms, 220–222
maturity trap, 668
maximizer, 643
means conflicts, 502, 504
means-oriented frustration, 505
mechanistic bureaucracy, 188
mechanistic organization, decision making in, 601
mechanistic structure, 180–181
mediation, 511
membership in group, 328
memory, 99–100, 473
  organizational, 666
mental maps, 14
mental models, 697, 869
mergers, 151
meritocracy, 63
metaparadigm theory building, 78
methodological incommensurability, 45
methodological subsystem, 335
Michigan, University of, on leadership, 850–851
micro level, 23
  change at, 808

micropolitics, 73, 573
middle-range theories, 466
mimetic conformity, 142–143
miner metaphor, 56–57
mixed approaches (structural and processual), to conflict management, 521–522
modernism, postmodern era contrasted with, 68–69
modes, decision, 633
motivation, 292, 465
  applied to behavior in organizations, 282–283
  defined, 281–282
  extrinsic, 282
  intrinsic, 282
  management and, 309
  potential and, 304–305
motivation in higher education workplace, 278–310
  ERG theory, 292–294
  feminist theory and, 307–308
  management and, 309
  need theories, 284–294
    for achievement, 288–289
    hierarchy of, 284–288
    two-factor theory of needs and satisfaction, 289–292
  process theories, 294–306
    equity, 299–302
    expectancy, 294–296
    goal, 296–299
    job characteristics, 302–306
  social construction and motivation theory, 306–307
motivators, 290
muddling through, 137
multifocus person, 643–644
multinational corporations, 66–67
multiparadigm research, 78
multiparadigm reviews, 77–78
multiple constituency model, 766

National Association of Independent Colleges and Universities (NAICU), 134
National Education Association (NEA), 133
natural selection, 138
  model of, 139

need(s)
  for achievement, 288–289, 856
  for affiliation, 856
  belonging and social, 286
  deficiency, 287
  esteem, 286
  growth, 287
  hierarchy of, 284–288
  higher, 287
  lower, 287
  physiological, 285
  psychological, 832
  safety, 285–286
  satisfaction and, 289–292
  self-actualization, 286
  social, 286
  theories of, 284–294, 306
negotiation, 511
  cooperative, 506–507
  culture and, 377
neo-institutional perspective, 144
network organization, 229
neutrality, 556
niche, environmental, 138
nomothetic approaches to understanding
    leadership, 843–847
nomothetic dimension in social systems the-
    ory, 474, 835, 836
nomothetic influences
  proportionate contribution of, versus idio-
      graphic, 114–116
  strengths of, on behavior, 115
nonconformity to norms, sanctions for, 342
non-decision making, 650–653
nonroutine technologies, 188
nonsubstitutability, 553
normal schools, 101–102
normative conformity, 143
normative power, 565
norming stage, 337
norms, 332, 367–368
  college, 207–208
  conditions of conformity to, 341–342
  development of, 339–340
  group, 338–339
  norms about, 341
  organizational, 465

sanctions for nonconformity to, 342
    variety of, 340–341
noxicity, 645

objective role ambiguity, 265
objectivist epistemology, 56–57, 65
observational incommensurability, 45
observed behavior, 110
offices as roles, 247
official goals, 759
Ohio State University, studies of leadership,
    848–849
  model, 862
one-dimensional view of power, 542
ontology, dualistic, 55–56, 56, 65
open learning stage, 674
open systems, 95–96, 472
  metaphor of, 493–494
  sources of conflict in, 496
operational decisions, 598
operational goals, 759–760
opinion leadership method of identifying
    stakeholders, 716
opportunistic surveillance, 139
  potential effect of, 140
organic organizational design, 180
organization(s), 112
  colleges and universities as complex, 2–5
  conflict in, 487–530
  conflict settings in, 495
  culture in academic, 362
  decision making in mechanistic, 601
  faculty in academic, 27–28
  feminist perspectives on, 64–65
  focal, 130
  formal, 101, 330–332, 565
  informal, 329–345
  mass production, 187
  network, 229
  patriarchal, 260
  personal power tactics in, 566, 568
  position in, 255–256
  power use in different kinds of, 568
  relation to its environment, 370–371
  role theory in, 246–247
  virtual, 229
organizational analysis
  approaches to, 38–79

organizational authorities, 555
organizational challenges, emerging, in
    higher education, 890–891
organizational change in higher education,
    790–820
    defining change, 796–798
    emergent change framework, 808–810
    planned change models, 798–808
    synthesis of models, 810–813
organizational climate, 338, 390–393
    types of, 394
Organizational Climate Description Ques-
    tionnaire (OCDQ), 392
    dimensions in, 393
organizational coalition participants, games
    played by, 567
organizational conflict, 519
organizational culture, 5, 190, 358–396,
    465–566
    critical theory and, 385–386
    framework for studying, 382
    organizational functions and, 372–375
    positivist research on, 375–376
    postmodern perspectives on, 386–388
    questions to guide an analysis of, 391
    Schein's framework for, 364–372
    social constructionist perspectives on,
        381–382
    symbolic leadership and, 867–869
organizational decision making, 475–478,
    583–620
    by compromise, 603–604
    by computation, 602–603
    by consensus, 603
    contrasted with problem solving, 590–592
    defined, 589–590
    effective styles, 645
    by inspiration, 604
    key questions in, 592–593
    modes of, 602–605
    participation theories of, 605–615
    procedural models in, 601–602
    as process, 594–597
    risky shift, polarization, and social loafing
        in, 616–617
    routinization of, 590–591
    shared, 608–614

social constructionist perspectives on
    group, 617–620
    as structure, 597–605
    technology and, 591–596
    zone of acceptance, 614–615
organizational design, 366, 403, 464–465
    alternative modes of, 178–181
    defined, 174–175
    dependent variable of, 194
    determinants of, 181–194
        culture, 183, 190–191
        external environment, 183–184
        goals, 182–183, 189–190
        interdependence, 191–194
        size, 183, 191
        technology, 184, 186–189
        technology/tasks, 182
    differentiation and integration in, 176–178
    effects of, on change process, 803–804
    goals and, 760–761
    organic, 180
    postmodern views on, 228–231
organizational determinants of power,
    549–550
    personal determinants of power versus,
        548–549
organizational development, 818
organizational effectiveness, social construc-
    tion model of, 774–777
organizational efficiency, 779–781
organizational environments, 126–165, 402–
    403, 464
    positivist theories of relations, 134–158
        contingency theory, 145–148
        dependency reduction, 149–150
        deterministic model, 136–137
        enactment of new external, 151–152
        exploitive/strategic model, 138
        external linkages, 150–151
        institutional theory, 141–144
        passive interactants model, 137
        population ecology theory, 138–141
        random transformation model, 144–145
        resource dependence theory, 148–152
        symbiotic relationship model, 137–138
    postmodern perspectives on, 158–161
    proximate, 132–134

social construction perspectives on, 152–158
  importance of sensemaking, 154–155
  institutional identity and image, 155–158
systems theory and, 130–134
  general, 131–132
organizational goals
  benefits of, 760–761
  effectiveness, and efficiency, 750–781
    competing values model, 770–771
    conceptualization of, 755–758
    "fit" models, 767–770
    goal model, 758–763
    internal process model, 765–766
    organizational efficiency, 779–781
    other models of, 773–774
    phase models, 767
    postmodern perspectives on, 777–779
    quality model, 771–773
    social construction model of, 774–777
    strategic constituencies model, 766–767
    system resource model, 764
organizational improvisation, 692–693
organizational inputs, 98
organizational leadership
  symbols as tools for, 368–369
  theories as tools in, 466–467
organizational learning, 478–479, 660–698, 670–673
  challenges associated with, 670
  conceptualizations of, 665–670
  cultural, 478, 686–689
  contingencies governing use of alternative models, 694–696
  dialectical perspectives on cultural learning, 689–693
  dialectical tensions in, 692–693
  learning organization, 696–698
  linkages among individual, group and, 684–685
  linking individual learning with, 678–686
  nexus between individual learning and, 680–686
  postmodern interpretations of, 478–479, 693–694
  processes and stages of, 670–678

strategies associated with differing environmental conditions, 695
organizational memory, 666
organizational method of identifying stakeholders, 716
organizational norms, 465
organizational paradigms, 44, 364, 467–471
organizational roles, 239–269, 465
  ambiguity, 265–266
  benefits and detriments of precise definition, 245–246
  conflict, 262–265
  as expected behavior, 249–257
    intervening variables, 254–257
    modes of inquiry, 249–250
    received role, 254
    response of focal person, 257
    role episode, 250
    role senders, 250, 252
    sent expectations, 252–253
    sent roles, 253–254
  as functional positions in bureaucracies, 247–249
  postmodern and feminist perspectives on, 260–262
  social construction conceptualization of, 258–260
  supplementary concepts
    diffuseness-specificity, 268
    manifest-latent, 267–268
    quality-performance orientation, 269
    universalism-particularism, 268–269
  theory of, 246–247
organizational set theory, 51
organizational strategy, 479, 706–742
  adaptive model of, 726–730
  curriculum as, 736–738
  emergent model of, 730–732
  external and internal coalitions in, 716–721
  external environment and, 714–723
  heuristics for choosing model of, 738–741
  higher education and, 714–715
  linear model of, 723–726
  postmodern models on, 734–736
  symbolic model of, 732–734
organizational structure, social construction of, 222–228

organizational subcultures, 382–384
organizational subsystems, 105
organizational theory, 6, 10–12, 407–424,
        466–467
    application of, to research, 412–418
    fragmentation of field, 887
    identification of patterns, 10–11
    in positivist mode, 407–418
    positivist perspective on, 12–14
    in postmodernist mode, 422–424
    postmodern perspective on, 14–16
    reflective practice in, 11
    in social construction mode, 418–422
    social construction perspective on, 14
    systemic thinking in, 11
    tools for analysis in, 11–12
organization-environment relations, positiv-
        ist theories of, 134–158
organization-wide change, complexities and
        challenges associated with, 480–481
organized anarchies, 634
orthogonal subculture, 384
outcomes, 522
outputs, 105, 178, 473
output set, 51
overall cost leadership, 729
overboundedness, 96–97
over-efficient organization, programming of
        decisions by, 591
overt behavior of organizational culture,
        367–368

paradigms
    approaches to, 43–46
    defined, 42–43, 467
    functionalist, 44
    in higher education, 48–50
    interpretivist, 44
    multiple, 46
    organizational, 44, 364, 467–471
    positivist, 50–54, 468
    radical humanist, 44
    radical structuralist, 44
    social constructionist, 54–65, 478
participation, 212–214, 559–560, 635
    internally, 719
    theories of, 605–615

participative leadership, 856
particularism, 268–269
part-time faculty, 30–31
passive external coalition, 718
passive interactants model, 137
path-goal leadership theory, 481, 854–856
    contingencies in, 858
    types of leadership in, 856
patriarchal construction of gender, 65
patriarchal organization, 260
patriarchy, 64–65, 873–874
patterns, identification of, in organizational
        theory, 10–11
perceived choice, 135–136
perceived inequity in resource allocation, 518
perceptual frames, 14
perceptual role ambiguity, 265
performance orientation, 269
performance standards, lack of common, 503
performing stage, 337
personal determinants of power, organiza-
        tional determinants of power versus,
        548–549
personality, 565
    decisions as manifestations of, 639–643
personalized alliance, 719
personal mastery, 697
personal power, 561, 563–571
    tactics in organization, 566, 568
personal roles in groups, 333–334
personnel decisions, 29–34
person-role conflict, 262
persuasion, 558, 800
phase models, 767
physical environment, 132
physiological needs, 285
place forms of structure, 219
planned change models, 797, 798–808
planning
    academic, 629–633
    individual, 509–510
    strategic, 308, 479, 708–711
    tactical, 514–515
polarization, 345, 616
policy decisions, 21
political culture, 377
political forces for change, 808

political model of organizational behavior, comparison of rational model of organizational behavior and, 547
political trends, 131
politicized alliance, 719
politics, 475, 545, 719
  in higher education organizations, 535–576
  power, unions and, 574–575
polity, politics in, 545
polyvocality, 777
pooled interdependence, 192, 327
population ecology, 137
  theory of, 138–141
positional method of identifying stakeholders, 716
position in organization, 255–256
position power, 861
positive organizational scholarship, 324–325
positivism, 46–47, 364, 407–418, 468
  alternatives to, 54
  conflict management and, 523
  in higher education, 49
  key terms in, 409–412
  organization-environment relations and, 134–158
  using, 389–390
positivist organizational theory, 308
positivist paradigm, 50–54, 468
  foundations of, 50–53
positivist perspective, 471
  applying, 15
  implications for leadership using, 53–54
  on organizational theory, 12–14
positivist research, 469
  basic approach of, 375–376
  on organizational culture, 375–376
  purpose of, 12–13, 468
postmodernism, 47, 422–424, 469–470
  applying, 15–16
  change and, 816–817
  conflict and, 524–526
  contrasted with modernism, 68–69
  effectiveness and, 777–779
  environment and, 158–161
  groups and, 349–350
  in higher education, 49
  as historical era, 66–68

implications for higher education, 74–76
  on individual decision making, 653–655
  as intellectual perspective, 69–72
  interpretations of organizational learning and, 693–694
  leadership and, 76–77
  models on strategy, 734–736
  on organizational culture, 386–388
  on organizational design, 228–231
  on organizational learning, 478–479
  on organizational theory, 14–16
  on organizations, 65–77
  perspectives of and challenges to, 889–890
  roles and, 260–262
  on teams, 349–350
  theorists, 713–714
  using, 389–390
potential partisans, 475, 555
power, 72–73, 475
  bases of, 565
  coercive, 563, 564
  defined, 541
  distribution of, 503
  equating, 573
  excessive uses of, 540
  expert, 563, 564
  in higher education organizations, 535–576
  horizontal, 550
  legitimate, 563, 564
  Marxism, 572–573
  normative, 565
  one-dimensional view of, 542
  organizational determinants of, 549–550
  personal, 561, 563–571
  politics, unions and, 574–575
  rationality and, 546–548
  referent, 563, 564
  reward, 563
  social constructionist perspectives on, 568–571
  three-dimensional view of, 542–543
  trust and, 556–557
  two-dimensional view of, 542
  use of, in different kinds of organizations, 568
  vertical, 550

power holders
  identifying, 568
  modes of identifying, 570
practitioner knowledge, 57
president, role of, in colleges and universities, 23–25
pressure campaigns, 719
primacy, 339
primary socialization, 59
prioritization, norms of, 340
private research universities, funding for, 20
probabilities, 647
problem(s), 635
  identification of, 53
  importance of solving right, 600–601
problem latency, 516
problem solving, decision making contrasted with, 590–592
procedural conflicts, 502
procedural specification, 206–208
process
  conflict as, 500–501, 503–522
  organizational decision making as, 594–597
process approaches
  to conflict management, 518–521
  to organizational decision making, 592–593
process theories, 284, 294–306, 306
product forms of structure, 217–219
production, 212, 214
production subsystems, 100
professional alliance, 719
progress toward tenure, 31
proliferating events, 801
promotion
  criteria for, 33–34
  selection based on technical competence and, 209–210
  tenure requirements for faculty and, 63
propinquity trap, 668
proximate environment, 131, 132–134
psychological frame, 571–572
psychological needs, 832
public research universities, 20
public service outreach, 102
punctuated equilibrium, 337
puzzle solving, scientific, 43

quality model of organizational effectiveness, 771–773
quality orientation in production, 269
quasi group, 555–556

radical humanist paradigm, 44
radical structuralist paradigm, 44
random transformation model, 144–145
rational approaches to conflict management, 524
rational goal model, 771
rationality, 497
  power and, 546–548
rational-legal authority, 210
rational model of organizational behavior, comparison between political models of organizational behavior and, 547
reality
  nature of, 371
  social construction of, 57–61
received role, 249, 254
reciprocal interdependence, 193–194
reciprocal linkages, 282
recognition-based decision making, 633
recruitment of students, to graduate school, 29–30
referent power, 563, 564
reflective practice in organizational theory, 11
refreezing, 807
regional accreditation, 129
regulatory agencies, 133–134
relationship, norms of, 340
relearning, 688
reporting relationships, designation of formal, 175
reputational method of identifying stakeholders, 716
required and emergent activities, 329
research
  action, 693–694
  development team and, 327–328
  expectations for productivity, 173–174
  multiparadigm, 78
  positivist, 12–13, 375–376, 468, 469
  vice president for, 26
research knowledge, 57
research universities, 20, 146
  image of top 10, 156–157

private, 20
public, 20
resource dependence theory, 138, 148–152
resources, 227
  acquisition of, 212, 214
  allocation of, 212, 213–214, 639
    perceived inequity in, 518
response of focal person, 249
response uncertainty, 727
results, knowledge of, 303
revelatory analysis, 773
reward power, 563
rewards
  extrinsic, 295
  intrinsic, 295
risk, 646–647
  taking and rewards in decision making,
    648
risky shift, 616–617
rituals, 368, 369
rival camps game, 567
role(s), 112
  conflict, 243–244, 262–265, 465
  diffuseness of, 268
  enactment, 258
  episode, 250
  as expected behavior, 249–257
  as functional positions in bureaucracies,
    247–249
  overload, 264–265
  playing, decisions as, 637–639
  postmodern and feminist perspectives on,
    260–262
  routinization, 258
  senders, 249, 250, 252
  separation, 517–518
  social construction conceptualizations of,
    258–260
  socialization, 258
  specificity of, 268
  theory in organizations, 246–247
role ambiguity, 243–244, 265–266, 465
  balance between role clarity and, 266
role-based decision mode, 633
role behavior, 249
  ambiguity and misinterpretation of ex-
    pected, 244

role clarity
  balance between role ambiguity and, 266
routine technologies, 187–188
routinization, 206, 207
  of decision making, 590–591
rule-based decisions, 590, 633
rules, 226–227
  function of, 207–208

sabbatical leaves, 34
safety needs, 285–286
saga, 367
salient alternatives, calculation of, 506
sanctions, 328, 338
  for nonconformity to norms, 342
satisfaction, 292
  needs and, 289–292
satisficing, 592
scalar chain of command, 210
scarcity, 149, 551–552
  of resources, 503
sciences, 60
  hard, 45
  soft, 45
scientific experimentation, 44
scientific management, 322
scientific puzzle solving, 43
screening, 597
searching and scanning, 672
secondary socialization, 59
selection, 596
  based on technical competence, promo-
    tion and, 209–210
self-actualization needs, 286
self-efficacy, 297, 298
self-esteem, 286
self-managed teams, 230, 325, 346
self-presentation, norms of, 340
semantic incommensurability, 45
sensemaking, 154
  importance of, 154–155
sent expectations, 249, 252–253
sentiments, 329
sent role, 253–254
separate spheres, 64
sequential interdependence, 192–193
sequential linkages, 282

setback events, 801
sex and gender issues in leadership, 871–874
shared commitments, 384
  identification of, 521
shared decision making, 608–614
  using model for, 611–614
shared group consciousness, 617, 619–620
shared mental models, 680–686
shared vision, 697
shocking events, 801
signal inputs, 98–99, 99, 473
signs, 253
single-loop learning, 674–678
situational dimension of leadership, 835, 836
situational leadership, 852–853
size, 183, 191, 254
skill variety, 303
small-batch organizations, 187
small group theory, 845–846
small wins, 691–692
social cognitive theory, 306
social construction, 346–349
  conceptualizations of roles, 258–260
  leadership and, 866–871
  motivation theory and, 306–307
social constructionism, 418–422, 469
  in higher education, 49
  using, 389–390
social constructionist paradigm, 54–65, 478
  assumptions, 55–57
  of reality, 57–61
social constructionist perspectives, 380
  applying, 15
  on conflict, 522–524
  critical theory, 62–64
  on environment, 152–158
  feminist, on organizations, 64–65
  on group decision, 617–620
  implications for applying, 61–62
  limitations of effectiveness, 776–777
  on organizational culture, 381–382
  on organizational theory, 14
  on power, 568–571
social constructionists, 47, 364, 481, 523
  contributions of, 890
  organizational learning and, 667
social construction model of organizational
  effectiveness, 774–777

social construction of organizational structure, 222–228
socialization
  primary, 59
  secondary, 59
social loafing, 342–343, 616–617
social milieu, 391–392
social needs, 286
social norms, 719
social participation method of identifying
  stakeholders, 716
social process, sensemaking as, 155
social science, 60
social structure, 392
social systems, 45
social systems model, 111–113, 831
  expanded, 113
  idiographic dimension, 112–113
  nomothetic dimension, 111–112
social systems theory, 91, 109–111, 474
social trends, 131
sociograms, 335
sociological consensus, 44
sociometric analysis of groups, 335–336
sociotechnical theories, 801–805
soft sciences, 45
solidary group, 555
solutions, 635
  development of, 596
solutions generated, 643
span of control, 211
special interest groups, 134
specialization, 4, 101–102, 205
specificity, 253
  of role, 268
speculatives, 641
sponsorship game, 567
stability, maintaining balance between
  change and, 799
staff morale, problem of low, 7
stakeholders
  external, 281
  identifying, 715–716
  model of, 766
standardization, 206–207
state of the system, 103, 473
state uncertainty, 727

statewide governing boards, 23, 129
status
    hierarchy within group, 335–336
    unequal rewards for, 503
storage, 99–100
storming stage, 336–337
strategic candidates game, 567
strategic constituencies model, 766–767
strategic contingencies theory, 550, 551–554
strategic decisions, 597–598
strategic leniency, 208
strategic outcomes assessment, 510, 512–514
strategic planning, 308, 479
strategy
    adaptive model of, 712, 726–730, 739–740
    criticisms of, 729–730
Strengths, Weaknesses, Opportunities, and
    Threats (SWOT) analysis, 728–729
structural approach to organizational deci-
    sion making, 593
structural challenges for colleges and univer-
    sities, 4
structural interdependence, 180–181
structural questions, associated decision-
    making variables and, 593
structural transitions, 571
structuration, 227
    theory of, 226–228, 347
structures, 100–101, 226, 473
    conflict as, 500, 501–503
    organizational decision making as,
        597–605
student affairs, vice president for, 25–27
student integration, 423
student market, segmentation of, 173
student participation in decision making,
    35–36
subcultures
    counterculture, 384
    enhancing, 383
    organizational, 382–384
    orthogonal, 384
suboptimization, 496
substantive theories, 466
subsystems, 100, 473
    adaptive, 100
    exchanges across interfaces, 97–98

in groups, 335
    maintenance, 100
    managerial, 100
    organizational, 105
    production or technical, 100
    supportive, 100
superstitious learning, 667
suppliers, 132–133
supportive leadership, 856
supportive subsystems, 100
surface structure, 62–63
Survey Research Center at University of
    Michigan on leadership, 849–850
symbiotic relationship model, 137–138
symbolic convergence, 58
    theory of, 617, 619
symbolic leadership, organizational culture
    and, 867–869
symbolic models, 740
    of strategy, 713, 732–734
symbols of organizational culture, 368–369
synthesis of change models, 810–813
systematics, 641
systemic thinking in organizational theory, 11
system resource model, 764
systems, 94, 472
    closed, 472
    "fit" between and among components,
        116–118
    individual as, 110
    open, 472
systems theory, 51–52, 129–130, 402, 494, 589
    central theme of, 471
    extensions of, 118
    as grand theory, 471–472
    history of, 91–93
    key concepts in, 472–474
    organizational environments and, 130–134
    overview of, 471–472
systems thinking, 697

tactical decisions, 598
tactical planning, 514–515
tactics development, 510
task identity, 303–304
task significance, 304
task structure, 861

teams, 217, 404–405
  as groups, 345–346
  learning as, 697
  postmodern perspectives on, 349–350
  self-managed, 230
technical competence, promotion and selection based on, 209–210
technical level of roles, 248
technical subsystems, 100
technological advances, 132
technological choice, 366
technological imperative, 186
technologies, 184, 186–189
  categories of, 186–187
  core, 186
  customized craft, 188
  engineering, 188
  nonroutine, 188
  organizational decision making and, 591–596
  rapid changes in, 67–68
  routine, 187–188
technology/tasks, 182
tenure
  academic freedom and, 34–35
  criteria for, 33–34
theories, 7–8, 466
  definition of, 9–10
  grand, 466
  middle-range, 466
  organizational, 466–467
  positivist, 468
  substantive, 466
  usefulness of, 8–9
Theory X, 309, 369, 371, 842
Theory Y, 309, 369, 371, 842
third party conciliators, 521–522
three-dimensional view of power, 542–543
tightly coupled structures, 225
time forms of structure, 219
tools for analysis in organizational theory, 11–12
total quality management, 771–772
trait theory, 835, 838–840
transactional leadership, 481–482, 838, 841–842
transformational leadership, 481, 838, 840–841

transformations, 102, 473
traveler metaphor, 57
trial-and-error learning, 713
triple-loop learning, 677
trust, power and, 556–557
truth, nature of, 371
turbulence, 160
two-dimensional view of power, 542
two-factor theory, 289–292

uncertainty, 503, 552, 645, 647–649
  decision making under degrees of, 477–478
underboundedness, 96–97
unfreezing, 805–806
unifocus person, 643
unions, 133
  power, politics and, 574–575
units of analysis, 53
unity of command, 210–211
universalism, 268–269
universities. *See* Colleges and universities
unresolvable joint outcome space, 508–509
upward influence, 557–559
  politics of, 558

valence, 294, 295–296
values, 365, 369–370
  cultural, 367
  decision making and, 589
variables, 409–410
  cultural, 190
  types of, 410
vertical coordination, 177
vertical power, 550
  partisans and authorities, 554–561
vicarious learning, 672
Vienna Circle, 50
virtual organization, 229

web of inclusion, 230
web of meaning, 478
well-defined hierarchy of authority, 210–212
Western Electric, 323–324
whistle blowing game, 567
women-affirming structures, importance of creating, 874

work, experienced meaningfulness of, 303
worker behavior, characteristics of, 393
work facilitation, 851
workflow centrality, 552–553
work groups, 321
work outcomes, experienced responsibility
    for, 303
work restriction norm, 324

work team, 345–346

young Turks game, 567

zero-sum relationship, effectiveness and effi-
    ciency in, 756
zero-sum scenario, 506–507
zone of acceptance, 564, 614–615

Abrahamson, E., 46, 92, 712, 730
Abramis, D. J., 265
Acker, J., 65, 874
Ackoff, R. L., 592
Adams, J. S., 51, 255, 299
Adler, P. S., 207
Agor, W. H., 637
Ahearne, M., 854
Ahlstrand, B., 713
Ahuja, G., 668
Albanese, R., 616
Albert, A., 156
Albert, S., 809
Aldag, R. J., 345
Alderfer, C. P., 292–294, 302, 328
Aldrich, H. E., 517
Alesina, A., 554
Alexander, F. K., 129
Alfred, R., 676, 689, 714, 715, 766
Allan, G., 401–402
Allen, R. W., 544, 558
Allen, V. L., 246
Allison, G., 495
Allmendinger, J., 161
Allport, G. W., 113
Alstete, J. W., 759
Alt, J. E., 554
Alvesson, M., 778
Amason, A. C., 493, 499
Ames, D. R., 633, 634
Amey, M., 358
Ancona, D. G., 255, 672
Anderson, J., 50
Anderson, M., 45
Anderson, S., 67
Andrews, F. M., 845
Angle, H. L., 544, 558
Ansoff, H. I., 712
Antonakis, J., 833
Aquinas, Thomas, 371
Argote, L., 671
Argyris, C., 43, 106, 324, 370, 674–678, 697

Armenakis, A. A., 244
Arthur, J., 671
Astley, W. G., 140
Atkinson, J. W., 281, 305
Atwater, L., 833
Austin, A. E., 244, 259
Avolio, B. J., 840, 843
Awbrey, S., 665, 696

Bacharach, S., 564–566, 568
Bachrach, P., 62, 523, 542, 590, 592, 652
Bachmann, R., 347
Bacon, Francis, 68
Baden-Fuller, C., 809
Baehr, T. A., 262
Baez, B., 260, 386, 535, 817
Bailey, D. E., 325
Bailey, K. D., 92
Baird, I., 591
Baker, E. L., 780
Balbastre, F., 665, 677, 686
Balderston, F., 48, 151, 225, 374, 809
Baldridge, J. V., 48
Bales, R. F., 64, 641, 850, 864, 873
Ball, M. A., 619
Balogun, J., 730
Bandura, A., 295, 306, 307
Banta, T. W., 759, 780, 781
Bapuji, H., 665, 672
Barak, R., 189, 759
Baratz, M. S., 62, 523, 542, 590, 592, 652
Bargh, J. A., 297
Barker, R. G., 183
Barnard, C. I., 176, 192, 325, 545, 559, 614
Barney, J., 673
Baron-Cohen, S., 871, 872
Barrett, F. J., 669
Barrick, M. R., 639
Barrow, J., 835
Barsky, A. E., 492
Bartos, O. J., 504
Bartunek, J. M., 516

Bass, B. M., 594, 831, 840, 841
Bass, D. J., 345
Bastein, D., 810, 867
Bauman, G., 421, 422, 694, 774, 779
Baxter, L., 76, 522
Bazerman, M. H., 590, 591
Bedeian, A. G., 184, 186, 193, 244, 246, 760
Behn, R. D., 594
Beil, C., 871
Belasco, J., 571
Belenky, M., 287, 308
Bell, C. H., 818
Benjamin, R., 177, 698, 810
Benne, K., 499, 797
Bennis, W., 499, 797, 840, 841
Bensimon, E. M., 16, 49, 73, 244, 260, 261,
    262, 348, 421, 422, 423, 470, 589, 665,
    694, 725, 735, 774, 775, 779, 830, 867,
    873, 874
Benson, J. K., 522
Benton, D. A., 327
Berger, P. L., 14, 55, 469, 867, 870
Bergquist, W., 48, 229, 377, 470
Berman, J. E., 770
Berrien, F. K., 92, 99, 104, 472
Bertalanffy, L. von, 92, 95
Bess, J. L., 19, 26, 48, 76, 108, 190, 206, 211,
    302, 367, 470–471, 594, 619–620, 655,
    765, 833, 859
Betz, D., 759
Beyer, J., 98
Biddle, B., 246
Bigelow, B., 574
Biglan, A., 45, 383
Birch, J. B., 551
Bird, C., 839
Birnbaum, R., 19, 48, 98, 154, 182, 225, 270,
    376, 377, 383, 405, 500, 549, 667, 675,
    866
Black, J. S., 289
Black, M., 386
Blackburn, R. S., 192
Blackburn, R. T., 244
Blackman, D., 677
Blais, A-R., 633, 634
Blake, R. R., 834, 849–850
Blanchard, K. H., 852
Blau, P., 52, 183, 208, 212, 255, 270, 284
Bloland, H., 48, 49, 65, 67, 68, 69, 71, 159,
    349, 387, 478, 480, 525, 693, 734, 816,
    817

Bloom, M., 302
Blum, D. E., 574
Bobko, P., 75
Bogart, D. H., 106
Bogue, E., 780
Bokeno, R. M., 677
Boland, R., 780
Bolman, L., 4, 14, 60, 155, 228, 346, 868
Bommer, W. H., 854
Borden, V. M. H., 780
Bormann, E., 14, 58, 224, 524, 617, 618, 713
Borys, B., 207
Bossert, S., 869
Boulding, K., 92, 93–94
Bourdieu, P., 840
Bourgeois, L., 672
Bowers, D. G., 606, 850
Boyatzis, R. E., 839
Boyce, M., 694
Boyer, E., 102, 244, 793
Brady, G., 866
Braskamp, L., 133, 794
Brass, D. J., 549
Braverman, H., 76, 572, 778
Breaugh, J. A., 265
Brehmer, B., 634
Bricmont, J., 888
Bridges, E. M., 614
Bridwell, L. G., 285
Bromiley, P., 591
Brooks, D., 671
Brown, L. D., 492, 498
Brown, R. H., 229, 401
Brown, S., 188, 690, 810, 812, 845
Brown, W. R., 540, 780
Browning, L., 794
Bruehl, M. E., 496
Buchanan, D., 778, 779, 816
Buckley, W., 92, 104
Burawoy, M., 76
Burke, J. C., 780, 781, 888
Burkhardt, M. E., 549
Burnes, B., 795, 807, 811, 812, 819
Burnham, D., 288
Burns, J. M., 544, 840, 841
Burns, T., 52, 145–146, 471, 694–695, 801
Burrell, G., 42, 44, 45, 92, 181
Burton, R. M., 93
Butler, R. J., 595
Byrne, J. A., 220

Cahn, D. D., 507, 511, 526
Calas, M. B., 64, 307, 385, 845
Caldwell. D. F., 93, 255, 672
Callister, R. R., 493
Cameron, K. S., 324, 641, 757, 767, 768, 769, 770, 771, 774, 841, 864, 865
Campbell, J., 296
Campbell, R. F., 111, 112, 114
Cannella, A. A., Jr., 678, 865
Cannon-Bowers, J. A., 865
Carducci, R., 46, 325, 469, 870
Carlson, O., 136, 140, 144, 740
Carlyle, Thomas, 838
Carr, A., 730
Carroll, J. S., 673–674
Carroll, S., 177, 698, 810
Cartwright, D., 350
Castro, S., 859
Casu, B., 780
Cavanaugh, J., 67
Caza, A., 324
Cazale, L., 869
Chaffee, E. E., 67, 133, 170, 479, 712, 726, 732, 733, 737
Chaison, G., 574
Champoux, J. E., 372
Chandler, A., 712, 723–726
Chatman, J., 93
Chemers, M. M., 859
Chickering, A., 669
Chin, R., 499, 797
Chisholm, D., 324
Chonko, L. B., 255
Choppin, J., 772
Christensen, C. R., 765
Chun, J., 678
Chung, K., 866
Churchman, C. W., 92
Cistone, P., 521
Clark, B. R., 367, 845
Clark, S., 155
Claxton, C. S., 679
Clegg, S. R., 230, 551, 777
Clery, S., 133, 574
Clinchy, B., 287, 308
Coaldrake, W., 365
Cohen, D., 840
Cohen, M. D., 118, 186, 245, 377, 477, 545, 636, 654, 730
Cohen, S. G., 325, 870

Colbeck, C., 182, 244, 265
Colihan, J. P., 265
Collins, J. M., 262
Collins, R., 501
Collinson, D. L., 833
Colquitt, J. A., 840, 870
Comer, D. R., 616
Comte, Auguste, 50
Conger, J. A., 571, 832, 834, 865
Conlon, E., 766
Connelly, J., 677
Connolly, T., 766
Contreras-McGavin, M., 46, 325, 469, 870
Conway, M. E., 92
Cook, S., 47, 680, 682, 687, 688–689, 693
Coons, A., 848
Cooper, C. L., 765
Corak, K., 29, 48, 725
Corbin, J., 9, 418–419, 420, 421
Corea, S., 92
Coser, L., 522
Costantino, C. A., 495, 511, 512
Couger, J., 805
Cragan, J. F., 617, 713
Cray, D., 595
Crenson, M. A., 543
Creswell, J. W., 421, 422, 466, 467
Croft, D., 392
Crossan, M., 665, 666, 672, 678, 680–685
Crosson, P., 98
Crutchfield, J. P., 402
Csikszentmihalyi, M., 289
Cummings,, J. N., 833, 843
Cummings, T. G., 331
Cunliff, E., 759
Cutright, M., 20, 87, 160, 186, 231, 470, 725, 730, 733, 735
Cyert, R. M., 516, 596, 759, 761, 767

Daft, R. L., 136, 140, 144, 174, 179, 184, 185, 205, 363, 368, 517, 546, 740, 757, 763, 772
Dahl, R. A., 541
Dale, B. G., 772
Daly, C., 264
Damanpour, F., 796, 802
Dansereau, F., 678, 833
Darkenwald, G., 496
Darwin, Charles, 68, 466
Davies, J., 401
Davis, G. F., 130

Davis, J. H., 362, 556
Davis, K., 328
Davis, S. M., 220
Dawson, P., 778
Day, A. L., 246
Day, G., 479, 672, 726
Deal, T., 4, 14, 60, 155, 228, 346, 364, 375, 389, 868
Dean, D., 317
DeCew, J. W., 575
Deci, E., 285, 304
de Dreu, C., 493
Dee, J., 49, 75, 224, 264, 384, 521, 571, 733, 777, 794
Deephouse, D., 141
Deetz, S., 61, 62, 77, 154, 350, 368, 385, 545, 571, 589, 652, 713, 734, 778, 818
de Geus, A. P., 669
Delanty, G., 77
Del Favero, M., 98, 384, 470, 500, 628, 725
De Meuse, K. P., 325
Denis, J.-L., 869
Denison, D., 364, 374, 375
Denzin, N., 777
Derrida, J., 69–71, 75, 524–525, 683
Descartes, René, 68
DeShon, R. P., 297
Deutsch, M., 504
Deutsch, S., 766
Deutscher, I., 370
Dewey, J., 504, 678
Diana, M., 840
Dickens, D. R., 229, 470, 889
Dickson, W. J., 52, 321, 323
Diener, E., 343
Dill, D., 140, 142, 664, 676, 683, 694
DiMaggio, P. J., 142, 807
Dionne, S., 678
Doise, W., 616
Donaldson, L., 45–46, 93, 401, 403, 724, 739
Donnellon, A., 325
Donnelly, J. H., 266
Dorfman, P. W., 132, 846
Dougherty, K, J, 780
Downey, D., 174, 215
Downs, A., 730
Drazin, R., 54, 105, 117, 410
Driver, M., 477, 643–646
Druckman, D., 497
D'Souza, D., 74

Dubin, R., 372
Duchon, D., 859
Duemer, L., 571
Duguid, P., 667, 670, 682, 684, 686
Dukerich, J. M., 156, 780, 809
Duncan, R. B., 146, 147, 148, 216, 219, 591, 796
Durant, R., 730
Dutton, J. E., 139, 156, 167, 760, 786, 809, 823
Dutton, J. M., 504, 534
Dvir, T., 853

Eagly, A. H., 871
Easton, D., 545
Eckel, P., 48, 381, 419, 420, 733, 795, 797, 812, 842, 870
Eckensberger, L. H., 46
Eisenhardt, K., 188, 672, 690, 810, 812, 845
Elizur, D., 289
Elliot, Charles W., 846
Ellul, J., 186
Elron, C. F., 759
Emery, F. E., 130
Emmett, D. C., 135
Engledow, J. L., 139
Erbert, L., 321
Erez, A., 246
Etzioni, A., 256, 344, 555, 758, 763
Evan, W. M., 51, 248, 721, 796
Evans, M., 854
Evans, P., 869
Eve, R. A., 231
Ewell, P., 766

Fagen, R. E., 94
Fairhurst, G. T., 56
Farmer, R. N., 759
Fayol, H., 322
Feather, N. T., 305
Feldman, D. D., 339
Ferguson, K., 260
Ferren, A. S., 870
Ferry, D. L., 757
Festinger, L. A., 299
Feurig, P., 665, 696
Fiedler, F. E., 327, 639, 859, 860
Fincher, C., 831
Fincher, R. D., 511
Finkelstein, M., 30, 174
Fiol, C. M., 666–667, 817

Fisher, H., 780
Fisher, J., 48
Fisher, R., 76, 520
Fitzpatrick, A. R., 345
Fligstein, N., 776
Flink, J. J., 589
Flood, R., 677
Floyd, S. W., 249
Follett, M. P., 246, 322–323, 499, 608, 844, 870
Fombrun, C., 95
Fontana, A., 229, 470, 889
Ford, R. C., 346
Foucault, M., 70, 72–73, 479, 544, 568–569, 570, 573, 693, 889
Fox, D., 373
Fox, S., 633
Frankel, M., 818
Franklin, P., 694
Freedman, R., 139
Freeman, J., 138
French, J., 549–564
French, W. L., 818
Fretwell, E., 11, 715, 731
Friedan, B., 64, 873
Friedman, R. A., 255, 256
Froosman, J., 149
Fukuyama, F., 556
Fuller, S. R., 345
Fulmer, R. M., 865
Futrell, D., 325

Gabarro, J., 865
Gaffney, M., 129
Gailliers, R., 92
Galbraith, J. R., 76, 174, 205, 215
Galton, F., 838
Gamson, W. A., 475, 549, 550, 554, 555, 557, 558, 559, 566, 574, 766
Garcia, J. E., 327
Gardner, W. L., 843
Geertz, C., 56, 364
Gellerman, W., 818
George, J. M., 349, 616, 840
Gergen, K., 66, 69
Gersick, C., 337–338
Gerstein, M., 174
Getzels, J. W., 111, 112, 114
Ghiselli, E. E., 839
Gibb, C. A., 832–833
Gibson, C. B., 334

Giddens, A., 50, 55, 226, 347, 651, 817
Gilbert, J. A., 840
Gilbreth, F. B., 322
Gillespie, J. Z., 297
Gilligan, C., 287n, 308
Gioia, D. A., 46, 78, 95, 155, 156, 157, 713, 733, 738, 761, 809
Giroux, H., 389
Glazer, J. S., 287n, 307–308
Glazer, S., 262
Glazer-Raymo, J., 64, 826, 873
Gmelch, W., 27, 244
Goddard, R. D., 281–282, 295
Gogliser, C. C., 859
Goldberger, N., 287, 308
Goldstein, W. M., 477, 634, 646, 647
Goleman, D., 840
Goltz, S., 551
Gonzales, R., 228, 794
Gonzalez, K., 389
Gooding, R. Z., 183
Goodwin, P., 649
Gordjin, J., 229
Gordon, R., 480, 734
Gorman, D., 865
Gouldner, A., 207, 245, 267, 340, 591
Gouran, D. S., 548
Graen, G. B., 256, 258, 832
Graff, G., 498
Graham, S., 28
Grandy, G., 480, 734
Grant, D., 480, 734
Graves, L., 65, 872, 873
Gray, P. H., 590
Gray, P. J., 781
Green, M., 795, 797, 812
Green, S. G., 859
Greene, C. N., 244
Gresov, C., 105
Griffin, R. W., 302
Griffith, T. L., 513
Grimes, A., 42, 46, 77, 467
Grimshaw, D., 402
Grinyer, P., 158, 224, 384, 521, 797
Gross, N. C., 246, 262
Grusky, O., 865
Guetzkow, H., 500
Gueverra, J., 139
Guinn, D., 759

Gully, S. M., 865
Gump, P. V., 183
Gumport, P. J., 129, 173, 308
Gupta, V., 132
Gyr, J. R., 500

Haber, S., 780
Hackman, J. R., 161, 217, 291, 302–306, 321, 342, 343, 346, 760, 802, 830
Hall, A. D., 94
Hall, R., 678
Halpin, A., 392
Halsey, W. F., 846
Hamm, R. E., 378–380, 761
Hancock, N., 770
Hanges, P., 132
Hanna, D. P., 220
Hannan, M., 138
Harden, G., 548, 684
Hardy, C., 551, 713, 730, 732, 777, 798, 811
Hardy, M. E., 246
Hargadon, A. B., 668
Harkins, S., 616
Harquail, C. V., 780
Harris, T. M., 655
Harrison, E. F., 590
Hart, J. W., 616
Harter, J. K., 281
Hartley, M., 60–61, 63, 156, 688, 689, 795, 868
Haslam, S. A., 322
Hassard, J., 44, 693
Hastie, R., 648
Hatakenaka, S., 673–674
Hatch, M. J., 61, 76, 132, 153, 162, 226, 380, 383–384, 479, 635, 667, 676, 712, 729, 732, 808
Hatfield, J., 299
Hatherly, D., 758
Hawaii, University of (Hilo), 772
Hayes, T. L., 281
Hearn, J., 45, 126
Hebein, R., 512
Heck, R., 239
Helgesen, S., 230, 871
Hellawell, D., 770
Heller, F., 606
Hellriegel, D., 216, 221, 334, 338, 350, 495, 500–501, 594
Helmich, D., 866
Helsabeck, R. E., 212, 213

Hemphill, J. K., 848
Henderson, G., 322
Henderson, S., 677
Henkin, A., 521, 571
Heraty, N., 670
Herden, R. P., 640, 766
Herman, R. D., 755
Hermann, T., 494
Herriott, S., 668
Hersey, P., 834, 852, 855, 859
Hertz, H. S., 771
Herzberg, F., 289, 290, 291, 293, 302, 802
Heskett, J., 364, 375
Hickson, D. J., 207, 494, 551, 595
Hietapelton, A., 551
Higgins, L., 805
Hill. B., 795, 797, 812
Hill, M. A., 832
Hills, R. J., 92, 472n
Hinds, P., 346, 830
Hinings, C. R., 494, 551
Hirokawa, R. Y., 321, 548
Hirschhorn, L., 15, 66, 77, 350, 470, 526, 872
Hitt, M. A., 711, 721
Hobbes, Thomas, 68, 371
Hodgkinson, M., 694
Hogarth, R. M., 595
Hogg, M. A., 862
Hollander, E. P., 571, 832
Hollenbeck, J. R., 606
Homans, G., 329
Hong, E., 780
Horsfall, S., 231
Hoskisson, R. E., 721
Hostager, T., 810, 867
Hot, W., 267
House, R. J., 132, 246, 262, 289n, 843, 854
Howell, I. P., 846
Hoy, A. W., 104–105, 281–282, 295
Hoy, W. K., 7, 191, 207, 231, 281–282, 290, 295, 297, 392, 556, 564, 614, 615
Hoyle, J. R., 243
Hrebiniak, L. G., 136, 140, 144, 740
Huber, G. P., 478, 591, 595, 666, 667, 686
Huber, O., 476, 589, 590
Hudgins, J., 766
Hughes, M., 140, 229
Hughey, A. W., 831
Hulin, C. L., 184
Hunt, J. G., 831, 840

Huntley, C., 671
Hurrell, J. J., 266
Hurst, A., 321
Huseman, R., 299
Hutcheon, L., 71
Huxham, C., 265

Ibarra, R., 388, 424
Ilgen, D. R., 262, 606
Ilies, R., 849
Ireland, R. D., 711, 721
Ivancevi, J. M., 266

Jackson, J., 790
Jackson, M., 92
Jackson, S. W., 262
Jacob, P.E., 589
Jacobson, S., 732
Jago, A. G., 608, 609, 610, 862
Jalomo, R., 389
James, W., 422
Jameson, F., 889
Janis, I. L., 60, 344, 495
Janz, B., 870
Jarzabkowski, P., 712
Javidan, M., 132
Jeffcutt, P., 321
Jehn, K. A., 499, 519, 522
Jensen, M. A., 336
Jermeir, J. M., 846
Jick, T., 807, 808
Jobs, Steve, 681, 682, 864–865
Johnson, B. T., 871
Johnson, D., 246
Johnson, G., 730
Johnson, J. F., 840
Johnson, T., 256
Johnsrud, L., 262
Jones, E., 255
Jones, G., 349
Joyce, W. F., 136, 140, 144, 740
Judd, C. M., 755
Judge, T. A., 849
Jung, C. G., 639

Kabanoff, B., 864
Kahn, R. L., 52, 100, 102, 107, 131, 245, 246,
    247, 249, 250, 252, 254, 255, 256, 258,
    757, 765, 798, 849
Kahneman, D., 616, 645
Kakabadse, A., 590

Kanigel, R., 780
Kanter, R. M., 526, 807, 808, 872
Kanungo, R. N., 571, 834
Kaplan, A. R., 285, 286, 288, 466
Kaplan, R. E., 594
Karaosmanoglu, E., 732
Karau, S. J., 616
Kartseva, V., 229
Kast, F., 282
Kates, A., 174, 215
Katz, D., 52, 100, 102, 107, 131, 245, 247, 249,
    250, 252, 254, 256, 258, 757, 798, 831,
    846, 849
Katzenbach, E. L., 780
Katzenbach, J., 869, 871
Keating, D. E., 325
Kelemen, M., 44
Keller, G., 48, 715, 725, 726, 728–729, 730,
    794, 796, 798
Kelley, H. H., 606, 608
Kelloway, E. K., 246
Kelly, D., 282
Kemery, E. R., 246
Kennedy, A., 364, 375, 389
Kennedy, John F., 344–345
Kerber, L., 64, 872
Keren, G., 590
Kerlinger, F. N., 466
Kerr, C., 829–830
Kerr, N. A., 616
Kerr, N. L., 606
Kerr, S., 846
Kesner, I. F., 865
Kessler, E., 226
Kezar, A. J., 28, 46, 48, 49, 63, 64, 129, 177,
    325, 381, 419, 420, 469, 470, 670–673,
    725, 733, 794, 795, 812, 842, 867, 870,
    875
Kiesler, S., 346, 830, 833, 843
Kilbourne, L., 302
Kilmann, R. H., 336, 477, 634, 639–643, 757,
    766
Kim, D., 677, 678, 680, 685–686
Kim, J. E., 780
King, D. G., 346
King, D. W., 265
King, L. A., 265
Kirkman, B. L., 325, 871
Kirkpatrick, S. A., 839

Klein, H. J., 297
Klein, K. J., 678
Klir, G. J., 103
Knezevich, S. J., 9
Kniker, C., 189, 759
Ko, J., 572
Koch, J., 48
Koenig, R., Jr., 135
Kogan, N., 616
Kolb, D. A., 677–680
Kolb, D. M., 516, 523, 526
Kolodny, H. F., 221
Kontoghiorghes, C., 665, 696
Koot, W., 321
Korman, A. K., 848
Kornberger, M., 308
Kotter, J., 364, 375
Kozlowski, S. W. J., 865
Kramer, M. W., 770
Kramer, R. M., 556
Kuh, G. D., 770
Kuhn, A., 95
Kuhn, T. S., 43–46, 119, 573
Kumar, E. S., 262
Kund, G., 368
Kushner, R., 736–737
Kvale, S., 56–57, 418, 421

Labaree, D., 67
Ladenson, R., 818
Lamm, H., 345
Lampel, J., 713
Lampert, C., 668
Landy, F., 293n
Lane, H., 666, 678, 680–685
Lane, J., 583
Lane, P. J., 249
Langley, A., 713, 730, 798, 811
Latane, B., 616
Latham, G. P., 297, 298n, 839, 854
Lattuca, L., 194
Lawler, E., 294, 564–566, 568, 760
Lawrence, J. H., 244
Lawrence, P. R., 101, 176, 220, 471, 517
Layzell, T., 759
Leana, C. R., 606
Lee, C. A., 494, 551
Lee, J., 133, 574, 770
Lee, M. E., 231
Lee, Y. S., 755
Leisink, P., 321

Lenning, O., 755
Lenz, R. T., 139
LePine, J. A., 332
Leslie, D. W., 11, 712, 715, 731, 809
Leslie, L., 150, 888
Levinson, H., 404
Levinthal, D., 668, 672
Levitt, B., 667
Levy, A., 799
Lewicki, R. J., 516, 518
Lewin, A. Y., 758
Lewin, K., 294, 474, 511, 805–808, 831, 845, 848
Lewis, M., 42, 46, 77, 467, 677
Liddell, W. W., 264
Liden, R. C., 832, 859
Lieberman, D., 666
Lincoln, Y., 42, 777
Lindblom, C. E., 594, 796
Lindholm, J., 244
Lindsley, D. H., 345
Linton, R., 248
Lipham, J. M., 111, 112, 114
Lippitt, R., 350, 845, 848
Lipsky, D. B., 511
Lirtzman, S. I., 246, 262
Liska, L. Z., 854
Litterer, J. A., 518
Locke, E. A., 297, 298n, 606, 839, 854
Locke, John, 68
Loke, W. H., 603
Lopes, L. L., 589
Lorber, J., 64, 874
Lorenz, E., 119, 159, 160
Lorsch, J. W., 101, 176, 471, 517
Losey, M. R., 533
Louis, K. S., 795
Low, M. B., 712
Lubatkin, M., 866
Lubinescu, E., 129
Luce, R. D., 590
Luckmann, T., 14, 55, 469, 867, 870
Lueder, D. C., 852
Luhmann, N., 92, 94, 101, 798
Lukes, S., 523, 542, 543, 544, 652, 817
Lulofs, R. S., 507, 511, 526
Luthans, F., 285, 345, 843
Luther, Martin, 371
Lutz, F., 225, 763
Lyles, M., 666–667

Lynton, E., 102
Lyotard, J.-F., 104, 734
Lysons, A., 758

Maccoby, M., 287, 404, 832
MacKenzie, S. B., 854
Maguire, M. A., 221
Mahar, L., 859
Major, D., 606
Mallory, G. R., 595
Manning, K., 715, 797
Manz, C. C., 325
March, J. G., 101, 118, 144, 186, 207, 208, 245,
    292, 377, 477, 493, 516, 518, 545, 590,
    593, 596, 634, 657, 667, 668, 681, 683,
    690, 730, 759, 761, 762, 767
Marchese, T., 48
Marchington, M., 402
Marrow, A. J., 606
Marsick, V., 686
Martin, J., 46, 78, 260, 321, 349, 359, 362,
    364, 387, 390, 389, 390, 526–527, 554,
    571, 573, 652, 653, 654, 778, 779
Martin, P. Y., 307
Martin, R. O., 715, 759, 797
Martz, A. E., 548
Marx, Karl, 366
Masland, A. T., 364
Maslow, A. H., 279, 284–288, 289, 291, 292,
    293, 302
Mason, W. S., 246, 262
Match, J., 730
Maule, A. J., 644
Mausner, B., 290, 802
May, D. R., 843
Mayer, R. C., 362, 556
Mayo, E., 52, 322, 323
McCaffery, P., 504
McCall, M. W., 594
McCanse, A. A., 834
McClelland, D. C., 288, 289, 839
McClenney, K., 766
McDaniel, R. R., 591, 595
McDermott, M., 655
McEachern, A. W., 246, 262
McGee, R. J., 19, 500, 672
McGowan, R., 230
McGregor, D., 288–289, 309, 369–370, 371,
    842
McHugh, P. P., 865
McIntyre, S., 805

McKelvey, B., 336, 757
McKersie, R. B., 513
McLaughlin, D. J., 588
McLendon, M., 21
McLuhan, M., 366
McNamara, G., 591
McNamara, J. F., 243
McPhee, R., 227, 347
Medin, D. L., 590
Mednick, M. T., 308, 309
Melewar, T., 732
Merchant, C. S., 495, 511
Mercier, J., 230
Merrell, V. D., 346
Merton, R., 246, 247, 258
Meyer, J., 368
Meyer, M. W., 208, 212
Meyerson, D., 386
Micek, S. S., 755
Michalski, W. J., 346
Middlemist, R. D., 711
Mihata, K., 402
Milam, J., 694
Miles, E., 299
Miles, R. H., 244, 255, 262, 552
Miller, A. N., 655
Milliken, F. J., 99, 726
Mills, A., 480, 734
Mills, M., 777
Minassians, H. P., 780, 781
Mingers, J., 92
Minor, J. B., 556, 706, 846
Minton, J. W., 758
Mintzberg, H., 160, 176, 178, 193, 245, 247,
    477, 479, 502, 549, 566, 574, 589, 590,
    594, 597, 604, 634, 637–639, 713, 716–
    721, 725, 730, 731, 732, 737, 763, 798, 811
Miskel, C. G., 7, 104–105, 207, 231, 267, 290,
    297, 392, 564, 614, 615
Mitchell, T. R., 854
Mitroff, I., 477, 634, 639–643, 715
Mohrman, A., 870
Mohrman, S., 870
Moment, D., 832
Monane, J., 92
Mone, M. A., 282
Montez, J., 244
Montgomery, B., 76, 522
Montgomery, J. D., 259
Moore, W. L., 552

Moreno-Luzón, M., 665, 677, 686
Morgan, G., 44, 45, 49, 92, 155, 181, 545, 666
Morgenstern, O., 590, 647
Morphew, C., 143
Morrison, J. L., 182
Mort, P., 800
Moscovici, S., 615
Mossholder, K. W., 246
Moultrie, J., 677
Mouton, J. S., 849–850
Mudrack, P. W., 344
Mumby, D., 61–62, 154, 385, 713, 818
Mumford, L., 366
Mumford, M. D., 840
Murphy, J. T., 837
Murphy, L. R., 765
Murrell, P. H., 679
Myers, D. G., 345
Myers, S. L., 260

Nadler, D. A., 13, 98, 116, 117, 174, 472n, 739, 767–768, 811
Nagel, E., 402
Nanus, B., 840, 841
Narver, J., 665
Nauta, A., 344
Naylor, J. C., 262
Neal, M. A., 499
Neilson, E. H., 517
Nelson, D. L., 266, 345
Nelson, R. B., 852
Neumann, A., 49, 55, 62, 348, 469, 774, 830, 867, 868, 869
Newton, Isaac, 50, 68
Nixon, Richard, 846
Noe, R. A., 179, 870
Nonaka, I., 673
Nora, A., 389
Nord, W. R., 633
Norris, W. R., 852
Northcraft, G. B., 499, 513
Nunez, W., 715
Nutt, P. C., 588, 600, 641
Nyhan, R., 572
Nystrom, P. C., 326

O'Banion, T., 190, 665, 694
Obert, S. L., 336
Offermann, L. R., 571, 832, 871
Ogawa, R., 869
Ogren, C., 93, 102

Oldham, G. R., 302–306, 802
O'Leary-Kelly, P., 302
Olsen, J. P., 101, 144, 207, 245, 477, 606, 636, 654, 730, 762
Olsen, M. E., 93
O'Meara, K., 260
O'Reilly, C. A., III, 93
Organ, D. W., 244
Orris, J., 256
Ortiz, F., 228
Orton, J. D., 222, 223, 225, 266, 797
Ostroff, C., 292, 758
Ouchi, W. G., 221, 364, 373, 830
Owers, J., 866

Padilla, A., 835
Palmer, I., 732
Park, W. W, 345
Parkay, F., 244
Parker, G. M., 346
Parsons, T., 52, 64, 69, 92, 107–108, 113, 246, 248, 268, 366, 372–373, 374–375, 594, 597, 598, 599–600, 641, 758, 834, 864, 873
Patchen, M., 606
Paterson, D., 732
Paul, D. A., 794
Pelz, D. C., 845
Pennings, J. M., 494, 551
Perlman, M., 776, 780
Perreault, W. D., Jr., 244, 255, 262
Perrow, C., 132, 182, 187, 188, 189, 689, 759, 761, 773–774
Peters, T. J., 362, 730
Peterson, M., 98, 140, 339, 393, 732, 771, 845
Petrides, L., 660, 694
Pettigrew, A. M., 363, 548, 551, 590, 712
Pfeffer, J., 45, 149, 188, 191, 225, 545, 549, 551, 552, 561, 568, 764, 776, 889
Phillipchuk, J., 289n
Phillips, F. P., 511
Phillips, N., 732
Piccolo, R. F., 840, 849
Pinkley, R. L., 513
Pitre, E., 46, 78
Platt, G., 594
Pneuman , R. W., 496
Podolny, J., 255
Podsokoff, P. M., 854
Poindexter, S., 798
Polkinghorne, D., 421, 422, 694, 774, 779

Pondy, L. R., 504, 522, 570, 571
Poole, M. S., 227, 347
Poropat, A., 77
Porter, L. W., 294, 372, 544, 558, 760
Porter, M. E., 479, 726, 729
Porterfield, T., 572
Posner, B. Z., 589
Poulantzas, N., 572
Powell, G., 65, 872, 873
Powell, T. C., 772
Powell, W. W., 130, 142, 807
Presley, J. B., 712
Price, J. L., 207
Price, K. H., 342
Pritchard, R. D., 262, 296
Prusak, L., 840
Pugh, D. S., 183, 207
Pusic, E., 606
Putnam, L., 523, 654

Quick, J. C., 326
Quinn, R. E., 246, 250, 254, 480, 584, 767, 771

Raffel, S., 256
Ragan, J. W., 862
Rahim, M. A., 495, 527
Rahman, S., 772
Raiffa, H., 590
Raisinghani, D., 477, 590, 597
Rallis, S., 422
Ramaley, J., 715, 797
Randolph, W., 346
Rangarajan, D., 255
Rankin, D., 865
Ratcliff, J., 129
Ravasi, D., 157, 158
Raven, B., 549–564
Reagans, R., 671
Reason, P., 422
Reciniello, S., 874
Reed, M., 140, 229
Rendón, L., 389
Renz, D. O., 755
Rettinger, D. A., 648
Reynolds, P. D., 467
Rhoades, G., 731, 732, 794
Rhoads, R., 74–75, 259, 260, 386
Rice, R. E., 259
Richman, B. M., 759
Riesman, D., 142, 403, 672, 761

Rivkin, J., 106, 672
Rizzo, J. R., 246, 262
Robbins, S. P., 205, 220, 499, 516, 520, 522
Roberts, H., 810
Roberts, J. A., 255
Roberts, K., 617
Roberts, L., 779
Rockart, J. F., 758
Roe, A., 110
Roethlisberger, F. J., 52, 321, 323, 765
Rogers, E., 800
Rogers, M., 866
Rohrbaugh, J., 480, 771
Romanelli, E., 795
Romm, N., 677
Romme, A. G. L., 676
Roome, N., 665, 677
Roos, L. L., 258
Rorty, R., 891
Rose, J., 713, 730, 798, 811
Rosen, B., 325, 871
Rosenzweig, J., 282
Rosovsky, H., 724
Rosser, V., 292
Rossman, G., 422
Ross-Smith, A., 308
Rost, J. C., 56, 837, 869
Rousseau, D. M., 678
Rousseau, Jean-Jacques, 68, 371
Rowan, B., 368
Rowe, W. G., 865
Roznowksi, M., 184
Rubery, J., 402
Rudolph, F., 498
Rudolph, J. W., 673–674
Rudolph, L., 780
Ruizendaal, G., 220
Ruppert, S. S., 780
Ryan, A. M., 639
Ryan, R., 285, 304

Sackmann, S., 363, 381
Sagie, A., 289
Salancik, G. R., 149, 225, 551, 776
Salas, E., 865
Samson, F. L., 655
Sandberg, J., 55, 56, 57, 58, 59, 70, 833
Sanders, K., 344
Sandfort, J. R., 764
Sandole, D., 494
Sarbin, T. R., 246

Sarr, R. A., 56
Sawyer, J. E., 265
Sawyer, O., 672
Sayles, L., 324, 328
Scandura, T. A., 258, 859
Schein, E., 190, 359, 363, 364–372
Scherer, A., 45
Schick, A. G., 551
Schmidt, F. L., 281
Schmidt, W. H., 589
Schmitt, N., 758
Schneck, R. E., 494, 551
Schoemaker, P., 479, 672, 726
Schoenherr, R. A., 183
Schön, D., 43, 154, 370, 674–678
Schoorman, F. D., 362, 556
Schriescheim, C. A., 859
Schuchman, H. L., 589
Schuler, R. S., 255, 262, 264
Schultz, M., 157, 158, 732
Schuster, J., 21, 29, 30, 48, 99, 174, 725
Schweiger, D. M., 499, 606
Scott, W. G., 324
Scott, W. R., 103, 144, 184, 774
Seashore, S. E., 343, 606, 764, 850
Sebora, T. C., 865
Seeber, R. L., 511
Seely-Brown, J. S., 667, 670, 682, 684, 686
Sego, D. J., 606
Seibold, D., 227, 347
Selden, S. C., 764
Selznick, P., 842, 875
Senge, P., 14, 55, 106, 346, 666, 680, 697
Sergiovanni, T., 373
Service, A. L., 755
Seymour, D., 797
Shamir, B., 843, 853
Shanley, M., 95
Shapira, Z., 591
Shaw, R., 174
Shearer, R. E., 765
Sheppard, B. H., 518
Shields, D. C., 617, 713
Shils, E. A., 113, 641
Shoemaker, F., 800
Short, L., 832
Shrivastava, P., 159, 225, 666
Siegelman, M., 110
Sifferman, J. J., 262
Siggelkow, N., 672

Simmel, G., 498
Simmons, B. L., 266
Simon, H. A., 207, 208, 292, 493, 516, 518, 564, 590, 592, 767
Simsek, H., 795
Singh, J., 255
Sitkin, S. B., 345, 668, 669
Slater, P. E., 850
Slater, S., 665
Slaughter, S., 150, 794, 888
Slocum, J. W., Jr., 216, 221, 264, 334, 338, 350, 495, 500–501, 594
Slovic, P., 645
Slusher, E. A., 549
Smart, J. C., 378–380, 759, 761
Smart, J. M., 104
Smircich, L., 64, 307, 385, 845
Smith, Adam, 68
Smith, B. L., 831
Smith, D., 29, 48, 725, 869, 871
Smyth, J., 888
Snoek, J. D., 246, 250, 254, 255, 256
Snyderman, B., 290, 802
Sokal, A., 888
Sorcinelli, M. D., 259
Sowa, J. E., 764
Spalding, W. B., 104
Spencer, M., 339, 393, 845
Spender, J.-C., 158, 224, 226, 384, 521, 797
Sporn, B., 750
Sproull, L., 680, 682, 687, 688–689, 693
Stajkovic, A. D., 285, 345
Stake, R., 418
Stalker, G., 52, 145–146, 471, 694–695, 801
Stanton, W. W., 870
Stanton-Salazar, R., 63, 388
Starbuck, W., 258, 664
Starke, F. A., 258
Stasson, M. F., 616
Staw, B., 158, 224, 384, 521
Steers, R. M., 189, 289, 501, 517, 759
Stein, B., 807, 808
Steiner, I. D., 326
Steinmann, H., 45
Stewart, J., 694
Stilwell, D., 859
Stogdill, R. M., 343, 344, 832, 839
Stohl, C., 654
Stoner, J. A. F., 616
Stopford, J., 809

Strauss, A., 9, 418–419, 420, 421
Strauss, G., 324, 328, 606
Straussman, J. D., 594
Strayer, R., 571
Streuffer, S., 648
Sturnick, J. A., 500
Sullivan, P. A., 712
Sundstrom, E., 325
Sutcliffe, K. M., 591
Sutton, R. I., 641
Svenson, O., 644
Sweetland, S., 191

Taber, T. D., 859
Tagiuri, R., 391–392
Takeuchi, H., 673
Tan, Y-H., 229
Tarule, J., 287, 308
Taylor, F. W., 52, 322, 780
Thanassoulis, E., 780
Thaxter, L., 28
Theoret, A., 477, 590, 597
Thibaut, J. W., 606, 608
Thierry, H., 294
Thomas, C. R., 780
Thomas, E., 246
Thomas, H., 591, 712
Thomas, J. B., 95, 155, 156, 157, 345, 713, 733,
    738, 761, 809
Thomas, K. W., 500, 504, 509, 510, 514, 515,
    520
Thompson, D. P., 243
Thompson, G., 374
Thompson, J. D., 52, 192, 193, 471, 476, 601,
    602, 604, 608
Thompson, V. A., 206, 208, 210
Thomson, S. C., 772
Threlfall, K. V., 840
Tiberius, R. G., 373
Tidd, S. T., 256
Tierney, W., 49, 73, 76, 129, 190, 244, 259,
    260, 261, 262, 364, 381–382, 423, 523,
    556, 733, 735, 737, 763, 794, 866, 867,
    873, 874
Tindale, R. S., 606
Tinto, V., 423–424
Tjosvold, D., 499
Tolman, E., 294
Toma, J. D., 129, 382
Tonn, J., 322
Tosi, H., 678

Touliatos, J., 246
Trice, H., 98
Tricker, R. I., 780
Tripp, R. E., 551
Trist, E. L., 130
Tschannen-Moran, M., 556
Tubre, T. C., 262
Tuckman, B. W., 336, 337
Tuden, A., 476, 601, 604, 608
Turner, C. S., 260, 389
Tushman, M. L., 13, 98, 116, 117, 472*n*, 541,
    739, 767–768, 795, 811
Tversky, A., 616, 645
Tyler, T. R., 556

Ulh-Bien, M., 832
Ulrich, D. O., 841
Ury, W., 76, 520

Vallejo, E., 421, 422, 694, 774, 779
Van der Wiele, T., 772
Van de Ven, A. H., 54, 117, 135, 140, 410, 757,
    796, 801
Van de Vliert, E., 493
van Dijk, E., 616
Van Dyke, J., 780
Van Dyne, L., 332
Van Eerde, W., 294
Van Fleet, D. D., 616
Vangen, S., 265
van Knippenberg, B., 616
van Knippenberg, D., 616
Van Maanen, J., 258, 368, 524
Van Slyke, E. J., 502
Van Witteloostujin, A., 676
Vecchio, R. P., 852
Ventimiglia, L., 795
Verweel, P., 321
Victor, B., 192
von Neumann, J., 590, 647
Vroom, V. H., 292, 294, 608, 609, 610

Wagner, J. A., III, 183
Wahba, M. A., 285
Waldman, D. A., 833
Walker, C., 278
Wall, J., 493
Wallach, M. A., 616
Walton, E. J., 403
Walton, R. E., 504, 513
Walumbwa, F. O., 843

Washburn, J., 888
Wasley, P., 574
Waterman, R. H., Jr., 362
Waters, J. A., 479, 604, 713
Watkins, K. E., 670, 686
Wayne, S. J., 832, 859
Weber, E. U., 477, 633, 634, 646, 647
Weber, M., 52, 68–69, 142, 203–205, 210, 212, 541
Webster, D., 19
Wegner, G., 204, 210, 221
Wehr, P., 504
Weick, K. E., 14, 55, 60, 136, 140, 144, 147, 154, 155, 222, 223, 224, 225, 266, 346, 380, 469, 617, 667, 680, 687, 689, 690–692, 730, 733, 740, 773, 775, 797, 830, 866, 867, 869
Weiermair, K., 776, 780
Weimer-Jehle, W., 92
Welbourne, T., 246
Welsh, J., 715
Welsh, M. A., 549
Wergin, J., 133, 794
Westley, F., 224, 687, 689, 690–692
Wexley, K. N., 343
Wheatley, M., 387
Whetten, D. A., 156, 244, 255, 641, 757, 768, 771, 809, 864, 865
White, G., 545
White, L., 819
White, R. K., 666, 678, 680–685, 845, 848
Whitt, E. J., 770
Whittaker, J., 289n
Whittington, R., 712
Whyte, G., 344
Whyte, W. F., 324, 332–333
Wigdor, L. A., 289n
Wijen, F., 665, 677
Wilkins, A. L., 364, 373

Williams, A. R. T., 772
Williams, K., 616
Wilmott, H., 402
Wilpert, B., 606
Wilson, D. C., 595
Wilson, I., 182
Wofford, J. C., 854
Wolf, B., 869
Wolfe, D. M., 246, 250, 254, 255, 256
Wolff, K. H., 326
Wolff, R. P., 540
Wolverton, M., 244
Woodman, R. W., 216, 221, 334, 350, 495, 500–501, 594
Woodward, J., 186–187
Wooten, K., 819
Wright, G., 649
Wu, P. Y., 772

Yamada, M., 29, 48, 725
Yamagishi, M., 556
Yamagishi, T., 556
Yammarino, F. J., 678, 833
Yang, P., 780
Yanow, D., 47, 680, 682, 687, 688–689, 693
Yetton, P. W., 608, 609
Young, O. R., 92
Yuchtman, E., 764
Yukl, G. A., 343, 563

Zaccaro, S. J., 840
Zairi, M., 772
Zaleznik, A., 765, 832
Zaltman, G., 796
Zammuto, R. F., 184, 186, 193, 760
Zand, D. E., 329
Zavalloni, M., 616
Zigarmi, D., 852
Znaniecki, F., 258

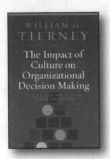

The Impact of Culture on Organizational Decision-Making
Theory and Practice in Higher Education
William G. Tierney

"At a time when institutions recognize the need for change but may be unsure of how to make that change happen, I found *The Impact of Culture on Organizational Decision-Making*, by William G. Tierney, a must-read. I would recommend it to business officers and other leaders engaging their campuses in improvement and prioritization processes. Understanding the culture of the institution—and of higher education in general—is vital to the success of any change plan, particularly for business officers coming from private industry. Tierney's call to look beyond the structure of American research institutions and use a cultural model to understand organizational decision making is a needed wake-up call to college and university administrators who wish to lead their organizations to success and excellence in the 21st century."—***Business Officer Magazine***

Community College Leadership
A Multidimensional Model for Leading Change
Pamela L. Eddy
Foreword by George R. Boggs

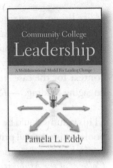

"Pamela L. Eddy's *Community College Leadership: A Multidimensional Model for Leading Change* deserves our time for two simple reasons: first, the multidimensional model for leading change transcends community colleges and is applicable broadly within and beyond education; and, second, the author's thoughtful inclusion of vignettes and case studies provides the day-today grounding to make her model relevant to readers of all professions. Yes, community college readers have the advantage of knowing many of the leadership challenges firsthand and will be more interested than most in sections such as 'Challenges of Community College Leadership,' but this book adds sufficiently to leadership literature that it should find itself on the bookshelves of professionals across education and the private sector."—***The Department Chair***

Sty/us

22883 Quicksilver Drive
Sterling, VA 20166-2102

Subscribe to our e-mail alerts: www.Styluspub.com

Also available from Stylus

Cautionary Tales
Strategy Lessons from Struggling Colleges
Alice W. Brown
With Elizabeth R. Hayford, Richard R. Johnson, Susan Whealler Johnston,
Richard K. Kneipper, Michael G. Puglisi and Robert Zemsky

"A roadmap for organizational health, for spotting and avoiding problems before they become overwhelming, and for becoming sustainable, not just surviving. There is rich material here for all the key players: trustees, presidents, faculty members, and administrative staff on the roles they play and the responsibilities they often share for both the onset of survival threats and for their successful (or unsuccessful) resolution."—*Patrick T. Terenzini*

"Alice Brown's new study of colleges on the brink of closure provides a fascinating resource for college planners. The book's case studies of a half dozen such colleges, told from the vantage points of key participants in the decisions that proved most critical, gives texture to our understanding of the ways in which institutional histories actually unfold. The accompanying essays by several informed observers provide a broader context for the case studies. In a field that is often dominated by jargon, Brown's clear prose makes for engaging reading."—**Richard Ekman,** *President, Council of Independent Colleges*

"This volume could be useful for students as they prepare for careers in higher education. The essays in this book focus on small private institutions, but they contain useful lessons for students who will often be working in larger universities or community colleges."—**Elizabeth Hayford,** *former President of the Associated Colleges of the Midwest*

Rethinking Leadership Practices in a Complex, Multicultural, and Global Environment
New Concepts and Models for Higher Education
Edited by Adrianna Kezar

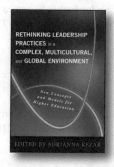

"Indeed *Rethinking Leadership Practices* is an excellent compilation of the concepts, models, and good practices to develop the contemporary leadership capacity so needed in a new generation of college leaders. . . . The audience for this book is any administrator accountable to develop talent and capacity for faculty and staff in the leadership pipeline. With the admonition that old models of training will not develop leadership capacities so needed in today's times, Kezar and her authors present successful models that have developed women and professionals of color over the years. . . . Each chapter is well written, rich in context and detail, well researched with useful resources, and anchored by direct practical applications. The chapters are uniformly of high quality. Many students tell me they usually skip the 'preface', but in this book, that would be a big mistake! This preface is a substantive contribution to the evolution of leadership development programs and framework for the argument for the book."—**The Review of Higher Education**

"Many resources on higher education leadership are of only passing relevance to department chairs. Not this one. While not all of the chapters will be of interest to the typical chair, most of them will, particularly the introductory overview and the chapters on complexity, activism, and ethics. Here even the most jaded consumer of 'airport leadership' books will find provocative and maybe even inspiring material."
—**The Department Chair**